FOURTH EDITION

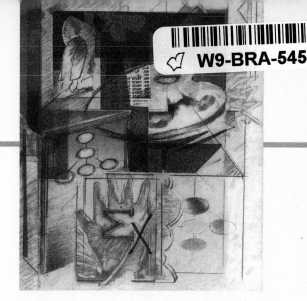

Reframing Organizations

Artistry, Choice, and Leadership

Lee G. Bolman • Terrence E. Deal

JOSSEY-BASS
A Wiley Imprint
www.josseybass.com

Published by Jossey-Bass
A Wiley Imprint
989 Market Street, San Francisco, CA 94103-1741—www.josseybass.com

Credits are on page 528.

Readers should be aware that Internet Web sites offered as citations and/or sources for further information may have changed or disappeared between the time this was written and when it is read.

Jossey-Bass books and products are available through most bookstores. To contact Jossey-Bass directly call our Customer Care Department within the U.S. at 800-956-7739, outside the U.S. at 317-572-3986, or fax 317-572-4002.

Jossey-Bass also publishes its books in a variety of electronic formats. Some content that appears in print may not be available in electronic books.

Library of Congress Cataloging-in-Publication Data

Bolman, Lee G.
    Reframing organizations : artistry, choice, and leadership / Lee G. Bolman, Terrence E. Deal.—4th ed.
      p.   cm.—(The Jossey-Bass business & management series)
    Includes bibliographical references and index.
    ISBN 978-0-7879-8798-5 (cloth)
    ISBN 978-0-7879-8799-2 (pbk.)
    1. Management. 2. Organizational behavior. 3. Leadership. I. Deal, Terrence E. II. Title.
  HD31.B6135   2008
  658.4'063—dc22

                                                                   2008022738

Printed in the United States of America
FOURTH EDITION
HB Printing   10 9 8 7 6 5 4 3 2
PB Printing   10 9 8 7 6 5 4 3 2

The Jossey-Bass Business & Management Series

An updated online Instructor's Guide with test bank
is available at **www.wiley.com/college/bolman**

Available in spring 2009: New with this fourth edition of *Reframing Organizations*
is an online assessment program that runs in Blackboard, WebCT, and Vista. Each
chapter includes 15–20 multiple choice, true/false, matching, and essay questions
designed to assess understanding of the key concepts presented in the text. Multiple
choice, matching, and true/false questions will include detailed feedback for incorrect answers, and students will also be provided references to the text for incorrect
answers. Please consult your sales representative for further details.

CONTENTS

PREFACE

This is the fifth release of a work that began in 1984 as *Modern Approaches to Understanding and Managing Organizations*. We're grateful to readers around the world who have told us the book gave them ideas that make a difference—at work and elsewhere in their lives.

It is time for an update, and we're gratified to be back by popular demand. Like everything else, organizations and their leadership challenges have been changing rapidly in recent years, and scholars have been running hard to keep up. This edition tries to capture the current frontiers of both knowledge and art.

The four-frame model, with its view of organizations as factories, families, jungles, and temples, remains the book's conceptual heart. But much else has changed. We have updated our case examples extensively to keep up with the latest developments in managerial practice. We have updated a feature we inaugurated in the third edition, "greatest hits in organization studies." These features offer pithy summaries of key ideas from the some of the most influential works in the scholarly literature (as indicated by a citation analysis, described in the Appendix at the end of the book). As a counterpoint to the scholarly works, we have also added occasional summaries of recent management best-sellers.

Life in organizations has also produced many new examples, and there is new material throughout the book. At the same time, we worked zealously to minimize bloat by tracking down and expunging every redundant sentence, marginal concept, or extraneous example. We are proud that, despite new material in every chapter, this edition is actually a bit shorter than the last one. At the same time, we've tried to keep it fun. Collective life is an endless source of examples as entertaining as they are instructive, and we've sprinkled them throughout the text. We apologize to anyone who finds that an old favorite fell to the cutting-room floor, but we think most readers will find the book an even clearer and more efficient read.

As always, our primary audience is managers and future leaders. We have tried to answer the question, What do we know about organizations and leadership that is genuinely relevant and useful to practitioners? We have worked to present a large, complex body of theory, research, and practice as clearly and simply as possible. We tried to avoid watering it down or presenting simplistic views of how to solve managerial problems. Our goal is to offer not solutions but powerful and provocative ways of thinking about opportunities and pitfalls.

We continue to focus on both management *and* leadership. Leading and managing are different, but they're equally important. If an organization is overmanaged but underled, it eventually loses any sense of spirit or purpose. A poorly managed organization with a strong, charismatic leader may soar briefly—only to crash shortly thereafter. Malpractice can be as damaging and unethical for managers and leaders as for physicians. Myopic managers or overzealous leaders usually harm more than just themselves. The challenges of modern organizations require the objective perspective of managers as well as the brilliant flashes of vision that wise leadership provides. We need more people in managerial roles who can find simplicity and order amid organizational confusion and chaos. We need versatile and flexible leaders who are artists as well as analysts, who can reframe experience to discover new issues and possibilities. We need managers who love their work, their organizations, and the people whose lives they affect. We need leaders and managers who appreciate management as a moral and ethical undertaking. We need leaders who combine hard-headed realism with passionate commitment to larger values and purposes. We hope to encourage and nurture such qualities and possibilities.

As in the past, we have tried to produce a clear and readable synthesis and integration of the field's major theoretical traditions. We concentrate mainly on organization theory's implications for practice. We draw on examples from every sector and around the globe. Historically, organization studies have been divided into several intellectual camps, often isolated from one another. Works that seek to give a comprehensive overview of organization theory and research often drown in social science jargon and abstraction and have little to say to practitioners. We try to find a balance between misleading oversimplification and mind-boggling complexity.

The bulk of work in organization theory has focused almost exclusively on either the private *or* the public sector, but not both. We think this is a mistake. Managers need to understand similarities and differences among all types of organizations. The public and private sectors increasingly interpenetrate one another. Public administrators who regulate airlines, nuclear power plants, or pharmaceutical companies face the problem of "indirect management" every day. They struggle to influence the behavior of organizations over which they have very limited authority. Private firms need to manage relationships with multiple levels of government. The situation is even more complicated for managers in multinational companies coping with the subtleties of governments with very different systems and traditions. Across sectors and cultures, managers often harbor narrow, stereotypic conceptions of one another that impede effectiveness on both sides. We need common ground and a shared understanding that can help strengthen public and private organizations in the United States and throughout the world. The dialogue between public and private, domestic and multinational organizations has become increasingly important. Because of their generic application, the frames offer an ecumenical language for the exchange. Our work with a variety of organizations around the world has continually reinforced our confidence that the frames are relevant everywhere. Political issues, for example, are universally important, even though the specifics vary greatly from one country or culture to another.

The idea of *reframing* continues to be a central theme. Throughout the book, we show how the same situation can be viewed in at least four ways. In Part Six, we include a series of chapters on reframing critical organizational issues such as leadership, change, and ethics. Two chapters are specifically devoted to reframing real-life situations.

We also continue to emphasize artistry. Overemphasizing the rational and technical side of an organization often contributes to its decline or demise. Our counterbalance emphasizes the importance of art in both management and leadership. Artistry is neither exact nor precise; the artist interprets experience, expressing it in forms that can be felt, understood, and appreciated. Art fosters emotion, subtlety, and ambiguity. An artist represents the world to give us a deeper understanding of what is and what might be. In modern organizations, quality, commitment, and creativity are highly valued but often hard to find. They can be developed and encouraged by leaders or managers who embrace the expressive side of their work.

OUTLINE OF THE BOOK

The first part of the book, "Making Sense of Organizations," tackles a perplexing question about management: Why is it that smart people so often do dumb things? Chapter One, "The Power of Reframing," explains why: Managers often misread situations. They have not learned how to use multiple lenses to get a better sense of what they're up against and what they might do. Chapter Two, "Simple Ideas, Complex Organizations," uses several famous cases (9/11, Hurricane Katrina, and a friendly-fire tragedy in the skies over Iraq in 1994) to show how managers' everyday thinking and theories can lead to catastrophe. We explain basic factors that make organizational life complicated, ambiguous, and unpredictable; discuss common fallacies in managerial thinking; and spell out criteria for more effective approaches to diagnosis and action.

Part Two, "The Structural Frame," explores the key role that social architecture plays in the functioning of organizations. Chapter Three, "Getting Organized," describes basic issues managers must consider in designing structure to fit an organization's goals, tasks, and context. It demonstrates why organizations—from Harvard University to McDonald's—need different structures in order to be effective in their unique environments. Chapter Four, "Structure and Restructuring," explains major structural pathologies and pitfalls. It presents guidelines for aligning structures to situations, along with several cases illustrating successful structural change. Chapter Five, "Organizing Groups and Teams," shows that structure is a key to high-performing teams.

Part Three, "The Human Resource Frame," explores the properties of both people and organizations, and what happens when the two intersect. Chapter Six, "People and Organizations," focuses on the relationship between organizations and human nature. It shows how a manager's practices and assumptions about people can lead either to alienation and hostility or to commitment and high motivation. It contrasts two strategies for achieving effectiveness: "lean and mean," or investing in people. Chapter Seven, "Improving Human Resource

Management," is an overview of practices that build a more motivated and committed workforce—including participative management, job enrichment, self-managing workgroups, management of diversity, and organization development. Chapter Eight, "Interpersonal and Group Dynamics," presents an example of interpersonal conflict to illustrate how managers can enhance or undermine relationships. It also discusses how group members can increase their effectiveness by attending to group process, including informal norms and roles, interpersonal conflict, leadership, and decision making.

Part Four, "The Political Frame," views organizations as arenas. Individuals and groups compete to achieve their parochial interests in a world of conflicting viewpoints, scarce resources, and struggles for power. Chapter Nine, "Power, Conflict, and Coalition," analyzes the tragic loss of the space shuttles *Columbia* and *Challenger,* illustrating the influence of political dynamics in decision making. It shows how scarcity and diversity lead to conflict, bargaining, and games of power; the chapter also distinguishes constructive and destructive political dynamics. Chapter Ten, "The Manager as Politician," illustrates basic skills of the constructive politician: diagnosing political realities, setting agendas, building networks, negotiating, and making choices that are both effective and ethical. Chapter Eleven, "Organizations as Political Arenas and Political Agents," highlights organizations as both arenas for political contests and political actors influencing broader social, political, and economic trends. Case examples such as Wal-Mart and Ross Johnson explore political dynamics both inside and outside organizations.

Part Five explores the symbolic frame. Chapter Twelve, "Organizational Symbols and Culture," spells out basic symbolic elements in organizations: myths, heroes, metaphors, stories, humor, play, rituals, and ceremonies. It defines organizational culture and shows its central role in shaping performance. The power of symbol and culture is illustrated in cases as diverse as Harley-Davidson, the U.S. Congress, Nordstrom department stores, the Air Force, and an odd horse race in Italy. Chapter Thirteen, "Culture in Action," uses the case of a computer development team to show what leaders and group members can do collectively to build a culture that bonds people in pursuit of a shared mission. Initiation rituals, specialized language, group stories, humor and play, and ceremonies all combine to transform diverse individuals into a cohesive team with purpose, spirit, and soul. Chapter Fourteen, "Organization as Theater," draws on dramaturgical and institutional theory to reveal how organizational structures, activities, and events serve as secular dramas, expressing our fears and joys, arousing our emotions, and kindling our spirit. It also shows how organizational structures and processes, such as planning, evaluation, and decision making, are often more important for what they express than for what they accomplish.

Part Six, "Improving Leadership Practice," focuses on the implications of the frames for central issues in managerial practice, including leadership, change, and ethics. Chapter Fifteen, "Integrating Frames for Effective Practice," shows how managers can blend the frames to improve their effectiveness. It looks at organizations as multiple realities and gives guidelines for aligning frames with situations. Chapter Sixteen, "Reframing in Action," presents four scenarios, or scripts, derived from the frames. It applies the scenarios to the harrowing experience of a young manager whose first day in a new job turns out to be far more challenging than she expected. The discussion illustrates how leaders can expand their options and enhance their effectiveness by considering alternative approaches. Chapter Seventeen, "Reframing Leadership," discusses limitations in traditional views of leadership and proposes a more comprehensive view of how leadership works in organizations. It summarizes and critiques current knowledge on the characteristics of leaders, including the relationship of leadership and gender. It shows how frames generate distinctive images of effective leaders as architects, servants, advocates, and prophets.

Chapter Eighteen, "Reframing Change in Organizations," describes four fundamental issues that arise in any change effort: individual needs, structural alignment, political conflict, and existential loss. It uses cases of successful and unsuccessful change to document key strategies, such as training, realigning, creating arenas, and using symbol and ceremony. Chapter Nineteen, "Reframing Ethics and Spirit," discusses four ethical mandates that emerge from the frames: excellence, caring, justice, and faith. It argues that leaders can build more ethical organizations through gifts of authorship, love, power, and significance. Chapter Twenty, "Bringing It All Together," is an integrative treatment of the reframing process. It takes a troubled school administrator through a weekend of reflection on critical difficulties he faces. The chapter shows how reframing can help managers move from feeling confused and stuck to discovering a renewed sense of clarity and confidence. The Epilogue (Chapter Twenty-One) describes strategies and characteristics needed in future leaders. It explains why they will need an artistic combination of conceptual flexibility and commitment to core values. Efforts to prepare future leaders have to focus as much on spiritual as on intellectual development.

ACKNOWLEDGMENTS

As we noted in our first edition, "Book writing often feels like a lonely process, even when an odd couple is doing the writing." This odd couple keeps getting older (both closing in on seventy)—and, some would say, even odder and more grumpy. Yet the process seems less lonely because of our close friendship and our contact with many other colleagues and friends. The best thing about teaching is that you learn so much from your students. Students at Harvard, Vanderbilt, the University of Missouri–Kansas City, and the University of Southern California have given us invaluable criticism, challenge, and support over the years. We're grateful to the many readers who have responded to our invitation to write and ask questions or share comments. Their input has made the book better in many ways. (The invitation is still open—our contact information is in "The Authors" section.) We wish we could personally thank all of the leaders and managers from whose experience we have profited in seminars, workshops, and consultations. Their knowledge and wisdom are the foundation and touchstone for our work.

As in the past, we owe much to our colleagues. Thanks again to all who helped us in the prior editions; your contribution still lingers in this work. But we particularly want to mention those who have made more recent contributions.

We have learned much from collaboration with a number of teaching fellows and graduate assistants at the University of Missouri–Kansas City; in particular, we are very grateful for the help of Mary Yung, Hooilin Chan, Vera Stoykova, and Zhou Yongjie. They all did an outstanding job helping us develop the citation analysis that appears in the Appendix, and Vera did excellent work on developing a test bank.

We wish we could thank all the colleagues and readers in the United States and around the world who have offered valuable comments and suggestions, but the list is long and our memories keep getting shorter. Elena Granell de Aldaz of the Institute for Advanced Study of Management in Caracas collaborated with us on developing a Spanish-language adaptation of *Reframing Organizations* as well as on a more recent project that studied frame orientations among managers in Venezuela. We are proud to consider her a valued colleague and wonderful friend. Bob Marx, of the University of Massachusetts, deserves special mention as a charter member of the frames family. Bob's interest in the frames, creativity in developing teaching designs, and eye for video material have aided our thinking and teaching immensely. Cdr. Gary Deal, USN; Maj. Kevin Reed, USAF; Dr. Peter Minich, a transplant surgeon; and Jan and Ron Haynes of FzioMed all provided valuable case material. The late Peter Frost of the University of British Columbia continues to inspire our work. Peter Vaill of the Antioch Graduate School has been a continuing source of ideas, support, and inspiration. Kent Peterson, University of Wisconsin at Madison, and Sharon Conley, University of California at Santa Barbara, are continuing sources of ideas and support. A number of individuals, including many friends and colleagues at the Organizational Behavior Teaching Conference, have given us helpful ideas and suggestions. We apologize for any omissions, but we want to thank Anke Arnaud, Carole K. Barnett, Max Elden, Kent Fairfield, Olivier Hermanus, Jim Hodge, Earlene Holland, Scott Johnson, Mark Kriger, Larry Levine, Hyoungbae Lee, Mark Maier, Magid Mazen, Thomas P. Nydegger, Dave O'Connell, Lynda St. Clair, Susan Twombly, and Pat Villeneuve. We only wish we had succeeded in implementing all the wonderful ideas we received from these and other colleagues.

Bill Eddy, dean emeritus of the Bloch School at the University of Missouri–Kansas City, gets special thanks for nurturing an environment that helps scholarship flourish. His successors on the leadership team at the Bloch School, including Al Page, Homer Erekson, Karyl Leggio and Lanny Solomon, have kept that tradition alive. Other current or former Bloch School colleagues who have helped more than they know are Dave Bodde, Nancy Day, Dick Heimovics, Bob Herman, Doranne Hudson, Deborah Noble, Stephen Pruitt, David Renz, Beth Smith, and Marilyn Taylor. Lee's colleagues in the Department of Organization, Leadership, and Marketing at the Bloch School have done their part, and he is grateful to Raj Arora, Gene Brown, Rita Cain, Pam Dobies, Mark Parry, Michael Song, and Rob Waris. Colleagues Carl Cohn, Stu Gothald, and Gib Hentschke of the University of Southern California offer both intellectual stimulation and moral support.

Others to whom our debt is particularly clear are Chris Argyris, Sam Bacharach, Cliff Baden, Estella Bensimon, Margaret Benefiel, Bob Birnbaum, Barbara Bunker, Tom Burks, Ellen Castro, Norma Saba Corey, Carlos Cortés, Linton Deck, Jim Honan, Tom Johnson (always a source of creative ideas), Bob Kegan, Grady McGonagill, Judy McLaughlin, John Meyer, Harrison Owen, Michael Sales, Dick Scott, Joan Vydra, Roy Williams, and Karl Weick. Thanks again to Dave Brown, Phil Mirvis, Barry Oshry, Tim Hall, Bill Kahn, and Todd Jick of the Brookline Circle, now in its third decade of searching for joy and meaning in lives devoted to the study of organizations.

Outside the United States, we are grateful to Poul Erik Mouritzen in Denmark; Rolf Kaelin, Cüno Pumpin, and Peter Weisman in Switzerland;

Ilpo Linko in Finland; Tom Case in Brazil; Einar Plyhn and Haakon Gran in Norway; Peter Normark and Dag Bjorkegren in Sweden; Ching-Shiun Chung in Taiwan; Anastasia Vitkovskaya in Russia; and H.R.H. Prince Philipp von und zu Lichtenstein.

Closer to home, Lee is very grateful to physical therapist Scott Knoche, whose intervention in a debilitating case of cervical radiculopathy produced near-miraculous results. Lee also owes more than he can say to Bruce Kay, whose genial and unflappable approach to work, coupled with high levels of organization and follow-through, have all had a wonderfully positive impact since he took on the challenge of bringing a modicum of order and sanity to Lee's professional functioning. We also continue to be grateful for the long-term support and friendship of Linda Corey, who still serves as our resident representative at Harvard, and Homa Aminmadani, who now lives part-time in Teheran.

Couples of the Edna Ranch Vintners Guild—the Schnackenbergs, Pescatores, Hayneses, and Beadles—link efforts with Terry in exploring the ups, downs, and mysteries of the art and science of wine making. Three professional wine makers, Bob Schiebelhut of Tolosa, Romeo "Meo" Zuech of Piedra Creek Winery, and Brett Escalera of Consilience and TresAnelli, offer advice that applies to leadership as well as wine making. Meo reminds us, "Never overmanage your grapes," and Brett prefaces answers to all questions with "It all depends."

We're delighted to be well into the third decade of our partnership with Jossey-Bass. We're grateful to the many friends who have helped us over the years, including Bill Henry, Steve Piersanti, Lynn Lychow, Bill Hicks, Debra Hunter, Cedric Crocker, Byron Schneider, and many others. In recent years, Kathe Sweeney has been a wonderful editor and even better friend, and we're delighted to be working with her again. Rob Brandt has done superb work keeping us organized enough for the editorial process to move forward. Beverly Peavler's keen eye, editorial judgment, and willingness to crack the whip gently have made for a much stronger manuscript.

We received many valuable suggestions from a diverse, knowledgeable, and talented team of outside reviewers: Hannah Carter (University of Florida), Matthew Eriksen (University of Tampa), James "Jae" Espey (Clemson), Chris Foley (University of Pennsylvania), Frank Hamilton (Eckerd College), Robert "Bob" Innes (Vanderbilt), and Kristi Loescher (University of Texas, Austin). We did not succeed in implementing all of their many excellent ideas, and they did not always agree among themselves, but the manuscript benefited in many ways from their input.

Lee's six children—Edward, Shelley, Lori, Scott, Christopher, and Bradley—all continue to enrich his life and contribute to his growth. He still wishes he could give them as much as they have given him. Brad has become a creative source of new ways to think about reframing, and Chris served as our consultant on contemporary music. Janie Deal Rice has delighted her father in becoming a fascinating and independent entrepreneur, running (with husband Jake, also mayor of Hagerman, Idaho) a catering business and bed and breakfast, Ein Tisch Inn. Janie has a rare talent of almost magically transforming simple ingredients into fine cuisine. Special mention also goes to Terry's parents, Bob and Dorothy Deal. His father is deceased and his mother is now in her nineties, but both lived long enough to be pleasantly surprised that their oft-wayward son could write a book.

We dedicate the book to our wives, who have more than earned all the credit and appreciation that we can give them. Joan Gallos, Lee's spouse and closest colleague, combines intellectual challenge and critique with support and love. She has been an active collaborator in developing our ideas, and her teaching manual for previous editions was a frame-breaking model for the genre. Her contributions have become so integrated into our own thinking that we are no longer able to thank her for all the ways that the book has gained from her wisdom and insights.

Sandy Deal's psychological training enables her to approach the field of organizations with a distinctive and illuminating slant. Her successful practice produces examples that have helped us make some even stronger connections to the concepts of clinical psychology. She is one of the most gifted diagnosticians in the field, as well as a delightful partner whose love and support over the long run have made all the difference. She is a rare combination of courage and caring, intimacy and independence, responsibility and playfulness.

To Joan and Sandy, thanks again. As the years accumulate, we love you even more.

June 2008

Lee G. Bolman
Kansas City, Missouri

Terrence E. Deal
San Luis Obispo, California

PART ONE

Making Sense of Organizations

Introduction

The Power of Reframing

Bob Nardelli expected to win the three-way competition to succeed management legend Jack Welch as CEO of General Electric. He was stunned when Welch told him late in 2000 that he'd never run GE. The next day, though, he found out that he'd won the consolation prize. A director of Home Depot called to tell him, "You probably could not feel worse right now, but you've just been hit in the ass with a golden horseshoe" (Sellers, 2002, p. 1).

Within a week, Nardelli hired on as Home Depot's new CEO. He was a big change from the free-spirited founders, who had built the wildly successful retailer on the foundation of an uninhibited, entrepreneurial "orange" culture. Managers ran their stores using "tribal knowledge," and customers counted on friendly, knowledgeable staff for helpful advice. Nardelli revamped Home Depot with a heavy dose of command-and-control management, discipline, and metrics. Almost all the top executives and many of the frontline managers were replaced, often by ex-military hires. At first, it seemed to work—profits improved, and management experts hailed the "remarkable set of tools" Nardelli used to produce "deep, lasting culture change" (Charan, 2006, p. 1). But the lasting change included a steady decline in employee morale and customer service. Where the founders had successfully promoted "make love to the customers," Nardelli's toe-the-line stance pummeled Home Depot to last place in its industry for customer satisfaction.

A growing chorus of critics harped about everything from the declining stock price to Nardelli's extraordinary $245 million in compensation. At Home Depot's 2006 shareholders' meeting, Nardelli hoped to keep naysayers at bay by giving them little time to say anything and refusing to respond to anything they did say: "It was, as even Home Depot executives will concede, a 37-minute fiasco. In a basement hotel ballroom in Delaware, with the board nowhere in sight and huge time displays on stage to cut off angry investors, Home Depot held a hasty annual meeting last year that attendees alternately described as 'appalling' and 'arrogant' " (Barbaro, 2007, p. C1). The outcry from shareholders and the business press was scathing. Nardelli countered with metrics to show that all was well. He seemed unaware or unconcerned that he had embarrassed his board, enraged his shareholders, turned off his customers, and reinforced his reputation for arrogance and a tin ear. Nardelli abruptly left Home Depot at the beginning of 2007 (Grow, 2007).

Nardelli's old boss, Jack Welch, called him the best operations manager he'd ever seen. Yet, as talented and successful as he was, Nardelli flamed out at Home Depot because he was only seeing part of the picture. He was a victim of one of the most common afflictions of leaders: seeing an incomplete or distorted picture as a result of overlooking or misinterpreting important signals. An extensive literature on business blunders attests to the pervasiveness of this lost-at-sea state (see, for example, Adler and Houghton, 1997; Feinberg and Tarrant, 1995; Ricks, 1999; Sobel, 1999).

Enron's demise provides another example of floundering in a fog. In its heyday, Enron proclaimed itself the "World's Leading Company"—with some justification. Enron had been a perennial honoree on *Fortune*'s list of "America's Most Admired Companies" and was ranked as the "most innovative" six years in a row (McLean, 2001, p. 60). Small wonder that CEO Kenneth W. Lay was among the nation's most admired and powerful business leaders. Lay and Enron were on a roll. What could be wrong with such a big, profitable, innovative, fast-growing company?

The trouble was that the books had been cooked, and the outside auditors were asleep at the switch. In December 2001, Enron collapsed in history's then-largest corporate bankruptcy. In the space of a year, its stock plunged from eighty dollars to eighty cents a share. Tens of billions of dollars in shareholder wealth evaporated. More than four thousand people lost their jobs and, in many cases, their savings and retirement funds.[1] The auditors also paid a steep price. Andersen Worldwide, a hundred-year-old firm with a once-sterling reputation, folded along with Enron.

What went wrong? After the cave-in, critics offered a profusion of plausible explanations. Yet Enron's leaders seemed shocked and baffled by the abrupt free fall. Former CEO Jeffrey K. Skilling, regarded as the primary architect of Enron's high-flying culture, was described by associates as "the ultimate control freak. The sort of hands-on corporate leader who kept his fingers on all the pieces of the puzzle" (Schwartz, 2002, p. C1). Skilling resigned for unexplained "personal reasons" only three months before Enron imploded. Many wondered if he had jumped ship because he foresaw the iceberg looming dead ahead. But after Enron's crash, he claimed, "I had no idea the company was in anything but excellent shape" (p. C1). Ultimately, in October 2006, both he and Lay were convicted of multiple counts of fraud for their role in Enron's disintegration. During their trials both steadfastly contended that they had done nothing wrong. Enron, they insisted, had been a sound and successful company brought down by forces they either weren't aware of or couldn't control. Despite public opinion to the contrary, both seemed to genuinely believe that they were victims rather than villains.

Skilling and Lay were both viewed as brilliant men, yet both sought refuge in cluelessness. It is easy to argue they claimed ignorance only because they had no better defense. Even so, they were out of touch at a deeper level. Lay and Skilling were passionate about building Enron into the "World's Leading Company." They staunchly believed that they had created a mold-breaking company with a revolutionary business model. They knew risks were involved, but you have to bend or break old rules when you're exploring uncharted territory. Investors bought the stock, and business professors wrote articles about the management lessons behind Enron's success. The snare was that Lay and Skilling had misread their world and had no clue that they were destroying the company they loved.

The curse of cluelessness is not limited to corporations—government provides its share of examples. In August 2005, Hurricane Katrina devastated New Orleans. Levees failed, and much of the city was underwater. Tens of thousands of people, many poor and black, found themselves stranded for days in desperate circumstances. Government agencies bumbled aimlessly, and help was slow to arrive. As Americans watched television footage of the chaos, they were stunned to hear the nation's top disaster official, the secretary of Homeland Security, tell reporters that he "had no reports" of things viewers had seen with their own eyes. It seemed he might have been better informed if he had relied on CNN rather than his own agency.

Homeland Security, Enron, and Home Depot represent only a few examples of an endemic challenge: how to know if you're getting the right picture or tuning in to the wrong channel. Managers often fail this test. Cluelessness is a fact of life, even for very smart people. Sometimes, the information they need is fuzzy or hard to get. Other times, they ignore or misinterpret information at hand. Decision makers too often lock themselves into flawed ways of making sense of their circumstances. For Lay and Skilling, it was a mistaken view that "we're different from everyone else—we're smarter." For Nardelli, it was his conviction that his metrics gave him the full picture.

In the discussion that follows, we explore the origins and symptoms of cluelessness. We introduce *reframing*—the conceptual core of the book and our basic prescription for sizing things up. Reframing requires an ability to think about situations in more than one way. We then introduce four distinct frames—structural, human resource, political, and symbolic—each logical and powerful in its own right. Together, they help us decipher the full array of significant clues, capturing a more comprehensive picture of what's going on and what to do.

VIRTUES AND DRAWBACKS OF ORGANIZED ACTIVITY

Before the emergence of the railroad and the telegraph in the mid-nineteenth century, individuals managed their own affairs—America had no multiunit businesses and no need for professional managers (Chandler, 1977). Explosive technological and social changes have produced a world that is far more interconnected, frantic, and complicated than it was in those days. Humans struggle to catch up, at continual risk of drowning in complexity that puts us "in over our heads" (Kegan, 1998). Forms of management and organization effective a few years ago are now obsolete. Sérieyx (1993) calls it the organizational big bang: "The information revolution, the globalization of economies, the proliferation of events that undermine all our certainties, the collapse of the grand ideologies, the arrival of the CNN society which transforms us into an immense, planetary village—all these shocks have overturned the rules of the game and suddenly turned yesterday's organizations into antiques" (pp. 14–15).

The proliferation of complex organizations has made most human activities collective endeavors. We grow up in families and then start our own families. We work for business or government. We learn in schools and universities. We worship in synagogues, churches, and mosques. We play sports in teams, franchises, and leagues. We join clubs and associations. Many of us will grow old and die in hospitals or nursing homes. We build these human enterprises because of what they can do for us. They offer goods, entertainment, social services, health care, and almost everything else that we use, consume, or enjoy.

All too often, however, we experience a darker side. Organizations can frustrate and exploit people. Too often, products are flawed, families are dysfunctional, students fail to learn, patients get worse, and policies backfire. Work often has so little meaning that jobs offer nothing beyond a paycheck. If we can believe mission statements and public pronouncements, every company these days aims to nurture its employees and delight its customers. But many miss the mark. Schools are blamed for social ills, universities are said to close more minds than they open, and government is criticized for red tape and rigidity. The private sector has its own problems. Automakers drag their feet about recalling faulty cars. Producers of food and pharmaceuticals make people sick with tainted products. Software companies deliver bugs and "vaporware." Industrial accidents dump chemicals, oil, toxic gas, and radioactive materials into the air and water. Too often, corporate greed and insensitivity create havoc for individual lives and communities. The bottom line: we seem hard-pressed to manage organizations so that their virtues exceed their vices. The big question: Why?

The Curse of Cluelessness

Year after year, the best and brightest managers maneuver or meander their way to the apex of enterprises great and small. Then they do really dumb things. How do bright people turn out so dim? One theory is that they're too smart for their own good. Feinberg and Tarrant (1995) label it the "self-destructive intelligence syndrome." They argue that smart people act stupid because of personality flaws—things like pride, arrogance, and unconscious desires to fail. It's true that psychological flaws have been apparent in such brilliant, self-destructive individuals as Adolph Hitler, Richard Nixon, and Bill Clinton. But on the whole, intellectually challenged people have as many psychological problems as the best and brightest. The primary source of cluelessness is not personality or IQ. We're at sea whenever our sense-making efforts fail us. If our image of a situation is wrong, our actions will be wide of the mark as well. But if we don't realize our image is incorrect, we won't understand why we don't get what we hoped for. So, like Bob Nardelli, we insist we're right even when we're off track.

Vaughan (1995), in trying to unravel the causes of the 1986 disaster that destroyed the *Challenger* space shuttle and killed its crew, underscored how hard it is for people to surrender their entrenched mental models: "They puzzle over contradictory evidence, but usually succeed in pushing it aside—until they come across a piece of evidence too fascinating to ignore, too clear to misperceive, too painful to deny, which makes vivid still other signals they do not want to see, forcing them to alter and surrender the world-view they have so meticulously constructed" (p. 235).

All of us sometimes construct our own psychic prisons, and then lock ourselves in. When we don't know what to do, we do more of what we know. This helps explain a number of unsettling reports from the managerial front lines:

- Hogan, Curphy, and Hogan (1994) estimate that the skills of one-half to three-quarters of American managers are inadequate for the demands of their jobs. But most probably don't realize it: Kruger and Dunning (1999) found that the more incompetent people are, the more they overestimate their performance, partly because they don't know what good performance looks like.

- About half of the high-profile senior executives companies hire fail within two years, according to a 2006 study (Burns and Kiley, 2007).

- In 2003, the United States was again the world's strongest economy, yet corporate America set a new record for failure with two of history's top three bankruptcies—WorldCom at $104 billion and Conseco at $61 billion. Charan and Useem (2002) trace such failures to a single source: "managerial error" (p. 52).

Small wonder that so many organizational veterans nod assent to Scott Adams's admittedly unscientific "Dilbert principle": "the most ineffective workers are systematically moved to the place where they can do the least damage—management" (1996, p. 14).

Strategies for Improving Organizations: The Track Record

We have certainly made an effort to improve organizations. Legions of managers report to work each day with that hope in mind. Authors and consultants spin out a flood of new answers and promising solutions. Policymakers develop laws and regulations to guide organizations on the right path.

The most common improvement strategy is upgrading management. Modern mythology promises that organizations will work splendidly if well managed. Managers are supposed to have the big picture and look out for their organization's overall health and productivity. Unfortunately, they have not always been equal to the task, even when armed with computers, information systems, flowcharts, quality programs, and a panoply of other tools and techniques. They go forth with this rational arsenal to try to tame our wild and primitive workplaces. Yet in the end, irrational forces too often prevail.

When managers cannot solve problems, they hire consultants. Today, the number and variety of advice givers is overwhelming. Most have a specialty: strategy, technology, quality, finance, marketing, mergers, human resource management, executive search, outplacement, coaching, organization development, and many more. For every managerial challenge, there is a consultant willing to offer assistance—at a price.

For all their sage advice and remarkable fees, consultants have yet to make a significant dent in problems plaguing organizations—businesses, public agencies, military services, hospitals, and schools. Sometimes the consultants are more hindrance than help, though they often lament clients' failure to implement their profound insights. McKinsey & Co., "the high priest of high-level consulting" (Byrne, 2002a, p. 66), worked so closely with Enron that managing partner Rajat Gupta sent his chief lawyer to Houston after Enron's collapse to see if his firm might be in legal trouble. The lawyer reported that McKinsey was safe, and a relieved Gupta insisted bravely, "We stand by all the work we did. Beyond that, we can only empathize with the trouble they are going through. It's a sad thing to see" (p. 68).

When managers and consultants fail, government frequently responds with legislation, policies, and regulations. Constituents badger elected officials to "do something" about a variety of ills: pollution, dangerous products, hazardous working conditions, and chaotic schools, to name a few. Governing bodies respond by making "policy." A sizable body of research records a continuing saga of perverse ways in which the implementation process distorts policymakers' intentions (Bardach, 1977; Elmore, 1978; Freudenberg and Gramling, 1994; Peters, 1999; Pressman and Wildavsky, 1973). Policymakers, for example, have been trying for decades to reform U.S. public schools. Billions of taxpayer dollars have been spent. The result? About the same as America's switch to the metric system. In the 1950s Congress passed legislation mandating adoption of the metric standards and measures. To date, progress has been minimal (see Chapter Eighteen). If you know what a hectare is, or can visualize the size of a three-hundred-gram package of crackers, you're ahead of most Americans. Legislators did not factor into their solution what it would take to get their decision implemented.

In short, difficulties surrounding improvement strategies are well documented. Exemplary intentions produce more costs than benefits. Problems outlast solutions. It is as if tens of thousands of hard-working, highly motivated pioneers keep hacking at a swamp that persistently produces new growth faster than the old can be cleared. To be sure, there are reasons for optimism. Organizations have changed about as much in the past few decades as in the preceding century. To survive, they had to. Revolutionary changes in technology, the rise of the global economy, and shortened product life cycles have spawned a flurry of activity to design faster, more flexible organizational forms. New organizational models flourish in companies such as Pret à Manger (the socially conscious U.K. sandwich shops), Google (a hot American company), and Novo-Nordisk (a Danish pharmaceutical company that includes environmental and social metrics in its bottom line). The dispersed collection of enthusiasts and volunteers who provide content for Wikipedia and the far-flung network of software engineers who have developed the Linux operating system provide dramatic examples of possibilities in the digital world. But despite such successes, failures are still too common. The nagging key question: How can leaders and managers improve the odds for themselves as well for their organizations?

FRAMING

Goran Carstedt, the talented executive who led the turnaround of Volvo's French division in the 1980s, got to the heart of a challenge managers face every day: "The world simply can't be made sense of, facts can't be organized, unless you have a mental model to begin with. That theory does not have to be the right one, because you can alter it along the way as information comes in. But you can't begin to learn without some concept that gives you expectations or hypotheses" (Hampden-Turner, 1992, p. 167). Such mental models have many labels—maps, mind-sets, schema, and cognitive lenses, to name a few.[2] Following the work of Goffman, Dewey, and others, we have chosen the label *frames*. In describing frames, we deliberately mix metaphors, referring to them as windows, maps, tools, lenses, orientations, filters, prisms, and perspectives, because all these images capture part of the idea we want to convey.

A frame is a mental model—a set of ideas and assumptions—that you carry in your head to help you understand and negotiate a particular "territory." A good frame makes it easier to know what you are up against and, ultimately, what you can do about it. Frames are vital because organizations don't come with computerized navigation systems to guide you turn-by-turn to your destination. Instead, managers need to develop and carry accurate maps in their heads.

Such maps make it possible to register and assemble key bits of perceptual data into a coherent pattern—a picture of what's happening. When it works fluidly, the process takes the form of "rapid cognition," the process that Gladwell (2005) examines in his best-seller *Blink*. He describes it as a gift that makes it possible to read "deeply into the narrowest slivers of experience. In basketball, the player who can take in and comprehend all that is happening around him or her is said to have 'court sense' " (p. 44).

Dane and Pratt (2007) describe four key characteristics of this intuitive "blink" process:

- It is nonconscious—you can do it without thinking about it and without knowing how you did it.

- It is very fast—the process often occurs almost instantly.

- It is holistic—you see a coherent, meaningful pattern.

- It results in "affective judgments"—thought and feeling work together so you feel confident that you know what is going on and what needs to be done.

The essence of this process is matching situational clues with a well-learned mental framework—a "deeply-held, nonconscious category or pattern" (Dane and Pratt, 2007, p. 37). This is the key skill that Simon and Chase (1973) found in chess masters—they could instantly recognize more than fifty thousand configurations of a chessboard. This ability enables grand masters to play twenty-five lesser opponents simultaneously, beating all of them while spending only seconds on each move.

The same process of rapid cognition is at work in the diagnostic categories physicians rely on to evaluate patients' symptoms. The Hippocratic Oath— "Above all else, do no harm"—requires physicians to be confident that they know what they're up against before prescribing a remedy. Their skilled judgment draws on a repertoire of categories and clues, honed by training and experience. But sometimes they get it wrong. One source of error is anchoring: doctors, like leaders, sometimes lock on to the first answer that seems right, even if a few messy facts don't quite fit. "Your mind plays tricks on you because you see only the landmarks you expect to see and neglect those that should tell you that in fact you're still at sea" (Groopman, 2007, p. 65).

Treating individual patients is hard, but managers have an even tougher challenge because organizations are more complex and the diagnostic categories less well defined. That means that the quality of your judgments depends on the information you have at hand, your mental maps, and how well you have learned to use them. Good maps align with the terrain and provide enough detail to keep you on course. If you're trying to find your way around downtown San Francisco, a map of Chicago won't help, nor one of California's freeways. In the same way, different circumstances require different approaches.

Even with the right map, getting around will be slow and awkward if you have to stop and study at every intersection. The ultimate goal is fluid expertise, the sort of know-how that lets you think on the fly and navigate organizations as easily as you drive home on a familiar route. You can make decisions quickly and automatically because you know at a glance where you are and what you need to do next.

There is no shortcut to developing this kind of expertise. It takes effort, time, practice, and feedback. Some of the effort has to go into learning frames and the ideas behind them. Equally important is putting the ideas to use. Experience, one often hears, is the best teacher, but that is only true if you reflect on it and extract its lessons. McCall, Lombardo, and Morrison (1988, p. 122) found that a key quality among successful executives was an "extraordinary tenacity in extracting something worthwhile from their experience and in seeking experiences rich in opportunities for growth."

Frame Breaking

Framing involves matching mental maps to circumstances. *Reframing* requires another skill—the ability to break frames. Why do that? A news story from the summer of 2007 illustrates. Imagine yourself among a group of friends enjoying dinner on the patio of a Washington, D.C., home. An armed, hooded intruder suddenly appears and points a gun at the head of a fourteen-year-old guest. "Give me your money," he says, "or I'll start shooting." If you're at that table, what do you do? You could try to break frame. That's exactly what Cristina "Cha Cha" Rowan did.

> "We were just finishing dinner," [she] told the man. "Why don't you have a glass of wine with us?"
>
> The intruder had a sip of their Chateau Malescot St-Exupéry and said, "Damn, that's good wine."
>
> The girl's father . . . told the intruder to take the whole glass, and Rowan offered him the bottle.
>
> The robber, with his hood down, took another sip and a bite of Camembert cheese. He put the gun in his sweatpants. . . .
>
> "I think I may have come to the wrong house," the intruder said before apologizing. "Can I get a hug?"
>
> Rowan . . . stood up and wrapped her arms around the would-be robber. The other guests followed.
>
> "Can we have a group hug?" the man asked. The five adults complied.
>
> The man walked away a few moments later with a filled crystal wine glass, but nothing was stolen, and no one was hurt. Police were called to the scene and found the empty wine glass unbroken on the ground in an alley behind the house [Associated Press, 2007].

In one stroke, Cha Cha Rowan redefined the situation from "we might all be killed" to "let's offer our guest some wine." Like her, artistic managers frame and reframe experience fluidly, sometimes with extraordinary results. A critic once commented to Cézanne, "That doesn't look anything like a sunset." Pondering his painting, Cézanne responded, "Then you don't see sunsets the way I do." Like Cézanne and Rowan, leaders have to find new ways to shift points of view when needed.

Like maps, frames are both windows on a territory and tools for navigation. Every tool has distinctive strengths and limitations. The right tool makes a job easier, but the wrong one gets in the way. Tools thus become useful only when a situation is sized up accurately. Furthermore, one or two tools may suffice for simple jobs, but not for more complex undertakings. Managers who master the hammer and expect all problems to behave like nails find life at work confusing and frustrating. The wise manager, like a skilled carpenter, wants at hand a diverse collection of high-quality implements. Experienced managers also understand the difference between possessing a tool and knowing when and how to use it. Only experience and practice bring the skill and wisdom to take stock of a situation and use suitable tools with confidence and skill.

The Four Frames

Only in the last half century have social scientists devoted much time or attention to developing ideas about how organizations work, how they should work, or why they often fail. In the social sciences, several major schools of thought have evolved. Each has its own concepts and assumptions, espousing a particular view of how to bring social collectives under control. Each tradition claims a scientific foundation. But a theory can easily become a theology that preaches a single, parochial scripture. Modern managers must sort through a cacophony of voices and visions for help.

Sifting through competing voices is one of our goals in writing this book. We are not searching for the one best way. Rather, we consolidate major schools of organizational thought into a comprehensive framework encompassing four perspectives. Our goal is usable knowledge. We have sought ideas powerful enough to capture the subtlety and complexity of life in organizations yet simple enough to be useful. Our distillation has drawn much from the social sciences—particularly sociology, psychology, political science, and anthropology. Thousands of managers and scores of organizations have helped us sift through social science research to identify ideas that work in practice. We have sorted insights from both research and practice into four major frames—structural, human resource, political, and symbolic (Bolman and Deal, 1984). Each is used by academics and practitioners alike and found on the shelves of libraries and bookstores.

Four Frames: As Near as Your Local Bookstore   Imagine a harried executive browsing in the management section of her local bookseller on a brisk winter day in 2008. She worries about her company's flagging performance and fears that her job might soon disappear. She spots the black-on-white spine of *The Last Link: Closing the Gap That Is Sabotaging Your Business* (Crawford, 2007). Flipping through the pages, she notices chapter titles like "Data," "Discipline," and "Linking It Together." She is drawn to phrases such as "It all comes down to one thing, doesn't it. Are you making your numbers?" and "a new formula for 21st-century business success." "This stuff may be good," the executive tells herself, "but it seems a little stiff."

Next, she finds *The SPEED of Trust: The One Thing That Changes Everything* (Covey and Merrill, 2006). Glancing inside, she reads, "Take communication. In a high-trust relationship, you can say the wrong thing and people will still get your meaning. In a low-trust relationship, you can be very measured, even precise, and they'll still misinterpret you." "Sounds nice," she mumbles, "but a little touchy-feely. Let's look for something more down to earth."

Continuing her search, she picks up *Secrets to Winning at Office Politics: How to Achieve Your Goals and Increase Your Influence at Work* (McIntyre, 2005). She scans chapter titles: "Forget Fairness, Look for Leverage," "Political Games: Moves and Countermoves," "Power, Power, Who Has the Power?" She chews over the book's key message—that we all engage in politics every day at work, even though we don't like to admit it. "Does it really all come down to politics?" she wonders. "It seems too cynical. Isn't there something more uplifting?"

She spots *The Starbucks Experience: 5 Principles for Turning Ordinary into Extraordinary* (Michelli, 2006). She ponders the five basic principles the book credits for the success of Starbucks: Make it your own. Everything matters. Surprise and delight. Embrace resistance. Leave your mark. She reads that these principles "remind all of us—you, me, the janitor, and the CEO—that we are responsible for unleashing a passion that ripples outward from behind the scenes, through the customer experience, and ultimately out into our communities" (p. 1). She wonders if such fervor can be sustained for long.

In her local bookstore, our worried executive has rediscovered the four perspectives at the heart of this book. Four distinct metaphors capture the essence of each of the books she examined: organizations as factories, families, jungles, and temples or carnivals.

Factories   The first book she stumbled on, *The Last Link,* provides counsel on how to think clearly and get organized, extending a long tradition that treats an organization as a factory. Drawing from sociology, economics, and management science, the structural frame depicts a rational world and emphasizes organizational architecture, including goals, structure, technology, specialized roles, coordination, and formal relationships. Structures—commonly depicted by organization charts—are designed to fit an organization's environment and technology. Organizations allocate responsibilities ("division of labor"). They then create rules, policies, procedures, systems, and hierarchies to coordinate diverse activities into a unified effort. Problems arise when structure doesn't line up well with current circumstances. At that point, some form of reorganization or redesign is needed to remedy the mismatch.

Families Our executive next encountered *The SPEED of Trust,* with its focus on interpersonal relationships. The human resource perspective, rooted in psychology, sees an organization as an extended family, made up of individuals with needs, feelings, prejudices, skills, and limitations. From a human resource view, the key challenge is to tailor organizations to individuals—finding ways for people to get the job done while feeling good about themselves and their work.

Jungles *Secrets to Winning at Office Politics* is a contemporary application of the political frame, rooted in the work of political scientists. It sees organizations as arenas, contests, or jungles. Parochial interests compete for power and scarce resources. Conflict is rampant because of enduring differences in needs, perspectives, and lifestyles among contending individuals and groups. Bargaining, negotiation, coercion, and compromise are a normal part of everyday life. Coalitions form around specific interests and change as issues come and go. Problems arise when power is concentrated in the wrong places or is so broadly dispersed that nothing gets done. Solutions arise from political skill and acumen—as Machiavelli suggested centuries ago in *The Prince* ([1514] 1961).

Temples and Carnivals Finally, our executive encountered *The Starbucks Experience,* with its emphasis on culture, symbols, and spirit as keys to organizational success. The symbolic lens, drawing on social and cultural anthropology, treats organizations as temples, tribes, theaters, or carnivals. It abandons assumptions of rationality prominent in other frames and depicts organizations as cultures, propelled by rituals, ceremonies, stories, heroes, and myths rather than rules, policies, and managerial authority. Organization is also theater: actors play their roles in the drama while audiences form impressions from what they see on stage. Problems arise when actors don't play their parts appropriately, symbols lose their meaning, or ceremonies and rituals lose their potency. We rekindle the expressive or spiritual side of organizations through the use of symbol, myth, and magic.

The FBI and the CIA: A Four-Frame Story

A saga of two squabbling agencies illustrates how the four frames provide different views of the same situation. Riebling (2002) documents the long history of head-butting between America's two intelligence agencies, the Federal Bureau of Investigation and the Central Intelligence Agency. Both are charged with combating espionage and terrorism, but the FBI's authority is valid within the United States, while the CIA's mandate covers everywhere else. Structurally, the FBI is housed in the Department of Justice and reports to the attorney general. The CIA reported through the director of central intelligence to the president until 2004, when a reorganization put it under a new director of national intelligence.

At a number of major junctures in American history (including the assassination of President John F. Kennedy, the Iran-Contra scandal, and the 9/11 terrorist attacks), each agency held pieces of a larger puzzle, but coordination snafus made it hard for anyone to see all the pieces, much less put them together. After 9/11, both agencies came under heavy criticism, and each blamed the other for lapses. The FBI complained that the CIA had known, but had failed to inform the FBI, that two of the terrorists had entered the United States and had been living in California since 2000 (Seper, 2005). But an internal Justice Department investigation also concluded that the FBI didn't do very well with the information it did get. Key signals were never "documented by the bureau or placed in any system from which they could be retrieved by agents investigating terrorist threats" (Seper, 2005, p. 1).

Structural barriers between the FBI and the CIA were exacerbated by the enmity between the two agencies' patron saints, J. Edgar Hoover and "Wild Bill" Donovan. When he first became FBI director in the 1920s, Hoover reported to Donovan, who didn't trust him and tried to get him fired. When World War II broke out, Hoover lobbied to get the FBI identified as the nation's worldwide intelligence agency. He fumed when President Franklin D. Roosevelt instead created a new agency and made Donovan its director. As often happens, cooperation between two units was chronically hampered by a rocky personal relationship between two top dogs who never liked one another.

Politically, the relationship between the FBI and CIA was born in turf conflict because of Roosevelt's decision to give responsibility for foreign intelligence to Donovan instead of Hoover. The friction persisted over the decades as both agencies vied for turf and funding from Congress and the White House.

Symbolically, different histories and missions led to very distinct cultures. The FBI, which built its image with the dramatic capture or killing of notorious gang leaders, bank robbers, and foreign agents, liked to pounce on suspects quickly and publicly. The CIA preferred to work in the shadows, believing that patience and secrecy were vital to its task of collecting intelligence and rooting out foreign spies.

Senior U.S. officials have recognized for many years that the conflict between the FBI and CIA damages U.S. security. But most initiatives to improve the relationship have been partial and ephemeral, falling well short of addressing the full range of issues.

Multiframe Thinking

The overview of the four-frame model in Exhibit 1.1 shows that each of the frames has its own image of reality. You may be drawn to some and repelled by others. Some perspectives may seem clear and straightforward, while others seem puzzling. But learning to apply all four deepens your appreciation and understanding of organizations. Galileo discovered this when he devised the first telescope. Each lens he added contributed to a more accurate image of the heavens.

Exhibit 1.1.
Overview of the Four-Frame Model.

	FRAME			
	STRUCTURAL	HUMAN RESOURCE	POLITICAL	SYMBOLIC
Metaphor for organization	Factory or machine	Family	Jungle	Carnival, temple, theater
Central concepts	Rules, roles, goals, policies, technology, environment	Needs, skills, relationships	Power, conflict, competition, organizational politics	Culture, meaning, metaphor, ritual, ceremony, stories, heroes
Image of leadership	Social architecture	Empowerment	Advocacy and political savvy	Inspiration
Basic leadership challenge	Attune structure to task, technology, environment	Align organizational and human needs	Develop agenda and power base	Create faith, beauty, meaning

Successful managers take advantage of the same truth. Like physicians, they reframe, consciously or intuitively, until they understand the situation at hand. They use more than one lens to develop a diagnosis of what they are up against and how to move forward.

This claim about the advantages of multiple perspectives has stimulated a growing body of research. Dunford and Palmer (1995) found that management courses teaching multiple frames had significant positive effects over both the short and long term—in fact, 98 percent of their respondents rated reframing as helpful or very helpful, and about 90 percent felt it gave them a competitive advantage. Other studies have shown that the ability to use multiple frames is associated with greater effectiveness for managers and leaders (Bensimon, 1989, 1990; Birnbaum, 1992; Bolman and Deal, 1991, 1992a, 1992b; Heimovics, Herman, and Jurkiewicz Coughlin, 1993, 1995; Wimpelberg, 1987).

Multiframe thinking requires moving beyond narrow, mechanical approaches for understanding organizations. We cannot count the number of times managers have told us that they handled some problem the "only way" it could be done. Such statements betray a failure of both imagination and courage and reveal a paralyzing fear of uncertainty. It may be comforting to think that failure was unavoidable and we did all we could. But it can be liberating to realize there is always more than one way to respond to any problem or dilemma. Those who master reframing report a sense of choice and power. Managers are imprisoned only to the extent that their palette of ideas is impoverished.

Akira Kurosawa's classic film *Rashomon* recounts the same event through the eyes of several witnesses. Each tells a different story. Similarly, organizations are filled with people who have their own interpretations of what is and should be happening. Each version contains a glimmer of truth, but each is a product of the prejudices and blind spots of its maker. No single story is comprehensive enough to make an organization truly understandable or manageable. Effective managers need multiple tools, the skill to use each, and the wisdom to match frames to situations.[3]

Lack of imagination—Langer (1989) calls it "mindlessness"—is a major cause of the shortfall between the reach and the grasp of so many organizations—the empty chasm between noble aspirations and disappointing results. The gap is painfully acute in a world where organizations dominate so much of our lives. The commission appointed by President George W. Bush to investigate the terrorist attacks of September 11, 2001, concluded that the strikes "should not have come as a surprise" but did because the "most important failure was one of imagination." Taleb (2007) depicts events like the 9/11 attacks as "black swans"— novel events that are unexpected because we have never seen them before. If every swan we've observed is white, we expect the same in the future. But fateful, make-or-break events are more likely to be situations we've never experienced before. Imagination is our best chance for being ready when a black swan sails into view, and multiframe thinking is a powerful stimulus to the broad, creative mind-set imagination requires.

Engineering and Art

Exhibit 1.2 presents two contrasting approaches to management and leadership. One is a rational-technical mind-set emphasizing certainty and control. The other is an expressive, artistic conception encouraging flexibility, creativity, and

---

Exhibit 1.2.
Expanding Managerial Thinking.

HOW MANAGERS THINK	HOW MANAGERS MIGHT THINK
They often have a limited view of organizations (for example, attributing almost all problems to individuals' flaws and errors).	They need a holistic framework that encourages inquiry into a range of significant issues: people, power, structure, and symbols.
Regardless of a problem's source, managers often choose rational and structural solutions: facts, logic, restructuring.	They need a palette that offers an array of options: bargaining as well as training, celebration as well as reorganization.
Managers often value certainty, rationality, and control while fearing ambiguity, paradox, and "going with the flow."	They need to develop creativity, risk taking, and playfulness in responses to life's dilemmas and paradoxes, focusing as much on finding the right question as the right answer, on finding meaning and faith amid clutter and confusion.
Leaders often rely on the "one right answer" and the "one best way"; they are stunned at the turmoil and resistance they generate.	Leaders need passionate, unwavering commitment to principle, combined with flexibility in understanding and responding to events.

---

interpretation. The first portrays managers as technicians; the second sees them as artists.

Artists interpret experience and express it in forms that can be felt, understood, and appreciated by others. Art embraces emotion, subtlety, ambiguity. An artist reframes the world so others can see new possibilities. Modern organizations often rely too much on engineering and too little on art in searching for quality, commitment, and creativity. Art is not a replacement for engineering but an enhancement. Artistic leaders and managers help us look beyond today's reality to new forms that release untapped individual energies and improve collective performance. The leader as artist relies on images as well as memos, poetry as well as policy, reflection as well as command, and reframing as well as refitting.

SUMMARY

As organizations have become pervasive and dominant, they have also become harder to understand and manage. The result is that managers are often nearly as clueless as the Dilberts of the world think they are. The consequences of myopic management and leadership show up every day, sometimes in small and subtle ways, sometimes in organizational catastrophes. Our basic premise is that a primary cause of managerial failure is faulty thinking rooted in inadequate ideas. Managers and those who try to help them too often rely on constricted models that capture only part of organizational life.

Learning multiple perspectives, or frames, is a defense against thrashing around without a clue about what you are doing or why. Frames serve multiple functions. They are filters for sorting essence from trivia, maps that aid navigation, and tools for solving problems and getting things done. This book is organized around four frames rooted in both managerial wisdom and social science knowledge. The structural approach focuses on the architecture of organization—the design of units and subunits, rules and roles, goals and policies. The human resource lens emphasizes understanding people, their strengths and foibles, reason and emotion, desires and fears. The political view sees organizations as competitive arenas of scarce resources, competing interests, and struggles for power and advantage. Finally, the symbolic frame focuses on issues of meaning and faith. It puts ritual, ceremony, story, play, and culture at the heart of organizational life.

Each of the frames is both powerful and coherent. Collectively, they make it possible to reframe, looking at the same thing from multiple lenses or points of view. When the world seems hopelessly confusing and nothing is working, reframing is a powerful tool for gaining clarity, regaining balance, generating new options, and finding strategies that make a difference.

NOTES

1. Enron's reign as history's greatest corporate catastrophe was brief. An even bigger behemoth, WorldCom, with assets of more than $100 billion, thundered into Chapter 11 seven months later, in July 2002. Stock worth more than $45 a share two years earlier fell to nine cents.

2. Among the possible ways of talking about frames are schemata or schema theory (Fiedler, 1982; Fiske and Dyer, 1985; Lord and Foti, 1986), representations (Frensch and Sternberg, 1991; Lesgold and Lajoie, 1991; Voss, Wolfe, Lawrence, and Engle, 1991), cognitive maps (Weick and Bougon, 1986), paradigms (Gregory, 1983; Kuhn, 1970), social categorizations (Cronshaw, 1987), implicit theories (Brief and Downey, 1983), mental models (Senge, 1990), definitions of the situation, and root metaphors.

3. A number of scholars (including Allison, 1971; Bergquist, 1992; Birnbaum, 1988; Elmore, 1978; Morgan, 1986; Perrow, 1986; Quinn, 1988; Quinn, Faerman, Thompson, and McGrath, 1996; and Scott, 1981) have made similar arguments for multiframe approaches to groups and social collectives.

Simple Ideas, Complex Organizations

Amerca's East Coast welcomed a crisp, sunny fall morning on September 11, 2001. For airline passengers in the Boston–Washington corridor, the perfect fall weather offered prospects of on-time departures and smooth flights. The promise would be broken for four flights, all bound for California. Like Pearl Harbor, 9/11 was a day that will live in infamy, a tragedy that changed America's sense of itself and the world. If we probe the how and why of 9/11, we find determined and resourceful terrorists, but we also find vulnerability and errors in organizations charged with detecting and preventing such catastrophes.

American Airlines flight 11 was first in the air, departing from Boston on time at 8:00 AM. United 175 followed at 8:15, ten minutes behind schedule. American 77, after a twenty-minute delay, left Washington-Dulles at 8:20 AM. Delayed forty minutes by congestion at Newark, United flight 93 departed at 8:42 AM.

The first sign that something was amiss for American 11 came less than fifteen minutes into the flight, when pilots stopped responding to input from air traffic controllers. For United 175, signs surfaced when the aircraft changed beacon codes, deviated from its assigned altitude, and failed to respond to New York air traffic controllers. American 77 departed from its assigned course at 8:54 AM, and attempts to communicate with the plane were futile. The last flight, United 93, followed a routine trajectory until the aircraft dropped precipitously. The captain radioed "Mayday," and controllers heard sounds of a violent struggle in the cockpit.

All four planes had been hijacked by teams of Al Quaeda terrorists who had managed to board the planes in spite of a security checkpoint system aimed at preventing such occurrences. In a meticulously planned scheme, the terrorists turned commercial aircraft into deadly missiles. Each aircraft was aimed at a high-profile target—New York's World Trade Center, the Pentagon, and the nation's Capitol. One by one, the planes slammed into their targets with devastating force. Only United 93 failed to reach its objective. A heroic passenger effort to regain control of the plane failed but thwarted the terrorists' intentions to ram the White House or Capitol building.

Why did no one foresee such a catastrophe? In fact, some had. As far back as 1993, security experts had envisioned an attempt to destroy the World Trade Center using airplanes as weapons. Such fears were reinforced when a suicidal pilot crashed a small private plane onto the White House lawn in 1994. But the mind-set of principals in the national security network was riveted on prior hijacks, which had almost always ended in negotiations. The idea of a suicide mission, using commercial aircraft as missiles, was never incorporated into homeland defense procedures.

America's homeland air defense system fell primarily under the jurisdiction of two government agencies: the Federal Aviation Administration (FAA) and the North American Aerospace Defense Command (NORAD). As the events of 9/11 unfolded, it became clear that these agencies' procedures to handle hijackings were inadequate. The controller tracking American 11, for example, began to suspect a hijacking early on and relayed the information to regional FAA headquarters, which began to follow its hijack protocol. As part of that protocol, a designated hijack coordinator could have requested a military fighter escort for the hijacked aircraft—but none was requested until too late.

At the same time, communication channels fell behind fast-moving events. Confusion at FAA headquarters resulted in a delay in informing NORAD about United 93. An interagency teleconference to provide coordination between the military and the FAA was hastily put together, but technical delays kept the FAA from participating. When NORAD asked for FAA updates, they got either no answer or incorrect information. Long after American 11 crashed into the World Trade Center, NORAD thought the flight was still headed toward Washington, D.C.

In the end, nineteen young men were able to outwit America's homeland defense systems. We can explain their success in part by pointing to their fanatical determination, meticulous planning, and painstaking preparation. Looking deeper, we can see a dramatic version of an old story: human error leading to tragedy. But if we look deeper still, we find that even the human-error explanation is too simple. In organizational life, there are almost always systemic causes upstream of human failures, and the events of 9/11 are no exception.

The nation had a web of procedures and agencies aimed at detecting and monitoring potential terrorists. Those systems failed, as did procedures designed to respond to aviation crises. Similar failures have marked other well-publicized disasters: nuclear accidents at Chernobyl and Three Mile Island, for example, and the botched response to Hurricane Katrina on the Gulf Coast in 2005. Each event illustrates a chain of error, miscommunication, and misguided actions.

Events like 9/11 and Katrina make headlines, but similar errors and failures happen every day. They rarely make front-page news, but they are all too familiar to people who work in organizations. The problem is that organizations are complicated, and communication among them adds another tangled layer. Reading messy situations accurately is not easy. In the remainder of this chapter, we explain why. We discuss how the fallacies of human thinking can obscure what's really going on and lead us astray. Then we describe some peculiarities of organizations that make them so difficult to figure out and manage.

COMMON FALLACIES IN EXPLAINING ORGANIZATIONAL PROBLEMS

Albert Einstein once said that a thing should be made as simple as possible, but no simpler. When we ask students and managers to analyze cases like 9/11 they often make things simpler than they really are. They do this by relying on one of three misleading, oversimplified one-size-fits-all concepts.

The first and most common is *blaming people.* This approach casts everything in terms of individual blunders. Problems result from bad attitudes, abrasive personalities, neurotic tendencies, stupidity, or incompetence. It's an easy way to explain anything that goes wrong. Once Enron went bankrupt, the hunt was on for someone to blame, and the top executives became the target of reporters, prosecutors, and talk-show comedians. One CEO said, "We want the bad guys exposed and the bad guys punished" (Toffler and Reingold, 2004, p. 229).

As children, we learned it was important to assign blame for every broken toy, stained carpet, or wounded sibling. Pinpointing the culprit is comforting. Assigning blame resolves ambiguity, explains mystery, and makes clear what must be done next: punish the guilty. Enron had its share of culpable individuals, some of whom eventually went to jail. But there is a larger story about the organizational and social context that set the stage for individual malfeasance. Targeting individuals while ignoring larger system failures oversimplifies the problem and does little to prevent its recurrence.

GREATEST HITS FROM ORGANIZATION STUDIES

Hit Number 10: James G. March and Herbert A. Simon, *Organizations* (New York: Wiley, 1958)

March and Simon's pioneering 1958 book *Organizations* sought to define a new field by offering a structure and language for studying organizations. It was part of the body of work that helped to earn Simon the 1978 Nobel Prize for economics.[1]

No brief summary can cover the range of topics March and Simon considered. They offered a cognitive, social-psychological view of organizational behavior with an emphasis on thinking, information processing, and decision making. The book begins with a model of behavior that presents humans as continually seeking to satisfy motives based on their aspirations. Aspirations at any given time are a function of both individuals' history and their environment. When aspirations are unsatisfied, people search until they find better, more satisfying options. Organizations influence individuals primarily by managing the information and options, or "decision premises," that they consider.

March and Simon followed Simon's earlier work (1947) in critiquing the economic view of "rational man," who maximizes utility by considering all available options and choosing the best. Instead, they argue that both individuals and organizations have limited information and restricted ability to process what is available. They never will know all the options. Instead, they gradually alter their aspirations as they search for alternatives. Instead of looking for the best option, "maximizing," individuals and organizations "satisfice," choosing the first option that is good enough.

Organizational decision making is additionally complicated because the environment is complex. Resources (time, attention, money, and so on) are scarce, and conflict among individuals and groups is constant. Organizational design happens through piecemeal bargaining that holds no guarantee of optimal rationality. Organizations simplify the environment to reduce the pressure on limited information-processing and decision-making capacities. They simplify by developing "programs"—standardized routines for performing repetitive tasks. Once a program is in place, the incentive is to stay with it as long as the results are marginally satisfactory. Otherwise, the organization is forced to expend time and energy to innovate. Routine tends to drive out innovation, because individuals find it easier and less taxing to devote limited time and energy to programmed tasks (which are automatic, well practiced, and more certain of success). Thus, a student facing a term-paper deadline may find it easier to "fritter"—make tea, rearrange the desk, check e-mail, and browse the Web—than to figure out how to write a good opening paragraph. A manager may sacrifice quality to avoid changing a well-established routine.

March and Simon's book falls primarily within the structural and human resource views. But their discussions of scarce resources, power, conflict, and bargaining recognize the reality of organizational politics. Although they do not use the term *framing*, March and Simon reaffirm its logic as an essential component of choice. Decision making, they argue, is always based on a simplified model of the world. Organizations develop unique vocabulary and classification schemes, which determine what people are likely to see and respond to. Things that don't fit an organization's mind-set are likely to be ignored or reframed into terms the organization can understand.

When it is hard to identify a guilty individual, a second popular option is *blaming the bureaucracy*. Things go haywire because organizations are stifled by rules and red tape—or because a lack of clear goals and roles creates chaos. One or the other explanation almost always applies. If things are out of control, then the system needs clearer rules and procedures, as well as tighter job descriptions. The 9/11 terrorist attacks could have been thwarted if agencies had had better protocols for such a terrorist attack. Tighter financial controls could have prevented Enron's free fall. The problem is that piling on rules and regulations typically leads to bureaucratic rigidity. Rules inhibit freedom and flexibility, stifle initiative, and generate reams of red tape. Could Enron have achieved its status as America's most innovative company if it had played by the old rules? When things become too tight, the solution is to "free up" the system so red tape and rigid rules don't stifle creativity and bog things down. But many organizations vacillate endlessly between being too loose and too tight.

A third fallacy attributes problems to *thirsting for power*. In the case of Enron, key executives were more interested in getting rich and expanding their turf than in advancing the company's best interests. The various agencies dealing with 9/11 all struggled prior to the disaster for their share of scarce federal resources. This view sees organizations as jungles teeming with predators and prey. Victory goes to the more adroit, or the more treacherous. Political games and turf wars cause most organizational problems. You need to play the game better than your opponents—and watch your backside.

Each of these three perspectives contains a kernel of truth but oversimplifies a knottier reality. Blaming people points to the perennial importance of individual responsibility. Some problems *are* caused by personal characteristics: rigid bosses, slothful subordinates, bumbling bureaucrats, greedy union members, or insensitive elites. Much of the time, though, condemning individuals blocks us from seeing system weaknesses and offers few workable options. If, for example, the problem really is someone's abrasive or pathological personality, what do we do? Even psychiatrists find it hard to alter character disorders, and firing everyone with a less-than-ideal personality is rarely a viable option. Training can go only so far in preparing people to carry out their responsibilities perfectly every time.

The blame-the-bureaucracy perspective starts from a reasonable premise: organizations are created to achieve specific goals. They are most effective when goals and policies are clear (but not excessive), jobs are well defined (but not constricting), control systems are in place (but not oppressive), and employees behave prudently (but not callously). If organizations always behaved that way, they would presumably work a lot better than most do. In practice, this perspective is better at explaining how organizations should work than why they often don't. Managers who cling to facts and logic become discouraged and frustrated when confronted by intractable irrational forces. Year after year, we witness the introduction of new control systems, hear of new ways to reorganize, and are dazzled by emerging management methods and gurus. Yet old problems persist, seemingly immune to every rational cure we devise. As March and Simon point out, rationality has limits.

The thirst-for-power view highlights enduring, below-the-surface features of organizations. Its dog-eat-dog logic offers a plausible analysis of almost anything that goes wrong. People both seek and despise power but find it a convenient way to explain problems. Within hours of the 9/11 terror attacks, a senior FBI official called Richard Clarke, America's counterterrorism czar, to tell him that many of the terrorists were known members of Al Quaeda. "How the f__k did they get on board then?" Clarke exploded. "Hey, don't shoot the messenger. CIA forgot to tell us about them." In the context of the long-running battle between the FBI and CIA, the underlying message of blame was clear: the CIA's self-interested concern with its own power caused this catastrophe.

The tendency to blame what goes wrong on people, the bureaucracy, or the thirst for power is part of our mental wiring. But there's much more to understanding a complex situation than assigning blame. Certain universal peculiarities of organizations make them especially difficult to sort out.

PECULIARITIES OF ORGANIZATIONS

Human organizations can be exciting and challenging places. At least, that's how they are often depicted in management texts, corporate annual reports, and fanciful managerial thinking. But in reality they can be deceptive, confusing, and demoralizing. It is a mistake to assume that organizations are either snake pits or rose gardens (Schwartz, 1986). Managers need to recognize characteristics of life at work that create opportunities for the wise as well as traps for the unwary. A case from the public sector provides a typical example:

DECEPTION AT WORK

Helen Demarco arrived in her office to discover a clipping from the local paper. The headline read, "Osborne Announces Plan." Paul Osborne had arrived two months earlier as Amtran's new chief executive. His mandate was to "revitalize, cut costs, and improve efficiency." After twenty years, Demarco had achieved a senior management position at the agency. She had little contact with Osborne, but her boss reported to him. Along with long-term colleagues, Demarco had been waiting apprehensively to learn what the new chief had in mind. She was startled as she read the newspaper account. Osborne's plan made technical assumptions directly related to her area of expertise. He might be a change agent, she thought, but he doesn't know much about our technology. She saw immediately the new plan's fatal flaws. *If he tries to implement this, it'll be the worst management mistake since the Edsel,* she thought to herself.

Two days later, Demarco and her colleagues received a memo instructing them to form a committee to work on the revitalization plan. When the group convened, everyone agreed the plan was crazy.

"What do we do?" someone asked.

"Why don't we just tell him it won't work?" said one hopeful soul.

"He's already gone public! You want to tell him his baby is ugly?"

"Not me. Besides, he already thinks a lot of us are deadwood. If we tell him it's no good, he'll just think we're defensive."

"Well, we can't just go ahead with it. We'd be throwing away money and it'll never work!"

"That's true," said Demarco thoughtfully. "But what if we tell him we're conducting a study of how to implement the plan?"

Her suggestion was approved overwhelmingly. The group informed Osborne that a study was under way. They even got a substantial budget to support their "research." No one mentioned the study's real purpose: buy time and find a way to minimize the damage without alienating the boss.

Over time, the group developed a strategy. Members assembled a lengthy technical report, filled with graphs, tables, and impenetrable jargon. The report offered Osborne two options. Option A, his original plan, was presented as technically feasible but expensive—well beyond anything Amtran could afford. Option B, billed as a "modest downscaling" of the original plan, was projected as a more cost-effective alternative.

When Osborne pressed the group on the huge cost disparity between the two proposals, he received a barrage of technical language and complicated cost-benefit projections. No one mentioned that even Option B offered few benefits at a very high cost. Osborne argued and pressed for more information. But given the apparent facts, he agreed to proceed with Option B. The plan required several years to implement, and Osborne moved on before it became operational. Even so, the "Osborne plan" was widely heralded as another instance of Paul Osborne's talent for revitalizing ailing organizations.

Helen Demarco came away with deep feelings of frustration and failure. The Osborne plan, in her view, was a wasteful mistake, and she had knowingly participated in a charade. "But," she rationalized to herself, "I really didn't have much choice. Osborne was determined to go ahead. It would have been career suicide to try to stop him."

Demarco had other options, but she couldn't see them. She and Paul Osborne both thought they were on track. They were tripped up in part by human fallibility, but even more important, by how hard it can be to understand organizations. The first step in managerial wisdom and artistry is to recognize key characteristics of organizations. Otherwise, managers are persistently surprised and caught off guard.

First, *organizations are complex.* They are populated by people, whose behavior is notoriously hard to predict. Large organizations in particular include a bewildering array of people, departments, technologies, and goals. Moreover, organizations are open systems dealing with a changing, challenging, and erratic environment. Things can get even more knotty across multiple organizations. The 9/11 disaster resulted from a chain of events that involved several separate systems. Almost anything can affect everything else in collective activity, generating causal knots that are hard to untangle. After an exhaustive investigation, our picture of 9/11 is woven from sundry evidence, conflicting testimony, and conjecture.

Second, *organizations are surprising.* What you expect is often not what you get. Paul Osborne saw his plan as a bold leap forward; Helen and her group considered it an expensive albatross. In their view, Osborne made matters *worse* by trying to improve them. He might have achieved better results by spending more time with his family and leaving things at work alone. And imagine the shock of Enron's executives when things fell apart. Until shortly before the bottom fell out, the company's leadership team appeared confident they were building a pioneering model of corporate success. Many analysts and management professors shared their optimism.

The solution to yesterday's problems often creates future obstacles. A friend of ours was president of a retail chain. In the firm's early years, he had a problem with two sisters who worked in the same store. To prevent this from recurring, he established a nepotism policy prohibiting members of the same family from working for the company. Years later, two key employees met at work, fell in love, and began to live together. The president was stunned when they asked if they could get married without being fired. As in this case, today's sensible choice may turn into tomorrow's regret. Taking action in a cooperative venture is like shooting a wobbly cue ball into a scattered array of self-directed billiard balls. Balls career in so many directions that it is impossible to know how things will eventually sort out.

Third, *organizations are deceptive.* They camouflage mistakes and surprises. After 9/11, America's homeland defense organizations tried to conceal their lack of preparedness and confusion for fear of revealing strategic weaknesses. Enron raised financial camouflage to an art form with a series of sophisticated partnerships (carrying *Star Wars* names like Chewco, Jedi, and Kenobe). Helen Demarco and her colleagues disguised obfuscation as technical analysis in hopes of fooling the boss.

It is tempting to blame deceit on individual character flaws. Yet Helen Demarco disliked fraud and regretted cheating—she simply believed she had no other alternative. Sophisticated managers know that what happened to Paul Osborne happens all the time. When a quality initiative fails or a promising product tanks, subordinates often either clam up or cover up. They fear that the boss will not listen or will punish them for being insubordinate. Thus early warnings that terrorists might commandeer commercial airliners went unvoiced or unheeded. Internal naysayers at Enron were silenced until dissenters "blew the whistle" publicly. A friend in a senior position in a large government agency put it simply: "Communications in organizations are rarely candid, open, or timely."

Fourth, *organizations are ambiguous.* Complexity, unpredictability, and deception generate rampant ambiguity, a dense fog that shrouds what happens from day to day. Figuring out what is really going on in businesses, hospitals, schools, or public agencies is not easy. It is hard to get the facts and, if you pin them down, even harder to know what they mean or what to do about them. Helen Demarco never knew how Paul Osborne really felt, how receptive he was to other points of view, or how open he was to compromise. She and her peers piled on more mystery by conspiring to keep him in the dark. As the 9/11 case illustrates, when you incorporate additional organizations into the human equation, uncertainty mushrooms.

Ambiguity has many sources. Sometimes available information is incomplete or vague. Different people may interpret the same information in a variety of ways, depending on mind-sets and organizational doctrines. At other times, ambiguity is intentionally manufactured as a smoke screen to conceal problems or steer clear of conflict. Much of the time, events and processes are so intricate, scattered, and uncoordinated that no one can fully understand—let alone control—the real truth. Exhibit 2.1 lists some of the most important sources of organizational uncertainty.

Exhibit 2.1.
Sources of Ambiguity.

- We are not sure what the problem is.
- We are not sure what is really happening.
- We are not sure what we want.
- We do not have the resources we need.
- We are not sure who is supposed to do what.
- We are not sure how to get what we want.
- We are not sure how to determine if we have succeeded.

Source: Adapted from McCaskey (1982).

ORGANIZATIONAL LEARNING

How can lessons be extracted from surroundings that are complex, surprising, deceptive, and ambiguous? It isn't easy. Yet turbulent, rapidly shifting situations require organizations to learn better and faster. Michael Dell, founder and CEO of Dell Computer Corporation, explained it this way: "In our business, the product cycle is six months, and if you miss the product cycle, you've missed the opportunity. In this business, there are two kinds of people, really: the quick and the dead" (Farkas and De Backer, 1996).

With stakes so high, how organizations learn from experience has become a timely topic. Decades ago, scholars debated whether the idea of organizational learning made sense: Could organizations actually learn, or was learning inherently individual? That debate lapsed as experience verified instances where individuals learned and organizations didn't, or vice versa. Complex firms such as Microsoft, Toyota, and British Airways have "learned" capabilities far beyond individual knowledge. Lessons are enshrined in acknowledged protocols and shared cultural codes and traditions. At the same time, individuals often learn when systems cannot.

From the late 1980s onward, senior officials in China recognized that the nation was heading in two contradictory directions, promoting capitalism economically while defending communism politically. Behind the scenes, party members began an urgent search for a way to bridge the gap between rival ideologies. Publicly, though, the party tamped down dissent and argued that capitalism was one more sign of socialist progress (Kahn, 2002). Most knew the party was on the road to perdition, but the system obscured that reality.

Several perspectives on organizational learning are exemplified in the work of Peter Senge (1990), Barry Oshry (1995), and Chris Argyris and Donald Schön (1978, 1996). Senge sees a core learning dilemma: "We learn best from our experience, but we never directly experience the consequences of many of our decisions" (p. 23). Learning is relatively easy when the link between cause and effect is clear. But complex systems often sever that connection: causes remote from effects, solutions detached from problems, and feedback delayed or misleading (Cyert and March, 1963; Senge, 1990). At home, you flip a switch and the light goes on. In an organization, you flip the switch and nothing happens—or a toilet may flush in a distant building. You are still in the dark, and the user of the toilet is unpleasantly surprised. To understand what is going on, you need to master the system's circular causality.

Senge emphasizes the value of "system maps" that clarify how a system works. Consider the system created by "Chainsaw Al" Dunlap, CEO of Scott Paper in the early 1990s. Dunlap was proud of his nickname and his turnaround at Scott. He raised profits and market value substantially by slashing head count and cutting frills such as research and development. But he rarely acknowledged Scott's steady loss of market share (Byrne, 1996). It is one of many examples of actions that look good until long-term costs become apparent. A corresponding systems model might look like Exhibit 2.2. The strategy might be cutting training to improve short-term profitability, drinking martinis to relieve stress, offering rebates to

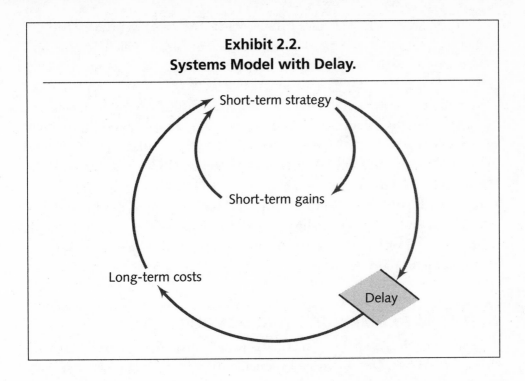

Exhibit 2.2.
Systems Model with Delay.

Short-term strategy

Short-term gains

Long-term costs

Delay

entice customers, or borrowing from a loan shark to cover gambling debts. In each case, what seems to work in the moment creates long-term costs down the line.

Oshry (1995) agrees that system blindness is widespread but highlights causes rooted in troubled relationships between groups that have little grasp of what's above or below their level. Top managers feel overwhelmed by complexity, responsibility, and overwork. They are chronically dissatisfied with subordinates' lack of initiative and creativity. Middle managers, meanwhile, feel trapped between contradictory signals and pressures. The top tells them to take risks but then punishes mistakes. Their subordinates expect them to shape up the boss and improve working conditions. Top and bottom tug in opposite directions, causing those in between to feel pulled apart, confused, and weak. At the bottom, workers feel helpless, unacknowledged, and demoralized. "They give us lousy jobs and pay, and order us around—never telling us what's really going on. Then they wonder why we don't love our work." If you cannot step back and see how system dynamics create these patterns, you muddle along blindly, unaware of better options.

Both Oshry and Senge argue that our failure to read system dynamics traps us in a cycle of blaming and self-defense. Problems are always caused by someone else. Unlike Senge, who sees gaps between cause and effect as primary barriers to learning, Argyris and Schön (1978, 1996) emphasize individuals' fears and defenses. As a result, "the actions we take to promote productive organizational learning actually inhibit deeper learning" (1996, p. 281).

According to Argyris and Schön, our behavior obstructs learning because we avoid undiscussable issues and tiptoe around organizational taboos. Our actions often seem to work in the short run because we avoid conflict and discomfort, but we create a double bind. We can't solve problems without dealing with problems we have tried to hide, but tackling them would expose our cover-up. Facing that double bind, Helen Demarco and her colleagues chose to disguise their scheme. The end result is escalating games of sham and deception. This is what happened at Enron, where desperate maneuvers to obscure the truth made the day of reckoning more catastrophic.

COPING WITH AMBIGUITY AND COMPLEXITY

Organizations deal with a complicated and uncertain environment by trying to make it simpler. One approach to simplification is to develop better systems and technology to collect and process information. Another is to break complex issues into smaller chunks and assign slices to specialized individuals or units. Still another approach is to hire or develop professionals with sophisticated expertise in handling thorny problems. These and other methods are helpful but not always sufficient. Despite the best efforts, unanticipated—and sometimes appalling—events still happen. The key in dealing with these events is developing better mental maps to anticipate complicated and unforeseeable problems.

You See What You Expect

On April 14, 1994, three years after the first Gulf War ended, two U.S. F-15C fighter jets took off from a base in Turkey to patrol the no-fly zone in northern Iraq. Their mission was to "clear the area of any hostile aircraft" (Snook, 2000, p. 4). The zone had not been violated in more than two years, but Iraqi antiaircraft fire was a continuing risk, and the media speculated that Saddam Hussein might be moving a large force north. At 10:22 AM, the fighter pilots reported to AWACS (Airborne Warning and Control System) controllers that they had made radar contact with two slow, low-flying aircraft. Unable to identify the aircraft electronically, the pilots descended for visual identification. The lead pilot,

Tiger 01, spotted two "Hinds"—Soviet-made helicopters used by the Iraqis. He reported his sighting, and an AWACS controller responded, "Copy, 2 Hinds" (p. 6). The fighters circled back to begin a firing run. They informed AWACS they were "engaged," and, at 10:30 AM, shot down the two helicopters.

Destroying enemy aircraft is the fighter pilots' grail. Only later did the two learn that they had destroyed two American UH-60 Black Hawk helicopters, killing all twenty-six U.N. relief workers aboard. How could experienced, highly trained pilots make such an error? Snook (2000) offers a compelling explanation. The two types of aircraft had different paint colors—Hinds tan, Black Hawks forest green—and the Black Hawks had American flags painted on the fuselage. But the Black Hawks' camouflage made them difficult to see against the terrain, particularly for fighters flying very fast at high altitudes. Visual identification required flying at a dangerously low altitude in a mountain-walled valley. The fighter pilots were eager to get above the mountains as quickly as possible. An extensive postmortem confirmed that the Black Hawks would have been difficult to identify. The pilots did the normal human thing in the face of ambiguous perceptual data: they filled in gaps based on what they knew, what they expected, and what they wanted to see. "By the time Tiger 01 saw the helicopters, he already *believed* that they were enemy. All that remained was for him to selectively match up incoming scraps of visual data with a reasonable cognitive scheme of an enemy silhouette" (p. 80).

Recall that in Chapter One, we described the "blink" process of rapid cognition. The essence of this process is matching situational cues with a well-learned mental model—a "deeply-held, nonconscious category or pattern" (Dane and Pratt, 2007, p. 37). While necessary and useful, quick judgments are not foolproof. Their accuracy depends on available clues, expectations, and patterns in the decision maker's repertory. All of these presented problems for the fighter pilots. The perceptual data were hard to read, and expectations were prejudiced by a key missing clue—no mention of friendly helicopters. Even though situation analysis plays a pivotal role in their training, pilots lacked adequate diagnostic schemata for distinguishing Hinds from Black Hawks. All this made it easy for them to conclude that they were seeing enemy aircraft.

Making Sense of What's Going On

Some events are so clear and unambiguous that it is easy for people to agree on what is going on. Determining if a train is on schedule, if a plane landed safely, or if a clock is keeping accurate time is straightforward. But most of the important issues confronting managers are not so clear-cut. Solid facts and simple problems in everyday life at work are scarce. Will a reorganization work? Was a meeting successful? Why did a consensual decision backfire? In trying to make sense of complicated and ambiguous situations, we—like the F-15C fighter pilots—depend very much on our frames, or mind-sets, to give us a full reading of what we are up against. But snap judgments work only if we have adequately sized up the situation.

Since our interpretations depend so much on our cognitive repertoires, expectations, beliefs, and values, our internal world is as important as what is outside—sometimes more so. The fuzziness of everyday life makes it easy for people to shape the world to conform to their favored internal schemata. As noted by DeBecker, "Many experts lose the creativity and imagination of the less informed. They are so intimately familiar with known patterns that they may fail to recognize or respect the importance of a new wrinkle" (1997, p. 30). In such cases, snap judgments work against, rather than for, the person who is trying to figure things out.

Managers regularly face an unending barrage of puzzles or "messes." To act without creating more trouble, they must first grasp an accurate picture of what is happening. Then they must move quickly to a deeper level, asking, "What is *really* going on here?" That's the main objective of teaching pilots the art of situational analysis. But this important step in reading a situation is often overlooked. As a result, managers too often form superficial analyses and leap on the solutions nearest at hand or most in vogue. Market share declining? Try strategic planning. Customer complaints? Put in a quality program. Profits down? Time to reengineer or downsize.

A better alternative is to think, to probe more deeply into what is really going on, and to develop an accurate diagnosis. The process is more intuitive than analytic: "[It] is in fact a cognitive process, faster than we recognize and far different from the step-by-step thinking we rely on so willingly. We think conscious thought is somehow better, when in fact, intuition is soaring flight compared to the plodding of logic" (DeBecker, 1997, p. 28). The ability to size up a situation quickly is at the heart of leadership. Admiral Carlisle Trost, former chief of naval operations, once remarked, "The first responsibility of a leader is to figure out what is going on. . . . That is never easy to do because situations are rarely black or white, they are a pale shade of gray . . . they are seldom neatly packaged."

It all adds up to a simple truth that is easy to overlook. The world we perceive is, for the most part, constructed internally. The ideas, or theories, we hold determine whether a given situation is foggy or clear, mildly interesting or momentous, a paralyzing disaster or a genuine learning experience. Personal theories are essential because of a basic fact about human perception: in any situation, there is simply too much happening for us to attend to everything. To help us understand what is going on and what to do next, well-grounded, deeply ingrained personal theories offer two advantages: they tell us what is important and what can be safely ignored, and they group scattered bits of information into manageable patterns.

The Dilemma of Changing or Conserving

To a nonpilot, a commercial airliner's cockpit is a confusing array of controls, switches, and gauges. Yet an experienced pilot can discern the aircraft's status at a glance. Like other professionals, a pilot learns patterns that cluster seemingly fragmented bits of information into a clear picture. The patterns take many hours to learn, but once learned, they help the pilot size things up with ease, speed, and accuracy. In the same way, an experienced manager can read a situation very rapidly, decide what needs to be done, and make it happen.

The good and bad news is that, right or wrong, our theories shield us from confusion, uncertainty, and anxiety. Tiger 01, for example, knew exactly what to do because he believed what he saw. We rely on the theories we have, and, in the heat of the moment, it's not easy to recognize when we are making a big mistake if we feel confident in our judgment. But, as Gladwell writes: "Our snap judgments and first impressions can be educated and controlled" to shift the odds in our favor (2005, p. 15).

This learning needs to happen before we find ourselves in make-or-break situations. When the stakes are high, we have tried every lens we know, and nothing works, we get anxious and stuck. We are caught in a dilemma: holding on to old patterns is ineffective, but developing new mental models is difficult. It is also risky; it might lead to analysis paralysis and further erosion of our confidence and effectiveness.

This dilemma exists even if we see no flaws in our current mind-set, because our theories are self-sealing filters—they block us from recognizing our errors. Extensive research documents the many ways in which individuals spin reality to protect existing beliefs (see, for example, Garland, 1990; Kühberger, 1995; Staw and Hoang, 1995). This helps to explain why Enron's Ken Lay insisted he had done the right thing, even though his company collapsed. Heath and Gonzalez (1995) found that decision makers rely on others more to strengthen preconceived thinking than to gain new information. Tetlock (2000) showed that managers' judgments of performance were influenced by cognitive preferences and political ideologies. Extensive research on the "framing effect" (Kahneman and Tversky, 1979) shows how powerful subtle cues can be. Relatively modest changes in how a problem or decision is framed can have a dramatic impact on how people respond (Shu and Adams, 1995; Gegerenzer, Hoffrage, and Kleinbölting, 1991). Decision makers, for example, tend to respond more favorably to an option that has a "70 percent chance of success" than one that has a "30 percent chance of failure," even though they are statistically identical.

Many of us recognize that our mental maps influence how we interpret the world. Less widely understood is that what we expect often determines what we get. Rosenthal and Jacobson (1968) studied schoolteachers who were told that certain students in their classes were "spurters"—students who were "about to bloom." The so-called spurters had been randomly selected but still achieved above-average gains on achievement tests. They really *did* spurt. Somehow the teachers' expectations were communicated to and assimilated by the students. Modern medical science is still trying to understand the power of the placebo effect—the power of sugar pills to make people better. Results are attributed to an unexplained change in the patient's belief system. Patients believe they will get better; therefore they do. Similar effects have been replicated in countless reorganizations, new product launches, and new approaches to performance appraisal. All these examples show how hard it is to disentangle the reality out there from the models in our minds.[2]

In Western cultures, particularly, there is a tendency to embrace one theory or ideology and to try to make the world conform. If it works, we persist in our view. If discrepancies arise, we try to rationalize them away. If people challenge our view, we ignore them or put them in their place. Only poor results over a long period of time call our theories into question. Even then, we often simply entrench ourselves in a new worldview, triggering the cycle again.

Japan has four major religions, each with unique beliefs and assumptions: Buddhism, Confucianism, Shintoism, and Taoism. Though the religions differ greatly in history, traditions, and basic tenets, many Japanese feel no need to choose only one. They use all four, taking advantage of the strengths of each for suitable purposes or occasions. The four frames can play a similar role for managers in modern organizations. Rather than portraying the field of organizational theory as fragmented, we present it as pluralistic. Seen this way, the field offers a rich assortment of lenses for viewing organizations. Each theoretical tradition is helpful. Each has blind spots. Each tells its own story about organizations. The ability to shift nimbly from one to another helps redefine situations so they become understandable and manageable. The ability to reframe is one of the most powerful capacities of great artists. It can be equally powerful for managers. Undergraduates at Vanderbilt University captured this in a class-initiated rap (for best results, rap fans might imagine the rapper Common doing these lines in a neo-soul, hip-hop style):

Reframe, reframe, put a new spin on
the mess you're in.
Reframe, reframe, try to play a different game.
Reframe, reframe, when you're in a tangle,
shoot another angle;
look at things a different way.

SUMMARY

Because organizations are complex, surprising, deceptive, and ambiguous, they are formidably difficult to comprehend and manage. Our preconceived theories and images determine what we see, what we do, and how we judge what we accomplish. Narrow, oversimplified perspectives become fallacies that cloud rather than illuminate managerial action. The world of most managers and administrators is a world of messes: complexity, ambiguity, value dilemmas, political pressures, and multiple constituencies. For managers whose images blind them to important parts of this chaotic reality, it is a world of frustration and failure. For those with better theories and the intuitive capacity to use them with skill and grace, it is a world of excitement and possibility. A mess can be defined as both a troublesome situation and a group of people who eat together. The core challenge of leadership is to move an organization from the former to something more like the latter.

In succeeding chapters, we look at four perspectives, or frames, that have helped managers and leaders find clarity and meaning amid the confusion of organizational life. The frames are grounded in cool-headed management science and tempered by the heat of actual practice. We cannot guarantee your success as a manager or a change agent. We believe, though, that you can improve your odds with an artful appreciation of how to use the four lenses to understand and influence what's really going on.

NOTES

1. We used citation analysis (how often a work is referenced in the scholarly literature) to develop a list of "scholars' greatest hits"—the works that organizational scholars rely on most. The Appendix shows our results and discusses how we developed our analysis. At appropriate points in the book (where the ideas are most relevant, as here), we present a brief summary of key ideas from works at the top of our list.

2. These examples all show thinking influencing reality. A social constructivist perspective goes a step further to say that our thinking *constructs* social reality. In this view, an organization exists not "out there" but in the minds and actions of its constituents. This idea is illustrated in an old story about a dispute among three baseball umpires. The first says, "Some's balls, and some's strikes, and I calls 'em like they are." The second counters, "No, you got it wrong. Some's balls, and some's strikes, and I calls 'em the way I sees them." The third says, "You guys don't really get it. Some's balls, and some's strikes, but they ain't nothing until I call them." The first umpire is a realist who believes that what he sees is exactly what is. The second recognizes that reality is influenced by his own perception. The third is the social constructivist—his call makes them what they are. This distinction is particularly important in the symbolic frame, which we return to in Chapter Twelve.

The Structural Frame

A frame, as explained in Chapter Two, is a coherent set of ideas forming a prism or lens that enables you to see and understand more clearly what goes on from day to day. In Part Two, we embark on the first stage of a tour of four different ways of making sense of life at work—or anywhere else. Each frame is presented in three chapters: one that introduces the basic concepts and two that focus on key applications and extensions. We begin with one of the oldest and most popular ways of thinking about organizations, the structural frame.

If someone asked you to describe your organization—your workplace, your school, or even your family—what image would come to mind? A likely possibility is a traditional organization chart: a series of boxes and lines depicting job responsibilities and levels. The chart might be shaped roughly like a pyramid, with a small number of authorities at the top and a much larger number of grunts at the bottom. Such a chart is only one of many images that reflect the structural view. The frame is rooted in traditional rational images but goes much deeper to develop versatile and powerful ways to understand social architecture and its consequences.

We begin Chapter Three with two cases contrasting the structural features of a highly disciplined aircraft carrier with the structural lapses that hampered rescue efforts in New York City's 9/11 terrorist attacks. We then highlight the basic assumptions of the structural view with emphasis on two key dimensions: dividing work and coordinating it thereafter. We emphasize how structural design depends on an organization's circumstances, including its goals, technology, and environment. In addition, we show why tightly controlled, top-down forms may work in simple, stable situations but fall short in more fluid and ambiguous ones.

In Chapter Four, we turn to issues of structural change and redesign. We describe basic structural tensions, explore alternatives to consider when new circumstances require revisions, and discuss challenges of the restructuring process. We close the chapter with examples of successful structural change.

Finally, in Chapter Five, we apply structural concepts to groups and teams. When teams work poorly, members often blame one another for problems that reflect configuration rather than individual failings. We begin by examining structural arrangements in five-person teams. Then we contrast the games of baseball, American football, and basketball to show how optimal structure depends on what a team is trying to do and under what conditions. We close by examining the architectural design of high-performance teams.

Getting Organized

"I t might have looked like chaos, but we always knew what was going on," says Commander Gary Deal about his service on the aircraft carrier *USS Kennedy*.[1] In Commander Deal's panoramic view from the bridge, a complex, fast-moving flight deck was relatively easy to read and manage. When fully equipped for deployment, the *Kennedy* was home to more than five thousand men and women. About half were assigned to the ship and half to the carrier's air wing. The ship was organized into nineteen departments, while the air wing had nine squadrons. The flight deck was responsible for the safe and efficient launch and recovery of the aircraft. Fifty functional roles were involved in the process. Individuals' functions were immediately obvious from their uniforms: blue for "grunts," red for weapons and fire-control personnel, brown for aircraft traffic directors, and purple for fuelers (affectionately referred to as "grapes"). Supervisory personnel wore yellow, safety personnel wore white, and officers on the bridge dressed in standard khaki. The officer of the deck wore a gold-emblazoned baseball cap. The captain had overall command of the ship, while the commander of the air group was in charge of the pilots and aircraft.

In combat, the *USS Kennedy*'s primary goal was clear: bombs on target. To reach that objective, all functions had to work together. Anyone's actions could affect everyone aboard, especially in close quarters under battle conditions. Individuals knew their own jobs even if they were less clear about the big picture. A carrier succeeded only if roles were clear and everybody responded to the chain of command. The performance of the carrier fleet in the Gulf War in the early 1990s and a decade later in Afghanistan, as well as in the more recent 2003 campaign in Iraq, gave ample evidence that warships like the *Kennedy* can do their job.

A naval carrier can plan for most combat contingencies. The same was not true for New York City's fire and police departments when they confronted the 9/11 terrorist strikes on the World Trade Center. That day saw countless inspiring examples of individual heroism and personal sacrifice. At the risk of their own lives, emergency personnel rescued thousands of people. Many died in the effort. But extraordinary individual efforts were hindered or thwarted by breakdowns in communication, command, and control. Police helicopters near the north tower radioed that it was near collapse more than twenty minutes before it fell. Police officers got the warning, and most escaped. But the word reached very few firefighters. There was no link between fire and police radios, and the commanders in the two departments could not communicate because their command posts were three blocks apart. It might not have helped if they had talked, because the fire department's radios were notoriously unreliable in high-rise buildings. The breakdown of communication and coordination magnified the death toll—including 121 firefighters who died when the north tower collapsed. The absence of a clear, workable structure seriously impaired the effectiveness of highly dedicated, skilled professionals who gave their all in an unprecedented catastrophe (Dwyer, Flynn, and Fessenden, 2002).

Comparing the situation aboard the *USS Kennedy* with rescue efforts at the World Trade Center points to a core premise of the structural lens: clear, well-understood goals, roles, and relationships and adequate coordination are essential to organizational performance. This is true of all organizations: families, clubs, hospitals, businesses, and public agencies. The right structure forms a solid underpinning to combat the risk that individuals, however talented, will become confused, ineffective, apathetic, or hostile. The purpose of this chapter and the next two is to identify the basic ideas and inner workings of a perspective that is fundamental to social endeavors.

We begin our examination of the structural frame by highlighting its core assumptions, origins, and basic forms. The possibilities for designing an organization's structure, or social architecture, are almost limitless, but any option must address two key questions: How do we allocate responsibilities across different units and roles? And, once we've done that, how do we integrate diverse efforts in pursuit of common goals? In this chapter, we explain these basic issues, describe the major options, and discuss imperatives to consider when designing a structure to fit the challenges of a unique situation.

STRUCTURAL ASSUMPTIONS

The assumptions of the structural frame are reflected in current approaches to organizational design. These suppositions reflect a belief in rationality and a faith that a suitable array of formal roles and responsibilities will minimize distracting personal static and maximize people's performance on the job. Where the human resource approach (to be discussed in Chapters Six through Eight) emphasizes dealing with issues by changing people (through training, rotation, promotion, or dismissal), the structural perspective argues for putting people in the right roles and relationships. Properly designed, these formal arrangements can accommodate both collective goals and individual differences.

Six assumptions undergird the structural frame:

1. Organizations exist to achieve established goals and objectives.

2. Organizations increase efficiency and enhance performance through specialization and appropriate division of labor.

3. Suitable forms of coordination and control ensure that diverse efforts of individuals and units mesh.

4. Organizations work best when rationality prevails over personal agendas and extraneous pressures.

5. Structures must be designed to fit an organization's current circumstances (including its goals, technology, workforce, and environment).

6. Problems arise and performance suffers from structural deficiencies, which can be remedied through analysis and restructuring.

ORIGINS OF THE STRUCTURAL PERSPECTIVE

The structural view has two main intellectual roots. The first is the work of industrial analysts bent on designing organizations for maximum efficiency. The most prominent of these, Frederick W. Taylor (1911), was the father of time-and-motion studies; he founded an approach that he labeled "scientific management." Taylor broke tasks into minute parts and retrained workers to get the most from each motion and every second spent at work. Other theorists who contributed to the scientific management approach (Fayol, [1919] 1949; Urwick, 1937; Gulick and Urwick, 1937) developed principles focused on specialization, span of control, authority, and delegation of responsibility.

A second ancestor of structural ideas is the German economist and sociologist Max Weber. Weber wrote around the beginning of the twentieth century. At the time, formal organization was a relatively new phenomenon. Patriarchy, rather than rationality, was still the primary organizing principle. Patriarchal organizations were dominated by a father figure, a ruler with almost unlimited authority and boundless power. He could reward, punish, promote, or fire on personal whim. Seeing an evolution of new models in late-nineteenth-century Europe, Weber described "monocratic bureaucracy" as an ideal form that maximized norms of rationality. His model outlined several major features:

- A fixed division of labor
- A hierarchy of offices
- A set of rules governing performance
- A separation of personal from official property and rights
- The use of technical qualifications (not family ties or friendship) for selecting personnel
- Employment as primary occupation and long-term career

After World War II, Weber's work was rediscovered, inspiring a substantial body of theory and research. Blau and Scott (1962), Perrow (1986), Thompson (1967), Lawrence and Lorsch (1967), and Hall (1963), among others, amplified the bureaucratic model. Their work examined relationships among the elements of structure, looked closely at why organizations choose one structure over another, and analyzed the effects of structure on morale, productivity, and effectiveness.

Hit Number 4: James D. Thompson, *Organizations in Action: Social Science Bases of Administrative Theory* (New York: McGraw-Hill, 1967)

"Organizations act, but what determines how and when they will act?" (p. 1). That guiding question opens Thompson's compact, tightly reasoned book. He answers that "organizations do some of the basic things they do because they must—or else! Because they are expected to produce results, their actions are expected to be reasonable, or rational" (p. 1). As Thompson sees them, organizations operate under "norms of rationality," but rationality is no easy thing to achieve because of the central challenge of uncertainty. "Uncertainties pose major challenges to rationality, and we will argue that technologies and environments are basic sources of uncertainty for organizations. How these facts of organizational life lead organizations to design and structure themselves needs to be explored" (p. 1).

Thompson looked for a way to meld two distinct ways of thinking about organizations. One was to see them as closed, rational systems (as in Taylor's scientific management and Weber's theory of bureaucracy). A second viewed them as open, natural systems in which "survival of the system is taken to be the goal, and the parts and their relationships are presumably determined through evolutionary processes" (p. 6). In melding the two, he tried to build on a "newer tradition" emerging from the work of March and Simon (1958, number 10 on our scholars' list) and Cyert and March (1963, number 2). This tradition viewed organizations as "problem facing and problem solving" in a context of limited information and capacities.

With these premises, Thompson developed a series of propositions about how organizations design and manage themselves as they seek rationality in an uncertain world. The two primary sources of uncertainty, in his view, are technology and the environment. He distinguishes three kinds of technology—pooled, sequential, and reciprocal—each making different demands on communication and coordination. Since demands and intrusions from the environment threaten efficiency, organizations try to increase their ability to anticipate and control the environment and attempt to insulate their technical core from environmental fluctuations. Still another source of uncertainty is the "variable human." The more uncertainty an organization faces, the more discretion individuals need to cope with it, but greater discretion creates a challenge of controlling its use. "Paradoxically, the administrative process must reduce uncertainty but at the same time search for flexibility" (pp. 157–158).

STRUCTURAL FORMS AND FUNCTIONS

How does structure influence what happens in the workplace? Essentially, it is a blueprint for officially sanctioned expectations and exchanges among internal players (executives, managers, employees) and external constituencies (such as customers and clients). Like an animal's skeleton or a building's framework, structural form both enhances and constrains what an organization can accomplish. The alternative design possibilities are virtually infinite, limited only by human preferences and capacity.

We often assume that people prefer structures with more choices and latitude (Leavitt, 1978). But this is not always the case. A study by Moeller (1968), for example, explored the effects of structure on teacher morale in two school systems. One was structured loosely and encouraged wide participation in decision making. The other was tightly controlled, with centralized authority and a clear chain of command. Moeller found the opposite of what he expected: faculty morale was higher in the district with a tighter structure.

United Parcel Service, "Big Brown," provides a current example of Moeller's finding. In the company's early days, UPS delivery employees were "scampering messenger boys" (Niemann, 2007). Since then, computer technology has replaced employee discretion, and every step from pickup to delivery is highly routinized. Detailed instructions specify where and in what order packages are to be placed on delivery trucks. Drivers follow computer-generated routes (which minimize mileage and left turns, to save time and gas). Newly scheduled pickups are automatically inserted into the nearest driver's route plan. If a driver sees you as he trots to your door, you'll get a friendly greeting. Look carefully and you'll notice the truck keys on the ring finger of the left hand. Given such a tight leash, you might expect demoralized employees. But the technology makes the job easier and enables drivers to be more productive. As one remarked with a smile, "We're happy robots."

Do these examples prove that a tighter structure is better? Not necessarily. Adler and Borys (1996) argue that the type of structure is as important as the amount or rigidity. There are good rules and bad ones. Formal structure enhances morale if it helps us get our work done. It has a negative impact if it gets in our way, buries us in red tape, or makes it too easy for management to control us. Equating structure to rigid bureaucracy confuses "two very different kinds of machine—machines designed to de-skill work and those designed to leverage users' skills" (p. 69).

Structure, then, need not be machinelike or inflexible. Structures in stable environments are often hierarchical and rules-oriented. But recent years have witnessed remarkable inventiveness in designing structures emphasizing flexibility, participation, and quality. A prime example is BMW, the luxury automaker whose success formula relies on a combination of stellar quality and rapid innovation. "Just about everyone working for the Bavarian automaker—from the factory floor to the design studios to the marketing department—is encouraged to speak out. Ideas bubble up freely, and there is never a penalty for proposing a new way of doing things, no matter how outlandish. Detroit's rigid and bloated bureaucracies are slow to respond to competitive threats and market trends, while BMW's management structure is flat, flexible, entrepreneurial—and fast. That explains why, at the very moment GM and Ford appear to be in free fall, BMW is more robust than ever. The company has become the industry benchmark for high-performance premium cars, customized production, and savvy brand management" (Edmondson, 2006, p. 72).

Dramatic changes in technology and the business environment have rendered old structures obsolete at an unprecedented rate, spawning a new interest in organizational design (Nadler, Gerstein, and Shaw, 1992; Bryan and Joyce, 2007). Pressures of globalization, competition, technology, customer expectations, and workforce dynamics have prompted organizations worldwide to rethink and redesign structural prototypes. A swarm of items compete for managers' attention—money, markets, people, and technological competencies, to name a few. But a significant amount of time and attention must be devoted to social architecture—designing structure that allows people to do their best:

> CEOs typically opt for the ad hoc structural change, the big acquisition, or a focus on where and how to compete. They would be better off focusing on organizational design. Our research convinces

us that in the digital age, there is no better use of a CEO's time and energy than making organizations work better. Most companies were designed for the industrial age of the past century, when capital was the scarce resource, interaction costs were high, and hierarchical authority and vertically integrated structures were the keys to efficient operation. Today superior performance flows from the ability to fit these structures into the present century's very different sources of wealth creation [Bryan and Joyce, 2007, p. 1].

BASIC STRUCTURAL TENSIONS

Two issues are central to structural design: how to allocate work *(differentiation)* and how to coordinate diverse efforts once responsibilities have been parceled out *(integration)*. Even in a group as small and intimate as a family, it's important to settle issues concerning who does what, when the "what" gets done, and how individual efforts mesh to ensure harmony. Every family will find an arrangement of roles and synchronization that works—or suffer the fallout.

Division of labor—or allocating tasks—is the keystone of structure. Every living system creates specialized roles to get important work done. Consider an ant colony: "Small workers . . . spend most of their time in the nest feeding the larval broods; intermediate-sized workers constitute most of the population, going out on raids as well as doing other jobs. The largest workers . . . have a huge head and large powerful jaws. These individuals are . . . soldiers; they carry no food but constantly run along the flanks of the raiding and emigration columns" (Topoff, 1972, p. 72).

Like ants, humans long ago discovered the virtues of specialization. A job (or position) channels behavior by prescribing what someone is to do—or not do—to accomplish a task. Prescriptions take the form of job descriptions, procedures, routines, protocols, or rules (Mintzberg, 1979). On one hand, these formal constraints can be burdensome, leading to apathy, absenteeism, and resistance (Argyris, 1957, 1964). On the other hand, they help to ensure predictability, uniformity, and reliability. If manufacturing standards, airline maintenance, hotel housekeeping, or prison sentences were left solely to individual discretion, problems of quality and equity would abound.

Once an organization spells out positions or roles, managers face a second set of key decisions: how to group people into working units. They have several basic options (Mintzberg, 1979):

- Functional groups based on *knowledge or skill,* as in the case of a university's academic departments or the classic industrial units of research, engineering, manufacturing, marketing, and finance.

- Units created on the basis of *time,* as by shift (day, swing, or graveyard shift).

- Groups organized by *product:* detergent versus bar soap, wide-body versus narrow-body aircraft.

- Groups established around *customers or clients,* as in hospital wards created around patient type (pediatrics, intensive care, or maternity), computer sales departments organized by customer (corporate, government, education, individual), or schools targeting students in particular age groups.

- Groupings around *place or geography,* such as regional offices in corporations and government agencies or neighborhood schools in different parts of a city.

- Grouping by *process:* a complete flow of work, as with "the order fulfillment process. This process flows from initiation by a customer order, through the functions, to delivery to the customer" (Galbraith, 2001, p. 34).

Creating roles and units yields the benefits of specialization but creates problems of coordination and control—how to ensure that diverse efforts mesh. Units tend to focus on their separate priorities and strike out on their own, as New York's police and fire departments did on 9/11. The result is *suboptimization,* an emphasis on achieving unit goals rather than focusing on the overall mission. Efforts become fragmented, and performance suffers.

This problem plagued Tom Ridge, who was named by President George W. Bush as the director of homeland security in the aftermath of the terrorist attacks. Ridge struggled to pull together previously autonomous agencies. But he was more salesman and preacher than boss—he lacked the authority to compel compliance. Ridge's slow progress led President Bush to create a cabinet-level Department of Homeland Security. The goal was to cluster independent security agencies under one central authority. Unfortunately, the new structure created its own problems. Folding the Federal Emergency Management Agency into the mix reduced FEMA's autonomy and shifted its priorities toward more focus on security and less on disaster management. The same agency that had responded nimbly to hurricanes and earthquakes in the 1990s was slow and ponderous in the aftermath of Hurricane Katrina and lacked authority and budget to move without a formal okay from the new secretary of homeland security (Cooper and Block, 2006).

Successful organizations employ a variety of methods to coordinate individual and group efforts and to link local initiatives with corporation-wide goals. They do this in two primary ways: *vertically,* through the formal chain of command, and *laterally,* through meetings, committees, coordinating roles, or network structures. We next look at each of these strategies in detail.

VERTICAL COORDINATION

With vertical coordination, higher levels coordinate and control the work of subordinates through authority, rules and policies, and planning and control systems.

Authority

The most basic and ubiquitous way to harmonize the efforts of individuals, units, or divisions is to designate a boss with formal authority. Authorities—executives, managers, and supervisors—are officially charged with keeping action aligned with goals and objectives. They accomplish this by making decisions, resolving conflicts, solving problems, evaluating performance and output, and distributing rewards and sanctions. A chain of command is a hierarchy of managerial and supervisory strata, each with legitimate power to shape and direct the behavior of those at lower levels. It works best when authority is both endorsed by subordinates and authorized by superiors (Dornbusch and Scott, 1975). On the *USS Kennedy,* for example, the chain of command was crystal clear and universally accepted. It is one reason that the ultimate goal—bombs on target—was consistently attained.

Rules and Policies

Rules, policies, standards, and standard operating procedures limit individual discretion and help ensure that behavior is predictable and consistent. Rules and policies govern conditions of work and specify standard ways of completing tasks, handling personnel issues, and relating to customers and other key players in the outer environment. This helps ensure that similar situations are handled in comparable ways. It reduces "particularism" (Perrow, 1986)—responding to specific issues on the basis of personal whims or political pressures unrelated to organizational goals. Two citizens' complaints about a tax bill are supposed to be treated similarly, even if one citizen is a prominent politician and the other a shoe clerk. Once a situation is defined as one where a rule applies, the course of action is clear, straightforward, and, in an ideal world, almost automatic.

A standard is a benchmark to ensure that goods and services maintain a specified level of quality. Measurement against the standard makes it possible to identify and fix problems. During the 1970s and 1980s, American manufacturing standards lagged, while Japanese manufacturers were scrupulous in ensuring that high standards were widely known and universally accepted. In one case, an American company ordered ball bearings from a Japanese plant. The Americans insisted on what they saw as an unusually high standard—only twenty defective parts per thousand. When the order arrived, it included a separate bag of twenty defective bearings, and a note: "We were not sure why you wanted these, but here they are." Pressure for world-class quality spawned growing interest in "Six Sigma," a statistical standard of near perfection (Pyzdek, 2003). Although Six Sigma has raised quality standards in many companies around the world, its laser focus on measurable aspects of work processes and outcomes has sometimes hampered creativity in innovative companies such as 3M (Hindo, 2007, pp. 8–12). Safer, more measurable options may crowd out the elusive breakthroughs a firm needs.

Standard operating procedures (SOPs) reduce variance in routine tasks that have little margin for error. Commercial airline pilots typically fly with a different crew every month. Cockpit actions are tightly intertwined, the need for coordination is high, and mistakes can kill. SOPs consequently govern much of the work of flying a plane. Pilots are trained extensively in the procedures and seldom violate them. But a significant percentage of aviation accidents occur in the rare case that someone does. More than one airplane has crashed on takeoff because the crew missed a required checklist item.

SOPs can fall short, however, in the face of "black swans" (Taleb, 2007)—freak surprises that the SOPs were never designed to handle. In the 9/11 terrorist attacks, pilots followed standard procedures for dealing with hijackers: cooperate with their demands and try to get the plane on the ground quickly. These SOPs were based on a long history of hijackers who wanted to make a statement, not wreak destruction on a suicide mission. Passengers on United Airlines flight 93, who had learned via cell phones that the hijackers were using aircraft as bombs rather than bully pulpits, abandoned this approach. They lost their lives fighting to regain control of the plane, but theirs was the only one of four hijacked jets that failed to devastate a high-profile building.

Planning and Control Systems

Reliance on planning and control systems—forecasting and measuring—has mushroomed since the dawn of the computer era. Retailers, for example, need to know what's selling and what isn't. Point-of-sale terminals now yield that information instantly. Data flow freely up and down the hierarchy, greatly enhancing management's ability to oversee performance and respond in real time.

Mintzberg (1979) distinguishes two major approaches to control and planning: performance control and action planning. *Performance control* imposes concrete outcome objectives (for example, "increase sales by 10 percent this year") without specifying how the results are to be achieved. Performance control measures and motivates individual efforts, particularly when targets are reasonably clear and calculable. Locke and Latham (2002) make the case that clear and challenging goals are a powerful incentive to high performance. Performance control is less successful when goals are ambiguous, hard to measure, or of dubious relevance. A notorious example was the use of enemy body counts by the U.S. Army to measure combat effectiveness in Vietnam; field commanders became obsessed with "getting the numbers up." The numbers painted a picture of progress, even as the war was being lost.

Action planning specifies methods and time frames for decisions and actions, as in "increase this month's sales by using a companywide sales pitch" (Mintzberg, 1979, pp. 153–154). Action planning works best when it is easier to assess *how* a job is done than to measure its product. This is often true of service jobs. McDonald's has very clear specifications for how counter employees are to greet customers (for example, with a smile and a cheerful welcome). United Parcel Service has a detailed policy manual that specifies how a package should be delivered. The objective is customer satisfaction, but it is easier to monitor employees' behavior than customers' reactions. An inevitable risk in action planning is that the link between action and outcome may fail. When that happens, employees may get bad results by doing just what they're supposed to do.

LATERAL COORDINATION

People's behavior is often remarkably untouched by commands, rules, and systems. Lateral techniques—formal and informal meetings, task forces, coordinating roles, matrix structures, and networks—pop up to fill the void. Lateral forms are typically less formal and more flexible than authority-bound systems and rules. They are often simpler and quicker as well.

Meetings

Formal gatherings and informal exchanges are the cornerstone of lateral coordination. All organizations have regular meetings. Boards confer to make policy. Executive committees gather to make strategic decisions. In some government agencies, review committees (sometimes known as "murder boards") convene to examine proposals from lower levels. Formal meetings provide a lion's share of lateral harmonization in relatively simple, stable organizations—for example, a railroad with a predictable market, a manufacturer with a stable product, or a life insurance company selling standard policies.

But informal contacts and exchanges are vital to take up slack and glue things together in fast-paced, turbulent environments. Pixar, the animation studio whose series of hits has included *Toy Story, Finding Nemo, The Incredibles,* and *Cars,* relies on a constant stream of informal connections among managers and engineers in its three major groups. Technologists develop graphic tools, artists create stories and pictures, and production experts knit the pieces together in the final film. "What makes it all work is [Pixar's] insistence that these groups constantly talk to each other. So a producer of a scene can deal with the animator without having to navigate through higher-ups" (Schlender, 2004, p. 212).

Task Forces

As organizations become more complex, the demand for lateral communication mushrooms. Additional face-to-face coordination devices are needed. Task forces assemble when new problems or opportunities require collaboration of diverse specialties or functions. High-technology firms rely heavily on project teams or task forces to synchronize the development of new products or services.

Coordinating Roles

Coordinating roles or units use persuasion and negotiation to help others dovetail their efforts. These are essentially boundary-spanners, individuals or groups with diplomatic status who are artful in dealing across specialized turfs. For example, a product manager in a consumer goods company, responsible for the performance of a laundry detergent or low-fat snack, has what is primarily a coordinating role, spending much of the day pulling together functions essential to the product's success: research, manufacturing, marketing, and sales.

Matrix Structures

Beginning in the 1960s, many organizations in unwieldy environments developed matrix structures. By the mid-1990s, Asea Brown Boveri (ABB), the electrical engineering giant, had grown to encompass some thirteen hundred separate companies and more than two hundred thousand employees worldwide. To hold this complex collection together, ABB developed a matrix structure crisscrossing approximately a hundred countries with about sixty-five business sectors (Rappaport, 1992). Each subsidiary reported to both a country manager (Sweden, Germany, and so on) and a sector manager (power transformers, transportation, and the like). The design carried the inevitable risk of confusion, tension, and conflict between sector and country managers. ABB tried to create structural cohesion at the top with a small executive coordinating committee (thirteen individuals from eight countries), an elite cadre of some five hundred global managers, and a policy of communicating in English, even though it was a second language for most employees.

The structure worked through the 1990s, and ABB became one of Europe's most admired companies. But the inherent tensions eventually took a toll, and after a business downturn in 2000, ABB began to generate more bad news than good (Reed and Sains, 2002). Nonetheless, variations on ABB's structure—a matrix with business or product lines on one axis and countries or regions on the other—are common in global corporations.

Networks

Networks have always been around, more so in some places than others. Cochran (2000) describes how both Western and Japanese firms doing business in China in the nineteenth and twentieth centuries had to adapt their hierarchical structures to accommodate powerful social networks of merchants and workers deeply embedded in Chinese culture. One British firm tried for years, with little success, to limit the control of "Number Ones" (who headed local networks based on kinship and birthplace) over the hiring and wages of its workforce. The proliferation of information technology beginning in the 1980s led to an explosive growth of computer networks—everything from small local grids to the global Internet. These powerful new lateral communication devices often supplanted vertical strategies and spurred the development of network structures within and between organizations (Steward, 1994). Powell, Koput, and Smith-Doerr (1996) describe the mushrooming of "interorganizational networks" in fast-moving fields like biotechnology, where knowledge is so complex and widely dispersed that no organization can go it alone. They give an example of research on Alzheimer's disease that was carried out by thirty-four scientists from three corporations, a university, a government laboratory, and a private research institute.

Many large global corporations have evolved into interorganizational networks (Ghoshal and Bartlett, 1990). Horizontal linkages supplement and sometimes supplant vertical coordination. Such a firm is multicentric: initiatives and strategy emerge from many places, taking shape through a variety of partnerships and joint ventures.

DESIGNING A STRUCTURE THAT WORKS

In designing a structure that works, managers have a set of options for dividing up the work and coordinating multiple efforts. Structure needs to be designed with an eye toward desired ends, the nature of the environment, the talents of the workforce, and the available resources (such as time, budget, and other contingencies). The options are summarized in Exhibit 3.1.

Vertical or Lateral?

As noted, vertical coordination rests on top-down command and control. It is efficient but not always effective, and it depends on employees' willingness to follow directives from above. More decentralized and interactive lateral forms of coordination are often needed to keep top-down control from stifling initiative and creativity. Lateral coordination is often more effective but costlier than its vertical counterparts. A meeting, for example, provides an opportunity for face-to-face dialogue and decision making, but risks squandering time and energy. Personal and political agendas often undermine the meeting's purpose. A task force fosters creativity and integration around pressing problems but may divert attention from ongoing operating issues. The effectiveness of coordinators who span boundaries depends on their credibility and skills in handling others. Coordinators are also prone to schedule meetings that take still more time from actual work (Hannaway and Sproull, 1979). Matrix structures provide lateral linkage and integration but are notorious for creating conflict and confusion. Networks are inherently difficult to manage.

Exhibit 3.1.
Basic Structural Options.

Division of labor: Options for differentiation	Function
	Time
	Product
	Customers or clients
	Place (geography)
	Process
Coordination: Options for integration	
Vertical	Authority
	Rules and policies
	Planning and control systems
Lateral	Meetings
	Task forces
	Coordinating roles
	Matrix structures
	Networks

Organizations have to use both vertical and horizontal procedures for coordination. The optimal blend of the two depends on the unique challenges in a given situation. Vertical coordination is generally superior if an environment is stable, tasks are well understood and predictable, and uniformity is essential. Lateral communications work best when a complex task is performed in a turbulent, fast-changing environment. Every organization must find a design that works for its circumstances. Consider the contrasting structures of two highly successful organizations: McDonald's and Harvard University.

MCDONALD'S AND HARVARD: A STRUCTURAL ODD COUPLE

McDonald's, the company that made the Big Mac a household word, has been enormously successful. For forty years after its founding in the 1950s, the company was an unstoppable growth engine that came to dominate the worldwide fast-food business. McDonald's has a relatively small staff at its world headquarters near Chicago; the vast majority of its employees are salted across the world in more than 31,000 local outlets. But despite its size and geographic reach, McDonald's is a highly centralized, tightly controlled organization. Most major decisions are made at the top.

Managers and employees of McDonald's restaurants have limited discretion about how to do their jobs. Their work is controlled by technology; machines time french fries and measure soft drinks. The parent company uses powerful systems like its "Global Restaurant Operations Improvement Process" to ensure that customers get what they expect and a Big Mac tastes about the same whether purchased in New York, Beijing, or Moscow. Guaranteed standard quality inevitably limits the discretion of people who own and work in individual outlets. Cooks are not expected to develop creative new versions of the Big Mac or Quarter Pounder. Creative departures from standard product lines are neither encouraged nor tolerated on a day-to-day basis, though the company has adapted to growth and globalization by increasing its receptivity to new ideas from the field—the Egg McMuffin was created by a local franchisee, and burgers-on-wheels home delivery was pioneered in traffic-choked cities like Cairo and Taipei (Arndt, 2007).

All that structure might sound oppressive, but one of the major McDonald's miscues in the 1990s resulted from trying to loosen up. Responding to pressure from some frustrated franchisees, McDonald's in 1993 stopped sending out inspectors to grade restaurants on service, food, and ambience. When left to police themselves, some restaurants slipped badly. Customers noticed, and the company's image sagged. Ten years later, a new CEO brought the inspectors back to correct lagging standards (David, 2003).

Harvard University is also highly successful. Like McDonald's, it has a very small administrative group at the top, but in most other respects the two organizations diverge. Even though Harvard is more geographically concentrated than McDonald's, it is significantly more decentralized. Nearly all of Harvard's activities occur within a few square miles of Boston and Cambridge, Massachusetts. Most employees are housed in the university's several schools: Harvard College (the undergraduate school), the graduate faculty of arts and sciences, and various professional schools. Each school has its own dean and its own endowment and, in accordance with Harvard's philosophy of "every tub on its own bottom," largely controls its own destiny. Schools have fiscal autonomy, and individual professors have enormous discretion. They have substantial control over what courses they teach, what research they do, and which university activities they pursue, if any. Faculty meetings are typically sparsely attended. If a dean or a department head wants a faculty member to chair a committee or offer a new course, the request is more often a humble entreaty than an authoritative command.

The contrast between McDonald's and Harvard is particularly strong at the level of service delivery. No one expects individual personality to influence the quality of McDonald's hamburgers. But everyone expects each course at Harvard to be the unique creation of an individual professor. Two schools might offer courses with the same title but different content and widely divergent teaching styles. Efforts to develop standardized core curricula founder on the autonomy of individual professors.

Structural Imperatives

Why do McDonald's and Harvard have such radically different structures? Is one more effective than the other? Or has each evolved to fit its unique circumstances? In fact, there is no such thing as an ideal structure. Every organization needs to respond to a universal set of internal and external parameters (outlined in Exhibit 3.2). These parameters include the organization's size, age, core process, environment, strategy and goals, information technology, and workforce characteristics. All these characteristics combine to dictate the optimal social architecture.

Size and Age Size and age affect structural shape and character. Problems crop up if growth (or downsizing) is not matched with fine-tuning of roles and relationships. A small, entrepreneurial organization typically has very simple, informal architecture. Growth spawns formality and complexity (Greiner, 1972; Quinn and Cameron, 1983). If carried too far, this leads to the suffocating bureaucratic rigidity often seen in large, mature enterprises.

Exhibit 3.2.
Structural Imperatives.

DIMENSION	STRUCTURAL IMPLICATIONS
Size and age	Complexity and formality increase with size and age.
Core process	Core processes or technologies must align with structure.
Environment	Stable environment rewards simpler structure; uncertain, turbulent environment requires a more complex, flexible structure.
Strategy and goals	Variation in clarity and consistency of goals requires appropriate structural adaptations.
Information technology	Information technology permits flatter, more flexible, and more decentralized structures.
Nature of the workforce	More educated and professional workers need and want greater autonomy and discretion.

In the beginning, McDonald's was not the tightly controlled company it is today. It began as a single hamburger stand in San Bernardino, California, owned and managed by the McDonald brothers. They virtually invented the concept of fast food and their stand was phenomenally successful. The two tried to expand by selling franchise rights, with little success. They were making more than enough money, disliked travel, and had no heirs. If they were richer, said one brother, "we'd be leaving it to a church or something, and we didn't go to church" (Love, 1986, p. 23).

The concept took off when Ray Kroc arrived on the scene. He had achieved modest success selling milk shake machines to restaurants. When many of his customers began to ask for the McDonald's milk shake mixer, he decided to visit the brothers. Seeing the original stand, Kroc realized the potential: "Unlike the homebound McDonalds, Kroc had traveled extensively, and he could envision hundreds of large and small markets where a McDonald's could be located. He understood the existing food services businesses, and understood how a McDonald's unit could be a formidable competitor" (Love, 1986, pp. 39–40). Kroc persuaded the McDonald brothers to let him take over the franchising effort. The rest is history.

Core Process   Structure is ideally built around an organization's basic method of transforming raw materials into finished products. Every organization has a core technology that includes at least three elements: raw materials, activities that turn inputs into outputs, and underlying beliefs about the links among inputs, activities, and outcomes (Dornbusch and Scott, 1975).

Core technologies vary in clarity, predictability, and effectiveness. Assembling a Big Mac is relatively routine and programmed. The task is clear, most potential problems are known in advance, and the probability of success is high. Its relatively simple core technology allows McDonald's to rely mostly on vertical coordination.

In contrast, Harvard's two core processes—research and teaching—are far more complex and less predictable. Teaching objectives are knotty and amorphous. Unlike hamburger buns, students are active agents. Which teaching strategies best yield desired results is more a matter of faith than of fact. Even if students could be molded predictably, mystery surrounds the knowledge and skills they will need to succeed in life. This uncertain technology, greatly dependent on the skills and knowledge of highly educated professionals, is a key source of Harvard's loosely coordinated structure.

Core technologies often evolve, and significant technical innovation calls for corresponding structural alterations (Barley, 1990). In recent decades, struggles to integrate new technologies have become a fateful reality for many firms (Henderson and Clark, 1990). Existing arrangements often get in the way. Companies are tempted to mold innovative technologies to fit their existing operations. A change from film to digital photography, slide rules to calculators, or "snail mail" to e-mail gives an advantage to start-ups less committed to the old ways. Christensen (1997) found this in his study of the disk drive industry from 1975 to 1994, for example. Innovation in established firms was often blocked not by technical challenges but by marketers who argued, "Our customers don't want it."

Organizations try to insulate internal operations from outside pressures, but changing environments are a potent force. Organizations depend on the environment to provide raw materials and consume products and services. Stable, mature businesses—such as railroads, furniture manufacturers, and elementary schools—deal with slow-changing and predictable external pressures. As a result, they rely on simpler forms of organizing. Organizations with rapidly changing technologies or markets—such as high-technology electronics firms—confront a much higher degree of uncertainty. New products may be obsolete in six months or less. Uncertainty and turbulence press for new roles and more elaborate, flexible approaches to vertical and lateral coordination.

Some organizations are more susceptible to outside influences than others. Public schools, for example, are highly vulnerable to external pressures because they have so little capacity to claim the resources they need or to shape the results they are supposed to produce. In contrast, an institution like Harvard is insulated from such intrusions by its size, elite status, and large endowment. The university can therefore afford to offer low teaching loads, generous salaries, and substantial autonomy to its faculty. A Harvard diploma is taken as sufficient evidence that instruction is having its desired effect.

Strategy and Goals Strategic decisions are future oriented, concerned with long-term direction (Chandler, 1962; Mintzberg, 1994). Across sectors, a major task of organizational leadership is "the determination of long-range goals and objectives of an enterprise, and the adoption of courses of action and allocation of resources necessary for carrying out these goals" (Chandler, 1962, p. 13).

A variety of goals are embedded in strategy. In business firms, goals such as profitability, growth, and market share are relatively specific and easy to measure. Goals of educational or human services organizations are typically much more diffuse: "producing educated men and women" or "improving individual well-being." This is another reason Harvard adopts a more decentralized, loosely integrated system of roles and relationships.

Historically, McDonald's had fewer, more easily quantifiable, and less controversial goals than those of Harvard. This aligned well with the McDonald's centralized, top-down structure. But that structure has become more complex as the company's size and global reach have fostered levels of decentralization that allowed outlets in India to offer vegetarian cuisine and those in France to run ads attacking Americans and American beef (Tagliabue, 1999; Stires, 2002; Arndt, 2007).

To complicate matters still further, stated goals are not the only ones an organization pursues. Westerlund and Sjostrand (1979) suggest various others:

- *Honorific:* Fictitious goals with desirable qualities.
- *Taboo:* Goals pursued but not talked about.

- *Stereotypical:* Goals any reputable organization should have.

- *Existing:* Goals quietly pursued even though inconsistent with stated values and self-image.

Understanding linkages among goals, structure, and strategy requires a look beyond formal statements of purpose. Schools, for example, are often criticized if structure does not coincide with the official goal of scholastic achievement. But schools have other, less visible goals. One is character development, often espoused with little follow-through. Another is the taboo goal of certification and selection, as schools channel students into tracks and sort them into careers. Still a third goal is custody and control—keeping kids off the streets and out from underfoot. Finally, schools often herald honorific goals such as excellence. Strategy and goals shape structure, but the process is often complex and subtle (Dornbusch and Scott, 1975).

Information Technology New technologies continue to revolutionize the amount of information available and the speed at which it travels. Once accessible exclusively to top-level or middle managers, information is now easy to get and widely shared. E-mail has made communication immediate and far reaching. With the press of a key, anyone can reach another person—or an entire network. All this makes it possible to move decisions closer to the action.

In the 2003 invasion of Iraq, for example, U.S. and British forces had an obvious advantage in military hardware. They also had a powerful structural advantage because their superior information technology let them develop a much more flexible and decentralized command structure. Commanders in the field could change their plans immediately in response to new developments. Iraqi forces, meanwhile, had a much slower, more vertical structure that relied on decisions from the top. A major reason that Iraqi resistance was lighter than expected in early weeks was that commanders had no idea what to do when they were cut off from their chain of command (Broder and Schmitt, 2003).

Later, however, the structure and technology so effective against Iraq's military had much more difficulty with the rising resistance movement, which evolved a loosely connected structure of entrepreneurial local units that could adapt quickly to U.S. tactics. New technologies like the Internet and cell phones enabled the resistance to structure itself as a network, or "complex adaptive system" (Waldrop,

1992, p. 145)—a set of loosely connected units, each pursuing its own agenda in response to local conditions. The absence of strong central control in such networks can be a virtue because local units can adapt very fast to new developments and because the loss of any one outpost does little damage to the whole.

By increasing the flow of information, improved technology reduces uncertainty. Galbraith (1973) defines uncertainty as the difference between the information an organization has and the information it needs. One way that organizations reduce this gap is by increasing their ability to process information (with information systems, for example). A second alternative is to reduce the need for information by creating self-contained units (which can work on their own using information at hand) or by adding slack resources (extra copying machines or support staff, for example, so that people don't have to fight over access).

Information technology has made flatter structures both possible and inevitable because "the information-based organization needs far fewer levels of management than the traditional command-and-control model" (Drucker, 1989, p. 20). As technology spread in the late twentieth century, organizations around the world made deep cuts in both management levels and support staff, a process that still continues.

Nature of the Workforce   Human resource requirements have changed dramatically in recent decades. Many lower-level jobs now require higher levels of skill. A better-educated workforce expects and often demands more discretion in daily work routines. Increasing specialization has professionalized many functions. Professionals typically know more than their supervisors about technical aspects of their work. They expect autonomy and prefer reporting to professional colleagues. Trying to tell a Harvard professor what to teach is an exercise in futility. In contrast, giving too much discretion to a youthful, low-skilled McDonald's worker could become a disaster for both employee and customers.

Dramatically different structural forms are emerging as a result of changes in workforce demographics. Deal and Kennedy (1982) predicted early on the emergence of the atomized or network organization, made up of small, autonomous, often geographically dispersed work groups tied together by information systems and organizational symbols. Drucker makes a similar observation in noting that businesses increasingly "move work to where the people are, rather than people to where the work is" (1989, p. 20).

Challenges of Global Organization

In sum, numerous forces affecting structural design create a knotty mix of challenges and tensions. It is not simply a matter of deciding whether we should be centralized like McDonald's or decentralized like Harvard. Many organizations find that they have to do both and somehow accommodate the competing structural tensions.

Two electronics giants, Matsushita in Japan and Philips in the Netherlands, have competed with one another around the globe for half a century. Over time, Matsushita developed a strong headquarters, while Phillips was more decentralized, with strong units in different countries. The pressures of global competition pushed both to become more alike (Bartlett, 2006). Philips struggled to gain the efficiencies that come from selling the same products around the world. Meanwhile, as Matsushita gradually discovered, "No company can operate effectively on a global scale by centralizing all key decisions and then farming them out for implementation. It doesn't work. . . . No matter how good they are, no matter how well supported analytically, the decision-makers at the center are too far removed from individual markets and the needs of local customers" (Ohmae, 1990, p. 87).

SUMMARY

The structural frame looks beyond individuals to examine the social architecture of work. Though sometimes equated with red tape, mindless memos, and rigid bureaucrats, the approach is much broader and more subtle. It encompasses the freewheeling, loosely structured entrepreneurial task force as well as the more tightly controlled railway company or postal department. If structure is overlooked, an organization often misdirects energy and resources. It may, for example, waste time and money on massive training programs in a vain effort to solve problems that have much more to do with social architecture than people's skills or attitudes. It may fire managers and bring in new ones, who then fall victim to the same structural flaws that doomed their predecessors.

At the heart of organizational design are the twin issues of differentiation and integration. Organizations divide work by creating a variety of specialized roles, functions, and units. They must then use both vertical and horizontal procedures to lash the many elements together. There is no one best way to organize. The right structure depends on prevailing circumstances and considers an organization's goals, strategies, technology, people, and environment. Understanding the complexity and variety of design possibilities can help create formal prototypes that work for, rather than against, both people and collective purposes.

NOTE

1. The supercarrier *USS Kennedy* was decommissioned in May 2007 after almost forty years of service.

Structure and Restructuring

L arry Summers took the helm as president of Harvard in 2001. An economist and former U.S. treasury secretary, Summers concluded that the venerable university needed an overhaul. From the president's office, he issued a series of authoritative new directives. He attacked the undergraduate grading system, in which half of the students received A's and 90 percent graduated with honors. He stiffened standards for awarding tenure, encouraged more foreign study, and asked faculty (especially senior professors) to spend more time with students. He stepped across curricular boundaries to call for an emphasis on educational reform and more interdisciplinary courses. He proposed a center for medicine and science to encourage more applied research. Finally, he announced a bold move to build an additional campus across the Charles River to house new growth and development. Summers's initiatives aimed to tighten Harvard's famously decentralized structure and to imbue the president's office with more clout.

How did his plans pan out? Prior experience with restructuring teaches that a crash was likely, and, in this instance, it was a big one. Summers was forced out after the shortest term for a Harvard president in more than a century.

Major initiatives to redesign structure and processes have often proved neither durable nor beneficial. Moving from designing a structure to putting all the parts in place and satisfying every interested party is difficult and hazardous. The attempt after the 9/11 attacks to bring related agencies under the Homeland Security umbrella provides another example of the perils of restructuring. We can get an idea of the effects of this attempt by looking at one organization—the Federal Emergency Management Agency (FEMA).

Before 9/11, FEMA was an autonomous operation. Its main goal was to respond to domestic disasters caused by hurricanes, earthquakes, and other whims of Mother Nature. FEMA was created in 1979 by a stroke of President Jimmy Carter's official pen. It was an effort to integrate separate emergency agencies—hurricane, earthquake, flood—under a single authority. The hitch was that the blend also included Mount Weather, a super-secret national counterespionage group that was housed in separate quarters, replete with guards and other accoutrements shrouding a clandestine operation. This self-styled elite dismissed their colleagues in the rest of FEMA as a "bunch of weenies who went out and chased storms" (Cooper and Block, 2006, p. 55). In fact, FEMA was a two-headed agency. Structurally, as a disaster relief agency, it was itself a disaster, provoking an insider's comment, "How can you help others when you can't even take care of yourself?" (p. 56).

Enter James Lee Witt, a political appointee tapped to head FEMA in 1993, who promised to remake the agency into an integrated organization capable of delivering the goods when disaster struck. He envisioned catastrophes as political opportunities to showcase taxpayers' dollars at work. One of his first actions was to restructure FEMA to focus on disaster relief rather than splitting its mission to encompass national security. He also developed the agency's role in preparing for rather than just responding to national tragedies.

FEMA demonstrated its new configuration in responding successfully to earthquakes in Seattle and in Northridge, California, as well as other national disasters of the new millennium. But after September 11, 2001, terrorism rather than national disasters topped the federal agenda. FEMA was folded into a new agency, the Department of Homeland Security. Tom Ridge was appointed to head the mix of diverse, previously independent operations. The overarching goal: stop terrorism.

Structurally, the change gave FEMA another reporting level and left its funding for disaster relief vulnerable to the new emphasis on terrorism. The flaws in this arrangement became evident when Hurricane Katrina scored a bull's-eye on

New Orleans. FEMA's response to the unparalleled disaster sometimes looked like an episode of the Keystone Kops or the Three Stooges. Who was in charge, who reported to whom, and basic logistical decisions appeared more happenstance than planned. More could be learned from CNN than from the official chain of command.

In the usual political blame game, FEMA's head, Michael Brown, took the hit. But the real culprit was not an individual. It was a restructuring plan that didn't work out. The core assumptions of the structural frame were overlooked or ignored. The costs in property damage and human lives were enormous, and the reputation of a previously successful government agency was tarnished.

Reorganizing, or restructuring, is a powerful but high-risk approach to improvement. An organization's structure at any moment represents its resolution of an enduring set of basic tensions or dilemmas. We begin this chapter by describing these dilemmas. Then, drawing on the work of Henry Mintzberg and Sally Helgesen, we describe two unique views of the alternatives organizations may consider in aligning structure with mission and environment. We conclude with several case examples illustrating both opportunities and challenges managers encounter when attempting to create a more workable structural design.

STRUCTURAL DILEMMAS

Finding a satisfactory system of roles and relationships is an ongoing, universal struggle. Managers rarely face well-defined problems with clear-cut solutions. Instead, they confront enduring structural dilemmas, tough trade-offs without easy answers.

Differentiation Versus Integration

The tension between allocating work and coordinating sundry efforts creates a classic dilemma, as we saw in Chapter Three. The more complex a role structure (lots of people doing many different things), the harder it is to sustain a focused, tightly coupled enterprise. Think about the challenge facing Larry Summers as he tried to bring a higher level of coordination to a highly decentralized university. As complexity grows, organizations need more sophisticated—and more costly—coordination strategies. Rules, policies, and commands have to be augmented by lateral strategies.

Gap Versus Overlap

If key responsibilities are not clearly assigned, important tasks fall through the cracks. Conversely, roles and activities can overlap, creating conflict, wasted effort, and unintended redundancy. A patient in a prestigious teaching hospital, for example, called her husband and pleaded with him to rescue her before she went crazy. At night, she couldn't sleep because hospital staff kept waking her up, often to repeat what someone else had already done. Conversely, when she wanted something, her call button rarely produced any response.

As we have seen, the new cabinet-level Department of Homeland Security, created in the wake of the 9/11 terrorist attacks, was intended to reduce gaps and overlaps among the many agencies responsible for responding to domestic threats. Activities incorporated into the new department included immigration, border protection, emergency management, and intelligence analysis. Yet, as noted in Chapter One, the two most prominent antiterrorism agencies, the FBI and the CIA—with their long history of mutual gaps, overlaps, and bureaucratic squabbling—remained separate and outside the new agency (Firestone, 2002).

Underuse Versus Overload

If employees have too little work, they become bored and get in other people's way. In one physician's office, for example, members of the clerical staff were able to complete most of their tasks during the morning. After lunch, they filled their time talking to family and friends. As a result, the office's telephone lines were constantly busy, making it difficult for patients to ask questions and schedule appointments. Meanwhile, nurses were swamped with clients and routine paperwork. Too busy for informal talk with patients, they were often brusque and curt. Patients complained about impersonal care. A better structural balance was accomplished by reassigning many of the nurses' clerical duties to office staff.

Lack of Clarity Versus Lack of Creativity

If employees are unclear about what they are supposed to do, they often tailor their roles around personal preferences instead of systemwide goals, frequently leading to trouble. Most McDonald's customers are not seeking novelty and surprise in their burgers and fries. But when responsibilities are overdefined, people conform to prescribed roles and protocols in "bureaupathic" ways. They rigidly follow job descriptions regardless of how much the service or product suffers. "You lost my bag!" an angry passenger shouted, confronting an airline manager.

The manager's response was to inquire, "How was the flight?" "I asked about my bag," the passenger said. "That's not my job," the manager replied. "See someone in baggage claim." The passenger did not leave a happy customer.

Excessive Autonomy Versus Excessive Interdependence

When individuals or groups are too autonomous, people often feel isolated. Schoolteachers working in self-contained classrooms and rarely seeing other adults may feel lonely and unsupported. Yet efforts to create closer teamwork have repeatedly run aground because of teachers' difficulties in working together. In contrast, if units and roles are too tightly linked, people are distracted from work and waste time on unnecessary coordination. IBM lost an early lead in the personal computer business in part because new initiatives required so many approvals—from levels and divisions alike—that new products were overdesigned and late to market. Hewlett-Packard's ability to innovate in the late 1990s was hindered by the same problem.

Too Loose Versus Too Tight

A critical structural challenge is how to hold an organization together without holding it back. If structure is too loose, people go their own way or get lost, with little sense of what others are doing. Structures that are too tight stifle flexibility and cause people to spend much of their time trying to beat the system.

We can see some of the perils of too loose a structure in the former accounting firm Andersen Worldwide, indicted in 2002 for its role in the Enron scandal. Andersen's Houston office shredded documents and altered memos to cover up its role in Enron's questionable accounting procedures. At its Chicago headquarters, Andersen had an internal audit team, the Professional Standards Group, which was charged with reviewing the work of regional offices. But unlike other big accounting firms, Andersen let frontline partners closest to the clients overrule its internal audit team. This loose control permitted local discretion, which was a selling point to customers, but it came back to haunt the firm. The lax controls created a situation where "the rainmakers were given the power to overrule the accounting nerds" (McNamee and Borrus, 2002, p. 33).

The opposite problem is common in managed health care. Medical decisions are reviewed by insurance companies, giving clerks far removed from patient's bedside the authority to approve or deny treatment. Many physicians lament spending more time talking on the phone with insurance representatives than seeing patients. As a result of these tight controls, insurance providers sometimes deny treatments that physicians might see as urgent. In one case, a hospital-based psychologist diagnosed an adolescent as a likely perpetrator of sexual assault. The insurer questioned the diagnosis and denied hospitalization. The next day, the teenager raped a five-year-old girl.

Goalless Versus Goalbound

In some situations, few people know what the goals are; in others, people cling to goals long after they have become irrelevant or outmoded. That spells trouble unless an organization can find or invent a substitute. In the sixties, for example, polio was virtually eradicated by new vaccines. This eliminated the goal of the March of Dimes organization, which for years championed finding a cure for the crippling disease. The organization chose to shift its purpose to focus on preventing birth defects.

Irresponsible Versus Unresponsive

If people abdicate their responsibilities, performance suffers. However, adhering too rigidly to policies or procedures can be equally harmful. In public agencies, "street-level bureaucrats" (Lipsky, 1980) who deal with the public are often asked, "Could you do me this favor?" or "Couldn't you bend the rules a little bit in this case?" Turning down every request, no matter how reasonable, alienates the public and perpetuates images of bureaucratic rigidity and red tape. But agency workers who are too accommodating create problems of inconsistency and favoritism.

GREATEST HITS FROM ORGANIZATION STUDIES

Hit Number 5: Michael C. Jensen and William H. Meckling, "Theory of the Firm: Managerial Behavior, Agency Costs, and Ownership Structure," *Journal of Financial Economics*, 1976, *3*, 305–360

This classic article, fifth on our list of works most often cited by scholars, focuses on two central questions:

- What are the implications of the "agency problem"—that is, the conflicts of interest between principals and their agents?

- Given those conflicts, why do corporations even exist?

An agency relationship is a structural arrangement created whenever one party engages another to undertake some task. Jensen and Meckling's particular focus is the relationship between a corporation's owners (shareholders) and their agents, the managers. Principals and agents both seek to maximize utility, but their interests often diverge. If you are a sole proprietor, a dollar of the firm's money is a dollar of yours as well. But if you are an employee with no ownership interest, you have an incentive to pad your expense account or schedule a business meeting at an expensive resort because you're spending someone else's money.

One rationale for linking executive compensation to the price of the company's stock is that it reduces the agency problem, but the impact is often marginal at best. A notorious example is Tyco's chief executive, Dennis Kozlowski, who reportedly spent more than $30 million of company money to buy, furnish, and decorate his palatial apartment in New York City (Sorkin, 2002). Nonexecutive shareholders hate this kind of thing, but it is difficult for them to stay abreast of everything management does, and they can't do it without incurring "monitoring costs," time and money spent on things like supervision and auditing.

One implication the authors draw is that the primary value of stock analysts is the sentinel function they perform. Analysts' ability to pick stocks is notoriously poor, but their oversight puts more heat on managers to serve shareholder interests. The article also concludes that, despite the agency conflicts, the corporate form still makes economic sense for the parties involved—managers cost more than owners wish, but they still earn their keep.

The authors see the agency problem as a pervasive feature of cooperative activity. The relationship between a team and individual members, or between a boss and a subordinate, is like that between principal and agent. If members of a team share rewards equally, for example, there is an incentive for "free riders" to let someone else do most of the work. Principals face a perennial problem of keeping agents in line and on task.

STRUCTURAL CONFIGURATIONS

Structural design rarely starts from scratch. Managers search for options among the array of possibilities drawn from their accumulated wisdom or the experiences of others. Abstract templates and frameworks can offer food for thought. Henry Mintzberg and Sally Helgesen offer two conceptions of structural possibilities.

Mintzberg's Fives

As the two-dimensional lines and boxes of a traditional organization chart have become increasingly archaic, students of organizational design have developed a variety of new structural images. One influential example is Mintzberg's five-sector "logo," depicted in Exhibit 4.1. Mintzberg's chief contribution is clustering various functions into groupings and showing their relative size and clout in response to different missions and external challenges. His schema does not provide details. It is a rough atlas of the structural terrain that helps managers get their bearings. It assists in sizing up the lay of the land before assembling a structure that conforms to the surroundings.

At the base of Mintzberg's image is the *operating core,* consisting of people who perform essential work. The core is made up of workers who produce or provide products or services to customers or clients: teachers in schools, assembly-line workers in factories, physicians and nurses in hospitals, and flight crews in airlines.

Directly above the operating core is the *administrative component:* managers who supervise, coordinate, control, and provide resources for the operators. School principals, factory foremen, and echelons of middle management fulfill this role. At the top of Mintzberg's figure, senior managers in the strategic apex track current developments in the environment, determine the mission, and shape the grand design. In school systems, the strategic apex includes superintendents and school boards. In corporations, the apex houses the board of directors and senior executives.

Two more components sit alongside the administrative component. The *technostructure* houses specialists, technicians, and analysts who standardize, measure, and inspect outputs and procedures. Accounting and quality control departments in industry, audit departments in government agencies, and flight standards departments in airlines perform such technical functions.

The *support staff* performs tasks that support or facilitate the work of others throughout the organization. In schools, for example, the support staff includes nurses, secretaries, custodians, food service workers, and bus drivers. These people often wield influence far greater than their station would suggest.

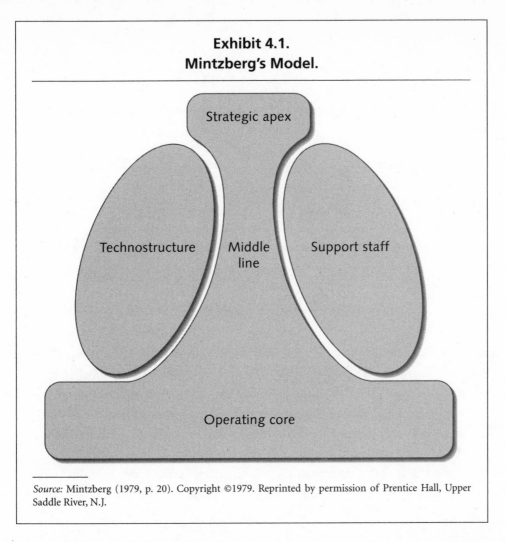

**Exhibit 4.1.
Mintzberg's Model.**

Strategic apex

Technostructure   Middle   Support staff
                        line

Operating core

Source: Mintzberg (1979, p. 20). Copyright ©1979. Reprinted by permission of Prentice Hall, Upper Saddle River, N.J.

From this basic blueprint, Mintzberg (1979) derived five structural configurations: simple structure, machine bureaucracy, professional bureaucracy, divisionalized form, and adhocracy. Each creates its unique set of management challenges.

Simple Structure   Most businesses begin as simple structures with only two levels: the strategic apex and an operating level (see Exhibit 4.2). Coordination is accomplished primarily through direct supervision and oversight, as in a small mom-and-pop operation. Mom or pop constantly monitors what is going on and exercises total authority over daily operations. William Hewlett and David Packard began their business in a garage, as did Apple Computer's Steve Jobs

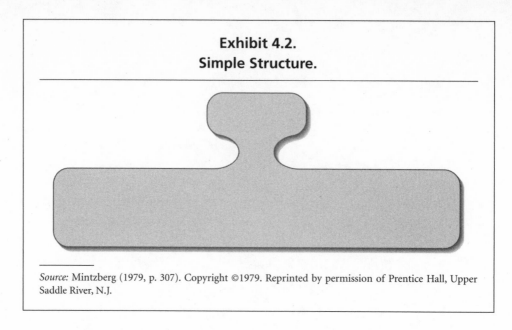

Exhibit 4.2.
Simple Structure.

Source: Mintzberg (1979, p. 307). Copyright ©1979. Reprinted by permission of Prentice Hall, Upper Saddle River, N.J.

and Steve Wozniak; General Electric had its humble beginnings in Thomas Edison's laboratory. The virtues of simple structure are flexibility and adaptability; one or two people control the entire operation. But virtues can become vices. Authorities block as well as initiate change, and they punish capriciously as well as reward handsomely. A boss too close to day-to-day operations is easily distracted by immediate problems, neglecting long-range strategic issues.

When a start-up company grows in size, a simple structure struggles to manage the accompanying complexity. Mintzberg's schema offer alternative possible routes, such as moving toward a machine or professional bureaucracy, or evolving into a divisionalized structure.

Machine Bureaucracy   McDonald's is a classic machine bureaucracy. Important decisions are made at the strategic apex; day-to-day operations are controlled by managers and standardized procedures. Machine bureaucracies have large support staffs and a sizable technostructure, with many layers between the apex and operating levels (see Exhibit 4.3).

For routine tasks, such as making hamburgers and manufacturing automotive parts, a machinelike operation is both efficient and effective. A key challenge is how to motivate and satisfy workers in the operating core. People tire quickly of

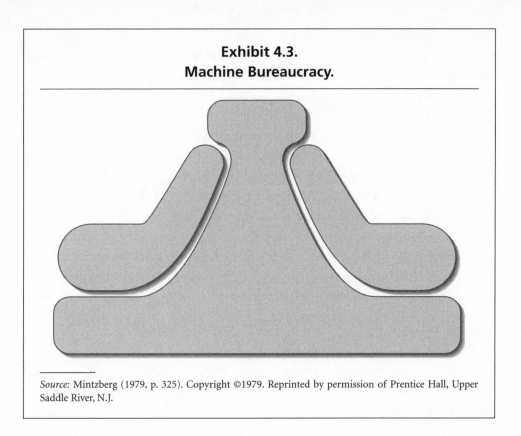

Exhibit 4.3.
Machine Bureaucracy.

Source: Mintzberg (1979, p. 325). Copyright ©1979. Reprinted by permission of Prentice Hall, Upper Saddle River, N.J.

repetitive work and standardized procedures. Yet offering too much creativity and personal challenge in, say, a McDonald's outlet could undermine consistency and uniformity—two keys to the company's success.

Like other machine bureaucracies, McDonald's deals constantly with tension between local managers and headquarters. Middle managers are heavily influenced by local concerns and tastes. Top executives, aided by analysts armed with computer printouts, rely more on generic and abstract information and pursue corporation-wide concerns. As a result, a solution from the top may not always match the needs of individual units. Faced with declining sales and market share, McDonald's introduced a new food preparation system in 1998 under the marketing banner "Made for you." CEO Jack Greenberg was convinced the new cook-to-order system would produce the fresher, tastier burgers the company needed to get back on the fast track. But franchisees soon complained that the new system led to long lines and frustrated customers. Unfazed by the criticism, Greenberg invited a couple of skeptical financial analysts to flip burgers at a McDonald's out-let in New Jersey so they could see firsthand that the concerns were unfounded. The experiment backfired. The analysts concluded that the system was too slow and decided to pass on the stock (Stires, 2002). Greenberg was replaced at the end of 2002.

Beginning with the precepts of scientific management in the early twen-tieth century, recurring efforts have been made to improve public schools by getting them to work more like machine bureaucracies in which teachers are the production workers. The initiatives have included "teacher-proof" curricula, incentive pay schemes, and the use of test scores or yearly performance indicators to measure how well a school is doing. Teachers, in contrast, see themselves as professionals who need sufficient autonomy to use their experience and judgment in finding the best way for students to learn. They often prefer to work in an orga-nization that mirrors another of Mintzberg's types, the professional bureaucracy.

Professional Bureaucracy   Harvard University affords a glimpse into the inner workings of a professional bureaucracy (see Exhibit 4.4). Its operating core is large relative to its other structural parts, particularly the technostructure. Each individual school, for example, has its own local approach to teaching evaluations; there is no university-wide profile developed by analysts. Few managerial levels exist between the strategic apex and the professors, creating a flat and decentralized profile.

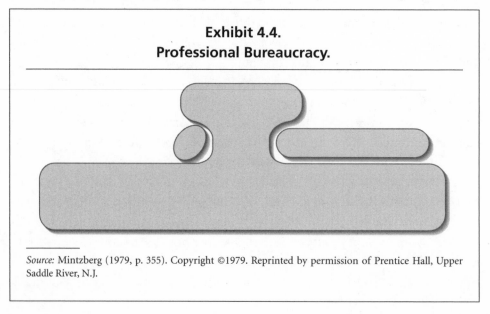

Exhibit 4.4.
Professional Bureaucracy.

Source: Mintzberg (1979, p. 355). Copyright ©1979. Reprinted by permission of Prentice Hall, Upper Saddle River, N.J.

Control relies heavily on professional training and indoctrination. Professionals are insulated from formal interference, freeing them to apply their expertise. Freeing highly trained experts to do what they do best produces many benefits but leads to challenges of coordination and quality control. Tenured professors, for example, are largely immune from formal sanctions. As a result, universities have to find other ways to deal with incompetence and irresponsibility.

A professional bureaucracy responds slowly to external change. Waves of reform typically produce little impact because professionals often view any change in their surroundings as an annoying distraction. The result is a paradox: individual professionals may strive to be at the forefront of their specialty, while the institution as a whole changes at a glacial pace. Professional bureaucracies regularly stumble when they try to exercise greater control over the operating core; requiring Harvard professors to follow standard teaching methods might do more harm than good.

In his efforts to achieve greater control over Harvard's fractious faculty, new president Larry Summers quickly ran into predictable challenges of a professional bureaucracy. In one famous case, he suggested that superstar African American studies professor Cornel West redirect his scholarly efforts. Summers's advice was given in private, but West's pique made the front page of the *New York Times*. Summers's profuse public apologies failed to deter the offended professor from decamping to Princeton. In professional bureaucracies, struggles between the strategic apex and the operating core are often won by the professionals, who are more tightly bonded to their field than to any specific institution. This is a lesson hospital administrators learn quickly in their dealings with physicians.

Divisionalized Form In a divisionalized organization (see Exhibit 4.5), the bulk of the work is done in quasi-autonomous units, as with free-standing campuses in a multi-campus university, areas of expertise in a large multi-specialty hospital, or independent businesses in a Fortune 500 firm (Mintzberg, 1979). Hewlett-Packard, for example, created separate divisions organized around different products and engineering expertise. Its printer division cornered the market to become a financial success, while its computer division struggled against intense competition. But the divisionalized structure gave the computer division time, resources, and a powerful brand that it leveraged to transform itself from also-ran to market leader.

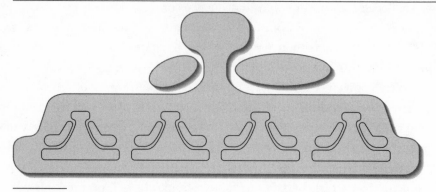

**Exhibit 4.5.
Divisionalized Form.**

Source: Mintzberg (1979, p. 393). Copyright ©1979. Reprinted by permission of Prentice Hall, Upper Saddle River, N.J.

One of the oldest businesses in the United States, Berwind Corporation, houses divisions in business sectors as diverse as manufacturing, financial services, real estate, and land management. Each division serves a distinct market and supports its own functional units. Division presidents are accountable to the corporate office in Philadelphia for specific results: profits, sales growth, and return on investment. As long as they deliver, divisions have relatively free rein. Philadelphia manages the strategic portfolio and allocates resources on the basis of its assessment of market opportunities.

Divisionalized structure offers economies of scale, resources, and responsiveness while controlling economic risks, but it creates other tensions. One is a cat-and-mouse game between headquarters and divisions. Headquarters wants oversight, while divisional managers try to evade corporate control:

> Our top management likes to make all the major decisions. They think they do, but I've seen one case where a division beat them. I received . . . a request from the division for a chimney. I couldn't see what anyone would do with a chimney. . . . [But] they've built and equipped a whole plant on plant expense orders. The chimney is the only indivisible item that exceeded the $50,000 limit we put on plant expense orders. Apparently they learned that a new plant wouldn't be formally received, so they built the damn thing" [Bower, 1970, p. 189].

Another risk in the divisionalized form is that headquarters may lose touch with operations. (As one manager put it, "Headquarters is where the rubber meets the air.") Divisionalized enterprises become unwieldy unless goals are measurable and reliable vertical information systems are in place (Mintzberg, 1979).

Adhocracy Adhocracy is a loose, flexible, self-renewing organic form tied together mostly through lateral means (see Exhibit 4.6). Usually found in a diverse, freewheeling environment, adhocracy functions as an "organizational tent," exploiting benefits that structural designers traditionally regarded as liabilities: "Ambiguous authority structures, unclear objectives, and contradictory assignments of responsibility can legitimize controversies and challenge traditions. Incoherence and indecision can foster exploration, self-evaluation, and learning" (Hedberg, Nystrom, and Starbuck, 1976, p. 45). Inconsistencies and contradictions in an adhocracy become paradoxes where a balance between opposites protects an organization from falling into an either-or trap.

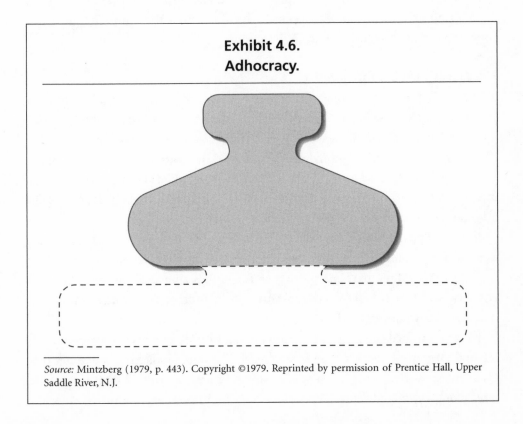

**Exhibit 4.6.
Adhocracy.**

Source: Mintzberg (1979, p. 443). Copyright ©1979. Reprinted by permission of Prentice Hall, Upper Saddle River, N.J.

Ad hoc structures are most often found in conditions of turbulence and rapid change. Examples are advertising agencies, think-tank consulting firms, and the recording industry. In the 1970s and 1980s, Digital Equipment was a well-known pioneer of adhocracy: "In many ways [DEC] is a big company in small company clothes. It doesn't believe much in hierarchy, rule books, dress codes, company cars, executive dining rooms, lofty titles, country club memberships, or most trappings of 'corporacy.' It doesn't even have assigned parking spots. Only the top half-dozen executives have sizable offices. Everyone else at the company headquarters in Maynard, Mass., makes do with dinky doorless cubicles" (Machan, 1987, p. 154).

Digital's structural arrangements helped it become the world leader in minicomputers. But the structural design became a problem when the market shifted toward personal computers, where aggressive new competitors like Compaq and Dell were dominant. "They flew so high and crashed so hard," said one observer, because "at DEC, the internal mattered so much. They spent their lives playing with each other" (Johnson, 1996, p. F11). The strength of Digital's adhocracy, a flowering of local creativity, became a liability when the company needed a timely organization-wide change in direction.

Helgeson's Web of Inclusion

Mintzberg's five-sector imagery adds a new dimension to the conventional line-staff organization chart but still retains much of the traditional portrait of structure as a clear-cut, top-down pyramid. Helgesen argues that the idea of hierarchy is primarily a male-driven depiction, quite different from structures created by female executives: "The women I studied had built profoundly integrated and organic organizations in which the focus was on nurturing good relationships; in which the niceties of hierarchical rank and distinction played little part; and in which lines of communication were multiplicitous, open, and diffuse. I noted that women tended to put themselves at the center of their organizations rather than at the top, thus emphasizing both accessibility and equality, and that they labored constantly to include people in their decision-making" (Helgesen, 1995, p. 10).

Helgesen coined the expression "web of inclusion" to portray an organic architectural form more circular than hierarchical. The web builds from the center out. Its architect works much like a spider, spinning new threads of connection and reinforcing existing strands. The web's center and periphery are interconnected;

action in one place ripples across the entire configuration, forming "an interconnected cosmic web in which the threads of all forces and events form an inseparable net of endless, mutually conditioned relations" (Fritjof Capra, quoted in Helgesen, 1995, p. 16). As a consequence, weaknesses in either the center or the periphery of the web undermine the strength of the natural network.

One of the most famous and important examples of web organization is "Linux, Inc.," the loose organization of individuals and companies that has formed around Linus Torvalds, the creator of the open-source operating system Linux, which has become Microsoft Windows's biggest competitor on servers and desktops. "Linux, Inc." is anything but a traditional company: "There's no headquarters, no CEO, and no annual report. And it's not a single company. Rather, it's a cooperative venture in which employees at about two dozen companies, along with thousands of individuals, work together to improve Linux software. . . . The Linux community, Torvalds says, is like a huge spider web, or better yet, multiple spider webs representing dozens of related open-source projects. His office is 'near where those webs intersect'" (Hamm, 2005).

The freewheeling web form encounters increasing challenges as an organization gets bigger. When Meg Whitman become CEO of Internet phenomenon eBay in 1998, she joined an organization of fewer than fifty employees configured in an informal web surrounding founder Pierre Omidyar. One of her first steps was to set up appointments with her new staff. She was surprised to learn that scheduled meetings were a foreign concept in a company where no one kept a calendar. Omidyar had built a company with a strong culture and powerful sense of community but no explicit strategy, no regular meetings, no marketing department, and almost no other identifiable structural elements. Despite the company's phenomenal growth and profitability, Whitman concluded that it was in danger of imploding without more structure and discipline. Omidyar agreed. He had worked hard to recruit Whitman because he believed she brought the big-company management experience that eBay needed to keep growing (Hill and Farkas, 2000).

GENERIC ISSUES IN RESTRUCTURING

Sooner or later, internal or external changes force every structure to remodel. When the time for restructuring comes, managers need to take account of tensions specific to each structural configuration. Consultants and managers often apply general principles and specific answers without recognizing key differences across architectural forms. Reshaping an adhocracy, for example, is radically different from restructuring a machine bureaucracy, and reweaving a web is a far cry from nudging a professional bureaucracy. Falling victim to the one-best-system or one-size-fits-all mentality is a surefire route to disaster. But the comfort of a well-defined prescription lulls too many managers into a temporary comfort zone. The iceberg looming ahead falls outside their field of vision.

Mintzberg's imagery suggests general principles to guide restructuring across a range of circumstances. Each major component of his model exerts its own pressures. Restructuring triggers a multidirectional tug-of-war that eventually determines the shape of the structure. Unless various pushes and pulls are acknowledged and managed effectively, the result may be a catastrophe.

The strategic apex—top management—tends to exert centralizing pressures. Through commands, rules, or less obtrusive means, top managers continually try to develop a unified mission or strategy. Deep down, they long for a simple structure they can control. By contrast, middle managers resist control from the top and tend to pull the organization toward balkanization. Navy captains, school principals, department heads, and bureau chiefs become committed to their own domain and seek to protect and enhance their unit's parochial interests. Tensions between centripetal forces from the top and centrifugal forces from middle management are especially prominent in divisionalized structures but are critical issues in any restructuring effort.

The technostructure exerts pressures to standardize; analysts want to measure and monitor the organization's progress against well-defined criteria. Depending on the circumstances, they counterbalance (or complement) top administrators, who want to centralize, and middle managers, who seek greater autonomy. Technocrats feel most at home in a machine bureaucracy.

The support staff pulls in the direction of greater collaboration. Its members usually feel happiest when authority is dispersed to small work units. There they can influence, directly and personally, the shape and flow of everyday decisions. They prefer adhocracy. Meanwhile, the operating core seeks to control its own destiny and minimize influence from the other components. Its members often look outside—to a union or to their professional colleagues—for support.

Attempts to restructure must acknowledge the natural tensions among various components. Depending on the configuration—machine bureaucracy, professional bureaucracy, simple structure, divisionalized form, or adhocracy—each component has more or less influence on the final outcome. In a simple structure, the boss has the edge. In machine bureaucracies, the technostructure and strategic apex possess the most clout. In professional bureaucracies, chronic conflict between administrators and professionals is the dominant tension, while members of the technostructure play an important role in the wings. In the adhocracy, a variety of actors can play a pivotal role in shaping the emerging structural patterns.

Beyond internal negotiations lurks a more crucial issue. A structure's workability ultimately depends on its fit with the organization's environment and technology. Natural selection weeds out the field, determining survivors and victims. The major players must negotiate a structure that meets the needs of each component and still works in the organization's environment.

Why Restructure?

Restructuring is a challenging process that consumes time and resources with no guarantee of success. Organizations typically embark on that path when they feel compelled to respond to major problems or opportunities. Various pressures can lead to that conclusion:

- *The environment shifts.* At American Telephone & Telegraph, a mandated shift from regulated monopoly to a market with multiple competitors required a massive reorganization of the Bell System that played out over decades. When AT&T split off its local telephone companies into regional "Baby Bells," few anticipated that eventually one of the children (Southwest Bell) would swallow up the parent and appropriate its identity.
- *Technology changes.* The aircraft industry's shift from piston to jet engines profoundly affected the relationship between engine and airframe. Some established firms faltered because they underestimated the complexities; Boeing rose to lead the industry because it understood them (Henderson and Clark, 1990).
- *Organizations grow.* Digital Equipment thrived with a very informal and flexible structure during the company's early years, but the same structure produced major problems when it grew into a multibillion-dollar corporation.
- *Leadership changes.* Reorganization is often the first initiative of new leaders. It is a way for them to try to put their stamp on the organization, even if no one else sees a need to restructure.

Miller and Friesen (1984) studied a sample of successful as well as troubled firms undergoing structural change and found that those in trouble typically fell into one of three configurations:

- *The impulsive firm:* A fast-growing organization, controlled by one individual or a few top people, in which structures and controls have become too primitive and the firm is increasingly out of control. Profits may fall precipitously, and survival may be at stake. Many once-successful entrepreneurial organizations stumble at this stage; they have failed to evolve beyond their simple structure.

- *The stagnant bureaucracy:* An older, tradition-dominated organization with an obsolete product line. A predictable and placid environment has lulled everyone to sleep, and top management is slavishly committed to old ways. Information systems are too primitive to detect the need for change, and lower-level managers feel ignored and alienated. Many old-line corporations and public bureaucracies fit this group of faltering machine bureaucracies.

- *The headless giant:* A loosely coupled, divisional organization that has turned into a collection of feudal baronies. The administrative core is weak, and most of the initiative and power resides in autonomous divisions. With little strategy or leadership at the top, the firm is adrift. Collaboration is minimal because departments compete for resources. Decision making is reactive and crisis-oriented. WorldCom is a recent example of how bad things can get in this situation. CEO Bernie Ebbers built the company rapidly from a tiny start-up in Mississippi to a global telecommunications giant through some sixty-five acquisitions. But "for all its talent in buying competitors, the company was not up to the task of merging them. Dozens of conflicting computer systems remained, local network systems were repetitive and failed to work together properly, and billing systems were not coordinated. 'Don't think of WorldCom the way you would of other corporations,' said one person who has worked with the company at a high level for many years. 'It's not a company, it's just a bunch of disparate pieces. It's simply dysfunctional'" (Eichenwald, 2002c, p. C4).

Miller and Friesen (1984) found that even in troubled organizations, structural change is episodic: long periods of little change are followed by brief episodes of major restructuring. Organizations are reluctant to make major changes because a stable structure reduces confusion and uncertainty, maintains internal consistency, and protects the existing equilibrium. The price of stability is a structure that grows increasingly misaligned with the environment. Eventually, the gap gets so big that a major overhaul is inevitable. Restructuring, in this view, is like spring cleaning: we accumulate debris over months or years until we are finally forced to face up to the mess.

Making Restructuring Work: Three Case Examples

In this section, we look at three case examples of restructuring. We focus particularly on examples of reengineering, which rose to prominence in the 1990s as an umbrella concept for emerging trends in structural thinking. Hammer and Champy promised a revolution in how organizations were structured: "When a process is reengineered, jobs evolve from narrow and task oriented to multidimensional. People who once did as they were instructed now make choices and decisions on their own instead. Assembly-line work disappears. Functional departments lose their reason for being. Managers stop acting like supervisors and behave more like coaches. Workers focus more on customers' needs and less on their bosses' whims. Attitudes and values change in response to new incentives. Practically every aspect of the organization is transformed, often beyond recognition" (1993, p. 65).

The process of reengineering and the results it produces vary significantly. As Champy admitted in his follow-up book, *Reengineering Management* (1995), "Reengineering is in trouble." He attributed the shortfall to flaws in senior management thinking. Essentially, for reengineering to succeed, managers need to be rewired. Some reengineering initiatives have indeed been catastrophic, a notorious example being the long-haul bus company, Greyhound Lines. As the company came out of bankruptcy in the early 1990s, a new management team announced a major reorganization, with sizable cuts in staffing and routes and development of a new, computerized reservation system. The new initiative played well on Wall Street, where the company's stock soared, but it fared very poorly on Main Street as both customer service and the new reservations system collapsed. Rushed, underfunded, and insensitive to both employees and customers, it was a textbook example of how not to restructure. Eventually, Greyhound's stock crashed, and management was forced out. One observer noted wryly, "They reengineered that business to hell" (Tomsho, 1994, p. A1). Across many organizations, reengineering was a cover for downsizing the workforce.

But while few in number compared to disasters, there have also been examples of notable restructuring success. Here we discuss three of them, drawn from different eras and industries. The first, from Citibank, dates back to the 1970s, well before the term *reengineering* was applied to structural change.

The "back room" at Citibank—the department that processed checks and other financial instruments—was in trouble when John Reed took charge in 1970 (Seeger, Lorsch, and Gibson, 1975). Productivity was disappointing, errors were frequent, and expenses were rising almost 20 percent every year. Reed soon determined that the area needed dramatic structural change. Traditionally, it was viewed as a service for the bank's customer-contact offices, though it was structured as a machine bureaucracy. Reed decided to think of it not as a support function but as a factory: an independent, high-volume production facility. To implement this concept, he imported high-level executives from the automobile industry. One was Robert White, who came from Ford to become the primary architect of new structure and systems for the back room.

White began by developing a "phase one action plan" that called for cutting costs, putting in new computer systems, and developing a financial control system capable of both forecasting and measuring performance. In effect, the strategy retained the machine bureaucracy but tightened it. After phase one was implemented, White concluded that "we hadn't gone back to the basics enough. We found that we did not really understand the present processes completely" (Seeger, Lorsch, and Gibson, 1975, p. 8). What followed was an intensive, detailed study of how the back room's processes worked, laid out in a detailed flowchart that covered the walls of a room. They realized that the current structure was, in effect, one very large functional pipeline. Everything flowed into "preprocessing" at the front end of the pipe, then to "encoding," and on through a series of functional areas until it eventually came out at the other end. Reed and White decided to break the pipe into several smaller lines, each carrying a different "product" and each supervised by a single manager with responsibility for an end-to-end process. The key insight was to change the structure from machine bureaucracy to a divisionalized form. Along with the change, White instituted extensive performance measures and tight accountability procedures—69 quality indicators and 129 different standards for time lines.

Not surprisingly, White's demanding, top-down approach produced fear and loathing among many old-timers in the back room and nearly led to rebellion. As Mintzberg's model predicts, the technical core strongly resisted this intrusion. Reed and White implemented the new structure virtually overnight, and the short-term result was chaos and a major breakdown in the system. It took two weeks to get things working again, and five months to recover from the problems generated by the transition. But once past that crisis, the new system led to a dramatic improvement in operating results: production was up, and costs and errors were down. The back room had unexpectedly become a major source of competitive advantage.

The revamp of the Citibank back room demonstrates again the value of managerial imagination. The basic concepts behind restructuring the back room were not new. The change from a functional bureaucracy to a divisionalized form first occurred in the 1920s at General Motors and DuPont. The key imaginative leap was to apply the concept of a divisionalized organization to the back room of a bank.

The Citibank restructuring was strongly driven from the top down and focused primarily on internal efficiencies. This has been true of many, but by no means all, reengineering efforts.

KODAK'S BLACK-AND-WHITE DIVISION

Eastman Kodak, a classic reengineering example portrayed by Hammer and Champy (1993), began with a push from the top but put much greater emphasis on customers and on empowering employees at multiple levels. Kodak traces its rich historic roots back to the late 1880s, when George Eastman began to manufacture wooden boxes capable of capturing one hundred personal images on film.

A century later, Kodak was a giant in trouble. Its name and film were known around the world, but the company had been rocked by intense competition, high costs, declining customer satisfaction, threats of a hostile takeover, and low employee morale. At a top management meeting in 1989, Kodak's normally gentle, soft-spoken CEO, Colby

Chandler, wielded a machete to hack a wooden lectern to pieces. The message was clear and dramatic: Kodak needed fundamental change, and its functional, "stovepipe" structure had to give way to an organization based on process—a seamless flow from raw materials to finished products (Hammer and Champy, 1993).

Kodak chose to reorganize into six flows, one of which was black-and-white film. Implementation was to begin immediately, and any laggard operations would be shut down. In the black-and-white division, a group of executives focused on creating three streams: graphics, health sciences, and solvent coatings. All other areas (financial services, human resources, and engineering support) would be "dedicated" to supporting these flows.

One of the first tasks was to create performance measures and standards for the flows (productivity, inventory, waste, quality, conformance to specifications). With the operating flow as the center of attention, managers and supervisors became coaches and cheerleaders. Frequent informal meetings were an opportunity to air concerns and identify problems. Employees were encouraged to develop local visions and determine priorities and improvement plans for everything from reducing inventory and cutting waste to establishing relationships with suppliers and speeding delivery time (Frangos, 1996).

The overall flow focused on satisfying external customers; each step in the process emphasized satisfying internal customers and building cooperation among employees. Cross-functional teams began to achieve breakthroughs in quality and cost reduction. Two years after the restructuring was launched, performance standards were being surpassed. The division was not only one of the company's shining stars in terms of profitability but also was widely heralded as one of the company's best places to work.

BETH ISRAEL HOSPITAL

Boston's Beth Israel Hospital is a restructuring effort in health care that sought to move toward greater autonomy and teamwork. When Joyce Clifford became Beth Israel's director of nursing, she found a top-down structure common in hospitals:

The nursing aides, who had the least preparation, had the most contact with the patients. But they had no authority of any kind. They had to go to their supervisor to ask if a patient could have an aspirin. The supervisor would then ask the head nurse, who would then ask a doctor. The doctor would ask how long the patient had been in pain. Of course the head nurse had absolutely no idea, so she'd have to track down the aide to ask her, and then relay that information back to the doctor. It was ridiculous, a ludicrous and dissatisfying situation, and one in which it was impossible for the nurse to feel any satisfaction at all. The system was hierarchical, fragmented, impersonal, and [overmanaged] [Helgesen, 1995, p. 134].

Within units, the responsibilities of nurses were highly specialized: some assigned to handling medications, others to monitoring vital signs, still others to taking blood pressure readings. Add to the list specialized housekeeping roles—bedpan, bed making, and food services—and a patient witnessed interruptions from a multitude of virtual strangers. No one really knew for sure what was going on with any individual patient.

With the support and cooperation of Mitchell Rabkin, Beth Israel's progressive CEO, Clifford instituted a major structural change, from a pyramid with nurses at the bottom to an inclusive web with nurses at the center. The concept, called primary nursing, has each primary nurse monitor the care of a specific patient. The nurse takes information when the patient is admitted, develops a comprehensive plan, assembles a team to provide round-the-clock care, and lets the family know what to expect. A nurse manager sets goals for the unit, deals with budget and administrative matters, and makes sure that primary nurses have ample resources to provide quality care.

As the primary nurse assumed more responsibility, connections with physicians and other hospital workers had to be revised. Instead of simply carrying out physicians' orders, the primary nurse became a professional partner, attending rounds and participating as an equal in treatment decisions. Housekeepers reported to primary nurses rather than to housekeeping supervisors. The same housekeeper was assigned to make a patient's bed, attend to the patient's hygiene, and deliver trays. Laundry workers brought in clean items on demand rather than making a once-a-day delivery. Beth Israel's inclusive web was further strengthened by sophisticated technology that gave all network points easy access to patient information and administrative data.

Primary nurses learned from performing a variety of heretofore menial tasks. Bed making, for example, became an opportunity to evaluate a patient's condition and assess how well a treatment plan was working. Joyce Clifford's role also was transformed from top-down supervisor to a web-centered coordinator. Rather than telling people what to do, she focused on keeping everyone informed:

> At the center of all patient care at Beth Israel, Joyce Clifford linked the various intersecting points of the inclusive web: "A big part of my job is to keep nurses informed on a regular basis of what's going on out there—what the board is doing, what decisions are confronting the hospital as a whole, what the issues are in health care in this country. I also let them know that I'm trying to represent what the nurses here are doing—to our vice-presidents, to our board, and people in the outside world . . . to the nursing profession and the health care field as a whole" [Helgesen, 1995, p. 158].

Beth Israel's primary nursing concept, initiated in the mid-1970s, produced significant improvement in both patient care and nursing morale. Nursing turnover declined dramatically (Springarn, 1982) and the model's success made it highly influential and widely copied both in the United States and abroad. But even successful change won't work forever. Over the years, changes in the health care system put Beth Israel's model under increasing pressure. More patients with more problems but shorter hospital stays made nurses' jobs much harder at the same time that cost pressures forced reductions in nursing staff. Beth Israel chose to update its approach by creating interdisciplinary "care teams." Instead of assembling an ad hoc collection of care providers for each new patient, ongoing teams of nurses, physicians, and support staff were created to provide interdisciplinary support to primary nurses (Rundall, Starkweather, and Norrish, 1998).

Principles of Successful Structural Change

The proportion of reengineering failures to successes is high. The Citibank, Kodak, and Beth Israel efforts succeeded by following several basic principles of successful structural change:

- The change architects developed a new conception of the organization's goals and strategies.
- They carefully studied the existing structure and process so that they fully understood how things worked. Many efforts at structural change fail because they start from an inadequate picture of current roles, relationships, and processes.
- They designed the new structure in response to changes in goals, technology, and environment.
- Finally, they experimented as they moved along, retaining things that worked and discarding those that did not.

SUMMARY

At a given moment, an organization's structure represents its best effort to align internal workings with outside concerns. Simultaneously, managers work to juggle and resolve enduring organizational dilemmas: Are we too loose, or too tight? Are employees underworked, or overwhelmed? Are we too rigid, or do we lack standards? Do people spend too much or too little time harmonizing with one another? Structure represents a resolution of contending claims from various groups.

Mintzberg differentiates five major components in organizational structure: strategic apex, middle management, operating core, technostructure, and support staff. These components configure in unique designs: machine bureaucracy, professional bureaucracy, simple structure, divisionalized form, and adhocracy. Helgesen adds a less hierarchical model, the web of inclusion.

Changes eventually require some form of structural adaptation. Restructuring or reengineering is a logical but high-risk response. In the short term, it invariably produces confusion, resistance, and even a decline in success. In the long run, success depends on how well the new model aligns with environment, task, and technology. It also hinges on the route for putting the new structure in place. Effective restructuring requires both a fine-grained, microscopic assessment of typical problems and an overall, topographical sense of structural options.

Organizing Groups and Teams

In Seattle, a seventeen-year-old girl is mortally injured in an automobile accident. She is pronounced brain-dead, and her parents give permission to harvest her organs. Her kidney tissue type is entered into a national database. In Nashville, a potential recipient is identified: a forty-two-year-old mother of three who will die without a new kidney.

Dr. Peter Minnich, the Nashville surgeon who will perform the transplant, contacts his counterpart in Seattle to check the condition of the kidney. Weighing several factors, he decides to accept the organ. A Seattle surgical team procures the kidney, checks for a tissue match, and transports the iced kidney to the airport for its flight to Nashville. Simultaneously, the Nashville transplant team hospitalizes the recipient. They also notify the hospital and give an estimate of how long the operation will take. The lab is alerted to perform the final cross-match once the kidney arrives, a procedure that takes three hours.

On arrival, the kidney is taken to the lab. Ninety minutes before the results of the cross-match are complete, nurses begin to prepare the operating room. The lab calls in a positive result, so the transplant can go forward. Members of the transplant team scrub in and go about their respective duties. The surgeon cleans up the kidney. The first assistant trims the fat and helps the surgeon pack the organ in fresh ice slush. A scrub nurse and a circulating nurse prepare the instrument table. The anesthesiologist and nurse assistant prepare the patient for surgery. During the transplant procedure, the circulating nurse brings instruments and sutures. The scrub nurse watches the surgery and anticipates which instruments the surgeon will need. The surgeon focuses on the procedure. The first assistant retracts tissue. The anesthesiologist monitors the patient's vital signs and supervises the nurse assistant.

Success in this life-saving procedure depends as much on the performance of the team as on the technical skills of the surgeon. Multiple roles are clearly defined, but team members also have the flexibility to cross role boundaries to do what needs to be done. The surgeon is in charge, but there is substantial lateral coordination. A good scrub nurse, for example, anticipates which instruments to hand off, with the discretion, as Dr. Minnich puts it, to "give me what I want, not what I'm asking for." He adds, "The more often team members work together the greater the chance for a successful outcome. Building a cohesive team is critical. The surgeon has to be a team leader as well as a good technician." The resulting teamwork has allowed Minnich to compile a perfect success record.

The impact of structure on a team's performance is not restricted to the operating suite. During World War II, a U.S. Army commando team compiled a distinctive record. It accomplished every mission it was assigned, including extremely high-risk operations behind the lines. Deaths and injuries were among the lowest of any U.S. military unit. A research team was charged with finding out what made the unit so successful. Were the enlisted men and officers especially talented? Was their training longer or more intensive than normal? Or was the group just plain lucky?

Researchers pinpointed the reason for the group's success: the ability to reconfigure its structure to fit the situation. Planning for missions, the group functioned democratically. Anyone could volunteer ideas and make suggestions. Decisions were reached by consensus, and the engagement strategy was approved by the group as a whole. The unit's planning structure resembled that of a research and development team or a creative design group. Amorphous roles, lateral coordination, and a flat hierarchy encouraged participation, creativity, and productive conflict. Battle plans reflected the group's best ideas.

Executing the plan was another story. The group's structure transformed from a loose, creative confederation to a well-defined, tightly controlled chain of command. Each individual had a specific assignment. Tasks had to be done with split-second precision. The commanding officer had sole responsibility for making operational decisions or revising the plan. Everyone else obeyed orders without question, though they were allowed to offer suggestions if time permitted. In battle, the group relied on the traditional military structure: clear-cut responsibilities and decisions made at the top and executed by the rank and file.

The group's ability to tailor its structure captured the best of two worlds. Participation encouraged creativity, ownership, and understanding of the battle plan. Authority, accountability, and clarity enabled the group to function with speed and efficiency during the operation.

Today, we see increasing reliance on self-organizing units or teams. A deadly example is Al Quaeda. Committed to uniting all Muslims under a new caliphate, Al Quaeda believes that only force can achieve this mission. Al Quaeda began in Afghanistan in the 1980s as a more centralized, top-down organization under the leadership of Osama bin Laden. Expelled from its safe haven and seriously damaged by the U.S. invasion of Afghanistan, it adapted to circumstances and became more decentralized and loosely structured. Communication between top leadership and local units moves through a clandestine labyrinth of secret couriers and codes. The logistics of a selected strike are worked out in concert with intermediaries who link strategy with operations. The strike is then carried out by the *mujahideen*, or brigade members. Until activated for a specified mission, members of these sleeper cells blend with the general populace. Cells within the same region operate autonomously. They can be, without knowing it, on parallel tracks for the same mission. This hydra-like team structure looms as a deadly threat that is difficult to combat with traditional command-and-control strategies. Teamwork cuts across organizational and national boundaries and can work either for or against us.

Much of the work in large organizations of every sort is now done in groups or teams. When these units work well, they elevate the performance of ordinary individuals to extraordinary heights. When teams malfunction, as too often happens, they erode the potential contributions of even the most talented members. What determines how well groups perform? As illustrated by the surgical team, the commando team, and Al Quaeda, the performance of a small group depends heavily on structure. A key ingredient of a top-notch team is an appropriate blueprint of roles and relationships set in motion to attain common goals.

In this chapter, we explore the structural features of small groups or teams and show how restructuring can improve group performance. We begin by describing various design options for teams, accenting the relationship between design and tasks. Next, using sports as an example, we discuss different patterns of team differentiation, coordination, and interdependence. Then we describe the characteristics of high-performing teams. Finally, we discuss the pros and cons of self-managing teams—a hot item in the early twenty-first century.

TASKS AND LINKAGES IN SMALL GROUPS

From a range of options, groups must develop a structure that maximizes individuals' contributions while minimizing the problems that often plague small groups. A key to group structure is the work to be done. Tasks vary in clarity, predictability, and stability. The task-structure relationship in small groups is parallel to that in larger organizations.

Contextual Variables

As suggested in Chapter Four, complex tasks present challenges different from simpler ones. Planning a commando mission or transplanting a kidney is not the same as painting a house or setting up a family outing. Simple tasks align with basic structures—clearly defined roles, elementary forms of interdependence, and coordination by plan or command. More complicated projects generally require more complex forms: flexible roles, reciprocal give-and-take, and synchronization through lateral dealings and communal feedback. If a situation becomes exceptionally ambiguous and fast-paced, particularly when time is a factor, more centralized authority often works best. Otherwise, a group may be unable to make decisions quickly enough. Without a workable structure, performance and morale suffer, and troubles multiply.

Ferreting out the appropriate group structure requires careful consideration of pertinent contextual variables, some vague or tough to assess:

- What is our goal?
- What needs to be done?
- Who should do what?
- How should we make decisions?
- Who is in charge?
- How do we coordinate efforts?
- What do individual members care about most: time, quality, participation?
- What are the special skills and talents of each group member?

- What is the relationship between this group and others?

- How will we determine success?

Some Fundamental Team Configurations

A high percentage of employees' and managers' time is spent in meetings and working groups of three to twelve people. To illustrate design options, we examine several fundamental structural configurations from studies of five-member teams. These basic patterns are too simple to apply to larger, more complex systems, but they help to illustrate the principle of how different structural forms respond to a variety of challenges.

The first is a one-boss arrangement; one person has authority over others (see Exhibit 5.1). Information and decisions flow from the top. Group members offer information to and communicate primarily with the official leader rather than with one another. Although this array is efficient and fast, it works best in a relatively simple and straightforward situation. More complicated circumstances overload the boss, producing delays or bad decisions, unless the person in charge has an unusual level of skill, expertise, and energy. Subordinates quickly become frustrated when directives they receive are poorly timed or ill-suited to the situation.

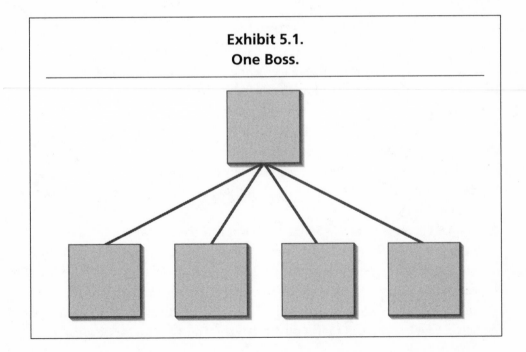

**Exhibit 5.1.
One Boss.**

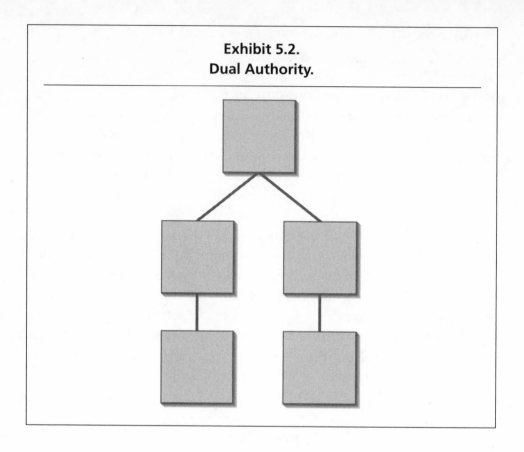

**Exhibit 5.2.
Dual Authority.**

A second alternative creates a management level below the boss (see Exhibit 5.2). Two individuals are given authority over specific areas of the group's work. Information and decisions flow through them. This arrangement works when a task is divisible; it reduces the boss's span of control, freeing up time to concentrate on mission, strategy, or relationships with higher-ups. But adding a new layer limits access from the lower levels to the boss. Communication becomes slower and more cumbersome, and may eventually erode morale and performance.

Another choice is to create, in effect, a simple hierarchy, with a middle manager who reports to the boss and in turn supervises and communicates with others (see Exhibit 5.3). This arrangement is used extensively at the White House. It frees the president to focus on mission and external relations while leaving operational details to the chief of staff. Though this further limits access to the top, it can be more efficient than a dual-manager arrangement. At the same time,

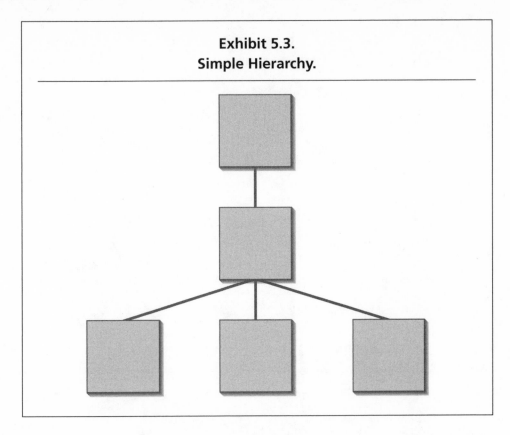

**Exhibit 5.3.
Simple Hierarchy.**

friction between operational and top-level managers is commonplace and can lead to attempts by the number two to usurp the number one's position.

A fourth option is a circle network, where information and decisions flow sequentially from one group member to another (see Exhibit 5.4). Each can add to or modify whatever comes around. This design relies solely on lateral coordination and simplifies communication. Each person has to deal directly with only two others; transactions are therefore easier to manage. But one weak link in the chain can undermine the entire enterprise. The circle can bog down with complex tasks that require more reciprocity.

A final possibility sets up what small group researchers call the all-channel, or star, network (see Exhibit 5.5). This design is similar to Helgesen's web of inclusion. It creates multiple connections so that each person can talk to anyone else. Information flows freely; decisions require touching multiple bases. Morale in an all-channel network is usually very high. The arrangement works well if a task is amorphous or complicated, but it is slow and inefficient for a

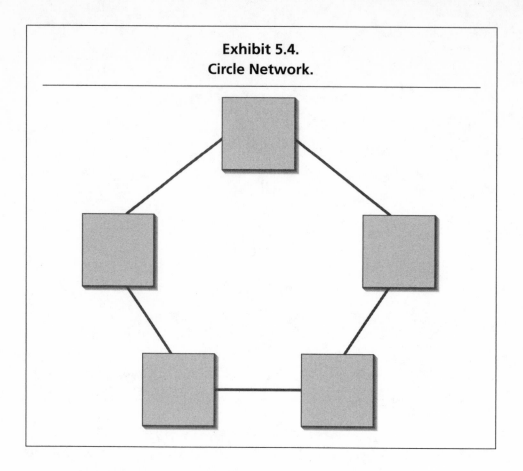

**Exhibit 5.4.
Circle Network.**

simpler undertaking. It works best when team members bring well-developed communication skills, enjoy participation, tolerate ambiguity, embrace diversity, and are able to manage conflict.

TEAMWORK AND INTERDEPENDENCE

Even in the relatively simple case of five-person groups, the formal network is critical to team functioning. In the give-and-take of larger organizations, things get more complicated. We can get a fresh perspective and sharpen our thinking about structure in groups by looking beyond work organizations. Making the familiar strange often helps the strange become familiar. Team sports, among the most popular pastimes around the world, offer a helpful analogy to clarify how teamwork varies depending on the tasks at hand. Every competition calls for its own unique patterns of interaction. Because of this, unique team structures

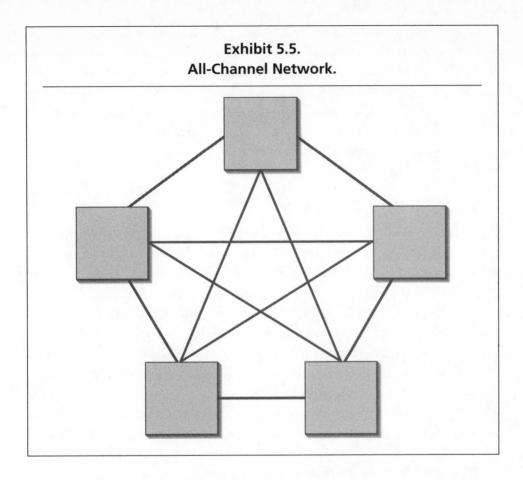

**Exhibit 5.5.
All-Channel Network.**

are required for different sports. Social architecture is thus remarkably different for baseball, football, and basketball.

Baseball

As baseball player Pete Rose once noted, "Baseball is a team game, but nine men who meet their individual goals make a nice team" (Keidel, 1984, p. 8). In baseball, as in cricket and other bat-and-ball games, a team is a loosely integrated confederacy. Individual efforts are mostly independent, seldom involving more than two or three players at a time. Particularly on defense, players are separated from one another by significant distance. The loose connections minimize the need for synchronization among the various positions. The pitcher and catcher must each know what the other is going to do, and at times, infielders must anticipate how a teammate will act. Managers' decisions are mostly tactical, normally involving individual substitutions or actions. Managers come and go without seriously disrupting the team's play. Players can transfer from one team to another with relative ease. A newcomer can do the job without major retuning. John Updike summed it up well: "Of all the team sports, baseball, with its graceful intermittence of action, its immense and tranquil field sparsely salted with poised men in white, its dispassionate mathematics, seemed to be best suited to accommodate, and be ornamented by, a loner. It is an essentially lonely game" (Keidel, 1984, pp. 14–15).

Football

Baseball is poles apart from American football. Unlike baseball players, football players perform in close proximity. Linemen and offensive backs hear, see, and often touch one another. Each play involves every player on the field. Efforts are sequentially linked in a prearranged plan. The actions of linemen pave the way for the movement of backs; a defensive team's field position becomes the starting point for the offense, and vice versa. In the transition from offense to defense, specialty platoons play a pivotal role. The efforts of individual players are not independent but instead are tightly coordinated. George Allen, former coach of the Washington Redskins, put it this way: "A football team is a lot like a machine. It's made up of parts. If one part doesn't work, one player pulling against you and not doing his job, the whole machine fails" (Keidel, 1984, p. 9).

Because of the tight connections among parts, a football team must be well integrated, mainly through planning and top-down control. The primary units are the offensive, defensive, and specialty platoons, each with its own coordinator. Under the direction of the head coach, the team uses scouting reports and other surveillance to develop a strategy or game plan in advance. During the game, strategic decisions are typically made by the head coach. Tactical decisions are made by assistants or by designated players on either offense or defense (Keidel, 1984).

A football team's tight-knit character makes it tougher to swap players from one team to another. Irv Cross, of the Philadelphia Eagles, once remarked, "An Eagles player could never make an easy transition to the Dallas Cowboys; the system and philosophies are just too different" (Keidel, 1984, p. 15). Unlike baseball, football requires intricate strategy and tightly meshed execution.

Basketball

Basketball players perform in even closer proximity to one another than football players. In quick, rapidly moving transitions, offense becomes defense—with the same players. The efforts of individuals are highly reciprocal; each player depends on the performance of others. Each may be involved with any of the other four. Anyone can handle the ball or attempt to score.

Basketball is much like improvisational jazz. Teams require a high level of spontaneous, mutual adjustment. Everyone is on the move, often in an emerging pattern rather than a predetermined course. A successful basketball season depends heavily on a flowing relationship among team members who read and anticipate one another's moves. Players who play together a long time develop a sense of what their teammates will do. A team of newcomers experiences difficulty in adjusting to individual predispositions or quirks. Keidel (1984) notes that coaches, who sit or roam the sidelines, serve as integrators. Their periodic interventions reinforce team cohesion, helping players coordinate laterally on the move. Unlike baseball teams, basketball teams cannot function as a collection of individual stars. Unlike football, basketball has no platoons. It is wholly a harmonized group effort.

A study of Duke University's successful women's basketball team in 2000 documented the importance of group interdependence and cohesion. The team won because players could anticipate the actions of others. The individual "I" deferred to the collective "we." Passing to a teammate was valued as highly as making the shot. Basketball is "fast, physically close, and crowded, 20 arms and legs in motion, up, down, across, in the air. The better the team, the more precise the passing into lanes that appear blocked with bodies" (Lubans, 2001, p. 1).

DETERMINANTS OF SUCCESSFUL TEAMWORK

In sports and elsewhere, structural profiles of successful teams at work depend on the game—on what a team is trying to do. Keidel (1984) suggests several important questions in designing an appropriate structure:

- What is the nature and degree of dealings among individuals?
- What is the spatial distribution of unit members?
- Given a group's objectives and constraints, where does authority reside?

- How is coordination achieved?

- Which word best describes the required structure: conglomerate, mechanistic, or organic?

- What sports expression metaphorically captures the task of management: filling out the line-up card, preparing the game plan, or influencing the game's flow?

Appropriate team structures can vary, even within the same organization. For example, a senior research manager in a pharmaceutical firm observed a structural progression in discovering and developing a new drug: "The process moves through three distinct stages. It's like going from baseball to football to basketball" (Keidel, 1984, p. 11). In basic research, individual scientists work independently to develop a body of knowledge. As in baseball, individual labors are the norm. Once identified, a promising drug passes from developmental chemists to pharmacy researchers to toxicologists. If the drug receives preliminary federal approval, it moves to clinical researchers for experimental tests. These sequential relationships are reminiscent of play sequences in football. In the final stage ("new drug application") physicians, statisticians, pharmacists, pharmacologists, toxicologists, and chemists work closely and reciprocally to win final approval from the Food and Drug Administration. Their efforts resemble the closely linked and flowing patterns of a basketball team (Keidel, 1984).

Jan Haynes, executive vice president of FzioMed, a California developer of new biomedical approaches to preventing scar tissue in surgical procedures, echoes the pharmaceutical executive's observations. But she adds, "In sports a game lasts only a short period of time. In our business, each game goes on for months, even years. It more closely resembles cricket. A single game can go on for days and still end in a draw. Our product has been in the trial stage for several years and now we have to shift the team to a new phase; working with the FDA to get final approval, which could take a long time." Ron Haynes, the firm's chairman, points out how difficult it is to change his leadership style as the rules of the game change: "I moved from manager to owner of an expansion team where we have several games being played simultaneously in the same stadium. If our leadership can't shift quickly from one to another, our operation won't get the job done right." Doing the right job requires a structure or structures well suited to what an organization is trying to accomplish.

TEAM STRUCTURE AND TOP PERFORMANCE

The importance of a clear and appropriate structure to team performance is well documented. Katzenbach and Smith (1993), for example, interviewed hundreds of people on more than fifty teams in developing their book *The Wisdom of Teams.* Their sample encompassed thirty enterprises in settings as diverse as Motorola, Hewlett-Packard, Operation Desert Storm, and the Girl Scouts. They drew a clear distinction between undifferentiated "groups" and sharply focused "teams": "A team is a small number of people with complementary skills, who are committed to a common purpose, set of performance goals and approach for which they hold themselves mutually accountable" (p. 112).

Katzenbach and Smith's research highlights six distinguishing characteristics of high-quality teams:

- *High-performing teams shape purpose in response to a demand or an opportunity placed in their path, usually by higher management.* Top managers clarify the team's charter, rationale, and challenge while giving the team flexibility to work out goals and plans of operation. By giving a team clear authority and then staying out of the way, management releases collective energy and creativity.

- *High-performing teams translate common purpose into specific, measurable performance goals.* Purpose yields an overall mission, but successful teams take the additional step of recasting purpose into specific and measurable performance goals: "If a team fails to establish specific performance goals or if those goals do not relate directly to the team's overall purpose, team members become confused, pull apart, and revert to mediocre performance. By contrast, when purpose and goals are built on one another and are combined with team commitment, they become a powerful engine of performance" (p. 113).

- *High-performing teams are of manageable size.* Katzenbach and Smith fix the optimal size for an effective team somewhere between two and twenty-five people: "Ten people are far more likely than fifty to work through their individual, functional, and hierarchical differences toward a common plan and to hold themselves jointly accountable for the results" (p. 114). More members mean more structural complexity, so teams should aim for the smallest size that can get the job done.

- *High-performing teams develop the right mix of expertise.* The structural frame stresses the critical link between specialization and expertise. Effective teams seek out the full range of necessary technical fluency; "product development teams that include only marketers or engineers are less likely to succeed than those with the complementary skills of both" (p. 115). In addition, exemplary teams find and reward expertise in problem solving, decision making, and interpersonal skills to keep the group focused, on task, and free of debilitating personal squabbles.

• *High-performing teams develop a common commitment to working relationships.* "Team members must agree on who will do particular jobs, how schedules will be set and adhered to, what skills need to be developed, how continuing membership in the team is to be earned, and how the group will make and modify decisions" (p. 115). Effective teams take time to explore who is best suited for a particular task as well as how individual roles come together. Achieving structural clarity varies from team to team, but it takes more than an organization chart to identify roles and pinpoint one's place in the official pecking order and layout of responsibilities. Most teams require a more detailed understanding of who is going to do what and how people relate to each other in carrying out diverse tasks.

One possibility is to use responsibility charting (Galbraith, 1977). Responsibility charting presents a framework and a language for hammering out how people work together. For a given task, responsibility is assigned to the individual or group with overall accountability. The next step is to outline how that role relates to others on the team. Does someone need to approve the actions of the responsible person? Are there people who need to be consulted? Are there others who must be kept informed? The acronym CAIRO summarizes the framework: C for *consults;* A for *approval;* I for *informed;* R for *responsibility;* and O for *out of the loop,* or not informed. Whatever form it takes, an effective team "establishes a social contract among members that relates to their purpose and guides and obligates how they will work together" (Katzenbach and Smith, 1993, p. 116).

• *Members of high-performing teams hold themselves collectively accountable.* Pinpointing individual responsibility is crucial to a well-coordinated effort, but effective teams find ways to hold the collective accountable: "Teams enjoying a common purpose and approach inevitably hold themselves responsible, both as individuals and as a team, for the team's performance" (p. 116).

Teams have become the rage but are often thrown together with little attention to what ensures success. In an influential article, Brian Dumaine (1994) highlights a common error: "Teams often get launched in a vacuum, with little or no training or support, no changes in the design of their work, and no new systems like e-mail to help communication between teams. Frustrations mount, and people wind up in endless meetings trying to figure out why they are a team and what they are expected to do." A focused, cohesive structure is a fundamental underpinning for high-performing teams. Even highly skilled people zealously pursuing a shared mission will falter and fail if group structure constantly generates inequity, confusion, and frustration.

SELF-MANAGING TEAMS: STRUCTURE OF THE FUTURE?

The sports team analogy discussed earlier assumed some role for a top-down team manager. But what about teams that manage themselves organically from the bottom up? Self-managing work teams have been defined as groups of employees with the following characteristics (Wellins and others, 1990):

- They manage themselves (plan, organize, control, staff, and monitor).
- They assign jobs to members (decide who works on what, where, and when).
- They plan and schedule work (control start-up and ending times, the pace of work, and goal setting).
- They make production- or service-related decisions (take responsibility for inventory, quality control decisions, and work stoppage).
- They take action to remedy problems (address quality issues, customer service needs, and member discipline and rewards).

Evidence suggests that self-directed teams often produce better results and higher morale than groups operating under more traditional top-down control (Cohen and Ledford, 1994; Emery and Fredendall, 2002). But getting such teams started and giving them the resources they need to be effective is a complex undertaking. Many well-known firms—such as Microsoft, Boeing, Google, W. L. Gore, Southwest Airlines, Harley-Davidson, Whole Foods, and Goldman Sachs—have stumbled successfully toward the benefits of self-directed teams without being overwhelmed by logistical snafus or reverting to the traditional command-and-control structure. A classic multidecade example is the Saturn division of General Motors.

In 1983, General Motors announced the launch of a revolutionary experiment: the Saturn project, which would produce automobiles in a new way. The Saturn experiment showed what can happen when you place people in a suitable structure of roles and relationships. After it was launched by its parent, Saturn quickly achieved levels of quality, consumer satisfaction, and customer loyalty that surpassed those of much of the U.S. automotive industry. What was the secret of the company's success?

Credit has been assigned to its sophisticated technology and its enlightened approach to managing people and its unique culture. On the technology side, Saturn made extensive use of computers and deployed robots for many repetitive or dangerous jobs. Its human resource practices emphasized training, conflict management, and extensive employee participation. Its unique way of doing things and cohesion are legendary. Yet it is easy to overlook Saturn's distinctive team structure as an important element of its achievements.

Company-wide, Saturn employees were granted authority to make team decisions, within a few flexible guidelines. Restrictive rules and ironclad, top-down work procedures were left behind as the company moved away from what employees call the "old world" of General Motors. Early in the company's history, a new manager imported from General Motors was walking the line and noticed an assembly worker standing beside a pile of parts. He asked the employee why the parts were not being used. The worker replied that they did not meet quality standards. The manager told him to use the parts anyway. The worker refused. "Very quickly the UAW [United Automobile Workers] president and a top manager came to the scene. They flat out told [the new manager] that things aren't done that way here at Saturn and that he'd better learn his job. To which the manager replied, 'What is my job?' The union president retorted, 'That's for you to discover'" (Deal and Jenkins, 1994, p. 244).

Saturn's engineers and assembly-line workers worked together to solve problems and design manufacturing processes. Quality was everyone's business, and any employee had the authority to stop the assembly line if something ran amiss. Relationships between UAW and Saturn management were cordial and cooperative, governed by an official agreement just one page in length.

Most of the actual assembly of the Saturn automobile was done by teams. More than 150 production teams of eight to fifteen cross-trained, highly interdependent workers assembled the cars on a half-mile-long assembly line. The traditional system of sequential, repetitive efforts by isolated individuals became a thing of the past. Saturn created "a work environment where people provide leadership for themselves and others. It is cooperation and self and team management that make Saturn tick. Problems are solved by people working together—they are not kicked upstairs for others to solve" (p. 230).

Saturn teams exemplified Katzenbach and Smith's (1993) profile of successful teams. The design of the car, corporate values, and quality standards came down from the executive suite, but each team translated broad objectives into measurable performance goals. Teams were empowered to deal with budget, safety procedures, ergonomics, vacations, time off, and other matters. In effect, each team managed its own business within general guidelines. An employee in body systems described how it worked on her team: "The working conditions are like running your own business. We decide when the shifts are, who starts where, break and eating times, and vacation schedules" (Deal and Jenkins, 1994, p. 242).

Saturn teams designated their own working relationships. Prior to the beginning of a shift, team members conferred in a team center for five or ten minutes. They determined the day's rotation. A team of ten would have ten jobs to do and typically rotated through them, except that rotation was more frequent for jobs involving heavy lifting or stress. Every week the plant shut down to let teams review quality standards, budget, safety, and the ergonomics of assembly. The level of responsibility teams assumed was illustrated by an interior design team that chose to eliminate sixteen team jobs. In looking for ways to trim costs, the team identified an inefficient practice: walking too far to pick up parts for the assembly. Moving the parts closer to the line eliminated the extra distance, but it also made the extra positions unnecessary. The team—including those who eventually moved to other positions at Saturn—made decisions about which positions to eliminate.

Group accountability became an accepted way of life for Saturn teams. Workers watched the numbers every day. At least $10,000 in salary was put at risk each year. If the company met its performance objectives, everyone gained. If it did not, the loss was also shared. Everyone at Saturn admitted that things were not perfect. But there was general agreement that teams were learning from mistakes and constantly refining the structure of teamwork.

Since its beginnings in the 1980s, Saturn has been through ups and downs. Today, the company is a division of GM and more closely aligned with the parent company. New presidents chosen in 1998 and 2000 both came from GM. Since 2004, Saturn vehicles have been designed to use parts from other GM divisions. Saturn's original independence as a company has been reduced by GM's rising control, and Saturn has struggled to achieve the market success and profitability its founders envisioned. But in spite of all the changes, the original team-based concept continues to produce a high-quality automobile assembled by self-directed employees. At last word, GM was still convinced that "Saturn definitely has a future."

SUMMARY

Every group evolves a structure as its members work together, but the design may help or hinder effectiveness. Conscious attention to structure and roles can make all the difference in group performance. A team structure emphasizing hierarchy and top-down control tends to work well for simple, stable tasks. As work becomes more complex or the environment gets more turbulent, structure must also develop more multifaceted and lateral forms of communication and coordination.

Sports analogies can help clarify teamwork options. It helps to understand whether the game you are playing is more like baseball, football, or basketball. Many teams never learn the lesson of the commando team: vary the structure in response to changes in task and circumstance. Leaders must know when the rules of the game change and redesign the structure accordingly.

PART THREE

The Human Resource Frame

O ur most important asset is our people."

"Organizations exploit people—chew them up and spit them out." Of these two contrasting views of the relationship between people and organizations, which is more accurate? How you answer affects everything you do at work.

The human resource frame centers on what organizations and people do to and for one another. We begin in Chapter Six by laying out basic assumptions, focusing on the fit between human needs and organizational requirements.

Organizations generally hope for a cadre of talented, highly motivated employees who give their best. Often, though, these same organizations rely on outdated assumptions and counterproductive practices that cause workers to give less and demand more.

After examining how organizations err in Chapter Six, we turn in Chapter Seven to a discussion of how smart managers and progressive organizations find better ways to manage people. We describe "high-involvement" or "high-commitment" practices that build and retain a talented and motivated workforce.

In Chapter Eight, we examine issues in interpersonal relations and small groups. We describe competing strategies for managing relationships and look at how interpersonal dynamics can make or break a group or team.

People and Organizations

Early afternoon, March 9, 2006. Three electricians who worked for Nucor Corporation got bad news. In Hickman, Arkansas, the company's steel mill was dead in the water because its electric grid had failed. All three employees dropped what they were doing to head for Arkansas. One drove from Indiana, arriving at nine that night. The other two flew from North Carolina to Memphis, then drove two more hours, arriving after midnight. All three camped out at the plant and worked twenty-hour shifts with local staff to get the grid back up.

The electricians volunteered—they didn't need a boss to tell them that Nucor had to have that mill back on line. Their Herculean effort brought them no immediate financial reward, even though it was a big help to the company. Their initiative helped Hickman post a quarterly record for tons of steel shipped (Byrnes and Arndt, 2006).

At Nucor, this story is not particularly unusual:

> In an industry as Rust Belt as they come, Nucor has nurtured one of the most dynamic and engaged workforces around. Its nonunion employees don't see themselves as worker bees waiting for instructions from above. Nucor's flattened hierarchy and emphasis on pushing power to the front line have given its employees the mindset of owner-operators. It's a profitable formula: Nucor's 387% return to

shareholders over the past five years soundly bests almost all other companies in the Standard & Poor's 500-stock index [Byrnes and Arndt, 2006, p. 58].

What's in it for the workers? Their base pay is nothing special—it's below the industry average. But when Nucor has a good year, as it usually does, they get big bonuses, based on their own output and the company's success. That's one reason electricians would grab a plane to help jump-start a plant in Arkansas. It's also why a new plant manager at Nucor can expect supportive calls from veteran managers who want to help out.

At Nucor, work is more than a job. It's about pride. Employees enjoy seeing their names listed on the covers of corporate publications. They're proud that their company, which turns scrap metal into steel, is the world's largest recycler. And they're exhilarated when they can draw on their intelligence and creativity to demonstrate that American workers can still compete.

Companies like Nucor belong, unfortunately, to a rare breed. Most companies give lip service to the idea that employees are the firm's most important asset. But few behave accordingly. In practice, employees are treated as pawns to be moved where needed and sacrificed when necessary.

Consider McWane, one of the world's largest manufacturers of cast-iron pipes, whose management philosophy, at least until recently, could have been lifted from a Dickens novel. As a former McWane plant manager put it, "The way you treat people would be awful. You know, the people, they're nothing', they're just a number. You move 'em in and out. If they don't do the job, you fire 'em. If they get hurt, or complain about safety, you put a 'bulls-eye' on them. They're not gonna have a job in the near future" (Frontline, 2003).

Not surprisingly, McWane had "by far the worst safety record in an industry that has itself the highest injury rate in the nation" (Barstow and Bergman, 2003c, p. A1). In 1995, McWane bought Tyler Pipe, a foundry in central Texas. Over the next two years, McWane cut nearly two-thirds of its employees, eliminating quality control and safety inspectors, while maintaining production at prior levels. Profits soared, but so did turnover and injuries (including at least three deaths). Workers were supposedly expected to work "as quickly and efficiently as possible without compromising safety rules or safe practices in any way" (Barstow and Bergman, 2003a, p. A14). But federal safety inspectors concluded that the safety program was a "charade"; the company routinely violated safety standards in its push to avoid production downtime. Since rookie employees often made mistakes, got hurt, and left, injuries and turnover fed one another. In 2002, McWane admitted in federal court that it had willfully ignored or violated safety rules (Barstow and Bergman, 2003a). The company has since promised to clean up its act.

Sacrificing people for profits reinvigorates age-old images of insensitive, heartless employers (Amar, 2004). That's still a very popular image of the workplace. One of America's most popular cartoon strips is *Dilbert,* whose white-collar, cubicle-class hero wanders mindlessly through a tortuous office landscape of bureaucratic inertia, corporate doublespeak, and callous, incompetent bosses.

In this chapter, we focus on the human side of organization. We start by summarizing the assumptions underlying the human resource view. Next, we examine how people's needs are either satisfied or frustrated at work. Then we look at today's changing employment contract and its impact on both people and organizations.

HUMAN RESOURCE ASSUMPTIONS

McWane and Nucor represent opposite poles in a perennial debate about the relationship between people and organizations. One side sees individuals as objects to be exploited by organizations. The opposing camp holds that the needs of individuals and organizations can be aligned, engaging people's talent and energy while the enterprise profits. This dispute has intensified with globalization and the growth in size and power of modern institutions. Can people find freedom and dignity in a world dominated by economic fluctuations and an emphasis on short-term results? Answers are not easy. They require a sensitive understanding of people and their symbiotic relationship with organizations.

The human resource frame evolved from early work of pioneers such as Mary Parker Follett (1918) and Elton Mayo (1933, 1945), who questioned a century-old, deeply held assumption—that workers had no rights beyond a paycheck. Their duty was to work hard and follow orders. Pioneers who laid the human resource frame's foundation criticized this view on two grounds: it was unfair, and it was bad psychology. They argued that people's skills, attitudes, energy, and commitment are vital resources that can make or break an enterprise. The human resource frame is built on core assumptions that highlight this linkage:

- Organizations exist to serve human needs rather than the converse.

- People and organizations need each other. Organizations need ideas, energy, and talent; people need careers, salaries, and opportunities.

- When the fit between individual and system is poor, one or both suffer. Individuals are exploited or exploit the organization—or both become victims.

- A good fit benefits both. Individuals find meaningful and satisfying work, and organizations get the talent and energy they need to succeed.

Organizations ask, "How do we find and retain people with the skills and attitudes to do the work?" Workers want to know, "How well will this place meet my needs?" These two questions are closely related, because "fit" is a function of at least three different things: how well an organization responds to individual desires for useful work; how well jobs enable employees to express their skills and sense of self; and how well work fulfills individual financial and life-style needs (Cable and DeRue, 2002).

Human Needs

The concept of need is controversial—at least in some academic circles. Some theorists argue that the idea is too vague and refers to something difficult to observe. Others say that people have needs that are so variable and strongly influenced by their surroundings that the concept offers little help in explaining behavior (Salancik and Pfeffer, 1977). Goal-setting theory (Locke and Latham, 2002, 2004) suggests that managers may do better by emphasizing specific performance goals than by worrying about employees' psychic needs. Economists like Jensen and Meckling (1994) argue that people's willingness to trade off one thing for another (time for money or sleep for entertainment) disproves the idea of need.

Despite this academic skepticism, needs are a central element in everyday psychology. Parents worry about the needs of their children, politicians promise to meet the needs of constituents, and managers make an effort to understand the needs of workers. Wegmans, a grocery chain that perennially finishes at or near the top of *Fortune* magazine's list of best places to work, states its philosophy in those terms: "We set our goal to be the very best at serving the needs of our customers.

Every action we take should be made with this in mind. We also believe that we can achieve our goal only if we fulfill the needs of our own people" (Wegmans, n.d.).

Common sense tells us that needs are important because we all have them. But identifying what needs we have at any given time is more elusive. A horticultural analogy may help clarify. A gardener knows that every plant has specific requirements. The right combination of temperature, moisture, soil, and sunlight allows a plant to grow and flourish. Plants do their best to get what they need. They orient leaves sunward to get more light and sink roots deeper in search of water. A plant's capabilities generally increase with maturity. Highly vulnerable seedlings become more self-sufficient as they grow (better able to fend off insects and competition from other plants). These capabilities decline as a plant nears the end of its life cycle.

Human needs are similar. Conditions or elements in the environment allow people to survive and grow. Basic needs for oxygen, water, and food are clear; the idea of universal psychic needs is more controversial. A genetic, or "nature," perspective posits that certain psychological needs are essential to being human (Maslow, 1954; McClelland, 1985; White, 1960). A "nurture" view, in contrast, suggests that people are so shaped by environment, socialization, and culture that it is fruitless to talk about common psychic needs.

In extreme forms, both nature and nurture arguments are misleading. An advanced degree in psychology is not required to recognize that people are capable of enormous amounts of learning and adaptation. Nor do we need specialized training in biology to recognize that many physical attributes and psychological characteristics, such as temperament, are present at birth.

A majority of scholars see human behavior as resulting from the interplay between heredity and environment. Genes initially determine potential and predispositions. Research has identified, for example, connections between certain genetic patterns and behavioral tendencies such as antisocial behavior. But learning profoundly modifies innate directives, and research in behavioral genetics regularly concludes that genes and environment interact in complex ways to determine how people act (Baker, 2004).

The nature-nurture seesaw suggests a more powerful way of thinking about human needs. A need can be defined as a genetic predisposition to prefer some experiences over others. Needs energize and guide behavior and vary in potency at different times. We enjoy the company of others, for example, yet sometimes want to be alone. Since genetic instructions cannot anticipate all situations, both the form and the expression of each person's inborn needs are significantly tailored by experiences after birth.

What Needs Do People Have? The existential psychologist Abraham Maslow (1954) developed one of the most influential theories about human needs. He started with the notion that people are motivated by a variety of wants, some more fundamental than others. The desire for food dominates the lives of the chronically hungry, but other motives drive people who have enough to eat. Maslow grouped human needs into five basic categories, arrayed in a hierarchy from lowest to highest (Exhibit 6.1).

In Maslow's view, basic needs for physical well-being and safety are "prepotent"; they have to be satisfied first. Once lower needs are fulfilled, individuals are motivated by social needs (for belongingness, love, and inclusion) and

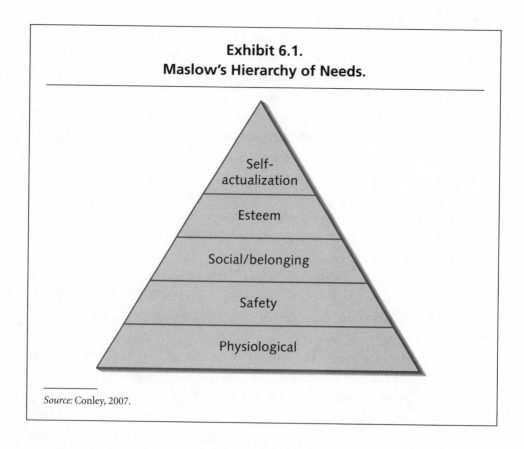

**Exhibit 6.1.
Maslow's Hierarchy of Needs.**

Self-actualization

Esteem

Social/belonging

Safety

Physiological

Source: Conley, 2007.

ego needs (for esteem, respect, and recognition). At the top of the hierarchy is self-actualization—developing to one's fullest and actualizing one's ultimate potential. The order is not ironclad. Parents may sacrifice themselves for their children, and martyrs sometimes give their lives for a cause. Maslow believed that such reversals occur when lower needs are so well satisfied early in life that they recede into the background later on.

Attempts to validate Maslow's theory have produced mixed results, partly because the theory is hard to test (Alderfer, 1972; Latham and Pinder, 2005; Lawler and Shuttle, 1973; Schneider and Alderfer, 1973; Wahba and Bridwell, 1976). Some research suggests that the theory is valid across cultures (Ajila, 1997; Rao and Kulkarni, 1998), but there is still little evidence to support the premise that people have the needs Maslow posited or that the satisfaction of one need leads to activation of another.

Despite the modest evidence, Maslow's view is still widely accepted and enormously influential in managerial practice. Take, for example, the advice that the *Manager's Guide* at Federal Express offers employees: "Modern behavioral scientists such as Abraham Maslow . . . have shown that virtually every person has a hierarchy of emotional needs, from basic safety, shelter, and sustenance to the desire for respect, satisfaction, and a sense of accomplishment. Slowly these values have appeared as the centerpiece of progressive company policies, always with remarkable results" (Waterman, 1994, p. 92). Chip Conley, founder of a California hotel chain, put it simply, "I came to realize my climb to the top wasn't going to be on a traditional corporate ladder; instead it was going to be on Maslow's Hierarchy of Needs pyramid" (Conley, 2007). Academic skepticism didn't prevent him, or FedEx, from building a highly successful management philosophy based on Maslow's theory, because the ideas carry a powerful message. If you manage solely by carrot and stick, you'll get only a part of the energy and talent that people have to offer.

Theory X and Theory Y   Douglas McGregor (1960) built on Maslow's theory by adding another important idea: that managers' assumptions about people tend to become self-fulfilling prophecies. McGregor argued that most managers harbor "Theory X" assumptions, believing that subordinates are passive and lazy, have little ambition, prefer to be led, and resist change. Most conventional management practices, in his view, had been built on either "hard" or "soft" versions of Theory X. The hard version emphasizes coercion, tight controls, threats, and punishments. Over time, it generates low productivity, antagonism, militant unions, and subtle sabotage—conditions that were turning up in workplaces across the United States at the time. Soft versions of Theory X try to avoid conflict and keep everyone happy. The usual result is superficial harmony with undercurrents of apathy and indifference.

McGregor's key point was that a hard or soft Theory X approach is self-fulfilling: if you treat people as if they're lazy and need to be directed, they conform to your expectations. Managers who say their experience proves that Theory X is the only way to get anything done are missing a key insight: the fact that people always respond to you in a certain way may say more about you than about them. McGregor advocated a different way to think about people that he called Theory Y. Maslow's hierarchy of needs was the foundation:

> We recognize readily enough that a man suffering from a severe dietary deficiency is sick. The deprivation of physiological needs has behavioral consequences. The same is true—although less well recognized—of deprivation of higher-level needs. The man whose needs for safety, association, independence, or status are thwarted is sick as surely as the man who has rickets. And his sickness will have behavioral consequences. We will be mistaken if we attribute his resultant passivity, hostility, and refusal to accept responsibility to his inherent human nature. These forms of behavior are symptoms of illness—of deprivation of his social and egoistic needs [McGregor, 1960, pp. 35–36].

Theory Y's key proposition is that "the essential task of management is to arrange conditions so that people can achieve their own goals best by directing efforts toward organizational rewards" (McGregor, 1960, p. 61). If individuals find no satisfaction in their work, management has little choice but to rely on Theory X and external control. Conversely, the more managers align organizational requirements with employee self-interest, the more they can rely on Theory Y's principle of self-direction.

Personality and Organization

Like his contemporary McGregor, Chris Argyris (1957, 1964) saw a basic conflict between human personality and prevailing management practice. Argyris argued that people have basic "self-actualization trends"—akin to the efforts of a plant to reach its biological potential. From infancy into adulthood, people advance from dependence to independence, from a narrow to a broader range of skills and interests. They move from a short time perspective (interests quickly developed and forgotten, with little ability to anticipate the future) to a much longer-term horizon. The child's impulsivity and limited self-knowledge are replaced by a more mature level of self-awareness and self-control.

Like McGregor, Argyris felt organizations often treated workers like children rather than adults—a view eloquently expressed in Charlie Chaplin's 1936 film *Modern Times*. In one scene, Chaplin's character works furiously on an assembly line, trying to tighten bolts on every piece that slides past. Skill requirements are minimal, and he has no control over the pace of his work. An efficiency expert uses Chaplin as the guinea pig for a new machine designed to feed him lunch while he continues to tighten bolts. It goes haywire and begins to assault Chaplin with food—pouring soup on his lap and shoving bolts into his mouth. The film's message is clear: industrial organizations abuse workers and treat them like infants.

Argyris and McGregor saw person-structure conflict built into traditional principles of organizational design and management. The structural concept of task specialization defines jobs as narrowly as possible to improve efficiency. But the rational logic often backfires. Consider the experience of autoworker Ben Hamper. His observations mirror a story many other U.S. workers could tell:

> I was seven years old the first time I ever set foot inside an automobile factory. The occasion was Family Night at the old Fisher Body plant in Flint where my father worked the second shift. If nothing else, this annual peepshow lent a whole world of credence to our father's daily grumble. The assembly line did indeed stink. The noise was very close to intolerable. The heat was one complete bastard.
>
> After a hundred wrong turns and dead ends, we found my old man down on the trim line. His job was to install windshields using this goofy apparatus with large suction cups that resembled an octopus being crucified. A car would nuzzle up to the old man's work area and he would be waiting for it, a cigarette dangling from his lip, his arms wrapped around the windshield contraption as if it might suddenly rebel and bolt off for the ocean. Car, windshield. Car, windshield. Car, windshield. No wonder my father preferred playin' hopscotch with barmaids [Hamper, 1992, pp. 1–2].

Following in his father's and grandfather's footsteps, Ben Hamper became an autoworker—the pay was good, and he didn't know anything else. He soon discovered a familiar pattern. Though his career began decades after Argyris and McGregor questioned the fallacies of traditional management, little had changed. Hamper held down a variety of jobs, each as mindless as the next: "The one thing that was impossible to escape was the monotony. Every minute, every hour, every truck, and every movement was a plodding replica of the one that had gone before" (1992, p. 41).

The specialization Ben Hamper experienced in the auto plant calls for a clear chain of command to coordinate discrete jobs. Bosses direct and control subordinates, thus encouraging passivity and dependence. The conflict worsens at lower levels of the hierarchy—narrower, more mechanized jobs, more directives, and tighter controls. As people mature, conflict intensifies. Leann Bies was forty-four with a bachelor's degree in business when she started work as a licensed electrician at a Ford truck plant in 2003, and "for two years they treated me as if I were dumber than a box of rocks. You get an attitude if you are treated that way" (Uchitelle, 2007, p. 10).

Argyris argued that employees try to stay sane by looking for ways to escape these frustrations. He identified six options:

• *They withdraw—through chronic absenteeism or simply by quitting.* Ben Hamper chronicled many examples of absenteeism and quitting, including this friend, who lasted only a couple of months:

> My pal Roy was beginning to unravel in a real rush. His enthusiasm about all the money we were makin' had dissipated and he was having major difficulty coping with the drudgery of factory labor. His job, like mine, wasn't difficult. It was just plain monotonous. . . .
>
> The day before he quit, he approached me with a box-cutter knife sticking out of his glove and requested that I give him a slice across the back of the hand. He felt sure this ploy would land him a few days off. Since slicing Roy didn't seem like a solid career move, I refused. Roy went down the line to the other workers where he received a couple of charitable offers to cut his throat, but no dice on the hand. He wound up sulking back to his job. After that night, I never saw Roy again [1992, pp. 40, 43].

- *They stay on the job but withdraw psychologically, becoming indifferent, passive, and apathetic.* Like many other workers, Ben Hamper didn't want to quit, so he looked for ways to cope with the tedium. His favorite was to "double up" by making a deal with another worker to take turns covering each other's job. This made it possible to get full pay for half a day's work:

> What a setup. Dale and I would both report to work before the 4:30 horn. We'd spend a half hour preparing all the stock we'd need for the evening. At 5:00, I would take over the two jobs while Dale went to sleep in a makeshift cardboard bed behind our bench. . . . I'd work the jobs from 5:00 until 9:24, the official lunch period. When the line stopped, I'd give Dale's cardboard coffin a good kick. It was time for the handoff. I would give my ID badge to Dale so that he could punch me out at quitting time [1992, p. 61].

If doubling up didn't work, workers invented other diversions, like Rivet Hockey (sailing rivets into a coworker's foot or leg) and Dumpster Ball (kicking cardboard boxes high enough to clear a dumpster). And there was always alcohol:

> Drinking right on the line wasn't something everyone cared for. But plenty did, and the most popular time to go snagging for gusto was the lunch break. As soon as that lunch horn blew, half of the plant put it in gear, sprinting out the door in packs of three or four, each pointed squarely for one of those chilly coolers up at one of the nearby beer emporiums [1992, p. 56].

- *They resist by restricting output, deception, featherbedding, or sabotage.*[1] Hamper reports what happened when the company removed a popular foreman because he was "too close to his work force" (1992, p. 205):

> With a tight grip on the whip, the new bossman started riding the crew. No music. No Rivet Hockey. No horseplay. No drinking. No card playing. No working up the line. No leaving the department. No doubling-up. No this, no that. No questions asked.
>
> No way. After three nights of this imported bullyism, the boys had had their fill. Frames began sliding down the line minus parts. Rivets became cross-eyed. Guns mysteriously broke down. The repairmen

began shipping the majority of the defects, unable to keep up with the repair load.

Sabotage was drastic, but it got the point across and brought the new foreman into line. To survive, the foreman had to fall into step. Otherwise, he would be replaced, and the cycle would start anew.

- *They try to climb the hierarchy to better jobs.* Moving up works for some, but there are rarely enough "better" jobs to go around. Many workers are reluctant to take promotions anyway. Hamper reports what happened to a coworker who tried to crack down after he was promoted to foreman:

> For the next eight days, we made Calvin Moza's short-lived career switch sheer hell. Every time he'd walk the aisle, someone would pepper his steps with raining rivets. He couldn't make a move without the hammers banging and loud chants of "suckass" and "brown snout" ringin' in his ears. He got everything he deserved [1992, p. 208].

Hamper himself found an escape: he started to moonlight as a writer during one of automaking's periodic layoffs. Styling himself "The Rivethead," he wrote a column about factory life from the inside. His writing eventually led to a best-selling book. Most of his buddies weren't as fortunate.

- *They form alliances (such as labor unions) to redress the power imbalance.* Union movements grow out of workers' desire for a more equal footing with management. Argyris cautioned, however, that leaders might run unions much like factories, because they knew no other way to manage. In the long run, employees' sense of powerlessness would change little. Ben Hamper, like most autoworkers, was a union member, yet the union is largely invisible in his accounts of life on the assembly line. He rarely sought union help and even less often got any. He appreciated wages and benefits earned at the bargaining table, but nothing in the labor agreement protected workers from boredom, frustration, or the feeling of powerlessness.

- *They teach their children to believe that work is unrewarding and hopes for advancement are slim.* Hamper's account of life on the line is a vivid illustration of Argyris's contention that organizations treat adults like children. The company assigned an employee to wander through the plant dressed in costume as "Howie Makem, the Quality Cat." (Howie was mostly greeted with groans, insults, and an occasional flying rivet.) Message boards were plastered with inspirational phrases such as "Riveting is fun." A plant manager would emerge from his usual invisibility to give an annual speech promising to talk more with workers. All this hypocrisy took its toll: "Working the Rivet Line was like being paid to flunk high school the rest of your life. An adolescent time warp in which the duties of the day were just an underlying annoyance" (Hamper, 1992, p. 185).

Researchers in the 1960s began to note that children of farmers grew up believing hard work paid off, while the offspring of urban blue-collar workers did not. As a result, many U.S. companies began to move facilities away from old industrial states like Michigan (where Ben Hamper worked) to more rural states like North Carolina and Tennessee, in search of employees who still embodied the work ethic. Argyris predicted, however, that industry would eventually demotivate even the most committed workforce unless management practices changed. In recent decades, manufacturing and service jobs have been moving offshore to low-wage enclaves around the world, continuing the search for employees who will work hard without asking for too much in return.

The powerlessness and frustration that Hamper experienced are by no means unique to factory work. Bosses who treat office workers like children are a pop culture staple—including the pointy-haired martinet in *Dilbert* and the pathetically clueless boss in the television series *The Office*. In public education, many teachers and parents lament that increasing emphasis on high-stakes standardized tests alienates teachers and turns them into "deskilled clerks" (Giroux, 1998). Batstone sees frustration as pervasive among workers at every level: "Corporate workers from the mailroom to the highest executive office express dissatisfaction with their work. They feel crushed by widespread greed, selfishness, and quest for profit at any cost. Apart from their homes, people spend more time on the job than anywhere else. With that kind of personal stake, they want to be part of something that matters and contribute to a greater good. Sadly, those aspirations often go unmet" (2003, p. 1).

Argyris and McGregor formed their views on the basis of observations of U.S. organizations in the 1950s and 1960s. Since then, investigators have documented similar conflicts between people and organizations around the world. Orgogozo (1991), for example, contended that typical French management practices caused workers to feel humiliation, boredom, anger, and exhaustion "because they have no hope of being recognized and valued for what they do" (p. 101). She depicted relations between superiors and subordinates in France as tense and distant because "bosses do everything possible to protect themselves from the resentment that they generate" (p. 73).

Early on, human resource ideas were often ignored by scholars and managers. The dominant "assembly-line" mentality enjoyed enough economic success to persist. The frame's influence has grown with the realization that misuse of human resources depresses profits as well as people. Legions of consultants, managers, and researchers now pursue answers to the vexing human problems of organizations.

HUMAN CAPACITY AND THE CHANGING EMPLOYMENT CONTRACT

In recent years, the person-organization relationship has become even more problematic as global trends have pushed organizations in two conflicting directions. On one hand, global competition, rapid change, and shorter product life cycles have produced a turbulent, intensely competitive world, placing an enormous premium on the ability to adapt quickly to shifts in the environment. One way to do that is to minimize fixed human assets. Beginning in the late twentieth century, more and more organizations turned to downsizing, outsourcing, and using part-time and temporary employees to cope with business fluctuations. Universities, for example, have shifted to more part-time adjunct instructors and fewer full-time faculty. Volkswagen opened a manufacturing plant in Brazil in which subcontractors employed 80 percent of the workforce. Even in Japan, traditional notions of lifetime careers have eroded in the face of "a bloated work force, particularly in the white collar sector, which proved to be an economic drag" (WuDunn, 1996, p. D8). Around the world, employees looking for career advice have been told to count on themselves rather than employers. Give up on job security, the advice often went, and focus instead on developing skills and flexibility that will make you marketable.

On the other hand, some of the same global forces push in another direction—toward growing dependence on well-trained, loyal human capital. Organizations have become more complex as a consequence of globalization and a more information-intensive economy. More decentralized structures, like the networks discussed in Chapter Three, have proliferated in response to greater complexity and turbulence. These new configurations depend on a higher level of skill, intelligence, and commitment across a broader spectrum of employees. A network of decentralized decision nodes is a blueprint for disaster if the dispersed decision makers lack the capacity or desire to make sensible choices. Skill requirements have been changing so fast that individuals are hard-pressed to keep up. The result is a troubling gap: organizations struggle to find people who bring the skills and qualities needed, while individuals with yesterday's skills face dismal job prospects. In 2006, telephone giant AT&T committed to bringing five thousand offshored jobs back to the U.S. Two years later, CEO Randall Stephenson said only fourteen hundred had come back, because "we're having trouble finding the numbers that we need with the skills that are required to do these jobs" (Forsyth, 2008). He blamed public schools for turning out a defective product.

The shift from a production-intensive to an information-intensive economy is not helping to close the gap. There used to be more jobs that involved *making things*. In the first three decades after World War II, high-paying jobs in developed nations were heavily concentrated in blue-collar work (Drucker, 1993). These jobs generally required little formal training and few specialized skills, but they afforded pay and benefits to sustain a comfortable and stable lifestyle. No more. Workers in manufacturing jobs accounted for more than a third of the U.S. workforce in the 1950s. By 2004, they were only a tenth of the workforce and their share was still declining (Congressional Budget Office, 2004).

Surviving production jobs often require much higher skill levels than in the past. When U.S. automobile manufacturers began to replace retiring workers in the mid-1990s, they emphasized quick minds more than strong bodies and put applicants "through a grueling selection process that emphasized mental acuity and communication skills" (Meredith, 1996, p. 1).

This skill gap is even greater in many developing nations. China's population of 1.4 billion people consists largely of farmers and workers with old-economy skills. Beginning in the 1980s, China began a gradual shift to a market economy, reducing regulations, welcoming foreign investment, and selling off fading state-owned enterprises. Results were dramatic: China's economy shifted from almost entirely state-owned in 1980 to 70 percent private by 2005. China became one of the world's fastest-growing economies, with compound growth at approximately 8 percent a year in the early twenty-first century, but unemployment mushroomed as state-owned enterprises succumbed to nimbler—and leaner—domestic and foreign competitors.

Pressures to increase flexibility and employee skills simultaneously create a vexing human resource dilemma. Should an organization seek adaptability (through a downsized, outsourced, part-time workforce) or loyalty (through a long-term commitment to people)? Should it seek high skills (by hiring the best and training them well) or low costs (by hiring the cheapest and investing no more than necessary)?

Lean and Mean: More Benefits Than Costs?

The advantages of a smaller, more flexible workforce seem compelling: lower costs, higher efficiency, and greater ability to respond to business fluctuations. Many analysts have argued that U.S. competitive success in recent decades is directly related to corporate willingness to shed unnecessary staff (Lynch, 1996). For some companies, downsizing has worked: "The formula of cutting staff and investing heavily in computerized equipment has paid off particularly in manufacturing, which enjoys a much greater productivity growth rate—more than 3 percent a year on average in the 1990s—than business as a whole" (Uchitelle, 1996, p. 1).

Downsizing works best when new technology and smart management combine to enable fewer people to do more. Yet even when downsizing works, it risks trading short-term gains for long-term decay. As mentioned in Chapter Two, "Chainsaw Al" Dunlap became a hero of the downsizing movement. As chief executive of Scott Paper, he more than doubled profits and market value. His strategy? Cut people—half of management, half of research and development, and a fifth of blue-collar workers. Financial outcomes were impressive, but employee morale sank, and Scott lost market share in every major product line. Dunlap did not stay around long enough to find out if he had sacrificed Scott's future for short-term gains. After less than two years on the job, he sold the company to its biggest competitor and walked away with almost $100 million for his efforts (Byrne, 1996).

Companies have eliminated millions of jobs in recent decades, yet many firms have found benefits elusive. Markels and Murray (1996) reported that downsizing has too often turned into "dumbsizing": "Many firms continue to make flawed decisions—hasty, across-the-board cuts—that come back to haunt, on the bottom line, in public relationships, in strained relationships with customers and suppliers, and in demoralized employees." In shedding staff, firms often found that they also sacrificed knowledge, skill, innovation, and loyalty (Reichheld, 1993, 1996). Recent research confirms that cutting people hurts more often than it helps performance (Cascio, Young, and Morris, 1997; Gertz and Baptista, 1995; Love and Kraatz, 2005; Mellahi and Wilkinson, 2006). Nevertheless, more than half of the companies in a 2003 survey admitted that they would make cuts that hurt in the long term if that's what it took to meet short-term earnings targets (Berenson, 2004).

Downsizing and outsourcing also have a corrosive effect on employee motivation and commitment. A 1996 poll found that 75 percent of U.S. workers felt that companies had become less loyal to their employees, and 64 percent felt that employees were less loyal to their companies (Kleinfeld, 1996). Workers reported that the mood in the workplace was angrier and colleagues were more competitive. A more recent study (Walker Information, 2005) found a modest uptick in loyalty—34 percent of employees said they were truly loyal, up from 30 percent in 2003—but there is still plenty of room for improvement.

Employee loyalty was a big issue during Robert Nardelli's roller-coaster tenure as chief executive of Home Depot from 2001 to 2007 (discussed in Chapter One). Home Depot's founders had built the company on fun, family, and decentralization. Managers ran their stores using experience and intuition, and customers counted on helpful, knowledgeable staff. But Nardelli was a dyed-in-the-wool structural-frame manager who put heavy emphasis on measurement and control. Where the founders had preached "make love to the customers," Nardelli cut staff, including many veterans who knew their way around paint and power tools. Customer complaints mushroomed, and by 2005 Home Depot's ratings of customer satisfaction were dead last among American retailers.

Nardelli's board pushed him out at the beginning of 2007 but cushioned the blow with a $210 million severance package. His successor, Frank Blake, reversed course in a hurry. Blake abolished the catered lunch for top executives that Nardelli had instituted, telling his colleagues to pay their own way in the employee cafeteria. He brought back the "inverted pyramid" organization chart that the founders liked but Nardelli didn't. It showed customers and employees on top and the CEO at the bottom. To reinvigorate Home Depot's playful spirit, he gave every store $3,000 for a "fun fund" to be spent at employee discretion (Barbaro, 2007).

Investing in People

Few employers invest the time and resources necessary to develop a cadre of committed, talented employees. Precisely for that reason, a number of authors (including Cascio and Boudreau, 2008; Lawler, 1996; Lawler and Worley, 2006; Pfeffer, 1994, 1998, 2007; and Waterman, 1994) have made the case that a skilled and motivated workforce is a powerful source of strategic advantage. Consistent with core human resource assumptions, high-performing companies do a better job of understanding and responding to the needs of both employees and customers. As a result, they attract better people who are motivated to do a superior job.

The most successful company in the U.S. airline industry in recent decades, Southwest Airlines, paid employees a competitive wage but had an enormous cost advantage because its highly committed workforce was so productive. Competitors tried to imitate Southwest's approach but rarely succeeded because "the real difference is in the effort Southwest gets out of its people. That is very, very hard to duplicate" (Labich, 1994, p. 52).

Ewing Kauffman started a pharmaceutical business in a Kansas City basement which he grew into a multibillion-dollar company (Morgan, 1995). His approach was heavily influenced by his personal experiences as a young pharmaceutical salesman:

> I worked on straight commission, receiving no salary, no expenses, no car, and no benefits in any way, shape, or form—just straight commission. By the end of the second year, my commission amounted to more than the president's salary. He didn't think that was right, so he cut my commission. By then I was Midwest sales manager and had other salesmen working for me under an arrangement whereby my commission was three percent of everything they sold. In spite of the cut in my commission, that year I still managed to make more than the president thought a sales manager should make. So this time he cut the territory, which was the same as taking away some of my income. I quit and started Marion Laboratories.
>
> I based the company on a vision of what it would be. When we hired employees, they were referred to as "associates," and they shared in the success of the company. Once again, the two principles that have guided my entire career, which were based on my experience working for that very first pharmaceutical company, are these: "Those who produce should share in the profits," and "Treat others as you would be treated" [Kauffman, 1996, p. 40].

Few managers in 1950 shared Kauffman's faith, and many are still skeptics. An urgent debate is under way about the future of the relationship between people and organizations. The battle of lean-and-mean versus invest-in-people continues. In pipe manufacturing, two of the dominant players are crosstown rivals in Birmingham, Alabama. One is McWane, discussed at the beginning of the chapter for its abysmal record on safety and environmental protection—9 deaths, 400 safety violations, and 450 environmental violations between 1995 and 2002 (Barstow and Bergman, 2003b). The other is American Cast Iron Pipe (Acipco), which has appeared on *Fortune*'s list of the best places to work in America (Levering and Moskowitz, 2003). Barstow and Bergman write that "several statistical measures show how different Acipco is from McWane. At some McWane plants, turnover rates approach 100 percent a year. Acipco—with a work force of about 3,000, three-fifths the size of McWane—has annual turnover of less than half a percent; 10,000 people recently applied for 100 openings. McWane has also been cited for 40 times more federal safety violations since 1995, OSHA records show" (2003c, p. A15).

Which of these two competing visions works better? Financially, it is difficult to judge, since both companies are privately held. Both companies have achieved business success for roughly a century. But in January 2003, at the same time that *Fortune* was lauding Acipco for its progressive human resource practices, the *New York Times* and a television documentary pilloried McWane for its callous disregard of both people and the law. Stay tuned for further updates; this story continues to evolve.

SUMMARY

The human resource frame highlights the relationship between people and organizations. Organizations need people (for their energy, effort, and talent), and people need organizations (for the many intrinsic and extrinsic rewards they offer), but their respective needs are not always well aligned. When the fit between people and organizations is poor, one or both suffer: individuals may feel neglected or oppressed, and organizations sputter because individuals withdraw their efforts or even work against organizational purposes. Conversely, a good fit benefits both: individuals find meaningful and satisfying work, and organizations get the talent and energy they need to succeed.

Global competition, turbulence, and rapid change have heightened an enduring organizational dilemma: Is it better to be lean and mean or to invest in people? A variety of strategies to reduce the workforce—downsizing, outsourcing, use of temporary and part-time workers—have been widely applied to reduce costs and increase flexibility. But they risk a loss of talent and loyalty that leads to organizations that are mediocre, even if flexible. Emerging evidence suggests that downsizing has often produced disappointing results. Many highly successful organizations have gone in another direction: investing in people on the premise that a highly motivated and skilled workforce is a powerful competitive advantage.

NOTE

1. *Featherbedding* is a colloquial term for giving people jobs that involve little or no work. This can occur for a variety of reasons: union pressures, nepotism (employing family members), or "kicking someone upstairs" (moving an underperformer into a job with no significant responsibilities).

Improving Human Resource Management

W ith more than five hundred applicants for every job opening in 2007, Google was harder to get into than Harvard. Its king-of-the-Internet image helped, but the search giant knew it took more to hire and keep the brainy, high-energy geeks who kept the place going and growing. So it made prospective hires an offer it hoped they couldn't refuse. Beyond the basics of generous pay, benefits, and time to work on their own projects, Google tried to anticipate its employees' needs to save them from wasting time on personal distractions. Medical care, gourmet cafeterias, child care, gym, lap pool, language classes, self-service laundry, shuttle bus service—the list went on. All were available on site. And all were free.

Few companies go as far as Google, but a growing number of enlightened companies are finding their own ways to attract and develop human capital. They see talent and motivation as business necessities. This thinking has taken a couple of centuries to gain traction, and a lot of companies still don't get it. Many adhere to the old view that anything given to employees siphons money from the bottom line—like having your pocket picked or your bank account cleaned out.

One of the pioneers of a more progressive approach was a Welshman, Robert Owen, who ran into fierce opposition. Born in 1771, Owen was in many ways the Bill Gates of his time. Like Microsoft's founder, Owen was a wildly successful entrepreneur before the age of thirty. He did it by exploiting the day's hot technology—in his case, spinning mills. Owen was as controversial as Gates, but for different reasons. Gates was faulted for his take-no-prisoners approach to competition. Owens was loathed because he was the only capitalist of his time who believed it bad for business to work eight-year-olds in thirteen-hour factory shifts. At his New Lanark, Scotland, knitting mill, bought in 1799, Owen took a new approach:

> Owen provided clean, decent housing for his workers and their families in a community free of contagious disease, crime, and gin shops. He took young children out of the factory and enrolled them in a school he founded. There he provided preschool, day care, and a brand of progressive education that stresses learning as a pleasurable experience (along with the first adult night school). The entire business world was shocked when he prohibited corporal punishment in his factory and dumbfounded when he retrained his supervisors in humane disciplinary practices. While offering his workers an extremely high standard of living compared to other workers of the era, Owen was making a fortune at New Lanark. This conundrum drew twenty thousand visitors between 1815 and 1820 [O'Toole, 1995, pp. 201, 206].

Owen tried to convince fellow capitalists that investing in people could produce a greater return than investments in machinery, but the business world dismissed him as a wild radical whose ideas would harm the people he wanted to help (O'Toole, 1995).

Owen was 150 years ahead of his time. Only in the late twentieth century did business leaders come to accept that investing in people is a key to successful financial performance. In recent years, periodic waves of restructuring and downsizing have raised age-old questions about the relationship between the individual and organization. A number of persuasive reports suggest Owen was right: one sure route to long-term success is investing in employees and responding to their needs (Applebaum, Bailey, Berg, and Kalleberg, 2000; Collins and Porras, 1994; Deal and Jenkins, 1994; Farkas and De Backer, 1996; Kotter and Heskett, 1992; Lawler, 1996; Levering and Moskowitz, 1993; Pfeffer, 1994, 1998; Waterman, 1994). Yet many organizations still don't believe it, and others only flirt with the idea:

Something very strange is occurring in organizational management. Over the past decade or so, numerous rigorous studies conducted both within specific industries and in samples across industries have demonstrated the enormous economic returns obtained through the execution of what are variously labeled as high involvement, high performance, or high commitment management practices. Much of this research validates earlier writing on participative management and employee involvement. But even as positive results pile up, trends in actual management practice are often moving exactly opposite to what the evidence advocates [Pfeffer, 1998, p. xv].

Why do managers persist in pursuing less effective strategies when better ones are at hand? One reason is that Theory X managers fear losing control or indulging workers. A second is that investing in people requires time and persistence to yield a payoff. Faced with relentless pressure for immediate results, managers often conclude that slashing costs, changing strategy, or reorganizing is more likely to produce a quick hit. Pfeffer (1998) believes another factor is the dominance of a "financial" perspective that sees the organization as simply a portfolio of financial assets. In this view, human resources are subjective, soft, and suspect in comparison to hard financial numbers.

GETTING IT RIGHT

Despite such barriers, many organizations get it right. Their practices are not perfect, but they're good enough. The organization benefits from a talented, motivated, loyal, and free-spirited workforce. Employees in turn are more productive, innovative, and willing to go out of their way to get the job done. They are less likely to make costly blunders or to jump ship when someone offers them a better deal. That's a potent edge—in sports, business, or anywhere. Every organization with productive people management has its unique approach, but most include variations on strategies summarized in Exhibit 7.1 and examined in depth in the remainder of the chapter.

Develop and Implement an HR Philosophy

Step one is developing a philosophy or credo that makes explicit an organization's core beliefs about managing people. The credo then has to be translated

---

Exhibit 7.1.
Basic Human Resource Strategies.

HUMAN RESOURCE PRINCIPLE	SPECIFIC PRACTICES
Build and implement an HR strategy.	Develop a shared philosophy for managing people.
	Build systems and practices to implement the philosophy.
Hire the right people.	Know what you want.
	Be selective.
Keep them.	Reward well.
	Protect jobs.
	Promote from within.
	Share the wealth.
Invest in them.	Invest in learning.
	Create development opportunities.
Empower them.	Provide information and support.
	Encourage autonomy and participation.
	Redesign work.
	Foster self-managing teams.
	Promote egalitarianism.
Promote diversity.	Be explicit and consistent about the organization's diversity philosophy.
	Hold managers accountable.

---

into specific management systems and practices. Most organizations have never developed a philosophy, or ignore the one they espouse. A philosophy provides direction; practices make it operational.

In the 1990s, Federal Express explained the company's philosophy in its *Manager's Guide:* "Take care of our people; they in turn will deliver the impeccable service demanded by our customers, who will reward us with the profitability necessary to secure our future. People—Service—Profit these three words are the very foundation of Federal Express." FedEx's philosophy might have been empty words if the company had not been diligent about reinforcing it. Managers were rated annually by subordinates on a leadership index with questions about how well they helped subordinates and listened to their ideas. Managers with subpar scores had to repeat the process in six months—a distinction no one wanted. If the collective index fell below the standard, the top three hundred managers lost their bonuses (Waterman, 1994).

Hire the Right People

Strong companies know the kinds of people they want and hire those who fit the mold. Southwest Airlines became the airline industry's most successful firm by hiring people with positive attitudes and well-honed interpersonal skills, including a sense of humor (Farkas and De Backer, 1996; Labich, 1994; Levering and Moskowitz, 1993). When a group of pilots applying for jobs at Southwest were asked to change into Bermuda shorts for the interviews, two declined. They weren't hired (Freiberg and Freiberg, 1998).

A focus on customer service enabled Enterprise Rent-a-Car to overtake Hertz and become the biggest firm in its industry. Enterprise wooed its midmarket clientele by deliberately hiring "from the half of the class that makes the top half possible"—college graduates more successful in sports and socializing than in class. Enterprise wanted people skills more than "book smarts" (Pfeffer, 1998, p. 71). In contrast, Microsoft's formidably bright CEO, Bill Gates, insisted on "intelligence or smartness over anything else, even, in many cases, experience" (Stross, 1996, p. 162). Google wants smarts too, but believes teamwork is equally important, one reason that hiring is team-based (Schmidt and Varian, 2005).

This same principle—the idea that selecting the right people gets results—was found in a study of successful midsized companies in Germany (Simon, 1996). Companies in Simon's sample had little employee turnover—except among new hires: "Many new employees leave, or are terminated, shortly after joining the work force, both sides having learned that a worker does not fit into the firm's culture and cannot stand its pace" (p. 199).

Keep Employees

To get people they want, companies like Google and Southwest Airlines offer attractive pay and benefits. To keep them, they protect jobs, promote from within, and give people a piece of the action. They recognize the high cost of turnover—which for some jobs and industries can run well over 100 percent a year. Beyond the cost of hiring and training replacements, turnover hurts performance because newcomers' lack of experience and skills increases errors and reduces efficiency (Kacmar and others, 2006).

Reward Well

In a cavernous, no-frills retail warehouse setting, where bulk sales determine stockholder profits, knowledgeable, dependable service usually isn't part of the low-cost package. Don't tell that to Costco Wholesale Corp., where employee longevity and high morale are as commonplace as overloaded shopping carts. "We like to turn over our inventory faster than our people," says Jim Sinegal, president and CEO of Costco, a membership warehouse store headquartered in Washington State with more than three hundred stores across the country (Montgomery, 2000).

Costco has a unique success formula: pay employees more and charge customers less than its biggest competitor, Sam's Club (a subsidiary of retail giant Wal-Mart). It sounds like a great way to fail, but in recent years Costco has been the industry's most profitable firm. How? In CEO Sinegal's view, the answer is easy: "If you pay the best wages, you get the highest productivity. By our industry standards, we think we've got the best people and the best productivity when we do that." Compared with competitors, Costco has achieved higher sales volumes, faster inventory turnover, and lower shrinkage (Boyle, 2006). It adds up to industry-leading profits and customer satisfaction (American Customer Satisfaction Index, 2007).

Costco is a specific example of a general principle: pay should reflect value added. Paying people more than they contribute is a losing proposition. But the reverse is also true: it makes sense to pay top dollar for exemplary contributions of skilled, motivated, and involved employees (Lawler, 1996).

To get and keep good people, selective organizations also offer attractive benefits. Osterman (1995) found, for example, that firms with "high-commitment" human resource practices were more likely to offer work and family benefits, such as day care and flexible hours.

Software powerhouse SAS is an example: In the software industry, where turnover rates hover around 20 percent, SAS maintains a level below 4 percent, which results in about $50 million a year in HR-related savings, according to a recent Harvard Business School study. In addition, the company believes that its stable workforce enables it to produce new versions of its data-mining and statistical-analysis software more cheaply and efficiently. "The well-being of our company is linked to the well-being of our employees," says SAS CEO Jim Goodnight (Stein, 2000, p. 133).

Protect Jobs

Job security seems anachronistic today, a relic of more leisurely, paternalistic times. In a turbulent, highly competitive world, how is long-term commitment to employees possible? It's not easy, and not always possible. Companies (and even countries) historically offering long-term security have abandoned their commitment in the face of severe economic pressures.

From the early 1980s to the mid-1990s, electronics retailer Circuit City was so successful that Collins (2001) identified it as one of his "good-to-great" companies. But success can be fickle. Circuit City subsequently faded from great to mediocre. After missing sales estimates and reporting losses for the third and fourth quarters in 2006, the company announced a layoff of 3,800 of its highest-paid retail staff. Archrival Best Buy reported big sales and profit gains in the same period, and its CEO, Brad Anderson, attributed success to a belief that it's "all about the customer—and the employees." Circuit City ranked last in its industry in customer satisfaction, and experts predicted the layoffs would make it even less competitive with the more customer-friendly Best Buy (Kavilanz, 2007).

Sometimes, an entire nation has to change employment practices. The largest downsizing process in history has been taking place in China. Economic reforms of the 1990s and early 2000s forced state-owned enterprises to sink or swim in a competitive market. Many foundered and abandoned the traditional guarantee of lifetime employment (Smith, 2002). In three years, from 1998 to 2001, a government report counted more than 25 million layoffs from these firms, many of them unskilled older workers ("China Says 'No' . . . ," 2002; Lingle, 2002; Smith, 2002). Many remained unemployed years later. Estimates of unemployment in China in 2005 ranged as high as a quarter of the workforce (Wolf, 2004).

Still, many firms continue to honor job security as a cornerstone of their human resource philosophy. Publix, an employee-owned, Fortune 500 super-market chain in the southeastern United States, has never had a layoff since its 1930 founding. Not coincidentally, in 2007, Publix had the highest rating of customer satisfaction in its industry for the twelfth consecutive year.

Similarly, Lincoln Electric, the world's largest manufacturer of arc welding equipment, has, since 1914, honored a policy that no employee with more than three years of service would be laid off. This commitment was tested in the

1980s, when the company experienced a 40 percent year-to-year drop in demand for its products. To avoid layoffs, production workers were converted to salespeople. They canvassed businesses rarely reached by the company's regular distribution channels. "Not only did these people sell arc welding equipment in new places to new users, but since much of the profit of this equipment comes from the sale of replacement parts, Lincoln subsequently enjoyed greater market penetration and greater sales as a consequence" (Pfeffer, 1994, p. 47).

Japan's Mazda, facing similar circumstances, had a parallel experience: "At the end of the year, when awards were presented to the best salespeople, the company discovered that the top ten were all former factory workers. They could explain the product effectively, and when business picked up, the fact that factory workers had experience talking to customers yielded useful ideas about product characteristics" (Pfeffer, 1994, p. 47).

Promote from Within

Costco promotes at least 80 percent of its managers from inside the company. Similarly, 90 percent of managers at FedEx started in a nonmanagerial job. Promoting from within offers several advantages (Pfeffer, 1998):

- It encourages both management and employees to invest time and resources in upgrading skills.
- It is a powerful performance incentive.
- It fosters trust and loyalty.
- It capitalizes on knowledge and skills of veteran employees.
- It avoids errors by newcomers unfamiliar with the company's history and proven ways.
- It increases the likelihood that employees will think for the longer term and avoid impetuous, shortsighted decisions. Collins and Porras (1994) found that highly successful corporations almost never hired a chief executive from the outside; less effective companies did so regularly.

Share the Wealth

Many employees feel little responsibility for an organization's performance. They expect gains in efficiency and profitability to benefit only executives and shareholders. People-oriented organizations have devised a variety of ways to align employee rewards more directly with business success. These include gain-sharing, profit-sharing, and employee stock ownership plans (ESOPs). Scanlon plans, first introduced in the 1930s, give workers an incentive to reduce costs and improve efficiency by offering them a share of gains. Profit-sharing plans at companies like Nucor give employees a bonus tied to overall profitability or to the performance of their local unit.

Both gain-sharing and profit-sharing plans have been shown to have a positive impact on performance and profitability. Kanter (1989a) suggests that gain-sharing plans have spread slowly because they require significant changes: cross-unit teams, suggestion systems, and more open communication of financial information to employees. Similar barriers have slowed the progress of ESOPs:

> Evidence shows that, to be effective, ownership has to be combined with ground-floor efforts to involve employees in decisions through schemes such as work teams and quality-improvement groups. Many companies have been doing this, of course, including plenty without ESOPs. But employee-owners often begin to expect rights that other groups of shareholders have: a voice in broad corporate decisions, board seats, and voting rights. And that's where the trouble can start, since few executives are comfortable with this level of power-sharing [Bernstein, 1996, p. 101].

Nevertheless, there have been many successful ESOPs. Rosen, Case, and Staubus (2005) estimate that thousands of firms participate in ESOPs. Evidence suggests that most of the plans have been successful (Blasi, Kruse, and Bernstein, 2003; Kruse, 1993; Blair, Kruse, and Blasi, 2000). Employee ownership tends to be a durable arrangement and to make the company more stable—less likely to go under, be sold, or lay off employees (Blair, Kruse, and Blasi, 2000). When first introduced, employee ownership tends to produce a 4 to 5 percent increase in productivity, and the increase persists over time (Kruse, 1993). Rosen and others (2005) argue that a plan's success depends on effective implementation of three elements of the "equity model" (p. 19):

- Employees must have a significant ownership share in the company.

- The organization needs to build an "ownership culture" (p. 34) by sharing financial data, involving employees in decisions, breaking down the hierarchy, emphasizing teams and cross-training, and protecting jobs.

- It is important that "employees both learn and drive the business disciplines that help their company do well" (p. 38). Depending on the company, the key discipline might be technical innovation, cost control, or customer service, but employees understand what it takes to make the company competitive and focus on making it work.

Bonus and profit-sharing plans spread rapidly in the boom years of the 1990s. Top managers were more likely than other employees to benefit, but many successful firms shared benefits more widely. Skeptics noted a significant downside risk to profit-sharing plans: they work when there are rewards but breed disappointment and anger if the company experiences a financial downturn. A famous example is United Airlines, whose employees took a 15 percent pay cut in return for 55 percent ownership of the company in 1994. Initially, it was a huge success. Employees were enthusiastic when the stock soared to almost $100 a share. But, like most airlines, United experienced financial difficulties after 9/11. Employees were crushed when bankruptcy left their shares worthless and their pensions underfunded.

Invest in Employees

As products, markets, and organizations become more complex, the value of people's specialized knowledge and skills increases. Undertrained workers harm organizations in many ways: shoddy quality, poor service, higher costs, and costly mistakes. Pfeffer (1994), for example, reports that a high proportion of petrochemical industry accidents involve contract employees. In post-invasion Iraq, some of America's more damaging mistakes were the work of private security contractors, who often had less training and discipline than their military counterparts.

Many organizations are reluctant to invest in developing human capital. The costs of training are immediate and easy to measure; the benefits are elusive and long-term. Training temporary or contract workers carries added disincentives. Yet many companies report a sizable return on their training investment. An internal study at Motorola, for instance, found a gain of twenty-nine dollars for every dollar invested in sales training (Waterman, 1994).

The human resource–oriented organization also recognizes that learning must occur on the job as well as in the classroom. Carnaud et Metal Box in France, the world's third-largest packaging company, puts great emphasis on creating a learning organization: "Learning in an organization takes place when three elements are in place: good mentors who teach others, a management system that lets people try new things as much as possible, and a very good exchange with the environment" (Aubrey and Tilliette, 1990, pp. 144–145). Carnaud's chief executive, Jean-Marie Descarpentries, has said that the biggest flaw in managers is their failure to be aggressive and systematic about learning.

Empower Employees

Progressive organizations give power to employees as well as invest in their development. Empowerment includes keeping employees informed, but it doesn't stop there. It also involves encouraging autonomy and participation, redesigning work, fostering teams, promoting egalitarianism, and infusing work with meaning.

Provide Information and Support A key factor in Enron's dizzying collapse was that few people fully understood its financial picture. Eight months before the crash, *Fortune* reporter Bethany McLean asked new CEO Jeffrey Skilling, "How, exactly, does Enron make money?" Her March 2001 article in *Fortune* pointed out that the company's financial reports were almost impenetrable and the stock price could implode if the company missed its earnings forecasts.

Over the last twenty years, a very different philosophy—called "open-book management"—has begun to take root in many progressive companies. This movement is inspired by the near-death experience of an obscure plant in Missouri, Springfield Remanufacturing (now SRC Holdings). SRC was created in 1983 when a group of managers and employees purchased it from International Harvester for about $100,000 in cash and $9 million in debt. It was one of history's most highly leveraged buyouts (Pfeffer, 1998; Stack and Burlingham, 1994). Less debt had strangled many companies, and CEO Jack Stack figured the business could make it only with everyone's best efforts. He developed the open-book philosophy as a way to survive. The system is built around three basic principles (Case, 1995):

- All employees at every level should see and learn to understand financial and performance measures. Important numbers should be readily available, and all employees should master Financial Literacy 101 so they know what the numbers mean.

- Employees are encouraged to think like owners, doing whatever they can to improve the numbers.

- Everyone gets a piece of the action—a stake in the company's financial success.

Open-book management works for several reasons. First, it sends a clear signal that management trusts people. Second, it creates a powerful incentive for employees to contribute. They can see the big picture—how their work affects the bottom line and how the bottom line affects them. Finally, it furnishes information they need to do a better job. If efficiency is dropping, scrap is increasing, or a certain product has stopped selling, employees can pinpoint the problem and correct it.

Encourage Autonomy and Participation   Information is necessary but not sufficient to fully engage employees. The work itself needs to offer opportunities for autonomy, influence, and intrinsic rewards. The Theory X approach, still alive and well, assumes that managers make decisions and employees follow orders. Treated like children, employees behave accordingly. As companies have faced up to the costs of this downward spiral in motivation and productivity, they have developed programs under the generic label of *participation*. This gives workers more opportunity to influence decisions about work and working conditions. The results have often been remarkable.

A classic illustration comes from a group of manual workers—all women—who painted dolls in a toy factory (Whyte, 1955). In a reengineered process, each woman took a toy from a tray, painted it, and put it on a passing hook. The women received an hourly rate, a group bonus, and a learning bonus. Although management expected little difficulty, production was disappointing and morale worse. Workers complained that the room was too hot and the hooks moved too fast.

Reluctantly, the foreman followed a consultant's advice and met face to face with the employees. After hearing the women's complaints, the foreman agreed to bring in fans. Though he and the engineer who designed the manufacturing process expected no benefit, morale improved. Discussions continued, and the employees came up with a radical suggestion: let them control the belt's speed. The engineer was vehemently opposed; he had carefully calculated the optimal speed. The foreman was also skeptical but agreed to give the suggestion a try. The employees developed a complicated production schedule: start slow at the beginning of the day, increase the speed once they had warmed up, slow it down before lunch, and so on.

Results of this inadvertent experiment were stunning. Morale skyrocketed. Production increased far beyond the most optimistic calculations. The women's bonuses escalated to the point that they were earning more than workers with more skill and experience. For that reason, the experiment ended unhappily. The women's production and high pay became a problem as other higher-skilled workers protested. To restore harmony, management reverted to the earlier recommendation: a fixed speed for the belt. Production plunged, morale plummeted, and most of the women quit.

Successful examples of participative experiments have multiplied across sectors and around the globe. A Venezuelan example is illustrative. Historically, the nation's health care was provided by a two-tier system: small-scale, high-quality private care for the affluent and a large public health care system for others. The public system, operated by the ministry of health, was in a state of perpetual crisis. It suffered from overcentralization, chronic deficits, poor hygiene, decaying facilities, and constant theft of everything from cotton balls to X-ray machines (Palumbo, 1991).

A small group of health care providers founded Ascardio to provide cardiac care in one rural area (Palumbo, 1991; Malavé, 1995). Participation was a key to remarkably high standards of patient care:

> The Ascardio style requires, beyond mastery of a technical specialty, the willingness to get involved in an environment of team decision making instead of working in isolation. This is particularly evident in the General Assembly, which brings together all key people: doctors, technical personnel, workers, board members, and community representatives (none of whom are physicians). In its monthly meetings, the Assembly discusses everything from the poor performance of an individual doctor to the system-wide repercussions of giving salary increases decreed by the President of Venezuela" [Malavé, 1995, p. 16].

Studies of participation show it to be a powerful tool to increase both morale and productivity (Appelbaum, Bailey, Berg, and Kalleberg, 2000; Blumberg, 1968; Katzell and Yankelovich, 1975; Levine and Tyson, 1990). A study of three industries—steel, apparel, and medical instruments—found participation consistently associated with higher performance (Appelbaum and others, 2000). Workers in high-performance plants had more confidence in management, liked their jobs better, and received higher pay. The authors suggested that participation improves productivity through two mechanisms: increasing effectiveness of individual workers and enhancing organizational learning (Appelbaum and others, 2000).

Even when it works, participation often creates the need for changes resisted by other parts of an organization, as in the toy-factory example. Another problem is that participation is often more rhetoric than reality (Argyris, 1998; Argyris and Schön, 1996), turning into "bogus empowerment" (Ciulla, 1998, p. 63). Efforts at fostering participation have failed for two main reasons: difficulty in designing workable systems, and managers' ambivalence—they like the idea but fear subordinates will abuse it. Without realizing it, managers mandate participation in a controlling, top-down fashion, sending mixed messages, "You make the decision, but do what I want." Such contradictions virtually guarantee failure.

Redesign Work   In the name of efficiency, many organizations spent much of the twentieth century trying to oust the human element by designing jobs to be simple, repetitive, and low skill. The analogue in education is "teacher-proof" curricula and prescribed teaching techniques. When such approaches dampen motivation and enthusiasm, managers and reformers habitually blame workers or teachers for being uncooperative. Only in the late twentieth century did opinion shift toward the view that problems might have more to do with jobs than with workers. A key moment occurred when a young English social scientist took a trip to a coal mine:

> In 1949 trade unionist and former coal miner Ken Bamforth made a trip back to the colliery where he used to work in South Yorkshire. At the time, he was a postgraduate fellow being trained for industrial fieldwork at the Tavistock Institute for Social Research in London and had been encouraged to return to his former industry to report any new perceptions of work organization. At a newly opened coal seam, Bamforth noticed an interesting development. Technical improvements in roof control had made it possible to mine "shortwall," and the men in the pits, with the support of their union, proposed to reorganize the work process. Instead of each miner being responsible for a separate task, as had become synonymous with mechanized "longwall" mining, workers organized relatively autonomous groups. Small groups rotated tasks and shifts among themselves with a minimum of

supervision. To take advantage of new technical opportunities, they reinvigorated a tradition of small group autonomy and responsibility dominant in the days before mechanization [Sirianni, 1995, p. 1].

Bamforth's observations helped to spur the "sociotechnical systems" approach (Rice, 1953; Trist and Bamforth, 1951). Trist and Bamforth noted that the long-wall method isolated individual workers and disrupted informal groupings that offered potent social support in the difficult and dangerous coal mine environment. They argued for the creation of "composite" work groups, in which individuals would be cross-trained in multiple jobs so each group could work relatively autonomously. Their approach made only modest headway in England in the 1950s but got a boost when two Tavistock researchers (Eric Trist and Fred Emery) were invited to Norway. The invitation came from Einar Thorsrud of the Norwegian Industrial Democracy Project, a joint labor-management effort to provide workers more impact.

At about the same time, in a pioneering American study, Frederick Herzberg (1966) asked employees about their best and worst work experiences. "Good feelings" stories featured achievement, recognition, responsibility, advancement, and learning; Herzberg called these *motivators.* "Bad feelings" stories clustered around company policy and administration, supervision, and working conditions; Herzberg labeled these *hygiene factors.* Motivators dealt mostly with work itself; hygiene factors bunched up around the work context. Attempts to motivate workers with better pay and fringe benefits, improved conditions, communications programs, or human relations training missed the point, said Herzberg. He saw job enrichment as central to motivation, but distinguished it from simply adding more dull tasks to a tedious job. Enrichment meant giving workers more freedom and authority, more feedback, and greater challenges.

Hackman and his colleagues extended Herzberg's ideas by identifying three critical factors in job redesign: "Individuals need (1) to see their work as meaningful and worthwhile, more likely when jobs produce a visible and useful 'whole,' (2) to use discretion and judgment so they can feel personally accountable for results, and (3) to receive feedback about their efforts so they can improve" (Hackman, Oldham, Janson, and Purdy, 1987, p. 320).

Experiments with job redesign have grown significantly in recent decades. Many efforts have been successful, some resoundingly so (Kopelman, 1985; Lawler, 1986;

Yorks and Whitsett, 1989; Pfeffer, 1994; Parker and Wall, 1998; Mohr and Zoghi, 2006). Typically, job enrichment has a stronger impact on quality than on productivity. There is more satisfaction in doing good work than in simply doing more (Lawler, 1986). Most workers prefer redesigned jobs, though some still favor old ways. Hackman emphasized that employees with "high growth needs" would welcome job enrichment, while others with "low growth needs" would not.

Recent decades have witnessed a gradual reduction in dreary, unchallenging jobs. Routine work is either redesigned or turned over to machines and computers. But significant obstacles block the progress of job enrichment, and monotonous jobs will not soon disappear. One barrier is the lingering belief that technical imperatives make simple, repetitive work efficient and cheap. Another barrier is the belief that workers produce more in a Theory X environment. A third barrier is economic; many jobs cannot be altered without major investments in redesigning physical plant and machinery. A fourth barrier is illustrated in the doll-manufacturing experiment: when it works, job enrichment leads to pressures for systemwide change. Workers with enriched jobs often develop higher opinions of themselves. They may demand more—sometimes increased benefits, other times career opportunities or training for new tasks (Lawler, 1986).

Foster Self-Managing Teams   From the beginning, the sociotechnical systems perspective emphasized a close connection between work design and teamwork. Another influential early advocate of teaming was Rensis Likert, who argued in 1961 that an organization chart should depict not a hierarchy of individual jobs but a set of interconnected teams.[1] Each team would be highly effective in its own right and linked to other teams via individuals who served as "linking pins." It took decades for such ideas to take hold, but an increasing number of firms now embrace the idea. One is Whole Foods Markets, a successful grocery chain based in Texas. Everyone who works at Whole Foods is a *team member.* The firm cites "featured team members" on its Web site, and its "Declaration of Interdependence" pledges, "We Support Team Member Excellence and Happiness."

Each Whole Foods store is a profit center, organized into about ten self-managed teams. Team leaders in each store make up another team, as do store leaders in each region and the company's six regional vice presidents. New hires have to be approved by two-thirds of team members. An elaborate system of peer review puts strong emphasis on people's learning from one another (Pfeffer, 1998).

The central idea in the autonomous team approach is giving groups respon- sibility for a meaningful whole—a product, subassembly, or complete service— with ample autonomy and resources and with collective accountability for results. Teams meet regularly to determine work assignments, scheduling, and current production. Supervision typically rests with a team leader, who either is appointed or emerges from the group itself. Levels of discretion vary. At one extreme, a team may have authority to hire, fire, determine pay rates, specify work methods, and manage inventory. In other cases, the team's scope of decision making is narrower, focusing on issues of production, quality, and work methods.

The team concept rarely works without ample training. Workers need group skills and a broader range of technical skills so that each member understands and can perform someone else's job. "Pay for skills" gives team members an incentive to keep expanding their range of competencies (Manz and Sims, 1995).

Promote Egalitarianism Egalitarianism implies a democratic workplace where employees participate in decision making. This idea goes beyond partici- pation, often viewed as a matter of style and climate rather than sharing author- ity. Managers—even in participative systems—still make key decisions. Broader, more egalitarian sharing of power is resisted worldwide. Managers have particu- larly opposed organizational democracy, the idea of building worker participa- tion into the formal structure to protect it from management interference. Most U.S. firms report a form of employee involvement, but many approaches (such as a suggestion box or quality circle) "do not fundamentally change the level of decision-making authority extended to the lowest levels of the organization" (Ledford, 1993, p. 148). Pfeffer (1998) and Ledford (1993) argue that American organizations make less use of workforce involvement than evidence of effective- ness warrants.

Formal efforts to democratize the workplace have been attempted in some parts of Europe. Norway legally mandated worker participation in decision mak- ing in 1977 (Elden, 1983, 1986). Major corporations pioneered efforts to democ- ratize and improve the quality of work life. Three decades later, the results of the "Norwegian model" look impressive—Norway is at or near top of rankings for "best country to live in," with a strong economy, broad prosperity, low unem- ployment, and excellent health care (Barstad, Ellingsen, and Hellevik, 2005).

The Brazilian manufacturer Semco offers a dramatic illustration of orga- nizational democracy in action (Killian, Perez, and Siehl, 1998; Semler, 1993).

Ricardo Semler took over the company from his father in the 1980s and gradually evolved an unorthodox philosophy of management:

> The key to management is to get rid of all the managers.
>
> The key to getting work done on time is to stop wearing a watch.
>
> The best way to invest corporate profits is to give them to the employees.
>
> The purpose of work is not to make money. The purpose of work is to make the employees, whether working stiffs or top executives, feel good about life [Ricardo Semler, cited in Killian, Perez, and Siehl, 1998, p. 2].

At Semco, workers hire new employees, evaluate bosses, and vote on major decisions. In one instance, employees voted to purchase an abandoned factory Semler didn't want and then proceeded to turn it into a remarkable success. Semco's experiments produced dramatic gains in productivity, and the company was repeatedly rated the best place to work in Brazil. Even after Semler no longer saw a need for his company to grow, it grew anyway because innovative employee groups kept inventing new businesses.

Harrison and Freeman (2004) ask, "Is organizational democracy worth the effort?" and conclude that the answer is yes. Even if it does not produce economic gains, it produces other benefits. Despite positive evidence, many managers and union leaders oppose the idea because they fear losing prerogatives they believe essential to success. Union leaders sometimes see democracy as a management ploy to get workers to accept gimmicks in place of gains in wages and benefits or as a wedge that might come between workers and their union.

Organizations that stop short of formal democracy can still become more egalitarian by reducing both real and symbolic status differences (Pfeffer, 1994, 1998). In most organizations, it is easy to discern an individual's place in the pecking order from such cues as office size and access to perks like limousines and corporate jets. Organizations that invest in people, by contrast, often reinforce participation and job redesign by replacing symbols of hierarchy with symbols of cooperation and equality. Semco, for example, has no organization chart, secretaries, or personal assistants. Top executives type letters and make their own photocopies. At Nucor, the chief executive "flies commercial, manages without an executive parking space, and really does make the coffee in the office when he takes the last cup" (Byrnes and Arndt, 2006, p. 60).

Reducing symbolic differences is helpful, but reducing material disparities is important as well. A controversial issue is the pay differential between workers and management. In the 1980s, Peter Drucker suggested that no leader should earn more than twenty times the pay of the lowest-paid worker. He reasoned that outsized gaps undermine trust and devalue workers. Corporate America paid little heed. In 2005, with an average annual compensation of $18.9 million, CEOs of large American companies earned more than four hundred times as much as the average factory worker (Strauss and Hansen, 2006). In the year it went bankrupt, Enron was a pioneer in the golden paycheck movement, handing out a total of $283 million to its five top executives (Ackman, 2002).

In contrast, a number of progressive companies, such as Costco, Whole Foods, and Southwest Airlines, have traditionally underpaid their CEOs by comparison with their competitors. Whole Foods Markets has had a policy limiting executives' pay to ten times the average salary of employees. It was newsworthy that Southwest's CEO received "less than $1 million in 2006 even as the carrier posted its 34th straight year of profits" (Roberts, 2007). Meanwhile, United Airlines, just out of bankruptcy, managed to unite all five of its unions in protest against the estimated take-home pay of $39 million for its CEO.

Promote Diversity

A good workplace is serious about treating everyone well—workers as well as executives; women as well as men; Asians, African Americans, and Hispanics as well as whites; gay as well as straight employees. Sometimes companies support diversity because they think it's the right thing to do. Others do it grudgingly because of bad publicity, a lawsuit, or government pressure.

In 1994, Denny's Restaurants suffered a public relations disaster and paid $54 million to settle discrimination lawsuits. The bill was even higher for Shoney's, at $134 million. Both restaurant chains got religion as a result (Colvin, 1999). So did Coca-Cola, which settled a class action suit by African American employees for $192 million in November 2000 (Kahn, 2001), and Texaco, after the company's stock value dropped by half a billion dollars in the wake of a controversy over racism (Colvin, 1999). Denny's transformation was so thorough that the company has regularly been at or near the top spot on *Fortune*'s list of the fifty best companies for minorities (Esposito, Garman, Hickman, Watson, and Wheat, 2002; Daniels and others, 2004).

The biggest discrimination suit in history—a class action on behalf of more than 1.5 million women hit Wal-Mart in 2003, with allegations of discrimination in pay and promotion. Wal-Mart tried to block the suit and force women to sue individually, but as of December 2007, federal courts had consistently ruled that the suit could go forward (*Dukes v. Wal-Mart,* 2007). So far, Wal-Mart has vigorously defended its human resource practices, but adverse publicity and liability risks are likely to pressure the retail giant to seek accommodation with its female and minority employees.

In the end, it makes good business sense for companies to promote diversity. If a company devalues certain groups, word tends to get out and alienate customers. In the United States, more than half of consumers and workers are female, and about a fourth are Asian, African American, or Latino. California, New Mexico, and Texas have become the first states in which non-Hispanic whites are no longer a majority. The same will eventually be true of the United States as a whole. When talent matters, it is tough to build a workforce if your business practices write off a sizable portion of potential employees. That's one reason so many public agencies in the United States have long-standing commitments to diversity. One of the most successful is the U.S. Army, as exemplified in Colin Powell's ability to rise through the ranks to head the Joint Chiefs of Staff and, subsequently, to become the nation's secretary of state.

Many private employers have also moved aggressively to accommodate gay employees:

> As a high-profile supporter of gay rights, Raytheon of course provides health-care benefits to the domestic partners of its gay employees. It does a lot more, too. The company supports a wide array of gay-rights groups, including the Human Rights Campaign, the nation's largest gay-advocacy group. Its employees march under the Raytheon banner at gay-pride celebrations and AIDS walks. And it belongs to gay chambers of commerce in communities where it has big plants. Why? Because the competition to hire and retain engineers and other skilled workers is so brutal that Raytheon doesn't want to overlook anyone. To attract openly gay workers, who worry about discrimination, a company like Raytheon needs to hang out a big welcome sign. "Over the next ten years we're going to need anywhere from 30,000 to 40,000 new employees," explains Heyward Bell,

Raytheon's chief diversity officer. "We can't afford to turn our back on anyone in the talent pool" [Gunther, 2006, p. 94].

Promoting diversity comes down to focus and persistence. Organizations have to take it seriously and build it into day-to-day management. They tailor recruiting practices to diversify the candidate pool. They develop a variety of internal diversity initiatives, such as mentoring programs to help people learn the ropes and get ahead. They tie executive bonuses to success in diversifying the workforce. They work hard at eliminating the glass ceiling. They diversify their board of directors. They buy from minority vendors. It takes more than lip service, and it doesn't happen overnight. Many organizations still don't get it. But many others have made impressive strides.

PUTTING IT ALL TOGETHER: TQM AND NUMMI

If human resource management strategies are implemented in a halfhearted, piecemeal fashion, they lead to predictable failure. Success requires a comprehensive strategy and long-term commitment that many organizations espouse but fewer deliver. One example of a comprehensive strategy that combines structural and human resource elements is total quality management (TQM), which swept across corporate America in the 1980s. Quality gurus such as W. Edwards Deming (1986), Joseph Juran (1989), Philip Crosby (1989), and Kaoru Ishikawa (1985) differed on specifics, but they all emphasized workforce involvement, participation, and teaming as essential components of a serious quality effort.

Hackman and Wageman (1995) analyzed the theory and practice of the quality movement and concluded that it represented a coherent and distinctive philosophy, consistent with existing research on effective human resource management. They summarized four core assumptions in TQM:

- High quality is actually cheaper than low quality.
- People want to do good work.
- Quality problems are cross-functional.
- Top management is ultimately responsible for quality.

In practice, many organizations diluted the philosophy by implementing only certain parts, usually the easiest and least disruptive. It is no surprise that a majority of quality programs failed to achieve their objectives (Gertz and

Baptista, 1995; Port, 1992), although many companies obtained extraordinary results (Engardio and DeGeorge, 1994; Greising, 1994; Waterman, 1994). One such company, Motorola, reported a total of $17 billion in savings from its quality initiatives as of 2006.

The power of an integrated approach to TQM is illustrated in the case of New United Motors Manufacturing, Inc. (NUMMI), a joint venture of General Motors and Toyota. In 1985, NUMMI reopened an old GM plant in Fremont, California, and began to build cars. It drew the workforce from five thousand employees laid off by GM the preceding year. These workers had a reputation at GM for militancy, poor attendance, alcohol and drug abuse, and even fistfights on the assembly line (Holusha, 1989; Lawrence and Weckler, 1990; Lee, 1988). Two years later, absenteeism had declined from 20 percent at GM to 2 percent at NUMMI, and the plant was producing cars of higher quality at a lower labor cost than any other GM plant. NUMMI's Chevrolets ranked second among cars sold in the United States in initial owner satisfaction; no other GM car was even in the top fifteen.

What accounted for this manufacturing miracle? The answer, in a word, was Toyota, GM's partner in the joint venture. GM provided the plant, the workers, and an American nameplate, but both car and production processes were designed in Japan. Toyota managed the plant, and production was split between Chevrolets and Toyotas. NUMMI's success was built on a comprehensive human resource philosophy. There was symbolic egalitarianism: workers and executives wore the same uniforms, parked in the same lots, and ate in the same cafeteria. Grouped in small, self-managing teams, employees designed their jobs and rotated through different jobs. NUMMI's motto was "There are no managers, no supervisors, only team members."

Both union and management stressed collaboration. If a worker complained to the union, the union representative was likely to be accompanied by a member of the company's human relations staff. The three would try to solve the problem on the spot. If workers fell behind, they could pull a cord to stop the line, and help would arrive quickly. NUMMI's president, Kan Higashi, saw the cord as a sign of trust between management and labor: "We had heavy arguments about installing the cord here. We wondered if workers would pull it just to get a rest. That has not happened." When car sales slumped in 1988, NUMMI laid off no one. Workers were sent at full pay to training sessions on problem solving and interpersonal relations. One worker commented, "With GM, if the line slowed down, some of us would have been on the street" (Holusha, 1989, p. 1).

Even union leaders liked NUMMI. Bruce Lee, a UAW official, said that the team system liberated workers by giving them more control over their jobs and was "increasing the plant's productivity and competitiveness while making jobs easier" (Holusha, 1989). UAW president Owen Bieber said when he toured the plant, "I was most struck that there is hardly any management here at all" (Lee, 1988, pp. 232–233).

NUMMI was not a trouble-free paradise. A dissident union group complained that the brisk pace of work amounted to "management by stress" and that the plant's policy on absenteeism was inhumane. But even dissidents conceded things were better than in the past. Most workers were happy simply for the chance to make automobiles. As one worker said, "We got a second chance here, and we are trying to take advantage of it. Many people don't get a second chance" (Holusha, 1989, p. 1).

GM was sufficiently impressed to try to transfer NUMMI techniques to other plants. Sometimes it worked. At one plant, innovations like self-managing teams doing their own quality audits led to higher quality and lower costs (Hampton and Norman, 1987). But transplants often failed to root because the NUMMI philosophy was implemented piecemeal, with predictably marginal results. "Team decision making" became a fad at GM but often backfired because managers dictated to the teams (Lee, 1988). Kochan, Lansbury, and MacDuffie concluded, "The NUMMI story is well known, so it will suffice to say that GM did a terrible job of learning from that experience" (1997, p. 28).

The NUMMI case illustrates that successful human resource applications are neither as idyllic as idealists might hope nor as soft as old-line managers fear. The NUMMI experiment combined creative human resource management with demanding work standards to produce an automobile highly competitive in terms of both cost and quality. Such combinations have become more and more common in recent decades.

GETTING THERE: TRAINING AND ORGANIZATION DEVELOPMENT

GM's difficulty in learning from NUMMI is one of countless examples of organizations that espouse but fail to apply noble human resource practices. Why? One problem is managerial ambivalence. Progressive practices cost money and alter the relationship between superiors and subordinates. Managers are skeptical about a compensatory return on investment and fearful of losing authority. Moreover, execution requires skill and understanding that are often in short supply. Beginning as far back as the 1950s, the chronic difficulties in improving life at work spurred the rise of the field of Organization Development (OD), an array of ideas and techniques designed to help managers convert intention to reality.

Group Interventions

Working in the 1930s and 1940s, social psychologist Kurt Lewin pioneered the idea that change efforts should emphasize the group rather than the individual (Burnes, 2006). His work was instrumental in the development of a provocative and historically influential group intervention: sensitivity training in "T-groups." The T-group (T for training) was a serendipitous discovery. At a conference on race relations in the late 1940s, participants met in groups, and researchers were stationed in each group to observe and take notes. In the evening, the researchers reported their observations to program staff. Participants asked to be included in these evening sessions. They were fascinated to hear things about themselves and their behavior that they hadn't known before. Researchers recognized that they had discovered something important and developed a program of "human relations laboratories." Trainers and participants joined in small groups, working together and learning from their work at the same time.

As word spread, T-groups began to supplant lectures as a way to develop human relations skills. But research indicated that T-groups were better at changing individuals than organizations (Gibb, 1975; Campbell and Dunnette, 1968). In light of this evidence, T-group trainers began to experiment with new approaches. "Conflict laboratories" were designed for situations involving friction among groups and organizational units. "Team-building" programs were created to help groups work more effectively. "Future search" (Weisbord and Janoff, 1995), "open space" (Owen, 1993, 1995), and other large-group designs (Bunker and Alban, 1996, 2006) brought together sizable numbers of people drawn from different constituencies to work on key issues or challenges. Mirvis (2006) observes that even though the T-group itself has become passé, it gave birth to an enormous range of workshops and training activities that are now a standard part of organizational life.

One famous example of a large-group intervention is the "Work-Out" conferences initiated by Jack Welch when he was CEO of General Electric. Frustrated by the slow pace of change in his organization, Welch convened a series of town hall meetings, typically with one hundred to two hundred employees, to identify and resolve issues "that participants thought were dumb, a waste of time, or needed to be changed" (Bunker and Alban, 1996, p. 170). The conferences were generally viewed as highly successful and spread throughout the company.

Survey Feedback

In the late 1940s, researchers at the University of Michigan began to develop surveys to measure patterns in human behavior. They focused on motivation, communication, leadership styles, and organizational climate (Burke, 2006). Rensis Likert helped found the Survey Research Center at the University of Michigan and produced a 1961 book, *New Patterns of Management,* that became a classic in the human resource tradition. Likert's survey data showed that "employee-centered" supervisors, who focused more on people and relationships, typically managed higher-producing units than "job-centered" supervisors, who ignored human issues, made decisions themselves, and dictated to subordinates.

Survey research paved the way for survey feedback as an approach to organizational improvement. The process begins with questionnaires aimed at human resource issues. The results are tabulated and then shown to managers. The results might show, for example, that information within a unit flows well but that decisions are made in the wrong place using bad information. Members of the work unit, perhaps with the help of a consultant, discuss the results and explore how to improve their effectiveness. A variant on the survey feedback model that has become increasingly standard in organizations is 360-degree feedback, in which managers get survey feedback about how they are seen by subordinates, peers, and superiors.

Evolution of OD

T-groups and survey research gave birth to the field of OD in the 1950s and 1960s. Since then, OD has continued to evolve as a discipline (Burke, 2006; Gallos, 2006; Mirvis, 1988, 2006). In 1965, few managers had heard of OD; thirty years later, few had not. Most major organizations (particularly in the United States) have experimented with OD: General Motors, the U.S. Postal Service, IBM, the Internal Revenue Service, Texas Instruments, Exxon, and the U.S. Navy have all employed their own brands.

Surveying the field in 2006, Mirvis depicts significant innovation and ferment emanating from both academic visionaries and passionate "disciples"

(Mirvis, 2006, p. 87). He also sees "exciting possibilities in the spread of OD to emerging markets and countries; its broader applications to peace making, social justice, and community building, and its deeper penetration into the mission of organizations" (p. 88).

SUMMARY

When individuals find satisfaction and meaning in work, the organization profits from effective use of their talent and energy. But when satisfaction and meaning are lacking, individuals withdraw, resist, or rebel. In the end, everyone loses. Progressive organizations implement a variety of "high-involvement" strategies for improving human resource management. Some approaches strengthen the bond between individual and organization by paying well, offering job security, promoting from within, training the workforce, and sharing the fruits of organizational success. Others empower workers and give work more significance through participation, job enrichment, teaming, egalitarianism, and diversity. No single strategy is likely to be effective by itself. Success typically requires a comprehensive strategy undergirded by a long-term human resource management philosophy. Ideas and practices from organization development often play a significant role in supporting the evolution of more comprehensive and effective human resource practices.

NOTE

1. Likert (pronounced *Lick-urt*) is also widely known for the "Likert Scale," a survey method he developed in the 1930s for measuring attitudes. A typical Likert Scale uses a range of numbers from 1 to 5 or 1 to 7, anchored by "Strongly agree" at one end, and "Strongly Disagree" at the other.

Interpersonal and Group Dynamics

ANNE BARRETA

Anne Barreta was excited but scared when she became the first woman and the first Hispanic American ever promoted to district marketing manager at the Hillcrest Corporation. She knew she could do the job, but expected to be under a microscope. Her boss, Steve Carter, was very supportive. Others were less enthusiastic—like the coworker who smiled as he patted her on the shoulder and said, "Congratulations! I just wish *I* was an affirmative action candidate."

Anne was responsible for one of two districts in the same city. Her counterpart in the other district, Harry Reynolds, was twenty-five years older and had been with Hillcrest twenty years longer. Some said that the term *good old boy* could have been invented to describe Harry. Usually genial, he had a temper that flared quickly when someone got in his way. Anne tried to maintain a positive and professional relationship but often found Harry to be condescending and arrogant.

Things came to a head one afternoon as Anne, Harry, and their immediate subordinates were discussing marketing plans. Anne and Harry were disagreeing politely. Mark, one of Anne's subordinates, tried to support her views, but Harry kept cutting him off. Anne saw Mark's frustration building, but she was still surprised when he angrily told Harry, "If you'd listen to anyone besides yourself, and think a little before you open your mouth, we'd make a lot more progress." With barely controlled fury, Harry declared that "this meeting is adjourned" and stormed out.

165

A day later, Harry phoned to demand that Anne fire Mark. Anne tried to reason with him, but Harry was adamant. Worried about the fallout, Anne talked to Steve, their mutual boss. He agreed that firing Mark was too drastic but suggested a reprimand. Anne agreed and informed Harry. He again became angry and shouted, "If you want to get along in this company, you'd better fire that guy!" Anne calmly replied that Mark reported to her. Harry's final words were, "You'll regret this!"

Three months later, Steve called Anne to a private meeting. "I just learned," he said, "that someone's been spreading a rumor that I promoted you because you and I are having an affair." Anne was stunned by a jumble of feelings—confusion, rage, surprise, shame. She groped for words, but none came.

"It's crazy, I know," Steve continued. "But the company hired a private detective to check it out. Of course, they didn't find anything. So they're dropping it. But some of the damage is already done. I can't prove it, but I'm pretty sure who's behind it."

"Harry?" Anne asked.

"Who else?"

Managers spend most of their time relating to other people—in conversations and meetings, in groups and committees, over coffee or lunch, on the phone, or on the Internet (Kanter, 1989b; Kotter, 1982; Mintzberg, 1973; Watson, 2000). The quality of their relationships figures prominently in how satisfied and how effective they are at work. But people bring patterns of behavior to the workplace that have roots in early life. These patterns do not change quickly or easily on the job. Thompson (1967) and others have argued that the socializing effects of family and society shape people to mesh with the workplace. Schools, for example, teach students to be punctual, complete assignments on time, and follow rules. But schools are not always fully successful, and future employees are shaped initially by family, a decentralized cottage industry that seldom produces raw materials exactly to corporate specifications.

People are imperfect cogs in the bureaucratic machinery. They form relationships to fit individual styles and preferences, often ignoring what the organization requires. They may work, but never *only* on their official assignments. They also express personal and social needs that often diverge from formal rules and requirements. A project falters, for example, because no one likes the manager's style. A committee bogs down because of interpersonal tensions that everyone notices but no one mentions. A school principal spends most days dealing with a handful of abrasive and vocal teachers who generate more than their share of discipline problems and parent complaints. Protracted warfare arises because of personal friction between two department heads.

This chapter begins by looking at basic sources of effective (or ineffective) interpersonal relations at work. We examine why individuals are often blind to self-defeating personal actions. We describe theories of interpersonal competence and emotional intelligence, explaining how they influence office relationships. We explore different ways of understanding individual style preferences. Finally, we discuss key issues in how groups and teams work (or don't): roles, norms, conflict, and leadership.

GREATEST HITS FROM ORGANIZATION STUDIES

Hit Number 6: M. S. Granovetter, "Economic Action and Social Structure: The Problem of Social Embeddedness," *American Journal of Sociology,* **1985,** *91*(3), 481–510

The central question in Granovetter's influential paper is a very broad one: "how behavior and institutions are affected by social relations." Much of his approach is captured in a quip from James Duesenberry: "Economics is all about how people make choices; sociology is all about how they don't have any choices to make" (1960, p. 233) Classical economic perspectives, Granovetter argues, are "undersocialized." They assume that economic actors are atomized individuals whose decisions are little affected by their relationships with others. "In classical and neoclassical economics, therefore, the fact that actors may have social relations with one another has been treated, if at all, as a frictional drag that impedes competitive markets" (Granovetter, 1985, p. 484). Conversely, Granovetter maintains that sociological models are often "oversocialized," because they depict "processes in which actors acquire customs, habits, or norms that are followed mechanically and automatically, irrespective of their bearing on rational choice (p. 485). The truth, in Granovetter's view, lies between these two extremes: "Actors do not behave or decide as atoms outside a social context, nor do they adhere slavishly to a script written for them by the particular intersection of social categories that they happen to occupy. Their attempts at purposive action are instead embedded in concrete, ongoing systems of social relations" (p. 487). Granovetter's argument may sound familiar, since it aligns with a central theme in our book: actors make choices, but their choices are inevitably shaped by social context.

To illustrate his argument, Granovetter critiques another influential perspective—Oliver Williamson's analysis of why some decisions get made in organizational hierarchies, and others are made in markets (Williamson, 1975, number 9 on our list of scholars' hits). Williamson proposed that repetitive decisions involving high uncertainty were more likely to be made in hierarchies because organizations had advantages of information and control—people had more knowledge and leverage over each another. Granovetter counters that Williamson underestimates the power of relationships in cross-firm transactions, and overemphasizes the advantages of hierarchy. A central point in Granovetter's argument is that relationships often trump structure:

"The empirical evidence that I cite shows . . . that even with complex transactions, a high level of order can often be found in the market—that is, across firm boundaries—and a correspondingly high level of disorder within the firm. Whether these occur, instead of what Williamson expects, depends on the nature of personal relations and networks of relations between and within firms. I claim that both order and disorder, honesty and malfeasance have more to do with structures of such relations than they do with organizational form" (p. 502).

INTERPERSONAL DYNAMICS

In organizations, as elsewhere in life, many of the greatest highs and lows stem from our relations with others. Three recurrent questions about relationships regularly haunt managers:

- What is really happening in this relationship?
- What motives are behind other peoples' behavior?
- What can I do about it?

All were key questions for Anne Barreta. What was happening between her and Harry Reynolds? Did he really start the rumor? If so, why? How should she deal with someone who seemed so difficult and devious? Should she talk to him? What options did she have?

To some observers, what's happening might seem obvious: Harry resents a young minority woman who has become his peer. He becomes even more bitter when she rejects his demand to fire Mark and seeks revenge through a sneak attack. The case resembles many others in which men dominate or victimize women. What should Anne, or any woman in similar circumstances, do? Confront the larger issues? That might help in the long run, but a woman who initiates confrontation risks being branded a troublemaker (Collinson and Collinson, 1989). Should Anne try to sabotage Harry before he gets her? If she does, will she kindle a war without winners?

Human resource theorists maintain that constructive personal responses are possible even in highly politicized situations. Argyris (1962), for example, emphasizes the importance of "interpersonal competence" as a basic managerial skill. He shows that managers' effectiveness is often impaired because they overcontrol, ignore feelings, and are blind to their impact on others.

Argyris and Schön's Theories for Action

Argyris and Schön (1974, 1996) carry the issue of interpersonal effectiveness a step further. They argue that individual behavior is controlled by personal theories for action—assumptions that inform and guide behavior. Argyris and Schön distinguish two kinds of theory. *Espoused theories* are accounts individuals provide whenever they try to describe, explain, or predict their behavior. *Theories-in-use* guide what people actually do. A theory-in-use is an implicit program or set of rules that specifies how to behave.

Argyris and Schön found significant discrepancies between espoused theories and theories-in-use, which means that individuals' self-descriptions are often disconnected from their actions. Managers typically see themselves as more rational, open, concerned for others, and democratic than they are seen by colleagues. Such blindness is persistent because people don't learn very well from their experience. The biggest block to learning is a self-protective model of interpersonal behavior that Argyris and Schön refer to as Model I (see Exhibit 8.1).

Exhibit 8.1.
Model I Theory-in-Use.

CORE VALUES (GOVERNING VARIABLES)	ACTION STRATEGIES	CONSEQUENCES FOR BEHAVIORAL WORLD	CONSEQUENCES FOR LEARNING
Define and achieve your goals.	Design and manage the environment unilaterally.	You will be seen as defensive, inconsistent, fearful, selfish.	Self-sealing (so you won't know about negative consequences of your actions).
Maximize winning, minimize losing.	Own and control whatever is relevant to your interests.	You create defensiveness in interpersonal relationships.	Single-loop learning (you don't question your core values and assumptions).
Minimize generating or expressing negative feelings.	Unilaterally protect yourself (from criticism, discomfort, vulnerability, and so on).	You reinforce defensive norms (mistrust, risk avoidance, conformity, rivalry, and so on).	You test your assumptions and beliefs privately, not publicly.
Be rational.	Unilaterally protect others from being upset or hurt (censor bad news, hold private meetings, and so on).	Key issues become undiscussable.	Unconscious collusion to protect yourself and others from learning.

Source: Adapted from Argyris and Schön (1996), p.93.

Model I Lurking in Model I is the core assumption that an organization is a dangerous place where you have to look out for yourself or someone else will do you in. This assumption leads individuals to follow a predictable set of steps in their attempts to influence others. We can see the progression in the exchanges between Harry and Anne:

1. Assume that the problem is caused by the other side. Harry seems to think that his problems are caused by Mark and Anne; Mark is insulting, and Anne protects him. Anne, for her part, blames Harry for being biased, unreasonable, and devious. This is the basic assumption at the core

of Model I: "I'm OK, you're not." So long as problems are someone else's fault, that person, not you, needs to change.

2. Develop a private, unilateral diagnosis and solution. Harry defines the problem and tells Anne how to solve it: fire Mark. When she declines, he apparently develops another, sneakier strategy: covertly undermine Anne.

3. Since the other person is the cause of the problem, get that person to change. Use one or more of three basic strategies: facts, logic, and rational persuasion (tell others why you're right); indirect influence (ease in, ask leading questions, manipulate the other person); or direct critique (tell the other person directly that a specific action pattern is wrong). Harry starts out logically, moves quickly to direct critique, and, if Steve's diagnosis is correct, finally resorts to subterfuge and sabotage.

4. If the other person resists or becomes defensive, it just confirms that the other person caused the problem. Anne's refusal to fire Mark presumably verifies Harry's perception of her as an ineffective troublemaker. Harry confirms Anne's perception that he's unreasonable by stubbornly insisting that firing is the only sufficient punishment for Mark.

5. Respond to resistance through some combination of intensifying pressure and protecting or rejecting the other person. When Anne resists, Harry intensifies the pressure. Anne tries to soothe him without firing Mark. Harry apparently concludes that Anne is impossible to deal with and that the best tactic is sabotage.

6. If your efforts are unsuccessful or less successful than hoped, it is the other person's fault. You need feel no personal responsibility. Harry does not succeed in getting rid of Mark or Anne. He stains Anne's reputation but damages his own in the process. Everyone is hurt. But Harry probably never realizes the error of his ways. The incident may confirm to Harry's colleagues that he is temperamental and devious. Such perceptions will probably block Harry's promotion to a more senior position. But Harry may persist in believing that he is right and Anne is wrong, because no one wants to confront someone as defensive and cranky as Harry.

The result of Model I assumptions is minimal learning, strained relationships, and deterioration in decision making. Organizations that operate on this model are rarely happy places.

Model II What else can be done about a situation like Anne's? Argyris and Schön (1996) propose Model II as an alternative. Here are Model II's basic guidelines:

1. Emphasize common goals and mutual influence. Even in a situation as difficult as Anne's, developing shared goals is possible. Deep down, Anne and Harry both want to be effective. Neither benefits from mutual destruction. At times, each needs help and might learn and profit from the other. To emphasize common goals, Anne might ask Harry, "Do we really want an ongoing no-win battle? Wouldn't we both be better off if we worked together to develop a better outcome?"

2. Communicate openly; publicly test assumptions and beliefs. Model II suggests that Anne talk directly to Harry and test her assumptions. She believes Harry deliberately started the rumor, but she is not certain. She suspects Harry will lie if she confronts him, another untested assumption. Anne might say, for example, "Harry, someone started a rumor about me and Steve. Do you know anything about how that story might have been started?" The question might seem dangerous or naive, but Model II suggests that Anne has little to lose and much to gain. Even if she does not get the truth, she lets Harry know she is aware of his game and is not afraid to call him on it.

3. Combine advocacy with inquiry. Advocacy includes statements that communicate what an individual actually thinks, knows, wants, or feels. Inquiry seeks to learn what others think, know, want, or feel. Exhibit 8.2 presents a simple model of the relationship between advocacy and inquiry.

Model II emphasizes integration of advocacy and inquiry. It asks managers to express openly what they think and feel and to actively seek understanding of others' thoughts and feelings. Harry's demand that Anne fire Mark combines *high* advocacy with *low* inquiry. He tells her what he wants while showing no interest in her point of view. Such behavior tends to be perceived as assertive at best, dominating or arrogant at worst. Anne's response is low in both advocacy and inquiry. In her discomfort, she tries to get out of the meeting without making concessions. Harry might see her as apathetic, unresponsive, or weak.

Model II counsels Anne to combine advocacy and inquiry in an open dialogue. She can tell Harry what she thinks and feels while testing her assumptions

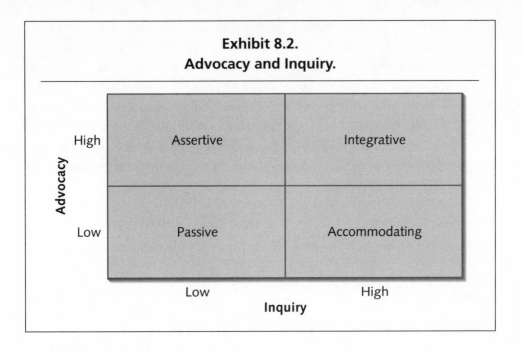

Exhibit 8.2.
Advocacy and Inquiry.

	Low Inquiry	High Inquiry
High Advocacy	Assertive	Integrative
Low Advocacy	Passive	Accommodating

and trying to learn from him. This is difficult to learn and practice. Openness carries risks, and it is hard to be effective when you are ambivalent, uncomfortable, or frightened. It gets easier as you become more confident that you can handle others' honest responses. Anne's ability to confront Harry depends a lot on her self-confidence and interpersonal skills. Beliefs can be self-fulfilling. If you tell yourself that it's too dangerous to be open and that you do not know how to deal with difficult people, you will probably be right. But a more optimistic prediction can be equally self-fulfilling.

The Perils of Self-Protection   When managers feel vulnerable, they revert to self-protection. They skirt issues or attack others and escalate games of camouflage and deception (Argyris and Schön, 1978). Feeling inadequate, they try to camouflage their inadequacy. To avoid detection, they pile subterfuge on top of camouflage. This generates even more uncertainty and ambiguity and makes it difficult or impossible to detect errors. As a result, an organization often persists in following a course everyone privately thinks is a path to disaster. No one wants to be the one to speak the truth. Who wants to be the messenger bearing bad news?

The result is often catastrophe because critical information never reaches decision makers. You might think it difficult to ignore a major gap between what we're doing and what we think we're doing, but it's easy because we get so much help from others. You can see this happening in the following conversation between Susan, a cubicle-dwelling supervisor in an insurance company, and one of her subordinates, Dale. Dale has been complaining that he's underpaid and overqualified for his mail clerk job. As he regularly reminds everyone, he is a *college graduate.* Susan has summoned Dale to offer him a new position as an underwriting trainee.

What Susan is thinking:	What Susan and Dale say:
I wonder if his education makes him feel that society owes him a living without any relationship to his abilities or productivity.	*Susan:* We're creating a new trainee position and want to offer it to you. The job will carry a salary increase, but let me tell you something about the job first.
	Dale: OK. But the salary increase has to be substantial so I can improve my standard of living. I can't afford a car. I can't even afford to go out on a date.
How can he be so opinionated when he doesn't know anything about underwriting? How's he going to come across to the people he'll have to work with? The job requires judgment and willingness to listen.	*Susan:* You'll start as a trainee working with an experienced underwriter. It's important work, because selecting the right risks is critical to our results. You'll deal directly with our agents. How you handle them affects their willingness to place their business with us.
	Dale: I'm highly educated. I can do anything I set my mind to. I could do the job of a supervisor right now. I don't see how risk selection is that difficult.
That's the first positive response I've heard.	*Susan:* Dale, we believe you're highly intelligent. You'll find you can learn many new skills working with an experienced underwriter. I'm sure many of the things you know today came from talented professors and teachers. Remember, one of the key elements in this job is your willingness to work closely with other people and to listen to their opinions.

Dale: I'm looking for something that will move me ahead. I'd like to move into the new job as soon as possible.

We owe him a chance, but I doubt he'll succeed. He's got some basic problems.

Susan: Our thought is to move you into this position immediately. We'll outline a training schedule for you. On-the-job and classroom, with testing at the end of each week.

Dale: Testing is no problem. I think you'll find I score extremely high in anything I do.

Dale is puzzled that no one seems to appreciate his talents. He has no clue that his actions continually backfire. He tries to impress Susan, but almost everything he says confirms his weaknesses and makes things worse. His constant self-promotion reinforces his public persona: opinionated, defensive, and a candidate for failure. But Dale doesn't know this because Susan doesn't tell him. At the moment that Susan is worrying that Dale will offend coworkers by not listening to them, she tells him, "We think you're intelligent." Susan has good reason to doubt Dale's ability to listen: he doesn't seem to hear her very well. If he can't listen to his boss, what's the chance he'll hear anyone else? But Susan ends the meeting still planning to move Dale into a new position in which she expects that he'll fail. She colludes in the likely disaster by skirting the topic of Dale's self-defeating behavior. In protecting herself and Dale from a potentially uncomfortable encounter, Susan helps to ensure that no one learns anything.

There's nothing unusual about the encounter between Susan and Dale—similar things happen every day in workplaces around the world. The Dales of the world dig themselves into deep holes. The Susans help them to remain oblivious as they dig. Argyris calls it "skilled incompetence"—using well-practiced skills to produce the opposite of what you intend. Dale wants Susan to recognize his talents. Instead, he strengthens her belief that he's arrogant and naive. Susan would like Dale to recognize his limitations but unintentionally reassures him that he's fine as he is.

Salovey and Mayer's Emotional Intelligence

The capacity that Argyris (1962) labeled *interpersonal competence* harked back to Thorndike's definition of *social intelligence* as "the ability to understand and manage men and women, boys and girls—to act wisely in human relations" (1920, p. 228). Salovey and Mayer (1990) updated Thorndike by coining the term *emotional intelligence* as a label for skills that include awareness of self and others and the ability to handle emotions and relationships. Salovey and Mayer found that individuals who scored relatively high in the ability to perceive accurately, understand, and appraise others' emotions could respond more flexibly to changes in their social environments and were better able to build supportive social networks (Cherniss, 2000; Salovey, Bedell, Detweiler, and Mayer, 1999). In the early 1990s, Daniel Goleman popularized Salovey and Mayer's work in his best-selling book *Emotional Intelligence*.

Interpersonal skills and emotional intelligence are vital because personal relationships are a central element of daily life. Many change efforts fail not because managers' intentions are incorrect or insincere but because the managers are unable to handle the social challenges of changing. Not long ago, a manufacturing organization proudly announced its "Put Quality First" program. A young manager was assigned to chair a quality team where she worked. She and her team began eagerly. But her plant manager dropped in on most team meetings and regularly dismissed suggestions for change as impractical or unworkable. The team's enthusiasm quickly faded. The plant manager intended to demonstrate accessibility and "management by walking around." No one had the courage to tell him he was killing the initiative.

MANAGEMENT BEST-SELLERS

Daniel Goleman, *Emotional Intelligence* (New York: Bantam, 1995)

Daniel Goleman didn't invent the idea of emotional intelligence, but he made it famous. His best-selling *Emotional Intelligence* focused more on children and education than on work, but it still attracted great interest from the business community. It was followed by articles in the *Harvard Business Review* and has led to a small industry producing books, exercises, and training programs aimed at helping people improve their emotional intelligence (EI). Goleman's basic argument is that EI, rather than intellectual abilities (or intelligence quotient, IQ), accounts for most of the variance in effectiveness among managers, particularly at the senior level.

In *Primal Leadership,* Goleman, McKee, and Boyatzis (2002) define four dimensions of emotional intelligence. Two are internal (self-awareness and self-management), and two are external (social awareness and relationship management). Self-awareness includes awareness of one's feelings and one's impact on others. Self-management includes a number of positive psychological characteristics, among them emotional self-control, authenticity, adaptability, drive for achievement, initiative, and optimism. Social awareness includes empathy (attunement to the thoughts and feelings of others), organizational awareness (sensitivity to the importance of relationships and networks), and commitment to service. The fourth characteristic, relationship management, includes inspiration, influence, developing others, catalyzing change, managing conflict, and teamwork.

Critics have two main complaints about Goleman's work: They say there's nothing new, just an updating of old ideas and common sense, and they maintain that Goleman is better at explaining why EI is important than at suggesting practical ideas for enhancing it. Both criticisms have some validity. Goleman borrowed the EI label from Salovey and Mayer, and the idea of multiple forms of intelligence was developed earlier by Howard Gardner (1993) at Harvard and Robert J. Sternberg (1985) at Yale. The dimensions of EI in *Primal Leadership* (inspiration, teamwork, and so forth) look as if they were culled from the leadership literature of the last few decades. But even if Goleman is offering old wine in new bottles, his work has found a large and receptive audience because of the way he has packaged and framed the issue. He has offered a way to think about the relative importance of intellectual and social skills, arguing that managers with high IQ but low EI are a danger to themselves and others.

MANAGEMENT STYLES

Argyris and Schön's work on theories for action and Salovey and Mayer's work on emotional intelligence focuses on universal competencies—qualities useful to anyone. Another research stream focuses on how individuals diverge in personality and style. A classic experiment (Lewin, Lippitt, and White, 1939) compared autocratic, democratic, and laissez-faire leadership in a study of boys' clubs. Leadership style had a powerful impact on both productivity and morale.

Under autocratic leadership, the boys were productive but joyless. Laissez-faire leadership led to aimlessness and confusion. The boys strongly preferred democratic leadership, which produced a more productive and positive group climate.

A number of subsequent studies have examined leadership in the work setting (Stogdill, 1974; Bass, 1990; Yukl, 2005). Fleishman and Harris (1962) examined two dimensions of interpersonal style: *consideration* (how much a manager shows concern for and sensitivity to people) and *initiating structure* (to what degree a manager actively structures subordinates' activity). Subsequent research has produced a complex pattern of findings. Higher consideration for employees is generally associated with lower turnover, fewer grievances, and less absenteeism. Overall, more effective supervisors tend to be high on both consideration and structure.

Countless theories, books, workshops, and tests have been devoted to helping managers identify their own and others' personal or interpersonal styles. Are leaders introverts or extroverts? Are they friendly helpers, tough battlers, or objective thinkers? Are they higher on dominance, influence, stability, or conscientiousness? Do they behave more like parents or like children? Are they superstars concerned for both people and production, "country club" managers who care only about people, or hard-driving taskmasters who ignore human needs and feelings (Blake and Mouton, 1969)?

In the 1980s, the Myers-Briggs Type Indicator (Myers, 1980) became (and has remained) a popular tool for examining management styles. Built on principles from Jungian psychology, the inventory assesses four dimensions: introversion versus extroversion, sensing versus intuition, thinking versus feeling, and perceiving versus judging. On the basis of scores on those dimensions, it categorizes an individual into one of sixteen types. The Myers-Briggs approach suggests that each style has its strengths and weaknesses and none is universally better than the rest. It also makes the case that interpersonal relationships are less confusing and frustrating if individuals understand and appreciate both their own style and those of coworkers.

One (and maybe both) of the authors of this book, for example, are ENFPs (extroverted, intuitive, feeling, perceiving). ENFPs tend to be warmly enthusiastic, high-spirited, ingenious, and imaginative. But they dislike rules and bureaucracy, their desks are usually messy, and they tend to be disorganized, impatient with details, and uninterested in planning. One of us was once paired with an

ISTJ (introverted, sensing, thinking, judging), who was true to her type—serious, quiet, thorough, practical, and dependable. The task was managing an educational program, but the relationship got off to a rocky start. The ISTJ arrived at meetings with a detailed agenda and a trusty notepad. Her ENFP counterpart arrived with enthusiasm and a few vague ideas. As decisions were reached, the ISTJ carefully wrote down both her assignments and his on a to-do list. Her counterpart made brief, semilegible notes on random scraps of paper. She followed through on all her tasks in a timely manner. He often lost the notes and did only the assignments that he remembered. She became distraught at his lack of organization. He found her bureaucratic rigidity annoying. The relationship might have collapsed had not the two discussed their respective Myers-Briggs styles and recognized that they needed one other; each brought something different but essential to the relationship and the undertaking.

A number of other measures of personality or style, in addition to the Myers-Briggs, are widely used in management development, but none is popular with academic psychologists. They prefer the "Big 5" model of personality on the ground that it has stronger research support (Goldberg, 1992; John, 1990; Judge, Bono, Ilies, and Gerhardt, 2002; Organ and Ryan, 1995). As its name implies, the model interprets personality in terms of five major dimensions. The labels for these dimensions vary from one author to another, but a typical list includes extroversion (displaying energy, sociability, and assertiveness), agreeableness (getting along with others), conscientiousness (a tendency to be orderly, planful, and hard-working), neuroticism (difficulty in controlling negative feelings), and openness to experience (preference for creativity and new experience). For popular use, though, the Big 5 has its disadvantages. Compared with the Myers-Briggs, it conveys stronger value judgments; it is hard to argue that being disagreeable and neurotic are desirable leadership qualities. Moreover, some of the labels (such as neuroticism) make more sense to psychologists than to laypeople.

Despite the risk of turning managers into amateur psychologists, it helps to have shared language and concepts to make sense of the elusive, complex world of individual differences. When managers are blind to their own preferences and personal style, they usually need help from others to learn about it. Their friends and colleagues may be more ready to lend a hand if they have some way to talk about the issues. Tests like the Myers-Briggs provide a shared framework and language.

GROUPS AND TEAMS IN ORGANIZATIONS

Anne Barreta's case shows how demanding even a two-person relationship can become. Managers face even more difficult challenges because they spend much of their time in groups. Groups, as we saw in Chapter Five, can take many forms: standing committees, boards, task forces, project teams, juries, advisory groups, and cliques, to name a few. Groups persistently challenge and frustrate participants. Cynics offer witty but jaundiced perspectives on committees as "a cul-de-sac down which ideas are lured and then quietly strangled" or "a group of the unwilling, chosen by the unfit, to do the unnecessary." Painful experience has led many managers to conclude that groups are almost invariably inefficient and frustrating. But even people who hate groups can often recall at least one peak experience.

Groups, in fact, have both assets and liabilities (Collins and Guetzkow, 1964; Hackman, 1989; McGrath, 1984; Cohen and Bailey, 1997). Groups have more knowledge, diversity of perspective, time, and energy than individuals working alone. Groups often improve communication and increase acceptance of decisions. On the downside, groups may overrespond to social pressure or individual domination, bog down in inefficiency, or let personal agendas smother collective purposes (Maier, 1967).

Groups can be wonderful or terrible, conformist or creative, productive or stagnant. Whether paradise or inferno, groups are indispensable in the workplace. They solve problems, make decisions, coordinate work, promote information sharing, build commitment, and negotiate disputes (Handy, 1993). As modern organizations rely less on hierarchical coordination, groups have become even more important in forms such as self-managing teams, quality circles, and virtual groups whose members are linked by technology.

Groups operate on two levels: an overt, conscious level focused on *task* and a more implicit level of *process,* involving group maintenance and interpersonal dynamics (Bales, 1970; Bion, 1961; Leavitt, 1978; Maier, 1967; Schein, 1969). Many people see only confusion in groups. The practiced eye sees much more. Groups, like modern art, are complex and subtle. A few basic dimensions offer a map for bringing clarity and order out of apparent chaos and confusion. Our map emphasizes four central issues in group process: informal roles, informal norms, interpersonal conflict, and leadership and decision making.

Informal Roles

In groups, as in organizations, the fit between the individual and the larger system is a central human resource concern. The structural frame emphasizes the importance of formal roles, traditionally defined by a title and a job description. In groups and teams, individual roles are often much more informal and implicit on both task and personal dimensions. The right set of *task roles* helps get work done and makes optimal use of each member's resources. But without a corresponding set of informal roles, individuals feel frustrated and dissatisfied, which may foster unproductive or disruptive behaviors.

Every work group needs a structure of task roles so members understand who is going to do what. The roles are often fluid, evolving over time as the group moves through phases of its task. Groups do better when task roles align with individual differences. Group members bring different interests (some love research but hate writing), skills (some are better at writing, while others are better presenters), and varying degrees of enthusiasm (some may be highly committed to the project, while others drag their feet). It is risky, for example, to assign the writing of a final report to a poor writer or to put the most insecure member on stage in front of a demanding group of senior executives.

Anyone who joins a group hopes to find a comfortable and satisfying personal role. Imagine a three-person task force. One member, Karen, is happiest when she feels influential and visible. Bob prefers to be quiet and inconspicuous. Teresa finds it hard to participate unless she feels liked and valued. In the early going in any new group, members send implicit signals about roles they prefer, usually without realizing they are doing it. In their first group meeting, Karen jumps in, takes the initiative, and pushes for her ideas. Teresa smiles, compliments other people, asks questions, and says she hopes everyone will get along. Bob mostly just watches.

If the three individuals' preferred roles dovetail, things may go well. Karen is happy to have Bob as a listener, and Bob is pleased that Karen lets him be inconspicuous. Teresa is content if she feels that Karen and Bob like her. Now suppose that Tony, who likes to be in charge, joins the group. Karen and Tony may collide—two alphas who want the same role. The prognosis looks bleak. But suppose that another member, Susan, signs on. Susan's mission in life is to help other people get along. If Susan can help Karen feel visible, Teresa feel loved, and Tony feel powerful while Bob is left alone, everyone will be happy—and the group should be productive.

Some groups are blessed with a rich set of resources and highly compatible individuals, but many are less fortunate. They have a limited supply of talent, skill, and motivation. They have areas of both compatibility and potential conflict. The challenge is to capitalize on their assets while minimizing liabilities. Unfortunately, many groups either never identify potential hurdles or avoid talking about them. Avoidance often backfires. Neglected challenges come back to haunt team performance, often at the worst possible moment, when a deadline looms and everyone feels the heat.

It usually works better to deal with issues early on. A major consulting firm produced a dramatic improvement in effectiveness and morale by conducting a team-building process whenever an "engagement team" formed to work on a new project. Members discussed the roles they preferred, how the group would operate, and the resources each individual brought. Initially, many skeptics viewed the team building as a waste of time with doubtful benefits. But the investment in group process at the beginning more than paid for itself in effectiveness down the road.

The absence of team building can be catastrophic. In the friendly-fire incident discussed in Chapter Two, where American fighter jets accidentally shot down two U.S. helicopters over Iraq, the post-accident investigation focused on what the pilots did (misidentified friendly helicopters and then shot them down) and on what the airborne AWACS controllers didn't do (failed to give pilots information or warnings about the presence of friendly helicopters in their vicinity). Snook (2000) attributes the controllers' errors of omission to a weak team, which, as luck would have it, was undertaking its maiden flight. All the individuals were technically trained and knew their jobs, but they had not yet jelled as a working team. Before going operational, the team was supposed to experience two full-mission simulations to test their functioning under real-time conditions. But because of last-minute assignments, they only got one, and three of the four key team leaders were not present. Some *individuals* got half the prescribed "spin-up" training. The *team as a whole* got none.

Informal Group Norms

Every group develops informal rules to live by—norms that govern how the group functions and how members conduct themselves. We once observed two families in adjacent sites in the same campground. At first glance, both were alike: two adults, two small children, California license plates. Further observation made it clear that the families had very different unwritten rules.

Family A practiced a strong form of "do your own thing." Everyone did what he or she wanted, and no one paid much attention to anyone else. Their two-year-old wandered around the campground until he fell down a fifteen-foot embankment. He lay there wailing while a professor of leadership pondered the risks and rewards of intervening in someone else's family. Finally, he rescued the child and returned him to his parents, who seemed oblivious and behaved as though they were indifferent to their son's mishap.

Family B, in contrast, was a model of interdependence and efficiency, operating like a well-oiled machine. Everything was done collectively; each member had a role. A drill sergeant would have admired the speed and precision with which they packed for departure. Even their three-year-old approached her assigned tasks with purpose and enthusiasm.

Like these two families, groups evolve informal norms for "how we do things around here." Eventually, such rules are taken for granted as a fixed social reality. The parents in Family A envied Family B. They were plainly puzzled as they asked, "How did they ever get those kids to help out like that? *Our* kids would never do that!"

With norms, as with roles, early intervention helps. Do we want to be task-oriented, no-nonsense, and get on with the job? Or would we prefer to be more relaxed and playful? Do we insist on full attendance at every meeting, or should we be more flexible? Must people be unerringly punctual, or would that cramp our style? If individuals fail to complete assignments, do we hang them or gently encourage them to do better? Do we prize boisterous debate or courtesy and restraint? Groups develop norms to answer such questions.

Informal Networks in Groups

Like informal norms, informal networks—patterns of who relates to whom—help to shape groups. *Remember the Titans,* a feel-good Hollywood film, tells a story of a football teams whose black and white players were suddenly thrust together as a result of school desegregation. Their coach took them off-site for a week of team-building camp where black and white players roomed together and soon developed bonds. Those relationships became a critical feature of the team's ability to win a state championship.

The Titans, like any team, can be viewed as an informal social network—a series of connections that link members to one another. When the team was first formed, it consisted of two different networks separated by suspicion and antagonism across racial boundaries. The coach intuitively understood something research has confirmed—informal bonds among members make a big difference. Balkundi and Harrison (2006) found that teams with more informal ties were more effective and more likely to stay together than teams in which members had fewer connections.

Interpersonal Conflict in Groups

The worst horror stories about group life concern personal conflict. Interpersonal strife can block progress and waste time. It can make things unpleasant at best, painful at worst. Some groups are blessed with little conflict, but most encounter predictable differences in goals, perceptions, preferences, and beliefs. The larger and more diverse the group, the greater the likelihood of conflict.

How can a group cope with interpersonal conflict? The Model I manager typically relies on two strategies: "pour oil on troubled waters" and "might makes right." As a result, things get worse instead of better. The oil-on-troubled-waters strategy views conflict as something to avoid at all costs: minimize it, deny its existence, smooth it over, bury it, or circumvent it. Suppose, for example, that Tony in our hypothetical group says that the group needs a leader and Karen counters that a leader would selfishly dominate the group. Teresa, dreading conflict, might rush to say, "I think we're all basically saying the same thing" or "We can talk about leadership later; right now, why don't we find out a little more about each other?"

Smoothing tactics may work if the issue is temporary or peripheral. In such cases, conflict may disappear on its own, much to everyone's relief. But conflict suppressed early in a group's life has a remarkable tendency to resurface again and again. If smoothing tactics fail and conflict persists, another option is might-makes-right. If Tony senses conflict between Karen and himself, he may employ Model I thinking: since we disagree, and I am right, she is the problem; I need to get her to shape up. Tony may try any of several strategies to change Karen. He may try to convince her he's right. He may push others in the group to side with him and put pressure on Karen. He may subtly, or not so subtly, criticize or attack her. If Karen thinks she is right and Tony is the problem, the two are headed for collision. The result may be painful for everyone.

If Model I is a costly approach to conflict, what else might a group do? Here are some guidelines that often prove helpful.

Develop skills. More and more organizations are recognizing that group effectiveness depends on members' ability to understand what is happening and contribute effectively. Skills like listening, communicating, managing conflict, and building consensus are critical building blocks in a high-performing group.

Agree on the basics. Groups too often plunge ahead without taking the time to agree on goals and procedures. Down the road, people continue to stumble over unresolved issues. Shared understanding and commitment around the basics are a powerful glue to hold things together in the face of the inevitable stress of group life.

Search for common interests. How does a group reach agreement if it starts out divided? It helps to keep asking, "What do we have in common? If we disagree on the issue at hand, how can we put it in a more inclusive framework where we can all agree?" If Tony and Karen clash on the need for a leader, where do they agree? Perhaps both want to do the task well. Recognizing commonalities makes it easier to confront differences. It also helps to remember that common ground is often rooted in complementary differences (Lax and Sebenius, 1986). Karen's desire to be visible is compatible with Bob's preference to be in the background. Conversely, similarity (as when Karen and Tony both want to lead) is often a source of conflict.

Experiment. If Tony is sure the group needs a leader (namely, him) and Karen is equally convinced it does not, the group could bog down in endless debate. Susan, the group's social specialist, might propose an experiment: since Karen sees it one way and Tony sees it another, could we try one meeting with a leader and one without to see what happens? Experiments can be a powerful response to conflict. They offer a way to move beyond stalemate without forcing either party to lose face or admit defeat. Parties may agree on a test even if they can't agree on anything else. Equally important, they may learn something that moves the conversation to a more productive plane.

Doubt your infallibility. This was the advice that Benjamin Franklin offered his fellow delegates to the U.S. constitutional convention in 1787: "Having lived long, I have experienced many instances of being obliged by better information, or fuller consideration, to change opinions even on important subjects, which I once thought right, but found to be otherwise. It is therefore that the older I grow, the more apt I am to doubt my own judgment, and to pay more respect to the judgment of others" (Rossiter, 1966).

Groups typically possess diverse resources, ideas, and outlooks. A group that sees diversity as an asset and a source of learning has a good chance for a productive discussion and resolution of differences. Conflict can be a good thing—research suggests that conflict about ideas promotes effectiveness, even though personal conflict gets in the way (Cohen and Bailey, 1997). In the heat of the moment, though, a five-person group can easily turn into five teachers in search of a learner, or a lynch mob in search of a victim. At such times, it helps if at least one person asks, "Are we all sure we're infallible? Are we really hearing one another?"

Treat differences as a group responsibility. If Tony and Karen are on a collision course, it is tempting for others to stand aside. But all will suffer if the team fails. The debate between Karen and Tony reflects personal feelings and preferences but also addresses leadership as an issue of shared importance.

Leadership and Decision Making in Groups

A final problem that every group must resolve is the question of navigation: "How will we set a course and steer the ship, particularly in stormy weather?" Groups often get lost. Meetings are punctuated with statements like "I'm not sure where we're going" or "We've been talking for an hour without getting anywhere" or "Does anyone know what we're talking about?"

Leadership helps groups develop a shared sense of direction and commitment. Otherwise, a group becomes rudderless or moves in directions that no one supports. Noting that teams are capable of very good and very bad performance, Hackman emphasizes that a key function of leadership is setting a compelling direction for the team's work that "is challenging, energizes team members and generates strong collective motivation to perform well" (2002, p. 72). Another key function of leadership in groups, as in organizations, is managing relationships with external constituents. Druskat and Wheeler found that effective leaders of self-managing teams "move back and forth across boundaries to build relationships, scout necessary information, persuade their teams and outside constituents to support one another, and empower their teams to achieve success" (2003, p. 435).

Though leadership is essential, it need not come from only one person. A single leader focuses responsibility and clarifies accountability. But the same individual may not be equally effective in all situations. Groups sometimes do better with a shared and fluid approach, regularly asking, "Who can best take charge in *this* situation?" Katzenbach and Smith (1993) found that a key characteristic of high-performance teams was mutual accountability, fostered when leaders were willing to step back and team members were prepared to share the leadership.

Leadership, whether shared or individual, plays a critical role in group effectiveness and individual satisfaction. Maier (1967) found that leaders who overcontrol or understructure tend to produce frustration and ineffectiveness. Good leaders are sensitive to both task and process. They enlist others actively in managing both. Effective leaders help group members communicate and work together, while less effective leaders try to dominate and get their own ideas accepted.

SUMMARY

Employees are hired to do a job but always bring social and personal baggage with them. At work, they spend much of their time interacting with others, one to one and in groups. Both individual satisfaction and organizational effectiveness depend heavily on the quality of interpersonal relationships.

An individual's social skills or competencies are a critical element in the effectiveness of relationships at work. Argyris and Schön argue that interpersonal dynamics are counterproductive as often as not. People frequently employ theories-in-use (behavioral programs) that emphasize self-protection and the control of others. Argyris and Schön developed an alternative model built on values of mutuality and learning. Salovey and Mayer, as well as Goleman, underscore the importance of emotional intelligence—social skills that include awareness of self and others and the ability to handle emotions and relationships.

Small groups are often condemned for wasting time while producing little, but groups *can* be both satisfying and efficient. In any event, organizations cannot function without them. Managers need to understand that groups always operate at two levels: task and process. Both levels need to be managed if groups are to be effective. Among the significant process issues that groups have to manage are informal roles, group norms, interpersonal conflict, and leadership.

PART FOUR

The Political Frame

When you ponder the word *politics*, what images come to mind? Are any of them positive or helpful? The answer is probably no.

Although they came from different persuasions, the last two American presidents, Bill Clinton and George W. Bush, were repeatedly accused of "being political." Critics complained that they responded to self-interest and political pressures rather than championing the common good. Politics and politicians are almost universally despised and viewed as an unavoidable evil. In organizations, phrases like "they're playing politics" or "it was all political" are invariably terms of disapproval.

Similar attitudes surround the idea of *power,* a concept that is central in political thinking. In her last interview, only days before she was assassinated in December 2007, Benazir Bhutto was asked if she liked power. Her response captured the mixed feelings many of us harbor: "Power has made me suffer too much. In reality I'm ambivalent about it. It interests me because it makes it possible to change things. But it's left me with a bitter taste" (Lagarde, 2008, p. 13).

A jaundiced view of politics constitutes a serious threat to individual and organizational effectiveness. Viewed from the political frame, politics is the realistic process of making decisions and allocating resources in a context of scarcity and divergent interests. This view puts politics at the heart of decision making.

We introduce the elements of the political frame in Chapter Nine. We begin by examining dynamics lurking in the background of the tragic loss of the space shuttles *Columbia* and *Challenger.* We also lay out the perspective's key assumptions and discuss basic issues of power, conflict, and ethics.

In Chapter Ten, we look at the constructive side of politics. The chapter is organized around basic skills of the effective organizational politician: setting agendas, mapping the political terrain, networking, building coalitions, and negotiating. We also offer four principles of moral judgment to guide in dealing with ethically slippery political issues.

Chapter Eleven moves from the individual to the organizational level. In the chapter, we look at organizations as both arenas for political contests and active political players or actors. As arenas, organizations have an important duty to shape the rules of the game. As players or actors, organizations are powerful tools for achieving the agenda of whoever controls them. We close with a discussion of the relative power of organizations and society. Will giant corporations take over the world? Or will other institutions channel and constrain their actions?

Power, Conflict, and Coalition

Early on the morning of February 1, 2003, the U.S. space shuttle *Columbia* was returning to earth from a smooth and successful mission when something went terribly wrong. The crew was suddenly flooded with emergency signals—the noise of alarms and the glare of indicator lights signaling massive system failure. The craft tumbled out of control before it was finally blown apart. Cabin and crew were destroyed (Wald and Schwartz, 2003a, 2003b).

After months of investigation, a blue-ribbon commission concluded that *Columbia*'s loss resulted as much from organizational as from technical failures. Organizational breakdowns included "the original compromises that were required to gain approval for the shuttle, subsequent years of resource-constraints, fluctuating priorities, schedule pressures, mischaracterization of the shuttle as operational rather than developmental, and lack of an agreed national vision for human space flight" (Columbia Accident Investigation Board, 2003, p. 9).

In short, politics brought down the shuttle. It all sounded sadly familiar, and the investigation board emphasized that there were many "echoes" of the loss of the space shuttle *Challenger* seventeen years earlier. Then, too, Congressional committees and a distinguished panel had spent months studying what happened and developing recommendations to keep it from happening again. But as the *Columbia* board said bluntly: "The causes of the institutional failure responsible for *Challenger* have not been fixed" (Columbia Accident Investigation Board, 2003, p. 195).

Flash back to 1986. After a series of delays, *Challenger* was set to launch on January 28. At sunrise, it was clear but very cold in Cape Canaveral, Florida. The weather was more like New Hampshire, where Christa McAuliffe was a high school teacher. Curtains of ice greeted ground crews as they inspected the shuttle. The temperature had plunged overnight to a record low of 24 degrees Fahrenheit (−4 degrees Celsius). The ice team removed as much as they could. Temperatures gradually warmed, but it was still brisk at 8:30 AM. *Challenger's* crew of seven astronauts noted the ice as they climbed into the capsule. As McAuliffe, the first teacher to venture into space, entered the ship, a technician offered her an apple. She beamed and asked him to save it until she returned. At 11:38 AM, *Challenger* lifted off. A minute later, there was a massive explosion in the booster rockets. Millions watched television screens in horror as the shuttle and its crew were destroyed.

On the eve of the launch, an emergency teleconference had been called between NASA and the Morton Thiokol Corporation, the contractor for the shuttle's solid-fuel rocket motor. During the teleconference, Thiokol engineers pleaded with superiors and NASA to delay the launch. They feared cold temperatures would cause a failure in synthetic rubber O-rings sealing the rocket motor's joints. If the rings failed, the motor could blow up. The problem was simple and familiar: rubber loses elasticity at cold temperatures. Freeze a rubber ball and it won't bounce; freeze an O-ring and it might not seal. Engineers recommended strongly that NASA wait for warmer weather. They tried to produce a persuasive engineering rationale, but their report was hastily thrown together, and the data seemed equivocal (Vaughan, 1995). Meanwhile, Thiokol and NASA both faced strong pressure to get the shuttle in the air:

> Thiokol had gained the lucrative sole source contract for the solid rocket boosters thirteen years earlier, during a bitterly disputed award process. It was characterized by some veteran observers as a low point in squalid political intrigue. At the time of the award, a relatively small Thiokol Chemical Company in Brigham City, Utah, had considerable political clout. Both the newly appointed chairman of the Senate Aeronautics and Space Science Committee, Democratic Senator Frank Moss, and the new NASA administrator, Dr. James Fletcher, were insiders in the tightly knit Utah political hierarchy. By summer 1985, however, Thiokol's monopoly was under attack,

and the corporation's executives were reluctant to risk their billion-dollar contract by halting shuttle flight operations long enough to correct flaws in the booster joint design [McConnell, 1987, p. 7].

Meanwhile, NASA managers were experiencing their own political pressures. As part of the effort to build congressional support for the space program, NASA had promised that the shuttle would eventually pay for itself in cargo fees, like a boxcar in space. Projections of profitability were based on an ambitious plan: twelve flights in 1984, fourteen in 1985, and seventeen in 1986. NASA had fallen well behind schedule—only five launches in 1984 and eight in 1985. The promise of "routine access to space" and self-supporting flights looked more and more dubious. With every flight costing taxpayers about $100 million, NASA needed a lot of cash from Congress, but prospects were not bright. NASA's credibility was eroding as the U.S. budget deficit soared.

That was the highly charged context in which Thiokol's engineers recommended canceling the next morning's launch. The response from NASA officials was swift and pointed. One NASA manager said he was "appalled" at the proposal, and another said, "My God, Thiokol, when do you want me to launch? Next April?" (McConnell, 1987, p. 196). Senior managers at Thiokol huddled and decided, against the advice of engineers, to recommend the launch. NASA accepted the recommendation and launched Flight 51-L the next morning. The O-rings failed almost immediately, and the flight was destroyed (Bell and Esch, 1987; Jensen, 1995; McConnell, 1987; Marx, Stubbart, Traub, and Cavanaugh, 1987; Vaughan, 1990, 1995).

It is disturbing to see political agendas corrupting technical decisions, particularly when lives are at stake. We might be tempted to explain *Challenger* by blaming individual selfishness and questionable motives. But such explanations are little help in understanding what really happened or avoiding a future catastrophe. As we saw in Chapter Two's friendly-fire case (where U.S. fighter jets mistakenly shot down two of their own helicopters), individual errors typically occur downstream from powerful forces channeling decision makers over a precipice no one sees until too late. With *Columbia* and *Challenger,* key decision makers were experienced, highly trained, and intelligent. If we tried to get better people, where would we find them? Even if we could, how could we ensure that they too would not become ensnared by parochial interests and political gaming? The *Columbia* investigating board recognized this reality, concluding, "NASA's problems cannot be solved simply by retirements, resignations, or transferring personnel" (Columbia Accident Investigation Board, 2003, p. 195).

Both *Columbia* and *Challenger* were extraordinary tragedies, but they illustrate political dynamics that are everyday features of organizational life. The political frame does not blame politics on individual characteristics such as selfishness, myopia, or incompetence. Instead, it proposes that interdependence, divergent interests, scarcity, and power relations inevitably spawn political activity. It is naive and romantic to hope organizational politics can be eliminated, regardless of individual players. Managers can, however, learn to acknowledge, understand, and manage political dynamics, rather than shy away from them. In government, politics is a way of life rather than dirty pool. Chris Matthews calls it *hardball:* "Hardball is clean, aggressive Machiavellian politics. It is the discipline of gaining and holding power, useful to any profession or undertaking, but practiced most openly and unashamedly in the world of public affairs" (1999, p. 13).

This chapter seeks to explain why political processes are universal, why they won't go away, and how they can be handled adroitly. We describe the political frame's basic assumptions and explain how they work. Next, we highlight organizations as freewheeling coalitions rather than formal hierarchies. Coalitions are tools for exercising power, and we contrast power with authority and highlight tensions between authorities (who try to keep things under control) and partisans (who try to influence a system to get what they want). We also delineate multiple sources of power. Since conflict is normal among members of a coalition, we underscore the role of conflict in organizations. Finally, we discuss an issue at the heart of organizational politics: Do political dynamics inevitably undermine principles and ethics?

POLITICAL ASSUMPTIONS

The political frame views organizations as roiling arenas hosting ongoing contests of individual and group interests. Five propositions summarize the perspective:

1. Organizations are coalitions of assorted individuals and interest groups.
2. Coalition members have enduring differences in values, beliefs, information, interests, and perceptions of reality.

3. Most important decisions involve allocating scarce resources—who gets what.

4. Scarce resources and enduring differences put conflict at the center of day-to-day dynamics and make power the most important asset.

5. Goals and decisions emerge from bargaining and negotiation among competing stakeholders jockeying for their own interests.

Political Propositions and the *Challenger*

All five propositions of the political frame came into play in the *Challenger* incident:

Organizations are coalitions. NASA did not run the space shuttle program in isolation. The agency was part of a complex coalition of contractors, Congress, the White House, the military, the media—even the American public. Consider, for example, why Christa McAuliffe was aboard. Her expertise as a teacher was not technically critical to the mission. But the American public was bored with seeing white male pilots in space. Human interest was good for NASA and Congress; it built public support for the space program. McAuliffe's participation was a media magnet because it made for a great human interest story. Symbolically, Christa McAuliffe represented all Americans. Everyone flew with her.

Coalition members have enduring differences. NASA's hunger for funding competed with the public's interest in lower taxes. Astronauts' concerns about safety were at odds with pressures on NASA and its contractors to maintain an ambitious flight schedule.

Important decisions involve allocating scarce resources. Time and money were both in short supply. Delay carried a high price—not just dollars, but also further erosion of support from key constituents. On the eve of the *Challenger* launch, key officials at NASA and Morton Thiokol struggled to balance these conflicting pressures. Everyone from President Ronald Reagan to the average citizen was clamoring for the first teacher to fly in space. No one wanted to tell the audience the show was off.

Scarce resources and enduring differences make conflict central and power the most important asset. The teleconference on the eve of the launch began as a debate between the contractor and NASA. As sole customer, NASA was in the driver's seat. When managers at Morton Thiokol sensed NASA's level of disappointment and frustration, the scene shifted to a tense standoff between engineers and managers. Managers relied on their authority to override the engineers' concerns and recommended the launch.

Goals and decisions emerge from bargaining, negotiation, and jockeying for position among competing stakeholders. Political bargaining and powerful allies had propelled Morton Thiokol into the rocket motor business. Thiokol's engineers had been attempting to focus management's attention on the booster joint problem for many months. But management feared that acknowledging a problem, in addition to costing time and money, would erode the company's credibility. A large and profitable contract was at stake.

Implications of the Political Propositions

The assumptions of the political frame also explain why organizations are inevitably political. A coalition forms because of interconnections among its members; they need one another, even though their interests may only partly overlap. The assumption of enduring differences implies that political activity is more visible and dominant under conditions of diversity than of homogeneity. Agreement and harmony are easier to achieve when everyone shares similar values, beliefs, and cultural ways.

The concept of scarce resources suggests that politics will be more salient and intense in difficult times. Schools and colleges, for example, have lived through alternating feast and famine in response to peaks and valleys in economic and demographic trends. When money and students are plentiful (as they were in the 1960s and again in the 1990s), administrators spend time designing new buildings and initiating innovative programs. Work is fun when you're delivering good news and constituents applaud. Conversely, when resources dry up, you may have to shutter buildings, close programs, and lay off staff. Conflict mushrooms, and administrators often succumb to political forces they struggle to understand and control.

Differences and scarce resources make power a key resource. Power in organizations is basically the capacity to make things happen. Pfeffer defines power as "the potential ability to influence behavior, to change the course of events, to overcome resistance, and to get people to do things they would not otherwise do" (1992, p. 30). Social scientists often emphasize a tight linkage between power and dependency: if A has something B wants, A has leverage. In much of organizational life, individuals and groups are interdependent; they need things from one another, and power relationships are multidirectional. From the view of the political frame, power is a "daily mechanism of our social existence" (Crozier and Friedberg, 1977, p. 32).

The final proposition of the political frame emphasizes that goals are not set by edict at the top but evolve through an ongoing process of negotiation and bargaining. Few organizations have a unitary apex. Who, for example, is at the head of a public company? The CEO? But the CEO reports to the board. The board is elected by and accountable to the shareholders. And the shareholders are typically a large and scattered group of absentee owners with little time, interest, or capacity to influence the organization in which each has a sliver of ownership. If a corporate raider or hedge fund acquires a major ownership stake, the stage is set for a battle over control of the company.

The dynamic of multiple constituents jockeying for influence is especially apparent in the public sector. Consider a commitment China made in 2001 to gain membership in the World Trade Organization. The Chinese government promised to get serious about protecting intellectual property, ensuring that products carrying brands such as Coca-Cola, Microsoft, Sony, and Rolex were authentic. The central government passed laws, threw the book at the occasional unlucky offender, blustered in the media, and put pressure on local governments. Yet years later, name-brand knockoffs and pirated music continued to be sold all over China. In late 2007, the Shanghai street price for the latest Hollywood movies on DVD was about sixty cents, and tourists in Beijing encountered countless vendors offering amazing bargains on Rolex watches (Powell, 2007). In response to numerous complaints from abroad, the government announced still another crackdown, promised stiffer fines for violators, and staged a nationwide burn-in at which 42 million pirated items were consigned to bonfires (Coonan, 2007).

Why have the anti-piracy efforts had so little impact? The Chinese government is far from monolithic and is only one of many players in a complex power game. Newly affluent Chinese consumers want foreign brands. Lots of large and small Chinese businesses know, for example, that a homemade carbonated fluid can fetch a better price if it carries an American brand name. The problem has been so widespread that Coca-Cola's Chinese affiliate has found itself not only raiding factories but also chasing pirates who slap Coke labels on bottles in delivery trucks en route to retail outlets.

Stopping piracy has run into a range of obstacles. Pirates are often local businesses with plenty of *guanxi* (connections) who generously share the loot with local government and police officials. As one *New York Times* reporter discovered when he was imprisoned for several hours in a toy factory, "Factory bosses can overrule the police, and Chinese government officials are not as powerful as you might suspect" (Barboza, 2007, p. 3). Moreover, the concept of intellectual property rights is new to many Chinese. They find it hard to see the merit of punishing a hard-working Chinese entrepreneur to protect a big foreign corporation. In short, multiple power centers and continuing divisions have seriously limited senior officials' ability to translate intention into action.

ORGANIZATIONS AS COALITIONS

Academics and managers alike have assumed that organizations have, or ought to have, clear and consistent goals set at the apex of authority. In a business, the owners or top managers set goals such as growth and profitability. Goals in a government agency are presumably set by the legislature and elected executives. The political frame challenges such views. Cyert and March articulate the difference between structural and political views of goals:

> To what extent is it arbitrary, in conventional accounting, that we call wage payments "costs" and dividend payments "profit" rather than the other way around? Why is it that in our quasi-genetic moments we are inclined to say that in the beginning there was a manager, and he recruited workers and capital? . . . The emphasis on the asymmetry has seriously confused the understanding of organizational goals. The confusion arises because ultimately it makes only slightly more sense to say that the goal of a business enterprise is to maximize profit than to say that its goal is to maximize the salary of Sam Smith, assistant to the janitor [1963, p. 30].

Cyert and March are saying something like this: Sam Smith, the assistant janitor; Jim Ford, the foreman; and Celeste Cohen-Peters, the company president are all members of a grand coalition, Cohen-Peters Enterprises. All make demands on resources and bargain to get as much of what they value as possible. Cohen-Peters has more authority than Jones or Ford and, in case of disagreement, she will often win—but not always. Her influence depends on how much power she mobilizes in comparison with that of Smith, Ford, and other members of the coalition. Xerox had a close brush with bankruptcy in 2001 under a CEO who had come from the outside and never mastered the politics at the top of the organization. The firm was adrift, and the captain had lost control of his ship. His successor, Anne Mulcahy, was a canny insider who built the relationships and alliances she needed to get Xerox back on course.

If political pressures on goals are visible in the private sector, they are blatant in the public arena. As in the *Challenger* incident, public agencies operate amid a welter of constituencies, each making demands and trying to get its way. The result is a confusing multiplicity of goals, many in conflict. Consider Gazprom, Russia's biggest company and the world's largest producer of natural gas. For a time in 2006, it ranked third in the world in market capitalization, behind only Exxon and General Electric. Gazprom supplies most of the natural gas in Eastern Europe and 25 percent or more in France, Germany, and Italy. It began as a state ministry under Mikhail Gorbachev, became a public stock company under Boris Yeltsin, and then turned semi-public under Vladimir Putin, with the Russian government the majority stockholder.

Many observers felt that Gazprom functioned as an extension of government policy. Prices for gas exports seemed to correlate with how friendly a government was to Moscow. "If people take us for the state, that doesn't make us unhappy," said Sergey Kouprianov, a company spokesman. "We identify with the state" (Pasquier, 2007, p. 43). Russian President Vladimir Putin returned the sentiment. Gazprom produced a quarter of Russia's government revenues, and Putin saw hydrocarbons substituting for the Red Army as a lever to project Russian power. At the same time, Russian consumers got their gas at about 20 percent of market price. When the company tried for a domestic price increase in 2006, it was blocked by a government that was thinking ahead to the next presidential election. Was this giant in business to benefit customers, management, stockholders, the Kremlin, or Russian citizens? All of the above and more, because all were participants in the grand and messy Gazprom coalition.

Hit Number 2: Richard M. Cyert and James G. March, *A Behavioral Theory of the Firm* (Upper Saddle River, N.J.: Prentice Hall, 1963)

Coming in at number two on the scholars' lists of greatest hits is a forty-year-old book by an economist, Richard Cyert, and a political scientist, James G. March. Cyert and March defined their basic purpose as developing a predictive theory of organizational decision making rooted in a realistic understanding of how decisions actually get made. They rejected as unrealistic the traditional economic view of a firm as a unitary entity (a corporate "person") with a singular goal of maximizing profits. Cyert and March chose instead to view organizations as coalitions made up of individuals and subcoalitions. This view implied a central idea of the political frame: goals emerge out of a bargaining process among coalition members. Cyert and March also insisted that "side payments" are critical, since preferences are only partly compatible and decisions rarely satisfy everyone. A coalition can survive only if it offers sufficient inducements to keep essential members on board. This is not easy, because resources—money, time, information, and decision-making capacity—are limited.

In analyzing decision making, Cyert and March developed four "relational concepts," implicit rules that firms use to make decisions more manageable:

1. *Quasi-resolution of conflict.* Instead of resolving conflict, organizations break problems into pieces and farm pieces out to different units. Units make locally rational decisions (for example, marketers do what they think is best for marketing). Decisions are never consistent but need only be good enough to keep the coalition functioning.

2. *Uncertainty avoidance.* Organizations employ a range of simplifying mechanisms—such as standard operating procedures, traditions, and contracts—that enable them to act as if the environment is clearer than it is.

3. *Problemistic search.* Organizations look for solutions in the neighborhood of the presenting problem and grab the first acceptable solution.

4. *Organizational learning.* Over time, organizations evolve their goals and aspiration levels, altering what they attend to and what they ignore, and changing search rules.

POWER AND DECISION MAKING

At every level in organizations, alliances form because members have interests in common and believe they can do more together than apart. To accomplish their aims, they need power. Power can be viewed from multiple perspectives. Structural theorists typically emphasize authority, the legitimate prerogative to make binding decisions. In this view, managers make rational decisions (optimal and consistent with purpose); monitor actions to ensure decisions are implemented; and calculate how well subordinates carry out directives. In contrast, human resource theorists place less emphasis on power and more on empowerment (Bennis and Nanus, 1985; Block, 1987). More than structuralists, they emphasize limits of authority and tend to focus on influence that enhances mutuality and collaboration. The implicit hope is that participation, openness, and collaboration substitute for power.

The political frame views authority as only one among many forms of power. It recognizes the importance of individual (and group) needs but emphasizes that scarce resources and incompatible preferences cause needs to collide. The political issue is how competing groups articulate preferences and mobilize power to get what they want. Power, in this view, is not evil: "We have to stop describing power always in negative terms: [as in] it excludes, it represses. In fact, power produces; it produces reality" (Foucault, 1975, p. 12).

Authorities and Partisans

Gamson (1968) describes the relationship between two antagonists—partisans and authorities—that are often central to the politics of both organizations and society. By virtue of their position, authorities are entitled to make decisions binding on their subordinates. Any member of the coalition who wants to exert bottom-up pressure is a potential partisan. Gamson describes the relationship in this way: "Authorities are the recipients or targets of influence, and the agents or initiators of social control. Potential partisans have the opposite roles—as agents or initiators of influence, and targets or recipients of social control" (p. 76).

In a family, parents function as authorities and children as partisans. Parents make binding decisions about bedtime, television viewing, or which child uses a particular toy. Parents initiate social control, and children are the recipients of parental decisions. Children in turn try to influence the decision makers. They argue for a later bedtime or point out the injustice of giving one child something another wants. They try to split authorities by lobbying one parent after the other has refused. They may form a coalition (with siblings, grandparents, and so on) in an attempt to strengthen their bargaining position.

Authority is essential to anyone in a formal position because social control depends on it. Officeholders can exert control only so long as partisans respect or fear them enough that their authority or power remains intact. If partisans are convinced that existing authorities are too evil or incompetent to continue, they will risk trying to wrest control—unless they regard the authorities as too formidable. Conversely, if partisans trust authority, they will accept and support it in the event of an attack (Gamson, 1968; Baldridge, 1971).

If partisan opposition becomes too powerful, authority systems may collapse. The process can be very swift, as events in Eastern Europe and China in 1989 illustrated. Established regimes had lost legitimacy years earlier but held on through coercion and control of access to decision making. When massive demonstrations erupted, authorities faced an unnerving choice: activate the police and army in the hope of preserving power or watch their authority fade away. Authorities in China and Romania chose the first course. It led to bloodshed in both cases, but only the Chinese were able to quash their opposition. In Eastern Europe, authorities' attempts to quell dissent with force were futile, and their legitimacy evaporated as swiftly as water in a desert.

The period of evaporation is typically heady but always hazardous. The question is whether new authority can reconstitute itself quickly enough to avoid chaos. Authorities and partisans both have reason to fear a specter such as Lebanon encountered in the 1980s and again in the early 2000s, Bosnia and Liberia in the 1990s, Somalia since 1991, and Iraq in the aftermath of U.S. intervention. All are dismal examples of chronic turmoil and misery, with no authority strong enough to bring partisan strife under control.

Sources of Power

Authority is far from the only source of power—partisans have other sources they can draw upon. A number of social scientists (Baldridge, 1971; French and Raven, 1959; Kanter, 1977; Pfeffer, 1981, 1992; Russ, 1994) have tried to identify the various wellsprings of power. The full list includes

- *Position power (authority).* Positions confer certain levels of legitimate authority. Professors assign grades, judges settle disputes. Positions also place incumbents in more or less powerful locations in communications and power networks. It helps as much to be in the right unit as to hold the right job. A lofty title in a backwater department may not mean much, but junior members of a powerful unit may have substantial clout (Pfeffer, 1992).

- *Control of rewards.* The ability to deliver jobs, money, political support, or other rewards brings power. There are many differences between Chicago Mayor Richard Daley and Iraqi cleric Muqtada al-Sadr, who heads the Mahdi army, but both cement their power base by delivering services and jobs to loyal supporters (Mihalopoulos and Kimberly, 2006; Rubin, 2007).

- *Coercive power.* Coercive power rests on the ability to constrain, block, interfere, or punish. A union's ability to walk out, students' capacity to sit in, and an army's ability to clamp down exemplify coercive power. A chilling example is the rise of suicide attacks in the last quarter-century. "Suicide attacks amount to just 3 percent of all terrorist incidents from 1980 to 2003, but account for 48 percent of all fatalities, making the average suicide attack twelve times deadlier than other forms of terrorism—even if the immense losses of September 11 are not counted" (Pape, 2006, p. 4).

- *Information and expertise.* Power flows to those with the information and know-how to solve important problems. It flows to marketing experts in consumer products industries, to the faculty in elite universities, and to political consultants who help politicians get elected.

- *Reputation.* Reputation builds on expertise. In almost every area of human performance, people develop track records based on their prior accomplishments. Opportunities and influence flow to people with strong reputations, like the Hollywood superstars whose presence in a new film sells tickets.

- *Personal power.* Individuals who are attractive and socially adept—because of charisma, energy, stamina, political smarts, gift of gab, vision, or some other characteristic—are imbued with power independent of other sources. French and Raven (1959) used the term *referent power* to describe influence that comes when people like you or want to be like you. John Kennedy and Ronald Reagan expanded their influence because they brought to the presidency levels of charm, humor, and ease that Jimmy Carter and George W. Bush lacked.

- *Alliances and networks.* Getting things done in an organization involves working through a complex network of individuals and groups. Friends and allies make things a lot easier. Kotter (1982) found that a key difference between more and less successful senior managers was attentiveness to building and cultivating ties with friends and allies. Managers who spent too little time building networks had much more difficulty getting things done.

- *Access and control of agendas.* A by-product of networks and alliances is access to decision arenas. Organizations and political systems typically give some groups more access than others. When decisions are made, the interests of those with "a seat at the table" are well represented, while the concerns of absentees are often distorted or ignored (Lukes, 1974; Brown, 1986).

- *Framing: control of meaning and symbols.* "Establishing the framework within which issues will be viewed and decided is often tantamount to determining the result" (Pfeffer, 1992, p. 203). Elites and opinion leaders often have substantial ability to shape meaning and articulate myths that express identity, beliefs, and values. Viewed positively, this fosters meaning and hope. Viewed cynically, elites can convince others to accept and support things not in their best interests (Brown, 1986; Frost, 1985; Lakoff, 2004). Lakoff argued that Republican electoral success in 2000 and 2004 owed much to skill in framing issues—recasting, for example, the "estate tax" (which sounds like a tax on the rich) into the "death tax" (which sounds like adding insult to injury).

Partisans' multiple sources of power constrain authorities' capacity to make binding decisions. Officeholders who rely solely on position power generate resistance and get outflanked, outmaneuvered, or overrun by others more versatile in exercising other forms of power. Kotter (1985) argues that managerial jobs come with a built-in "power gap" because position power is rarely enough to get the job done. Expertise, rewards, coercion, allies, access, reputation, framing, and personal power help close the gap.

Power can be very volatile, rising and falling with changes in circumstances. An organization that sets new profit records each year is rarely besieged by complaints and demands for change. As many company presidents have learned, however, the first bad quarter triggers a stream of calls and letters from board members, stockholders, and financial analysts. In the boom of the late 1990s, "everyone" was getting rich in the stock market, and charismatic CEOs such as Jack Welch of General Electric and Jean-Marie Messier of France's Vivendi became popular heroes. But when the economy, the market, and the image of business crashed in the first years of the new century, so did these heroic images. In 2002, Welch found himself deeply embarrassed by public revelation of the generous postretirement payouts his old company was bestowing on him. In the same year, Messier was booted out by board members dissatisfied with the company's stock price and his arrogant "American" leadership style.

Clark Kerr once remarked ruefully that his primary tasks as chancellor of the University of California at Berkeley seemed to be providing "sex for the students, parking for the faculty, and football for the alumni." The remark was half facetious but reflects an important grain of truth: a president's power lies particularly in *zones of indifference*—areas only a few people care much about. The zone of indifference can expand or contract markedly, depending on how an organization is performing in the eyes of its major constituents. In the late 1960s, many college presidents lost their jobs because they were blamed for student unrest. Among them was Kerr, who remarked that he left the job just as he entered it, "fired with enthusiasm." Managers need to track the shifting boundaries of zones of indifference so they do not blunder into decisions that seem safe but stir up unanticipated firestorms of criticism and resistance.

Distribution of Power: Overbounded and Underbounded Systems

Organizations and societies differ markedly in how power is distributed. Alderfer (1979) and Brown (1983) distinguish between overbounded and underbounded systems. In an *overbounded system,* power is highly concentrated and everything is tightly regulated. In an *underbounded system,* power is diffuse and the system is very loosely controlled. An overbounded system regulates politics with a firm hand; an underbounded system openly encourages conflict and power games.

If power is highly regulated, political activity is often forced under wraps. Before the emergence of Mikhail Gorbachev and glasnost ("openness") in the

1980s, it was common for Westerners to view Soviets as a vast, amorphous mass of like-minded people, brainwashed by decades of government propaganda. It was not true, but even so-called experts on Soviet affairs missed the underlying reality (Alterman, 1989). Ethnic, political, philosophical, and religious differences simmered quietly underground so long as the Kremlin maintained a tightly regulated society. Glasnost took the lid off, leading to an outpouring of debate and dissent that rapidly caused the collapse of the old order in the Soviet Union and throughout Eastern Europe. Almost overnight, much of Eastern Europe went from overbounded to underbounded.

The war in Iraq, beginning in 2003, produced a similar result. The collapse of the overbounded Saddam Hussein regime created a power vacuum that attracted a host of contenders vying for supremacy. By 2006, Iraq had the formal elements of a new government, including a constitution and an elected parliament, but it was still uncertain two years later when, or if, the state would have the capacity to bring conflict and chaos under control.

CONFLICT IN ORGANIZATIONS

The political frame stresses that the combination of scarce resources and divergent interests produces conflict as surely as night follows day. Conflict is not viewed as something that can or should be tamped down or stamped out. Other frames view conflict differently. The structural frame, in particular, views conflict as an impediment to effectiveness. Hierarchical conflict raises the possibility that lower levels will ignore or subvert management directives. Conflict among major partisan groups can undermine leadership's ability to function. Such dangers are precisely why the structural perspective finds virtue in a well-defined, authoritative chain of command.

From a political perspective, conflict is not necessarily a problem or a sign that something is amiss. Organizational resources are in short supply; there is rarely enough to give everyone everything they want. Individuals compete for jobs, titles, and prestige. Departments compete for resources and power. Interest groups vie for policy concessions. If one group controls the policy process, others may be frozen out. Conflict is normal and inevitable. It's a natural by-product of collective life.

The political prism puts more emphasis on strategy and tactics than on resolution of conflict. Conflict has benefits as well as costs: "a tranquil, harmonious organization may very well be an apathetic, uncreative, stagnant, inflexible, and unresponsive organization. Conflict challenges the status quo [and] stimulates interest and curiosity. It is the root of personal and social change, creativity, and innovation. Conflict encourages new ideas and approaches to problems, stimulating innovation" (Heffron, 1989, p. 185).

An organization can experience too much or too little conflict (Brown, 1983; Heffron, 1989; Jehn, 1995). Intervention may be needed to tamp down or stoke up the intensity, depending on the situation (Heifetz and Linsky, 2002). Even more important than the amount of conflict is how it is managed. Badly managed conflict leads to the infighting and destructive power struggle revealed in the *Challenger* and *Columbia* cases. But well-handled conflict can stimulate creativity and innovation that make an organization a livelier, more adaptive, and more effective place (Kotter, 1985).

Conflict is particularly likely to occur at boundaries, or interfaces, between groups and units. Horizontal conflict occurs in the boundary between departments or divisions; vertical conflict occurs at the border between levels. Cultural conflict crops up between groups with differing values, traditions, beliefs, and lifestyles. Cultural quarrels in the larger society often seep into the workplace, generating tension around gender, ethnic, racial, and other differences. But organizations also house their own value disputes. The culture of management is different from that of frontline employees. Workers who move up the ladder sometimes struggle with elusive adjustments required by their new role.

The management challenge is to recognize and manage interface conflict. Like other forms, it can be productive or debilitating. One of the most important tasks of unit managers or union representatives is to be a persuasive advocate for their group on a political field with many players representing competing interests. They need negotiation skills to develop alliances and cement deals that enable their group to move forward with "without physical or psychological bloodshed and with wisdom as well as grace" (Peck, 1998, p. 71).

MORAL MAZES: THE POLITICS OF GETTING AHEAD

Does a world of power, self-interest, conflict, and political games inevitably develop into a dog-eat-dog jungle in which the strong devour the weak? Is an unregulated organization invariably a nasty, brutish place where values and ethics are irrelevant? The corporate ethics scandals of recent years reinforced a recurrent suspicion that the morals of the marketplace amount to no morals at all.

Jackall (1988) views the corporation as a world of cabals and alliances, dominance and submission, conflict and self-interest, and "moral mazes." He suggests that "wise and ambitious managers resist the lulling platitudes of unity, though they invoke them with fervor, and look for the inevitable clash of interests beneath the bouncy, cheerful surface of corporate life" (p. 37). Moving up the ladder inevitably involves competition for the scarce resource of status. The favored myth is that free and fair competition ensures that better performers will win, at least in the long run.

But assessing performance in a managerial job is fraught with ambiguity. There are multiple criteria, some of which can be assessed only through subjective judgment (particularly by the boss and other superiors). It is often hard to separate individual performance from group performance or from a host of exogenous factors. It may also make a big difference who is doing the judging. When bright, creative energy traders at Enron developed clever techniques with names like "Get Shorty" and "Fat Boy" to exploit a crisis in California's electricity market in 2001, did they deserve commendation for boosting the bottom line? Or jail time? Did Thiokol engineers who fought to stop the launch of *Challenger* deserve a high grade for persistence and integrity, or a low grade because they failed to persuade their bosses? When some of those same engineers went public with their criticism, were they demonstrating courage or disloyalty? Whistleblowers are regularly lauded by the press, yet pilloried or banished by employers (Alford, 2001). This is exemplified by *Time* magazine's 2002 Person of the Year award, given to three women who blew the whistle on their employers: Enron, WorldCom, and the FBI. By the time they received the award, all had moved on from workplaces that viewed them more as traitors than as exemplars of courage and integrity.

Managers frequently learn that getting ahead is a matter of personal "credibility," which comes from doing what is socially and politically correct. Definitions of political correctness reflect tacit forms of power deeply embedded in organizational patterns and structure (Frost, 1986). Because getting ahead and making it to the top dominate the attention of many managers (Dalton, 1959; Jackall, 1988; Ritti and Funkhouser, 1982), both organizations and individuals need to develop constructive and positive ways to engage in the political game. The question is not whether organizations will have politics but rather what kind of politics they will have. Jackall's view is bleak:

> Bureaucracy breaks apart the ownership of property from its control, social independence from occupation, substance from appearances, action from responsibility, obligation from guilt, language from meaning, and notions of truth from reality. Most important, and at the bottom of all these fractures, it breaks apart the traditional connection between the meaning of work and salvation. In the bureaucratic world, one's success, one's sign of election, no longer depends on an inscrutable God, but on the capriciousness of one's superiors and the market; and one achieves economic salvation to the extent that one pleases and submits to new gods, that is, one's bosses and the exigencies of an impersonal market [1988, pp. 191–192].

This is not a pretty picture, but it is often accurate. Productive politics is a possible alternative although hard to achieve. In the next chapter, we explore ways that a manager can become a constructive politician.

SUMMARY

The traditional view sees organizations as created and controlled by legitimate authorities who set goals, design structure, hire and manage employees, and ensure pursuit of the right objectives. The political view frames a different world: Organizations are coalitions composed of individuals and groups with enduring differences who live in a world of scarce resources. That puts power and conflict at the center of organizational decision making.

Authorities have position power, but they must vie with many other contenders for other forms of leverage. Contenders bring their own beliefs, values, and interests. They seek access to various forms of power and compete for their share of scarce resources in a finite organizational pie.

From a political perspective, goals, structure, and policies emerge from an ongoing process of bargaining and negotiation among major interest groups. Sometimes legitimate authorities are the dominant members of the coalition, as is often true in small, owner-managed organizations. But large corporations are often controlled by senior management rather than by stockholders or the board of directors. Government agencies may be controlled more by the permanent civil servants than by the political leaders at the top. The dominant group in a school district may be the teachers' union instead of the school board or the superintendent. In such cases, rationalists see the wrong people setting the agenda. But the political view suggests that exercising power is a natural part of ongoing contests. Those who get and use power to their advantage will be winners.

There is no guarantee that those who gain power will use it wisely or justly. But power and politics are not inevitably demeaning and destructive. Constructive politics is a possibility—indeed, a necessary option if we are to create institutions and societies that are both just and efficient.

The Manager as Politician

B ill Gates was standing in the right place in the early 1980s when IBM's fledgling personal computer business came looking for an operating system. Gates didn't have one, but his partner, Paul Allen, knew someone who did. Gates paid $75,000 for QDOS (Quick and Dirty Operating System) in the deal—or steal—of the twentieth century. Gates changed the name to DOS and resold it to IBM, but shrewdly retained the right to license it to anyone else. DOS quickly became the primary operating system for most of the world's personal computers. Gates himself was on the road to becoming one of the world's richest men (Manes and Andrews, 1994; Zachary, 1994).

Windows, a graphic interface riding atop DOS, fueled another great leap forward for the Microsoft empire. But by the late 1980s, Gates had a problem. He and everyone else knew that DOS was obsolete and woefully deficient. The solution was supposed to be OS/2, a new operating system developed jointly by Microsoft and IBM, but it was a tense partnership. IBMers saw "Microsofties" as undisciplined adolescents. Microsoft folks moaned that "Big Blue" was a hopelessly bureaucratic producer of "poor code, poor design, and poor process" (Manes and Andrews, 1994, p. 425). Increasingly pessimistic about the viability of OS/2, Gates decided to hedge his bets by developing a new operating system to be called Windows NT. Gates recruited the brilliant but crotchety Dave Cutler from Digital Equipment to head the effort. Cutler had led the development of the operating system that helped DEC dominate the minicomputer industry.

Gates recognized that Cutler was known "more for his code than his charm" (Zachary, 1993, p. A1). Things started well, but Cutler insisted on keeping his team small and wanted no responsibility beyond the "kernel" of the operating system. He figured someone else could worry about details like the user interface. Gates began to see a potential disaster looming, but issuing orders to the temperamental Cutler was as promising as telling Picasso how to paint. So Gates put the calm, understated Paul Maritz on the case. Born in South Africa, Maritz had studied mathematics and economics in Cape Town before deciding that software was his destiny. He joined Microsoft in 1986 and became the leader of its OS/2 effort. When he was assigned informal oversight of Windows NT, he got a frosty welcome:

> As he began meeting regularly with Cutler on NT matters, Maritz often found himself the victim of slights. Once Maritz innocently suggested to Cutler that "We should—" Cutler interrupted, "We! Who's we? You mean you and the mouse in your pocket?" Maritz brushed off such retorts, even finding humor in Cutler's apparently inexhaustible supply of epithets. He refused to allow Cutler to draw him into a brawl. Instead, he hoped Cutler would "volunteer" for greater responsibility as the shortcomings of the status quo became more apparent [Zachary, 1994, p. 76].

Maritz enticed Cutler with tempting challenges. In early 1990, he asked Cutler if he could put together a demonstration of NT for COMDEX, the industry's biggest trade show. Cutler took the bait. Maritz knew that the effort would expose NT's weaknesses (Zachary, 1994). When Gates subsequently seethed that NT was too late, too big, and too slow, Maritz scrambled to "filter that stuff from Dave" (p. 208). Maritz's patience eventually paid off when he was promoted to head all operating systems development:

> The promotion gave Maritz formal and actual authority over Cutler and the entire NT project. Still, he avoided confrontations, preferring to wait until Cutler came to see the benefits of Maritz's views. Increasingly Cutler and his inner circle viewed Maritz as a powerhouse, not an empty suit. "He's critical to the project," said [one of Cutler's most loyal lieutenants]. "He got into it a little bit at a time.

Slowly he blended his way in until it was obvious who was running the show. Him" [p. 204].

⌖

Chapter Nine's account of the *Columbia* and *Challenger* cases drives home a chilling lesson about political pressures sidetracking momentous decisions. The implosion of firms such as Enron and WorldCom shows how the unfettered pursuit of self-interest by powerful executives can bring even a huge corporation to its knees. Many believe that the antidote is to get politics out of management. But this is unrealistic so long as politics is inseparable from social life. Enduring differences lead to multiple interpretations of what's true and what's important. Scarce resources trigger contests about who gets what. Interdependence means that people cannot ignore one another; they need each other's assistance, support, and resources. Under such conditions, efforts to eliminate politics are futile and counterproductive. In our search for more positive images of the manager as constructive politician, Paul Maritz's deft combination of patience, persistence, and diplomacy offers an instructive example.

Kotter (1985) contends that too many managers are either naive or cynical about organizational politics. Pollyannas view the world through rose-colored glasses, insisting that most people are good, kind, and trustworthy. Cynics believe the opposite: everyone is selfish, things are always cutthroat, and "get them before they get you" is the best survival tactic. Brown and Hesketh (2004) documented similar contrasting stances among college job seekers. The naive "purists" believe that hiring is fair and that, if they present themselves honestly, they'll be rewarded on their merits. The more cynical "players" game the system and try to present the self they think employers want. In Kotter's view, neither extreme is realistic or effective: "Organizational excellence . . . demands a sophisticated type of social skill: a leadership skill that can mobilize people and accomplish important objectives despite dozens of obstacles; a skill that can pull people together for meaningful purposes despite the thousands of forces that push us apart; a skill that can keep our corporations and public institutions from descending into a mediocrity characterized by bureaucratic infighting, parochial politics, and vicious power struggles" (p. 11).

Organizations now more than ever need "benevolent politicians" who can find a middle course: "Beyond the yellow brick road of naïveté and the mugger's lane of cynicism, there is a narrow path, poorly lighted, hard to find, and even harder to stay on once found. People who have the skill and the perseverance to take that path serve us in countless ways. We need more of these people. Many more" (Kotter, 1985, p. xi).

In a world of chronic scarcity, diversity, and conflict, the nimble manager has to walk a tightrope: developing a direction, building a base of support, and cobbling together working relations with both allies and opponents. In this chapter, we discuss why this is vital and then lay out the basic skills of the manager as politician. Finally, we tackle ethical issues, the soft underbelly of organizational politics. Is it possible to be political and still do the right thing? We discuss four instrumental values to guide ethical choice.

POLITICAL SKILLS

The manager as politician exercises four key skills: agenda-setting (Kanter, 1983; Kotter, 1988; Pfeffer, 1992; Smith, 1988), mapping the political terrain (Pfeffer, 1992; Pichault, 1993), networking and forming coalitions (Kanter, 1983; Kotter, 1982, 1985, 1988; Pfeffer, 1992; Smith, 1988), and bargaining and negotiating (Bellow and Moulton, 1978; Fisher and Ury, 1981; Lax and Sebenius, 1986).

Agenda Setting

Structurally, an agenda outlines a goal and a schedule of activities. Politically, an agenda is a statement of interests and a scenario for getting the goods. In reflecting on his experience as a university president, Warren Bennis arrived at a deceptively simple observation: "It struck me that I was most effective when I knew what I wanted" (1989, p. 20). Kanter's study of internal entrepreneurs in American corporations (1983), Kotter's analysis of effective corporate leaders (1988), and Smith's examination of effective U.S. presidents (1988) all reached a similar conclusion: whether you're a middle manager or the CEO, the first step in effective political leadership is setting an agenda.

The effective leader creates an "agenda for change" with two major elements: a vision balancing the long-term interests of key parties, and a strategy for achieving the vision while recognizing competing internal and external forces (Kotter, 1988). The agenda must convey direction while addressing concerns of major stakeholders. Kanter (1983) and Pfeffer (1992) underscore the intimate tie between gathering information and developing a vision. Pfeffer's list of key political attributes includes "sensitivity"—knowing how others think and what they care about so that your agenda responds to their concerns: "Many people think of politicians as arm-twisters, and that is, in part, true. But in order to be a successful arm-twister, one needs to know which arm to twist, and how" (p. 172).

Kanter adds: "While gathering information, entrepreneurs can also be 'planting seeds'—leaving the kernel of an idea behind and letting it germinate and blossom so that it begins to float around the system from many sources other than the innovator" (1983, p. 218). Paul Maritz did just that. Ignoring Dave Cutler's barbs and insults, he focused on getting information, building relationships, and formulating an agenda. He quickly concluded that the NT project was in disarray and that Cutler had to take on more responsibility. Maritz's strategy was attuned to his quarry: "He protected Cutler from undue criticism and resisted the urge to reform him. [He] kept the peace by exacting from Cutler no ritual expressions of obedience" (Zachary, 1994, pp. 281–282).

A vision without a strategy remains an illusion. A strategy has to recognize major forces working for and against the agenda. Smith's point about U.S. presidents is relevant to managers at every level:

> The paramount task and power of the president is to articulate the national purpose: to fix the nation's agenda. Of all the big games at the summit of American politics, the agenda game must be won first. The effectiveness of the presidency and the capacity of any president to lead depend on focusing the nation's political attention and its energies on two or three top priorities. From the standpoint of history, the flow of events seems to have immutable logic, but political reality is inherently chaotic: it contains no automatic agenda. Order must be imposed [1988, p. 333].

Agendas never come neatly packaged. The bigger the job, the harder it is to wade through the clutter and find order amid chaos. Contrary to Woody Allen's dictum, success requires more than just showing up. High office, even if the incumbent enjoys great personal popularity, is no guarantee. In his first year as president, Ronald Reagan was remarkably successful following a classic strategy for winning the agenda game: "First impressions are critical. In the agenda game, a swift beginning is crucial for a new president to establish himself as leader—to show the nation that he will make a difference in people's lives. The first one hundred days are the vital test; in those weeks, the political community and the public measure a new president—to see whether he is active, dominant, sure, purposeful" (Smith, 1988, p. 334).

Reagan began with a vision but without a strategy. He was not gifted as a manager or a strategist, despite extraordinary ability to portray complex issues in broad, symbolic brushstrokes. Reagan's staff painstakingly studied the first hundred days of four predecessors. They concluded that it was essential to move with speed and focus. Pushing competing issues aside, they focused on two: cutting taxes and reducing the federal budget. They also discovered a secret weapon in David Stockman, the only person in the Reagan White House who understood the federal budget process. "Stockman got a jump on everyone else for two reasons: he had an agenda and a legislative blueprint already prepared, and he understood the real levers of power. Two terms as a Michigan congressman plus a network of key Republican and Democratic connections had taught Stockman how to play the power game" (Smith, 1988, p. 351). Reagan and his advisers had the vision; Stockman provided strategic direction.

Mapping the Political Terrain

It is foolhardy to plunge into a minefield without knowing where explosives are buried, yet managers unwittingly do it all the time. They launch a new initiative with little or no effort to scout and master the political turf. Pichault (1993) suggests four steps for developing a political map:

1. Determine channels of informal communication.

2. Identify principal agents of political influence.

3. Analyze possibilities for mobilizing internal and external players.

4. Anticipate counterstrategies that others are likely to employ.

Pichault offers an example of planned change in a large government agency in Belgium. The agency wanted to replace antiquated manual records with a fully automated paperless computer network. But proponents of the new system had virtually no understanding of how work got done. Nor did they anticipate the interests and power of key middle managers and frontline bureaucrats. It seemed obvious to the techies that better data meant higher efficiency. In reality, frontline bureaucrats made little use of the data. They applied standard procedures in 90 percent of cases and asked their bosses what to do about the rest. Their queries were partly to get the "right" answer, but even more to get political cover. Since they saw no need for the new technology, frontline bureaucrats were likely to ignore or work around it. After a consultant clarified the political map, a new battle erupted between unrepentant techies, who insisted their solution was correct, and senior managers who argued for a less ambitious approach. The two sides ultimately compromised.

A simple way to develop a political map for any situation is to create a two-dimensional diagram mapping players (who is in the game), power (how much clout each player is likely to exercise), and interests (what each player wants). Exhibits 10.1 and 10.2 present two hypothetical versions of the Belgian bureaucracy's political map. Exhibit 10.1 shows the map as the techies saw it. They expected little opposition and assumed they held all the high cards; that implied a quick and easy win. Exhibit 10.2, a more objective map, paints a very different picture. Resistance is more intense and opponents more powerful. This view forecasts a stormy process with protracted conflict. Though less comforting, the second map has an important message: success requires substantial effort to

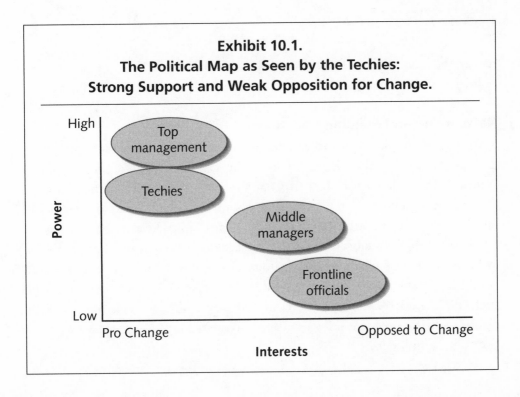

Exhibit 10.1.
The Political Map as Seen by the Techies:
Strong Support and Weak Opposition for Change.

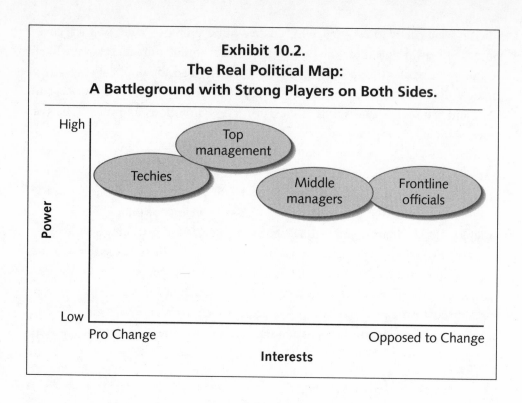

Exhibit 10.2.
The Real Political Map:
A Battleground with Strong Players on Both Sides.

realign the political force field. The third and fourth key skills of the manager as politician, discussed in the next two sections, include strategies for doing that.

Networking and Building Coalitions

Managers often fail to get things done because they rely too much on reason and too little on relationships. In both the *Challenger* and *Columbia* space shuttle catastrophes (discussed in Chapter Nine), engineers pitched careful, data-based arguments to their superiors about potentially lethal safety risks—and failed to dent their bosses' resistance (Glanz and Schwartz, 2003; Vaughn, 1995). Six months before the *Challenger* accident, for example, an engineer at Morton Thiokol wrote to management: "The result [of an O-ring failure] would be a catastrophe of the highest order—loss of human life" (Bell and Esch, 1987, p. 45). A memo, if it is clear and powerful, may work, but is often a sign of political innocence. Kotter (1985) suggests four basic steps for exercising political influence:

1. Identify relevant relationships. (Figure out which players you need to influence.)

2. Assess who might resist, why, and how strongly. (Determine where the leadership challenges will be.)

3. Develop, wherever possible, links with potential opponents to facilitate communication, education, or negotiation. (Hold your enemies close.)

4. If step three fails, carefully select and implement either more subtle or more forceful methods. (Save your big guns until you really need them, but have a Plan B in case Plan A falls short.)

These steps underscore the importance of developing a power base. Moving up the managerial ladder confers authority but also creates more dependence, because success requires the cooperation of many others (Kotter, 1985, 1988; Butcher and Clarke, 2001). People rarely give their best efforts and fullest cooperation simply because they have been ordered to do so. They accept direction better when they perceive the people in authority as credible, competent, and sensible.

The first task in building networks and coalitions is to figure out whose help you need. The second is to develop relationships so people will be there when you need them. Successful middle-management change agents typically begin by getting their boss on board (Kanter, 1983). They then move to "preselling," or "making cheerleaders": "Peers, managers of related functions, stakeholders in the issue, potential collaborators, and sometimes even customers would be approached individually, in one-on-one meetings that gave people a chance to influence the project and [gave] the innovator the maximum opportunity to sell it. Seeing them alone and on their territory was important: the rule was to act as if each person were the most important one for the project's success" (p. 223).

Once you cultivate cheerleaders, you can move to "horse trading": promising rewards in exchange for resources and support. This builds a resource base that helps in "securing blessings," or getting the necessary approvals and mandates from higher management (Kanter, 1983). Kanter found that the usual route to success in securing blessings is to identify critical senior managers and to develop a polished, formal presentation to nail down their support. The best presentations respond to both substantive and political concerns. Senior managers typically care about two questions: Is it a good idea? How will my constituents react? Once innovators get a nod from higher management, they can formalize the coalition with their boss and make specific plans for pursuing the project.

The basic point is simple: as a manager, you need friends and allies to get things done. To sew up their support, you need to build coalitions. Rationalists and romantics sometimes react with horror to this scenario. Why should you have to play political games to get something accepted if it's the right thing to do? One of the great works in French drama, Molière's *The Misanthrope*, tells the story of a protagonist whose rigid rejection of all things political is destructive for him and everyone close by. The point that Molière made four centuries ago still holds: it is hard to dislike politics without also disliking people. Like it or not, political dynamics are inevitable under three conditions most managers face every day: ambiguity, diversity, and scarcity.

Informal networks perform a number of functions that formal structure may do poorly or not at all—moving projects forward, imparting culture, mentoring, and creating "communities of practice." Some organizations use measures of social networking to identify and manage who's connected to whom. When Procter & Gamble studied linkages among its twenty-five research and development units around the world, it discovered its unit in China was relatively isolated from all the rest—a clear signal that linkages needed to be improved to corner a big and growing market (Reingold and Yang, 2007).

Ignoring or misreading people's roles in networks is costly. Consider the mistake that undermined John LeBoutillier's political career. Shortly after he was elected to Congress from a wealthy district in Long Island, LeBoutillier fired up his audience at the New York Republican convention with the colorful quip that Speaker of the House Thomas P. O'Neill, was "fat, bloated and out of control, just like the Federal budget." Asked to comment, Tip O'Neill was atypically terse: "I wouldn't know the man from a cord of wood" (Matthews, 1999, p. 113). Two years later, LeBoutillier unexpectedly lost his bid for reelection to an unknown opponent who didn't have the money to mount a real campaign—until a mysterious flood of contributions poured in from all over America. When LeBoutillier later ran into O'Neill, he admitted sheepishly, "I guess you were more popular than I thought you were" (Matthews, 1999, p. 114). LeBoutillier learned the hard way that it is dangerous to underestimate or provoke people when you don't know how much power they have or who their friends are.

Bargaining and Negotiation

We often associate bargaining with commercial, legal, and labor relations transactions. From a political perspective, though, bargaining is central to decision making. The horse trading Kanter describes as part of coalition building is just one of many examples. Negotiation is needed whenever two or more parties with some interests in common and others in conflict need to reach agreement. Labor and management may agree that a firm should make money and offer good jobs to employees but part ways on how to balance pay and profitability. Engineers and managers in the NASA space program had a common interest in the success of the shuttle flights, but at key moments differed sharply on how to balance technical and political trade-offs.

A fundamental dilemma in negotiations is choosing between "creating value" and "claiming value" (Lax and Sebenius, 1986). Value creators believe that successful negotiators must be inventive and cooperative in searching for a win-win solution. Value claimers see "win-win" as naively optimistic. For them, bargaining is a hard, tough process in which you have to do what it takes to win as much as you can.

One of the best-known win-win approaches to negotiation was developed by Fisher and Ury (1981) in their classic *Getting to Yes*. They argue that people too often engage in "positional bargaining": they stake out positions and then reluctantly make concessions to reach agreement. Fisher and Ury contend that positional bargaining is inefficient and misses opportunities to create something that's better for everyone. They propose an alternative: "principled bargaining," built around four strategies.

The first strategy is to separate people from the problem. The stress and tension of negotiations can easily escalate into anger and personal attack. The result is that a negotiator sometimes wants to defeat or hurt the other party at almost any cost. Because every negotiation involves both substance and relationship, the wise negotiator will "deal with the people as human beings and with the problem on its merits." Paul Maritz demonstrated this principle in dealing with the prickly Dave Cutler. Even though Cutler continually baited and insulted him, Maritz refused to be distracted and persistently focused on getting the job done.

The second strategy is to focus on interests, not positions. If you get locked into a particular position, you might overlook better ways to achieve your goal. An example is the 1978 Camp David treaty between Israel and Egypt. The sides were at an impasse over where to draw the boundary between the two countries.

Israel wanted to keep part of the Sinai, while Egypt wanted all of it back. Resolution became possible only when they looked at underlying interests. Israel was concerned about security: no Egyptian tanks on the border. Egypt was concerned about sovereignty: the Sinai had been part of Egypt from the time of the Pharaohs. The parties agreed on a plan that gave all of the Sinai back to Egypt while demilitarizing large parts of it (Fisher and Ury, 1981). That solution led to a durable peace agreement.

Fisher and Ury's third strategy is to invent options for mutual gain instead of locking on to the first alternative that comes to mind. More options increase the chance of a better outcome. Maritz recognized this in his dealings with Cutler. Instead of bullying, he asked innocently, "Could you do a demo at COMDEX?" It was a new option that created gains for both parties.

Fisher and Ury's fourth strategy is to insist on objective criteria—standards of fairness for both substance and procedure. Agreeing on criteria at the beginning of negotiations can produce optimism and momentum, while reducing the use of devious or provocative tactics that get in the way of a mutually beneficial solution. When a school board and a teachers' union are at loggerheads over the size of a pay increase, they can look for independent standards, such as the rate of inflation or the terms of settlement in other districts. A classic example of fair procedure finds two sisters deadlocked over how to divide the last wedge of pie between them. They agree that one will cut the pie into two pieces and the other will choose the piece that she wants.

Fisher and Ury devote most of their attention to creating value—finding better solutions for both parties. They downplay the question of claiming value. Yet there are many examples in which shrewd value claimers have come out ahead. In 1980, Bill Gates offered to license an operating system to IBM about forty-eight hours before he had one to sell. Then he neglected to mention to QDOS's owner, Tim Paterson of Seattle Computer, that Microsoft was buying his operating system to resell it to IBM. Gates gave IBM a great price: only $30,000 more than the $50,000 he'd paid for it. But he retained the rights to license it to anyone else. At the time, Microsoft was a flea atop IBM's elephant. Almost no one except Gates saw the possibility that consumers would want an IBM computer made by anyone but IBM. IBM negotiators might well have thought they were stealing candy from babies in buying DOS royalty-free for a measly $80,000. Meanwhile, Gates was already dreaming about millions of computers running his code. As it turned out, the new PC was an instant hit, and IBM couldn't make enough of them. Within a year, Microsoft had licensed MS-DOS to fifty companies, and the number kept growing (Mendelson and Korin, n.d.). Twenty years later, onlookers who wondered why Microsoft was so aggressive and unyielding in battling government antitrust suits might not have known that Gates had always been a dogged value claimer.

A classic treatment of value claiming is Schelling's 1960 essay *The Strategy of Conflict,* which focuses on how to make a credible threat. Suppose, for example, that I want to buy your house and am willing to pay $250,000. How can I convince you that I'm willing to pay only $200,000? Contrary to a common assumption, I'm not always better off if I'm stronger and have more resources. If you believe that I'm very wealthy, you might take my threat less seriously than if I can get you to believe that $200,000 is the furthest I can go. Common sense also suggests that I should be better off if I have considerable freedom of action. Yet I may get a better price if I can convince you my hands are tied—for example, I'm negotiating for a very stubborn buyer who won't go above $200,000, even if the house is worth more. Such examples suggest that the ideal situation for a bargainer is to have substantial resources and freedom while convincing the other side of the opposite. Value claiming provides its own slant on the bargaining process:

- *Bargaining is a mixed-motive game.* Both parties want an agreement but have differing interests and preferences, so that what seems valuable to one is insignificant to the other.

- *Bargaining is a process of interdependent decisions.* What each party does affects the other. Each player wants to be able to predict what the other will do while limiting the other's ability to reciprocate.

- *The more player A can control player B's level of uncertainty, the more powerful A is.* The more A can keep private—as Bill Gates did with Seattle Computer and IBM—the better.

- *Bargaining involves judicious use of threats rather than sanctions.* Players may threaten to use force, go on strike, or break off negotiations. In most cases, they prefer not to bear the costs of carrying out the threat.

- *Making a threat credible is crucial.* A threat works only if your opponent believes it. Noncredible threats weaken your bargaining position and confuse the process.

- *Calculation of the appropriate level of threat is also critical.* If I underthreaten, you may think I'm weak. If I overthreaten, you may not believe me, may break off the negotiations, or may escalate your own threats.

Creating value and claiming value are both intrinsic to the bargaining process. How does a manager decide how to balance the two? At least two questions are important: How much opportunity is there for a win-win solution? And will I have to work with these people again? If an agreement can make everyone better off, it makes sense to emphasize creating value. If you expect to work with the same people in the future, it is risky to use scorched-earth tactics that leave anger and mistrust in their wake. Managers who get a reputation for being manipulative, self-interested, or untrustworthy have a hard time building the networks and coalitions they need for future success.

Axelrod (1980) found that a strategy of conditional openness works best when negotiators need to work together over time. This strategy starts with open and collaborative behavior and maintains the approach if the other responds in kind. If the other party becomes adversarial, however, the negotiator responds accordingly and remains adversarial until the opponent makes a collaborative move. It is, in effect, a friendly and forgiving version of tit for tat—do unto others as they do unto you. Axelrod's research discovered that this conditional openness approach worked better than even the most fiendishly diabolical adversarial strategy.

A final consideration in balancing collaborative and adversarial tactics is ethics. Bargainers often deliberately misrepresent their positions—even though lying is almost universally condemned as unethical (Bok, 1978). This leads to a tricky question for the manager as politician: What actions are ethical and just?

MORALITY AND POLITICS

Block (1987), Burns (1978), Lax and Sebenius (1986), and Messick and Ohme (1998) explore ethical issues in bargaining and organizational politics. Block's view asserts that individuals empower themselves through understanding: "The process of organizational politics as we know it works against people taking responsibility. We empower ourselves by discovering a positive way of being political. The line between positive and negative politics is a tightrope we have to walk" (1987, p. xiii).

Block argues that bureaucratic cycles often leave individuals feeling vulnerable, powerless, and helpless. If we confer too much power on the organization or others, we fear that the power will be used against us. Consequently, we develop manipulative strategies to protect ourselves. To escape the dilemma, managers need to support organizational structures, policies, and procedures that promote empowerment. They must also empower themselves.

Block urges managers to begin by building an "image of greatness"—a vision of what their department can contribute that is meaningful and worthwhile. Then they need to build support for their vision by negotiating a binding pact of agreement and trust. Block suggests treating friends and opponents differently. Adversaries, he says, are simultaneously the most difficult and most interesting people to deal with. It is usually ineffective to pressure them; a better strategy is to "let go of them." He offers four steps for letting go: (1) tell them your vision, (2) state your best understanding of their position, (3) identify your contribution to the problem, and (4) tell them what you plan to do without making demands. It's a variation on Axelrod's strategy of conditional openness.

Although this strategy may work in favorable conditions, it can backfire with a formidable, hard-headed opponent in a situation of scarce resources and durable differences. Bringing politics into the open may make conflict more obvious and overt but offer little hope of resolution. Block argues that "war games in organizations lose their power when brought into the light of day" (1987, p. 148), but wise managers will test that assumption against their circumstances.

Burns's conception of positive politics (1978) draws on examples as diverse and complex as Franklin Roosevelt and Adolph Hitler, Gandhi and Mao, Woodrow Wilson and Joan of Arc. He sees conflict and power as central to leadership. Searching for firm moral footing in a world of cultural and ethical diversity, Burns turned to Maslow's (1954) theory of motivation and Kohlberg's (1973) treatment of ethics.

From Maslow, he borrowed the hierarchy of motives (see Chapter Six). Moral leaders, he argued, appeal to higher-order human needs. Kohlberg supplied the idea of stages of moral reasoning. At the lowest, "preconventional" level, moral judgment is based primarily on perceived consequences: an action is right if you are rewarded and wrong if you are punished. In the intermediate or "conventional" level, the emphasis is on conforming to authority and established rules. At the highest, "postconventional" level, ethical judgment rests on general principles: the greatest good for the greatest number, or universal moral principles.

Maslow and Kohlberg intertwined gave Burns a foundation for constructing a positive view of politics: "If leaders are to be effective in helping to mobilize and elevate their constituencies, leaders must be whole persons, persons with full functioning capacities for thinking and feeling. The problem for them as educators, as leaders, is not to promote narrow, egocentric self-actualization, but to extend awareness of human needs and the means of gratifying them, to improve the larger social situation for which educators or leaders have responsibility and over which they have power" (1978, pp. 448–449).

Burns's view provides two expansive criteria: Does your leadership rest on general moral principles? And does it appeal to the "better angels" in your constituents' psyches? Lax and Sebenius (1986) see ethical issues as inescapable quandaries but provide a concrete set of questions for assessing leaders' actions:

- *Are you following rules that are mutually understood and accepted?* In poker, for example, everyone understands that bluffing is part of the game but pulling cards from your sleeve is not.

- *Are you comfortable discussing and defending your choices?* Would you want your colleagues and friends to know what you're doing? Your spouse, children, or parents? Would you be comfortable if your deeds appeared in your local newspaper?

- *Would you want to be on the receiving end of your own actions?* Would you want this done to a member of your family?

- *What if everyone acted as you did? Would the impact on society be desirable?* If you were designing an organization, would you want people to follow your example? Would you teach your children the ethics you have embraced?

- *Are there alternatives you could consider that rest on firmer ethical ground?* Could you test your strategy with a trusted adviser and explore other options?

Although these questions may not tally up to a comprehensive ethical framework, they embody four important principles of moral judgment. They are instrumental values—guidelines about right actions rather than right outcomes. Four solidly anchored principles do not guarantee success, but they reduce ethical risks of taking a particular course of action.

Mutuality. Are all parties to a relationship operating under the same understanding about the rules of the game? Enron's Ken Lay was talking up the company's stock to analysts and employees even as he and others were selling their shares. In the period when WorldCom improved its profits by cooking the books, it made its competitors look bad. Top executives at competing firms such as AT&T and Sprint felt the heat from analysts and shareholders and wondered, "Why can't we get the results they're getting?" Only later did they learn the answer: "They're cheating, and we're not."

Generality. Does a specific action follow a principle of moral conduct applicable to comparable situations? When Enron and WorldCom violated accounting principles to inflate their results, they were secretly breaking the rules, not adhering to a broadly applicable rule of conduct.

Openness. Are we willing to make our thinking and decisions public and confrontable? As Justice Oliver Wendell Holmes observed many years ago, "Sunlight is the best disinfectant." Keeping others in the dark was a consistent theme in the corporate ethics scandals of 2001–2002. Enron's books were almost impenetrable, and the company attacked analysts who questioned the numbers. Enron's techniques for manipulating the California energy crisis had to be clandestine to work. One device involved creating the appearance of congestion in the California power grid and subsequently getting paid for "moving energy to relieve congestion without actually moving any energy or relieving any congestion" (Oppel, 2002, p. A1).

Caring. Does this action show concern for the legitimate interests and feelings of others? Enron's effort to protect its share price by locking in employees so they couldn't sell the Enron shares in their retirement accounts, even as the value of the shares plunged, put the interests of senior executives ahead of everyone else's.

The scandals of the early 2000s were not unprecedented; such a wave is a predictable feature of the trough following every business boom. The 1980s, for example, gave us Ivan Boesky and the savings and loan crisis. There was another wave of corporate scandals in the 1970s. In the 1930s, the president of the New York Stock Exchange went to jail in his three-piece suit (Labaton, 2002). There will always be temptation whenever gargantuan egos and large sums of money are at stake. Top managers too rarely think or talk about the moral dimension of management and leadership. Porter notes the dearth of such conversation:

> In a seminar with seventeen executives from nine corporations, we learned how the privatization of moral discourse in our society has created a deep sense of moral loneliness and moral illiteracy; how the absence of a common language prevents people from talking about

and reading the moral issues they face. We learned how the isolation of individuals—the taboo against talking about spiritual matters in the public sphere—robs people of courage, of the strength of heart to do what deep down they believe to be right [1989, p. 2].

If we choose to banish moral discourse and leave managers to face ethical issues alone, we invite dreary and brutish political dynamics. An organization can and should take a moral stance. It can make its values clear, hold employees accountable, and validate the need for dialogue about ethical choices. Positive politics without an ethical framework and moral dialogue is as unlikely as bountiful harvests without sunlight or water.

SUMMARY

The question is not whether organizations are political but what kind of politics they will encompass. Political dynamics can be sordid and destructive. But politics can also be a vehicle for achieving noble purposes. Organizational change and effectiveness depend on managers' political skills. Constructive politicians know how to fashion an agenda, map the political terrain, create a network of support, and negotiate with both allies and adversaries. In the process, they will encounter a predictable and inescapable ethical dilemma: when to adopt an open, collaborative strategy or when to choose a tougher, more adversarial approach. In making the decision, they have to consider the potential for collaboration, the importance of long-term relationships, and, most important, their own values and ethical principles.

Organizations as Political Arenas and Political Agents

S am Walton started his merchant career in 1945 as proprietor of the second-best variety store in a small rural Arkansas town. From that humble beginning, he built the world's largest retail chain. With close to 2 million "associates," Wal-Mart is by far the largest employer and, for both better and worse, one of the most powerful companies on the globe. More than 90 percent of American households shop at Wal-Mart every year, expecting the company to keep its promise of "always low prices" (Fishman, 2006).

Wal-Mart's impact is both subtle and pervasive, as is illustrated in a story about deodorant packaging. Deodorant containers used to come packed in cardboard boxes until Wal-Mart decision makers concluded in the early 1990s that the boxes were wasteful and costly—about a nickel apiece for something consumers would just throw away. When Wal-Mart told suppliers to kill the cardboard, the boxes disappeared from retail shelves across America. Good enough for Wal-Mart was okay for everyone else. The story is but one of countless examples of the "Wal-Mart effect"—an umbrella term for multiple ways Wal-Mart influences consumers, vendors, employees, communities, and the environment (Fishman, 2006).

Yet, for all its power and influence, Wal-Mart has struggled in recent years with a budding assortment of critics and image problems. The company has been accused of abusing workers, discriminating against women, busting unions, destroying small businesses, and damaging the environment. Circled by enemies,

229

it has mounted major public relations campaigns in defense of its image, with limited success (Bianco, 2007).

Like all organizations, Wal-Mart is both an arena for internal conflict and a political agent or player operating on a field crammed with competitors pursuing parochial interests. As arenas, organizations house an ongoing interplay of players and agendas. As agents, organizations are powerful tools for achieving the purposes of those calling the shots. Wal-Mart's enormous size and power have made its political maneuvers widely visible; almost everyone has strong feelings about Wal-Mart, one way or another. To be sure, the company's historic penchant for secrecy and its secluded location in Bentonville, Arkansas, have sometimes shielded its internal politics from the spotlight, but tales of political skullduggery still emerge. Vintage 2007 scandals included a titillating story of a recently recruited superstar marketing executive who was fired amid rumors of conflict with her conservative bosses and an office romance. The same year also spawned the strange tale of a Wal-Mart techie who claimed he'd been secretly recording the deliberations of the board of directors.

This chapter explores organizations like Wal-Mart as both arenas and political agents. Viewing organizations as political arenas is a way to reframe many organizational processes. Organizational design, for example, can be viewed not as a rational expression of an organization's goals but as a political embodiment of contending claims. In our discussion of organizations as arenas, we examine the political dimensions of organizational change, contrasting directives from the top with pressures from below. As political agents, organizations operate in complex ecosystems—interdependent networks of autonomous organizations engaged in related activities and occupying particular niches. We illustrate several forms ecosystems can take—business itself, public policy, the interface between business and government, and society. Finally, we look at the dark side of organizational power. We explore the concern that large global organizations represent a growing risk to the world because they are too powerful for anyone to control.

ORGANIZATIONS AS ARENAS

From a political view, "happily ever after" exists only in fairy tales. In reality, today's winners may quickly become tomorrow's losers or vice versa. Change and stability are paradoxical: organizations constantly change and yet never change. As in any competitive sport, players come and go, but the game goes on.

Jockeying for position is constant, and yesterday's elite may be tomorrow's also-ran. In the annals of organizational politics, few have illustrated these precepts as well as Ross Johnson, who once made the cover of *Time* magazine as the emblem of corporate greed and insensitivity. In *Barbarians at the Gate*, Bryan Burrough and John Helyar (1990) explain how.

BARBARIANS AT THE GATE

Ross Johnson began his career in the 1960s. His charm, humor, and charisma moved him ahead, and by the mid-1970s he was second in command to Henry Weigl at the consumer products firm Standard Brands. Johnson's lavish spending (on limousines and sumptuous entertainment, for example) soon put him on a collision course with his tightfisted boss, who tried to get him fired. But Johnson had wooed members of Standard's board of directors so successfully that he had more friends on the board than Weigl. Johnson argued that Weigl's conservative style was strangling the company, and the board bought his pitch. Weigl was kicked upstairs, and Johnson took over. He fired many of Weigl's people and enjoyed a spectacular period of lavish spending on executive perks. After four years of mediocre business results, an unexpected call came from the chairman of the food giant Nabisco, who proposed a merger of the two companies. Within two weeks, the transaction was done: a $1.9 billion stock swap—a big deal in 1981.

Everyone knew Nabisco would be in charge after the deal, since it was by far the stronger player. But they underestimated Ross Johnson. He was so successful at ingratiating himself with Nabisco's chairman while quietly forcing out the old Nabisco executives that after a few years, he was able to take over the company. Once in charge, Johnson showed more interest in hobnobbing with celebrities than in running the company. And then, in 1985, he received another call: Tylee Wilson, chief executive of R. J. Reynolds, the huge tobacco company, called to talk merger. Wilson needed a corporate partner to help Reynolds reduce its heavy dependence on the controversial cigarette business. Johnson held out for more than Wilson wanted to pay, but the deal was soon done: Reynolds coughed up $4.9 billion for Nabisco.

Though more than one of his friends warned him about Johnson, Wilson figured it was his deal, and he would be in charge. But Wilson, who lacked Johnson's awesome skills at ingratiation, had alienated some members of his board. After cultivating alliances with board members, Johnson used the same gambit that had worked at Standard Brands. He told friends on the board that he would be leaving because there was only room for one CEO. A few weeks later, Wilson was startled when his board pushed him out.

Political Dimensions of Organizational Processes

As arenas, organizations house contests and set parameters for the players, as well as the stakes and the rules of the game. In this light, every organizational process has a political dimension. Consider the task of shaping and structuring an organization. Most theories built on structural premises (as discussed in preceding chapters) assume that the best design is the one that contributes most to efficient strategy and successful attainment of goals. Pfeffer offers an explicitly political conception as an alternative: "Since organizations are coalitions, and the different participants have varying interests and preferences, the critical question becomes not how organizations should be designed to maximize effectiveness, but rather, whose preferences and interests are to be served by the organization. . . . What is effective for students may be ineffective for administrators. . . . Effectiveness as defined by consumers may be ineffectiveness as defined by stockholders. The assessment of organizations is dependent upon one's preferences and one's perspective" (1978, p. 223).

Even though groups have conflicting preferences, they have a shared interest in avoiding incessant conflict. So they agree on ways to distribute power and resources, producing settlements reflected in organizational design. Structures are "the resolution, at a given time, of the contending claims for control, subject to the constraint that the structures permit the organization to survive" (Pfeffer, 1978, p. 224).

An example is a controversial decision made by Ross Johnson when he headed RJR Nabisco. Johnson moved RJR's headquarters from Winston-Salem, where it had been for a century, to Atlanta. Reynolds was the commercial heart of Winston-Salem. It engendered fierce pride and loyalty among the citizenry, many of whom were substantial stockholders. Structural logic suggests putting your headquarters in a location that best serves the business, but Johnson and his key lieutenants saw the small city in the heart of tobacco country as boring and provincial. The move to Atlanta had scant business justification, was unpopular with the RJR board, and made Johnson the most hated man in Winston-Salem. But he headed the dominant coalition. He got what he wanted.

Sources of Political Initiative

Gamson's distinction (1968) between authorities and partisans (see Chapter Nine) implies two major sources of political initiative: bottom-up, relying on mobilization of groups to assert their interests; and top-down, relying on authorities' capacity to influence subordinates. We discuss examples of both to illustrate some of the basic premises of political action.

Bottom-Up Political Action   The rise of trade unions, the emergence of the American civil rights movement, the antiwar movement of the 1970s, and environmental activism in recent decades all exemplify the process of bottom-up change. In every case, the impetus for change was a significant disruption in old patterns. Trade unions developed in the context of the industrial revolution, rapid urbanization, and the decline of family farms. The civil rights movement arose after massive occupational and geographic shifts for black citizens. The antiwar movement emerged from the juxtaposition of an unpopular war with a draft lottery that affected every eighteen-year-old male in the United States. "Green" activism developed as the costs of growing prosperity—including pollution, destruction of habitats and species, and global warming—became increasingly visible and hard to discount. In each case, changing conditions intensified dissatisfaction for disenfranchised groups. Each reflected a classic script for revolutions: a period of rising expectations followed by widespread disappointment.

The initial impetus for change came from grassroots mobilizing and organizing—the formation of trade unions, civil rights groups, student movements, or environmental groups. Elites bitterly contested the legitimacy of grassroots action and launched coercive blocking tactics. At various points, employers used everything from lawsuits to violence to resist unions. The civil rights movement, particularly in its early stages, experienced violent repression by whites. Efforts to suppress the antiwar movement reached their apogee at Kent State University, when members of the Ohio National Guard fired on student demonstrators. Greens have been engaged in a long battle against business and political leaders who dispute the significance of environmental threats and resist what they see as the excessive costs of proposed remedies. Despite intense opposition, grassroots groups fought to have their rights embodied in law or policy. Each movement might have failed had it been weaker or its opposition stronger. Each suffered profound setbacks but mobilized enough power to survive and grow.

Compared with many grassroots change efforts, the ones just mentioned were relatively successful. Most such initiatives fail. After the U.S. invasion of Iraq in 2003, for example, another antiwar movement arose. But political conditions were different: The 9/11 terrorist attacks had intensified Americans' fears of dangers from abroad. Equally important, fewer American troops were involved, and no one was being drafted. Particularly on college campuses, the movement never gained the momentum of opposition to the Vietnam War.

Barriers to Control from the Top The difficulties of grassroots political action lead many people to believe that you have to begin at the top to get anything done. Yet research on mandated efforts also catalogues many failures.

Deal and Nutt (1980), for example, conducted a revealing analysis of local school districts that received generous, long-term federal funding to develop experimental programs for comprehensive changes in rural education. A typical scenario for these projects included these phases:

1. The central administration learned of the opportunity to obtain a sizable chunk of government funding.

2. A small group of administrators met to develop a proposal for improving some aspect of the educational program. (Tight deadlines meant that the process was usually rushed with only a few people involved.)

3. When funding was approved, the administration announced with pride and enthusiasm that in a national competition, the district had won an award that would bring substantial funds to support an exciting new project to improve instruction.

4. Teachers were dismayed to learn that the administration had committed to new teaching approaches without faculty input. Administrators were startled and perplexed when teachers greeted the news with resistance, criticism, and anger.

5. Caught in the middle between teachers and the funding agency, administrators interpreted teacher resistance as a sign of defensiveness and unwillingness to change.

6. The new program became a political football, producing more disharmony, mistrust, and conflict than tangible improvement in education.

The programs studied by Deal and Nutt represented examples of top-down change efforts under comparatively favorable circumstances. The districts were not in crisis. The change efforts were well funded and blessed by the federal government. Yet across the board, the new initiatives set off heated political battles. In many cases, administrators found themselves outgunned. Only one superintendent survived over the program's five-year funding cycle.

In most instances, administrators never anticipated a major political battle. They were confident their proposed programs were progressive, effective, and good for everyone. They overlooked the risks in proposing change that someone else was expected to carry out. As a result, they were showered with antagonism instead of the expected huzzahs.

A similar pattern appears repeatedly in other attempts at change from above. Innumerable efforts mounted by chief executives, frustrated managers, hopeful study teams, and high-status management consultants end in failure. The usual mistake is assuming that the right idea (as perceived by the idea's champions) and legitimate authority ensure success. This assumption neglects the agendas and power of the "lowerarchy"—partisans and groups in midlevel and lower-level positions, who devise creative and maddening ways to resist, divert, undermine, ignore, or overthrow innovative plans.

ORGANIZATIONS AS POLITICAL AGENTS

Organizations are lively arenas for internal politics. They are also active political agents in larger arenas, or "ecosystems" (Moore, 1993). Since organizations depend on their environment for resources they need to survive, they are inevitably enmeshed with external constituents whose expectations or demands must be heeded. These constituents often speak with loud but conflicting voices, adding to the challenge of managerial work (Hoskisson, Hitt, Johnson, and Grossman, 2002). As political actors, organizations need to master many of the basic skills of individual managers as politicians: develop an agenda, map the environment, manage relationships with both allies and enemies, and negotiate compacts, accords, and alliances.

Many of an organization's key constituents are other enterprises. Just as frogs, flies, and lily pads co-evolve in a swamp, organizations develop in tandem in a common environment. Moore (1993) illustrates with two ecosystems in the personal computer business, one pioneered by Apple Computer and the other by IBM. Apple's ecosystem dominated the PC industry before IBM's entry. But IBM's ecosystem rapidly surpassed Apple's. IBM had a very powerful brand, and the open architecture of its PC induced new players to flock to it. Some of these players competed head-on (for example, Compaq and Dell in hardware, Microsoft and Lotus in software). Others were related much like bees and flowers, each performing an indispensable service to the other. One symbiotic pairing was particularly fateful. As Microsoft gained control of the operating system and Intel of the microprocessor in the IBM ecosystem, the two increasingly became mutually indispensable. More sophisticated software needed faster microprocessors, and vice versa, so the two had every reason to cheer each other on. "Intel giveth, and Microsoft taketh away," as some cynics put it. Two companies that began as servants to IBM eventually took over what became the "Wintel" ecosystem. Industry terminology changed to reflect the shift in power—what were once called "IBM clones" and proudly advertised as "100-percent IBM compatible!" became simply "Windows PCs."

POLITICAL DYNAMICS OF ECOSYSTEMS

The same factors that spawn politics inside organizations also create political dynamics within and between ecosystems. Organizations have parochial interests and compete for scarce resources. Ross Johnson again provides an example. After he became CEO of RJR Nabisco, Johnson made a fateful decision to engage in a management craze of the time—a leveraged buyout (LBO). The basic idea of an LBO is to find an undervalued company, buy up shares with someone else's money, fix it up or break it up, and sell it at a profit. It's a high-risk venture.

Johnson's idea was to use a leveraged buyout to take RJR Nabisco private. But once he had announced the LBO, the company was in play; it was open season for anyone to enter the bidding. *Anyone* in this case meant Henry Kravis and his secretive firm, KKR, with some $45 billion in buying power. Johnson thought Kravis would stay out because the deal was so big, but he underestimated a dangerous adversary. What followed was one of business history's biggest six-week poker games. Huge coalitions formed around both players. Millions of dollars in fees gushed into the laps of bankers, lawyers, and brokers. When the dust cleared, Henry Kravis and KKR had won by a nose. RJR Nabisco was theirs for a cool $25 billion.

The bidding war created a fluid, temporary ecosystem illustrating many of the complexities of such arrangements. Dozens of individuals, groups, and organizations were involved, but the big prize in the contest, RJR Nabisco, was largely a bystander; its board was on the sidelines for most of the game. Johnson and his allies pursued their private interests more than the corporation's. Financial stakes were enormous, yet the game was often driven by issues of power, reputation, and personal animosity. Everyone wanted the prize, but you could win by losing and lose by winning. In the competitive frenzy, both sides bid too much, and the winner was stuck with an overpriced albatross.

The RJR Nabisco LBO ecosystem lasted only until the brutal bidding war was over. But many ecosystems, like Wintel's and Wal-Mart's, are durable, lasting for decades. In such cases, an organization's role in the ecosystem is an important determinant of how it can best balance pursuit of its own interests with the overall well-being of the ecosystem. This may not be a major concern for small players with only marginal influence, but Iansiti and Levien argue that this issue is vital for "keystone" firms like Wal-Mart that sit at the hub of an ecosystem:

> Wal-Mart is successful because it figured out how to create, manage and evolve an incredibly powerful business ecosystem. Over the years Wal-Mart took advantage of its ability to gather consumer information to coordinate the distributed assets of its vast network of suppliers. Wal-Mart made a point of tracking demand information in real time. The key was that it decided to share this information with its supplier network. It introduced Retail Link, the system that still delivers the most accurate, real-time sales information in the industry to Wal-Mart partners. Wal-Mart was unique in the retail space in offering this kind of service, turning Retail Link into a critical supply chain hub [2004, pp. 1–2].

Fishman agrees but sees less rosy results:

> The ecosystem isn't a metaphor; it is a real place in the global economy where the very metabolism of business is set by Wal-Mart.

The fear of Wal-Mart isn't just the fear of losing a big account. It's the fear that the more business you do with Wal-Mart, the deeper you end up inside the Wal-Mart ecosystem, and the less you are actually running your own business. Wal-Mart's leadership virtually never acknowledges this control, but the company clearly understands it, and even takes a sly pride in it [2006, p. 16].

But Wal-Mart's ecosystem is not a gated preserve. Much as it might like to, Wal-Mart has limited ability to exclude other players—including the firm's many competitors and critics—who choose to spend time in its neighborhood, even if uninvited. Wal-Mart initiatives to build new stores are routinely countered by opponents who decry the economic and environmental costs they claim the new outlet would create.

Organizational ecosystems come in many forms and sizes. Some, like Wal-Mart's, are huge and global. Others are small and local (like the ecosystem of laundries in Oslo or policing in Omaha). Next, we examine several significant types of ecosystems to illustrate the dynamics involved.

Public Policy Ecosystems

In the public sector, policy arenas form around virtually every government activity. One example is the air carriers, airplane manufacturers, travelers, legislators, and regulators who are all active participants in the commercial aviation ecosystem. In the United States, the Federal Aviation Administration has been a troubled key player for decades. Charged with divergent goals of defending safety, promoting the economic health of the industry, and keeping its own costs down, the FAA has perennially come under heavy fire from virtually every direction. Feeble oversight permitted marginal carriers to shortcut safety but continue flying. An air traffic modernization plan rang up billions of dollars in bills, but twenty years later had yielded few results:

> When Marion C. Blakey took over at the Federal Aviation Administration in 2002, she was determined to fix an air travel system battered by terrorism, antiquated technology, and the ever-turbulent finances of the airline industry. Five years later, as she prepares to step down on Sept. 13, 2007, it's clear she failed. Almost everything about flying is worse than when she arrived. Greater are the risks, the passenger headaches, and the costs in lost productivity.

Almost everyone has a horror story about missed connections, lost baggage, and wasted hours on the tarmac [Palmeri and Epstein, 2007, p. 1].

Some of the FAA's troubles were internal. An earlier report from what was then called the General Accounting Office had faulted the agency's lack of a "performance-oriented culture essential to establishing a culture of accountability and coordination" (Dillingham, 2001). But almost every move it made to solve one constituency's problem created trouble for others. Much of the fault lay in its ecosystem: "Nobody is in charge. The various players in the system, including big airlines, small aircraft owners, labor unions, politicians, airplane manufacturers, and executives with their corporate jets, are locked in permanent warfare as they fight to protect their own interests. And the FAA, a weak agency that needs congressional approval for how it raises and spends money, seems incapable of breaking the gridlock" (Palmeri and Epstein, 2007).

Education is another illustration of a complex policy ecosystem. Everyone thinks good schools are important. Families want their children to acquire the ingredients for success. Businesses need well-trained, literate graduates. Economists and policy analysts stress the importance of human capital. Teachers want better pay and working conditions. Taxpayers want to cut frills and keep costs down. Almost no one believes that American schools are as good as they should be, but there is little agreement about how to make them better. One popular remedy, enshrined in federal law in the "No Child Left Behind" Act, emphasizes tests and incentives. Measure how well schools are doing, reward the winners, and penalize the losers. But many teachers and parents argue that overemphasis on metrics and sanctions is crippling teachers and driving out essential learning opportunities.

Another cure for educational ills is granting parents more choice about which schools their children attend. One version of school choice is vouchers, grants that families can use to send their children to private schools. Another is charter schools, publicly funded, quasi-independent educational enterprises. Proponents of choice argue that parents would obviously choose the best school for their children and that the ensuing competition would have an invigorating effect on public schools. But school administrators maintain that vouchers and charter schools drain away resources and exacerbate the challenges of the neediest students. Coalitions have formed on both sides of the choice issue and have lobbied vigorously at the state and national levels. Available research suggests that, on the whole, choice programs enhance student achievement and parent satisfaction (Robinson, 2005), but opponents question the evidence, and the battle goes on. No Child Left Behind has been even more controversial; research evidence is equivocal, and strenuous opposition in many states has forced the federal Department of Education into state-by-state negotiations to modify the requirements, making valid assessments of success even more difficult (Sunderman, 2006). The debates continue.

Business-Government Ecosystems

Government and business inevitably intersect in a multitude of ecosystems. Perrow (1986) discusses one example: pharmaceutical companies, physicians, and government. A major threat to drug companies' profit margins is generic drugs, which sell at a much lower price than brand-name equivalents. In the United States, the industry trade association, an interorganization coalition, successfully lobbied many state legislatures to prohibit the sale of generic drugs, ostensibly to protect consumers. The industry also persuaded the American Medical Association (AMA) to permit drugs to be advertised by brand name in its journals. Consumers normally buy whatever the doctor prescribes, and drug companies wanted doctors to think brands rather than chemical names. As a result of the policy shift, the AMA's advertising income tripled in seven years, and the manufacturers strengthened the position of their respective brands (Perrow, 1986).

The ecosystem shifted with the rapid rise of a newly powerful group of players: insurers and managed care providers. The growing market dominance of a few large insurers dramatically reduced the bargaining power of physicians and drug companies. Insurers used their growing political leverage to push physicians to prescribe less expensive generic drugs. In an effort to save consumers' money, state legislatures began to require pharmacists to offer the generic equivalent when a brand name is prescribed. Pharmaceutical companies fought back with television advertising encouraging patients to ask their doctors for brand name drugs.

Drug companies are not alone in their attention to politics. Firms search feverishly for sources of competitive advantage. One such source is "government policy, which determines the rules of commerce; the structure of markets (through barriers to entry and changes in cost structures due to regulations, subsidies, and taxation); the offerings of goods and services that are permissible; and the sizes of markets based on government subsidies and purchases.

Consequently, gaining and maintaining access to those who make public policy may well be a firm's most important political goal" (Schuler, Rehbein, and Cramer, 2002, p. 659).

Schuler's group found that politically active firms use a range of strategies for influencing government agencies. FedEx illustrates the possibilities. In Chapter Seven, we noted the company's sophisticated approach to managing people. FedEx has been equally agile in managing its political environment. The *New York Times* described it as "one of the most formidable and successful corporate lobbies in the capital" (Lewis, 1996, p. A17). Its CEO, Fred Smith, "spends considerable time in Washington, where he is regarded as Federal Express's chief advocate. It was Mr. Smith who hit a lobbying home run in 1977 when he persuaded Congress to allow the fledgling company to use full-sized jetliners to carry its cargo, rather than the small planes to which it had been restricted. That was the watershed event that allowed the company to grow to its present dominating position with almost $10.3 billion in business" (p. A30).

FedEx's political action committee ranked among the nation's top ten, making generous donations to hundreds of congressional candidates. Its board was adorned with former legislative leaders from both major political parties. Its corporate jets regularly ferried officeholders to events around the country. All this generosity paid off. In October 1996, when FedEx wanted two words inserted into a 1923 law regulating railway express companies, the Senate stayed in session a few extra days to get it done, even with elections only a month away. A first-term senator commented, "I was stunned by the breadth and depth of their clout up here" (Lewis, 1996, p. A17).

A similar co-evolution of business and politics occurs around the world:

> No one would dispute that business and politics are closely intertwined in Japan. As one leading financial journalist puts it, "If you don't use politicians, you can't expand business these days in Japan— that's basic." Businessmen provide politicians with funds, politicians provide businessmen with information. If you wish to develop a department store, a hotel or a ski resort, you need licenses and permissions and the cooperation of leading local political figures. And it is always useful to hear that a certain area is slated for development, preferably several years before development starts, when land prices are still low [Downer, 1994, p. 299].

Society as Ecosystem

On a still grander scale, we find society: the massive, swirling ecosystem in which business, government, and the public are embedded. A critical question in this arena is the power relationship between organizations and everyone else. All organizations have power. Large organizations have a lot: "Of the 100 largest economies in the world, 51 are corporations, and only 49 are countries. Wal-Mart is bigger than Israel, Poland or Greece. Mitsubishi is bigger than Indonesia. General Motors is bigger than Denmark. If governments can't set the rules, who will? The corporations? But they're the players. Who's the referee?" (Longworth, 1996, p. 4).

This question is becoming more urgent as big companies get bigger. In 1954, it took more than sixty companies to equal 20 percent of the American economy; in 2005, it took only twenty. "We don't often talk about the concentration of corporate power, but it is almost unfathomable that the men and women who run just 20 companies make decisions every day that steer one-fifth of the U.S. economy" (Fishman, 2006, p. 22). A number of organizational scholars (including Korten, 1995; Perrow, 1986; and Stern and Barley, 1996) emphasize that whoever controls a multibillion-dollar tool wields enormous power. Korten's view is particularly gloomy:

> An active propaganda machinery controlled by the world's largest corporations constantly reassures us that consumerism is the path to happiness, government restraint of market excess is the cause of our distress, and economic globalization is both a historical inevitability and a boon to the human species. In fact, these are all myths propagated to justify profligate greed and mask the extent to which the global transformation of human institutions is a consequence of the sophisticated, well-funded, and intentional interventions of a small elite whose money enables them to live in a world of illusion apart from the rest of humanity. These forces have transformed once beneficial corporations and financial institutions into instruments of a market tyranny that is extending its reach across the planet like a cancer, colonizing ever more of the planet's living spaces, destroying livelihoods, displacing people, rendering democratic institutions impotent, and feeding on life in an insatiable quest for money [Korten, 1995, p. 12].

Hit Number 3: Jeffrey Pfeffer and Gerald Salancik, *The External Control of Organizations* (New York: HarperCollins, 1978)

Pfeffer and Salancik's book fell out of print for several years and is little known outside academic circles, but scholars love it; it occupies the third rung in our ranking of most-cited works. As its title suggests, the book's principal theme is that organizations are much more creatures than creators of their environment. In the authors' words: "The perspective [in this book] denies the validity of the conceptualization of organizations as self-directed, autonomous actors pursuing their own ends and instead argues that organizations are other-directed, involved in a constant struggle for autonomy and discretion, confronted with constraint and external control" (p. 257). The authors follow Cyert and March (1963) in viewing organizations as coalitions that are both "markets in which influence and control are transacted" (p. 259) and players that need to negotiate their relationships with a range of external constituents.

Pfeffer and Salancik emphasize that organizations depend on their environment for inputs that they need to survive. Much of the job of management is to understand and respond to demands of key external constituents whose support is vital to organizational survival. This job is made more difficult by two challenges:

- Organizations' understanding of their environment is often distorted or imperfect (because organizations only act on the information they're geared to collect and know how to interpret).

- Organizations confront multiple constituents whose demands are often inconsistent.

Organizations comply where they have to, but they also look for ways to increase their autonomy by making their environment more predictable and favorable. They may merge to gain greater market supremacy, form coalitions (alliances, joint ventures) to gain greater influence, or enlist government help (by seeking subsidies, tax breaks, or protective tariffs, for example). But there is a dilemma: every entanglement, even as it garners greater influence over a part of the environment, also produces erosion of the organization's autonomy. There's no free lunch.

Pfeffer and Salancik describe three roles for managers, two political and one symbolic. There is a responsive role in which managers adjust the organization's activities to comply with pressures from the environment. There is a discretionary role in which they seek to alter the organization's relationship with its environment. And there is a symbolic role arising from the widely accepted myth that managers make a difference. If a team is losing but you can't change the players, you fire the coach, creating the appearance of change without actually changing anything (an important idea that we address in the next three chapters).

Do sophisticated consumer marketing firms create and control consumer tastes, or do they simply react to needs created by larger social forces? Critics like Korten are convinced that the advantage lies with the corporations, but Pfeffer and Salancik (1978) see it the other way around, as do many proponents of "the marketing concept":

> The marketing concept of management is based on the premise that over the longer term all businesses are born and survive or die because people (the market) either want them or don't want them. In short, the market creates, shapes, and defines the demand for all classes of products and services. Almost needless to say, many managers tend to think that they can design goods and services and then create demand. The marketing concept denies this proposition. Instead, the marketing concept emphasizes that the creative aspect of marketing is discovering, defining, and fulfilling what people want or need or what solves their life-style problems [Marshall, 1984, p. 1].

Proponents of this view note that even the most successful marketers have had their share of Edsels—products released with great fanfare and a huge marketing budget that fluttered briefly and then sank like stones.

Are large multinational corporations so powerful that they have become a law unto themselves, or are they strongly shaped by the need to respond to the customers, culture, and governments in the countries where they operate? An ecological view suggests that the answer is some of both. Ecosystems and competitors within them rise and fall. Power relations are never static, and even the most powerful have no guarantee of immortality. Of the top twenty-five U.S. companies at the beginning of the twentieth century, all but one had dropped off the list or vanished altogether when the century came to a close. The lone survivor? General Electric.

Fishman frames both sides of this issue in the case of Wal-Mart:

> The easiest response to the Wal-Mart critics comes from people who shrug and say, the United States economy is capitalistic and market-based. Wal-Mart is large and ubiquitous—and powerful—because it does what it does so well. Wal-Mart is winning for no other reason than personal choice: Customers vote for Wal-Mart with their wallets; suppliers vote for Wal-Mart with their products. Any consumer, any businessperson who doesn't care for the way Wal-Mart does business is free to buy and sell products somewhere else.
>
> The problem is that this free choice has become an illusion. In many categories of products it sells, Wal-Mart is now 30 percent or more of the entire market. It sells 31 percent of the pet food used in the United States, 37 percent of the fresh meat, 45 percent of the office and school supplies bought by consumers, and 24 percent of the bottled water. That kind of dominance at both ends of the spectrum—dominance across a huge range of merchandise and dominance of geographic consumer markets—means that market capitalism is being strangled with the kind of slow inexorability of a boa constrictor. It's not free-market capitalism; Wal-Mart is running the market. The newly merged Procter & Gamble and Gillette has sales in excess of $64 billion a year—not only bigger by far than any other consumer products company, but bigger than all but 20 public companies of any kind in the United States. But remember: Wal-Mart isn't just P&G's number-one customer; it's P&G's business. Wal-Mart is bigger than P&G's next nine customers combined. That's why businesspeople are scared of Wal-Mart. They should be. And if a corporation with the scale, vigor, and independence of P&G must bend to Wal-Mart's will, it's easy to imagine the kind of influence

Wal-Mart wields over the operators of small factories in developing nations, factories that just want work and have no leverage with Wal-Mart or Wal-Mart's vendors [2006, p. 20].

Wal-Mart's clout remains formidable, but it is hard to predict where it will go from here. It has been caught in an embattled, slow-growth mode in recent years. Will it catch a second wind and accelerate its growth? Or will it follow companies like Sears and General Motors into a long downhill slide from the pinnacle it once commanded? Whatever happens to Wal-Mart, the battle over corporate power will continue on a global scale. Large multinational companies have enormous power but must also cope with the demands of other powerful players: governments, labor unions, investors, and consumers. In a cacophonous global village, this is the biggest political contest of all.

SUMMARY

Organizations are both arenas for internal politics and political agents with their own agendas, resources, and strategies. As arenas, they house competition and offer a setting for the ongoing interplay of divergent interests and agendas. An arena's rules and parameters shape the game to be played, the players on the field, and the interests to be pursued. From this perspective, every significant organizational process is inherently political.

As agents, organizations are tools, often very powerful tools, for achieving the purposes of whoever controls them. But they are also inevitably dependent on their environment for needed support and resources. They exist, compete, and co-evolve in business or political ecosystems with clusters of organizations, each pursuing its own interests and seeking a viable niche. As in nature, relationships within and between ecosystems are sometimes fiercely competitive, sometimes collaborative and interdependent.

A particularly urgent and controversial question is the relative power of organizations and society. Giant multinational corporations have achieved scale and resources unprecedented in human history. Critics worry that they are dominating and distorting politics, society, and the environment. Others argue that organizations are inherently dependent on a changing and turbulent environment—they retain their clout only by adapting to larger social forces and responding to the needs and demands of customers and constituents.

PART FIVE

The Symbolic Frame

What images or associations come to mind when you think about each of these terms?

- American flag
- Nazi
- General Motors
- Princess Diana
- Abu Ghraib
- Declaration of Independence

- Al Quaeda
- McDonald's
- Pearl Harbor
- Paris

It is likely that you had emotional, even visceral, reactions to many of these familiar words. Each refers to a specific person, group, place, or event, but each has also acquired symbolic resonance. Symbols carry powerful intellectual and emotional messages; they speak to both the mind and the heart.

The symbolic frame focuses on how humans make sense of the chaotic, ambiguous world in which they live. Meaning, belief, and faith are its central concerns. Meaning is not given to us; we have to create it. There are, for example, many who revere the American flag and many others who burn it. The flag is symbolically powerful for both groups, but for different reasons. It represents patriotism for one group, oppression or imperialism for the other. Symbols are the basic building blocks of the meaning systems, or cultures we inhabit. We experience our way of life in the same way that fish live in water. Our own cultural ways are often invisible to us because we see them simply as the ways things are—and ought to be. But we can react with revulsion and horror to cultures that are alien or hostile to our own. Consider the following words from an Al Quaeda instruction manual captured in Europe:

> Committed to uniting all Muslims under a new caliphate, Al Qaeda believes that only force can achieve this mission: The confrontation that we are calling for . . . does not know Socratic debates, Platonic ideals, nor Aristotelian dialogues. But it knows the dialogue of bullets, the ideals of assassination, bombing and destruction, and the diplomacy of the cannon and the machine gun. Islamic governments have never been and will never be established through peaceful solutions and cooperative councils. They are established as they have always been by pen and gun, by word and bullet, by tongue and teeth [Al Quaeda, n.d.].

The message is appalling to most Westerners, yet inspiring to those who share its particular vision of a restored caliphate. As symbols often do, the words carry an emotional wallop that may be very positive or very negative, depending on your perspective.

In Chapter Twelve, we explore the many forms symbols take in social life, including myth, vision, story, heroes and heroines, ritual, and ceremony. We then use a variety of examples to demonstrate what culture is and why it is so important.

In Chapter Thirteen, we apply symbolic concepts to team dynamics. We use a detailed account of a highly successful computer development team to show that the essence of its success was cultural and spiritual. The team relied on initiation rituals, humor, play, specialized language, ceremony, and other symbolic forms to weld a diverse and fractious group of individuals into a spirited, successful team.

Chapter Fourteen highlights dramaturgical and institutional perspectives, viewing organizations as akin to theater companies that seek recognition and support by staging dramas that both please and influence their audiences. We show that many activities and processes in organizations, such as evaluation and strategic planning, rarely achieve supposed goals. Yet they persist because they project vital messages that internal and external audiences want to hear.

Organizational Symbols and Culture

For eight hundred years neighborhoods in Siena, Italy, have competed twice each summer in a horse race known as the *palio*. Each side has its club, hymn, costumes, museum, and elected head. A crowd of more than a hundred thousand gathers to witness a seventy-five-second event that people live for all year. Riding under banners of the goose, seashell, or turtle, jockeys attack one another with whips and hang on desperately around ninety-degree turns. The first horse to finish, with or without rider, wins. "The winners are worshipped. The losers embarrass their clan" (Saubaber, 2007, p. 42). In July 2007, twenty-two-year-old Giovanni Atzeni won in a photo finish. His followers were ecstatic. A young woman shouted, "We've waited eight years," as she showered him with kisses. An old man almost fainted with joy at the chance to see a victory before he died. The legendary Aceto, a fourteen-time winner, once said, "Palio is a drug that makes you a God . . . and then crucifies you." The rest of Italy considers the event barbaric, but locals are proudly unfazed. Unless you were born in Siena, they insist, you will never understand the *palio*. Rooted in a time when Siena was a proud and powerful republic, the occasion embodies the town's unique identity.

Building community around a brand name updates ancient traditions based on tribe and homeland, like those surrounding the *palio*. In 2002, for example, Harley-Davidson celebrated its hundredth birthday with festivities that lasted for fourteen months. In a culminating extravaganza, a million bikers roared into the company's headquarters in Milwaukee to showcase their bikes and revel in Harley-Davidson's unique culture. To the HOGs (Harley Owner's Groups), owning a Harley is a way of life, and many riders have the company logo tattooed on their skins.

> Despite their diversity, Harley riders have something in common: a fanatical dedication to their Harleys. It's a feeling that many cannot articulate, and for them there's a Harley T-shirt inscribed: "Harley-Davidson—If I Have To Explain You Wouldn't Understand" . . . One thing is certain: This incredible brand loyalty is emotional. It is based on a pattern of associations that includes the American flag and another American symbol, the eagle (which is also a Harley symbol), as well as camaraderie, individualism, the feeling of riding free, and the pride of owning a product that has become a legend. On the road, one Harley rider always helps another in distress—even though one may be a tattooed biker and the other a buttoned-down bank president [Reid, 1989, p. 5].

Harley-Davidson and Siena's *palio* are two examples of how symbols permeate every fiber of society and organizations. "A symbol is something that stands for or suggests something else; it conveys socially constructed means beyond its intrinsic or obvious functional use" (Zott and Huy, 2007, p. 72). Distilled to the essence, people seek meaning in life. Since life is mysterious, we create symbols to sustain hope and faith. These intangibles then shape our thoughts, emotions, and actions. Symbols cut deeply into the human psyche (Freud, [1899] 1980) and tap the collective unconscious (Jung, [1912] 1965).

Symbols and symbolic actions are part of everyday life and are particularly perceptible at weekly, monthly, or seasonal high points. Symbols stimulate energy in moments of triumph and offer solace in times of tribulation. After 9/11 Americans turned to symbols to cope with the aftermath of a devastating terrorist attack. Flags flew. Makeshift monuments honored victims and the heroic acts of police and firefighters who gave their lives. Members of Congress sang "God Bless America" on the Capitol steps. Across the country, people gathered in both formal and informal healing ceremonies. Especially in times of calamity or victory, we embrace the spiritual magic symbols represent.

The symbolic frame interprets and illuminates the basic issues of meaning and belief that make symbols so powerful. It depicts a world far different from canons of rationality, certainty, and linearity. This chapter journeys into the symbolic inner sanctum. We first discuss symbolic assumptions and then highlight various forms that symbols take in organizations. These are basic building blocks of culture that people shape to fit unique circumstances. We then move on to discuss organizations as unique cultures or tribes. Finally, we describe how three distinctive companies—BMW, Continental Airlines, and Nordstrom Department Stores—have successfully applied symbolic ideas.

SYMBOLIC ASSUMPTIONS

The symbolic frame forms an umbrella for ideas from several disciplines, including organization theory and sociology (Selznick, 1957; Blumer, 1969; Schutz, 1970; Clark, 1975; Corwin, 1976; March and Olsen, 1976; Meyer and Rowan, 1978; Weick, 1976; Davis and others, 1976; Hofstede, 1984); political science (Dittmer, 1977; Edelman, 1971); magic (O'Keefe, 1983); and neurolinguistic programming (Bandler and Grinder, 1975, 1977). Freud and Jung relied heavily on symbolic concepts to probe the human psyche and unconscious archetypes. Anthropologists have traditionally focused on symbols and their place in the lives of humans (Mead, 1989; Benedict, 1989; Goffman, 1974; Ortner, 1973; Bateson, 1972).

The symbolic frame distills ideas from diverse sources into five suppositions:

- What is most important is not what happens but what it means.

- Activity and meaning are loosely coupled; events and actions have multiple interpretations as people experience life differently.

- Facing uncertainty and ambiguity, people create symbols to resolve confusion, find direction, and anchor hope and faith.

- Events and processes are often more important for what is expressed than for what is produced. Their emblematic form weaves a tapestry of secular myths, heroes and heroines, rituals, ceremonies, and stories to help people find purpose and passion.

- Culture forms the superglue that bonds an organization, unites people, and helps an enterprise accomplish desired ends.

The symbolic frame sees life as figurative, more serendipitous than linear. Organizations are like constantly changing, organic pinball machines. Issues, actors, decisions, and policies carom through an elastic labyrinth of cushions, barriers, and traps. Managers turning to Peter Drucker's *Effective Executive* might do better seeking advice from Lewis Carroll's *Through the Looking Glass*. But apparent chaos has a pattern and an emblematic order increasingly appreciated in corporate life.

ORGANIZATIONAL SYMBOLS

An organization's culture is revealed and communicated through its symbols: Geico's gecko, Target's bull's-eye, or Budweiser's Clydesdales. McDonald's franchises are unified as much by golden arches, core values, and the legend of Ray Kroc as by sophisticated control systems. Harvard professors are bound less by structural constraints than by rituals of teaching, values of scholarship, and the myths and mystique of Harvard.

Symbols take many forms in organizations. Myth, vision, and values imbue an organization with purpose and resolve. Heroes and heroines, through words and deeds, serve as living logos. Fairy tales and stories tender explanations, reconcile contradictions, and resolve dilemmas (Cohen, 1969). Rituals and ceremonies offer direction, faith, and hope (Ortner, 1973). Metaphor, humor, and play loosen things up. We look at each of these symbolic forms in this section.

Myths, Vision, and Values

Myths, operating at a mystical level, are the story behind the story (Campbell, 1988). They explain, express, legitimize, and maintain solidarity and cohesion. They communicate unconscious wishes and conflicts, mediate contradictions, and offer a narrative anchoring the present in the past (Cohen, 1969). All organizations rely on myths or sagas of varying strength and intensity (Clark, 1975). Myths transform a place of work into a revered institution and an all-encompassing way of life.

Myths often originate in the launching of an enterprise. The original plan for Southwest Airlines, for example, was sketched on a cocktail napkin in a San Antonio bar. It envisioned connecting three Texas cities: Dallas, Houston, and San Antonio. As legend has it, Rollin King, one of the original founders, said to his counterpart Herb Kelleher, "Herb, let's start an airline." Kelleher, who later became Southwest's CEO, replied, "Rollin, you're crazy. Let's do it!" (Freiberg and Freiberg, 1998, p. 15).

As the new airline moved ahead, it met fierce resistance from established carriers. Four years of legal wrangling kept the upstart grounded. In 1971, the Texas Supreme Court ruled in Southwest's favor, and its planes were ready to fly. A local sheriff's threat to halt flights under a court injunction prompted a terse directive from Kelleher: "You roll right over the son of a bitch and leave our tire tracks on his uniform if you have to" (Freiberg and Freiberg, 1998, p. 21). (The order, of course, signaled resolve, not an actual intention to cause harm.) The persistence and zaniness of Southwest's mythologized beginnings shape its unique culture: "The spirit and steadfastness that enabled the airline to survive in its early years is what makes Southwest such a remarkable company today" (p. 14).

Myths undergird an organization's values. Values characterize what an organization stands for, qualities worthy of esteem or commitment. Unlike goals, values are intangible and define a unique distinguishing character. Values convey a sense of identity, from boardroom to factory floor, and help people feel special about what they do.

The values that count are those an organization lives, regardless of what it articulates in mission statements or formal documents. Southwest Airlines has never codified its values formally. But its Symbol of Freedom billboards and banners express the company's defining purpose: extending freedom to fly to everyone, not just the elite, and doing it with an abiding sense of fun. Other organizations make values more explicit. The Edina (Minnesota) School District, following the suicide of a superintendent, involved staff, parents, and students in formally articulating values in a document: "We care. We share. We dare." The values of the U.S. Marine Corps are condensed into a simple phrase: "Semper Fi" (short for *semper fidelis*—always faithful). It is more than a motto; it stands for the traditions, sentiments, and solidarity that are instilled into recruits and perpetuated by veteran Marines: "The values and assumptions that shape its members . . . are all the Marines have. They are the smallest of the U.S. military services, and in many ways the most interesting. Theirs is the richest culture: formalistic, insular, elitist, with a deep anchor in their own history and mythology" (Ricks, 1998, p. 19).

Vision turns an organization's core ideology, or sense of purpose, into an image of the future. It is a shared fantasy, illuminating new possibilities within the realm of myths and values. Martin Luther King's "I Have a Dream" speech, for example, articulated poetically a new future for race relations rooted in the ideals of America's founding fathers.

Vision is seen as vital in contemporary organizations. In *Built to Last,* Collins and Porras profile a number of extraordinary companies and conclude, "The essence of a visionary company comes in the translation of its core ideology and its own unique drive for progress into the very fabric of the organization" (1994, p. 201). Johnson & Johnson's commitment to the elimination of "pain and disease" and to "the doctors, nurses, hospitals, mothers, and all others who use our products" motivated the company to make the costly decision to pull Tylenol from store shelves when several tainted bottles were discovered. 3M's principle of "thou shalt not kill a new product idea" came to life when someone refused to stop working on an idea that became Scotch Tape. The same principle paved the way for Post-it notes, a product resurrected from a failed adhesive. A vision offers mental pictures linking historical legend and core precepts to future events. Shared, it imbues an organization with spirit, resolve, and élan.

Subtle distinctions among intangible myths, values, and visions are difficult to draw—these ideas often conjoin. Take eBay, which emerged as a highly visible success amid a sea of 1990s dot-com disasters. Its interplay of myth, values, and vision contributes to top performance, even in a tough economic environment. Much of eBay's success can be traced to its founder, Pierre Omidyar. He envisioned a marketplace where buyers would have equal access to products and prices, and sellers would have an open outlet for goods. Prices would be set by laws of supply and demand. But Omidyar's vision incorporated another element: community. Historically, people have used market stalls and cafés to swap gossip, trade advice, and pass the time of day. Omidyar wanted to combine virtual business site and caring community. That vision led to eBay's core values of commerce and community. Embedded in these are corollary principles: "Treat other people online as you would like to be treated, and when disputes arise, give other people the benefit of the doubt."

eBay is awash in myths and legends. Omidyar's vision is said to have taken root over dinner with his fiancée. She complained that their move from Boston to Silicon Valley severed her ties with fellow collectors of Pez dispensers. He obliquely came to her rescue by writing code laying the foundation for a new company. Did it happen this way? Not quite. This story was hatched by Mary Lou Song, an eBay publicist, in an effort to get media exposure. Her rationale: "Nobody wants to hear about a thirty-year-old genius who wanted to create a perfect market. They want to hear that he did it for his fiancée." Her version persists because myths are truer than truth.

Heroes and Heroines

In the wake of scandals at Enron and elsewhere, *Business Week* (Byrnes, Byrne, Edwards, and Lee, 2002) profiled six "good" CEOs. They were not media celebrities like Lee Iacocca and Jack Welch nor symbols of corporate greed like Ken Lay, Bernie Ebbers, and Dennis Kozlowski. They were solid leaders who built time-tested companies and delivered results.

Just as important, these six leaders modeled corporate values they hoped to instill. Colgate Palmolive's Ruben Mark, one of the six, refused to comment on the story. He felt that an interview would add little value to his company. Another, Costco's James Sinegal, took pride in his disdain for corporate perks. He answered his own phone and personally escorted guests to his spartan office—no bathroom, no walls, twenty-year-old furniture. He commented: "We're low-cost operators, and it would be a little phony if we tried to pretend that we're not and had all the trappings" (Byrnes, Byrne, Edwards, and Lee, 2002, p. 82).

All six executives seemed to embrace their symbolic role as cultural heroes. They were living logos, human icons, whose words and deeds exemplified and reinforced important core values. The impact of well-placed cultural heroes and heroines is underscored by Bernie Marcus, cofounder of Home Depot: "People watch the titular heads of companies, how they live their lives, and they know [if] they are being sold a bill of goods. If you are a selfish son-of-a-bitch, well that usually comes across fairly well. And it comes across no matter how many memos you send out [stating otherwise]" (Roush, 1999, p. 139).

Not all icons are at the top. Doing their jobs, ordinary people often perform exemplary deeds. The late Joe Vallejo, custodian at a California junior high school, kept the place immaculate. But he was also a liaison between the school and its community. His influence knew few limits. When emotions ran high, he attended parent conferences and often negotiated a compromise acceptable to all parties. He knew the students and checked report cards. He was not bashful about telling seasoned teachers how to tailor lessons. When he retired, a patio was named in his honor. It remains today, commemorating a hero who made a difference well beyond his formal assignment.

Some heroic exploits go unrecognized because they happen out of view. Southwest Airlines annually recognizes its behind-the-scenes employees in a

"Heroes of the Heart" award ceremony. The honor goes to the backstage group that contributes most to Southwest's unique culture and successful performance. The year following the award, a Southwest aircraft flies with the group's name on its fuselage. A song written for the occasion expresses the value Southwest places on its heroes and heroines whose important work is often hidden:

Heroes come in every shape and size;
Adding something very special to others in their lives
No one gives you medals and the world won't
know your name
But in Southwest's eyes you're heroes just the same.

The Twin Towers tragedy reminded Americans of the vital role heroism plays in the human spirit. New York City police officers and firefighters touched people's hearts by risking their lives to save others. Many perished as a result. Their sacrifices reaffirmed Americans' spirit and resolve in enduring one of the nation's most costly tragedies. But every day, less dramatic acts of courage come to light as people go out of their way to help customers or serve communities. *Newsweek* runs an "everyday heroes" feature showcasing the uncommon exploits of common people. NBC's *Nightly News* airs a Friday segment recognizing people who "have made a difference." In 2007, Colin Powell proposed an "Above the Call" citizen award, a recognition on par with the Congressional Medal of Honor.

Exploits of heroes and heroines are lodged in our psyches. We call on their examples in times of uncertainty and stress. American POWs in North Vietnamese prisons drew upon stories of the courage of Captain Lance Sijan, Admiral James Stockdale, and Colonel Bud Day, who refused to capitulate to Viet Cong captors. "[Their examples] when passed along the clandestine prison communications network . . . helped support the resolve that eventually defeated the enemy's efforts" (McConnell, 2004, p. 249). During the Bosnian conflict, the ordeal of Scott O'Grady, a U.S. Air Force fighter pilot, made headlines. To survive after being shot down, O'Grady drew on the example of Sijan: "His strong will to survive and be free was an inspiration to every pilot I knew" (O'Grady, 1998, p. 83). Although drawn from nightmares of warfare, these examples demonstrate how human models influence our decisions and actions. We carry lessons of teachers, parents, and others with us. Their exploits, animated through stories, serve as guides to choices we make in our personal lives and at work.

Stories and Fairy Tales

Stories, like folk or fairy tales, offer more than entertainment or moral instruction for small children. They grant comfort, reassurance, direction, and hope to people of all ages. They externalize inner conflicts and tensions (Bettelheim, 1977). Stories are sometimes dismissed as the last resort of people lacking substance—like a professor accused of telling "war stories." Yet stories convey information, morals, and myths vividly and convincingly (Mitroff and Kilmann, 1975; Denning, 2005). They perpetuate values and keep feats of heroes and heroines alive. This helps account for the recent proliferation of business books linking stories and leadership (Clark, 2004; Denning, 2005; Simmons, 2006, 2007; Seely Brown, Denning, Groh, and Prusak, 2004). Barry Lopez captures poetically why stories are significant:

> Remember only this one thing,
> The stories people tell have a way of taking care of them.
> If stories come to you, care for them.
> And learn to give them away where they are needed.
> Sometimes a person needs a story more than food to stay alive.
> That is why we put these stories in each other's memories.
> This is how people care for themselves [Lopez, 1998, p. 13].

An example from higher education shows the sentiments a story can transmit. Joe B. Wyatt (then chancellor of Vanderbilt University) took the podium at the university's annual convocation. Several hundred professors and staff members were assembled to kick off a new school year. Wyatt wended his way through facts and figures about the university's status, recognized professors with long-term service, and awarded chairs to professors who had retired. He closed his presentation with a story:[1]

> I'd like to share with you a story about a young second-grade teacher in Austin, Texas. Her name is Roberta Wright. Among her young students was a little girl who was stealing materials from the classroom. Ms. Wright noticed the recurring pilfering, called the mother and scheduled a parent conference. She told the mother about the daily

thefts and let her know that the stealing could not continue. The mother sat silent for a few seconds and then said, "Oh, Ms. Wright, you don't understand, do you? She comes home each afternoon and plays that she's still in school. She pretends she's you."

Chancellor Wyatt paused, his eyes moving from person to person. He concluded: "And ladies and gentleman, that does not stop in second grade." His story gave emphasis to the sacred side of teaching, one of the university's core values, in an unusually dramatic way.

Stories are deeply rooted in the human experience. They are told and retold around campfires and during family reunions (Clark, 2004). David Armstrong, CEO of Armstrong International, notes that storytelling has played a commanding role in history through the teachings of Jesus, the Buddha, and Mohammed, among many others. It can play an equally potent role in contemporary organizations: "Rules, either in policy manuals or on signs, can be intimidating. But the morals in stories are invariably inviting, fun and inspiring. Through story-telling our people can know very clearly what the company believes in and what needs to be done" (Armstrong, 1992, p. 6). To Armstrong, storytelling is a simple, timeless, and memorable way to have fun, train new people, recognize accomplishments, and spread the word. Denning (2005) puts the functions of stories into eight categories:

- Sparking action
- Communicating who you are
- Communicating who the company is—branding
- Transmitting values
- Fostering collaboration
- Taming the grapevine
- Sharing knowledge
- Leading people into the future

Effective organizations are full of good stories. They often focus on the legendary exploits of corporate heroes. Marriott Hotels founder J. W. Marriott Sr. died years ago, but his presence is still felt. Stories of his unwavering commitment to customer service are told and retold. His aphorism "Take good care of your employees and they'll take good care of your customers" is still part of Marriott's philosophy.

According to fable, Marriott visited new general managers and took them for a walk around the property. He pointed out broken branches, sidewalk pebbles, and obscure cobwebs. By tour's end, the new manager ended up with a long to-do list—and, more important, an indelible lesson in what mattered at Marriott.

Not all stories center on the founder or chief executive. Ritz-Carlton is famous for the upscale treatment it offers guests. "My pleasure" is employees' traditional response to requests, no matter how demanding or how trivial. One hurried guest jumped into a taxi to the airport but left his briefcase on the sidewalk. The doorman retrieved the briefcase, abandoned his post, sped to the airport, and delivered it to the panicked guest. Instead of being fired, the doorman became part of the legends and lore—a living example of the company's commitment to service (Deal and Jenkins, 1994).

Stories are a key medium for communicating corporate myths. They establish and perpetuate tradition. Recalled and embellished in formal meetings and informal coffee breaks, they convey an organization's values and identity to insiders, building confidence and support. Stories also transmit the appeal of products and services. A good story trumps data and abstractions in wooing consumers.

In the late 1990s, Subway launched an advertising campaign to establish itself as a healthful alternative to high-fat rivals: "7 under 6" summed up the message that seven of Subway's sandwiches had less than six grams of fat. But the next promotion, based on the story of Jared Fogel, worked even better. Fogel initially tipped the scales at 425 pounds. A health scare motivated him to slim down, and Subway's "7 under 6" campaign caught his attention. He created his Subway diet plan: a foot-long veggie sub for lunch, a six-inch turkey sub for dinner. His dramatic weight loss caught the attention of a franchisee as well as the national media. An advertising blitz took it from there. Subway had a 189-pound hero whose story cut a competitive edge that dramatically improved sales (Heath and Heath, 2007).

Ritual

As a symbolic act, ritual is routine that "usually has a statable purpose, but one that invariably alludes to more than it says, and has many meanings at once" (Moore and Meyerhoff, 1977, p. 5). Enacted, ritual connects an individual or group to something mystical, more than words can capture. At home and at work, ritual gives structure and meaning to each day: "We find these magical moments every day—drinking our morning coffee, reading the daily paper, eating lunch with a friend, drinking a glass of wine while admiring the sunset, or saying, 'Good night, sleep tight . . .' at bedtime. The holy in the daily; the sacred in the single act of living. . . . A time to do the dishes. And a time to walk the dog" (Fulghum, 1995, pp. 3, 254).

Humans create both personal and communal rituals. The ones that carry meaning become the dance of life. "Rituals anchor us to a center," Fulghum writes, "while freeing us to move on and confront the everlasting unpredictability of life. The paradox of ritual patterns and sacred habits is that they simultaneously serve as a solid footing and springboard, providing a stable dynamic in our lives" (1995, p. 261).

The power of ritual becomes palpable if one experiences the emptiness of losing it. Campbell (1988) underscores this loss: "When you lose rituals, you lose a sense of civilization; and that's why society is so out of kilter." When the Roman Catholic Church changed its liturgy from Latin to vernacular, many Catholics felt a profound loss of conviction and faith. Conversely, in 2001 and 2002, when the Catholic Church suffered a series of scandals involving sexual misbehavior by priests, shaken laypersons turned to rituals of the mass for comfort and reassurance. The Church in 2007 reversed its earlier position and gave local priests permission to conduct the mass in Latin.

Rituals of initiation induct newcomers into communal membership. "Greenhorns" encounter powerful symbolic pressures as they join a group or organization. A new member must gain entry to the inner sanctum. Transition from stranger to full-fledged member grants access to cherished organizational secrets. The key episode is the rite of passage affirming acceptance. In tribes, simply attaining puberty is insufficient for young males: "There must be an accompanying trial and appropriate ritual to mark the event. The so-called primitives had the good sense to make these trials meaningful and direct. Upon attaining puberty you killed a lion and were circumcised. After a little dancing and whatnot, you were admitted as a junior member and learned some secrets. The [men's] hut is a symbol of, and a medium for maintaining, the status quo and the good of the order" (Ritti and Funkhouser, 1982, p. 3).

We are not beyond the primitive drives, sexism, and superstition that gave rise to age-old institutions such as the men's hut. Consider the experience of a newly elected member of the U.S. House of Representatives:

> One of the early female novices was a representative who was a
> serious feminist. Soon after arriving in Congress, she broke propriety
> by audaciously proposing an amendment to a military bill of Edward
> Hebert, Chief of the Defense Clan. When the amendment received

only a single vote, she supposedly snapped at the aged committee chairman: "I know the only reason my amendment failed is that I've got a vagina." To which Herbert retorted, "If you'd been using your vagina instead of your mouth, maybe you'd have gotten a few more votes" [Weatherford, 1985, p. 35].

That last exchange seems particularly harsh and offensive, but its multiple interpretations take us to the heart of symbolic customs. A kinder and gentler anecdote would conceal what transpires in a multilayered transaction with multiple meanings. Let's look at some possible interpretations.

One version highlights the age-old battle between the sexes. The female representative raises the specter of sexual discrimination; Hebert uses a sexist jibe to put her in her place. Another view sees the exchange as a classic give-and-take. Newcomers bring new ideas as agents of evolution and reform. Old-timers are supposed to pass along time-tested values and traditions. If newcomers succumb, an organization risks stultification and decay; if old-timers fail to induct new arrivals properly, chaos and disarray lie ahead.

As an initiation ritual, the exchange is a predictable clash between a new arrival and an established veteran. The old-timer is reminding the rookie who's in charge. Newcomers don't get free admission. The price is higher for those who, because of race, gender, or ethnicity, question or threaten existing values, norms, or patterns. Yet only a weak culture accepts newcomers without some form of hazing.

The rite of passage reinforces the existing culture while testing the newcomer's ability to become a member. As a freshman, Hillary Rodham Clinton survived her initiation and achieved full membership in the U.S. Senate when she and Senator Don Nickles, a Republican from Oklahoma, partnered on an unemployment bill in early 2003. This was impressive, since Nickles had led the effort to impeach Clinton's husband when he was president.

Initiation is one important role of ritual. But rituals also bond a group together and imbue the enterprise with traditions and values. They prepare combat pilots to slip into a fighter cockpit knowing they may not return:

> For me, there can be no fighter pilots without fighter pilot rituals. The end result of these rituals is a culture that allows individuals to risk their lives and revel in it. If the normal American finds it difficult to understand the circumstances that compel individuals to

willingly hurtle their bodies through space encased in several tons of steel while determined people are actively trying to kill them, it is because the normal American has not been indoctrinated into the fighter pilot culture [Broughton, 1988, p. 131].

Some rituals become ceremonial occasions to recognize momentous accomplishments. When Captain Sijan, mentioned earlier, received his posthumous Medal of Honor, the president of the United States attended:

> In the large room, men in impressive uniforms and costly vested suits and women [in uniforms] and cheerful spring pastels stood motionless and silent in their contemplation of the words. The stark text of the citation contained a wealth of evocative imagery, some of it savage, some tender to the point of heartbreak. President Ford left the rostrum: a group of senior officers drew up beside him to hand forward the glass-covered walnut case containing the medal. There was a certain liturgical quality to this passing of a sanctified object among a circle of anointed leaders [McConnell, 2004, pp. 217].

Other rituals soften grief. Major Kevin Reed, a former F-16 pilot, has outlined the Air Force's comprehensive liturgy (2001). The most solemn of Air Force rituals is the death notification. Once a fatality has been confirmed, a team of three officers is dispatched to the home of the nearest relative. An officer of superior rank passes the news: "The Chief of Staff of the Air Force conveys his deep sympathies." A flight surgeon is there for physical support. A chaplain offers spiritual sustenance. The notification ritual is the first step in the consolation ceremony (p. 10).

At the other end of the scale are the numerous fun rituals, but even they have a serious side:

> On a Friday night at a base officers club, four Marine A-6 Intruder pilots joined a packed crowd of Air Force officers. One of the Marine aviators put his cap on the bar while fishing for some money to pay for his drink. The bartender rang a foot-tall bell and yelled "Hat on the bar!" This infraction automatically means the guilty party buys a round of drinks. Surveying the size of the crowd, the Marine . . . refused to pay. An Air Force colonel approached him

and asked him if he really intended to flout the tradition. When the Marine responded in the affirmative, the colonel called the base security and ordered the A-6 [aircraft] on the ramp impounded. The Marine left and called his superior to report the colonel's action. Shortly thereafter, he returned and asked sheepishly, "What's everyone having?"

Rituals also govern key relationships. In a fighter squadron, one of the most important relationships is that between a pilot and a crew chief. A preflight ritual transfers ownership between someone who cares for an aircraft on the ground and the one who will take it aloft. The ground ritual has several phases. "A first salute reinforces rank and signifies respect between mechanic and pilot. A handshake takes the formal greeting to a new level, cementing the personal bond between the two. A second salute after the pilot has checked the aircraft indicates the aircraft's airworthiness. It is now officially under the pilot's command. Finally, a thumbs-up is a personal gesture wishing the pilot a good flight. Interwoven, the many rituals of combat flying bond the participants and bind them to the service's traditions and values. The same is true for cohesive cultures in other sectors" [R. Mola, cited in Reed, 2001, p. 5].

Ceremony

Historically, cultures have relied on ritual and ceremony to create order, clarity, and predictability—particularly around mysterious and random issues or dilemmas. The distinction between ritual and ceremony is elusive. As a rule of thumb, ritual is more everyday. Ceremonies are more episodic—grander and more elaborate—convened at times of transition or special occasions. Rain dances, harvest celebrations, and annual meetings invoke supernatural assistance in critical, unpredictable tasks of raising crops or building market share. Annual conventions renew old ties and revive deep collective commitments. "Convention centers are the basilicas of secular religion" (Fulghum, 1995, p. 96).

Both ritual and ceremony are illustrated in an account from Japan:

It has been the same every night since the death in 1964 of Yasujiro Tsutsumi, the legendary patriarch of the huge Seibu real-estate and transportation group. Two employees stand an overnight vigil at his tomb. On New Year's, the weather is often bitter, but at dawn the vigil expands to include five or six hundred top executives—directors, vice presidents, presidents—arrayed by company and rank, the most senior in front. A limousine delivers Yasujiro's third son, Yoshiaki Tsutsumi, the head of the family business and Japan's richest man. A great brass bell booms out six times as Yoshiaki approaches his father's tomb. He claps his hands twice, bows deeply, and says, "Happy New Year, Father, Happy New Year." Then he turns to deliver a brief-but-stern sermon to the assembled congregation. The basic themes change little from year to year: last year was tough, this year will be even tougher, and you'll be washing dishes in one of the hotels if your performance is bad. Finally, he toasts his father with warm sake and departs (Downer, 1994).

Ceremonies serve four major roles: they socialize, stabilize, reassure, and convey messages to external constituencies. Consider the example of Mary Kay Cosmetics. Several thousand people gather at the company's annual seminars to hear (now posthumous) personal messages from Mary Kay, to applaud the achievements of star salespeople, to hear success stories, and to celebrate. The ceremony brings new members into the fold and helps maintain faith, hope, and optimism in the Mary Kay family. It is a distinctive pageant and makes the Mary Kay culture accessible to outsiders, particularly consumers. Failure recedes and obstacles disappear in the "you can do it" spirit of the company symbol of the bumblebee—a creature that, according to mythical aerodynamics experts, should not be able to fly. Unaware of its limitations, it flies anyway.

Some events, like retirement dinners and welcoming events for new employees, are clearly ceremonial. Other ceremonies happen at moments of triumph or transition. When Phil Condit took over the reins of Boeing, he invited senior managers to his home for dinner. Afterward, the group gathered around a giant fire pit to tell stories about Boeing. Condit asked them to toss negative stories into the flames. It was an emblematic way to banish the dark side of the company's past (Deal and Key, 1998).

Condit resigned under pressure as Boeing's chairman in 2003 but returned as part of the crowd to witness the ceremonial roll-out of an aircraft his team had begun work on a decade earlier—the 787 Dreamliner. As the *Seattle Times* reported (July 8, 2007), "With some 15,000 people gathered Sunday inside the world's largest building—Boeing's Everett factory—and tens of thousand more watching the event live around the world—Boeing opened the hanger doors to reveal the 787 Dreamliner, the first commercial passenger plane that will have a mostly composite airframe rather than aluminum. . . . Those 15,000 employees, past and current executives, airline customers and others crowded around the new jet for an up-close look."

Condit mingled with employees to give and receive congratulations. Tom Brokaw served as master of ceremonies. Rock music roused the crowd. The event gave VIPs and politicians an opportunity to bask in the glory of a momentous accomplishment. As those who had launched every plane from the 707 through the 747 rubbed elbows and swapped tales, the roots of the past were fused with the joy of the present and the promise of tomorrow's next leap forward.

Ceremonies do not have to be as lavish as Boeing's introduction of the Dreamliner, of course. Every organization has its moments of achievement and atonement. Expressive events provide order and meaning and bind an organization or a society together.

Ceremony is equally evident in other social arenas. In the United States, political conventions select candidates, even though there is rarely much suspense about the outcome. Then follow several months in which competing candidates trade clichés. The same pageantry unfolds each election year. Rhetoric and spontaneous demonstrations are staged in advance. Campaigning is repetitious and superficial, reporters play up the skirmish of the day, and voting often seems disconnected from the main drama.

Even so, the process of electing a president is a momentous ceremony. It entails a sense of social involvement. It is an outlet for expression of discontent and enthusiasm. It stages live drama for citizens to witness and debate and gives millions of people a sense of participating in an exciting adventure. It lets candidates reassure the public that there are answers to our important questions and solutions to our vexing problems. It draws attention to common social ties and to the importance of accepting whichever candidate eventually wins (Edelman, 1977).

When properly conducted and attuned to valued myths, both ritual and ceremony fire the imagination and deepen faith; otherwise, they become cold, empty forms that people resent and avoid. They can release creativity and transform meanings, but they can also cement the status quo and block adaptation and learning. In some organizations, whining and complaining can evolve as rituals of choice. Negative symbols perpetuate evil, just as positive symbols reinforce goodness. Symbols cut both ways.

Metaphor, Humor, and Play

Metaphor, humor, and play illustrate the important "as if" quality of symbols. Metaphors make the strange familiar and the familiar strange. They capture subtle themes normal language can obscure. Consider these metaphors from managers asked to depict their agency as it is and as they hope it might become:

As It Is	As It Might Become
A maze	A well-oiled wheel
Wet noodle	Oak tree
Aggregation of tribes with competing agendas	Symphony orchestra
Three-ring circus	Championship team
A puzzle no one can put together	A smooth-running machine
Twilight zone	Utopia
Herd of cattle on the rampage	Fleet of ships heading for the same port

Metaphors compress complicated issues into understandable images, influencing our attitudes and actions. A university head who views the institution as a factory leads differently from one who conceives of it as a craft guild, shopping center, or beloved alma mater.

Humor also serves important functions. Indeed, Hansot (1979) argues that rather than asking why people use humor in organizations, we should ask why they are so serious. Humor plays a number of important roles: it integrates, expresses skepticism, contributes to flexibility and adaptiveness, and signals status. Though a classic device for distancing, humor also draws people together. It establishes solidarity and facilitates face saving. Above all, it is a way to illuminate and break frames, indicating that any single definition of a situation is arbitrary.

In most work settings, play and humor are sharply distinguished from work. Play is what people do away from work. Images of play among managers typically connote aggression, competition, and struggle ("We've got to beat them at their own game"; "We dropped the ball on that one"; "We knocked that one out of the park") rather than relaxation and fun. But if play is viewed as a state of mind (Bateson, 1972; Goffman, 1974), any activity can become playful. Play relaxes rules to explore alternatives, encouraging experimentation, flexibility, and creativity. Many remarkable innovations have been crafted by playful people at work. March (1976) suggests some guidelines for play in organizations: treat goals as hypotheses, intuition as real, hypocrisy as transition, memory as an enemy, and experience as a theory.

ORGANIZATIONS AS CULTURES

Culture: What is it? What is its role in an organization? Both questions are contested. Some argue that organizations *have* cultures; others insist that organizations *are* cultures. Schein (1992, p. 12) offers a formal definition: "a pattern of shared basic assumptions that a group learned as it solved its problems of external adaptation and integration, that has worked well enough to be considered valid and therefore to be taught to new members as the correct way to perceive, think, and feel in relation to those problems." Deal and Kennedy (1982, p. 4) portray culture more succinctly as "the way we do things around here." Culture is both a product and a process. As a product, it embodies wisdom accumulated from experience. As a process, it is renewed and re-created as newcomers learn the old ways and eventually become teachers themselves.

There is a long-standing controversy about the relationship between culture and leadership. Do leaders shape culture, or are they shaped by it? Is symbolic leadership empowering or manipulative? Another debate swirls around the link between culture and results. Do organizations with robust cultures outperform those relying on structure and strategy? Does success breed a cohesive culture, or is it the other way around? Books like Kotter and Heskett's *Corporate Culture and Performance* (1992), Collins and Porras's *Built to Last* (1994), and Collins's *Good to Great* (2001) offer impressive longitudinal evidence linking culture to the financial bottom line.

Over time, an organization develops distinctive beliefs, values, and customs. Managers who understand the significance of symbols and know how to evoke spirit and soul can shape more cohesive and effective organizations—so long as the cultural patterns are aligned with the challenges of the marketplace. To be sure, culture can become a negative force, as it did at Enron. But the three examples that follow demonstrate how a positive, cohesive culture can be fashioned and perpetuated.

BMW's Dream Factory

In 1959, BMW was in a financial hole as deep as the one General Motors and Ford have occupied in recent years (Edmunson, 2006). During the 1950s, the company misjudged the consumer market, and customers shunned two new models—one too big and pricey even for the luxury market, the other a two-seater too small and impractical for the sporty crowd. BMW almost went bankrupt and came close to being acquired by Mercedes. A wealthy shareholder stepped in and, with concessions from the unions, bailed the company out. The memory of this close call is part of BMW's lore: "Near death experiences are healthy for companies. BMW has been running scared for years" (p. 4). The near-death story is continually retold and is one of the first things newcomers learn.

Old ways are particularly vulnerable in times of crisis. BMW shucked off its top-down mentality in 1959 and took on a new mind-set to guard against making the same mistake twice. A visit to BMW's Leipzig plant shows how far the company has come. The plant's modern, artsy, open-air feeling reflects the company's cultural values and demonstrates its commitment to breaking down barriers among workers, designers, engineers, and managers. Openness encourages chance encounters and a freewheeling exchange of ideas. People "meet simply because their paths cross naturally. And they say 'Ah, glad I ran into you, I have an idea'" (Edmunson, 2006, p. 1).

At BMW, the bedrock value is innovation:

> Just about everyone working for the Bavarian automaker—from the factory floor to the design studios to the marketing department—is encouraged to speak out. Ideas bubble up freely, and there is never a penalty for proposing a new way of doing things, no matter how outlandish. Much of BMW's success stems from an entrepreneurial culture that's rare in corporate Germany, where management is usually top-down and the gulf between workers and management is vast. BMW's 100,000 employees have become a nimble network of true believers with few barriers to hinder innovation [Edmunson, 2006, pp. 1–2].

Commitment to its workers is another core value of BMW. Getting a job is not easy at a company that fields two hundred thousand applications annually. Those who pass initial screening have to survive intense interviews and a day of working in teams. The goal: to screen out those who don't fit. The lucky few who are hired are thrown in the deep end of the pool, forced to rely on colleagues to learn the ropes. But once part of the BMW workforce, workers have unparalleled job security. Layoffs, a common occurrence at places like Ford and GM, don't happen at BMW. The company is loyal to its employees, and they respond in kind.

From the start, workers are indoctrinated into the BMW Way. They are steeped "with a sense of place, history and mission. Individuals from all strata of the corporation work elbow-to-elbow, creating informal networks where they can hatch even the most unorthodox ideas for making better Bimmers or boosting profits. The average BMW buyer may not know it, but he is driving a machine born of thousands of important brain-storming sessions. BMW, in fact, may be the chattiest company ever" (Edmunson, 2006, p. 2).

Rituals are a way of life at BMW—building bonds among diverse groups, connecting employees' hearts with the company's soul, and pooling far-flung ideas for better products. After BMW acquired Rolls-Royce, an assemblage of designers, engineers, marketers, and line workers was thrown together to redesign Rolls's signature Phantom. The result was a super-luxurious best-seller. When management decided to drop the Z3, a designer persuaded some other designers and engineers to join him in an "off the books, skunk-works" effort. The outcome of their collective endeavor: the successful Z4 sports car.

The flexibility of BMW's manufacturing process allows buyers to select engine types, interior configuration, and trim, customizing almost every key feature. They can change their minds up to five hours before the vehicle is assembled—and do. The assembly line logs 170,000 alterations a month. This level of personal attention lets assemblers visualize who the driver might be. Making an identical car only every nine months creates a sense of personal touch and creativity. That's a prime reason why work at BMW has meaning beyond a paycheck. Everyone's efforts are aimed at building a distinctive automobile that an owner will be proud to drive.

The vitality and cohesiveness of the idea-driven BMW culture is reflected in the company's bottom line. From its nadir in the 1950s, BMW has grown past Mercedes to become the world's largest premium carmaker (Vella, 2006). But that growth may also be its biggest vulnerability. "Losing its culture to sheer size is a major risk" (Edmunson, 2006, p. 3). The challenge is to keep nurturing recollections of 1959 as a defense against complacency.

Continental's Cultural Transformation

Across the Atlantic, the power of symbols and drama prevailed in Gordon Bethune's turnaround of Continental Airlines, once panned as the worst air carrier in the United States. In 1994, the airline ranked dead last in on-time performance, worst in mishandling luggage, highest in customer complaints, and near the bottom in overbooking. It was losing money so fast that each of Bethune's early meetings to develop plans for reform was labeled "the last supper" (Bethune and Huler, 1999).

GREATEST HITS FROM ORGANIZATION STUDIES

Hit Number 18: Geert Hofstede, *Culture's Consequences: International Differences in Work-Related Values* (Thousand Oaks, Calif.: Sage, 1984)

Geert Hofstede pioneered research on the impact of national culture on the workplace. Although other studies, such as GLOBE (House, Hanges, Javidan, Dorfman, and Gupta, 2004), are more current, his remains the most frequently cited work.

Defining culture as "the collective programming of the mind that distinguishes the members of one human group from another" (p. 21), he focused particularly on work-related values. The heart of Hofstede's book is a survey of a large U.S. multinational company's employees. Some 117,000 surveys were collected from workers and managers in forty countries and twenty languages. Data were collected in two waves, one in 1968 and another in 1972. Hofstede then identified variables that reliably differentiated managers of various nations. He ultimately settled on four dimensions of national culture:

1. *Power distance*—A measure of power inequality between bosses and subordinates. High power-distance countries (such as the Philippines, Mexico, and Venezuela) display more autocratic relationships between bosses and subordinates than low power-distance countries (including Denmark, Israel, and Austria) that show more democratic and decentralized patterns.

2. *Uncertainty avoidance*—level of comfort with uncertainty and ambiguity. Countries high on uncertainty avoidance (Greece, Portugal, Belgium, and Japan) tend to make heavy use of structure, rules, and specialists to maintain control. Those low on the index (Hong Kong, Denmark, Sweden, and Singapore) put less emphasis on structure and are more tolerant of risk taking.

3. *Individualism*—the importance of the individual versus the collective (group, organization, or society). Countries highest on individualism (the United States, Australia, Great Britain, and Canada) put emphasis on autonomous, self-reliant individuals who care for themselves. Countries lowest on individuality (Peru, Pakistan, Colombia, and Venezuela) emphasized mutual loyalty.

4. *Masculinity-femininity*—the degree to which a culture emphasizes ambition and achievement versus caring and nurture. In countries highest in masculinity (Japan, Austria, Venezuela, Italy), men tend to feel strong pressures for success, relatively few women hold high-level positions, and job stress is high. The opposite is true in countries low in masculinity (such as Denmark, Norway, the Netherlands, and Sweden).

Hofstede argues that management practices and theories are inevitably culture-bound. Most management theory has been developed in the United States, which is culturally similar to nations where people speak English and other northern European languages, but distinct from most countries in Asia (as well as those speaking Romance languages). To Hofstede, managers and scholars have too often assumed that what works in their culture will work anywhere, an assumption that can have disastrous results.

Hofstede also explores the relationship between national and organizational culture, noting that a common culture is a powerful form of organizational glue. This is most likely to occur in multinationals in which a home country culture reigns companywide, which in turn requires that managers from outside the home country become bicultural. Many American managers who work abroad, in Hofstede's view, tend to live in American enclaves and remain both monolingual and monocultural.

Hofstede's research was limited in many ways. His sample came from only one American company (IBM), and many nations were absent (China, Russia, most of Africa and Eastern Europe). His data are now some four decades old. But no other work has been as influential (in terms of citations) in demonstrating the pervasive impact of national culture on organizations.

Bethune quickly launched a series of symbolic actions to get the company headed in a new direction:

- He removed the security cameras and opened the doors to the executive suite, previously locked and accessible only with an ID.

- He convened open houses in the executive offices with food and drink for employees. He personally led tours of his office, opening a closet door to prove that his unloved predecessor, Frank Lorenzo, was really gone.

- He sat in a different chair at each management meeting.

- He gathered up old employee manuals full of rules and regulations and led a group of employees to the parking lot for a bonfire.

- He ordered a new paint scheme for Continental's fleet. When the operations managers complained the time frame was too short, Bethune told them, "I have a Beretta at home with a fifteen-round magazine, and if you don't get those airplanes painted by July 1 I'm going to come in here and empty the clip. You're wonderful people and I love you, but you're going to get those airplanes painted or I'm going to shoot every last one of you." (As with Herb Kelleher's threat to drive an airplane over a local sheriff, recipients understood that the real message was about passion and urgency, not physical violence.)

- He invited a hundred of the airline's best customers and their spouses to his home for dinner and apologized for what they had put up with prior to 1994.

- He used metaphors to illustrate principles of cultural cohesion. An example was the watch, which, Bethune noted with a flourish, requires every part to function.

- He backed up intangible values with tangible rewards. Reliability, for example, became a core value. This meant being on time all the time. When Continental's flights hit 71 percent, each employee received a check for $65;

when the company topped all other U.S. airlines in on-time performance, each employee received $100. But the true value of the money was illustrated in stories of how it was spent, often by employees buying something for themselves or giving their kids a treat.

As a result of these and other actions, Continental began to haul in prestigious awards. The company received the J. D. Power Award for customer satisfaction in 1996 and 1997 and was named 1996 Airline of the Year. The same distinction was bestowed by *OAG (Official Airline Guide)* in 2004, along with Best Airline Based in North America and Best Executive Business Class. In 2002, the company earned spots on several of *Fortune* magazine's A lists: number two on "most admired global airlines," number thirty on "most admired global corporations," and number forty-two on "100 best companies to work for in America." The magazine designated Continental the most admired global company in 2006. Equally important, the company became profitable in 1995 and has remained so despite a highly competitive airline market and the industry's chronic economic woes.

Nordstrom's Rooted Culture

Nordstrom department stores are renowned for customer service and employee satisfaction. Customers rave about its no-hassle, no-questions-asked commitment to high-quality service: "not service the way it used to be, but service that never was" (Spector and McCarthy, 1995, p. 1). Year after year, Nordstrom has been ranked at or near the top in retail service ratings (*Business Week,* 2007).

Founder John Nordstrom was a Swedish immigrant who settled in Seattle after an odyssey across America and a brief stint looking for gold in Alaska. He and Carl Wallin, a shoemaker, opened a shoe store. Nordstrom's sons Elmer, Everett, and Lloyd joined the business. Collectively, they anchored the firm in an enduring philosophical principle: the customer is always right. The following generations of Nordstroms expanded the business while maintaining a close connection with historical roots.

The company relies on acculturated "Nordies" to induct new employees into customer service the Nordstrom way. Newcomers begin in sales, learning traditions from the ground up: "When we are at our best, our frontline people are lieutenants because they control the business. Our competition has foot soldiers on the front line and lieutenants in the back" (Spector and McCarthy, 1995, p. 106).

Nordstrom's unique commitment to customer service is heralded in its "heroics"—tales of heroes and heroines going out of their way:

- A customer fell in love with a particular pair of pleated burgundy slacks on sale at Nordstrom's downtown Seattle store. Unfortunately, the store was out of her size. The sales associate got cash from the department manager, marched across the street, bought the slacks at full price from a competitor, brought them back, and sold them to the customer at Nordstrom's reduced price (Spector and McCarthy, 1995, p. 26).

- When a customer inadvertently left her airline ticket on a Nordstrom counter, the sales associate called the airline. When that didn't work, she hopped a cab, headed for the airport, and handed the ticket to a thankful customer (Spector and McCarthy, 1995, p. 125).

- According to legend, a Nordie once refunded a customer's payment for a set of automobile tires, even though the company had never stocked tires. In 1975, Nordstrom had acquired three stores from Northern Commercial in Alaska. The customer had purchased the tires from Northern Commercial, so Nordstrom took them back—as the story goes (Spector and McCarthy, 1995, p. 27).

Nordstrom's commitment to customer service is reinforced in storewide rituals. Newcomers encounter the company's values in the initial employee orientation. For many years, they were given a 5" × 8" card labeled the "Nordstrom Employee Handbook," which listed only one rule: *Use your sound judgment in all situations.* Although the no-rule rule is no longer part of the company's orientation, the emphasis on pleasing the customer is still dominant. At staff meetings, sales associates compare and discuss sales techniques and role-play customer encounters.

Periodic ceremonies reinforce the company's cherished values. From the company's early years, the Nordstrom family sponsored summer picnics and Christmas dance parties, and the company continues to create occasions to celebrate customer service: "We do crazy stuff. Monthly store pow-wows serve as a kind of revival meeting, where customer letters of appreciation are read and positive achievements are recognized, while co-workers whoop and cheer for one another. Letters of complaint about Nordstrom customer service are also read over the intercom (omitting the names of offending salespeople)" (Spector and McCarthy, 1995, pp. 120, 129).

At one spirited sales meeting, a regional manager asked all present to call out their sales targets for the year, which he posted on a large chart. Then the regional manager uncovered his own target for each person. Anyone whose target was below the regional manager's was roundly booed. Those whose individual goals were higher were acclaimed with enthusiastic cheers (Spector and McCarthy, 1995).

The delicate balance of competition, cooperation, and customer service has served Nordstrom well. Its stellar identity has created a sterling image. In a sermon titled "The Gospel According to Nordstrom," one California minister "praised the retailer for carrying out the call of the gospel in ways more consistent and caring than we sometimes do in the church" (Spector and McCarthy, 1995, p. 21).

But symbolic luster must be persistently buffed to prevent the accumulating tarnish of time and change. Even though the firm continues to do well in surveys, there have been sporadic complaints in recent years about rude clerks and poor service, suggesting that Nordstrom might be slipping. It can happen quickly. Starbucks, purveyor of coffee to the world, is also known for its heartfelt, high-spirited culture. A 2007 memo from founder and chairman Howard Schultz sounded a warning about the risk of cultural slippage resulting from growth and technological change.

Starbucks had been growing at a phenomenal rate (from one hundred to thirteen thousand stores in ten years) and had recently automated its espresso makers and begun storing its coffee beans in airtight containers. These decisions made rational sense but "sacrificed the 'romance and theater' of the coffee shop experience for efficiency and profit" (Neil, 2007, p. 46). Schultz wrote: "Some people even call our stores sterile, cookie cutter, no longer reflecting the passion our partners feel about our coffee. . . . Stores no longer have the soul of the past and reflect a chain of stores vs. the warm feeling of a neighborhood store" (Neil, 2007, p. 46). His memo called for stopping the cultural drift: "It's time to get back to the core and make the changes that are necessary to evoke the heritage, the tradition, and passion we all have for the Starbucks' experience" (Wayne, 2007).

SUMMARY

In contrast to traditional views emphasizing rationality, the symbolic frame highlights the tribal aspect of contemporary organizations. It centers on complexity and ambiguity and emphasizes the idea that symbols mediate the meaning of work and anchor culture. An organization's culture is built over time as members develop beliefs, values, practices, and artifacts that seem to work and are transmitted to new recruits. Defined as "the way we do things around here," culture anchors an organization's identity and sense of itself.

Myths, values, and vision bring cohesiveness, clarity, and direction in the presence of confusion and mystery. Heroes and heroines are role models for people to admire and emulate. Stories carry values and serve as powerful modes of communication and instruction. Rituals and ceremonies provide scripts for celebrating success and facing calamity. Metaphors, humor, and play offer escape from the tyranny of facts and logic; they stimulate creative alternatives to time-worn choices. Symbolic forms and activities are the basic building blocks of culture, accumulated over time to shape an organization's unique identity and character. In *The Feast of Fools,* Cox (1969, p. 13) summarizes: "Our links to yesterday and tomorrow depend also on the aesthetic, emotional, and symbolic aspects of human life—on saga, play, and celebration. Without festival and fantasy, man would not really be a historical being at all."

NOTE

1. Personal observation by author. Chancellor Joe B. Wyatt's opening convocation, Vanderbilt University, 1989.

Culture in Action

Prescriptions and theories for better teamwork often miss the deeper secret of how groups and teams reach the state of grace and peak performance. Former Visa CEO Dee Hock captured the heart of the issue: "In the field of group endeavor, you will see incredible events in which the group performs far beyond the sum of its individual talents. It happens in the symphony, in the ballet, in the theater, in sports, and equally in business. It is easy to recognize and impossible to define. It is a mystique. It cannot be achieved without immense effort, training, and cooperation, but effort, training, and cooperation alone rarely create it" (quoted in Schlesinger, Eccles, and Gabarro, 1983, p. 173).

With a population of only slightly more than two million people in the 1770s, how was the United States able to produce an extraordinary leadership team that included John Adams, Benjamin Franklin, Thomas Jefferson, and George Washington? In World War II, did anyone believe that Britain's Royal Air Force could defend the island nation against Hitler's Luftwaffe? As Winston Churchill later commented, "Never have so many owed so much to so few." Did anyone expect the Iraqi soccer team to take home the Asian Cup in 2007? With all the turmoil and strife in Iraq, it is hard to picture the country even fielding a team. And how could two graduate students who came from opposite ends of the earth

279

(Michigan and Moscow), and who initially didn't like one another, create a company whose name—Google—would become a household word?

Are such peak performances simply a great mystery—beautiful when they happen but no more predictable or controllable than California's next earthquake? In this chapter, we analyze a well-documented team that achieved a state of transcendence. The story takes us directly to the symbolic roots of flow, spirit, and magic.

THE EAGLE GROUP'S SOURCES OF SUCCESS

Tracy Kidder, in *The Soul of a New Machine* (1981), wrote a dazzling account of a small group of engineers at Data General who created a new computer in record time in the 1970s. Despite scant resources and limited support, the Eagle Group outperformed all other Data General divisions to produce a new state-of-the-art machine. The technology is now antiquated, but lessons from how they pulled it off are as current as ever.[1]

Why did the Eagle Group succeed? So many groups of engineers—or educators, physicians, executives, or graduate students—start out with high hopes but falter and fail. Were the project members extraordinarily talented? Not really. Each was highly skilled, but there were equally talented engineers working on other Data General projects. Were team members always treated with dignity and respect? Quite the contrary. As one engineer noted, "No one ever pats anyone on the back" (p. 179). Instead, the group experienced what they called mushroom management: "Put 'em in the dark, feed 'em shit, and watch 'em grow" (p. 109). For over a year, group members jeopardized their health, their families, and their careers: "I'm flat out by definition. I'm a mess. It's terrible. It's a lot of fun" (p. 119).

Were financial rewards a motivating factor? Group members said explicitly that they did not work for money. Nor were they motivated by fame. Heroic efforts were rewarded neither by formal appreciation nor by official applause. The group quietly dissolved shortly after completing the new computer, and most members moved unrecognized to other parts of Data General, or to other companies. Their experience fits later successes at Cisco Systems, where Paulson concludes, "All personnel are driven by the desire to be a part of a winning organization" (2001, p. 187).

Perhaps the group's structure accounted for its success. Were its members pursuing well-defined and laudable goals? The group leader, Tom West, offered the precept that "not everything worth doing is worth doing well." Pushed to translate his maxim, he elaborated, "If you can do a quick-and-dirty job and it works, do it" (p. 119). Did the group have clear and well-coordinated roles and relationships? According to Kidder, it kept no meaningful charts, graphs, or organization tables. One of the group's engineers put it bluntly: "The whole management structure—anyone in Harvard Business School would have barfed" (p. 116).

Can the political frame unravel the secret of the group's phenomenal performance? Perhaps group members were motivated more by power than by money: "There's a big high in here somewhere for me that I don't fully understand. Some of it's a raw power trip. The reason I work is because I win" (p. 179). They were encouraged to circumvent formal channels to advance group interests: "If you can't get what you need from some manager at your level in another department, go to his boss—that's the way to get things done" (p. 191). Group members were also unusually direct and confrontational: "Feeling sorely provoked, [David] Peck one day said to this engineer, 'You're an asshole.' Ordered by his boss to apologize, Peck went to the man he had insulted, looking sheepish, and said, 'I'm sorry you're an asshole'" (p. 224).

The group was highly competitive with others in the company: "There's a thing you learn at Data General, if you work here for any period of time . . . that nothing ever happens unless you push it" (p. 111). They also competed with one another. Their "tube wars" are a typical example. Carl Alsing, head of a subgroup known as the Microkids, returned from lunch one day to find that all his files had become empty shells: the names were there, but the contents had vanished. It took him an hour to find where the real files were hidden. Alsing counterattacked by creating an encrypted file and tantalizing the team, "There's erotic writing in there and if you can find it, you can read it" (p. 107).

Here we begin to encounter the secrets of the group's success. The tube wars—and other exchanges among group members—were more than power struggles. They were a form of play that released tensions, created bonds, and contributed to an unusual group spirit. A shared and cohesive culture, rather than a clear, well-defined structure, was the invisible force that gave the team its drive.

From the Eagle Group's experience we can distill several important tenets of the symbolic frame that are broadly applicable to groups and teams:

- How someone becomes a group member is important.

- Diversity supports a team's competitive advantage.

- Example, not command, holds a team together.
- A specialized language fosters cohesion and commitment.
- Stories carry history and values and reinforce group identity.
- Humor and play reduce tension and encourage creativity.
- Ritual and ceremony lift spirits and reinforce values.
- Informal cultural players make contributions disproportionate to their formal role.
- Soul is the secret of success.

Becoming a Member

Joining a team involves more than a rational decision. It is a mutual choice marked by some form of ritual. In the Eagle Group, the process of becoming a member was called "signing up." When interviewing recruits, Alsing conveyed the message that they were volunteering to climb Mount Everest without a rope despite lacking the "right stuff" to keep up with other climbers. When the new recruits protested they wanted to climb Mount Everest anyway, Alsing told them they would first have to find out if they were good enough. After the selections had been made, Alsing summed it up this way: "It was kind of like recruiting for a suicide mission. You're gonna die, but you're gonna die in glory" (p. 66).

Through the signing-up ritual, an engineer became part of a special effort and agreed to forsake family, friends, and health to accomplish the impossible. It was a sacred declaration: "I want to do this job and I'll give it my heart and soul" (p. 63).

Diversity Is a Competitive Advantage

Though nearly all the group's members were engineers, each had unique skills and style. Tom West, the group's leader, was by reputation a highly talented technical debugger. He was also aloof and unapproachable, the "Prince of Darkness." Steve Wallach, the group's computer architect, was a highly creative maverick. According to Kidder (p. 75), before accepting West's invitation to join the group, he went to Edson de Castro, the president of Data General, to find out precisely what he'd be working on:

"Okay," Wallach said, "what the fuck do you want?"

"I want a thirty-two-bit Eclipse," de Castro told him.

"If we can do this, you won't cancel it on us?" Wallach asked. "You'll leave us alone?"

"That's what I want, a thirty-two," de Castro assured him, "a thirty-two-bit Eclipse and no mode bit."

Wallach signed up. His love of literature, stories, and verse provided a literary substructure for the technical architecture of the new machine. Alsing, the group's microcode expert, was as warm and approachable as West was cold and remote. He headed the Microkids, the group of young engineers who programmed the new machine. Ed Rasala, Alsing's counterpart, headed the Hardy Boys, the group's hardware design team. Rasala was a solid, hyperactive, risk-taking, detail-oriented mechanic: "I may not be the smartest designer in the world, a CPU giant, but I'm dumb enough to stick with it to the end" (p. 142).

Diversity among the group's top engineers was institutionalized in specialized functions. One engineer, for example, was viewed as a creative genius who liked inventing an esoteric idea and then trying to make it work. Another was a craftsman who enjoyed fixing things, working tirelessly until the last bug had been tracked down and eliminated. West buffered the team from upper management interference and served as a group "devil." Wallach created the original design. Alsing and the Microkids created "a synaptic language that would fuse the physical machine with the programs that would tell it what to do" (p. 60). Rasala and the Hardy Boys built the physical circuitry. Understandably, there was tension among these diverse individuals and groups. Harnessing the resulting energy galvanized the parts into a working team.

Example, Not Command

Wallach's design generated modest coordination for Eagle's autonomous individuals and groups. The group had some rules but paid little attention to them. De Castro, the CEO, was viewed as a distant god. He was never there physically, but his presence was always felt. West, the group's official leader, rarely interfered with the actual work, nor was he particularly visible in the laboratory. One Sunday morning in January, however, when the team was supposed to be resting, a Hardy Boy happened to come by the lab and found West sitting in front of one of the prototypes. The next Sunday, West wasn't in the lab, and after that they rarely saw him. For a long time he did not hint that he might again put his hands inside the machine.

West contributed primarily by causing problems for the engineers to solve and making mundane events and issues appear special. He created an almost endless series of "brushfires" so he could inspire his staff to put them out. He had a genius for finding drama and romance in everyday routine. Other members of the group's formal leadership followed de Castro and West in creating ambiguity, encouraging inventiveness, and leading by example. Heroes of the moment gave inspiration and direction. Subtle and implicit signals rather than concrete and explicit guidelines or decisions held the group together and directed it toward a common goal.

Specialized Language

Every group develops words, phrases, and metaphors unique to its circumstances. A specialized language both reflects and shapes a group's culture. Shared language allows team members to communicate easily, with minimal misunderstanding. To the members of the Eagle Group, for example, a *kludge* was a poor, inelegant solution—such as a machine with loose wires held together with duct tape. A *canard* was anything false. *Fundamentals* were the source of enlightened thinking. The word *realistically* typically prefaced flights of fantasy. "Give me a *core dump*" meant tell me your thoughts. A *stack overflow* meant that an engineer's memory compartments were too full, and a *one-stack-deep mind* indicated shallow thinking. "Eagle" was a label for the project, while "Hardy Boys" and "Microkids" gave identity to the subgroups. Two prototype computers were named Woodstock and Trixie.

A shared language binds a group together and is a visible sign of membership. It also sets a group apart and reinforces unique values and beliefs. Asked about the Eagle Group's headquarters, West observed, "It's basically a cattle yard. What goes on here is not part of the real world." Asked for an explanation, West remarked, "Mm-hmm. The language is different" (p. 50).

Stories Carry History, Values, and Group Identity

In high-performing organizations and groups, stories keep traditions alive and provide examples to guide everyday behavior. Group lore extended and reinforced the subtle yet powerful influence of Eagle's leaders—some of them distant and remote. West's reputation as a "troublemaker" and an "excitement junkie" was conveyed through stories about computer wars of the mid-1970s. Alsing said of West that he was always prepared and never raised his voice, but conveyed intensity and the conviction that he knew the way out of whatever storm was currently battering the group. West also had the skills of a good politician. He knew how to develop agendas, build alliances, and negotiate with potential supporters or opponents. When he had a particular objective in mind, he would first go upstairs to sign up senior executives. Then he went to people one at a time, telling them the bosses liked the idea and asking them to come on board: "They say, 'Ah, it sounds like you're just gonna put a bag on the side of the Eclipse,' and Tom'll give 'em his little grin and say, 'It's more than that, we're really gonna build this fucker and it's gonna be fast as greased lightning.' He tells them, 'We're gonna do it by April'" (p. 44).

Stories of persistence, irreverence, and creativity encouraged others to go beyond themselves, adding new exploits and tales to Eagle's lore. For example, as the group neared completion, a debugging problem threatened the entire project. Jim Veres, one of the engineers, worked day and night to find the error. Ken Holberger, one of the Hardy Boys, drove to work early one morning, pondering the state of the project and wondering if it would ever get done. He was awakened from his reverie by an unexpected scene as he entered the lab. "A great heap of paper lies on the floor, a continuous sheet of computer paper streaming out of the carriage at [the] system console. Stretched out, the sheet would run across the room and back again several times. You could fit a fairly detailed description of American history . . . on it. Veres sits in the midst of this chaos, the picture of the scholar. He's examined it all. He turns to Holberger. 'I found it,' he says" (p. 207).

Humor and Play

Groups often focus single-mindedly on the task at hand, shunning anything not directly work-related. Seriousness replaces godliness as a cardinal virtue. Effective teams balance seriousness with play and humor. Surgical teams, cockpit crews, and many other groups have learned that joking and playful banter are essential sources of invention and team spirit. Humor releases tension and helps resolve issues arising from day-to-day routines as well as from sudden emergencies.

Play among the members of the Eagle project was an innate part of the group process. When Alsing wanted the Microkids to learn how to manipulate the computer known as Trixie, he made up a game. As the Microkids came on board, he told each of them to figure out how to write a program in Trixie's assembly language. The program had to fetch and print contents of a file stored inside the computer. The Microkids went to work, learned their way around the machine, and felt great satisfaction—until Alsing's perverse sense of humor tripped them up. When they finally found the elusive file, they were greeted with the message "Access Denied." Through such play, the Microkids learned to use the computer, coalesced into a team, and practiced negotiating their new technical environment. They also learned that their playful leader valued creativity.

Humor was a continuous thread as the team struggled with its formidable task. Humor often stretched the boundaries of good taste, but that too was part of the group's identity:

> [Alsing] drew his chair up to his terminal and typed a few letters—a short code that put him in touch with Trixie, the machine reserved for the use of his microcoding team. "We've anthropomorphized Trixie to a ridiculous extent," he said.
>
> He typed, WHO.
>
> On the dark-blue screen of the cathode-ray tube, with alacrity, an answer appeared: CARL.
>
> WHERE, typed Alsing.
>
> IN THE ROAD, WHERE ELSE! Trixie replied.
>
> HOW.
>
> ERROR, read the message on the screen.
>
> "Oh, yeah, I forgot," said Alsing, and he typed, PLEASE HOW.
>
> THAT'S FOR US TO KNOW AND YOU TO FIND OUT.
>
> Alsing seemed satisfied with that, and he typed, WHEN.
>
> RIGHT FUCKING NOW, wrote the machine.
>
> WHY, wrote Alsing.
>
> BECAUSE WE LIKE TO CARL [pp. 90–91].

Throughout the year and a half it took to build their new machine, engineers of the Eagle project relied on play and humor as a source of relaxation, stimulation, enlightenment, and spiritual renewal.

Ritual and Ceremony

Rituals and ceremonies are expressive occasions. As parentheses in an ordinary workday, they enclose and define special forms of behavior. What occurs on the surface is not nearly as important as the deeper meaning communicated beneath visible behavior. Despite the stereotype of narrowly task-focused engineers with little time for anything nonrational, the Eagle Group understood the importance of symbolic activity. From the beginning, leadership encouraged ritual and ceremony.

As one example, Rasala, head of the Hardy Boys, established a rule requiring that changes in the boards of the prototype be updated each morning. This activity allowed efforts to be coordinated formally. More important, the daily update was an occasion for informal communication, bantering, and gaining a sense of the whole. The engineers disliked the daily procedure, so Rasala changed it to once a week—on Saturday. He made it a point always to be there himself.

Eagle's leaders met regularly, but their meetings focused more on symbolic issues than on substance. "'We could be in a lot of trouble here,' West might say, referring to some current problem. And Wallach or Rasala or Alsing would reply, 'You mean you could be in a lot of trouble, right, Tom?' It was Friday, they were going home soon, and relaxing, they could half forget that they would be coming back to work tomorrow" (p. 132). Friday afternoon is a customary time to wind down and relax. Honoring such a tradition was all the more important for a group whose members often worked all week and then all weekend. West made himself available to anyone who wanted to chat. Near the end of the day, before hurrying home, he would lean back in his chair with his office door open and entertain any visitor.

In addition to recurring rituals, the Eagle Group convened intermittent ceremonies to raise their spirits and reinforce their sense of shared mission. Toward the end of the project, Alsing instigated a ceremony to trigger a burst of renewed energy for the final push. The festivities called attention to the values of creativity, hard work, and teamwork. A favorite pretext for parties was presentation of the Honorary Microcoder Awards that Alsing and the Microcoder Team instituted. Not to be outdone, the Hardy Boys cooked up the PAL Awards (named for the programmable array logic chips used in the machines). The first was presented after work at a local establishment called the Cain Ridge Saloon. The citation read as follows (p. 250):

HONORARY PAL AWARD

In recognition of unsolicited contributions to the advancement of Eclipse hardware above and beyond the normal call of duty, we hereby convey unto you our thanks and congratulations on achieving this "high" honor.

The same values and spirit were reinforced again and again in a continued cycle of celebratory events:

> Chuck Holland [Alsing's main submanager] handed out his own special awards to each member of the Microteam, the Under Extraordinary Pressure Awards. They looked like diplomas. There was one for Neal Firth, "who gave us a computer before the hardware guys did," and one to Betty Shanahan, "for putting up with a bunch of creepy guys." After dispensing the Honorary Microcoder Awards to almost every possible candidate, the Microteam instituted the All-Nighter Award. The first of these went to Jim Guyer, the citation ingeniously inserted under the clear plastic coating of an insulated coffee cup [p. 250].

The Contribution of Informal Cultural Players

Alsing was the main organizer and instigator of parties. He was also the Eagle Group's conscience and nearly everyone's confidant. For a time when he was still in college, Alsing had wanted to become a psychologist. He adopted that sort of role now. He kept track of his team's technical progress, but was more visible as the social director of the Microteam, and often of the entire Eclipse Group. Fairly early in the project, Chuck Holland had complained, "Alsing's hard to be a manager for, because he goes around you a lot and tells your people to do something else." But Holland also conceded, "The good thing about him is that you can go and talk to him. He's more of a regular guy than most managers" (p. 105).

Every group or organization has a "priest" or "priestess" who ministers to spiritual needs. Informally, these people hear confessions, give blessings, maintain traditions, encourage ceremonies, and intercede in matters of gravest importance. Alsing did all these things and, like the tribal priest, acted as a counterpart to and interpreter of the intentions of the chief:

> West warned him several times, "If you get too close to the people who work for you, Alsing, you're gonna get burned." But West didn't interfere, and he soon stopped issuing warnings.
>
> One evening, while alone with West in West's office, Alsing said: "Tom, the kids think you're an ogre. You don't even say hello to them."
>
> West smiled and replied. "You're doing fine, Alsing" [pp. 109–110].

The duties of Rosemarie Seale, the group's secretary, also went well beyond formal boundaries. If Alsing was the priest, she was the mother superior. She did all the usual secretarial chores—answering the phones, preparing documents, and constructing budgets. But she found particular joy in serving as a kind of den mother who solved minor crises that arose almost daily. When new members came on, it was Rosemarie Seale who worried about finding them a desk and some pencils. When paychecks went astray, she would track them down and get them to their intended recipients. She liked the job, she said, because she felt that she was doing something important.

In any group, a network of informal players deals with human issues outside formal channels. On the Eagle project, their efforts were encouraged, appreciated, and rewarded outside the formal chain of command; they helped keep the project on track.

Soul Is the Secret of Success

The symbolic side of the Eagle Group was the real secret of its success. Its soul, or culture, created a new machine: "Ninety-eight percent of the thrill comes from knowing that the thing you designed works, and works almost the way you expected it would. If that happens, part of you is in that machine" (p. 273). All the members of the Eagle Group put something of themselves into the new computer. Individual efforts went well beyond the job and were supported by a way of life that encouraged each person to commit to doing something of significance. This commitment was elicited through the ritual of signing up and then maintained and accentuated by shared diversity, exceptional leaders, common language, stories, rituals, ceremonies, play, and humor. In the best sense of the word, the Eagle Group was a team, and the efforts of the individual members were knitted together by a cohesive culture. Symbolic elements were at the heart of the group's success.

The experience of the Eagle Group is not unusual. After extensive research on high-performing groups, Vaill (1982) concluded that spirit was at the core of every such group he studied. Members of such groups consistently "felt the spirit," a feeling essential to the meaning and value of their work. Bennis could have been writing about the Eagle Group when he concluded, "All Great Groups believe that they are on a mission from God, that they could change the world, make a dent in the universe. They are obsessed with their work. It becomes not a job but a fervent quest. That belief is what brings the necessary cohesion and energy to their work" (1997, p. 1).

More and more teams and organizations, like the Eagle project, now realize that culture, soul, and spirit are the wellspring of high performance. The U.S. Air Force, in the aftermath of the Vietnam War, embarked on a vigorous effort to reaffirm traditions and rebuild its culture. "Cohesion is a principle of war" was added to the list of core values. Project Warrior brought heroes—living and dead—forward as visible examples of the right stuff. Rituals were revitalized and reinforced. For example, the Air Force instituted a "reblue-ing" ceremony to encourage recommitment to its traditions and values.

Countless other organizations have taken similar steps. Mitsubishi, with more than twenty-five thousand products ranging from "noodles to space satellites" (Lifson and Takagi, 1981, p. 11), uses an elaborate entrance ceremony for newly hired employees as part of its effort to reinforce a corporate culture that stresses professionalism, cooperation, and entrepreneurship. Jan Carlzon revitalized the culture of the Scandinavian Air System around the precepts that every encounter between a customer and an SAS employee was a "moment of truth" and that SAS "flies people, not planes" (Carlzon, 1987, p. 27). The commitment at Outback Steakhouse to "No rules, just right" has distinguished the company in the intensely competitive restaurant industry. Instilling in employees the theme of creating a cheerful, comfortable, enjoyable, and fun atmosphere has made the restaurant chain a huge success in an industry littered with failures (Taylor, Ramaya, and Puia, 2003).

SUMMARY

Symbolic perspectives question traditional views that building a team mainly means finding the right people and designing an appropriate structure. The essence of high performance is spirit. If we were to banish play, ritual, ceremony, and myth, we would destroy teamwork, not enhance it. There are many signs that contemporary organizations are at a critical juncture because of a crisis of meaning and faith. Managers wonder how to build team spirit when turnover is high, resources are tight, and people worry about losing their jobs. Such questions are important, but by themselves they limit managerial imagination and divert attention from deeper issues of faith and purpose. Managers are inescapably accountable for budget and bottom line; they have to respond to individual needs, legal requirements, and economic pressures. But they can serve a deeper and more durable function if they recognize that team building at its heart is a spiritual undertaking. It is both a search for the spirit within and creation of a community of believers united by shared faith and shared culture. Peak performance emerges as a team discovers its soul.

NOTE

1. Unless otherwise attributed, page number citations in this chapter are to Kidder's book.

Organization as Theater

Theater as an activity, as a staging of reality, depends on the ability of the audience to frame what they experience. It depends precisely on the audience recognizing, being aware, that they are an audience; they are witnesses to, not participants in, a performance. It depends further on a distinction between actors and the parts they play—characters may die on stage, but actors will live to take a bow. Finally, theater depends on a recognition that performances play with reality in such a way as to turn the taken-for-granted into a plausible appearance.

—Mangham and Overington, 1987, p. 49

All the world's a stage, And all the men and women merely players." So wrote Shakespeare some four hundred years ago, capturing an enduring truth we sometimes neglect in our modern love affair with facts and logic. Much of human behavior is aimed at getting things done, and the assumption of linear causality works when the connection between means and ends is clear and measurable. But the logic falters when results are hard to produce and pin down. A factory rises or falls on what it produces. But what about a church or temple? Budget and congregation size are measurable, but souls saved and lives enriched are elusive. Instead, shared faith and liturgy tie believers together and bestow legitimacy. As in theater, performance and appearance matter more than data and logic.

Even in technical environments, a dramaturgical view offers enlightenment. The story of the U.S. Navy's Polaris missile system is a fascinating example of show business at work. In its time, the project was heralded as an exemplar of effective, efficient government work. One of its attributes was reliance on modern management techniques such as PERT (Program Evaluation Review Techniques) charts and PPBS (Program Planning and Budgeting Systems)—both better known by their acronyms than by their names. The methods were embodied in specialist roles, technical divisions, management meetings, and the Special Projects Office. In the wake of the project's success—on time and under budget—analysts gave credit to the project's innovative management approach. The admiral in charge was recognized for bringing modern management techniques to the U.S. Navy. A team of visiting British experts recommended PERT to their Admiralty.

But a later study by Sapolsky (1972) revealed a symbolic explanation for the project's accomplishments. Management innovations were highly visible but only marginally connected to the actual work. Specialists' activities were loosely linked to other elements of the project. The plans and charts produced by the technical division were mostly ignored. Management meetings served as public arenas to chide poor performers and to stoke the project's religious fervor. The Special Projects Office served as an official briefing area. Visiting dignitaries were regaled with impressive diagrams and charts mostly unrelated to the project's progress. Upon its visit, the team from the British Navy apparently surmised all this—and still recommended a similar approach back home (Sapolsky, 1972).

Instead of serving intended rational purposes, modern management techniques contributed to a saga that built external legitimacy and support and kept critics at bay. This myth afforded breathing space for work to go forward and elevated participants' spirits and self-confidence. The Polaris story demonstrates the virtues of drama in engaging the attention and appreciation of both internal and external audiences: "An alchemist's combination of whirling computers, bright-colored charts, and fast-talking public relations officers gave the Special Projects Office a truly effective management system. It mattered not whether the parts of the system functioned, or even existed. It mattered only that certain people, for a certain period of time, believed that they did" (Sapolsky, 1972, p. 129).

Of course, not all theater has a happy ending. The dramatic stage features tragedies as well as triumphs. U2's music video "The Saints Are Coming" demonstrates the power of drama in driving home the meaning of an experience. The video, which focuses on the effects of Hurricane Katrina, opens with scenes of the storm's traumatic aftermath: New Orleans under water, survivors trapped on roofs pleading for help, the horror of conditions at the Superdome, widespread devastation. The music's lyrics plaintively call for the next act: When will aid arrive?

CNN news flashes appear periodically on the screen below images of the ravaged city, showing troops redeployed to the city from Iraq and U.S. Air Force aid missions. With the melancholic lyrics as musical background, the video shows swarms of Black Hawk helicopters arriving to pluck victims from roofs, and larger helicopters and Harrier fighters dropping food and medical supplies. The video fades and a large sign appears: "Not as seen on TV."

The U2 video packs a wallop for several reasons: Bono himself is a heroic symbol on the world stage. The opening acts reveal the pathos all Americans observed initially. The "troops to the rescue" imagery conveys what everyone wanted to see; the final scene transports us back to what viewers actually saw on their television sets.

During previous hurricanes, FEMA had been cast as a heroic rescuer. The script was clear. Hurricane hits, bringing devastation and suffering. FEMA arrives with symbolic fanfare to dispense aid and hope to victims. A world audience applauds the performance. In New Orleans, the drama went off-track. The hero missed the show. The audience waited for an appearance that never came— or came too late. The once-heroic agency was transformed into an inept performer in a bad play.

The juxtaposed theatrical masks of comedy and tragedy capture the different dramas played out by Polaris and FEMA. Polaris capitalized on a theatrical presentation to produce a smash hit. FEMA blew its performance and dismayed its audience.

The symbolic frame recasts organizational structures and processes as secular drama that expresses our fears, joys, and expectations. Theater arouses emotions and kindles our spirit or reveals our fears. It reduces bewilderment and soothes open wounds. It provides a shared basis for understanding the present and imagining a more promising tomorrow. Dramaturgical and institutional theorists have explored the role of theater in organizations, and we begin this chapter by discussing their views. We then look at structure as theater and do the same with a number of organizational processes.

DRAMATURGICAL AND INSTITUTIONAL THEORY

Institutional theory is a recent addition to the management literature that draws on ideas from earlier dramaturgical theories. We can identify two dramaturgical traditions (Boje, Luhman, and Cunliffe, 2003), one represented by the work of Erving Goffman (1959, 1974), who pioneered in use of theater as a metaphor for understanding organizations, and the other by the work of Kenneth Burke (1937, 1945, 1972), who drew his inspiration from philosophy and literary criticism. Goffman approached organizations *as if* they were theatrical; Burke saw them *as* theater. Despite their differences, both theorists opened a window for seeing organizations in a new way: "Most of our organizational life is carefully scripted, we play out our scenes in organizationally approved dress codes and play the game by acceptable roles of conduct" (Boje, Luhman, and Cunliffe, 2003, p. 4).

Whereas dramaturgical theorists focus on social interaction among individuals and on internal situations, institutional scholars extend theatrical examples like Polaris and FEMA to the interface between organizations and their publics: "In technical organizations, the development of a rational plan is a prelude to the reconstruction and reintegration of a pattern of production activities. In institutionalized organizations, the creation of a rational plan constitutes a dramaturgical alternative to actual changes. Plans are regarded as ends in themselves—as evidence that we are a humane and scientific people who have brought yet another problem under rational control" (Meyer and Rowan, 1983a, p. 126).

DiMaggio and Powell, for example, conclude that in some contexts organizations worry more about how innovations appear than what they add to effectiveness: "New practices become infused with value beyond the technical requirements of the task at hand. . . . As an innovation spreads, a threshold is reached beyond which adoption provides legitimacy rather than improves performance" (1983, p. 142). Staw and Epstein (2000) present evidence that adoption of modern management techniques accentuates a company's legitimacy and heightens CEO compensation, even if the methods are not fully implemented. Economic performance does not improve, but perceptions of innovativeness and confidence in management rise.

Institutional theory is not without its critics (see Scott and Davis, 2007). But the ideas provide a counterweight to traditional views of organizations as closed, rational systems. In such views, functional demands shape social architecture. The environment serves as a source of raw materials and a market for finished products. Efficiency, internal control of the means of production, and economic performance are key concerns. External fluctuations and production uncertainties are buffered by rational devices such as forecasting, stockpiling, leveling peaks and valleys of supply and demand, and growth (so as to get more leverage over the environment).

Institutional theorists present a dramaturgical retake on rational imagery. Organizations, particularly those with vague goals and weak technologies, cannot seal themselves off from external events and pressures. They are constantly buffeted by larger social, political, and economic trends. The challenge is sustaining isomorphism—that is, schools need to look like schools and churches like churches in order to project legitimacy and engender support, faith, and hope among constituents. Structure and processes must reflect widely held myths and expectations. When production and results are hard to measure, correct appearance and presentation become the prevailing gauge of effectiveness.

GREATEST HITS FROM ORGANIZATION STUDIES

Hit Number 1: Paul J. DiMaggio and Walter W. Powell, "The Iron Cage Revisited: Institutional Isomorphism and Collective Rationality in Organizational Fields," *American Sociological Review,* Apr. 1983, *48*, 147–160

At the top of our list of greatest hits (up from third place in the last edition) is an article by Paul J. DiMaggio and Walter W. Powell that parallels our view of organization as theater. *Isomorphism,* as DiMaggio and Powell use the word, refers to processes that cause organizations to become more like other organizations, particularly members of the same "organizational field." The authors define an organizational field as a set of organizations that "constitute a recognized area of institutional life: key suppliers, resource and product consumers, regulatory agencies, and other organizations that produce similar services or products" (p. 148). This is similar to the concept of an organizational ecosystem, discussed in Chapter Eleven. As an example, think about public schools. They are like each other but unlike most other kinds of organization. They have similar buildings, classrooms, curricula, staffing patterns, gyms, and parent-teacher organizations. The structural frame explains these similarities as resulting from the need to align structure with goals, task, and technology. DiMaggio and Powell counter that isomorphism occurs for reasons unrelated to efficiency or effectiveness.

They describe three kinds of isomorphism: coercive, mimetic, and normative. Coercive isomorphism occurs when organizations become more similar in response to outside pressures or requirements. For example, MBA programs tend to have similar admission requirements, curricula, and faculty credentials because so many of them are accredited by the same body using the same standards. Mimetic isomorphism occurs when one organization simply copies another, as when a university of modest reputation adopts a set of freshman requirements borrowed from those at Harvard or Yale. To DiMaggio and Powell imitation is particularly likely in the presence of fuzzy goals and uncertain technology. When uncertainty makes it hard to prove one approach better than another, imitation saves time and may buy legitimacy.

Normative isomorphism, the third type, occurs because professionals (such as lawyers, doctors, engineers, and teachers) bring shared ideas, values, and norms from their training to the workplace. DiMaggio and Powell argue that professionally trained individuals are becoming more numerous and predominant. Managers with MBAs from accredited business schools carry shared values, beliefs, and practices wherever they go. Latest ideas from business schools may or may not produce better results, but they spread rapidly because the newly minted professionals believe in them.

The primary benefit of isomorphism is to improve an organization's image rather than its products and services: "Each of the institutional isomorphic processes can be expected to proceed in the absence of evidence that they increase internal organizational efficiency. To the extent that organizational effectiveness is enhanced, the reason will often be that organizations are rewarded for being similar to other organizations in their fields. This similarity can make it easier for organizations to transact with other organizations, to attract career-minded staff, to be acknowledged as legitimate and reputable, and to fit into administrative categories that define eligibility for public and private grants and contracts" (p. 153).

The idea that presentation can be more important than tangible results may seem heretical. Such heresy can easily lead to cynicism, undercutting confidence in organizations and undermining faith and morale for those struggling to make a difference. Skepticism is spawned mainly by rationalists who champion a tidy cause-and-effect world where concrete outcomes matter most. The symbolic frame offers a more hopeful interpretation. Institutionalized structures, activities, and events become expressive components of organizational theater. They create ongoing drama that entertains, creates meaning, and portrays the organization to itself and outsiders. They undergird life's meaning. Geertz observed this phenomenon in Balinese pageants, where "the carefully crafted and scripted, assiduously enacted ritualism of court culture was . . . 'not merely the drapery of political order but its substance'" (Mangham and Overington, 1987, p. 39).

ORGANIZATIONAL STRUCTURE AS THEATER

Recall that the structural frame depicts a workplace as a formalized network of interdependent roles and units coordinated through a variety of horizontal and vertical linkages. Structural patterns align with purpose and are determined by goals, technologies, and environment (Lawrence and Lorsch, 1967; Perrow, 1979; Woodward, 1970). In contrast, a symbolic view approaches structure as stage design: an arrangement of space, lighting, props, and costumes that make the drama vivid and credible to its audience.

One dramaturgical role of structure is reflecting and conveying prevailing social values and myths. Settings and costumes should be appropriate: a church should have a suitable building, religious artifacts, and a properly attired member of the clergy. A clinic should have examination rooms, uniformed nurses, and licensed physicians with diplomas prominently featured on the wall. Meyer and Rowan (1978, 1983b) depict the structure of public schools as largely symbolic. A school has difficulty sustaining public support unless it offers fashionable answers to three questions: Does it offer appropriate topics (for example, third-grade mathematics or world history)? Are topics taught to age-graded students by certified teachers?

Does it look like a school (with classrooms, a gymnasium, a library, and a flag near the front door)?

An institution of higher education is judged by the age, size, and beauty of the campus, the amount of its endowment, its faculty-student ratio, and the number of professors who received doctorates from prestigious institutions. Kamens (1977) suggests that the major function of a college or university is to redefine novice students as graduates who possess special qualities or skills. The value of the status transformation must be negotiated with important constituencies. This is done through constant references to the quality and rigor of educational programs and is validated by the structural characteristics or appearance of the institution.

A valid structural configuration, in Kamens's view, depends on whether an institution is elite or not and whether it allocates graduates to a specific social or corporate group. Each type of institution espouses its own myth and dramatizes its own aspects of structure. Ivy League schools such as Harvard, Yale, and Princeton are known for producing graduates who occupy elite roles in society. Elite schools dramatize selectivity, maintain an attractive residential campus, advertise a favorable ratio of faculty to students, and develop a core curriculum that restrains specialization in favor of a unified core of knowledge.

If an institution or its environment changes, theatrical refurbishing is needed. New audiences require revisions in actors, scripts, or settings. Since legitimacy and worth are anchored primarily in the match between structural characteristics and prevailing myths, organizations alter appearances to mirror changes in social expectations. For example, if total quality management, reengineering, or Six Sigma becomes the fashionable badge of honor for progressive companies, corresponding programs and consultants spread like fire in a parched forest.

New structures reflect legal and social expectations and represent a bid for legitimacy and support from the attending audience. An organization without an affirmative action program, for example, is suspiciously out of step with prevailing concerns for diversity and equity. Nonconformity invites questions, criticism, and inspection. It is easier to appoint a diversity officer than to change hiring practices deeply embedded in both individual and institutional beliefs and practices. Since the presence of a diversity officer is more visible than revisions in hiring priorities, the addition of a new role may signal to external constituencies that there has been improvement, even if, in reality, the appointment is a formality and no real change has occurred.

In this light, government agencies serve mostly political and symbolic functions: "Congress passes on to these agencies a type of symbolic control; they represent our belief in the virtues of planning and the value of an integrated program of action. But the agencies are given no formal authority over the organizations whose services they are to control and few funds to use as incentives to stimulate the cooperation of these existing organizations" (Scott, 1983, p. 126).

In practice, agencies reduce tension and uncertainty and increase the public's sense of confidence and security. Only in a crisis—as when people or pets die from eating contaminated food—do people ask why regulators didn't do their job. The ensuing drama of reform calls for perpetrators to be identified and punished and the situation remedied so the problems never recur.

ORGANIZATIONAL PROCESS AS THEATER

Rationally, procedures produce results. Administrative protocols coordinate work. Technology improves efficiency. Professors lecture to impart knowledge and wisdom. Physicians treat patients to cure illness. Social workers manage cases and write reports to identify and remedy social ills.

People spend much of their time engaged in such endeavors. To justify their labor, they want to believe their efforts produce the intended outcomes. Of course, even the best intentions or the most sophisticated technologies do not always yield expected results. Regardless, these activities play a very important theatrical role. They serve as scripts and stage markings for self-expressive opportunities, forums for airing grievances, and get-togethers for negotiating new understandings. We illustrate these purposes in the context of meetings, planning, performance appraisals, collective bargaining, the exercise of power, and symbolic management.

Meetings

March and Olsen (1976) were ahead of their time in depicting meetings as improvisational "garbage cans." In this imagery, meetings are magnets attracting managers looking for something to do, problems seeking answers, and people with solutions in search of problems. The results of a meeting depend on a serendipitous interplay among items that show up: Who came to the meeting? What problems, concerns, or needs were on their minds? What solutions or suggestions did they bring?

Garbage-can scripts are likely to play out in meetings dealing with emotionally charged, symbolically significant, or technically fuzzy issues. The topic of mission, for example, attracts a more sizable collection of people, problems, and solutions than the topic of cost accounting. Meetings may not always produce rational discourse, sound plans, or radical improvements. But they serve as expressive occasions to clear the air and promote collective bonding. Some players come upon their role in the drama and are able to practice and polish their lines. Others revel in the chance to add excitement to work. Audiences feel reassured that issues are getting attention and better times may lie ahead.

Planning

An organization without a plan can be labeled as reactive, shortsighted, and rudderless. Planning, then, is an essential ceremony organizations conduct periodically to maintain legitimacy. A plan is a badge of honor displayed conspicuously and with pride. A strategic plan carries even higher status. Mintzberg's insightful book *The Rise and Fall of Strategic Planning* (1994) presents an array of survey and anecdotal evidence questioning the link between strategic planning and its stated objectives. He shows that the presumed linear progression from analysis to objectives to action to results is more fanciful than factual. Many executives recognize the shortcomings of strategic planning, yet continue to champion it: "Recently I asked three corporate executives what decisions they had made in the last year that they would not have made were it not for their corporate plans. All had difficulty identifying one such decision. Since each of their plans [was] marked 'secret' or 'confidential,' I asked them how their competitors might benefit from the possession of their plans. Each answered with embarrassment that their competitors would not benefit. Yet these executives were strong advocates of corporate planning" (Russell Ackoff, quoted in Mintzberg, 1994, p. 98).

Planning persists because it plays an eminent role in an organization's enduring drama. Quinn notes: "A good deal of the corporate planning I have observed is like a ritual rain dance; it has no effect on the weather that follows, but those who engage in it think it does. Moreover, it seems to me that much of the advice and instruction related to corporate planning is directed at improving the dancing, not the weather" (quoted in Mintzberg, 1994, p. 139).

Discussing universities, Cohen and March (1974) list four symbolic roles that plans play:

- *Plans are symbols.* Academic organizations have few real pieces of objective evidence to evaluate performance. They have nothing comparable to profit or sales figures. How are we doing? No one really knows. Planning is a signal that all is well or improvement is just around the corner. A school or university undergoing an accreditation review engages in a "self-study" and lays out an ambitious strategic plan, which can then gather a decade of dust until it is time to repeat the process.

- *Plans become games.* Especially where goals and technology are unclear, planning becomes a test of will. A department that wants a new program badly must justify the expenditure by substantial planning efforts. An administrator who wishes to avoid saying yes but has no real basis for saying no can test commitment by asking for a plan. Benefits lie more in the process than the result.

- *Plans become excuses for interaction.* Developing a plan forces discussion and may increase interest in and commitment to new priorities. Occasionally, interaction yields positive results. But rarely does it yield an accurate forecast. Conclusions about what will happen next year are notoriously susceptible to alteration as people, politics, policies, or preferences change, but discussions of the future often modify views of what should be done differently today.

- *Plans become advertisements.* What is frequently called a plan is more like an investment brochure. It is an attempt to persuade private and public donors of an institution's attractiveness. Plans are typically adorned with glossy photographs of beautiful people in pristine settings, official pronouncements of excellence, and a noticeable dearth of specifics.

Cohen and March (1974) asked college presidents their views of the linkage between plans and decisions. Responses fell into four main categories:

> "Yes, we have a plan. It is used in capital project and physical location decisions."
>
> "Yes, we have a plan. Here it is. It was made during the administration of our last president. We are working on a new one."
>
> "No, we do not have a plan. We should. We're working on one."
>
> "I think there's a plan around here someplace. Miss Jones, do we have a copy of our comprehensive, ten-year plan?" [p. 113].

Evaluation

Assessing the performance of individuals, departments, or programs is a major undertaking. Organizations devote considerable time, energy, and resources to appraising individuals, even though few believe that the procedures are closely connected to improvements. Organization-wide reviews yield lengthy reports presented with fitting pomp and ceremony. Universities convene visiting committees or accrediting teams to evaluate schools or departments. Government requires routine assessment of program efficacy. Social service agencies commission studies or audits whenever an important problem or issue arises. Once in a while, insights or recommendations are carried out. Sometimes they yield tangible improvements. Just as often, however, results disappear into recesses of people's minds or the far reaches of administrators' file cabinets. But, taking into account an organization's need to foster faith and confidence among constituents, evaluation plays a decisive role.

Evaluation assures spectators that an organization is responsible, serious, and well managed. It shows that goals are taken seriously, performance receives attention, and improvement is a high priority. The evaluation process gives participants an opportunity to share opinions and have them recognized publicly. It helps people relabel old practices, escape normal routine, and build new beliefs (Rallis, 1980). Although impact on decisions or behavior may be marginal, methodical evaluation with its magic numbers serves as a potent weapon in political battles or as a compelling justification for a decision already made (Weiss, 1980).

In public organizations, Floden and Weiner argue, "Evaluation is a ritual whose function is to calm the anxieties of the citizenry and to perpetuate an image of government rationality, efficiency, and accountability. The very act of requiring and commissioning evaluations may create the impression that government is seriously committed to the pursuit of publicly espoused goals, such as increasing student achievement or reducing malnutrition. Evaluations lend credence to this image even when programs are created to appease interest groups" (1978, p. 17).

Collective Bargaining

In collective bargaining, labor and management meet and confer to forge divisive standoffs into workable agreements. The process typically pits two sets of interests against each other: unions want better wages, benefits, and working conditions for members; management aims to keep costs down and maximize profits for shareholders. Negotiating teams follow a familiar script: "Negotiators have to act like opponents, representatives and experts, showing that they are aligned with teammates and constituents, willing to push hard to achieve constituent goals, and constantly in control. On the public stage, anger and opposition dominate; rituals of opposition, representation and control produce a drama of conflict. At the same time, there are mechanisms for private understanding between opposing lead bargainers, such as signaling and sidebar discussions" (Friedman, 1994, pp. 86–87).

On the surface, the negotiation process appears as a strife-ridden political brawl where persistence and power determine the distribution of scarce resources. On a deeper plane, negotiation is a carefully crafted ritual that delivers the performance various audiences demand. Going off script carries high risk: "A young executive took the helm of a firm with the intention of eliminating bickering and conflict between management and labor. He commissioned a study of the company's wage structure and went to the bargaining table to present his offer. He informed the union representatives what he had done, and offered them more than they had expected to get. The astonished union leaders berated the executive for undermining the process of collective bargaining and asked for another five cents an hour beyond his offer" (Blum, 1961, pp. 63–64).

Similar problems have been documented by Friedman in his studies of mutual gains bargaining (which emphasizes cooperation and a win-win outcome rather than conflict). A disillusioned participant in an abortive mutual gains process lamented: "It hurt us. We got real chummy. Everyone talked. Then in the final hours, it was the same old shit. Maybe we should have been pounding on the table" (Friedman, 1994, p. 216).

In theater, actors who deviate from the script disrupt everyone else's ability to deliver their lines. The bargaining drama is designed to convince each side that the outcomes were the result of a heroic battle—often underscored by desperate, all-night, after-the-deadline rituals of combat that produce a deal just when hope seems lost. If well performed, the drama conveys the message that two determined opponents fought hard and persistently for what they believed was right (Blum, 1961; Friedman, 1994). It obscures the reality that actors typically know in advance how the play will end.

Power

Power is usually viewed as a real commodity that individuals or systems possess—something that can be seized, exercised, or redistributed. But power is inherently ambiguous and slippery. It is rarely easy to determine what power is, who has it, or how to get it. Sometimes it is even harder to know when power is wielded. You are powerful if others think you are.

Power is often attributed to certain performances. People who talk a lot, belong to committees, and seem close to the action are typically perceived as powerful. Yet there may be little relationship between activity and impact. The relationship may even be negative; the frustrated may talk a lot, and the disgruntled may resort to futile political intrigue or posturing (Enderud, 1976).

Power is also often attributed to particular individuals or groups to account for observed outcomes. If the unemployment or crime rates drop, political incumbents take credit. If a firm's profits jump, we credit the chief executive. If a program is started as things are getting better, it inherits success. Myths of leadership attribute causality to individuals in high places. Whether things are going well or badly, we like to hold someone responsible. Cohen and March have this to say about college presidents:

> Presidents negotiate with their audiences on the interpretations of their power. As a result, during . . . years of campus troubles, many college presidents sought to emphasize the limitations of presidential control. During the more glorious days of conspicuous success, they solicited a recognition of their responsibility for events. This is likely to lead to popular impressions of strong presidents during good times and weak presidents during bad times. Persons who are primarily exposed to the symbolic presidency (for example, outsiders) will tend to exaggerate the power of the presidency. Those people who have tried to accomplish something in the institution with presidential support (for example, educational reforms) will tend to underestimate presidential power or presidential will [1974, pp. 198–199].

As Edelman puts it: "Leaders lead, followers follow, and organizations prosper. While this logic is pervasive, it can be misleading. Marching one step ahead of a crowd moving in a specific direction may realistically define the connection between leadership and followership. Successful leadership is having followers who believe in the power of the leader. By believing, people are encouraged to link positive events with leadership behaviors" (1977, p. 73).

Though reassuring, the assumption that powerful leaders make a difference is often misleading. Cohen and March compare the command and control of college presidents to the driver of a skidding automobile: "The marginal judgments he makes, his skill, and his luck will probably make some difference to the life prospects of his riders. As a result, his responsibilities are heavy. But whether he is convicted of manslaughter or receives a medal for heroism is largely outside his control" (1974, p. 203).

As with other processes, a leader's power is less a matter of action than of appearance. When a leader does make a difference, it is by enriching and updating the drama—constructing new myths that alter beliefs and generate faith.

Managing Impressions

Peter Vaill (1989) characterized management as a performing art. This rings especially true for those trying to launch a business. One of the chief challenges confronting entrepreneurs is acquiring the resources needed to get embryonic ideas to the marketplace. This requires convincing investors of the future worth of an idea or product. Entrepreneurs typically concentrate on developing a persuasive business plan that projects a rosy financial future, coupled with a PowerPoint presentation full of information about the new idea's potential.

Zott and Huy's two-year field study suggests that symbols may be more powerful than numbers in determining who gets funded (2007). They compared entrepreneurs who garnered a lion's share of resources with others who did not fare as well. Their results depict "the entrepreneur as an active shaper of perceptions and a potentially skilled user of cultural tool kits. . . . By enacting symbols effectively entrepreneurs can shape a compelling symbolic universe that complements the initially weak and uncertain quality of their ventures" (pp. 100–101).

Resources flowed to entrepreneurs who presented themselves, their companies, and their products with dramatic flair rather than relying solely on technical promise and financial analyses. The winners knew their audience, capitalized on credentials and business associations, wore appropriate costumes to blend with clients and investors, shone the spotlight on the symbolic value of their products, stressed the cultural vigor of their enterprises, called attention to unique processes, highlighted personal commitment, pointed to short-term achievements, and told good stories.

It has been said that giving is a matter of heart more than head. By invoking meaningful symbols, successful entrepreneurs were able to loosen the purse strings of investors. They skillfully managed impressions through carefully crafted theatrical performances.

SUMMARY

From a symbolic perspective, organizations are judged as much on appearance as outcomes. The right drama gives audiences the performance they expect. The production reassures, fosters belief in the organization's purposes, and cultivates hope and faith. Structures that do little to coordinate activity, and protocols that rarely achieve their intended outcomes still play a significant symbolic role. They provide internal glue. They help participants cope, find meaning, and play their roles without reading the wrong lines, upstaging the lead actors, or confusing tragedy with comedy. To outside audiences, they provide a basis for confidence and support.

Dramaturgical concepts sharply redefine organizational dynamics. Historically, theories of management and organization have focused on instrumental issues. We see problems, try to solve them, and then ask, "What did we accomplish?" Often, the answer is "nothing" or "not much." We find ourselves repeating the old saw that the more things change, the more they remain the same. Such a message can be disheartening and disillusioning. It often produces a sense of helplessness and a belief that things will never get much better. In *Hope Dies Last*, Studs Terkel says it well: "In all epochs, there were first doubts and the fear of stepping forth and speaking out, but the attribute that spurred the warriors on was hope. And the *act*. Seldom was there a despair or a sense of hopelessness. Some of those on the sidelines, the spectators, feeling hopeless and impotent, had by the very nature of the passionate act of others become imbued with hope themselves" (2004, p. xviii).

Theatrical imagery offers a hopeful note. For a variety of reasons, we may be restless, frustrated, lost, or searching to renew our faith. We commission a new play called *Change*. At the end of the pageant, we can ask: What was expressed? What was recast? And what was legitimized? A good play assures us that each day is potentially more exciting and full of meaning than the last. If things go badly, buff up the symbols, revise the drama, develop new myths—or dance to another tune.

PART SIX

Improving Leadership Practice

Up to now, we have emphasized the unique features of four distinctive ways to think about organizations. But making sense of a complex situation is not a single-frame activity. A messy, turbulent world rarely presents bounded, well-defined problems. In this part of the book, we focus on combining lenses to achieve multiframe approaches to managing and leading.

In Chapter Fifteen, we contrast a stereotype of crisp, orderly rationality with a more frantic, reactive reality of managerial life. We show how routine activities and processes such as strategic planning, decision making, and conflict take on different meanings depending on how they are viewed. We provide an example to illustrate the cacophony that arises when parties are seeing different realities. Finally, we look at studies of effective organizations and senior managers to examine how research aligns with our framework.

In Chapter Sixteen, we examine a case of a middle manager who encounters an unexpected crisis on the first day in a new job. We show how, in a situation where the stakes and risks are high, each lens spawns both helpful and unproductive scenarios for her response.

We turn in Chapter Seventeen to a discussion of leadership. We begin with an example of a prominent leader in crisis to examine the interaction between leader and circumstances. We explore the concept of leadership and review research on the characteristics of effective leaders. After dissecting some popular leadership models, we illustrate each frame's image of leaders and leadership.

Chapter Eighteen takes us to a perennial challenge: creating change. We examine predictable barriers each frame suggests and point out different remedies. We then integrate the frames with a stage model of change. The two in combination provide a powerful map.

Ethics and spirit are the focus of Chapter Nineteen. We begin with a look at what went wrong at Enron. While Enron had plenty of smart, aggressive people, it lacked wisdom and soul. We end by discussing four criteria for ethical behavior: authorship, love, justice, and significance.

Chapter Twenty presents an integrative case in which we zoom in on a new principal in his perilous early weeks at a troubled urban high school. We illustrate how the frames in tandem generate a more comprehensive diagnosis of the issues and offer more promising options for moving ahead.

Finally, in the Epilogue, we summarize the basic messages of the book and lay out implications for the development of future leaders.

Integrating Frames for Effective Practice

No one could have forecast what New York City Mayor Rudolph Giuliani would face on September 11, 2001. During a breakfast meeting, he learned that a plane had hit one of the World Trade Center's twin towers. He went directly to the scene, arriving in time to see the devastating strike on the second tower. It was now clear that this was planned terrorism, an unprecedented human tragedy and a deep symbolic wound for the city.

In the aftermath, the American public observed what many assumed was a transformed Giuliani—a sensitive, emotional, and deeply caring leader whose ubiquitous presence was a source of inspiration to New Yorkers, as well as to all Americans. But His Honor disputes his supposed personal makeover: "The events of September 11 affected me more deeply than anything I have ever experienced; but the idea that I somehow became a different person on that day—that there was a pre–September 11 Rudy and a wholly other post-September Rudy—is not true. I was prepared to handle September 11 precisely because I was the same person who had been doing his best to take on challenges my whole career. . . . You can't be paralyzed by any situation. It's about balance" (Giuliani and Kurson, 2002, pp. x, xiii).

In an unprecedented crisis, Giuliani found himself drawing upon different aspects of his cognitive and behavioral repertoire—lessons learned from prior experience. Both the mayor and his constituents faced dramatically

311

altered circumstances, which required new thinking and realignment of their perceptive lenses. Symbolism, for example, had always seemed prominent in Giuliani's leadership but became even more so after 9/11. Meanwhile, the political dynamics on which Giuliani had historically thrived receded in relative significance.

Harmonizing the frames, and crafting inventive responses to new circumstances, is essential to both management and leadership. This chapter considers the frames in combination. How do you choose a way to frame an event? How do you integrate multiple lenses in the same situation? We begin by revisiting the turbulent world of managers. We then explore what happens when people rely on different views of the same challenge. We offer questions and guidelines to stimulate thinking about which prisms are likely to apply in specific situations. Finally, we examine literature on effective managers and organizations to see which modes of thought dominate current theory.

LIFE AS MANAGERS KNOW IT

Prevailing mythology depicts managers as rational men and women who plan, organize, coordinate, and control activities of subordinates. Periodicals, books, and business schools paint a pristine image of modern managers: unruffled and well organized, with clean desks, power suits, and sophisticated information systems. Such "super managers" develop and implement farsighted strategies, producing predictable and robust results. It is a reassuring picture of clarity and order. Unfortunately, it's wrong.

An entirely different picture appears if you watch managers at work (Carlson, 1951; Kotter, 1982; Mintzberg, 1973; Luthans, 1988). It's a hectic life, shifting rapidly from one situation to another. Decisions emerge from a fluid, swirling vortex of conversations, meetings, and memos. Information systems ensure an overload of detail about what happened last month or last year. Yet they fail to answer a far more important question: What to do next? In Afghanistan, sophisticated systems make information from battle zones readily available all the way up the command structure. But a faster flow of information has slowed rather than sped up tactical decision making because top officers can now ponder decisions better made on the spot. After identifying a high-value target, Special Forces may wait days before receiving permission to fire. By then the target is long gone.

In deciding what to do next, managers operate largely on the basis of intuition, drawing on firsthand observations, hunches, and judgment derived from experience. Too swamped to spend much time thinking, analyzing, or reading, they get most of their information in meetings, through e-mail, or over the phone. They are hassled priests, modern muddlers, and corporate wheeler-dealers.

How does one reconcile the actual work of managers with the heroic imagery? "Whenever I report this frenetic pattern to groups of executives," says Harold Leavitt, "regardless of hierarchical level or nationality, they always respond with a mix of discomfiture and recognition. Reluctantly, and somewhat sheepishly, they will admit that the description fits, but they don't like to be told about it. If they were really good managers, they seem to feel, they would be in control, their desks would be clean, and their shops would run as smoothly as a Mercedes engine" (1996, p. 294). Led to believe that they should be rational and on top of things, managers may instead become bewildered and demoralized. They are supposed to plan and organize, yet they find themselves muddling around and playing catch-up. They want to solve problems and make decisions. But when problems are ill defined and options murky, control is an illusion and rationality an afterthought.

ACROSS FRAMES: ORGANIZATIONS AS MULTIPLE REALITIES

Life in organizations is packed with happenings that can be interpreted in a number of ways. Exhibit 15.1 examines familiar processes through four lenses. As the chart shows, any event can be framed in several ways and serve multiple purposes. Planning, for example, produces specific objectives. But it also creates arenas for airing conflict and becomes a sacred occasion to renegotiate symbolic meanings.

Multiple realities produce confusion and conflict as individuals look at the same event through different lenses. A hospital administrator once called a meeting to make an important decision. The chief technician viewed it as a chance to express feelings and build relationships. The director of nursing hoped to gain power vis-à-vis physicians. The medical director saw it as an occasion for reaffirming the hospital's distinctive approach to medical care. The meeting became a cacophonous jumble, like a group of musicians each playing from a different score.

Exhibit 15.1.
Four Interpretations of Organizational Processes.

PROCESS	STRUCTURAL FRAME	HUMAN RESOURCE FRAME	POLITICAL FRAME	SYMBOLIC FRAME
Strategic planning	Strategies to set objectives and coordinate resources	Gatherings to promote participation	Arenas to air conflicts and realign power	Ritual to signal responsibility, produce symbols, negotiate meanings
Decision making	Rational sequence to produce right decision	Open process to produce commitment	Opportunity to gain or exercise power	Ritual to confirm values and provide opportunities for bonding
Reorganizing	Realign roles and responsibilities to fit tasks and environment	Maintain a balance between human needs and formal roles	Redistribute power and form new coalitions	Maintain an image of accountability and responsiveness; negotiate new social order
Evaluating	Way to distribute rewards or penalties and control performance	Feedback for helping individuals grow and improve	Opportunity to exercise power	Occasion to play roles in shared ritual
Approaching conflict	Maintain organizational goals by having authorities resolve conflict	Develop relationships by having individuals confront conflict	Develop power by bargaining, forcing, or manipulating others to win	Develop shared values and use conflict to negotiate meaning

Goal setting	Keep organization headed in the right direction	Keep people involved and communication open	Provide opportunity for individuals and groups to make interests known	Develop symbols and shared values
Communication	Transmit facts and information	Exchange information, needs, and feelings	Influence or manipulate others	Tell stories
Meetings	Formal occasions for making decisions	Informal occasions for involvement, sharing feelings	Competitive occasions to win points	Sacred occasions to celebrate and transform the culture
Motivation	Economic incentives	Growth and self-actualization	Coercion, manipulation, and seduction	Symbols and celebrations

The confusion that can result when people view the world through different lenses is illustrated in this classic case:

DOCTOR FIGHTS ORDER TO QUIT MAINE ISLAND

Dr. Gregory O'Keefe found himself the focus of a fierce battle between 1,200 year-round residents of Vinalhaven, Maine (an island fishing community), and the National Health Service Corps (NHSC), which pays his salary and is insisting he take a promotion to an administrator's desk in Rockville, Maryland.

O'Keefe doesn't want to go, and his patients don't want him to either. The islanders are so upset that, much to the surprise of NHSC officials, they have enlisted the aid of Senator William Cohen

(R-Maine) and U.S. Health and Human Services Secretary Margaret Heckler to keep him here.

It's certainly not the prestige or glamour of the job that is holding O'Keefe, who drives the town's only ambulance and, as often as twice a week, takes critically ill patients to mainland hospitals via an emergency ferry run or a Coast Guard cutter, private plane, or even a lobster boat.

Apparently unyielding in their insistence that O'Keefe accept the promotion or resign, NHSC officials seemed startled last week by the spate of protests from angry islanders, which prompted nationwide media attention and inquiries from the Maine Congressional delegation. NHSC says it probably would not replace O'Keefe on the island, which, in the agency's view, is now able to support a private medical practice.

Cohen described himself as "frustrated by the lack of responsiveness of lower-level bureaucrats." But to the NHSC, O'Keefe is a foot soldier in a military organization of more than 1,600 physicians assigned to isolated, medically needy communities. And he's had the audacity to question the orders of a superior officer.

"It's like a soldier who wanted to stay at Ft. Myers and jumped on TV and called the Defense Secretary a rat for wanting him to move," Shirley Barth, press officer for the federal Public Health Service, said in a telephone interview Thursday [Goodman, 1983, p. 1].

The NHSC officials had trouble seeing beyond the structural frame; they had a task to do and a strategy for achieving it. O'Keefe's resistance was illegitimate. O'Keefe saw the situation in human resource terms. He felt the work he was doing was meaningful and satisfying, and the islanders needed him. For Senator Cohen, it was a political issue; could minor bureaucrats be allowed to harm his constituents through mindless abuse of power? For the hardy residents of Vinalhaven, O'Keefe was a heroic figure of mythic proportions: "If he gets one night's sleep out of twenty, he's lucky, but he's always up there smiling and working." The islanders were full of stories about O'Keefe's humility, skill, humaneness, dedication, wit, confidence, and caring.

With so many people peering through different filters, confusion and conflict were predictable. The inability of NHSC officials to understand and acknowledge the existence of other perspectives illustrates the costs of clinging to a single view of a situation. Whenever someone's actions seem to make no sense, it is worth asking if you and they are seeing contrasting realities. You know better what you're up against when you understand their perspective, even if you're sure they're wrong. Their mind-set—not yours—determines how they act.

MATCHING FRAMES TO SITUATIONS

In a given situation, one cognitive map may be more helpful than others. At a strategic crossroads, a rational process focused on gathering and analyzing information may be exactly what is needed. At other times, developing commitment or building a power base may be more critical. In times of great stress, decision processes may become a form of ritual that brings comfort and support. Choosing a frame to size things up, or understanding others' perspectives, involves a combination of analysis, intuition, and artistry. Exhibit 15.2 poses questions to facilitate analysis and stimulate intuition. It also suggests conditions under which each way of thinking is most likely to be effective.

Exhibit 15.2.
Choosing a Frame.

QUESTION	IF YES:	IF NO:
Are individual commitment and motivation essential to success?	Human resource Symbolic	Structural Political
Is the technical quality of the decision important?	Structural	Human resource Political Symbolic
Are there high levels of ambiguity and uncertainty?	Political Symbolic	Structural Human resource
Are conflict and scarce resources significant?	Political Symbolic	Structural Human resource
Are you working from the bottom up?	Political	Structural Human resource Symbolic

---

- *Are commitment and motivation essential to success?* The human resource and symbolic approaches need to be considered whenever issues of individual dedication, energy, and skill are vital to success. A new curriculum launched by a school district will fail without teacher support. Support might be strengthened by human resource approaches, such as participation and self-managing teams, or through symbolic approaches linking the innovation to values and symbols teachers cherish.

- *Is the technical quality important?* When a good decision needs to be technically sound, the structural frame's emphasis on data and logic is essential. But if a decision must be acceptable to major constituents, then human resource, political, or symbolic issues loom larger. Could the technical quality of a decision ever be unimportant? A college found itself embroiled in a three-month battle over the choice of a commencement speaker. The faculty pushed for a great scholar, the students for a movie star. The president was more than willing to invite anyone acceptable to both groups; she saw no technical criterion proving that one choice was better than the other.

- *Are ambiguity and uncertainty high?* If goals are clear, technology is well understood, and behavior is reasonably predictable, the structural and human resource approaches are likely to apply. As ambiguity increases, the political and symbolic perspectives become more relevant. The political frame expects that the pursuit of self-interest will often produce confused and chaotic contests that require political intervention. The symbolic lens sees symbols as a way of finding order, meaning, and "truth" in situations too complex, uncertain, or mysterious for rational or political analysis. In the R. J. Reynolds leveraged buyout (discussed in Chapter Eleven), the most critical unknown was what opposing bidders were doing and what it meant. Everyone scouted the competition intensely and tried to interpret and read meaning into even the weakest signals. At a key point in the endgame, Henry Kravis hinted that he might drop out. To make the hint credible, he went off for a long weekend in Colorado just before final bids were due. The opposition picked up the signals and concluded, "Henry's not bidding." It was, according to one member of the other team, "our fatal error."

- *Are conflict and scarce resources significant?* Human resource logic fits best in situations favoring collaboration—as in profitable, growing firms or highly unified schools. But when conflict is high and resources are scarce, dynamics of conflict, power, and self-interest regularly come to the fore. In situations like the Reynolds bidding war, sophisticated political strategies are vital to success. In other cases, skilled leaders may find that an overarching symbol helps potential adversaries transcend their differences and work together. In the early 1980s, Yale University was paralyzed by a clerical and technical workers' strike. No one, including Yale's president, A. Bartlett Giamatti, knew how to settle the dispute. Then Phil Donahue invited the Yale community to appear on his television show. Union members energetically presented their side, and Giamatti represented the administration. The audience was active and vocal but polarized. Near the end of the program, Giamatti told a story about his father, an Italian immigrant, who was admitted to the neighborhood university, which happened to be Yale. His father couldn't pay the tuition, but Yale had a core value of "admission by ability, support by need." The story and the invocation of a shared value helped bridge the chasm dividing the parties.

- *Are you working from the bottom up?* Restructuring is an option primarily for those in a position of authority. Human resource approaches to improvement—such as training, job enrichment, and participation—usually need support from the top to be successful. The political frame, in contrast, fits well for changes initiated from below. Because partisans—change agents lower in the pecking order—rarely can rely on formal clout, they must find other bases of power, such as symbolic acts to draw attention to their cause and embarrass opponents. The 9/11 terrorists could have picked from an almost unlimited array of targets, but the World Trade Towers and the Pentagon were deliberately selected for their symbolic value.

The questions in Exhibit 15.2 are no substitute for judgment and intuition in deciding how to size up or respond to a situation. But they can guide and augment the process of choosing the most promising course of action. Consider once again the Helen Demarco case (Chapter Two). Her boss, Paul Osborne, had a plan for major change. Demarco thought the plan was a mistake but did not feel she could directly oppose it. What should she do? The issue of commitment and motivation was important, both in terms of her lack of support for Osborne's plan and her concern about finding a solution he could accept. The table suggests that the human resource frame was worth considering, though Demarco never did. The quality of the plan was critical in her judgment, but she was convinced that Osborne was immune to technical arguments.

Ambiguity played a significant role in the case. Even if technical issues were reasonably clear, the key issue of how to influence Osborne was shrouded in haziness. Implicitly, Demarco acknowledged the importance of the symbolism in using a form of theater (research that wasn't really research, a technical report that was window dressing) as her key strategy. Above all, Exhibit 15.2

suggests that Demarco's plight aligns best with the political frame: resources were scarce, conflict was high, and she was trying to influence from the bottom up. The choice point pressed toward politics and symbols. She went with the flow.

The guidelines in Exhibit 15.2 cannot be followed mechanically. Arriving at an adequate response for every situation is a matter of playing probabilities. In some cases, your line of thinking might lead you to a familiar frame. If the tried-and-true approach shows signs of producing a shortfall, though, reframe again. You may discover an exciting and creative new lens for deciphering the situation. Then you face another problem: how to communicate your breakthrough to others who still champion the old reality.

EFFECTIVE MANAGERS AND ORGANIZATIONS

Does the ability to use multiple frames actually help managers decipher events and determine alternative ways to respond? If so, how are the frames embedded and integrated in everyday situations? We examine several strands of research to answer these questions. First, we look at three influential guides to organizational excellence: *In Search of Excellence* (Peters and Waterman, 1982), *Built to Last* (Collins and Porras, 1994), and *From Good to Great* (Collins, 2001). We then review three studies of managerial work, *The General Managers* (Kotter, 1982), *Managing Public Policy* (Lynn, 1987), and *Real Managers* (Luthans, Yodgetts, and Rosenkrantz, 1988). Finally, we look at recent studies of managers' frame orientations to see if current thinking is equal to present-day challenges.

Organizational Excellence

Peters and Waterman's spectacular best-seller *In Search of Excellence* (1982) explored the question, "What do high-performing corporations have in common?" Peters and Waterman studied more than sixty large companies in six major industries: high technology (Digital Equipment and IBM, for example), consumer products (Kodak, Procter & Gamble), manufacturing (3M, Caterpillar), service (McDonald's, Delta Airlines), project management (Boeing, Bechtel), and natural resources (Exxon, DuPont). The companies were chosen on the basis of both objective performance indicators (such as long-term growth and profitability) and the judgment of knowledgeable observers.

Collins and Porras (1994) attempted a similar study of what they termed "visionary" companies but tried to address two methodological limitations in the Peters and Waterman study. Collins and Porras included a comparison group (missing in Peters and Waterman) by matching each of their top performers with another firm in the same industry with a comparable history. Their pairings included Citibank with Chase Manhattan, General Electric with Westinghouse, Sony with Kenwood, Hewlett-Packard with Texas Instruments, and Merck with Pfizer. Collins and Porras emphasized long-term results by restricting their study to companies at least fifty years old with evidence of consistent success over many decades.

Collins (2001) used a comparative approach similar to that of Collins and Porras but focused on another criterion for success: instead of organizations that had excelled for many years, he identified a group of companies that had made a dramatic breakthrough from middling to superlative and compared them with similar companies that had remained ordinary.

Each of the three studies identified seven or eight critical characteristics of excellent companies, similar in some respects and distinct in others, as Exhibit 15.3 shows. All three suggest that excellent companies manage to embrace paradox. They are loose yet tight, highly disciplined yet entrepreneurial. Peters and Waterman's "bias for action" and Collins and Porras's "try a lot, keep what works" both point to risk taking and experimenting as ways to learn and avoid bogging down in analysis paralysis. All three studies emphasize a clear core identity that helps firms stay on track and be clear about what they will not do.

Two of the studies emphasized something they did not find: charismatic, larger-than-life leadership. Collins and Porras (1994) and Collins (2001) both highlighted leaders who were usually homegrown and focused on building their organization rather than their personal reputation. Collins's "level 5" leaders were driven but self-effacing, extremely disciplined and hardworking but consistent in attributing success to their colleagues rather than themselves.

As Exhibit 15.3 shows, all three studies produced three-frame models. Notice that none of the characteristics of excellence are political. Does an effective organization eliminate politics? Or did the authors miss something? By definition, their samples focused on companies with a strong record of growth and profitability. Infighting and backbiting tend to be less visible on a winning team than on a loser. When resources are relatively abundant, political dynamics are less prominent because slack assets can be used to buy off conflicting interests. Recall, too, that a strong culture tends to increase homogeneity—people think more alike. A unifying culture reduces conflict and political strife—or at least makes them easier to manage.

Exhibit 15.3.
Characteristics of Excellent or Visionary Companies.

FRAME	PETERS AND WATERMAN, 1982	COLLINS AND PORRAS, 1994	COLLINS, 2001
Structural	Autonomy and entrepreneurship; bias for action; simple form, lean staff	Clock building, not time telling; try a lot, keep what works	Confront the brutal facts; "hedgehog concept" (best in the world, economic engine); technology accelerators; "flywheel," not "doom loop"
Human resource	Close to the customer; productivity through people	Home-grown management	"Level 5 leadership"; first who, then what
Political			
Symbolic	Hands-on, value-driven; simultaneously loose and tight; stick to the knitting	Big hairy audacious goals; cultlike cultures; good enough never is; preserve the core, stimulate progress; more than profits	Never lose faith; hedgehog concept (deeply passionate); culture of discipline

Even in successful companies, it is likely that power and conflict are more important than these studies suggest. Ask a few managers, "What makes your organization successful?" They rarely talk about coalitions, conflict, or jockeying for position. Even if it is a prominent issue, politics is typically kept in the closet—known to insiders but not on public display. But if we change our focus from effective organizations to effective managers, we find a different picture.

The Effective Senior Manager

Kotter (1982) conducted an intensive study of fifteen corporate general managers (GMs). His sample included "individuals who hold positions with some multifunctional responsibility for a business" (p. 2); each managed an organization with at least several hundred employees. Lynn (1987) analyzed five sub-cabinet-level executives in the U.S. government, political appointees with responsibility for a major federal agency. Luthans, Yodgetts, and Rosenkrantz (1988) studied a larger but less elite sample of managers than Kotter and Lynn. With a sample of about 450 managers at a variety of levels, they examined managers' day-to-day activities and reported how those activities related to success and effectiveness. Exhibit 15.4 shows the characteristics that these studies emphasize as being the keys to effectiveness.

Exhibit 15.4.
Challenges in Managers' Jobs.

FRAME	KOTTER (1982)	LYNN (1987)	LUTHANS, YODGETTS, AND ROSENKRANTZ (1988)
Structural	Keep on top of large, complex set of activities	Attain intellectual grasp of policy issues	Communication* (paperwork, exchange routine information)
	Set goals and policies under conditions of uncertainty		Traditional management (planning, goal setting, controlling)
Human resource	Motivate, coordinate, and control large, diverse group of subordinates	Use own personality to best advantage	Human resource management* (motivating, managing conflict, staffing, and so on)
Political	Achieve "delicate balance" in allocating scarce resources	Exploit all opportunities to achieve strategic gains	Networking† (politics, interacting with outsiders)
	Get support from bosses		
	Get support from corporate staff and other constituents		
Symbolic	Develop credible strategic premises		
	Identify and focus on core activities that give meaning to employees		

* Most relevant to managers who were judged "effective" by their subordinates.

† Most relevant to managers who were considered "successful" (achieved rapid promotions to higher positions faster than peers).

Kotter and Lynn described jobs of enormous complexity and uncertainty, coupled with substantial dependence on networks of people whose support and energy were essential for the executives to do their job. Both focused on three basic challenges: setting an agenda, building a network, and using the network to get things done. Lynn's work is consistent with Kotter's observation: "As a result of these demands, the typical GM faced significant obstacles in both figuring out what to do and in getting things done" (Kotter, 1982, p. 122).

Kotter and Lynn both emphasized the political dimension in senior managers' jobs. Lynn described the need for a significant dose of political skill and sophistication: "building legislative support, negotiating, and identifying changing positions and interests" (1987, p. 248). Kotter's model includes elements of all four frames; Lynn's includes all but the symbolic.

A somewhat different picture emerges from the study by Luthans, Yodgetts, and Rosenkrantz. In their sample, middle- and lower-level managers spent about three-fifths of their time on structural activities (routine communications and traditional management functions like planning and controlling), about one-fifth on "human resource management" (people-related activities like motivating, disciplining, training, staffing), and about one-fifth on "networking" (political activities like socializing, politicking, and relating to external constituents). The results suggest that, compared with the senior executives Kotter and Lynn studied, middle managers spend less time grappling with complexity and more time on routine.

Luthans, Yodgetts, and Rosenkrantz distinguished between "effectiveness" and "success." The criteria for effectiveness were the quantity and quality of the unit's performance and the level of subordinates' satisfaction with their boss. Success was defined in terms of promotions per year—how fast people got ahead. Effective managers and successful managers used time differently. The most "effective" managers spent much of their time on communications and human resource management and relatively little time on networking. But networking was the only activity that was strongly related to getting ahead. "Successful" managers spent almost half their time on networking and only about 10 percent on human resource management.

At first glance, this might seem to confirm the cynical suspicion that getting ahead in a career is more about politics than performance. More likely, though, the results confirm that performance is in the eye of the beholder. Subordinates rate their boss primarily on criteria internal to the unit—effective communications and treating people well. Bosses, on the other hand, focus on how well a manager handles relations to external constituents, including, of course, the bosses themselves. The researchers found that the 10 percent or so of their sample high on both success and effectiveness had a balanced approach emphasizing both internal and external issues. They were, in effect, multiframe managers.

Comparing all six studies—those focusing on organizations and those focusing on managers—reveals both similarities and differences. All give roughly equal emphasis to structural and human resource considerations. But political issues are invisible in the organizational excellence studies, whereas they are prominent in all the studies of individual managers. Politics was as important for Kotter's corporate executives as for Lynn's political appointees and was the key to getting ahead for middle managers. Conversely, symbols and culture were more prominent in the studies of organizational excellence. For various reasons, each study tended to neglect one frame or another. In assessing any prescription for improving organizations, ask if any frame is omitted. The overlooked perspective could be the one that derails the effort.

MANAGERS' FRAME PREFERENCES

Yet another line of research has yielded additional data on how frame preference influences leadership effectiveness. Bolman and Deal (1991, 1992a, 1992b) and Bolman and Granell (1999) studied populations of managers and administrators in both business and education. They found that the ability to use multiple frames was a consistent correlate of effectiveness. Effectiveness as a manager was particularly associated with the structural frame, whereas the symbolic and political frames tended to be the primary determinants of effectiveness as a leader.

Bensimon (1989, 1990) studied college presidents and found that multiframe presidents were viewed as more effective than presidents wedded to a single frame. In her sample, more than a third of the presidents used only one frame, and only a quarter relied on more than two. Single-frame presidents tended to be less experienced, relying mainly on structural or human resource perspectives. Presidents who relied solely on the structural frame were particularly likely to be seen as ineffective leaders. Heimovics, Herman, and Jurkiewicz Coughlin (1993) found the same thing for chief executives in the nonprofit sector, and Wimpelberg (1987) found comparable results in a study of eighteen school principals. His study paired nine more effective and less effective schools. Principals of ineffective schools relied almost entirely on the structural frame, whereas principals in effective schools used multiple frames. When asked about hiring teachers, principals in less effective schools talked about standard procedures (how vacancies are posted, how the central office sends a candidate for an interview), while more effective principals emphasized "playing the system" to get the teachers they needed.

Bensimon found that presidents thought they used more frames than their colleagues observed. They were particularly likely to overrate themselves on the human resource and symbolic frames, a finding also reported by Bolman and Deal (1991). Only half of the presidents who saw themselves as symbolic leaders were perceived that way by others.

Despite the low image of organizational politics in the minds of many managers, political savvy appears to be a primary determinant of success in certain jobs. Heimovics, Herman, and Jurkiewicz Coughlin (1993, 1995) found this for chief executives of nonprofit organizations, and Doktor (1993) found the same thing for directors of family service organizations in Kentucky.

SUMMARY

The image of firm control and crisp precision often attributed to managers has little relevance to the messy world of complexity, conflict, and uncertainty they inhabit. They need multiple frames to survive. They need to understand that any event or process can serve several purposes and that participants are often operating from different views of reality. Managers need a diagnostic map that helps them assess which lenses are likely to be salient and helpful in a given situation. Among the key variables are motivation, technical constraints, uncertainty, scarcity, conflict, and whether an individual is operating from the top down or from the bottom up.

Several lines of research have found that effective leaders and effective organizations rely on multiple frames. Studies of effective corporations, of individuals in senior management roles, and of public and nonprofit administrators all point to the need for multiple perspectives in developing a holistic picture of complex systems.

Reframing in Action

Opportunities and Perils

A nother case in point:

REACH AND GRASP

Put yourself in the shoes of Cindy Marshall, headed to the office for your first day in a new job. Your company has transferred you to Kansas City to manage a customer service unit. It's a big promotion, with a substantial increase in pay and responsibility. You know you face a major challenge. You are inheriting a department with a reputation for slow, substandard service. Senior management credits much of the blame to your predecessor, Bill Howard, who is seen as too authoritarian and rigid. Howard is moving to another job, but the company asked him to stay on for a week to help you get oriented. One potential sticking point is that he hired most of your new staff. Many may still feel loyal to him.

When you arrive, you get a frosty hello from Susan Bond, the department secretary. As you walk into your new office, you see Howard behind the desk in a conversation with three other staff members. You say hello, and he responds by saying, "Didn't the secretary tell you that we're in a meeting right now? If you'll wait outside, I'll be able to see you in about an hour."

As Cindy Marshall, what would you do? You're in the glare of the spotlight, and the audience eagerly awaits your response. If you feel threatened or attacked—as most of us would—those feelings will push you toward either fight or flight. Fighting back and escalating the conflict is risky and could damage everyone. Backing away or fleeing could suggest that you are too emotional or not tough enough.

This is a classic example of a manager's nightmare: a totally unexpected situation that is headed for disaster. Howard's greeting is well designed to throw you off stride and put you in a bind. It carries echoes of historic patterns of male arrogance and condescension in relating to women (similar to those that surfaced in the Anne Barreta case in Chapter Eight). Whether or not he intended it that way, Howard's response appears ideal for disconcerting a younger female colleague. He makes it likely that, as Cindy, you will feel trapped and powerless, or you will do something rash and regrettable. Either way, he wins and you lose.

The frames suggest another set of possibilities. They offer the advantage of multiple angles to size up the situation. What's really going on here? What options do you have? What script does the situation demand? How might you reinterpret the scene to create a more effective scenario? Reframing is a powerful tool in a tough situation for generating possibilities other than fight or flight.

An immediate question facing you, as Cindy Marshall, is whether to respond to Howard on the spot or to buy time. If you're at a loss for what to say or if you fear you will make things worse instead of better, take time to "go to the balcony"—try to get above the confusion of the moment long enough to get a better perspective and develop a workable strategy. Even better, though, find an effective response on the spot.

Each of the frames generates its own possibilities that can be translated into alternative scenarios. They can also be misapplied or misused. Success depends on the skill and artistry of the person following a given script. In this chapter, we describe setups Marshall could compose showing that each the four lenses can produce both effective and ineffective reactions. We conclude with a summary of the power and risks of reframing and highlight its importance for outsiders and newcomers.

Structural Frame
A STRUCTURAL SCENARIO

A structural scenario casts managers and leaders in the fundamental roles of clarifying goals, attending to the relationship between structure and environment, and developing a clearly defined array of roles and relationships appropriate to what needs to be done. Without a workable structure, people become unsure about what they are supposed to be doing. The result is confusion, frustration, and conflict. In an effective organization, individuals understand their responsibilities and their contribution. Policies, linkages, and lines of authority are straightforward and accepted. With the right structure, the organization can achieve its goals, and individuals can see their role in the big picture.

The main job of a leader is to focus on task, facts, and logic, rather than personality and emotions. Most people problems stem from structural flaws, not personal limitation or liability. The structural leader is not rigidly authoritarian and does not attempt to solve every problem by issuing orders (though that is sometimes appropriate). Instead, the leader tries to design and implement a process or architecture appropriate to the circumstances.

You may wonder what structure has to do with a direct, personal confrontation, but the structural scenario in the box can be scripted to generate a variety of responses.

Here's one example:

Howard: Didn't the secretary tell you that we're in a meeting right now? If you'll wait outside, I'll be able to see you in about an hour.

Marshall: My appointment as manager of this office began at nine this morning. This is now my office, and you're sitting behind my desk. Either you relinquish the desk immediately, or I will call headquarters and report you for insubordination.

Howard: I was asked to stay on the job for one more week to try to help you learn the ropes. Frankly, I doubt that you're ready for this job, but you don't seem to want any help.

Marshall: I repeat, I am now in charge of this office. Let me also remind you that headquarters assigned you to stay this week to assist me. I expect you to carry out that order. If you don't, I will submit a letter for your file detailing your lack of cooperation. Now, [firmly] I want my desk.

Howard: Well, we were working on important office business, but since the princess here is more interested in giving orders than in getting work done, let's move our meeting down to your office, Joe. Enjoy the desk!

In this exchange, Cindy places heavy emphasis on her formal authority and the chain of command. By invoking her superiors and her legitimate authority, she takes charge and gets Howard to back down, but at a price. She risks long-term tension with her new subordinates, who surely feel awkward during this combative encounter. They may see their new boss as autocratic and rigid.

There are other options. Here's another example of how Marshall might exercise her authority:

Howard: Didn't the secretary tell you that we're in a meeting right now? If you'll wait outside, I'll be able to see you in about an hour.

Marshall: She didn't mention it, and I don't want to interrupt important work, but we also need to set some priorities and work out an agenda for the day anyway. Bill, have you developed a plan for how you and I can get to work on the transition?

Howard: We can meet later on, after I get through some pressing business.

Marshall: The pressing business is just the kind of thing I need to learn about as the new manager here. What issues are you discussing?

Howard: How to keep the office functioning when the new manager is not ready for the job.

Marshall: Well, I have a lot to learn, but I feel up to it. With your help, I think we can have a smooth and productive transition. How about if you continue your meeting and I just sit in as an observer? Then, Bill, you and I could meet to work out a plan for how we'll handle the transition. After that, I'd like to schedule a meeting with each manager to get an individual progress report. I'd like to hear from each of you about your major customer service objectives and how you would assess your progress. Now, what were you talking about before I got here?

This time, Marshall is still clear and firm in establishing her authority, but she does it without appearing harsh or dictatorial. She underscores the importance of setting priorities. She asks if Howard has a plan for making the transition productive. She emphasizes shared goals and defines a temporary role for herself as an observer. She focuses steadfastly on the task and not on Howard's provocations. In keeping the exchange on a rational level and outlining a transition plan, she avoids escalating or submerging the conflict. She also communicates to her new staff that she has done her homework, is organized, and knows what she wants. When she says she would like to hear their personal objectives and progress, she communicates an expectation that they should follow her example.

Human Resource Frame
A HUMAN RESOURCE SCENARIO

The human resource leader believes that people are the center of any organization. If people feel the organization is responsive to their needs and supportive of their personal goals, you can count on commitment and loyalty. Administrators who are authoritarian or insensitive, who don't communicate effectively, or who don't care can never be effective leaders. The human resource leader works on behalf of both the organization and its people, seeking to serve the best interests of both.

The job of the leader is support and empowerment. Support takes a variety of forms: showing concern, listening to people's aspirations and goals, and communicating personal warmth and openness. The leader empowers through participation and inclusion ensuring that people have the autonomy and support needed to do their job.

As indicated in the human resource box, this frame favors listening and responsiveness. Some people, though, go a little too far in trying to be responsive:

Howard: Didn't the secretary tell you that we're in a meeting right now? If you'll wait outside, I'll be able to see you in about an hour.

Marshall: Oh, gosh, no, she didn't. I just feel terrible about interrupting your meeting. I hope I didn't offend anyone because to me, it's really important to establish good working relationships right from the outset. While I'm waiting, is there anything I can do to help? Would anyone like a cup of coffee?

Howard: No. We'll let you know when we're finished.

Marshall: Oh. Well, have a good meeting, and I'll see you in an hour.

In the effort to be friendly and accommodating, Marshall is acting more like a waitress than a manager. She defuses the conflict, but her staff are likely to see their new boss as weak. She could instead capitalize on an interest in people:

Howard: Didn't the secretary tell you that we're in a meeting right now? If you'll wait outside, I'll be able to see you in about an hour.

Marshall: I'm sorry if I'm interrupting, but I'm eager to get started, and I'll need all your help. [She walks around, introduces herself, and shakes hands with each member of her new staff. Howard scowls silently.] Bill, could we take a few minutes to talk about how we can work together on the transition, now that I'm coming in to manage the department?

Howard: You're not the manager yet. I was asked to stay on for a week to get you started—though, frankly, I doubt that you're ready for this job.

Marshall: I understand your concern, Bill. I know how committed you are to the success of the department. If I were you, I might be worried about whether I was turning my baby over to someone who wouldn't be able to take care of it. But I wouldn't be here if I didn't feel ready.

I want to benefit as much as I can from your experience. Is it urgent to get on with what you were talking about, or could we take some time first to talk about how we can start working together?

Howard: We have some things we need to finish.

Marshall: Well, as a manager, I always prefer to trust the judgment of the people who are closest to the action. I'll just sit in while you finish up, and then we can talk about how we move forward from there.

Here, Marshall is unfazed and relentlessly cheerful; she avoids a battle and acknowledges Howard's perspective. When he says she is not ready for the job, she resists the temptation to debate or return his salvo. Instead, she recognizes his concern but calmly communicates her confidence and focus on moving ahead. She demonstrates an important skill of a human resource leader: the ability to combine advocacy with inquiry. She listens carefully to Howard but gently stands her ground. She asks for his help while expressing confidence that she can do the job. When he says they have things to finish, she responds with the agility of a martial artist, using Howard's energy to her own advantage. She expresses part of her philosophy—she prefers to trust her staff's judgment—and positions herself as an observer, thus gaining an opportunity to learn more about her staff and the issues they are addressing. By reframing the situation, she has gotten off to a better start with Howard and is able to signal to others the kind of people-oriented leader she intends to be.

Political Frame
A POLITICAL SCENARIO

The political leader believes that managers have to recognize political reality and know how to deal with conflict. Inside and outside any organization, a variety of interest groups, each with its own agenda, compete for scarce resources. There is never enough to give all parties what they want, so there will always be struggles.

The job of the leader is to recognize major constituencies, develop ties to their leadership, and manage conflict as productively as possible. Above all, leaders need to build a power base and use power carefully. They can't give every group everything it wants, but they can create arenas where groups can negotiate differences and come up with a reasonable compromise. They also need to work at articulating what everyone has in common. It is wasteful for people to expend energy fighting each other when there are plenty of enemies outside to battle. Any group that doesn't get its act together internally tends to get trounced by outsiders.

Some managers translate the political approach described in this box to mean management by intimidation and manipulation. It sometimes works, but the risks are high. Here's an example:

Howard: Didn't the secretary tell you that we're in a meeting right now? If you'll wait outside, I'll be able to see you in about an hour.

Marshall: In your next job, maybe you should train your secretary better. Anyway, I can't waste time sitting around in hallways. Everyone in this room knows why I'm here. You've got a choice, Bill. You can cooperate with me, or you can lose any credibility you still have in this company.

Howard: If I didn't have any more experience than you do, I wouldn't be so quick to throw my weight around. But if you think you know it all already, I guess you won't need any help from me.

Marshall: What I know is that this department has gone downhill under your leadership, and it's my job to turn it around. You can go home right now, if you want—you know where the door is. But if you're smart, you'll stay and help. The vice president wants my report on the transition. You'll be a lot better off if I can tell him you've been cooperative.

Moviegoers cheer when bullies get their comeuppance. It can be satisfying to give the verbal equivalent of a kick in the groin to someone who deserves it. In this exchange, Marshall establishes that she is tough, even dangerous. But such coercive tactics can be expensive in the long run. She is likely to win this battle because her hand is stronger. But she may lose the war. She increases Howard's antagonism, and her attack may offend him and frighten her new staff. Even if they dislike

Howard, they might see Marshall as arrogant and callous. She lays the ground for a counterattack, and may have done political damage that will be difficult to reverse.

Sophisticated political leaders prefer to avoid naked demonstrations of power, looking instead for ways to appeal to the self-interests of potential adversaries:

Howard: Didn't the secretary tell you that we're in a meeting right now? If you'll wait outside, I'll be able to see you in about an hour.

Marshall: [pleasantly] Bill, if it's OK with you, I'd prefer to skip the games and go to work. I expect this department to be a winner, and I hope that's what we all want. I also would like to manage the transition in a way that's good for your career, Bill, and for the careers of others in the room.

Howard: If I need advice from you on my career, I'll ask.

Marshall: OK, but the vice president has asked me to let him know about the cooperation I get here. I'd like to be able to say that everyone has been helping me as much as possible. Is that what you'd like, too?

Howard: I've known the vice president a lot longer than you have. I can talk to him myself.

Marshall: I know, Bill, he's told me that. In fact, I just came from his office. If you'd like, we could both go see him right now.

Howard: Uh, no, not right now.

Marshall: Well, then, let's get on with it. Do you want to finish what you were discussing, or is this a good time for us to develop some agreement on how we're going to work together?

In this politically based response, Marshall is both direct and diplomatic. She uses a light touch in dismissing Howard's opening salvo. ("I'd prefer to skip the games.") She speaks directly to Howard's interest in his career and her subordinates' interest in theirs. She deftly deflates his posturing by asking if he wants to go with her to talk to the vice president. Clearly, she is confident of her political position and knows that his bluster has little to back it up.

Note that in both political scenarios, Marshall draws on her power resources. In the first, she uses those resources to humiliate Howard, but in the second, her approach is subtler. She conserves her political capital and takes charge while leaving Howard with as much pride as possible, achieving something closer to a win-win than a win-lose outcome.

Symbolic Frame
A SYMBOLIC SCENARIO

The symbolic leader believes that the most important part of a leader's job is inspiration—giving people something they can believe in. People become excited about and committed to a place with a unique identity, a special place where they feel that what they do is really important. Effective symbolic leaders are passionate about making the organization unique in its niche and communicating that passion to others. They use dramatic symbols to get people excited and to give them a sense of the organization's mission. They are visible and energetic. They create slogans, tell stories, hold rallies, give awards, appear where they are least expected, and manage by wandering around.

Symbolic leaders are sensitive to an organization's history and culture. They seek to use the best in an organization's traditions and values as a base for building a culture that has cohesiveness and meaning. They articulate a vision that communicates the organization's unique capabilities and mission.

At first glance, Cindy Marshall's encounter with Bill Howard might seem a poor candidate for the symbolic approach outlined in this box. An ineffective effort could produce embarrassing results, making the would-be symbolic leader look foolish:

Howard: Didn't the secretary tell you that we're in a meeting right now? If you'll wait outside, I'll be able to see you in about an hour.

Marshall: It's great to see that you're all hard at work. It's proof that we all share a commitment to excellence in customer service. In fact, I've already made up buttons for all the staff. Here—I have one for each of you. They read, "The customer is always first." They look great, and they communicate the spirit that we all want in the department. Go on with your meeting. I can use the hour to talk to some of the staff about their visions for the department. [She walks out of the office.]

Howard: [to remaining staff] Did you believe that? I told you they hired a real space cadet to replace me. Maybe you didn't believe me, but you just saw it with your own eyes.

Marshall's symbolic direction might be on the right track, but symbols work only when they are attuned to the context—both people and place. As a newcomer to the department culture, she needs to pay close attention to her audience. Meaningless symbols antagonize, and empty symbolic events backfire.

Conversely, a skillful symbolic leader understands that a situation of challenge and stress can serve as a powerful opportunity to articulate values and build a sense of mission. Marshall demonstrates how, in a well-formed symbolic approach to Howard's gruffness:

Howard: Didn't the secretary tell you that we're in a meeting right now? If you'll wait outside, I'll be able to see you in about an hour.

Marshall: [smiling] Maybe this is just the traditional initiation ritual in this department, Bill, but let me ask a question. If one of our customers came through the door right now, would you ask her to wait outside for an hour?

Howard: If she just came barging in like you did, sure.

Marshall: Are you working on something that's more important than responding to our customers?

Howard: They're not your customers. You've only been here five minutes.

Marshall: True, but I've been with this company long enough to know the importance of putting customers first.

Howard: Look, you don't know the first thing about how this department functions. Before you go off on some customer crusade, you ought to learn a little about how we do things.

Marshall: There's a lot I can learn from all of you, and I'm eager to get started. For example, I'm very interested in your ideas on how we can make this a department where as soon as people walk in, they get the sense that this is a place where people care, are responsive, and genuinely want to be helpful. I'd like that to be true for anyone who comes in—a staff member, a customer, or just someone who got lost and came into the wrong office. That's not the message I got from my initiation a couple of minutes ago, but I'm sure we can think of lots of ways to change that. How does that fit with your image of what the department should be like?

Notice how Marshall recasts the conversation. Instead of engaging in a personal confrontation with Howard, she focuses on the department's core values. She brings her "customer first" commitment with her, but she avoids positioning that value as something imposed from outside. Instead, she grounds it in an experience everyone in the room has just shared: the way she was greeted when she entered. Like many successful symbolic leaders, she is attuned to the cues about values and culture that are expressed in everyday life. She communicates her philosophy, but she also asks questions to draw out Howard and her new staff members. If she can use the organization's history to an advantage in rekindling a commitment to customer service, she is off to a good start.

BENEFITS AND RISKS OF REFRAMING

The multiple replays of the Howard-Marshall incident illustrate both the power and the risks of reframing. The frames are powerful because of their ability to spur imagination and generate new insights and options. But each frame has limits as well as strengths, and each can be applied well or poorly.

Frames can be used as scripts, or scenarios, to guide action in high-stakes circumstances. By changing your script, you can change how you appear, what you do, and how your audience sees you. You can create the possibility of transformation in everyday life. Few of us have the dramatic skill and versatility of a professional actor, but you can alter what you do by choosing an alternative script or scenario. You have been learning how to do this since birth. Both men and women, for example, typically employ different scenarios for same-sex and opposite-sex encounters. Students who are guarded and formal when talking to a professor become energized and intimate when talking to friends. Managers who are polite and deferential with the boss may be gruff and autocratic with subordinates and then come home at night to romp playfully with their kids. The tenderhearted neighbor becomes a ruthless competitor when his company's market share is threatened. The tough-minded drill instructor bows to authority when faced by a colonel. Consciously or not, we all read situations to figure out what scene we're in and what role we've been assigned so that we can respond in character. But it's important to ask ourselves whether the drama is the one we want and to recognize that we have latitude as to which character to play and how to interpret the script.

The essence of reframing is examining the same situation from multiple vantage points. The effective leader changes lenses when things don't make sense or aren't working. Reframing offers the promise of powerful new options, but it cannot guarantee that every new strategy will be successful. Each lens offers distinctive advantages, but each has its blind spots and shortcomings.

The structural frame risks ignoring everything that falls outside the rational scope of tasks, procedures, policies, and organization charts. Structural thinking can overestimate the power of authority and underestimate the authority of power. Paradoxically, overreliance on structural assumptions and a narrow emphasis on rationality can lead to an irrational neglect of human, political, and cultural variables crucial to effective action.

Adherents of the human resource frame sometimes cling to a romanticized view of human nature in which everyone hungers for growth and collaboration. Human resource enthusiasts can be overly optimistic about integrating individual and organizational needs while neglecting structure and the stubborn realities of conflict and scarcity.

The political frame captures dynamics that other frames miss but has its own limits. A fixation on politics easily becomes a cynical self-fulfilling prophecy, reinforcing conflict and mistrust while sacrificing opportunities for rational discourse, collaboration, and hope. Political action is too often interpreted as amoral, scheming, and oblivious to the common good.

The symbolic frame offers powerful insight into fundamental issues of meaning and belief, as well as possibilities for bonding people into a cohesive group with a shared mission. But its concepts are also elusive; effectiveness depends on the artistry of the user. Symbols are sometimes mere fluff or camouflage, the tools of a scoundrel who seeks to manipulate the unsuspecting or an awkward attempt that embarrasses more than energizes people at work.

REFRAMING FOR NEWCOMERS AND OUTSIDERS

Marshall's initial encounter with Howard exemplifies many of the challenges and tests that managers confront as they move forward in their careers. The different scenarios offer a glimmer of what they might run into, depending on how they size up a situation. Managers feel powerless and trapped when they rely on only one or two frames. This is particularly true for newcomers, as well as for women and members of other groups who experience "the dogged frustration of people living daily in a system not made for them and with no plans soon to adjust for them or their differences" (Gallos, Ramsey, and Associates, 1997, p. 216). These outsiders are less likely to get a second or third chance when they fail.

Though progressive organizations have made heroic strides in building more just opportunity structures (Levering and Moskowitz, 1993; Morrison, 1992), the path to success is still fraught with obstacles blocking women and minorities. Judicious reframing can enable them to transform an imprisoning managerial trap into a promising leadership opportunity. And the more often individuals break through the glass ceiling or out of the corporate ghetto, the more quickly those barriers will disappear altogether. Career barriers can feel as foreboding and impenetrable as the Berlin Wall did—until it suddenly fell. The 2008 U.S. presidential race signaled that more walls were imploding when the Democratic nomination came down to an unprecedented contest between a woman and an African American—Hillary Clinton and Barack Obama.

SUMMARY

Managers can use frames as scenarios, or scripts, to generate alternative approaches to challenging circumstances. In planning for a high-stakes meeting or a tense encounter, they can imagine and try out novel ways to play their roles. Until reframing becomes instinctive, it takes more than the few seconds that Cindy Marshall had to generate an effective response in every frame. In practicing any new skill—playing tennis, flying an airplane, or handling a tough leadership challenge—the process is often slow and painstaking at first. But as skill improves, it gets easier, faster, and more fluid.

Reframing Leadership

Rudy Giuliani could have shrunk from the awesome burdens created by the terrorist attacks of 9/11. He woke up that morning a virtual has-been, a wounded, end-of-term mayor whose ratings in New York and elsewhere had been in steady decline. New Yorkers were tired of his arrogance and bullying. A messy, very public divorce was beginning to turn him into an object of ridicule (his estranged wife and their children were living at Gracie Mansion, the mayor's official residence, while His Honor bunked in a friend's spare bedroom). Yet, as discussed in Chapter Fifteen, Giuliani seemed transformed on New York's bloodiest day. He sped to the scene, arriving in time to see smoke, chaos, and bodies falling from the sky. He brought his hand to his mouth as he battled back tears, and then he went to work. He closed bridges and tunnels, ordered the evacuation of the disaster area, and postponed the primary elections. "By mid-day, he had all of the city's commissioners sitting at a makeshift conference table at a temporary command center reporting on how their agencies were responding. Not just the police and fire and emergency management agencies: Every agency was present. That process created an immediate sense of discipline for a government that otherwise might have spun in confusion" (Coles, 2002).

Giuliani appeared repeatedly on television to offer calm, reassuring accounts of complex and horrible news. He resisted pressure to speculate beyond what he knew about the death toll, saying simply that it would be "much more than any of us can bear." Wearing spattered boots and a New York Fire Department baseball cap, he gave tours to visiting dignitaries. Determined to prove New York's resilience, the mayor pushed relentlessly to get Broadway theaters and the New York Stock Exchange reopened as soon as possible, overriding naysayers who said it couldn't or shouldn't be done. "He attended funerals, comforted survivors, urged residents to dine out and tourists to come in, all the while exuding compassion and resolve. The man who had seemed so finished just a few weeks earlier was now greeted with cheers wherever he went: Rudy! Rudy!" (Barry, 2001, p. A1).

In times of crisis we expect leadership from people in high places, and we are grievously disappointed if they fail to provide it. But it is misleading to imagine that leadership comes only from people in high positions. Such a view causes us to ask too much of too few. Rudy Giuliani insisted that the real heroes of 9/11 were firefighters, police officers, and rescue workers who risked, and in many cases lost, their lives trying to help others. Under conditions of enormous danger and confusion, often cut off from communication with their commanding officers, they improvised and exercised on-the-spot leadership that significantly reduced the death toll. They demonstrated clearly that we need more leaders as well as better leadership.

We begin this chapter by exploring what leadership is, what it is not, and what it can and cannot accomplish. We look at the differences between leadership and power and between leadership and management, and we emphasize that leadership is always situated in both relationships and contexts. We then review research on effective leadership and explore two leadership models popular with practitioners. We also examine the issue of gender and leadership. Finally, we explore how each of the four frames generates its own image of leadership.

THE IDEA OF LEADERSHIP

Leadership is seen as a panacea for almost any social problem. Middle managers and workers often say their enterprise would thrive if senior management showed "real leadership." Conventional wisdom sees leadership as a good thing that we need more of, at least the right kind. "For many—perhaps for most—Americans, leadership is a word that has risen above normal workaday usage as a conveyer of meaning and has become a kind of incantation. We feel that if we repeat it often enough with sufficient ardor, we shall ease our sense of having lost our way, our sense of things unaccomplished, of duties unfulfilled" (Gardner, 1986, p. 1). Yet there is confusion and disagreement about what leadership means and how much difference it can make.

Sennett (1980, p. 197) writes, "Authority is not a thing; it is a search for solidity and security in the strength of others which will seem to be like a thing." The same is true of leadership. It is not tangible. It exists only in relationships and in the perception of the engaged parties. Most images suggest that leaders are powerful. Yet many examples of the use of power fall outside our image of leadership: armed robbers, extortionists, bullies, traffic cops. Implicitly, we expect leaders to persuade or inspire rather than to coerce. We also expect leaders to produce cooperative effort and to pursue goals that transcend narrow self-interest.

Leadership is distinct from authority and position, though authorities may be leaders. Weber (1947) linked authority to legitimacy. People choose to obey authority so long as they believe it is legitimate. Authority and leadership are both built on voluntary compliance. Leaders cannot lead without legitimacy. But many examples of authority fall outside the domain of leadership. As Gardner put it, "The meter maid has authority, but not necessarily leadership" (1989, p. 7).

Heifetz argues that authority often impedes leadership: "Authority constrains leadership because in times of distress, people expect too much. They form inappropriate dependencies that isolate their authorities behind a mask of knowing. [The leadership role] is played badly if authorities reinforce dependency and delude themselves into thinking that they have the answers when they do not. Feeling pressured to know, they will surely come up with an answer, even if poorly tested, misleading, and wrong" (1994, p. 180).

Leadership is often confused with management. But a person can be a leader without being a manager, and many managers could not "lead a squad of seven-year-olds to the ice-cream counter" (Gardner, 1989, p. 2). Bennis and Nanus (1985) suggest that "managers do things right, and leaders do the right thing" (p. 21)—managers focus on execution, leaders on purpose. A managerially oriented navy officer gave a ringing endorsement of his more leaderlike successor: "I go by the book; he writes the book."

Kotter (1988) sees management as being primarily about structural nuts and bolts: planning, organizing, and controlling. He views leadership as a change-oriented process of visioning, networking, and building relationships. But Gardner argues against contrasting leadership and management too sharply because leaders may "end up looking like a cross between Napoleon and the Pied Piper, and managers like unimaginative clods" (1989, p. 3). He suggests several dimensions for distinguishing leadership from management. Leaders think in the long term, look outside as well as inside, and influence constituents beyond their immediate formal jurisdiction. They emphasize vision and renewal and have the political skills to cope with the demands of multiple constituencies.

THE CONTEXT OF LEADERSHIP

In story and myth, leaders are often lonely heroes and itinerant warriors, wed only to honor and a noble cause. Think of Jason Bourne, Joan of Arc, the Lone Ranger, or Rambo. But images of solitary, heroic leaders mislead by suggesting that leaders go it alone and by focusing the spotlight too much on individuals and too little on the stage where they play their parts. Leaders make things happen, but things also make leaders happen. The transformation in Rudy Giuliani's image after 9/11 from has-been to hero in twenty-four hours is a perfect illustration. Giuliani found himself center stage in an unplanned theater of horror and delivered the performance of his life. Another scenario would have required a different leadership role. No single formula is possible for the great range of situations leaders encounter.

Heroic images of leadership convey the notion of a one-way transaction: leaders show the way and followers tag along. This view masks the mutual interplay between the two. Leaders are not independent actors; they both shape and are shaped by their constituents (Gardner, 1989; Simmel, 1950; Heifetz and Linsky, 2002). Leaders often promote a new initiative only after a large number of constituents favor it (Cleveland, 1985). Leaders' actions generate responses that in turn affect the leaders' capacity for taking further initiatives (Murphy, 1985). As Briand puts it, "A 'leader' who makes a decision and then attempts to 'sell' it is not wise and will likely not prove effective. The point is not that leaders should do less, but that others can and should do more. Everyone must accept responsibility for the people's well-being, and everyone has a role to play in sustaining it" (1993, p. 39).

Although it is tempting to equate leadership with position, this relegates others to a passive role. It also reinforces a tendency for senior executives to take on more responsibility than they can discharge (Oshry, 1995). Leadership does not come automatically with high position; conversely, it is possible to be a leader without a position of formal authority. In fact, good organizations encourage leadership from many quarters (Barnes and Kriger, 1986; Kanter, 1983).

Leadership is thus a subtle process of mutual influence fusing thought, feeling, and action. It produces cooperative effort in the service of purposes embraced by both leader and led. Single-frame managers are unlikely to understand and attend to the intricacies of this lively process.

WHAT DO WE KNOW ABOUT GOOD LEADERSHIP?

Two of the most widely accepted leadership propositions offer divergent perspectives. One asserts that all good leaders must have the right stuff—qualities like vision, strength, and commitment. The other holds that good leadership is situational; what works in one setting will not work in another. A proposition from the "effective schools" literature illustrates the right-stuff perspective: a good school is headed by a strong and visionary instructional leader. An example of the situational view is the belief that it takes a different kind of person to lead when you're growing and adding staff than when you're cutting budgets and laying people off.

Despite the tension between these one-best-way and contingency views, both capture part of the truth. Studies have found shared characteristics among effective leaders across sectors and situations. Another body of research has identified situational variables that determine the kind of leadership that works best.

One Best Way

Recent decades have produced a steady stream of studies of effective leadership (Bennis and Nanus, 1985, 2007; Clifford and Cavanagh, 1985; Collins, 2001; Collins and Porras, 1994; Conger, 1989; Farkas and De Backer, 1996; Kotter, 1982, 1988; Kotter and Cohen, 2002; Kouzes and Posner, 2007; Levinson and Rosenthal, 1984; Maccoby, 1981, 2003; Peters and Austin, 1985; Vaill, 1982). Many have been qualitative studies of leaders, primarily corporate executives. Methodology has varied from casual impressions to systematic interviews and observation.

No characteristic is universal in these studies, but vision and focus show up most often. Effective leaders help articulate a vision, set standards for performance, and create focus and direction. A related characteristic explicit in some reports (Clifford and Cavanagh, 1985; Kouzes and Posner, 2007; Peters and Austin, 1985) and implicit in others is the ability to communicate a vision effectively, often through the use of symbols. Another quality often mentioned is commitment or passion (Clifford and Cavanagh, 1985; Collins, 2001; Peters and Austin, 1985; Vaill, 1982). Good leaders care deeply about their work and the people who do it. Yet another characteristic is the ability to inspire trust and build relationships (Bennis and Nanus, 2007; Kotter, 1988; Maccoby, 1981).

Beyond vision, passion, and trust, consensus breaks down. The studies cited so far, along with extensive reviews of the literature (Bass, 1990; Gardner, 1987; Hollander, 1978; Yukl, 2005), generate a long list of attributes associated with effective leadership: risk taking, flexibility, self-confidence, interpersonal skills, managing by walking around, task competence, intelligence, decisiveness, understanding of followers, and courage, to name a few. Kouzes and Posner (2007) found that honesty came first on a list of traits that people most admired in a leader. Workers said of Pat Carrigan, a school psychologist who shifted to the auto industry and turned around two different General Motors parts plants: "She ain't got a phony bone in her body." Her truthfulness played a key role in gaining the cooperation of formerly disaffected employees. Collins, in his best-seller *Good to Great* (2001), insists that humility is a key quality of great leaders, while Maccoby (2003) argues for narcissism instead. The oldest reliable finding about effective leaders—they are smarter and work harder than other people—continues to find research support (O'Reilly and Chatman, 1994). But effort and IQ are found in people who are better at almost anything, and there are many brilliant hard workers who are hopeless leaders.

Blake and Mouton's "managerial grid" (1969, 1985) is a classic and still popular example of a one-best-way approach. Diffused through scores of books, articles, and training programs, the grid postulates two fundamental dimensions of leader effectiveness: concern for task and concern for people. The model arrays approaches to leadership on a two-dimensional grid shown in Exhibit 17.1. Theoretically, the grid contains eighty-one cells, though Blake and Mouton emphasize only five:

- 1, 1: The manager with little concern for task or people who simply goes through the motions.

- 1, 9: The friendly manager who likes people but has less concern for task.

- 9, 1: The hard-driving taskmaster.

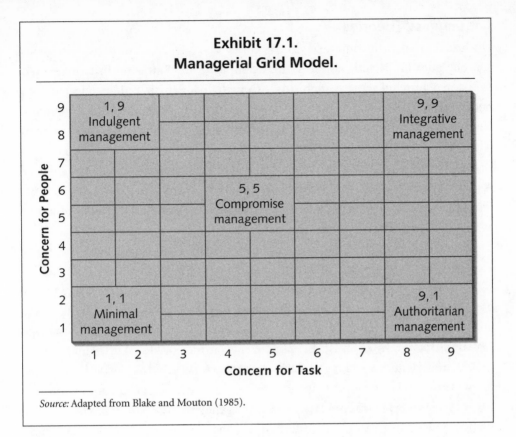

Exhibit 17.1.
Managerial Grid Model.

Source: Adapted from Blake and Mouton (1985).

- 5, 5: The compromising manager who tries to split the difference between task and people.

- 9, 9: The ideal manager who integrates task and people and produces outstanding performance.

Blake and Mouton have vigorously defended their conviction that a 9, 9 style is a leadership approach for all situations and all seasons (Blake and Mouton, 1982), but this claim has been heavily criticized. The grid approach focuses almost exclusively on task and people. It gives little attention to constituents other than direct subordinates and assumes that a leader who integrates concern for task with concern for people is effective in almost all circumstances. But if structure is unwieldy, political conflict is rampant, or culture is threadbare, the grid model has little to say.

Contingency Theories

Do leaders make the times, or do the times make leaders? In considering this age-old question, think about some examples. The Battle of Britain secured Winston Churchill's place in history, though the British public rejected him before the war and again right after. Much the same happened for Rudy Giuliani, who went from has-been before 9/11 to hero after it and then back to has-been when he ran for president in 2008. Jimmy Carter's intellect propelled him to success as a navy officer and governor, but could not save his presidency. Joan of Arc would not have rated a historical footnote without a war, a beleaguered king, and the dramatic circumstances of her death. Such examples argue for situation as the prime catalyst in leadership.

Several writers have offered situational theories of leadership (including Fiedler, 1967; Fiedler and Chemers, 1974; Hersey, 1984; Hersey and Blanchard, 1977; Reddin, 1970; and Vroom and Yetton, 1973), but most take a limited view of leadership and few have much empirical support. Many conflate leadership and management, typically treating leadership as synonymous with managing subordinates. In contrast, Burns (1978), Gardner (1986), Kotter and Cohen (2002), and Heifetz and Linsky (2002) argue persuasively that leaders need skill in managing relationships with all significant stakeholders, including superiors, peers, and external constituents. Contingency theories are a major area for further research. Almost everyone believes that widely varying circumstances require different forms of leadership, but evidence is still sparse.

These limitations have not kept approaches such as the Hersey and Blanchard notion of situational leadership (1977, 2007) from becoming widely popular in management development programs. Hersey and Blanchard use two dimensions of leadership similar to those in the managerial grid: task and people. Hersey defines task behavior as "the extent to which the leader engages in spelling out the duties and responsibilities of an individual or group" (1984, p. 31). Relationship behavior is "the extent to which the leader engages in two-way or multi-way communication." It includes "listening, encouraging, facilitating, providing clarification, and giving socioemotional support" (p. 32). Hersey combines task and people into a two-by-two chart that shows four possible "leadership styles." (See Exhibit 17.2.) The labels for three of those styles have evolved over the decades (from telling, selling, and participating to directing, coaching, and supporting), but the basic message has changed little.

Exhibit 17.2.
Situational Leadership Model.

High Relationship, Low Task: **Leadership Through Supporting** Use when followers are "able" but "unwilling" or "insecure"	*High Relationship, High Task:* **Leadership Through Coaching** Use when followers are "unable" but "willing" or "motivated"
Low Relationship, Low Task: **Leadership Through Delegation** Use when followers are "able" and "willing" or "motivated"	*Low Relationship, High Task:* **Leadership Through Directing** Use when followers are "unable" and "unwilling" or "insecure"

Source: Adapted from Hersey (1984, p. 63).

When is each style appropriate? It depends on subordinates' "maturity" (Hersey and Blanchard, 1977) or "readiness level" (Hersey, 1984). Hersey defines readiness in terms of subordinates' commitment (how willing they are to do a good job) and competence (how able they are to do the job well). Four levels of subordinate readiness determine the appropriate style.

For subordinates at the lowest level (low competence and low commitment), the model counsels managers to "direct": such people need their boss to tell them what to do. At the next level up (high commitment but low competence), subordinates want to do the job but lack skills—they need "coaching" from the boss. When subordinates are able but unwilling, the leader should "support" through a participative process of sharing ideas and discussing what to do. At the highest level, with subordinates who are both able and willing, the leader should simply "delegate": the subordinates will do fine on their own.

The model is very popular because it is intuitively plausible, but research has not provided strong support (Hambleton and Gumpert, 1982; Graeff, 1983; Blank, Weitzel, and Green, 1990). If, for example, managers give unwilling and unable subordinates high direction and low support, what would cause their motivation to improve? The manager of a computer design team told us ruefully, "I treated my group with a 'telling' [directing] management style and found that in fact they became both less able and less willing." Furthermore, like Blake and Mouton, Hersey and Blanchard focus mostly on the relationship between managers and immediate subordinates and say little about structure, politics, or symbols.

Leadership Models as Secular Myths

Dealing with people is a perennially perplexing aspect of managing. Managers are always looking for ideas to make the job easier. Too often, the search for simplicity overlooks important realities. Even so, a manager may conclude that any model or theory is better than nothing in the face of confusion and mystery. True believers may defend their faith with fervor, as the following case study illustrates.

WHEN FAITHS COLLIDE

A corporation was developing a new management training program for a group of two thousand technical managers. A task force with representatives from two divisions came together to decide what to teach. The representatives from Division A had participated in managerial grid seminars. They knew in their hearts that the grid was the one best way and that it should be the foundation of the seminar. The managers in Division B had attended situational leadership seminars, and their faith in the situational model was equally fervent.

Initially, the two sides engaged in polite talk and rational argument. When that failed, the conversation gradually became more heated. Eventually, the group found itself hopelessly deadlocked. An outside consultant came in to mediate the dispute. He listened while the representatives from each division reviewed the conversation. The consultant then said to the group, "I'm impressed by the passion on both sides. I'm curious about one thing. If you all believe so deeply in these models and if it makes a difference which model someone learns, why can't I see any difference in the behavior of your two groups?" Stunned silence fell over the room. Finally one member said, "You know, I think he's right. We don't use the damn models, we just preach them." That ended the impasse.

From the beginning, humans have sought explanations for occurrences that defied their capacity to make sense. Things happen and we can't explain why. To maintain our sanity we create myths to bolster our faith. Thereafter our beliefs sustain us in the face of doubt and confusion, shielding us from the reality of how little we know. That is true of our approaches to leadership—unless we are able to entertain more than one theology.

GENDER AND LEADERSHIP

Historically, research and writing on leadership focused mostly on men. The implicit, taken-for-granted assumption was that leadership is a male activity. More recent years, however, have seen a dramatic shift in women's roles and accomplishments. In breaking from masculine traditions and embracing more feminine conceptions of leadership, women have blazed new paths.

One example is Karren Brady, who became managing director of the Birmingham (England) City Football Club in 1993. At twenty-three, she was the youngest person, and the only woman, heading a professional English soccer team. As you might expect, she ran into a few challenges. There was the strapping forward who told her on the team bus that he liked her blouse because he could see her breasts through it. She looked him in the eye and replied, "Where I'm going to send you, you won't be able to see them from there." A week later, he was downgraded to a club a hundred miles away. There was the time the directors of another team told her how fortunate she was that they were willing to let her into their owners' box. She fired back, "The day I have to feel grateful for half a lager and a pork pie in a dump of a little box with a psychedelic carpet is the day I give up" (Hoge, 2002, p. A14).

Brady got plenty of media attention, but it often focused on her looks and wardrobe. One newspaper ran a full-page photo of her in a short skirt under the headline, "Sex Shooter." Another described her entry into a meeting: "Every inch the modern woman, she totters into the room on high-heeled strappy sandals and a short and sexy black suit." Brady was continually perplexed: "I came here to run a business, to put right a dilapidated, rundown operation with a series of business solutions. But the media, with the combination of my age, the way I look, and obviously the fact that I was a female—the first in a male-dominated world—went into a frenzy. It was unbelievable. I'd be in press conferences, and journalists would actually ask me my vital statistics" (Hoge, 2002, p. A14).

Still, Brady understood that publicity, even tinged with notoriety, was good for business. She took a team that had never shown a profit from the edge of bankruptcy to become one of the England's strongest teams, both on the field and at the cash register, with an estimated value in 2007 of more than $100 million. She even overcame the complications that might have arisen after she married one of her players. She bought and sold her husband twice, making over a million pounds in the process. She won businesswoman-of-the-year awards, and eventually even her fellow football executives recognized her talent, naming her to represent them in negotiations for the national television contract that yielded a big chunk of their revenue.

Women like Karren Brady have proven that they can lead in a man's world. But do men and women lead differently? Are they seen differently in leadership roles? Why do men still have such a disproportionate hold on positions of institutional and organizational power? Research on gender and leadership has asked these and other questions, and we turn next to some of the answers that have emerged.

Do Men and Women Lead Differently?

Helgesen (1990), Rosener (1990), and others have argued that women bring a "female advantage" to leadership. They believe that modern organizations need the leadership style that women are more likely to bring, including concern for people, nurturance, and willingness to share information. But the evidence is equivocal. We might expect, for example, that women would be higher on people attributes (warmth, support, participation) and lower on political characteristics (power, shrewdness, aggression). But examples like Karren Brady, Carly Fiorina as Hewlett-Packard CEO, and Margaret Thatcher as British Prime Minister tell us that things are not so simple. In fact, research gives such stereotypes limited support. Bolman and Deal (1991, 1992a) found no differences in frame orientation among men and women. Eagly and Johnson (1990) found no gender differences in emphasis on people versus task, though women tended to be somewhat more participative and less directive than men.

For the most part, the available evidence suggests that men and women in comparable positions are more alike than different, at least in the eyes of their subordinates (Carless, 1998; Komives, 1991; Morrison, White, and Van Velsor, 1987; Bolman and Deal, 1991, 1992a). When differences are detected, they generally show women scoring somewhat higher than men on a variety of measures of leadership and managerial behavior (Bass, Avolio, and Atwater, 1996; Eagly and

Carli, 2003; Edwards, 1991; Hallinger, Bickman, and Davis, 1990; Weddle, 1991; and Wilson and Wilson, 1991). But the differences are not large, and it is not clear whether they have practical significance.

Why the Glass Ceiling?

If women lead at least as well as men, why does the so-called glass ceiling cap their rise to top positions? Growing numbers are now in the pipeline leading to the executive suite. In the United States, they are a substantial majority of college students and an expanding presence in professional schools—more than half of education and law students and close to half in business and medical schools. This is a dramatic shift (except in education, where they have long been a majority).

Nevertheless, at the end of the twentieth century, women still represented less than 10 percent of senior executives in business (Ragins, Townsend, and Mattis, 1998). And in 2007, women made up less than 7 percent of senior executives and 2 percent of CEOs in *Fortune*'s Global 100 companies. More than half the companies did not have a single female officer. "In the race for talent, women are barely on the playing field in the most senior levels of the largest companies in the world," says Irene Natividad, co-chair of Corporate Women Directors International (Business Wire, 2007). "This is ironic, since the percentage of female workers, consumers, small business owners and investors continues to accelerate."

The story is similar in education. In American schools, women constitute the great majority of teachers and a growing percentage of middle managers, yet in 2007 they accounted for only 15 percent of school superintendents. That was about the same as in 1930, though it was up from only 2 percent in 1981 (Keller, 1999).

There is no consensus about what sustains the glass ceiling, but evidence points to several contributing factors:

• *Stereotypes associate leadership with maleness.* Schein (1975, 1990) found that both men and women tend to link leadership characteristics to men more than women.

• *Women walk a tightrope of conflicting expectations.* Simply put, high-level jobs are "powerful, but women, in the minds of many people, should not be. According to this set of beliefs, a powerful woman is distasteful, unfeminine, and even ludicrous. A strong woman can make both men and women uncomfortable by challenging the conventional understanding—unless, that is, she finds a way to exercise power that is recognizably different from the norm" (Keller, 1999; Belkin, 2007). For example, Brescoll and Uhlmann (2008) found that expressing anger was viewed as a positive for male executives, but a negative for women. Fisman, Iyengar, Kamenica, and Simonson (2006) found that women were attracted to intelligent men, but men tended not to like women who were smarter than they were.

The challenge for women is to be powerful and "feminine" at the same time, which is "an incredibly difficult role negotiation" (Brunner, cited in Keller, 1999). According to Eagly and Carli, women face pressures to "behave extremely competently while reassuring others that they conform to expectations concerning appropriate female behavior" (Eagly and Carli, 2003, p. 825). That was a distinctive challenge for Hillary Clinton as the one woman running for president in 2008. How could she demonstrate that she was tough enough to be commander-in-chief without seeming too aggressive or angry? How could she show feminine warmth and caring without seeming weak?

• *Women encounter discrimination.* In ancient fairy tales as well as modern films, powerful women often turn out to be witches (or worse). Shakespeare's *The Taming of the Shrew* is typical of many stories with the message that a strong woman is dangerous until tamed by a stronger man. The historical association of powerful men with leadership and of powerful women with evil produces unspoken and often unconscious bias. Valian (1999) argues that prevailing gender schemata tacitly shape our ways of thinking and associate competence with maleness. Even though these differences are subtle and unconscious, they accumulate over the course of individual careers to give men a competitive advantage. Eagly and Carli report that bias against women leaders varies by situation and that "women face discriminatory barriers mainly in male-dominated and masculine environments and with male evaluators. Because higher levels of authority and higher wages are concentrated in such environments and are controlled primarily by men, this prejudice is highly consequential for women's advancement" (2003, p. 822).

• *Women pay a higher price.* Shakeshaft (cited in Keller, 1999) argues that the rewards of senior positions may be lower for women for a reason. Compared with men, they have higher needs for success in their family and personal lives but lower needs for esteem and status. Almost 70 percent of women in one study named personal and family responsibilities as by far the biggest barrier to their career success (Morris, 2002). Executive jobs impose a crushing workload on incumbents. The burden is even more overwhelming for women, who still do the majority of the housework and child rearing in most dual-career families. That helps to explain why fast-track women are less likely to marry and, if they do marry, are more likely to divorce (Heffernan, 2002; Keller, 1999). It also clarifies why many women who do make it to the top are blessed with "trophy husbands"—those hard-to-find stay-at-home dads (Morris, 2002).

Women have made progress. Attitudes are changing, support mechanisms (such as day care) have increased, and cultural views have shifted. Perhaps the single strongest force for continued advancement is the tremendous talent pool that women represent—they make up more than half the population and have a growing educational edge over their male counterparts. In 1988, Benazir Bhutto became the first female prime minister in a Muslim country, and she might have returned to the job if not for her tragic assassination in 2007. In 2007, Nancy Pelosi became the first woman to occupy the powerful role of Speaker of the U.S. House of Representatives. Her home-state support network included both of California's senators, Democrats Barbara Boxer and Diane Feinstein. In the same year, Hillary Clinton became the first woman who was viewed as having a strong chance of becoming president of the United States. Between 1986 and 2006, the proportion of female presidents of American universities more than doubled—to almost one in four—and Harvard put a woman in the job for the first time in 2007. Princeton accepted no women until 1969, and thirty years later, some of its mostly male alumni worried that their beloved alma mater might be on the skids when the first woman president appointed the first female provost. But grumbling at alumni gatherings could not change the fact that women were making gains even in America's most elite academic institutions.

REFRAMING LEADERSHIP

Reframing offers a chance to get beyond constricted, oversimplified views of leadership. Each frame offers a distinctive image of the leadership process. Depending on leader and circumstance, each turn of the kaleidoscope can reveal compelling and constructive leadership opportunities, even though no one image is right for all times and seasons. In this section, we discuss the four images of leadership summarized in Exhibit 17.3. For each, we examine skills and processes and propose rules of thumb for successful leadership practice.

Exhibit 17.3.
Reframing Leadership.

	LEADERSHIP IS EFFECTIVE WHEN		LEADERSHIP IS INEFFECTIVE WHEN	
FRAME	LEADER IS:	LEADERSHIP PROCESS IS:	LEADER IS:	LEADERSHIP PROCESS IS:
Structural	Analyst, architect	Analysis, design	Petty bureaucrat or tyrant	Management by detail and fiat
Human resource	Catalyst, servant	Support, empowerment	Weakling, pushover	Abdication
Political	Advocate, negotiator	Advocacy, coalition building	Con artist, thug	Manipulation, fraud
Symbolic	Prophet, poet	Inspiration, meaning-making	Fanatic, charlatan	Mirage, smoke and mirrors

Architect or Tyrant? Structural Leadership

Structural leadership often evokes images of petty tyrants and rigid bureaucrats who never met a command or rule they didn't like. Compared with other frames, literature on structural leadership is sparse, and some structural theorists have contended that leadership is neither important nor basic (Hall, 1987). But the effects of structural leadership can be powerful and enduring, even if the style is subtler and more analytic than other forms. Collins and Porras (1994) reported that the founders of many highly successful companies, such as Hewlett-Packard and Sony, had neither a clear vision for their organization nor even a particular product in mind. They were "clock builders": social architects who focused on designing and building an effective organization.

One of the great architects in business history was Alfred P. Sloan Jr., who became president of General Motors in 1923 and remained a dominant force until his retirement in 1956. The structure and strategy he established made GM the world's largest corporation. He has been described as "the George Washington of the GM culture" (Lee, 1988, p. 42), even though his "genius was not in inspirational leadership, but in organizational structures" (p. 43).

At the turn of the twentieth century, some thirty manufacturers produced automobiles in the United States. In 1899, they produced a grand total of about six hundred cars. Most of these small carmakers stumbled out of the starting gate, leaving two late entries, the Ford Motor Company (founded by Henry Ford in 1903) and GM (founded by William Durant in 1908) as front-runners in the race to dominate the American automobile industry. Henry Ford's single-minded determination to build an affordable car pushed Ford into a commanding lead—until Sloan took over at GM.

Under Billy Durant, GM's founder, the company's divisions operated as independent fiefdoms. Durant had built GM by buying everything he could, forming a loose combination of previously independent firms. "GM did not have adequate knowledge or control of the individual operating divisions. It was management by crony, with the divisions operating on a horse-trading basis. The main thing to note here is that no one had the needed information or the needed control over the divisions. The divisions continued to spend lavishly, and their requests for additional funds were met" (Sloan, 1965, pp. 27–28).

Uncontrolled costs and a business slump in 1920 created a financial crisis. Chevrolet lost $5 million in 1921, and GM almost sank (Sloan, 1965). In 1923, Sloan's first year, matters got worse. GM's market share dropped from 20 percent to 17 percent, while Ford's increased to 55 percent. But change was afoot. Henry Ford had a disdain for organization and clung to his vision of a single low-priced, mass-market car. His cheap, reliable Model T—the "Tin Lizzie"—was a marketing miracle at a time when customers would buy anything with four wheels and a motor. But Ford stayed with the same design for almost twenty years. Ford dismissed the need for creature comforts in the Model T, but Sloan surmised that consumers would pay more for amenities like windows to keep out rain and snow. His strategy worked, and Chevrolet soon began to gnaw off large chunks of Ford's market share. By 1928, Model T sales had dropped so precipitously that Henry Ford was forced to close his massive River Rouge plant for a year to retool. General Motors took the lead in the great auto race for the first time in twenty years. For the rest of the twentieth century, no company ever sold more cars than General Motors.

The dominant structural model of the time was a centralized, functional organization, but Sloan felt that GM needed something better. He conceived one of the world's first decentralized organizations. The basic principle was simple: centralize planning and resource allocation; decentralize operating decisions. Under Sloan's model, divisions focused on making and selling cars, while top management did long-range strategy and made major funding decisions. Central staff provided the information and control systems senior management needed to make sound strategic decisions.

The structure worked. By the late 1920s, GM had a more versatile organization with a broader product line than Ford. With the founder still dominating his highly centralized company, Ford was poorly positioned to compete with GM's multiple divisions, each producing its own cars and chasing distinct market niches at different price points. GM's pioneering structural form eventually set the standard for others: "Although they developed many variations and although in very recent years they have been occasionally mixed into a matrix form, only two basic organizational structures have been used for the management of large industrial enterprises. One is the centralized, functional departmentalized type perfected by General Electric and Du Pont before World War I. The other is the multidivisional, decentralized structure initially developed at General Motors and also at Du Pont in the 1920s" (Chandler, 1977, p. 463).

In the 1980s, GM found itself with another structural leader, Roger Smith, at the helm. The results were less satisfying. Like Sloan, Smith ascended to the top job at a difficult time. In 1980, his first year as GM's chief executive, every American carmaker lost money. It was GM's first loss since 1921. Recognizing that the company had serious competitive problems, Smith banked on structure and technology to make it "the world's first 21st century corporation" (Lee, 1988, p. 16). He restructured vehicle operations and spent billions of dollars in a quest for paperless offices and robotized assembly plants. The changes were dramatic, but the results were dismal:

> [Smith's] tenure has been a tragic era in General Motors history. No GM chairman has disrupted as many lives without commensurate rewards, has spent as much money without returns, or has alienated so many along the way. An endless string of public relations and internal relations insensitivities has confused his organization and complicated the attainment of its goals. Few employees believe that [Smith] is in the least concerned with their well-being, and even fewer below executive row anticipate any measure of respect, or reward, for their contributions [Lee, 1988, pp. 286–287].

Why did Smith stumble where Sloan had succeeded? They were equally uncharismatic. Sloan was a somber, quiet engineer who habitually looked as if he were sucking a lemon. Smith's leadership aura was not helped by his blotchy complexion and squeaky voice. Neither had great sensitivity to human resource or symbolic issues. Why, then, was Sloan's structural contribution so durable and Smith's so problematic? The answer comes down to how well each implemented the right structural form. Structural leaders succeed not because of inspiration but because they have the right design for the times and are able to get their structural changes implemented. Effective structural leaders share several characteristics:

- *Structural leaders do their homework.* Sloan was a brilliant engineer who had grown up in the auto industry. Before coming to GM, he ran an auto accessories company where he implemented a divisional structure. When GM bought his firm in 1916, Sloan became a vice president and board member. Working under Durant, he devoted much of his energy to studying GM's structural problems. He pioneered the development of better information systems and market research. He was an early convert to group decision making and created a committee structure to make major decisions. Roger Smith had spent his entire career with General Motors, but most of his jobs were in finance. The numbers told him machines were cheaper than people, so much of his vision for General Motors involved changes in production technology, an area where he had little experience or expertise.

- *Structural leaders rethink the relationship of structure, strategy, and environment.* Sloan's new structure was intimately tied to a strategy for reaching the automotive market. He foresaw growing demand, better cars, and more discriminating consumers. In the face of Henry Ford's stubborn attachment to the Model T, Sloan initiated the "price pyramid" (cars for every pocketbook) and the annual introduction of new models. Automotive technology in the 1920s was evolving almost as fast as electronics and the Internet in recent years. New models every year soon became the industry norm.

For a variety of reasons, GM in the 1960s began to move away from Sloan's concepts. Fearing a government effort to break up the corporation, GM reduced the independence of the car divisions and centralized design and engineering. Increasingly, the divisions became marketing groups required to build and sell the cars that corporate gave them. "Look-alike cars" became the standard, and consumers became confused and angry when they found it hard to see the differences between a Chevrolet and a Cadillac.

Instead of addressing this central issue, Smith focused more on reducing costs than on selling cars. As he saw it, GM's primary competitive problem was high costs driven by high wages. He showed little interest in efforts already under way at GM to improve working conditions on the shop floor. Ironically, his two best investments—NUMMI and Saturn—succeeded precisely because of innovative approaches to managing people: "With only a fraction of the money invested in GM's heavily robotized plants, [the NUMMI plant at] Fremont is more efficient and produces better-quality cars than any plant in the GM system" (Hampton and Norman, 1987, p. 102).

• *Structural leaders focus on implementation.* Structural leaders often miscalculate the difficulties of putting their designs in place. They underestimate resistance, skimp on training, fail to build a political base, and misread cultural cues. Sloan was no human resource specialist, but he intuitively saw the need to cultivate understanding and acceptance of major decisions. He did that by continually asking for advice and by establishing committees and task forces to address major issues.

• *Effective structural leaders experiment.* Sloan tinkered constantly with GM's structure and strategy and encouraged others to do likewise. The Great Depression produced a drop of 72 percent in sales at GM between 1929 and 1932, but the company adapted adroitly to hard times. Sales fell, but GM increased its market share and made money every year. Sloan briefly centralized operations to survive the Depression but decentralized again once business began to recover. In the 1980s, Smith spent billions on his campaign to modernize the corporation and cut costs, yet GM lost market share every year and remained the industry's highest-cost producer: "Much of the advanced technology that GM acquired at such high cost hindered rather than improved productivity. Runaway robots started welding doors shut at the new Detroit-Hamtramck Cadillac plant. Luckily for Ford and Chrysler, poverty prevented them from indulging in the same orgy of spending on robots" ("On a Clear Day . . . ," 1989, p. 77).

Catalyst or Wimp? Human Resource Leadership

The tiny trickle of writing about structural leadership is swamped by a torrent of human resource literature (among the best: Argyris, 1962; Bennis and Nanus, 1985, 2007; Blanchard and Johnson, 1982; Bradford and Cohen, 1984; Boyatzis and McKee, 2005; Fiedler, 1967; Fiedler and Chemers, 1974; Goleman, Boyatzis, and McKee, 2004; Hersey, 1984; Hollander, 1978; House, 1971; Levinson, 1968; Likert, 1961, 1967; Vroom and Yetton, 1973; and Waterman, 1994). Human resource theorists typically advocate openness, caring, mutuality, listening, coaching, participation, and empowerment. They view the leader as a facilitator and catalyst who uses emotional intelligence to motivate and empower subordinates. The leader's power comes from talent, caring, sensitivity, and service rather than position or force. Greenleaf concludes that followers "will freely respond only to individuals who are chosen as leaders because they are proven and trusted as servants" (1973, p. 4). He adds, "The servant-leader makes sure that other people's highest priority needs are being served. The best test [of leadership] is: do those served grow as persons; do they, while being served, become healthier, wiser, freer, more autonomous, more likely themselves to become servants?" (p. 7).

Will managers who embrace such humanistic images be respected leaders who make a difference? Or will they be seen as naive and weak, carried along on the current of other people's ideas and energy? The Cindy Marshall case illustrates both sides. In one human resource encounter, Marshall seems more flunky than leader. In the other, she combines some of the virtues of both servant and catalyst. The leadership tightrope is challenging, and some managers hide behind participation and sensitivity as an excuse not to venture ahead.

There are also many human resource leaders whose skill and artistry produce extraordinary results. An example is Martín Varsavsky, an Argentine native who wound up in New York as a teenager after violence forced his family to flee the military dictatorship in his homeland. Over two decades, Varsavsky founded seven companies and picked up entrepreneur-of-the-year awards in both America and Europe. He made his first millions in New York City real estate before moving to Europe. There he founded two high-tech companies that he later sold for more than a billion dollars each. In 2005, he partnered with venture capitalists and Google to found FON, which soon became the world's largest WiFi network. His approach to managing people was pivotal to his success: "Martín developed management practices that would be keys throughout his career: create horizontal organizations without any hierarchy, communicate clearly what you intend before doing it, delegate as much as possible, trust your colleagues, and leave operating decisions in the hands of others" (Ganitsky and Sancho, 2002, p. 101).

Gifted human resource leaders such as Varsavsky typically apply a consistent set of people-friendly leadership principles.

• *Human resource leaders communicate their strong belief in people.* Human resource leaders are passionate about "productivity through people" (Peters and Waterman, 1982). They express this faith in both words and actions, often formalized in a core philosophy or credo. Fred Smith, founder and CEO of Federal Express, sees "putting people first" as the cornerstone of his company's success: "We discovered a long time ago that customer satisfaction really begins with employee satisfaction. That belief is incorporated in our corporate philosophy statement: "People—Service—Profit . . . In that order" (Waterman, 1994, p. 89).

William Hewlett, cofounder of electronics giant Hewlett-Packard, put it this way:

> The dignity and worth of the individual is a very important part of the HP Way. With this in mind, many years ago we did away with time clocks, and more recently we introduced the flexible work hours program. This is meant to be an expression of trust and confidence in people, as well as providing them with an opportunity to adjust their work schedules to their personal lives. Many new HP people as well as visitors often note and comment to us about another HP way—that is, our informality and our being on a first-name basis. I could cite other examples, but the problem is that none by [itself] really catches the essence of what the HP Way is all about. You can't describe it in numbers and statistics. In the last analysis, it is a spirit, a point of view. There is a feeling that everyone is part of a team, and that team is HP. It is an idea that is based on the individual [Peters and Waterman, 1982, p. 244].

• *Human resource leaders are visible and accessible.* Peters and Waterman (1982) popularized the notion of "management by wandering around"—the idea that managers need to get out of their offices and spend time with workers and customers. Patricia Carrigan—who, as noted earlier, was the first woman to be a plant manager at General Motors—modeled this technique in the course of turning around two manufacturing plants, each with a long history of union-management conflict (Kouzes and Posner, 1987). In both situations, she began by going to the plant floor to introduce herself to workers and ask how they thought the operation could be improved. One worker commented that before Carrigan, "I didn't know who the plant manager was. I wouldn't have recognized him if I saw him." When she left her first assignment after three years, the local union gave her a plaque. It concluded, "Be it resolved that Pat M. Carrigan, through the exhibiting of these qualities as a people person, has played a vital role in the creation of a new way of life at the Lakewood plant. Therefore, be it resolved that the members of Local 34 will always warmly remember Pat M. Carrigan as one of us" (Kouzes and Posner, 1987, p. 36).

- *Effective human resource leaders empower others.* People-oriented leaders often refer to their employees as "partners," "owners," or "associates." They make it clear that workers have a stake in the organization's success and a right to be involved in making decisions. In the 1980s, Jan Carlzon, CEO of Scandinavian Air Systems (SAS), turned around a sluggish business with the intent of making it "the best airline in the world for business travelers" (Carlzon, 1987, p. 46). To find out what the business traveler wanted, he turned to SAS's frontline service employees for their ideas and suggestions. Focus groups generated hundreds of ideas and emphasized the importance of frontline autonomy to decide on the spot what passengers needed. Carlzon concluded that SAS's image was built on countless "moments of truth": fifteen-second encounters between employees and customers.

> If we are truly dedicated toward orienting our company to each customer's individual needs, we cannot rely on rule books and instruction from distant corporate offices. We have to place responsibility for ideas, decisions, and actions with the people who are SAS during those 15 seconds. If they have to go up the organizational chain of command for a decision on an individual problem, then those 15 golden seconds will elapse without a response and we will have lost an opportunity to earn a loyal customer" [Carlzon, 1987, p. 66].

Advocate or Hustler? Political Leadership

Even in the results-driven private sector, leaders find that they have to plunge into the political arena to move their company where it needs to go. Consider two chief executives from quite dissimilar eras: Lee Iacocca, who became chief executive of Chrysler in the late 1970s when the company was near death, and Carleton "Carly" Fiorina, who became CEO of Silicon Valley giant Hewlett-Packard in July 1999.

Iacocca's career had taken him to the presidency of Ford Motor Company. But then, on July 1, 1978, his boss, Henry Ford II, fired him, reportedly with the simple explanation, "Let's just say I don't like you" (O'Toole, 1984, p. 231). Iacocca's unemployment was brief. Chrysler Corporation, desperate for new leadership, saw Iacocca as the answer to the company's business woes.

Even though Iacocca had done his homework before accepting Chrysler's offer, he found things were worse than he expected. Chrysler was losing money so fast that bankruptcy seemed almost inevitable. He concluded that the only way out was to persuade the U.S. government to guarantee massive loans. It was a tough sell; much of Congress, the media, and the American public were against the idea. Iacocca had to convince them all that government intervention was in their best interest as well as Chrysler's.

Like Iacocca, Fiorina came in to head a troubled giant. HP's problems were not as bad as Chrysler's; it was a profitable company with more than $40 billion in annual revenue. But *Business Week* included HP as part of "the clueless establishment" (Burrows and Elstrom, 1999, p. 76)—customer service was deteriorating, bureaucracy was stifling innovation, and HP seemed to be falling behind the technology curve. Fiorina's arrival was big news for more than one reason. She was only the fifth CEO in HP's sixty-year history and was the first to come from outside since Bill (Hewlett) and Dave (Packard) founded the company in a Palo Alto garage in 1938. She was also the first woman to head a company of HP's size in any industry. She brought many strengths, including "a silver tongue and an iron will" (Burrows and Elstrom, 1999, p. 76). But she faced daunting challenges, especially after she set her sights on a merger with Compaq, another floundering $40 billion company. Her board supported her initiative, but Bill and Dave's heirs, who controlled more than 15 percent of HP's stock, didn't. Fiorina had to win a massive gunfight at HP corral or lose her job.

Ultimately, Iacocca got his guarantees and Fiorina got her merger. Both won their battles by artfully employing a set of principles for political leaders.

- *Political leaders clarify what they want and what they can get.* Political leaders are realists. They avoid letting what they want cloud their judgment about possibilities. Iacocca translated Chrysler's survival into the realistic goal of getting enough help to eke through a couple of difficult years. He was always careful to ask not for money but for loan guarantees. He insisted that it would cost taxpayers nothing because Chrysler would pay back its loans. Fiorina, too, was realistic. Once she knew she faced a nasty public squabble, she zeroed in on one goal: getting enough votes to put the merger through.

• *Political leaders assess the distribution of power and interests.* Political leaders map the political terrain by thinking carefully about the key players, their interests, and their power, asking: Whose support do I need? How do I go about getting it? Who are my opponents? How much power do they have? What can I do to reduce or overcome their opposition? Is this battle winnable? Iacocca needed the support of Chrysler's employees and unions, but they had little choice. The key players were Congress and the public. Congress would vote for the guarantees only if Iacocca's proposal had sufficient popular support.

Fiorina needed the support of HP's board, analysts, and, in the end, a majority of voting shares. She first went after her board's support but ran into a stroke of bad luck. Walter Hewlett, board member and son of HP cofounder Bill Hewlett, missed the July 2001 board meeting at which McKinsey consultants made the case for merger. A month later, Hewlett voted reluctantly to approve the merger, but he had serious misgivings. Substantial layoffs were touted as one of the merger's "synergies," but in Hewlett's mind this amounted to abandoning the HP Way. HP's stock dropped some 40 percent after the merger announcement, buttressing his doubts. A few weeks later, he announced that he would vote against the merger (Burrows, 2001). Fiorina now faced an uphill battle. Her job and her vision for HP both hung on the outcome. The key was making a case persuasive enough to woo analysts and shareholders who were still on the fence.

• *Political leaders build linkages to key stakeholders.* Political leaders focus their attention on building relationships and networks. They recognize the value of personal contact and face-to-face conversations. Iacocca worked hard to build linkages with Congress, the media, and the public. He spent hours meeting with members of Congress and testifying before congressional committees. After he met with thirty-one Italian American members of Congress, all but one voted for the loan guarantees. Said Iacocca, "Some were Republicans, some were Democrats, but in this case they voted the straight Italian ticket. We were desperate, and we had to play every angle" (Iacocca and Novak, 1984, p. 221).

Fiorina's primary target was institutional shareholders, who held more than half the company's stock, and a few highly influential analysts. Armed with a fifty-page document that laid out the strategic and financial rationale for the merger, Fiorina and Compaq CEO Michael Capellas hit the road, speaking to every analyst they could find. Fiorina focused on the big picture while Capellas backed her up on the nitty-gritty details of integrating the two firms. A particularly vital target was Institutional Shareholders Services, an advisory firm whose clients held more than a fifth of HP's stock. ISS's recommendation could make or break the deal. Though initially skeptical, ISS's lead analyst for the merger, Ram Kumar, said that the Fiorina-Capellas team's persuasiveness and command of detail won him over. "They had a strong grasp of the technical aspects of the merger," Kumar said. "It was an exhaustive, detailed plan" ("Hewlett-Packard Merger Pitch . . . ," 2002).

• *Political leaders persuade first, negotiate second, and coerce only if necessary.* Wise political leaders recognize that power is essential to their effectiveness; they also know to use it judiciously. William P. Kelly, an experienced public administrator, put it well: "Power is like the old Esso [gasoline] ad—a tiger in your tank. But you can't let the tiger out, you just let people hear him roar. You use power terribly sparingly because it has a short half-life. You let people know you have it and hope that you don't have to use it" (Ridout and Fenn, 1974, p. 10).

Sophisticated political leaders know that influence begins with understanding others' concerns and interests. What is important to them? How can I help them get what they want? Iacocca knew that he had to address a widespread belief that federal guarantees would throw millions of taxpayer dollars down a rat hole. He used advertising to respond directly to public concerns. Does Chrysler have a future? Yes, he said, we've been here fifty-four years, and we'll be here another fifty-four years. Would the loan guarantees be a dangerous precedent? No, the government already carried $400 billion in other loan guarantees, and in any event, Chrysler was going to pay its loans back. Iacocca also spoke directly to Congressional concerns. Chrysler prepared computer printouts painting a grim picture of jobs lost in every district if Chrysler went under.

Fiorina knew her biggest hurdle was the spotty track record for big mergers, particularly in the computer industry. Hewlett, her most potent opponent, used Compaq's acquisition of fading giant Digital Equipment in 1998 as evidence that the deal would be a disaster, noting the 80 percent decline in Compaq's share value after the deal. Fiorina developed a threefold argument based on competitive scale, cost savings, and management strength. She took this story on the road in countless meetings with analysts and institutional shareholders. Her audiences generally found her very persuasive. HP buttressed the case with a blizzard of press releases, advertising, and direct mail.

As the battle intensified, Fiorina even resorted to the business equivalent of an attack ad. HP put out a press release designed to gently but firmly discredit Walter Hewlett as a semiclueless dilettante: "Walter Hewlett, an heir of HP co-founder Bill Hewlett, is a musician and academic who oversees the Hewlett family trust and foundation. While he serves on HP's board of directors, Walter has never worked at the company or been involved in its management" (Fried, 2002).

Iacocca and Fiorina, as mentioned, both won their battles. Chrysler pulled out of its tailspin, repaid its loans, ignited the minivan craze, and had many profitable years before the return of bad times in the 1990s led to a sale first to German automaker Daimler Benz in 1998 and then to a private equity firm in 2007. HP's merger fell short of expectations, and the company drifted for three years until HP's board forced Fiorina out early in 2005.

Prophet or Zealot? Symbolic Leadership

The symbolic frame represents a fourth turn of the leadership kaleidoscope, portraying organization as both theater and temple. As theater, an organization creates a stage on which actors play their roles and hope to communicate the right impression to their audience. As temple, an organization is a community of faith, bonded by shared beliefs, traditions, myths, rituals, and ceremonies.

Symbolically, leaders lead through both actions and words as they interpret and reinterpret experience. What are the real lessons of history? What is really happening in the world? What will the future bring? What mission is worthy of our loyalty and investment? Data and analysis offer few compelling answers to such questions. Symbolic leaders interpret experience so as to impart meaning and purpose through phrases of beauty and passion. Franklin D. Roosevelt reassured a nation in the midst of its deepest economic depression that "the only thing we have to fear is fear itself." At almost the same time, Adolph Hitler assured Germans that their severe economic and social problems were the result of betrayal by Jews and communists. Germans, he said, were a superior people who could still fulfill their nation's destiny of world mastery. Though many saw the destructive paranoia in Hitler's message, millions of fearful citizens were swept up in Hitler's bold vision of German preeminence.

Burns (1978) was mindful of leaders such as Franklin Roosevelt, Mohandas Gandhi, and Martin Luther King Jr., when he drew a distinction between "transforming" and "transactional" leaders. According to Burns, transactional leaders "approach their followers with an eye to trading one thing for another: jobs for votes, subsidies for campaign contributions" (p. 4). Transforming leaders are rarer. As Burns describes them, they evoke their constituents' "better angels" and move them toward higher and more universal needs and purposes. They are visionary leaders whose leadership is inherently symbolic.

Symbolic leaders follow a consistent set of practices and scripts.

• *Symbolic leaders lead by example.* They demonstrate their commitment and courage by plunging into the fray. In taking risks and holding nothing back, they reassure and inspire others. New York Mayor Rudy Giuliani's leadership in the aftermath of the 9/11 terrorist attacks is again a dramatic case in point. Risking his own life, he moved immediately to the scene. When the first tower collapsed, he was trapped for fifteen minutes in the rubble alongside other New Yorkers.

• *They use symbols to capture attention.* When Diana Lam became principal of the Mackey Middle School in Boston in 1985, she faced a substantial challenge. Mackey had the usual problems of an urban school: decaying physical plant, poor discipline, racial tension, disgruntled teachers, and limited resources (Kaufer and Leader, 1987a). In such a situation, a symbolic leader looks for something visible and dramatic to signal that change is on the way. During the summer before assuming her duties, Lam wrote a personal letter to every teacher requesting an individual meeting. She met teachers wherever they wanted (in one case driving two hours). She asked them how they felt about the school and what changes they wanted. Then she recruited her family to repaint the school's front door and some of the most decrepit classrooms. "When school opened, students and staff members immediately saw that things were going to be different, if only symbolically. Perhaps even more important, staff members received a subtle challenge to make a contribution themselves" (Kaufer and Leader, 1987b, p. 3).

When Iacocca became president of Chrysler, one of his first steps was to announce that he was reducing his salary from $360,000 to $1 a year. "I did it for good, cold pragmatic reasons. I wanted our employees and our suppliers to be thinking: 'I can follow a guy who sets that kind of example,'" Iacocca explained in his autobiography (Iacocca and Novak, 1984, pp. 229–230).

- *Symbolic leaders frame experience.* In a world of uncertainty and ambiguity, a key function of symbolic leadership is to offer plausible and hopeful interpretations of experience. President John F. Kennedy channeled youthful exuberance into the Peace Corps and other initiatives with his stirring Inaugural challenge: "Ask not what your country can do for you; ask what you can do for your country." When Martin Luther King Jr. spoke at the March on Washington in 1963 and gave his extraordinary "I Have a Dream" speech, his opening line was, "I am happy to join with you today in what will go down in history as the greatest demonstration for freedom in the history of our nation." He could have interpreted the event in a number of other ways: "We are here because progress has been slow, but we are not ready to quit yet"; "We are here because nothing else has worked"; "We are here because it's summer and it's a good day to be outside." Each version is about as accurate as the next, but accuracy is not the real issue. King's assertion was bold and inspiring; it told members of the audience that they were making history by their presence at a momentous event.

- *Symbolic leaders communicate a vision.* One powerful way in which a leader can interpret experience is by distilling and disseminating a vision—a persuasive and hopeful image of the future. A vision needs to address both the challenges of the present and the hopes and values of followers. Vision is particularly important in times of crisis and uncertainty. When people are in pain, when they are confused and uncertain, or when they feel despair and hopelessness, they desperately seek meaning and hope.

Where does such vision come from? One view is that leaders create a vision and then persuade others to accept it (Bass, 1985; Bennis and Nanus, 1985). An alternative view is that leaders discover and articulate a vision that is already there, even if in an inchoate and unexpressed form (Cleveland, 1985). Kouzes and Posner put it well: "Corporate leaders know very well that what seeds the vision are those imperfectly formed images in the marketing department about what the customers really wanted and those inarticulate mumblings from the manufacturing folks about the poor product quality, not crystal ball gazing in upper levels of the corporate stratosphere. The best leaders are the best followers. They pay attention to those weak signals and quickly respond to changes in the corporate course" (1987, p. 114).

Lou Gerstner let it be known on his arrival as the new CEO of a troubled IBM in 1993, "The last thing IBM needs is a vision." People expected him to tighten and shake things up as he had done earlier at RJR Nabisco. But instead of making wholesale changes, he looked through a rear-view mirror to trace IBM's history. He found what he was looking for: old values and practices, now forgotten, that were just what IBM needed to revive its spirit and performance. His new vision artfully restored the gloss on tarnished symbolic commitments that had once made IBM the world's most admired corporation.

Leadership is a two-way street. No amount of charisma or rhetorical skill can sell a vision that reflects only the leader's values and needs. Effective symbolic leadership is possible only for those who understand the deepest values and most pressing concerns of their constituents. But leaders still play a critical role in articulating a vision by bringing a unique, personal blend of history, poetry, passion, conviction, and courage in distilling and shaping direction. Most important, they can choose which stories to tell as a means of communicating a shared quest.

• *Symbolic leaders tell stories.* Symbolic leaders often embed their vision in a mythical story—a story about "us" and about "our" past, present, and future. "Us" could be a school's faculty, a plant's employees, the people of Thailand, or any other audience a leader hopes to reach. The past is usually golden, a time of noble purposes, of great deeds, of legendary heroes and heroines. The present is troubled, a critical moment when we have to make fateful choices. The future is a dreamlike vision of hope and greatness, often tied to past glories.

A version of this story line helped Ronald Reagan, a master storyteller, become America's thirty-ninth president. Reagan's golden past was rooted in the frontier, a place of rugged, sturdy, self-reliant men and women who built a great nation. They took care of themselves and their neighbors without interference from a monstrous national government. It was an America of small towns and volunteer fire departments. America had fallen into crisis, said Reagan, because "the liberals" had created a federal government that levied oppressive taxes and eroded freedom through bureaucratic regulation and meddling. Reagan offered a promising new vision: a return to American greatness by "getting government off the backs of the American people" and restoring traditional values of freedom and self-reliance. The story line worked for Reagan and resurfaced twenty years later for a Reagan acolyte, George W. Bush.

Such stories succeed because we want to believe them rather than to scrutinize their historical validity or empirical support. Even a flawed story will work if it taps persuasively into the experience, values, and hopes of listeners. Mohammed Said Sahaf, Saddam Hussein's information minister at the time of the 2003 U.S. invasion of Iraq, was dismissed by most Westerners as an unreliable source of lies and misinformation. He repeatedly predicted Iraqi victories that never materialized. Two days before Baghdad fell, he brazenly told reporters that there were no American forces in the city, despite the conspicuous presence of an American armored battalion at a presidential palace less than half a mile away.

But Sahaf became a media star in much of the Arab world, where many viewers saw him as more interesting and credible than the colorless U.S. military sources. His military uniform, pistol on hip, and rakish cocked beret expressed spirit and élan. Arabs admired his creative and pungent insults for the Americans ("bloodsucking worms," "sick dogs," "donkeys"). They particularly relished the story Sahaf told with such flair and conviction: the infidel invaders were aimlessly plunging deeper into a trap and would soon be destroyed by heroic Iraqi fighters. Sahaf's star fizzled abruptly with the collapse of Saddam's government. But for a time, millions of Arabs who felt enraged and humiliated by the invasion of Iraq took great delight in a man who told the story they wanted to believe (Alderson, 2003).

Good stories are truer than true: this reflects both the power and the danger of symbolic leadership. In the hands of a Gandhi or a King, the constructive power of stories is immense. Told by a Hitler, their destructive power is almost incalculable.

• *Symbolic leaders respect and use history.* When leaders assume that history started with their arrival, they typically misread their circumstances and alienate their constituents. Wise leaders attend to history and link their initiatives to the values, stories, and heroes of the past. Even as she unleashed massive changes at HP, Carly Fiorina told Bill and Dave stories and insisted on her fidelity to the HP Way. It might have worked had she not displayed a tin ear for the deeper values and folkways of HP's culture.

Sometimes the use of history is deliberately selective. When Hu Jintao became chief of the Chinese Communist Party in the fall of 2002, many wondered whether he would ever escape the long shadow of his predecessor, Jiang Zemin, who had bequeathed a party leadership stacked with his loyalists. Hu was unstinting in his praise of Jiang's legacy but began to differentiate himself symbolically (Eckholm, 2003). Hu enlisted a symbolic ally, Mao Zedong, the supreme hero of the Chinese Communist revolution. In December 2002, only a month after coming to power, Hu traveled to a small rural town that had been Mao's headquarters just before he took over China. In contrast to Jiang, who consistently touted the economic successes of his reign, Hu emphasized the need to help the poor and dispossessed deal with the changes sweeping over China. He referred often to Mao and rarely to Jiang, repeating Mao's call to the faithful to practice "plain living and arduous struggle" more than sixty times. As the editor of a party paper commented, "He showed that his legitimacy comes ultimately from Mao, not Jiang" (Eckholm, 2003, p. A6).

SUMMARY

Though leadership is universally accepted as a cure for all organizational ills, it is also widely misunderstood. Many views of leadership fail to recognize its relational and contextual nature and its distinction from power and position. Shallow ideas about leadership mislead managers. A multiframe view provides a more comprehensive map of a complex and varied terrain.

Each frame highlights significant possibilities for leadership, but each by itself is incomplete. A century ago, models of managerial leadership were narrowly rational. In the 1960s and 1970s, human resource leadership became fashionable. In recent years, symbolic and political leadership have become more prominent, and the literature abounds with advice on how to become a powerful or visionary leader. Ideally, managers combine multiple frames into a comprehensive approach to leadership. Wise leaders understand their own strengths, work to expand them, and build diverse teams that can offer an organization leadership in all four modes: structural, political, human resource, and symbolic.

Reframing Change in Organizations

chapter
EIGHTEEN

Training, Realigning, Negotiating, and Grieving

For years, the United States has been urged to align its weights and measures with the rest of the world, but in 2007, it was one of only three nations that had not yet officially converted to the metric system. This seems odd, given that the United States has little in common with the other two holdouts—Liberia and Myanmar. It also seems strange because, as far back as 1958, the *Federal Register* contained provisions that "all calibrations in the U.S. customary system of weights and measurements carried out by the National Bureau of Standards will continue to be based on metric measurement and standards." And seems even more peculiar because in 1996 all federal agencies were ordered to adopt the metric system. Adhering to a thousand-year-old English system that even the English have been abandoning imposes many disadvantages. It handicaps international commerce, for example, and it led to measurement confusion in the design of the Hubble space telescope that cost taxpayers millions of dollars. Yet little progress has been made in converting to a different system.

373

America's metric inertia illustrates pervasive and predictable realities of change that repeatedly scuttle promising innovations. Organizations spend millions of dollars on change strategies that produce little improvement or make things worse. Mergers fail. Technology falls short of its potential. Strategies that are vital to success never wend their way into practice. In U.S. presidential elections, nearly all candidates promise change, but the winners struggle to deliver on even a fraction of their pledges.

To shrink the gap between change agents' intentions and outcomes, a voluminous body of literature has flourished. The sheer volume of change models, case studies, and prescriptive remedies is overwhelming. Some contain productive insights. Beer and Nohria (2001), for example, compare two distinct change models—a hard, top-down approach that emphasizes shareholder value (Theory E) and a softer, more participative strategy (Theory O) that targets organizational culture. Kanter, Stein, and Jick's "Big Three" model (1992) helps managers sort through the interplay of change strategies, change implementers, and change recipients. But despite growing knowledge, the same mistakes repeat themselves. It's like reading the latest books on dieting but never losing weight. The desired target is never easy to reach, and almost everyone wants change as long as they don't have to do anything differently. An old adage summarizes the predicament: *Plus ça change, plus c'est la même chose* (The more things change, the more they stay the same; Karr, 1849).

This chapter opens by examining the innovation process at two different companies. It then moves to a multiframe analysis to show how participation, training, structural realignment, political bargaining, and symbolic rituals of letting go can help achieve more positive outcomes. It concludes with a discussion integrating the frames with John Kotter's influential analysis of the stages of change.

THE INNOVATION PROCESS

What makes organizational change so difficult? Comparing a typically flawed change effort with an atypical success story offers some answers.

Six Sigma at 3M: A Typical Scenario

Beginning at Motorola in 1986 and later enhanced at General Electric, Six Sigma evolved from a statistical concept to a range of metrics, methods, and management approaches intended to reduce defects and increase quality in products and services (Pande, Neuman, and Cavanagh, 2000). It became the new corporate shibboleth in the 1990s after its successful, widespread use at GE. Essentially the approach has two components, one emphasizing metrics and control and the other emphasizing systems design. It has spawned acronyms like DMAIC (define, measure, analyze, improve, and control) and DFSS (design for Six Sigma—by building quality in the from the start). GE executives groomed in the Six Sigma way brought the techniques with them when they moved to other corporations. One was James McNerney, who missed the chance to succeed Jack Welch as GE's CEO but was snapped up by 3M in 2001 to bring some discipline to a legendary enterprise that seemed to be losing its edge. Profit and sales growth were erratic, and the stock price had languished.

McNerney got people's attention by slashing eight thousand jobs (11 percent of the workforce), putting teeth in the performance review process, and tightening the free-flowing spending spigot. Thousands of 3M workers were trained to earn the Six Sigma title of "Black Belt." These converts pioneered company-wide Six Sigma initiatives such as boosting the tempo of production by reducing variation and eliminating pointless steps in manufacturing. The Black Belts trained rank-and-file employees as "green belts," in charge of local Six Sigma initiatives. The Black Belt elite maintained metrics that tracked both overall and "neighborhood" efforts to systematize and streamline all aspects of work—including research and development.

In the short run, McNerney's strategy paid off. Indicators of productivity improved, costs were trimmed, and the stock price soared. But Six Sigma's standardization began to intrude on 3M's historical emphasis on innovation. Prior to McNerney's arrival, new ideas were accorded almost unlimited time and funding to get started. Fifteen percent of employees' on-the-clock time was devoted to developing groundbreaking products—with little accountability. This approach had given birth to legendary products like Scotch Tape and Post-it notes.

Six Sigma systematized the research and development process. Sketchy, bluesky projects gave way to scheduled, incremental development. Funds carried an expiration date, and progress through a planned pipeline was measured and charted. Development of new products began to wane. "The more you hardwire a company on total quality management, [the more] it is going to hurt breakthrough innovation," says Vijay Govindarajan, a management professor at Dartmouth. "The mindset that is needed, the capabilities that are needed, the metrics that are needed, the whole culture that is needed for discontinuous innovation, are fundamentally different." Art Fry, the inventor of the Post-it, agreed. "We all came to the conclusion that there was no way in the world that anything like a Post-it note would ever emerge from this new system" (Hindo, 2007, p. 9).

The lethargy ended, but the damage done, McNerney left 3M in 2005 to become the new CEO of Boeing. Fry added, "What's remarkable is how fast a culture can be torn apart. [McNerney] didn't kill it because he wasn't here long enough. But if he had been here much longer, I think he would have." George Buckley, McNerney's successor, observed in retrospect, "Perhaps one of the mistakes that we made as a company—it's one of the dangers of Six Sigma—is that when you value sameness more than you value creativity, I think you potentially undermine the heart and soul of a company like 3M" (Hindo, 2007, p. 9).

The progression of change at 3M reveals a familiar scenario: New CEO introduces modern management techniques and scores a short-term victory; political pressures and cultural resistance start to mount; CEO leaves to try again; organization licks its wounds and moves both backward and onward. In short, optimistic beginning, tumultuous middle, and controversial conclusion. Robert Nardelli, one of McNerney's contemporaries at GE, followed a similar script in his six years as Home Depot's CEO.

Microsoft: An Atypical Case

Changes launched from the top often aim for standardization, measurement, tightening things up, and enhancing profitability. Less often do efforts burble up from below with an aim to loosen things up and emphasize more spiritual concerns. In 2007, Microsoft took the less traveled path.

Steve Ballmer, Microsoft's CEO, was perplexed. The company's stock was slipping sideways, products were delayed, and many insiders perceived the company as "flabby, middle-aged and un-hip"—especially in contrast to Google (Conlin and Greene, 2007). The standard fix-it response would be to hire a new human resource chief to come up with a company-driven antidote to the malaise. Instead, Ballmer reached down into the ranks and promoted a maverick to rekindle the company's spirit. He picked Lisa Brummel, a product manager beloved for her unconventional ways and dress.

One of Brummel's first initiatives might seem strange to structural thinkers— she brought back the towels that had been a feature of employee locker rooms until removed to cut costs. The lost towels had become a heated subject in internal blogs, primarily as symbols of how little the company cared. Beyond helping with Seattle's chronic drizzle, the towels were a small but treasured perk of working at Microsoft. Brummel also replaced the self-service "industrial sludge" coffeemakers with Starbucks machines that fit Seattle's barista ethos.

The next target for Brummel's magic wand was Microsoft's dreaded performance review procedure. Devised by Ballmer himself, the ranking system was a zero-sum game in which employees competed for their individual shares of a limited purse. Managers could give only so many A's, even if several employees had performed exceptionally well. It was a touchy issue pitting Brummel against Ballmer, but she won and implemented a system that gave managers more discretion and tied raises and bonuses to a combination of pay grade and annual performance.

Brummel opened up communications by moving the internal "underground" blog into the public spotlight. She changed the company's office décor from institutional drab to modern chic and created a mobile medicine service to dispatch company physicians to employees' homes for emergencies. Brummel's initiatives raised morale, cut attrition, and, in many instances, one-upped Google. Brummel combined human resource, political, and symbolic ideas as a catalyst for change rather than as a barrier. Instead of taking things away or imposing something unwanted, she gave people things they welcomed.

How Frames Can Help

Comparing the stories of change at 3M and Microsoft illustrates an iron law: changes rationally conceived at the top often fail. More versatile approaches have a better chance. Organizations today face a persistent dilemma. Changes in their environment or leadership pressure them to adapt, yet the more they try to change, the more likely their performance is to deteriorate (Nickerson and Silverman, 2003; Barnett and Freeman, 2001). Ormerod (2007) argues that "things usually fail" because decision makers don't understand their environment well enough to anticipate the consequences of their actions. So they march blindly down their preferred path despite warning signs that they are headed in the wrong direction. And in studying scores of innovations, we continue to see managers whose strategies are limited because their thinking is limited to one or two cognitive lenses.

As Machiavelli observed many years ago in *The Prince,* "It must be realized that there is nothing more difficult to plan, more uncertain of success, or more dangerous to manage than the establishment of a new order of [things]; for he who introduces [change] makes enemies of all those who derived advantage from the old order and finds but lukewarm defenders among those who stand to gain from the new one" ([1514] 1961, p. 27).

Machiavelli's trenchant observations are as timely as ever. Think about the challenges of rebuilding Iraq. The architects of the U.S. invasion foresaw a relatively quick and painless transition to democratic stability. Instead, removing the Saddam Hussein regime opened a Pandora's box of political and symbolic issues that had been seething beneath the surface. It is much better to see quicksand before rather than after you're mired in it. The frames can help change agents see pitfalls and roadblocks ahead, thereby increasing their odds of success.

Organizational change is a complex systemic undertaking. It rarely works to retrain people without revising roles or to revamp roles without retraining. Planning without broad-based participation that gives voice to the opposition almost guarantees stiff resistance later on. Change alters power relationships and undermines existing agreements and pacts. Even more profoundly, it intrudes on deeply rooted symbolic forms, traditional ways, and customary behavior. Below the surface, the organization's social tapestry begins to unravel, threatening both time-honored traditions and prevailing cultural values and ways.

In the remainder of the chapter, we look at the human resource, structural, political, and symbolic aspects of organizational change and integrate them with Kotter's model of the change process. Exhibit 18.1 summarizes the views of major issues in change that each frame offers. The human resource view focuses on needs, skills, and participation, the structural approach on alignment and clarity, the political lens on conflict and arenas, and the symbolic frame on loss of meaning and the importance of creating new symbols and ways. Each mode of thought highlights a distinctive set of barriers and offers possibilities for making change stick.

CHANGE, TRAINING, AND PARTICIPATION

It sounds simplistic to point out that investment in change calls for collateral outlays in training and developing active channels for employee input. Yet countless innovations falter and flop because managers neglect to spend time and money to develop needed knowledge and skills and to involve people throughout

Exhibit 18.1.
Reframing Organizational Change.

FRAME	BARRIERS TO CHANGE	ESSENTIAL STRATEGIES
Structural	Loss of direction, clarity, and stability; confusion, chaos	Communicating, realigning, and renegotiating formal patterns and policies
Human resource	Anxiety, uncertainty; people feel incompetent and needy	Training to develop new skills; participation and involvement; psychological support
Political	Disempowerment; conflict between winners and losers	Create arenas where issues can be renegotiated and new coalitions formed
Symbolic	Loss of meaning and purpose; clinging to the past	Create transition rituals; mourn the past, celebrate the future

the process. The human resource department is too often an afterthought no one takes seriously.

In one large firm, for example, top management decided to purchase state-of-the-art technology. They expected a decisive competitive advantage from a 50 percent cut in cycle time from customer order to delivery. Hours of careful analysis went into crafting the strategy. The new technology was launched with great fanfare. The CEO assured a delighted sales force it would now have a high-tech competitive edge. After the initial euphoria faded, though, the sales force realized that its old methods and skills were obsolete; years of experience were useless. Veterans felt like neophytes. When the CEO heard that the sales force was shaky about the new technology, he said, "Then get someone in human resources to throw something together. You know, what's-her-name, the new vice president. That's why we hired her." A year later, the new technology had failed to deliver. The training never materialized. Input from the front lines never reached the right ears. The company's investment ultimately yielded a costly, inefficient process and a demoralized sales force. The window of opportunity was lost to the competition.

Spencer Johnson, *Who Moved My Cheese? An A-Mazing Way to Deal with Change in Your Work and Your Life* (New York: Putnam, 1998)

Spencer Johnson's brief (ninety-four-page) parable about mice, men, and change topped *Business Week*'s best-seller list for three consecutive years (1999, 2000, and 2001), making it one of the most successful management books ever.

The essence of the book is a story about a maze and its four inhabitants: two mice named Sniff and Scurry and two "little people" named Hem and Haw. Life is good because they have found a place in the maze where they reliably discover a plentiful supply of high-quality cheese. But then the quality and quantity of cheese decline, and eventually the cheese disappears altogether.

The mice, being relatively simple creatures, figure "No cheese here? Let's go look somewhere else." Sniff is very good at sniffing out new supplies, and Scurry excels in scurrying after them once they're found. Before long, they're both back in cheese heaven.

But Hem and Haw, being human, are reluctant to abandon old ways. They figure someone has made a mistake because they're entitled to get cheese where they have always gotten it. They're confident that, if they wait, the cheese will return. It doesn't. As they get hungrier, Hem and Haw gripe and complain about the unfairness of it all. Eventually, Haw decides it's time to explore and look for something better. Hem, however, insists on staying where he is until the cheese comes back.

As he searches, Haw develops a new outlook. He posts signs on the walls to express his new thinking, with messages such as "Old beliefs do not lead you to new cheese." Haw's explorations eventually reunite him with Sniff, Scurry, and the new cache of cheese. Hem continues to starve.

Cheese, as the book points out, is a metaphor for whatever you might want in life. The maze represents the context in which you work and live; it could be your family, your workplace, or your life. The basic message is simple and clear: clinging to old beliefs and habits when the world around you has changed is self-defeating. Flexibility, experimentation, and the willingness to try on new beliefs are critical to success in a fast-changing world.

The book certainly has critics, particularly from those who worry that the story downplays the possibility that some change is wrongheaded and deserves to be resisted. But *Cheese* has far more fans, for whom its simplicity is a virtue. The parable often enables its ardent readers to see aspects of themselves and their own experience—times when, like Hem, they have hurt themselves by refusing to adapt to new circumstances.

A happier example occurred in a large hospital that invested millions of dollars in a new integrated information system. The goal was to improve patient care by making updates quickly available to everyone involved in a treatment plan. Widespread involvement ensured that relevant ideas and concerns were folded into the innovative system. Terminals linked patients' bedsides to nursing stations, attending physicians, pharmacy, and other services. To ensure that the new system would work, hospital administrators created a simulation lab. Individual representatives from all groups were brought into a room and seated at terminals. Hypothetical scenarios gave them a chance to practice and work out the kinks. Many staff members, particularly physicians, needed to improve their computer skills. Coaches were there to help. Each group became its own self-help support system. Skills and confidence improved in the training session. Relationships that formed as a result of extensive involvement and participation were invaluable as the new technology went into operation.

From a human resource perspective, people have good reason to resist change. Sometimes resistance is sensible because the new methods are a management mistake that would take the organization in the wrong direction. But in any event, no one likes feeling anxious, voiceless, and incompetent. Changes in routine practice and protocol undermine existing knowledge and skills and undercut people's ability to perform with confidence and success. When asked to do something they don't understand, haven't had a voice in developing, don't know how to do, or don't believe in, people feel puzzled, anxious, and insecure. Lacking skills and confidence to implement the new ways, they resist or even engage in sabotage, awaiting the return of the good old days. Or they may comply superficially while covertly dragging their feet. Even if they try to do what they are told, the results are predictably dismal. Training, psychological support, and participation all increase the likelihood that people will understand and feel comfortable with the new methods.

Often overlooked in the training loop are the change agents responsible for promoting and guiding the change. Kotter presents a vivid example of how training can prepare people to communicate the rationale for a new order of things. A company moving to a team-based structure developed at the top was concerned about how workers and trade unions would react. To make sure people would understand and accept the changes, the managers went through an intensive training regimen: "Our twenty 'communicators' practiced and practiced. They learned the responses, tried them out, and did more role plays until they felt comfortable with nearly anything that might come at them. Handling 200 issues well may sound like too much, but we did it. . . . I can't believe that what we did is not applicable nearly everywhere. I think too many people wing it" (Kotter and Cohen, 2002, p. 86). Taking the time to hear people's ideas and concerns and to make sure that all involved have the talent, confidence, and expertise necessary to carry out their new responsibilities is a requisite of successful innovation.

CHANGE AND STRUCTURAL REALIGNMENT

Involvement and training will not ensure success unless existing roles and relationships are realigned to fit the new initiative. As an example, a school system created a policy requiring principals to assume a more active role in supervising classroom instruction. Principals were trained in how to observe and counsel teachers. When they set out to apply their new skills, morale problems and complaints soon began to surface. No one had anticipated how changes in principals' duties might affect teachers and impinge on existing agreements about authority. Did teachers believe it was legitimate for principals to spend time in classrooms observing and suggesting ways to improve teaching? Most important, no one had asked who would handle administrative duties for which principals no longer had time. As a result, supplies were delayed, parents felt neglected, and discipline deteriorated. By midyear, most principals had gone back to their administrative duties and were leaving teachers alone.

Change undermines existing structural arrangements, creating ambiguity, confusion, and distrust. People no longer know what is expected of them or what they can expect from others. Everyone may think someone else is in charge when, in fact, no one is. As a result of changes in health care, for example, a hospital was experiencing substantial employee turnover and absenteeism, a shortage of nurses, poor communication, and low staff morale. There were rumors of an impending effort to organize a union. A consultant's report identified several structural problems:

> One set related to top management. Members of the executive committee seemed to be confused about their roles and authority. Many believed all important decisions were made (prior to the meetings) by Rettew, the hospital administrator. Many shared the perception that major decisions were made behind closed doors, and that Rettew often made "side deals" with different individuals, promising them special favors or rewards in return for support at the committee meetings. People at this level felt manipulated, confused, and dissatisfied.
>
> Major problems also existed in the nursing service. The director of nursing seemed to be patterning her managerial style after that of Rettew. . . . Nursing supervisors and head nurses felt that they had no authority, while staff nurses complained about a lack of direction and openness by the nursing administration. The structure of the organization was unclear. Nurses were unaware of what their jobs were, whom they should report to, and how decisions were made [McLennan, 1989, p. 231].

As the school and hospital examples both illustrate, when things start to shift, people become unsure of what their duties are, how to relate to others, and who has authority to decide what. Clarity, predictability, and rationality give way to confusion, loss of control, and a sense that politics trumps policy. To minimize such difficulty, innovators must anticipate structural issues and work to redesign the existing architecture of roles and relationships. In some situations, this can be done informally. In others, structural arrangements need to be renegotiated more formally (through some version of responsibility charting, discussed in Chapter Five).

Hit Number 8: Richard R. Nelson and Sidney G. Winter, *An Evolutionary Theory of Economic Change* (Cambridge, Mass.: Harvard University Press, 1982)

How do economists think about change in organizations? Nelson and Winter's book represents one side of a debate within economics that pits the dominant neoclassical view against a range of heretical perspectives. In essence, the neoclassical view sees both humans and organizations as rational decision makers who maximize their own interests (utility) in the face of available options and incentives. The problem of change is simple: rational maximizers will change if their preferences change, or if the environment changes the options and incentives they face.

An example of the neoclassical approach is Jensen and Meckling's paper on agency theory, discussed in Chapter Four as Greatest Hit Number 5. Nelson and Winter are dissenters. (So are the authors of two other works on our hit list: Number 2, Cyert and March, discussed in Chapter Nine, and Number 10, March and Simon, discussed in Chapter Two.)

Nelson and Winter criticize maximization on the ground that "firms have but limited bases for judging what will work best; they may even have difficulty establishing the plausible range of alternatives to be considered" (p. 399). In other words, decision makers find it hard to know their options and hard to evaluate the alternatives they see. Borrowing from Darwinian concepts of evolution, Nelson and Winter develop a theory of change that is intended to conform more closely to how change works in practice. Three concepts are central:

- *Routine:* A regular and predictable pattern of behavior, a way of doing something that a firm uses repeatedly. This is akin to what March and Simon (1958) refer to as "programmed activity."

- *Search:* The process of assessing current options, acquiring new information, and altering routines. "Routines play the role of genes in our evolutionary theory. Search routines stochastically generate mutations" (p. 400).

- *Selection environment:* The set of considerations determining whether an organization adopts an innovation and how an organization learns about an innovation from others.

Nelson and Winter see an organization as combining ongoing behavior patterns, which produce stability and continuity, with activities for scouting new options. When an organization finds promising new alternatives, it tries them out. As with natural selection, mutations that work are kept; others are discarded. Nelson and Winter's view is distinct from the "population ecology" perspective in organization theory, even though both borrow from Darwin. Nelson and Winter see selection affecting the routines that live or die within organizations; population ecologists see selection determining which organizations survive or fail.

CHANGE AND CONFLICT

Change invariably creates conflict. It typically turns into a tug-of-war between innovators and traditionalists to determine winners and losers. Change almost always benefits some people while neglecting or harming others. That ensures that some individuals and groups support the change while others oppose it, sit on the fence, or become isolated. Often, clashes go underground and smolder beneath the surface. Occasionally, they burst open as eruptions of unregulated warfare.

A classic case in point comes from a U.S. government initiative to improve America's rural schools.

THE EXPERIMENTAL SCHOOLS PROJECT

The Experimental Schools Project provided funds for comprehensive changes. It also carefully documented experiences of ten participating districts over a five-year period. The first year—the planning period—was free of conflict. But as plans became actions, hidden issues boiled to the surface. A Northwest school district illustrates a common pattern:

In the high school, a teacher evaluator explained the evaluation process while emphasizing the elaborate precautions to insure the raters would be unable to connect specific evaluations with specific teachers. He also passed out copies of the check-list used to evaluate the [evaluation forms]. Because of the tension the subject aroused, he joked that teachers could use the list to "grade" their own [forms]. He got a few laughs; he got more laughs when he encouraged teachers to read the evaluation plan by suggesting, "If you have fifteen minutes to spare and are really bored, you should read this section." When another teacher pointed out that her anonymity could not be maintained because she was the only teacher in her subject, the whole room broke into laughter, followed by nervous and derisive questions and more laughter.

When the superintendent got up to speak shortly afterwards, he was furious. He cautioned teachers for making light of the teacher evaluators who, he said, were trying to protect the staff. Several times he repeated that because teachers did not support the [project] they did not care for students. "Your attitude," he concluded, "is damn the children and full speed ahead!" He then rushed out of the room. . . . As word of the event spread through the system, it caused reverberations in other buildings as well [Firestone, 1977, pp. 174–175].

After the heated exchange, conflict between the administration and teachers intensified. The issue was broader than evaluation or anonymity. Teachers were angry about the entire project. The school board got involved and reduced the superintendent's authority. Rumors he might be fired undermined his clout even more.

Such a scenario is predictable. As changes emerge, camps form: supporters, opponents, and fence-sitters. Conflict is avoided or smoothed over until it explodes in divisive battles. Coercive power, rather than legitimate authority, often determines the victor. Typically, the status quo prevails and change agents lose.

From a political perspective, conflict is natural. It is best managed through processes of negotiation and bargaining, where settlements and agreements can be hammered out. If ignored, disputes explode into street fights—no rules, anything goes. People get hurt, and scars linger for years. The alternative to street fights is arenas with rules, referees, and spectators. Arenas create opportunities to forge divisive issues into shared agreements. Through bargaining, compromises can be worked out between the status quo and innovative ideals. Welding new ideas onto existing practices is essential to successful change. One hospital administrator said, "The board and I had to learn how to wrestle in a public forum."

Mitroff (1983) describes a drug company facing competitive pressure on its branded prescription drug from generic substitutes. Management was split into three factions: one group wanted to raise the price of the drug, another wanted to lower it, and still another wanted to keep it the same but cut costs. Each group collected information, constructed models, and developed reports showing that its solution was correct. The process degenerated into a frustrating spiral. Mitroff intervened to get each group to identify major stakeholders and articulate assumptions about them. All agreed that the most critical stakeholders were physicians prescribing the drug. Each group had its own suppositions about how physicians would respond to a price change. But no one really knew. The three groups finally agreed to test their assumptions by implementing a price increase in selected markets.

The intervention worked through convening an arena with a more productive set of rules. Similarly, experimental school districts that created arenas for resolving conflict were more successful than others in bringing about comprehensive change. In the school district cited earlier, teachers reacted to administrative coercion with a power strategy of their own:

> Community members initiated a group called Concerned Citizens for Education in response to a phone call from a teacher who noted that parents should be worried about what the [administrators] were doing to their children. The superintendent became increasingly occupied with responding to demands and concerns of the community group. Over time, the group joined in a coalition with teachers to defeat several of the superintendent's supporters on the school board and to elect members who were more supportive of their interests. The turnover in board membership reduced the administrator's power and authority, making it necessary to rely more and more on bargaining and negotiation strategies to promote the intended change [Deal and Nutt, 1980, p. 20].

Successful change requires an ability to frame issues politically, build coalitions, and establish arenas in which disagreements can be hammered into workable pacts. One insightful executive remarked: "We need to confront, not duck, and face up to disagreements and differences of opinions and conflicting objectives. . . . All of us must make sure—day in and day out—that conflicts are aired and resolved before they lead to internecine war."

CHANGE AND LOSS

In the early 1980s, America's Cola wars—a battle between Coke and Pepsi—reached a fever pitch. A head-to-head taste test called the Pepsi Challenge was making inroads in Coca-Cola's market share. In blind tests, even avowed Coke drinkers preferred Pepsi. Pepsi won narrowly in a Coke counterchallenge held at its corporate headquarters in Atlanta. Coca-Cola executives became more nervous when Pepsi stunned the industry by signing Michael Jackson to a $5 million celebrity advertising campaign. Coke struck back with one of the most startling announcements in the company's ninety-nine-year history: Old Coke would be replaced with New Coke:

> Shortly before 11:00 AM [on Tuesday, April 23, 1985], the doors of the Vivian Beaumont Theater at Lincoln Center opened to two hundred newspaper, magazine, and TV reporters. The stage was aglow with red. Three huge screens, each solid red and inscribed with the company logo, rose behind the podium and a table draped in red. The lights were low; the music began: "We are. We will always be. Coca-Cola. All-American history." As the patriotic song filled the theater, slides of Americana flashed on the center screen—families and kids, Eisenhower and JFK, the Grand Canyon and wheat fields, the Beatles and Bruce Springsteen, cowboys, athletes, and the Statue of Liberty—and interspersed throughout, old commercials for Coke. Robert Goizueta [CEO of Coca-Cola] came to the podium. He first congratulated the reporters for their ingenuity in already having reported what he was about to say. And then he boasted, "The best has been made even better." Sidestepping the years of laboratory research that had gone into the program, Goizueta claimed that in the process of concocting Diet Coke, the company flavor chemists had "discovered" a new formula. And research had shown that consumers preferred this new one to old Coke. Management could then do one of two things: nothing, or buy the world a new Coke.

Goizueta announced that the taste-test results made management's decisions "one of the easiest ever made" [Oliver, 1986, p. 132].

The rest is history. Coke drinkers overwhelmingly rejected the new product. They felt betrayed; many were outraged:

> Duane Larson took down his collection of Coke bottles and outside of his restaurant hung a sign, "They don't make Coke anymore." . . . Dennis Overstreet of Beverly Hills hoarded 500 cases of old Coke and advertised them for $30 a case. He is almost sold out. . . . *San Francisco Examiner* columnist Bill Mandel called it "Coke for wimps." . . . Finally, Guy Mullins exclaimed, "When they took old Coke off the market, they violated my freedom of choice—baseball, hamburgers, Coke— they're all the fabric of America" [Morganthau, 1985, pp. 32–33].

Even bottlers and Coca-Cola employees were aghast: "By June the anger and resentment of the public was disrupting the personal lives of Coke employees, from the top executives to the company secretaries. Friends and acquaintances were quick to attack, and once-proud employees now shrank from displaying to the world any association with the Coca-Cola company" (Oliver, 1986, pp. 166–167).

Coca-Cola rebounded quickly with Classic Coke. Indeed, the company's massive miscalculation led to one of the strangest serendipitous triumphs in marketing history. All the controversy, passion, and free publicity stirred up by the New Coke fiasco ultimately helped Coca-Cola regain its dominance in the soft drink industry. A brilliant stratagem, if anyone had planned it.

What led Coke's executives into such a quagmire? Several factors were at work. Pepsi was gaining market share. As the newly appointed CEO of Coca-Cola, Goizueta was determined to modernize the company. A previous innovation, Diet Coke, had been a huge success. Most important, Coca-Cola's revered long-time "Boss," Robert Woodruff, had just passed away. On his deathbed, he reportedly gave Goizueta his blessing for the new recipe.

In their zeal to compete with Pepsi, Coke's executives overlooked a central tenet of the symbolic frame. The meaning of an object or event can be far more powerful than the reality. Strangely, Coke's leadership had lost touch with their product's significance to consumers. To many people, old Coke was a piece of Americana. It was linked to cherished memories. Coke represented something far deeper than just a soft drink.

In introducing New Coke, company executives unintentionally announced the passing of an American symbol. Symbols create meaning, and when one is destroyed or vanishes people experience emotions akin to those at the passing of a spouse, child, old friend, or pet. When a relative or close friend dies, we feel a deep sense of loss. We harbor similar feelings when a computer replaces old procedures, a logo changes after a merger, or an old leader is replaced by a new one. When these transitions take place in the workplace rather than in a family, feelings of loss are often denied or attributed to other causes.

Rituals of Loss

Any significant change in an organization may trigger two conflicting symbolic responses. The first is to keep things as they were, to replay the past. The second is to ignore the loss and plunge into the future. Individuals or groups can get stuck in either form of denial or bog down vacillating between the two.

Four years after AT&T was forced to divest its local phone operations, an executive remarked: "Some mornings I feel like I can set the world on fire. Other mornings I can hardly get out of bed to face another day." Nurses in one hospital's intensive care unit were caught in a loss cycle for ten years following their move from an old facility. Loss is an unavoidable by-product of improvement. As change accelerates, executives and employees get caught in endless cycles of unresolved grief.

In our personal lives, the pathway from loss to healing is culturally prescribed. Every culture outlines a sequence for transition rituals following significant loss: always a collective experience in which pain is expressed, felt, and juxtaposed against humor and hope. (Think of Irish actor Malachy McCourt who, as his mother lay dying, said to her distressed physician, "Don't worry, Doctor, we come from a long line of dead people.")

In many societies, the sequence of ritual steps involves a wake, a funeral, a period of mourning, and some form of commemoration. From a symbolic perspective, ritual is an essential companion to significant change. A Naval change-of-command ceremony, for example, is informally scripted by tradition. A wake is held for the outgoing commander. The mantle of command is passed to the new commander in a full-dress ceremony attended by friends, relatives, and assembled officers and sailors. The climactic moment of transition occurs with the incoming and outgoing skippers at attention facing each other. The new commander salutes and says, "I relieve you, sir." The retiring commander salutes and responds, "I stand relieved." During the ceremony, the new commander's name is posted on the unit's entrance. After a time, the old commander's face or name is displayed in a picture or plaque.

Transition rituals initiate a sequence of steps that help people let go of the past, deal with a painful present, and move into a meaningful future. The form of these rites varies widely, but they are essential to the ability to face and transcend loss. Otherwise, people vacillate between clinging to the old and rushing to the future. An effective ritual helps them let go of old ways and embrace a new beginning.

The Rebirth of Delta Corporation

Owen (1987) vividly documents these issues in his description of change at "Delta Corporation." An entrepreneur named Harry invented a product that sold well enough to support a company of thirty-five hundred people. After a successful public stock offering, the company experienced soaring costs, flattened sales, and a dearth of new products. Facing stockholder dissatisfaction and charges of mismanagement, Harry passed the torch to a new leader.

Harry's replacement was very clear about her vision: she wanted "engineers who could fly." But her vision was juxtaposed against a history of "going downhill." A further complication was that various parts of the company were governed by distinct stories representing different Delta themes. Finance division stories exemplified the new breed of executives brought in following Harry's departure. Research and development stories varied by organizational level. At the executive level, "Old Harry" stories extolled the creative accomplishments of the former CEO. Middle management stories focused on the Golden Fleece award given monthly behind the scenes to the researcher who developed the idea with the least bottom-line potential. On the production benches, workers told of Serendipity Sam, winner of more Golden Fleece awards than anyone else, exemplar of the excitement and innovation of Harry's regime.

Across the levels and divisions, the tales clustered into two competing themes: the newcomers' focus on management versus the company's tradition of innovation. The new CEO recognized the importance of blending old and new to build a company where "engineers could fly." She brought thirty-five people from across the company to a management retreat where she surprised everyone:

> She opened with some stories of the early days, describing the intensity of Old Harry and the Garage Gang (now known as the Leper

Colony). She even had one of the early models of Harry's machine out on a table. Most people had never seen one. It looked primitive, but during the coffee break, members of the Leper Colony surrounded the ancient artifact, and began swapping tales of the blind alleys, the late nights, and the breakthroughs. That dusty old machine became a magnet. Young shop floor folks went up and touched it, sort of snickering as they compared this prototype with the sleek creations they were manufacturing now. But even as they snickered, they stopped to listen as the Leper Colony recounted tales of accomplishment. It may have been just a "prototype," but that's where it all began [Owen, 1987, p. 172].

After the break, the CEO divided the group into subgroups to share their hopes for the company. When the participants returned, their chairs had been rearranged into a circle with Old Harry's prototype in the center. With everyone facing one another, the CEO led a discussion, linking the stories from the various subgroups. Serendipity Sam's account of a new product possibility came out in a torrent of technical jargon:

The noise level was fierce, but the rest of the group was being left out. Taking Sam by the hand, the CEO led him to the center of the circle right next to the old prototype. There it was the old and the new—the past, present, and potential. She whispered in Sam's ear that he ought to take a deep breath and start over in words of one syllable. He did so, and in ways less than elegant, the concept emerged. He guessed about applications, competitors, market shares, and before long the old VP for finance was drawn in. No longer was he thinking about selling [tax] losses, but rather thinking out loud about how he was going to develop the capital to support the new project. The group from the shop floor . . . began to spin a likely tale as to how they might transform the assembly lines in order to make Sam's new machine. Even the Golden Fleece crowd became excited, telling each other how they always knew that Serendipity Sam could pull it off. They conveniently forgot that Sam had been the recipient of a record number of their awards, to say nothing of the fact that this new idea had emerged in spite of all their rules [Owen, 1987, pp. 173–174].

In one intense event, part of the past was buried, yet its spirit was resurrected and revised to fit the new circumstances. Disparaging themes and stories were merged into a company where "engineers could fly" profitably.

Releasing a Negative Past

Many find it hard to understand how villains can hold a culture together. But negative symbols are attractive when people lack more positive glue. In such cultural voids, griping can become the predominant ritual. The new owners of a newspaper realized that their acquisition was mired in a negative past. Letting go of old tyrants and wounds was essential to a new, more positive start.

Needing something dramatic, the new owners invited all employees to an event. They arrived to a room filled with black balloons. Pictures of the reviled managers were affixed to the lid of an open coffin positioned prominently in the front. Startled employees silently took their places. The new CEO opened the ceremony: "We are assembled today to say farewell to the former owners of this newspaper. But it only seems fitting that we should say a few words about them before they leave us forever."

On cue, without prompting or rehearsal, individuals rose from their seats, came forward, and, one by one, grabbed a picture. Each then described briefly life under the sway of "the bastards," tore up the person's photograph, and threw it into the coffin. When all the likenesses had been removed, a New Orleans style group of jazz musicians filed in playing a mournful dirge. Coffin bearers marched the coffin outside. Employees followed and released the black balloons into the sky. A buffet lunch followed, festooned by balloons with the colors of the new company logo.

The CEO admitted later, "What a risk. I was scared to death. But it came off without a hitch and the atmosphere is now completely different. People are talking and laughing together. Circulation has improved. So has morale. Who would have 'thunk' it?"

CHANGE STRATEGY

The frames offer a checklist of issues that change agents must recognize and respond to. But how can they be combined into an integrated model? How does the change process move through time? John Kotter, an influential student of leadership and change, has studied both successful and unsuccessful change efforts in organizations around the world. In his book *The Heart of Change* (2002, written with Dan S. Cohen), he summarizes what he has learned. His basic message is very much like ours. Too many change initiatives fail because they rely too much on "data gathering, analysis, report writing, and presentations" instead of a more creative approach aimed at grabbing the "feelings that motivate useful action" (p. 8). In other words, change agents fail when they rely mostly on reason and structure while neglecting human, political, and symbolic elements.

Kotter describes eight stages that he repeatedly found in successful change initiatives:

1. Creating a sense of urgency

2. Pulling together a guiding team with the needed skills, credibility, connections, and authority to move things along

3. Creating an uplifting vision and strategy

4. Communicating the vision and strategy through a combination of words, deeds, and symbols

5. Removing obstacles, or empowering people to move ahead

6. Producing visible symbols of progress through short-term victories

7. Sticking with the process and refusing to quit when things get tough

8. Nurturing and shaping a new culture to support the emerging innovative ways

Kotter's stages depict a dynamic process moving through time, though not necessarily in a linear sequence. In the real world, stages overlap, and change agents sometimes need to cycle back to earlier phases.

Combining Kotter's stages with the four frames generates the model presented in Exhibit 18.2. The table lists each of Kotter's stages and illustrates actions that change agents might take. Not every frame is essential to each stage, but all are critical to overall success. Consider, for example, Kotter's first stage, developing a sense of urgency. Strategies from the human resource, political, and symbolic strategies all contribute. Symbolically, leaders can construct a persuasive story by painting a picture of the current challenge or crisis and emphasizing why failure to act would be catastrophic. Human resource techniques of skill building, participation, and open meetings can help to get the story out and gauge

Exhibit 18.2.
Reframing Kotter's Change Stages.

KOTTER'S STAGE OF CHANGE	STRUCTURAL FRAME	HUMAN RESOURCE FRAME	POLITICAL FRAME	SYMBOLIC FRAME
1. Sense of urgency		Involve people throughout organization; solicit input	Network with key players; use power base	Tell a compelling story
2. Guiding team	Develop coordination strategy	Run team-building exercises for guiding team	Stack team with credible, influential members	Put commanding officer on team
3. Uplifting vision and strategy	Build implementation plan		Map political terrain; develop agenda	Craft a hopeful vision of future rooted in organization history
4. Communicate vision and strategy through words, deeds, and symbols	Create structures to support change process	Hold meetings to communicate direction, get feedback	Create arenas; build alliances; defuse opposition	Visible leadership involvement; kickoff ceremonies
5. Remove obstacles and empower people to move forward	Remove or alter structures and procedures that support the old ways	Provide training, resources, and support		Stage public hangings of counterrevolutionaries
6. Early wins	Plan for short-term victories		Invest resources and power to ensure early wins	Celebrate and communicate early signs of progress
7. Keep going when going gets tough	Keep people on plan			Hold revival meetings
8. New culture to support new ways	Align structure to new culture	Create a "culture" team; broad involvement in developing culture		Mourn the past; celebrate heroes of the revolution; share stories of the journey

audience reaction. Behind the scenes, leaders can meet with key players, assess their interests, and negotiate or use power as necessary to get people on board.

As another example, Kotter's fifth step calls for removing obstacles and empowering people to move forward. Structurally, this is a matter of identifying rules, roles, procedures, and patterns that block progress and then working to realign them. Meanwhile, the human resource frame counsels training, support, and resources to enable people to master new behaviors. Symbolically, a few "public hangings" (for example, firing, demoting, or exiling prominent opponents) could reinforce the message. Public celebrations could honor successes and herald a new beginning.

Exhibit 18.2 is intended as an illustration, not an exhaustive plan. Every situation and change effort is unique. Creative change agents can use the ideas to stimulate thinking and spur imagination as they develop an approach that fits local circumstances.

SUMMARY

Innovation inevitably generates four issues. First, it affects individuals' ability to feel effective, valued, and in control. Without support, training, and a chance to participate in the process, people become powerful anchors, embedded in the past, that block forward motion. Second, change disrupts existing patterns of roles and relationships, producing confusion and uncertainty. Structural patterns need to be revised and realigned to support the new direction. Third, change creates conflict between winners and losers—those who benefit from the new direction and those who do not. This conflict requires creation of arenas where the issues can be renegotiated and the political map redrawn. Finally, change creates loss of meaning for recipients of the change. Transition rituals, mourning the past, and celebrating the future help people let go of old attachments and embrace new ways of doing things. Kotter's model of successive change includes eight stages. Integrated with the frames, it offers a well-orchestrated, integrated design for responding to needs for participative learning, realignment, negotiation, and grieving.

Reframing Ethics and Spirit

What shall an organization profit if it should gain the world but lose its soul?[1] For Starbucks chairman Howard Schultz, the answer is "not a lot," which is why he raised exactly that question in a memo to everyone in his company in 2007, as described in Chapter Twelve. In the case of Enron, the answer was evidently "nothing at all"; the company eventually lost both its soul and the world it hoped to gain. Enron was America's largest gas pipeline company when Kenneth Lay took over as chief executive in 1985. At the time, it was a solid but pedestrian business. It was a strong competitor in its industry, but demand was flat, and profits cycled with fluctuations in the price of gas (Bodily and Bruner, 2002). Deregulation loomed, creating both threats and opportunities. Lay, as smart as he was genial, did what CEOs are expected to do: look for ways to grow the business and boost the share price. For more than fifteen years, he was remarkably successful. A once-sleepy company morphed into world's largest energy-trading business, and Enron's market value grew from $2 billion in 1985 to $70 billion in mid-2001.

Most of the excitement at Enron was generated by a new and unique business model. Instead of just pumping gas through pipes, the company redefined itself as a trader, a deal maker in a variety of commodities. Initially, the focus was energy, but Enron gradually expanded into areas as diverse as broadband and an esoteric form of weather insurance. By 2000, the old pipelines represented only about a fifth of Enron's revenues and profits. Much of the rest came from the new "merchant" businesses, which attracted a new breed of Enron employee: bright young fast-trackers with advanced degrees in business and finance.

The stable pipeline business was run by managers with years of industry experience. Reliability and operating efficiency were the keys to success. Pay was linked to seniority. The new trading operations carried much higher risks, which brought Enron into the business equivalent of the Wild West. Big rewards awaited aggressive gunslingers with the guts and smarts to grab whatever loot they could find. Enron's old pay system gave way to huge bonuses and generous stock options for high-performers. This was topped off with corporate jets and lavish parties adorned by $500 bottles of champagne and strippers who cost even more (Roberts and Thomas, 2002). As James O'Toole put it, "At Enron, you had a bunch of kids running loose without adult supervision" (Byrne, France, and Zellner, 2002, p. 1).

It's easy to catch gold fever in a mining town during a boom, and many of Enron's aggressive young pioneers were stricken. One was Timothy Belden, thirty-four-year-old head of Enron's energy trading office in Portland, Oregon. Belden earned bonuses totaling close to $5 million in 2001. A year later, he agreed to give some of it to the state of California, pleading guilty to illegal manipulation of California's energy crisis: "In the plea Belden admitted to working with others on trading tactics that effectively transformed California's complex system for buying and transmitting energy into a fictional world, complete with bogus transmission schedules, imaginary congestion on power lines and fraudulent sales of 'out of state' energy that in fact came from California itself" (Eichenwald and Richtel, 2002, p. C1).

When some of Enron's new mines produced only fool's gold, the company's financial wizards tried to keep the game going. Fancy financial maneuvers inflated revenue and hid debt, mostly by selling assets to supposedly independent partnerships that were controlled by Enron's chief financial officer, Andrew Fastow. Partnerships borrowed the money from banks or brokerages, and Enron guaranteed the loans (Eichenwald, 2002b). Moving money from one pocket to another bumped up Enron's financial statements in the short run, but eventually the off-balance-sheet shenanigans came home to roost, and the company imploded.

At the heart of this tragedy, the company lost track of what it was or stood for. As Arie De Geus puts it, companies "need profits in the same way as any living being needs oxygen. It is a necessity to stay alive, but it is not the purpose of life" (De Geus, 1995, p. 29). Enron's story is far from unique. Over the years, corporate flame-outs have recurred around the world. What can managers and organizations do about this abysmal state of moral lapse? We argue in this chapter that ethics must reside in *soul,* a sense of bedrock character that harbors core beliefs and values. We discuss why soul is important and how it sustains spiritual conviction and ethical behavior. We then present a variegated picture of leadership ethics.

SOUL AND SPIRIT IN ORGANIZATIONS

What Enron lacked becomes obvious if we compare it to the pharmaceutical giant Merck, one of America's most successful firms. Merck states its core purpose as preserving and improving human life, above making a profit. A noble sentiment, but is it reflected in key decisions and everyday behavior? Mostly, though Merck has sustained legitimate criticism in recent years for being slow to acknowledge health risks with some of its best-selling drugs like Vioxx (Fielder, 2005). But Merck can also point to a number of instances of selling a drug at a loss or giving it away to fulfill the company's core value of putting patients first. In one well-known instance, Merck had to decide whether to develop and distribute a drug for river blindness, an affliction of poor people in many Third World countries. From a cost-benefit viewpoint, the choice was clear: the drug had little chance of making money. For bottom-line-driven companies, such a decision would be a no-brainer. Merck, true to its emphasis on health, developed the drug and then gave it away. The company's commitment to its values made the decision easy, the CEO said afterward.

In contrast, "the woods were filled with smart people at Enron, but there were really no wise people, or people who could say 'this is enough'" (John Olson, cited in Eichenwald, 2002a, p. A26). Some of us have such strong ethical convictions that it matters little where we work, but many of us are more inclined to shilly-shally, attuned to cues and expectations from our colleagues at work about what to do and not to do. Enron lost track of its redeeming moral purpose and failed to provide ethical guardrails for its employees. Some went to jail, and many others suffered damage to careers and self-worth.

Many dispute the notion that organizations possess soul, but there is growing evidence that spirituality is a critical element in long-run success. A dictionary definition of *soul* uses terms such as "animating force," "immaterial essence," and "spiritual nature." For an organization, group, or family, soul can also be viewed as a resolute sense of character, a deep confidence about who we are, what we care about, and what we deeply believe in. Merck had it. Enron did not. Starbucks is concerned about losing it.

Why should an organization—a company, a school, or a public agency—be concerned about soul? Many organizations and most management writers either scoff at or ignore the matter. As an example, two best-sellers on strategy, Treacy and Wiersema's *The Discipline of Market Leaders* (1995) and Hamel and Prahalad's *Competing for the Future* (1994), link the enormous success of Southwest Airlines to its strategic prowess. But founder Herb Kelleher offered a very different explanation for what makes Southwest work, one that features people, humor, love, and soul. "Simply put, Kelleher 'cherishes and respects' his employees, and his 'love' is returned in what he calls 'a spontaneous, voluntary overflowing of emotion'" (Farkas and De Backer, 1996, p. 87). Kelleher's style was certainly unique: "On Easter, he walked a plane's aisle clad in an Easter bunny outfit, and for St. Patrick's Day he dressed as a leprechaun. When Southwest started a new route to Sacramento, Kelleher sang a rap song at a press conference with two people in Teenage Mutant Ninja costumes and two others dressed as tomatoes" (Levering and Moskowitz, 1993, p. 413).

But Kelleher's hijinks are only part of the Southwest success story. Soul, the heart of the "Southwest spirit," is shared throughout the company. Kelleher claimed that the most important group in the company was the "Culture Committee," a seventy-person cross-section of employees established to perpetuate the company's values and spirit. His charge to the committee was to "carry the spiritual message of Southwest Airlines" (Farkas and De Backer, 1996, p. 93). There were plenty of skeptics, and a competing airline executive grumbled, "Southwest runs on Herb's bullshit" (Petzinger, 1995, p. 284). But year after year, Southwest's growth and profitability topped its industry.

A growing number of successful leaders embrace a philosophy much like Kelleher's. Ben Cohen, cofounder of the ice cream company Ben and Jerry's Homemade, observes: "When you give love, you receive love. I maintain that there is a spiritual dimension to business just as there is to the lives of individuals"

(Levering and Moskowitz, 1993, p. 47). Lou Gerstner of IBM and Howard Schultz of Starbuck's echo his sentiments in their emphasis on culture and heart.

Evidence suggests that tapping a deeper level of human energy pays off. Collins and Porras (1994) and De Geus (1995) both found that a central characteristic of corporations succeeding over the long haul was a core ideology emphasizing "more than profits" and offering "guidance and inspiration to people inside the company" (Collins and Porras, 1994, pp. 48, 88). When authentic and part of everyday life, such core ideologies—love at Southwest, preserving human life at Merck—give a company soul.

Soul and ethics are inextricably intertwined. Recent decades have regularly produced highly public scandals of major corporations engaging in unethical, if not illegal, conduct. It happened in the 1980s, a decade of remarkable greed and corruption in business. It happened again with the spate of scandals in 2001 and 2002, as well as in the sub-prime mortgage mess of 2007–2008. Efforts to do something about the ethical void in management have ebbed and flowed as dishonor comes and goes. One proposed remedy is more emphasis on ethics in professional training programs. A second has sparked a flurry of corporate ethics statements. A third has pushed for stronger legal and regulatory muscle, such as the Foreign Corrupt Practices Act, forbidding U.S. corporations from bribing foreign officials to get or retain business, and "SOX"—the Sarbanes-Oxley Act of 2002[2]—which mandated a variety of measures to combat fraud and increase corporate transparency.

These are important initiatives, but they only skim the surface. Solomon calls for a deeper "Aristotelian ethic":

> There is too little sense of business as itself enjoyable (the main virtue of the "game" metaphor), that business is not a matter of vulgar self-interest but of vital community interest, that the virtues on which one prides oneself in personal life are essentially the same as those essential to good business—honesty, dependability, courage, loyalty, integrity. Aristotle's central ethical concept, accordingly, is a unified, all-embracing notion of "happiness" (or, more accurately, eudaimonia, perhaps better translated as "flourishing" or "doing well"). The point is to view one's life as a whole and not separate the personal and the public or professional, or duty and pleasure [1993, p. 105].

Solomon settled on the term *Aristotelian* because it makes no pretensions of imparting the latest cutting-edge theory or technique of management. Rather, he reminds us of a perspective and debate reaching back to ancient times. The central motive is not to commission a new wave of experts and seminars or to kick off one more downsizing bloodbath. "It is to emphasize the importance of continuity and stability, clearness of vision and constancy of purpose, corporate loyalty and individual integrity" (1993, p. 104). Solomon reminds us that ethics and soul are essential for living a good life as well as managing a fulfilling organization. Since the beginning, the world's philosophical and spiritual traditions have proffered wisdom to guide our search for better ways to accomplish both.

We have emphasized the four frames as cognitive lenses for understanding and tools for influencing collective endeavors. Our focus has been the heads and hands of leaders. Both are vitally important. But so are hearts and souls. The frames also carry implications for creating ethical communities and for reviving the moral responsibilities of leadership. Exhibit 19.1 summarizes our view.

		ORGANIZATIONAL	LEADERSHIP
Exhibit 19.1.			
Reframing Ethics.			
FRAME	**METAPHOR**	**ETHIC**	**CONTRIBUTION**
Structural	Factory	Excellence	Authorship
Human resource	Extended family	Caring	Love
Political	Jungle	Justice	Power
Symbolic	Temple	Faith	Significance

The Factory: Excellence and Authorship

One of our oldest images of organizations is that of factories engaged in a production process. Raw materials (steel, peanuts, or five-year-olds) come in the door and leave as finished products (refrigerators, peanut butter, or educated graduates). The ethical imperative of the factory is excellence: ensuring that work is done as effectively and efficiently as possible to produce high-quality yields. Since the 1982 publication of Peters and Waterman's famous book, almost everyone has been searching for excellence, though flawed products and mediocre services keep reminding us that the hunt does not always bring home the quarry.

One source of disappointment is that excellence requires more than pious sermons from top management; it demands commitment and autonomy at all levels of an enterprise. How do leaders foster such dedication? As we've said before, "Leading is giving. Leadership is an ethic, a gift of oneself" (Bolman and Deal, 2001, p. 106). Critical for creating and maintaining excellence is the gift of authorship:

> Giving authorship provides space within boundaries. In an orchestra, musicians develop individual parts within the parameters of a musical score and the interpretative challenges posed by the conductor. Authorship turns the pyramid on its side. Leaders increase their influence and build more productive organizations. Workers experience the satisfactions of creativity, craftsmanship and a job well done. Gone is the traditional adversarial relationship in which superiors try to increase control while subordinates resist them at every turn. Trusting people to solve problems generates higher levels of motivation and better solutions. The leader's responsibility is to create conditions that promote authorship. Individuals need to see their work as meaningful and worthwhile, to feel personally accountable for the consequences of their efforts, and to get feedback that lets them know the results [Bolman and Deal, 2001, pp. 111–112].

Southwest Airlines offers a compelling example of authorship. Its associates are encouraged to be themselves, have fun, and above all use their sense of humor. Only on Southwest are you likely to hear required FAA safety briefings sung to the music of a popular song or delivered as a stand-up comedy routine. ("Those of you who wish to smoke will please file out to our lounge on the wing, where you can enjoy our feature film, *Gone with the Wind*.") Too frivolous for something as serious as a safety announcement? Just the opposite: it's a way to get passengers to pay attention to a message they usually ignore. Surely, it's also a way for flight attendants to have fun and feel creative rather than being mechanically scripted by routine.

The Family: Caring and Love

Caring—one person's compassion and concern for another—is both the primary purpose and the ethical glue that holds a family together. Parents care for children and, eventually, children care for their parents. A compassionate family or community requires servant-leaders concerned with the needs and wishes of members and stakeholders. This creates a challenging obligation for leaders to understand and to provide stewardship of the collective well-being. The gift of the servant-leader is love.

Love is largely absent from most modern corporations. Most managers would never use the word in any context more profound than their feelings about food, family, films, or games. They shy away from love's deeper meanings, fearing both its power and its risks. Caring begins with knowing; it requires listening, understanding, and accepting. It progresses through a deepening sense of appreciation, respect, and ultimately love. Love is a willingness to reach out and open one's heart. An open heart is vulnerable. Confronting vulnerability allows us to drop our mask, meet heart to heart, and be present for one another. We experience a sense of unity and delight in those voluntary, human exchanges that mold "the soul of community" (Whitmyer, 1993, p. 81).

They talk openly about love at Southwest Airlines. As president Colleen Barrett reminisced, "Love is a word that isn't used often in Corporate America, but we used it at Southwest from the beginning." The word *love* is woven into the culture. They fly out of Love Field in Dallas; their symbol on the New York Stock Exchange is LUV; the employee newsletter is called *Luv Lines;* and their twentieth anniversary slogan was "Twenty Years of Loving You" (Levering and Moskowitz, 1993). They hold an annual "Heroes of the Heart" ceremony to honor members of the Southwest family who have gone above and beyond even Southwest's high call of duty. There are, of course, ups and downs in any family, and the airline industry certainly experiences both. Through life's peaks and valleys, love holds people—both employees and passengers—together in a caring community.

For Levi Strauss, the issue of caring came to a head in trying to apply the company's ethical principles (honesty, fairness, respect for others, compassion, promise keeping, and integrity) to the thorny dilemmas of working with foreign subcontractors. How should the company balance concern for domestic employees with concern for overseas workers? Even if pay and working conditions at foreign subcontractors are below those in the United States, are inferior jobs better than no jobs? A task force set to work to collect data and formulate guidelines for ethical practice. Ultimately, the company wound up making some tough decisions. It became the first American clothing company to develop a set of standards for working conditions in overseas plants. It pulled out of China for five years beginning in 1993 because of human rights abuses, despite the huge market potential there. In a factory in Bangladesh employing underage children, Levi's arranged for the children to go back to school while the contractor continued to pay their salaries (Waterman, 1994).

The Jungle: Justice and Power

We turn now to a third image: the organization as jungle. Woody Allen captured the competitive, predator-prey imagery succinctly: "The lion and the calf shall lie down together, but the calf won't get much sleep" (1986, p. 28). As the metaphor suggests, the jungle is a politically charged environment of conflict and pursuit of self-interest. Politics and politicians are routinely viewed as objects of scorn—often for good reason. Their behavior tends to prompt the question: Is there any ethical consideration associated with political action? We believe there is: the commitment to justice. In a world of competing interests and scarce resources, people are continually compelled to make trade-offs. No one can give everyone everything they want, but it is possible to honor a value of fairness in making decisions about who gets what. Solomon (1993, p. 231) sees justice as the ultimate virtue in corporations, because fairness—the perception that employees, customers, and investors are all getting their due—is the glue that holds things together.

Justice is never easy to define, and disagreement about its application is inevitable. The key gift that leaders can offer in pursuit of justice is sharing power. People with a voice in key decisions are far more likely to feel a sense of fairness than those with none. Leaders who hoard power produce powerless organizations. People stripped of power look for ways to fight back: sabotage, passive resistance, withdrawal, or angry militancy. Giving power liberates energy for more productive use. If people have a sense of efficacy and an ability to influence their world, they are more likely to direct their energy and intelligence toward making a contribution rather than making trouble. The gift of power enrolls people in working toward a common cause. It also creates difficult choice points. If leaders clutch power too tightly, they activate old patterns of antagonism. But if they cave in and say yes to anything, they put an organization's mission at risk.

During the Reagan administration, House Speaker "Tip" O'Neil was a constant thorn in the side of the president, but they carved out a mutually just agreement: they would fight ferociously for their independent interests but stay civil and find fairness wherever possible. Their rule: "After six o'clock, we're friends, whatever divisiveness the political battle has produced during working hours." Both men gave each other the gift of power. During one acrimonious public debate between the two, Regan reportedly whispered, "Tip, can we pretend it's six o'clock?" (Neuman, 2004, p. 1).

Power and authorship are related; autonomy, space, and freedom are important in both. Still, there is an important distinction between the two. Artists, authors, and craftspeople can experience authorship even working alone. Power, in contrast, is meaningful only in relation to others. It is the capacity to wield influence and get things to happen on a broader scale. Authorship without power is isolating and splintering; power without authorship can be dysfunctional and oppressive.

The gift of power is important at multiple levels. As individuals, people want power to control their immediate work environment and the factors that impinge on them directly. Many traditional workplaces still suffocate their employees with time clocks, rigid rules, and authoritarian bosses. A global challenge at the group level is responding to ethnic, racial, and gender diversity. Gallos, Ramsey, and their colleagues get to the heart of the complexity of this issue:

> Institutional, structural and systemic issues are very difficult for members of dominant groups to understand. Systems are most often designed by dominant group members to meet their own needs. It is then difficult to see the ways in which our institutions and structures systematically exclude others who are not "like us." It is hard to see and question what we have always taken for granted and painful to confront personal complicity in maintaining the status quo. Privilege enables us to remain unaware of institutional and social forces and their impact [1997, p. 215].

Justice requires that leaders systematically enhance the power of subdominant groups—ensuring access to decision making, creating internal advocacy groups, building diversity into information and incentive systems, and strengthening career opportunities (Cox, 1994; Gallos, Ramsey, and Associates, 1997; Morrison, 1992). All this happens only with a rock-solid commitment from top management, the one condition that Morrison (1992) found to be universal in organizations that led in responding to diversity.

Justice also has important implications for the increasingly urgent question of "sustainability": How long can a production or business process last before it collapses as a result of the resource depletion or environmental damage it produces? Decisions about sustainability inevitably involve trade-offs among the interests of constituencies that differ in role, place, and time. How do we balance our company's profitability against damage to the environment, or current interests against those of future generations? Organizations with a commitment to justice will take these questions seriously and look for ways to engage and empower diverse stakeholders in making choices.

The Temple: Faith and Significance

An organization, like a temple, can be seen as a hallowed place, an expression of human aspirations, a monument to faith in human possibility. A temple is a gathering place for a community of people with shared traditions, values, and beliefs. Members of a community may be diverse in many ways (age, background, economic status, personal interests), but they are tied together by shared faith and bonded by a sanctified spiritual covenant. In work organizations, faith is strengthened if individuals feel the organization is characterized by excellence, caring, and justice. Above all, people must believe that the organization is doing something worth doing—a calling that adds something of value to the world. Significance is partly about the work itself, but even more about how the work is embraced. This point is made by an old story about three stonemasons giving an account of their work. The first said he was "cutting stone." The second said that he was "building a cathedral." The third said simply that he was "serving God."

Temples need spiritual leaders. This does not mean promoting religion or a particular theology; rather, it means bringing a genuine concern for the human spirit. The dictionary defines spirit as "the intelligent or immaterial part of man," "the animating or vital principal in living things," and "the moral nature of humanity." Spiritual leaders help people find meaning and faith in work and help them answer fundamental questions that have confronted humans of every time and place: Who am I as an individual? Who are we as a people? What is the purpose of my life, of our collective existence? What ethical principles should we follow? What legacy will we leave?

Spiritual leaders offer the gift of significance, rooted in confidence that the work is precious, that devotion and loyalty to a beloved institution can offer hard-to-emulate intangible rewards. Work is exhilarating and joyful at its best; arduous, frustrating, and exhausting in less happy moments. Many adults embark on their careers with enthusiasm, confidence, and a desire to make a contribution. Some never lose that spark, but many do. They become frustrated with sterile or toxic working conditions and discouraged by how hard it is to make a difference, or even to know if they have made one. Tracy Kidder puts it well in writing about teachers: "Good teachers put snags in the river of children passing by, and over time, they redirect hundreds of lives. There is an innocence that conspires to hold humanity together, and it is made up of people who can never fully know the good they have done" (Kidder, 1989, p. 313). The gift of significance helps people sustain their faith rather than burn out and retire from a meaningless job.

Significance is built through the use of many expressive and symbolic forms: rituals, ceremonies, stories, and music. An organization without a rich symbolic life grows empty and barren. The magic of special occasions is vital in building significance into collective life. Moments of ecstasy are parentheses that mark life's major passages. Without ritual and ceremony, transition remains incomplete, a clutter of comings and goings; "life becomes an endless set of Wednesdays" (Campbell, 1983, p. 5).

When ritual and ceremony are authentic and attuned, they fire the imagination, evoke insight, and touch the heart. Ceremony weaves past, present, and future into life's ongoing tapestry. Ritual helps us face and comprehend life's everyday shocks, triumphs, and mysteries. Both help us experience the unseen web of significance that ties a community together. When inauthentic, such occasions become meaningless, repetitive, and alienating—wasting our time, disconnecting us from work, and splintering us from one another. "Community must become more than just gathering the troops, telling the stories, and remembering things past. Community must also be rooted in values that do not fail, values that go beyond the self-aggrandizement of human leaders" (Griffin, 1993, p. 178).

Stories give flesh to shared values and sacred beliefs. Everyday life in organizations brings many heartwarming moments and dramatic encounters. Transformed into stories, these events fill an organization's treasure chest with lore and legend. Told and retold, they draw people together and connect them with the significance of their work.

Music captures and expresses life's deeper meaning. When people sing or dance together, they bond to one another and experience emotional connections otherwise hard to express. The late Harry Quadracci, chief executive officer of the printing company Quadgraphics, convened employees once a year for an annual gathering. A management chorus sang the year's themes. Quadracci himself voiced the company philosophy in a solo serenade.

Max DePree, famed both as both a business leader and an author of elegant books on leadership, is clear about the role of faith in business: "Being faithful is more important than being successful. Corporations can and should have a redemptive purpose. We need to weigh the pragmatic in the clarifying light of the moral. We must understand that reaching our potential is more important than reaching our goals" (1989, p. 69). Spiritual leaders have the responsibility of sustaining and encouraging faith in themselves and in recalling others to the faith when they have wandered from it or lost it.

SUMMARY

Ethics ultimately must be rooted in soul: an organization's commitment to its deeply rooted identity, beliefs, and values. Each frame offers a perspective on the ethical responsibilities of organizations and the moral authority of leaders. Every organization needs to evolve for itself a profound sense of its own ethical and spiritual core. The frames offer spiritual guidelines for the quest.

Signs are everywhere that institutions in many developed nations suffer from a crisis of meaning and moral authority. Rapid change, high mobility, globalization, and racial and ethnic conflict tear at the fabric of community. The most important responsibility of managers is not to answer every question or get every decision right. Though they cannot escape their responsibility to track budgets, motivate people, respond to political pressures, and attend to culture, they serve a deeper, more powerful, and more enduring role if they are models and catalysts for such values as excellence, caring, justice, and faith.

NOTES

1. The question paraphrases Matthew 16:26: "For what is a man profited, if he shall gain the whole world, and lose his own soul?" (King James version).

2. Officially, the Public Company Accounting Reform and Investor Protection Act of 2002.

Bringing It All Together
Change and Leadership in Action

Life's daily challenges rarely arrive clearly labeled or neatly pack-aged. Instead, they immerse us in a murky, turbulent, and unre-lenting flood. The art of reframing uses knowledge and intuition to make sense of the current and to find sensible and effective ways to channel the flow.

In this chapter, we illustrate the process by following a new principal through his first week in a deeply troubled urban high school.[1] Had this been a corporation in crisis, a struggling hospital, or an embattled public agency, the basic leadership issues would be much the same. We assume that our protagonist is familiar with the frames and with reframing and is committed to the view of leadership and ethics described in Chapter Nineteen. How might he use what he knows to figure out what's going on? What strategies can he mull over? What will he do?

Read the case thoughtfully. Ask yourself what you think is going on and what options you would consider. Then compare your reflections with his.

ROBERT F. KENNEDY HIGH SCHOOL

On July 15, David King became principal of Robert F. Kennedy High School, the newest of six high schools in Great Ridge, Illinois. The school had opened two years earlier amid national acclaim as one of the first schools in the country designed and built on the "house system" concept. Kennedy High was organized into four "houses," each with three hundred students, eighteen faculty, and a housemaster. Each house was in a separate building connected to the "core facilities"—cafeteria, nurse's room, guidance offices, boys' and girls' gyms, offices, shops, and auditorium—and other houses by an enclosed outside passageway. Each had its own entrance, classrooms, toilets, conference rooms, and housemaster's office.

Hailed as a major innovation in inner-city education, Kennedy High was featured during its first year in a documentary on a Chicago television station. The school opened with a carefully selected staff of teachers, many chosen from other Great Ridge schools. At least a dozen were specially recruited from out of state. King knew that his faculty included graduates from several elite East Coast and West Coast schools, such as Yale, Princeton, and Stanford, as well as several of the very best Midwestern schools. Even the racial mix of students had been carefully balanced so that blacks, whites, and Latinos each comprised a third of the student body (although King also knew—perhaps better than its planners—that Kennedy's students were drawn from the toughest and poorest areas of the city). The building itself was also widely admired for its beauty and functionality and had won several national architectural awards.

Despite careful and elaborate preparations, Kennedy High School was in serious trouble by the time King arrived. It had been racked by violence the preceding year—closed twice by student disturbances and once by a teacher walkout. It was also widely reported (although King did not know for sure) that achievement scores of its ninth- and tenth-grade students had declined during the last two years, and no significant improvement could be seen in the scores of the eleventh and twelfth graders' tests. So far, Kennedy High School had fallen far short of its planners' hopes and expectations.

David King

David King was born and raised in Great Ridge, Illinois. His father was one of the city's first black principals. King knew the city and its school system well. After two years of military service, King followed in his father's footsteps by going to Great Ridge State Teachers College, where he received B.Ed. and M.Ed. degrees. King taught English and coached in a predominantly black middle school for several years until he was asked to become the school's assistant principal. He remained in that post for five years, when he was asked to take over a large middle school of nine hundred pupils—believed at the time to be the most "difficult" middle school in the city. While there, King gained a citywide reputation as a gifted and popular administrator. He was credited with changing the worst middle school in the system into one of the best. He had been very effective in building community support, recruiting new faculty, and raising academic standards. He was also credited with turning out basketball and baseball teams that had won state and county championships.

The superintendent made it clear that King had been selected for the Kennedy job over several more senior candidates because of his ability to handle tough situations. The superintendent had also told him that he would need every bit of skill and luck he could muster. King knew of the formidable credentials of Jack Weis, his predecessor at Kennedy High. Weis, a white man, had been the superintendent of a small local township school system before becoming Kennedy's first principal. He had written one book on the house system concept and another on inner-city education. Weis held a Ph.D. from the University of Chicago and a divinity degree from Harvard. Yet despite his impressive background and ability, Weis had resigned in disillusionment. He was described by many as a "broken man." King remembered seeing the physical change in Weis over that two-year period. Weis's appearance had become progressively more fatigued and strained until he developed what appeared to be permanent dark rings under his eyes and a perpetual stoop. King remembered how he had pitied the man and wondered how Weis could find the job worth the obvious personal toll it was taking on him.

History of the School

The First Year

The school's troubles began to manifest themselves in its first year. Rumors of conflicts between the housemasters and the six subject-area department heads spread throughout the system by the middle of the year. The conflicts stemmed from differences in interpretations of curriculum policy on required learning and course content. In response,

Weis had instituted a "free market" policy: subject-area department heads were supposed to convince housemasters why they should offer certain courses, and housemasters were supposed to convince department heads which teachers they wanted assigned to their houses. Many felt that this policy exacerbated the conflicts.

To add to the tension, a teacher was assaulted in her classroom in February. The beating frightened many of the staff, particularly older teachers. A week later, eight teachers asked Weis to hire security guards. This request precipitated a debate in the faculty about the desirability of guards in the school. One group felt that the guards would instill a sense of safety and promote a better learning climate. The other faction felt that the presence of guards in the school would be repressive and would destroy the sense of community and trust that was developing. Weis refused the request for security guards because he believed they would symbolize everything the school was trying to change. In April, a second teacher was robbed and beaten in her classroom after school hours, and the debate was rekindled. This time, a group of Latino parents threatened to boycott the school unless better security measures were implemented. Again, Weis refused the request for security guards.

The Second Year

The school's second year was even more troubled than the first. Financial cutbacks ordered during the summer prevented Weis from replacing eight teachers who resigned. Since it was no longer possible for each house to staff all of its courses with its own faculty, Weis instituted a "flexible staffing" policy. Some teachers were asked to teach a course outside their assigned house, and students in the eleventh and twelfth grades were able to take elective and required courses in other houses. Chauncey Carver, one of the housemasters, publicly attacked the new policy as a step toward destroying the house system. In a letter to the *Great Ridge Times,* he accused the board of education of trying to subvert the house concept by cutting back funds.

The debate over the flexible staffing policy was heightened when two of the other housemasters joined a group of faculty and department heads in opposing Carver's criticisms. This group argued that interhouse cross-registration should be encouraged because the fifteen to eighteen teachers in each house could never offer the variety of courses that the schoolwide faculty of sixty-five to seventy could.

Further expansion of the flexible staffing policy was halted, however, because of difficulties in scheduling fall classes. Errors cropped up in the master schedule developed during the preceding summer. Scheduling problems persisted until November, when the vice principal responsible for developing the schedule resigned. Burtram Perkins, a Kennedy housemaster who had formerly planned the schedule at Central High, assumed the function on top of his duties as housemaster. Scheduling took most of Perkins's time until February.

Security again became an issue when three sophomores were assaulted because they refused to give up their lunch money during a shakedown. The assailants were believed to be outsiders. Several teachers approached Weis and asked him to request the board of education to provide security guards. Again, Weis declined, but he asked Bill Smith, a vice principal at the school, to secure all doors except for the entrances to each of the four houses, the main entrance to the school, and the cafeteria. This move seemed to reduce the number of outsiders roaming through the school.

In May of the second year, a fight in the cafeteria spread and resulted in considerable damage, including broken classroom windows and desks. The disturbance was severe enough for Weis to close the school. A number of teachers and students reported that outsiders were involved in the fight and in damaging the classrooms. Several students were taken to the hospital for minor injuries, but all were released. A similar disturbance occurred two weeks later, and again the school was closed. The board of education ordered a temporary detail of municipal police to the school against Weis's advice. In protest to the assignment of police, thirty of Kennedy's sixty-eight teachers staged a walkout, joined by over half the student body. The police detail was removed, and an agreement was worked out by an ad hoc subcommittee composed of board members and informal representatives of teachers who were for and against a police detail. The compromise called for the temporary stationing of a police cruiser near the school.

King's First Week at Kennedy High

King arrived at Kennedy High on Monday, July 15, and spent most of his first week individually interviewing key administrators (see box):

ADMINISTRATIVE ORGANIZATION OF ROBERT F. KENNEDY HIGH SCHOOL

Principal: David King, 42 (black)
    B.Ed., M.Ed., Great Ridge State Teachers College
Vice principal: William Smith, 44 (black)
    B.Ed., Breakwater State College;
    M.Ed., Great Ridge State Teachers College
Vice principal: Vacant
Housemaster, A House: Burtram Perkins, 47 (black)
    B.S., M.Ed., University of Illinois
Housemaster, B House: Frank Czepak, 36 (white)
    B.S., University of Illinois;
    M.Ed., Great Ridge State Teachers College
Housemaster, C House: Chauncey Carver, 32 (black)
    A.B., Wesleyan University;
    B.F.A., Pratt Institute; M.A.T., Yale University
Housemaster, D House: John Bonavota, 26 (white)
    B.Ed., Great Ridge State Teachers College;
    M.Ed., Ohio State University
Assistant to the principal: Vacant
Assistant to the principal for community affairs: Vacant

On Friday, he held a meeting with all administrators and department heads. King's purpose in these meetings was to familiarize himself with the school, its problems, and its key people. His first interview was with Bill Smith, a vice principal. Smith was black and had worked as a counselor and then vice principal of a middle school before coming to Kennedy. King knew Smith's reputation as a tough disciplinarian who was very much disliked by many of the younger faculty and students. King had also heard from several teachers whose judgment he respected that Smith had been instrumental in keeping the school from "blowing apart" the preceding year. It became clear early in the interview that Smith felt that more stringent steps were needed to keep outsiders from wandering into the buildings. Smith urged King to consider locking all the school's thirty doors except for the front entrance so that everyone would enter and leave through one set of doors. Smith also told him that many of the teachers and pupils were scared and that "no learning will ever begin to take place until we make it so people don't have to be afraid anymore." At the end of the interview, Smith said he had been approached by a nearby school system to become its director of counseling but that he had not yet made up his mind. He said he was committed enough to Kennedy High that he did not want to leave, but his decision depended on how hopeful he felt about the school's future.

As King talked with others, he discovered that the "door question" was highly controversial within the faculty and that feelings ran high on both sides of the issue. Two housemasters in particular, Chauncey Carver, who was black, and Frank Czepak, who was white, were strongly against closing the house entrances. The two men felt such an action would symbolically reduce house "autonomy" and the feeling of distinctness that was a central aspect of the house concept.

Carver, master of House C, was particularly vehement on this issue and on his opposition to allowing students in one house to take classes in another house. Carver contended that the flexible staffing program had nearly destroyed the house concept. He threatened to resign if King intended to expand cross-house enrollment. Carver also complained about what he described as "interference" from department heads that undermined his teachers' autonomy.

Carver appeared to be an outstanding housemaster from everything King had heard about him—even from his many enemies. Carver had an abrasive personality but seemed to have the best-operating house in the school and was well liked by most of his teachers and pupils. His program appeared to be the most innovative, but it was also the one most frequently attacked by department heads for lacking substance and ignoring requirements in the system's curriculum guide. Even with these criticisms, King imagined how much easier it would be if he had four housemasters like Chauncey Carver.

During his interviews with the other three housemasters, King discovered that they all felt infringed upon by the department heads, but only Carver and Czepak were strongly against locking the doors. The other two housemasters actively favored cross-house course enrollments. King's fourth interview was with Burtram Perkins, also a housemaster. Perkins, mentioned earlier, was a black man in his late forties who had served as assistant to the principal of Central High before coming to Kennedy. Perkins spent most of the interview discussing how schedule pressures could be relieved. Perkins was currently developing the schedule for the coming school year until a vice principal could be appointed to perform that job (Kennedy High had allocations for two vice principals and two assistants in addition to the housemasters).

Two bits of information concerning Perkins came to King during his first week at the school. The first was that several teachers were circulating a letter requesting Perkins's removal as a housemaster. They felt that he could not control the house or direct the faculty. This surprised King because he had heard that Perkins was widely respected within the faculty and had earned a reputation for supporting high academic standards and for working tirelessly with new teachers. As King inquired further, he discovered that Perkins was genuinely liked but was also widely acknowledged as a poor housemaster. The second piece of information concerned how Perkins's house compared with the others. Although students had been randomly assigned to each house, Perkins's house had the highest absence rate and the greatest number of disciplinary problems. Smith had told him that Perkins's dropout rate the preceding year was three times that of the next highest house.

While King was in the process of interviewing his staff, he was called on by David Crimmins, chairman of the history department. Crimmins was a native of Great Ridge, white, and in his late forties. Though scheduled for an appointment the following week, he had asked King if he could see him immediately. Crimmins had heard about the letter asking for Perkins's removal and wanted to present the other side. He became very emotional, saying that Perkins was viewed by many of the teachers and department chairmen as the only housemaster trying to maintain high academic standards; his transfer would be seen as a blow to those concerned with quality education. Crimmins also described in detail Perkins's devotion and commitment to the school. He emphasized that Perkins was the only administrator with the ability to straighten out the schedule, which he had done in addition to all his other duties. As Crimmins departed, he threatened that if Perkins was transferred, he would write a letter to the regional accreditation council decrying the level to which standards had sunk at Kennedy. King assured Crimmins that such a drastic measure was unnecessary and offered assurance that a cooperative resolution would be found. King knew that Kennedy High faced an accreditation review the following April and did not wish to complicate the process unnecessarily.

Within twenty minutes of Crimmins's departure, King was visited by Tim Shea, a young white teacher. He said he had heard that Crimmins had come in to see King. Shea identified himself as one of the teachers who had organized the movement to get rid of Perkins. He said that he liked and admired Perkins because of the man's devotion to the school but that Perkins's house was so disorganized and that discipline there was so bad that it was nearly impossible to do any good teaching. Shea added, "It's a shame to lock the school up when stronger leadership is all that's needed."

King's impressions of his administrators generally matched what he had heard before arriving at the school. Carver seemed to be a very bright, innovative, and charismatic leader whose mere presence generated excitement. Czepak came across as a highly competent though not very imaginative administrator who had earned the respect of his faculty and students. Bonavota, at twenty-six, seemed smart and earnest but unseasoned and unsure of himself. King felt that with a little guidance and training, Bonavota might have the greatest promise of all; at the moment, however, the young housemaster seemed confused and somewhat overwhelmed. Perkins impressed King as a sincere and devoted person with a good mind for administrative details but an incapacity for leadership.

King knew that he had the opportunity to make several administrative appointments because of the three vacancies that existed. Indeed, should Smith resign as vice principal, King could fill both vice principal positions. He also knew that his recommendations for these positions would carry a great deal of weight with the central office. The only constraint King felt was the need to achieve some kind of racial balance among the Kennedy administrative group. With his own appointment as principal, black administrators outnumbered white administrators two to one, and Kennedy did not have a single Latino administrator, even though a third of its pupils were Hispanic.

The Friday Afternoon Meeting

In contrast to the individual interviews, King was surprised to find how quiet and conflict-free these same people seemed in the staff meeting he called on Friday. He was amazed at how slow, polite, and friendly the conversation was among people who had so vehemently expressed negative opinions of each other in private. After about forty-five minutes of discussion about the upcoming accreditation review, King broached the subject of housemaster–department head relations. There was silence until Czepak made a joke about the uselessness of discussing the topic. King probed further by asking if everyone was happy with the current practices. Crimmins suggested that the topic might be better discussed in a smaller group. Everyone seemed to agree—except for Betsy Dula, a white woman in her late twenties who chaired the English department. She said that one of the problems with the school was that no one was willing to tackle tough issues until they exploded. She added that relations between housemasters and department heads were terrible, and that made her job very difficult. She then attacked Chauncey Carver for impeding her evaluation of a nontenured teacher in Carver's house. The two argued for several minutes about the teacher and the quality of an experimental sophomore English course the teacher was offering. Finally, Carver, by now quite angry, coldly warned Dula that he would "break her neck" if she stepped into his house again. King intervened in an attempt to cool both their tempers, and the meeting ended shortly thereafter.

The following morning, Dula called King at home and told him that unless Carver publicly apologized for his threat, she would file a grievance with the teachers' union and take it to court if necessary. King assured Dula that he would talk with Carver on Monday. King then called Eleanor Debbs, a Kennedy High math teacher he had known well for many years, whose judgment he respected. Debbs was a close friend of both Carver and Dula and was also vice president of the city's teachers' union. Debbs said that the two were longtime adversaries but both were excellent professionals.

She also reported that Dula would be a formidable opponent and could muster considerable support among the faculty. Debbs, who was black, feared that a confrontation between Dula and Carver might stoke racial tensions in the school, even though both Dula and Carver were generally popular with students of all races. Debbs strongly urged King not to let the matter drop. She also told him that she had overheard Bill Smith, the vice principal, say at a party the night before that he felt King didn't have the stomach or the forcefulness to survive at Kennedy. Smith said that the only reason he was staying was that he did not expect King to last the year, in which case Smith would be in a good position to be appointed principal.

David King inherited a job that had broken his predecessor and could easily destroy him as well. His new staff greeted him with a jumble of problems, demands, maneuvers, and threats. His first staff meeting began with an undercurrent of tension and ended in outright hostility. Sooner or later, almost every manager will encounter situations this bad—or worse. The results are often devastating, leaving the manager feeling confused, overwhelmed, and helpless. Nothing makes any sense, and nothing seems to work. No good options are apparent. Can King escape such a dismal fate?

There is one potential bright spot. As the case ends, King is talking to Eleanor Debbs on a Saturday morning. She is a supportive colleague. He also has some slack—the rest of the weekend—to regroup. Where should he begin? We suggest that he might start by actively reflecting and reframing. A straightforward way to do that is to examine the situation one frame at a time asking two simple questions: From this perspective, what's going on? And what options does this angle suggest? This reflective process deserves ample time and careful thought. It requires "going to the balcony" (see Heifetz, 1994) to get a panoramic view of the scene below. Ideally, King would include one or more other people—a valued mentor, principals in other schools, close friends, his spouse—for alternative perceptions in pinpointing the problem and developing a course of action. We present a streamlined version of the kind of thinking that David King might entertain.

STRUCTURAL ISSUES AND OPTIONS

King sits down at his kitchen table with a cup of coffee, a pen, and a fresh yellow pad. He starts to review structural issues at Kennedy High. He recalls the "people-blaming" approach (Chapter Two), in which individuals are blamed for everything that goes wrong. He smiles and nods his head. That's it! Everyone at Kennedy High School is blaming everyone else. He recalls the lesson of the structural frame: we blame individuals when the real problems are systemic.

So what structural problems does Kennedy High have? King thinks about the two cornerstones of structure, differentiation and integration. In a flash of insight, he sees that Kennedy High School has an ample division of labor but weak overall coordination. He scribbles on his pad, trying to sketch the school's organization chart. He gradually realizes that the school has a matrix structure— teachers have an ill-defined dual reporting relationship to both department chairs and housemasters. He remembers the downside of the matrix structure: it's built for conflict (teachers wonder which authority they're supposed to answer to, and administrators bicker about who's in charge). The school has no integrating devices to link the approaches of housemasters like Chauncey Carver (who wants a coherent, effective program for his house) with those of department chairs like Betsy Dula (who is concerned about the schoolwide English curriculum and adherence to district guidelines). It's not just personalities; the structure is pushing Carver and Dula toward each other's throats. Goals, roles, and responsibilities are all vaguely defined. Nor is there a workable structural protocol (say, a task force or a standing committee) to diagnose and resolve such problems. If King had been in the job longer, he might have been able to rely more heavily on the authority of the principal's office. It helps that he's been authorized by the superintendent to fix the school. But so far, he's seen little evidence that the Kennedy High staff is endorsing his say-so with much enthusiasm.

King's musings are making sense, but it isn't clear what to do about the structural gaps. Is there any way to get the school back under control based on reason when it is teetering on the edge of irrational chaos? It doesn't help that his authority is shaky. He is having trouble controlling the staff, and they are having the same problem with the students. The school is an underbounded system screaming for structure and boundaries.

King notes, ruefully, that he made things worse in the Friday meeting. "I knew how these people felt about one another," he thinks. "Why did I push them to talk about something they were trying to avoid? We hadn't done any homework. I didn't give them a clear purpose for the conversation. I didn't set any ground rules for how to talk about the issue. When it started to heat up, I just watched. Why didn't I step in before it exploded?" He stops and shakes his head. "Live and learn, I guess. But I learned these lessons a long time ago—they served me well in turning the middle school around. In all the confusion, I forgot that even good people can't function very well without some structure. What did I do the last time around?"

King begins to brainstorm options. One possibility is responsibility charting (Chapter Five): bring people together to define tasks and responsibilities. It has worked before. Would it work here? He reviews the language of responsibility charting. The acronym CAIRO helps him remember. *Who's responsible? Who has to approve? Who needs to be consulted? Who should be informed? Who doesn't need to be in the loop?* As he applies these questions to Kennedy High, the overlap between the housemasters and the department chairs is an obvious problem. Without a clear definition of roles and relationships, conflict and confusion are inevitable. He wonders about a total overhaul of the structure: "Is the house system viable in its current form? If not, is it fixable? Maybe we need a process to look at the structure: What if I chaired a small task force to examine it and develop recommendations? I could put Dula and Carver on it—let them see firsthand what's causing their conflict. Get them involved in working out a new design. Give each authority over specific areas. Develop some policies and procedures."

It is clear even from a few minutes' reflection that Kennedy High School has major structural problems that have to be addressed. But what to do about the immediate crisis between Dula and Carver? The structure helped create the problem in the first place, and fixing it might prevent stuff like this in the future. But Dula's demand for an immediate apology didn't sound like something a rational approach would easily fix. King is ready to try another angle. He turns to the human resource frame for counsel.

HUMAN RESOURCE ISSUES AND OPTIONS

"How ironic," King muses. "The original idea behind the school was to respond better to students. Break down the big, bureaucratic high school. Make the house a community, a family even, where people know and care about each other. But it's drifted off course. Everyone's marooned on the bottom of Maslow's needs hierarchy: no one even feels safe. Until they do, they'll never focus on caring. The problem isn't personalities. Everyone's frustrated because no one is getting needs met. Not me, not Carver, not Dula. We're all so needy, we don't realize everyone else is in the same boat."

King shifts his thoughts from individual needs to interpersonal relationships. It's hard not to turn that way, with the Dula-Carver mess staring him in the face. Tense relationships everywhere. People talking only to people who agree with them. Why? How to get a handle on it? He remembers reading, "Lurking in Model I is the core assumption that an organization is a dangerous place where you have to look out for yourself or someone else will do you in" (Chapter Eight). "That's it!" he says. "That's us. Too bad they don't give a prize for the most Model I school in America. We'd win hands down. Everything here is win-lose. Nothing is discussed openly, and if it is, people just attack each other. If anything goes wrong, we blame others and try to straighten them out. They get defensive, which proves we were right. But we never test our assumptions. We don't ask questions. We just harbor suspicions and wait for people to prove us right. Then we hit them over the head. We've got to find better ways to deal with one another.

"How do you get better people management?" King wonders. "Successful organizations start with a clear human resource philosophy. We don't have one, but it might help. Invest in people? We've got good people. They're paid pretty well. They've got job security. We're probably OK there. Job enrichment? Jobs here are plenty challenging. Empowerment? That's a big problem. Everyone claims to be powerless, yet somehow everyone expects me to fix everything. Is there something we could do to get people's participation? Get them to own more of the problem? Convince them we've got to work together to make things better? The trouble is, if we go that way, people probably don't have the group skills they'd need. Staff development? With all the conflict, mediation skills might be a place to start." Conflict. Politics. Politics is normal in an organization. He's read it, and he knows it's true. "But we don't seem to have a midpoint between getting along and getting even."

POLITICAL ISSUES AND OPTIONS

King reluctantly shifts to a political lens. It isn't easy for him. He knows it's relevant; but he doesn't like to play the political game. Still, he's never seen a school with more intense political strife. His old school is beginning to seem tame by comparison; he tackled some things head-on there. Kennedy is a lot more volatile, with a history of explosions. Coercive force seems to be the power tactic of choice. But that's not an option he's comfortable with.

Things might get even more vicious if he tackles the conflict openly. He mulls over the basic elements of the political frame: enduring differences, scarce resources, conflict, and power. "Bingo! We've got 'em all—in spades. We've got factions for and against the house concept. Housemasters want to run their houses and guard their turf. Department chairs want to run the faculty and expand their territory. One group wants to close the doors and bring in guards to keep outsiders away. Another wants to keep out the guards and throw open the doors. We've got race issues simmering under the surface. No Latino administrators. This Carver-Dula thing could blow up the school. Black male says he'll break white female's neck. A recipe for disaster. We need some damage control.

"Then we've got all those outside folks looking over our shoulder. Parents worry about safety. The school board doesn't trust us. All they care about is test scores. The media are looking for a story. Accreditation is coming in the spring. Maybe there's some way to get people thinking about the enemies outside instead of inside. A common devil might pull people together—for a little while anyway.

"Scarce resources? They're getting scarcer. We lost 10 percent of our teachers— that got us into the flexible staffing mess. Housemasters and department chairs are fighting over turf. Bill Smith wants my job. It's a war zone. We need some kind of peace settlement. But who's going to take the diplomatic lead? We don't seem to have any neutral parties. Eleanor Debbs would respond to the call. People respect her. But she's not an administrator."

King's attention turns to the two faces of power. "Power can be used to do people in. That's what we're doing right now. But you can also use power to get things done. That's the constructive side of politics. Too bad no one here seems to have a clue about it. If I'm going to be a constructive politician, what can I do? First, I need an agenda. Without that, I'm dead in the water. Basically, I want everyone working in tandem to make the school better for kids. Most people could rally behind that. I also need a strategy. Networking—I need good relationships with key folks like Smith, Carver, and Dula. The interviews were a good place to start. I learned a lot about who wants what. The Friday meeting was a mistake, a collision of special interests with no common ground. It's going to take some horse trading. We need a deal the housemasters and the department chairs can both buy into. And I need some allies—badly."

He smiles as he remembers all the times he's railed against analysis paralysis. But he feels he's getting somewhere. He turns to a clean sheet on his pad. "Let's lay this thing out," he says to the quiet, empty kitchen. Across the top he labels three columns: allies, fence-sitters, and opponents. At the top left, he writes "High power." At the bottom left, "Low power." Over the next half-hour, he creates a political map of Kennedy High School, arranging individuals and groups in terms of their interests and their power. When he finishes, he winces. Too many powerful opponents. Too few supportive allies. A bunch of people waiting to choose sides. He begins to think about how to build a coalition and reshape the school's political map.

"No doubt about it," King says, "I have to get on top of the political mess. Otherwise they'll carry me out the same way they did Weis. But it's a little depressing. Where's the ray of hope?" He smiles. He's ready to think about symbols and culture. "Where's Dr. King when I need him?" He recalls the famous words from 1963: "For even though we face the difficulties of today and tomorrow, I still have a dream." What happened to Kennedy High's dream?

He decides to take a break, get some fresh air. He takes stock of his surroundings. Moonlit night. Crowded sidewalks. Young and old, poor and affluent, black, white, and Latino. Merchandise pours out of stores into sidewalk bins: clothes, toys, electronic gear, fruit, vegetables—you name it. It makes him feel better. King runs into some students from his old school. They're at Kennedy now. "We're tellin' our friends we got a *good* principal now," they say. He thanks them, hoping they're right.

SYMBOLIC ISSUES AND OPTIONS

Back to the kitchen and the yellow pad. Buoyed by the walk and another cup of coffee, he reviews the school's history. "Interesting," he observes. "That's one of the problems: the school's too new to have many roots or traditions. What we have is mostly bad. We've got a hodgepodge of individual histories people brought from someplace else. Deep down, everyone is telling a different story. Maybe that's why Carver is so attached to his house and Dula to her English department. There's nothing schoolwide for people to bond to. Just little pockets of meaning."

He starts to think about symbols that might create common ground. Robert Kennedy, the school's namesake. He has only vague recollection of Bobby Kennedy's speeches. Anything there? He remembers the man. What was he like? What did he stand for? What were the founders thinking when they chose his name for the school? What signals were they trying to send? Any unifying theme? Then it comes to him—words from Bobby Kennedy's eulogy for his brother: "Some people see things as they are, and say why? I dream things that never were, and say why not?"

"That's the kind of thinking we need here," King realizes. "We need to get above all the factions and divisions. We need a banner or icon that we all can rally around. Celebrate Kennedy's legacy now? Can we have a ceremony in the midst of warring chaos? It could backfire, make things worse. But it seems the school never had any special occasions—even at the start. No rituals, no traditions. The only stories are downbeat ones. The high road might work. We've got to get back to the values that launched the school in the first place. Rekindle the spark. What if I pull some people together? Start from scratch—this time paying more attention to symbols and ceremony? We need some glue to weld this thing together."

Meaning. Faith. He rolls the words around in his mind. Haunting images. Ideas start to tumble out. "We're supposed to be pioneers, but somehow we got lost. A lighthouse where the bulb burned out. Not a beacon anymore. We're on the rocks ourselves. A dream became a nightmare. People's faith is pretty shaky. There's a schism—folks splitting into two different faiths. Like a holy war between the church of the one true house system and the temple of academic excellence. We need something to pull both sides together. Why did people join up in the first place? How can we get them to sign up again—renew their vows?" He smiles at the religious overtones in his thoughts. His mother and father would be proud.

He catches himself. "We're not a church; we're a school, in a country that separates religion and state. But maybe the symbolic concept bridges the gap. Organization as temple. A lot of it is about meaning. What's Kennedy High School really about? Who are we? What happened to our spirit? What's our soul, our values? That's what folks are fighting over! Deep down, we're split over two versions of what we stand for. Department chairs promoting excellence.

Housemasters pushing for caring. We need both. That was the original dream. Bring excellence and caring together. We'll never get either if we're always at war with one another."

He thinks about why he got into public education in the first place. It was his calling. Why? Growing up in a racist society was tough, but his father had it a lot tougher—he was a principal when it was something black men didn't do. King had always admired his dad's courage and discipline. More than anything, he remembered his father's passion about education. The man was a real champion for kids—high standards, deep compassion. Growing up with this man as a role model, there was never much question in King's mind. As far back as he could remember, he'd wanted to be a principal too. It was a way to give to the community and to help young people who really needed it. To give everyone a chance. In the midst of a firefight, it was easy to forget his mission. It felt good to remember.

A FOUR-FRAME APPROACH

Before going further, King senses that it is a good time for a review. Over yet another cup of coffee, he goes back over his notes. They strike him as stream of consciousness, with some good stuff and a little whining and self-pity. He smiles as he remembers himself in graduate school, fighting against all that theory. "Don't think; do! Be a leader!" Now, here he is, thinking, reflecting, struggling to pull things together. In a strange way, it feels natural.

He organizes his ideas into a chart (see Exhibit 20.1). He's starting to feel better now. The picture is coming into focus. He feels he has a better sense of what he's up against. It's reassuring to see he has options. There are plenty of pitfalls, but some real possibilities. He knows he can't do everything at once; he needs to set priorities. He needs a plan of action, an agenda anchored in basic values. Where to begin? Soul? Values? He has to find a rallying point somewhere.

He has already embraced two values: excellence and caring. He turns his attention to leadership as gift giving. "I've mostly been waiting for others to initiate. What about me? What are my gifts? If I want excellence, the gift I have to offer is authorship. That's what people want. They don't want to be told what to do. They want to put their signature on this place. Make a contribution. They're fighting so hard because they care so much. That's what brought them to Kennedy in the first place. They wanted to be a part of something better. Create

Exhibit 20.1.
Reframing Robert F. Kennedy High School.

FRAME	WHAT'S GOING ON?	WHAT OPTIONS ARE AVAILABLE?
Structural	Weak integration—goals, roles, responsibilities, linkages unclear	Responsibility charting
	Ill-defined matrix structure	Task force on structure
	Underbounded	
Human resource	Basic needs not met (safety, and so on)	Improve safety, security
	Poor conflict management	Training in communication, conflict management
	People feel disempowered	Participation
		Teaming
Political	House-department conflict	Create arenas for negotiation
	Doors and guards issue	Damage control
	Carver-Dula and racial tension	Unite against outside threats
	Outside constituents—parents, board, media, and so on	Build coalitions, negotiate
Symbolic	No shared symbols (history, ceremony, ritual)	Hoist a banner (common symbol: RFK?)
	Loss of faith, religious schism	Develop symbols (meld excellence and caring?)
	Lack of identity (What is RKF's soul?)	Ceremony, stories
		Leadership gifts

something special. They all want to do a good job. How can I help them do it without tripping over or maiming each other?

"What about caring? The leadership gift is love. No one's getting much of that around here." (He smiles as a song fragment comes to mind: "Looking for love in all the wrong places.") "I've been waiting for someone else to show caring and compassion," he realizes. "I've been holding back."

The thought leads him to pick up the phone. He calls Betsy Dula. She is out, but he leaves a message on the machine: "Betsy, Dave King. I've been thinking a lot about our conversation. One thing I want you to know is that I'm glad you're part of the Kennedy High team. You bring a lot, and I sure hope I can count on your help. We can't do it without you. We need to finish what we started out to do. I care. I know you do, too. I'll see you Monday."

He senses he's on a roll. But it's one thing to leave a message on someone's machine and another to deliver it in person—particularly if you don't know how receptive the other person will be. *She may think I'm just shining on, faking it.*

On his next call, to Chauncey Carver, King takes a deep breath. He gets through immediately. "Chauncey? Dave King. Sorry to bother you at home, but Betsy Dula called me this morning. She's upset about what you said yesterday. Particularly the part about breaking her neck."

King listens patiently as Carver makes it clear that he was only defending himself against Dula's unprovoked and inappropriate public attack. "Chauncey, I hear you. . . . Yeah, I know you're mad. So is she." King listens patiently through another one-sided tirade. "Yes, Chauncey, I understand. But look, you're a key to making this school work. I know how much you care about your house and the school. The word on the street is clear—you're a terrific housemaster. You know it, too. I need your help, man. If this thing with Betsy blows up and goes public, what's it going to do to the school? . . . You're right, we don't need it. Think about it. Betsy's pushing hard for an apology."

He feared that the word *apology* might set Carver off again, and it does. This is getting tough. He reminds himself why he made the call. He shifts back into listening mode. After several minutes of venting, Chauncey pauses. Softly, King tries to make his point. "Chauncey, I'm not telling you what to do. I'm just asking you to think about it. I don't know the answer. Two heads might be better than one. Let me know what you come up with. Can we meet first thing Monday? . . . Thanks for your time. Have a good weekend."

King puts down the phone. Things are still tense, but he hopes he's made a start. Carver is a loose cannon with a short fuse. But he's also smart, and he cares about the school. Get him thinking, King figures, and he'll see the risks in his comment to Dula. Push him too hard, and he'll fight like a cornered badger. With some space; he might just figure out something on his own. The gift of authorship. Would Chauncey bite? Or would the problem wind up back on the principal's doorstep—with prejudice?

After the conversation with Chauncey, King needs another breather. He goes back to his yellow pad, which has become something of a security blanket. More than that, it's helping him find his way to the balcony. It has given him a better view of the situation. He's made notes about excellence and caring. Is he making progress or just musing? It doesn't matter. He feels better; the situation seems to be getting clearer and his options more promising.

King's thoughts move on to justice. "Do people feel the school is fair?" he asks. "I'm not hearing a lot of complaints about injustice. But it wouldn't take much to set off another war. The Chauncey-Betsy thing is scary. A man physically threatening a woman could send a terrible message. There's too much male violence in the community already. Make it a black man and a white woman, and it gets worse. The fact that Chauncey and I are black men is good and bad: it makes for a better chance of getting Chauncey's help—brothers united and all that. But it could be devastating if people think I'm siding with Chauncey against Betsy— sisters in defiance. It's like being on a tightrope: one false step and I'm history. And the school too. All the more reason to encourage Chauncey and Betsy to work this out. If I could get the two together, what a symbol of unity that would be! Maybe just what we need. A positive step at least."

Finally, King thinks about the ethic of faith and the gift of significance. Symbols again, revisited in a deeper way. "How did Kennedy High go from high hopes to no hope in two years? How do we rekindle the original faith? How do we recapture the dream that launched the school? Well," he sighs, "I've been around this track before. My last school was a snake pit when I got there. Not as bad as Kennedy, but still pretty awful. We turned that one around, and I learned some things in the process—including being patient, while hanging tough. It's gonna be hard. But maybe fun, too. And it *will* happen. That's why I took this job in the first place. So what am I moaning about? I knew what I was getting into. It's just that knowing it in my head is one thing. Feeling it in my gut is another."

By Sunday night, King has twenty-five pages of notes. They help—but not as much as his conversation with himself in an empty kitchen. Going to the gallery, getting a fresh look, reflecting instead of just fretting. The inner dialogue has led to new conversations with others, on a deeper level. He's made a lot of phone calls, talked to almost every administrator in the building. A lot of them have been surprised—a principal who calls on the weekend is unusual.

He is making headway. He needs to hear from Betsy but has some volunteers for a task force on structural issues. He's done some relationship building. A second call to Chauncey to commend him for devotion to the mission. A deeper connection. Crediting Frank Czepak for excellent counsel, even if the principal isn't smart enough to pay attention—a frank admission.

Some has been pure politics. Negotiating a deal with Bill Smith: "I *could* help you, Bill, next time the district needs a principal, but only if you help me. You scratch my back, I'll scratch yours." Gently persuading Burt Perkins that his calling was scheduling, not running a house, and that moving to assistant principal would be a step up. A call to Dave Crimmins to tell him Perkins has decided to make a change. An encouraging conversation with Luz Hernandez, a stalwart in his previous school. She is at least willing to think about coming to Kennedy High as a housemaster. Planting seeds with everyone about ways to resolve the door problem.

Above all, King has worked on creating symbolic glue, renewing the hopes and dreams people felt at the time the school was founded. A cohesive group pulling together for a common purpose, a school everyone can feel proud of. His to-do list is ambitious. But at least he has one. A month and a half until the first day of school and a lot to accomplish. He isn't sure what the future will bring, but he feels a little more hope in the air. The knot in his stomach is mostly gone. So are the images of being carried off like his predecessor, a broken man with a shattered career.

The phone rings. It's Betsy Dula. She's been away for the weekend but wants to thank King for his message. It was important to know he cared, she told him. "By the way," she says, "Chauncey Carver called me. Said he felt bad about Friday. Told me he'd lost his temper and said some things he didn't really mean. He invited me to breakfast tomorrow."

"Are you going?" King asks, as nonchalantly as possible. He holds his breath, thinking, *If she declines, we could be back to square one.*

"Yes," she says. "Even a phone call is a big step for Chauncey. He's a proud and stubborn man. But we're both professionals. It's worth a try."

A sigh of relief. "One more question," King says. "When you came to the school, you knew it wouldn't be easy. Why did you sign up for this in the first place?"

She is silent for a long time. He can almost hear her thinking. "I love English and I love kids," she says. "And I want kids to love English."

"And now?" he asks.

"Can't we get past all the bickering and fighting? That's not why we launched this noble experiment. Let's get back to why we're here. Work together to make this a good school for our kids. They really need us."

"How about a great school we can all be proud of?" he asks.

"Sounds even better," she says. Maybe she doesn't grasp what he means. But they are beginning to read from the same page. It will take time, but they can work it out.

At the end of a very busy weekend, David King is still a long way from solving all the problems of Kennedy High. "But," he tells himself, "I made it through the valley of confusion and I'm feeling more like my old self. The picture of what I'm up against is a lot clearer. I'm seeing a lot more possibilities than I was seeing on Friday. In fact, I've got some exciting things to try. Some may work; some may not. But deep down, I think I know what's going on. And I know which way is west. We're now moving roughly in that direction."

He can't wait for Monday morning.

CONCLUSION: THE REFRAMING PROCESS

A different David King would probably raise other questions and see other options. Reframing, like management and leadership, is more art than science. Every artist brings a distinctive vision and produces unique works. King's reframing process necessarily builds on a lifetime of skill, knowledge, intuition, and wisdom. Reframing guides him in accessing what he already knows. It helps him feel less confused and overwhelmed by the doubt and disorder around him. A cluttered jumble of impressions and experiences gradually evolves into a manageable image. His reflections help him see that he is far from helpless—he has a rich array of actions to choose from. He has also rediscovered a very old truth: reflection is a spiritual discipline, much like meditation or prayer. A path to faith and heart. He knows the road ahead is still long and difficult. There is no guarantee of success. But he feels more confident and more energized than when he started. He is starting to dream things that never were and say, "Why not?"

NOTE

1. The case in this chapter was adapted from case no. 9-474-183, *Robert F. Kennedy High School*, ©1974 by the President and Fellows of Harvard College. Used by permission of the Harvard Business School. The case was prepared by John J. Gabarro as a basis for class discussion rather than to illustrate the effective or ineffective handling of an administrative situation.

Epilogue
Artistry, Choice, and Leadership

We hope *Reframing Organizations* continues to inspire inventive management and wise leadership. Both managers and leaders require high levels of personal artistry if they are to respond to today's challenges, ambiguities, and paradoxes. They need a sense of choice and personal freedom to find new patterns and possibilities in everyday life at work. They need versatility in thinking that fosters flexibility in action. They need capacity to act inconsistently when uniformity fails, diplomatically when emotions are raw, nonrationally when reason flags, politically in the face of vocal parochial self-interests, and playfully when fixating on task and purpose backfires.

Managers face a leadership paradox: maintaining integrity and mission without making organizations rigid and intractable. Leading requires walking a fine line between rigidity and spinelessness. Rigidity saps energy, stifles initiative, misdirects resources, and leads ultimately to catastrophe. This pattern can be seen graphically in the decline of great corporations and in the escalation of chronic ethnic violence and terrorism. In a world of "permanent white water" (Vaill, 1989), nothing is fixed and everything is in flux. It is tempting to track familiar paths in a shifting terrain and to summon time-worn solutions, even when problems have changed. Doing what's familiar is comforting. It helps us

435

believe that our world is orderly and that we are in command. But when old ways fail, managers often flip-flop: they cave in and try to appease everyone. The result is aimlessness and anarchy, which kill or maim concerted, purposeful action. Collins and Porras (1994) made it extremely clear. "Visionary" companies have the paradoxical capacity to stimulate change and pursue high-risk new ventures while simultaneously maintaining their commitment to core ideology and values.

Good managers and leaders sustain a tension-filled poise between extremes. They combine core values with elastic strategies. They get things done without being done in. They know what they stand for and what they want and communicate their vision with clarity and power. But they also understand and respond to the vortex of forces that propel organizations in conflicting trajectories. They think creatively about how to make things happen. They develop strategies with enough elasticity to respond to the twists and turns of the path to a better future.

There is a misguided notion that a leader ventures into uncharted terrain with omniscient foresight and unlimited courage. Keller comes closer to the reality: "The greatest leaders are often, in reality, skillful followers. They do not control the flow of history, but by having the good sense not to stand in its way, they seem to. So it is with Mikhail S. Gorbachev. Mr. Gorbachev's achievement was having the vision to see the inevitable, and adopting it as his program rather than applying the repressive apparatus at his command to suppress it" (1990, p. 1).

Gorbachev's extraordinary rise and rapid fall illustrate many of the daunting challenges that all leaders confront. Leaders need confidence to confront gnarly problems and deep divisions. They must expect conflict, knowing their actions may unleash forces beyond their control. They need courage to follow uncharted routes, expecting surprise and pushing ahead when the ultimate destination is dimly foreseeable. Most important, they need to be in touch with their hearts as well as their heads. It has been said that the heart has a mind of its own. Good leaders listen.

COMMITMENT TO CORE BELIEFS

Poetry and philosophy are rare topics in managerial training, and business schools seldom ask if spiritual development is central to their mission. It is no wonder that managers are often viewed as chameleons who can adapt to anything, guided only by expediency. Analysis and agility are necessary, but not enough. Organizations need leaders who can provide a durable sense of purpose and direction, rooted deeply in values and the human spirit. "We have a revolution to make, and this revolution is not political, but spiritual" (Guéhenno, 1993, p. 167).

Leaders need to be deeply reflective and dramatically explicit about core values and beliefs. Many of the world's legendary corporate heroes articulated their philosophies and values so strikingly that they are still visible in today's behavior and operations. In government, Franklin Delano Roosevelt, Charles de Gaulle, Margaret Thatcher, and Lee Kuan Yew were controversial, but each espoused enduring values and beliefs. These served as a guiding beacon for their respective nations.

MULTIFRAME THINKING

Commitment to both resilient values and elastic strategies involves a paradox. Franklin Roosevelt's image as lion and fox, Mao's reputation as tiger and monkey, and Mary Kay Ash's depiction as both fairy godmother and pink panther were not so much inconsistencies as signs that they could embrace contradiction. They intuitively recognized the multiple dimensions of society and moved flexibly to implement their visions. The use of multiple frames permits leaders to see and understand more—*if* they are able to employ the different logics that accompany diverse ways of thinking.

Leaders fail when they take too narrow a view. Unless they can think flexibly and see organizations from multiple angles, they will be unable to deal with the full range of issues they inevitably encounter. Jimmy Carter's preoccupation with details and rationality made it hard for him to marshal support for his programs or to capture the hearts of most Americans. Even FDR's multifaceted approach to the presidency—he was a superb observer of human needs, a charming persuader, a solid administrator, a political manipulator, and a master of ritual and ceremony—miscarried when he underestimated the public reaction to his plan to enlarge the Supreme Court.

Multiframe thinking is challenging and often counterintuitive. To see the same organization as machine, family, jungle, and theater requires the capacity to think in different ways at the same time about the same thing. Like surfers, leaders must ride the waves of change. Too far ahead, they will be crushed. If they fall behind, they will become irrelevant. Success requires artistry, skill, and the ability to see organizations as organic forms in which needs, roles, power, and symbols must be integrated to provide direction and shape behavior. The power to reframe is vital for modern leaders. The ability to see new possibilities and to create new opportunities enables leaders to discover alternatives when options seem severely constrained. It helps them find hope and faith amid fear and despair. Choice is at the heart of freedom, and freedom is essential to achieving the twin goals of commitment and flexibility.

Organizations everywhere are struggling to cope with a shrinking planet and a global economy. The accelerating pace of change continues to produce grave political, economic, and social discontinuities. A world ever more dependent on organizations now finds them evolving too slowly to meet pressing social demands. Without wise leaders and artistic managers to help close the gap, we will continue to see misdirected resources, massive ineffectiveness, and unnecessary human pain and suffering. All these afflictions are already here, and there is no guarantee that they will not get worse—unless we can enlarge our palette of options.

We see prodigious challenges ahead for organizations and those who guide them, yet we remain optimistic. We want this revised volume to lay the groundwork for a new generation of managers and leaders who recognize the importance of poetry and philosophy as well as analysis and technique. We need pioneers who embrace the fundamental values of human life and the human spirit. Such leaders and managers will be playful theorists who can see organizations through a complex prism. They will be negotiators able to design resilient strategies that simultaneously shape events and adapt to changing circumstances. They will understand the importance of knowing and caring for themselves and the people with whom they work. They will be architects, catalysts, advocates, and prophets who lead with soul.

The Best of Organizational Studies

Scholars' Hits and Popular Best-Sellers

One of our goals is to cover the most important and influential works in the field and cite or summarize them where appropriate. There is no perfect way to determine the best or most important books and articles, but we can assess which ones seem to be most often read by scholars and by the general public. We developed two different lists: the greatest hits as rated by scholars, and the popular favorites as represented in *Business Week*'s annual list of business best-sellers.

SCHOLARS' HITS

Our list of scholars' "greatest hits" relies on citation analysis—how often a work is cited in the scholarly literature. This method is often used to measure scholarly impact. We began by conducting a citation analysis of the two journals that Trieschmann, Dennis, and Northcraft (2000) cited as the most visible and influential in the field of management: *Academy of Management Journal* (AMJ; for the years 1996 to 2004) and the *Administrative Science Quarterly* (ASQ; for the years 1993 to 2004). We combined the analyses from those two journals to get a list of the top articles and books based on citation frequency. (In identifying our top works, we excluded purely methodological works that dealt with statistical analysis or research methods.)

We then conducted an additional analysis using Google Scholar (GS), which provides a broadly inclusive analysis of citation data for scholarly work. This gave us three separate rankings: AMJ, ASQ, and GS. The first two are specific to the field of organization studies. The GS data provide a broader indication of influence both within and beyond the management field. For the items in our top twenty-five, the correlations among AMJ, ASQ, and GS are positive but low (ranging between .09 for AMJ/ASQ to .16 for ASQ/GS). We believe this reflects reality. Scholars who publish in different journals or come from different disciplines have different tastes and prefer different sources. It also suggests that our results are partly arbitrary, since a different set of journals might have produced different results. The results for the top twenty are shown in Exhibit A.1.

The results are not definitive, but they provide a broad estimate of the works that have had the greatest influence on scholars. To reduce our list to a single rank order, we averaged the rankings across the three separate data bases. For example, our highest ranking went to an article by DiMaggio and Powell (1983) that ranked first in AMJ and ASQ and tenth in GS.

Though the citation analysis is based on articles published in the 1990s and early 2000s, many of the works that appear at the high end of the list were published much earlier, in the 1960s, 1970s, and 1980s. The oldest item in the top twenty was published in 1958; the newest, in 1989. The results suggest that there is typically a lag of a decade or more before a new work can become a widely cited "classic."

POPULAR BEST-SELLERS

What scholars like and what the public reads are two very different things. For each of the years 1996 to 2006, we have identified a book at or near the top of the *Business Week* best-seller list (see Exhibit A.2). Normally, we chose a book that occupied the number one position on the hardcover or paperback list. But we chose books at a lower rank under two conditions: the top rank focused on topics outside the field of management and organizations (for example, works on personal finance), or the same book had held the top position for more than one year (which was particularly the case with *Who Moved My Cheese?* by Spencer Johnson).

Exhibit A.1.
Top 20 "Scholars' Hits" from Citation Analysis.

AMJ RANK	ASQ RANK	GS RANK	OVERALL RANK	AUTHOR	YEAR	TITLE
1	1	10	1	DiMaggio, P. J., & Powell, W. W.	1983	"The Iron Cage Revisited: Institutional Isomorphism and Collective Rationality in Organizational Fields"
3	3	9	2	Cyert, R. M., & March, J. G.	1963	A Behavioral Theory of the Firm
2	2	11	3	Pfeffer, J., & Salancik, G.	1978	The External Control of Organizations: A Resource Dependence Perspective
7	6	8	4	Thompson, J. D.	1967	Organizations in Action: Social Science Bases of Administrative Theory
4	15	3	5	Jensen, M. C., & Meckling, W. H.	1976	"Theory of the Firm: Managerial Behavior, Agency Costs, and Ownership Structure"
11	8	6	6	Granovetter, M. S.	1985	Economic Action and Social Structure: The Problem of Social Embeddedness
8	4	13	7	Meyer, J., & Rowan, B.	1977	"Institutionalized Organizations: Formal Structure as Myth and Ceremony"
9	20	5	8	Nelson, R. R., & Winter, S. G.	1982	An Evolutionary Theory of Economic Change

(Continued)

Exhibit A.1. (Continued)

AMJ RANK	ASQ RANK	GS RANK	OVERALL RANK	AUTHOR	YEAR	TITLE
16	17	4	9	Williamson, O. E.	1975	*Markets and Hierarchies*
10	21	7	10	March, J. G., & Simon, H. A.	1958	*Organizations*
20	18	2	11	Williamson, O. E.	1985	*The Economic Institutions of Capitalism*
15	7	19	12	Hannan, M. T., & Freeman, J.	1989	*Organizational Ecology*
6	22	15	13	Scott, W. R.	1985	*Institutions and Organizations*
17	11	16	14	Levitt, B., & March, J. G.	1988	"Organizational Learning"
13	13	19	15	Hannan, M. T., & Freeman, J.	1984	"Structural Inertia and Organizational Change"
19	14	16	16	Levinthal, D. A., & March, J. G.	1993	"The Myopia of Learning"
12	35	21	17	Burt, R. S.	1992	*Structural Holes: The Social Structure of Competition*
7	62	31	18	Hofstede, G.	1980	*Culture's Consequences: International Differences in Work-Related Values*
28	31	29	19	Kanter, R. M.	1977	*Men and Women of the Corporation*
5	43	22	20	Hambrick, D. C., & Mason, R. A.	1984	"Upper Echelons: The Organization as a Reflection of Its Top Managers"

Note: Italicized titles are books. Titles in quotation marks are journal articles.

Exhibit A.2.
Business Week Best-Sellers.

YEAR	BUSINESS BEST-SELLER	RANK ON *BUSINESS WEEK* LIST
2006	Friedman, T. L., *The World Is Flat*	#1 on hardcover list
2005	Gladwell, M., *Blink*	#1 on hardcover list
2004	Trump, D., *How to Get Rich*	#2 on hardcover list behind *The Automatic Millionaire*
2003	Bossidy, L., and Charan, R., *Execution*	#2 on hardcover list behind *Good to Great*
2002	Collins, J., *Good to Great*	#1 on hardcover list
2001	Welch, J., *Jack: Straight from the Gut*	#2 on hardcover list (behind *Who Moved My Cheese?*)
2000	Gladwell, M., *The Tipping Point*	#3 on hardcover list behind *Who Moved My Cheese?* and *The Millionaire Mind*
1999	Johnson, S., *Who Moved My Cheese?*	#1 on hardcover list (for 1999, 2000, and 2001)
1998	Chernow, R., *Titan*	#3 on hardcover list (behind two personal finance titles)
1997	Covey, S., *The 7 Habits of Highly Effective People*	#1 on paperback list for many years
1996	Adams, S., *The Dilbert Principle*	#1 on hardcover list

Not surprisingly, the popular best-sellers are often shorter and simpler than the scholars' picks. They are pragmatic and often emphasize people issues that fall in the human resource or symbolic frames, whereas the scholars' top choices emphasized symbolic, political, and structural issues. Typically, the popular best-sellers are upbeat. The message is, "You can make a difference." The scholars often prefer works with the opposite message: "You probably won't make much difference because you and your organization are controlled by much larger social and economic forces."

REFERENCES

Ackman, D. "Pay Madness at Enron." *Forbes,* Mar. 22, 2002. Available online: www.forbes. com/2002/03/22/0322enronpay.html. Access date: Feb. 3, 2008.

Adams, S. *The Dilbert Principle.* New York: HarperBusiness, 1996.

Adler, B., and Houghton, J. *Business Decisions: 101 Blunders, Flops, and Screwups.* New York: HarperCollins, 1997.

Adler, P. S., and Borys, B. "Two Types of Bureaucracy: Enabling and Coercive." *Administrative Science Quarterly,* 1996, *41,* 61–89.

Ajila, C. O. "Maslow's Hierarchy of Needs Theory: Applicability to the Nigerian Industrial Setting." *IFE Psychologia,* 1997, *5,* 162–74.

Al Quaeda. "The Al Quaeda Manual." Washington, D.C.: U.S. Department of Justice, no date. Available online: www.usdoj.gov/ag/manualpart1_1.pdf. Access date: Feb. 3, 2008.

Alderfer, C. P. *Existence, Relatedness, and Growth.* New York: Free Press, 1972.

Alderfer, C. P. "Consulting to Underbounded Systems." In C. P. Alderfer and C. Cooper (eds.), *Advances in Experiential Social Processes,* Vol. 2. New York: Wiley, 1979.

Alderson, A. "'True lies' make web star out of Saddam's mouthpiece." *Telegraph,* Apr. 13, 2003. Available online: http://tiny.cc/sahaf. Access date: Apr. 21, 2008.

Alford, C. F. *Whistleblowers: Broken Lives and Organizational Power.* Ithaca, N.Y.: Cornell University Press, 2001.

Allen, W. *Without Feathers.* Cambridge, Mass.: Ballantine, 1986.

Allison, G. *Essence of Decision: Explaining the Cuban Missile Crisis.* New York: Little, Brown, 1971.

Alterman, E. "Wrong on the Wall, and Most Else." *New York Times,* Nov. 12, 1989, p. E23.

Amar, V. *Pouvoir et leadership: Enquête sur les archétypes culturels du management* [Power and Leadership: An Inquiry into the Cultural Archetypes of Management]. Paris: Village Mondial, 2004.

American Customer Satisfaction Index, 2007. Available online: http://tiny.cc/ACSI. Access date: Apr. 23, 2008.

Applebaum, E., Bailey, T., Berg, P., and Kalleberg, A. L. *Manufacturing Advantage: Why High-Performance Work Systems Pay Off.* New York: Cornell University Press, 2000.

Argyris, C. *Personality and Organization.* New York: HarperCollins, 1957.

Argyris, C. *Interpersonal Competence and Organizational Effectiveness.* Homewood, Ill.: Irwin, 1962.

Argyris, C. *Integrating the Individual and the Organization.* New York: Wiley, 1964.

Argyris, C. "Empowerment: The Emperor's New Clothes." *Harvard Business Review,* 1998, *76*(3), 98.

Argyris, C., and Schön, D. A. *Theory in Practice: Increasing Professional Effectiveness.* San Francisco: Jossey-Bass, 1974.

Argyris, C., and Schön, D. A. *Organizational Learning: A Theory of Action Perspective.* Reading, Mass.: Addison-Wesley, 1978.

Argyris, C., and Schön, D. A. *Organizational Learning II: Theory, Method, and Practice.* Reading, Mass.: Addison-Wesley, 1996.

Armstrong, D. *Managing by Storying Around: A New Method of Leadership.* New York: Currency/Doubleday, 1992.

Arndt, M. "Knock Knock, It's Your Big Mac: From São Paulo to Shanghai, McDonald's Is Boosting Growth with Speedy Delivery." *Business Week,* July 12, 2007. Available online: www.businessweek.com/globalbiz/content/jul2007/gb20070712_387164.htm?chan=search. Access date: Feb. 4, 2008.

Associated Press. "Robber Demands Cash—but Settles for a Glass of Wine and a Group Hug." *International Herald Tribune on-line,* July 13, 2007. Available online: www.iht.com/articles/ap/2007/07/13/america/NA-ODD-US-Robber-Group-Hug.php. Access date: Feb. 4, 2008.

Aubrey, B., and Tilliette, B. *Savoir faire savoir: L'apprentissage de l'action en entreprise* [Knowing and teaching: Action learning in the enterprise]. Paris: InterÉditions, 1990.

Axelrod, R. "More Effective Choice in the Prisoner's Dilemma." *Journal of Conflict Resolution,* 1980, *24,* 379–403.

Baker, C. *Behavioral Genetics: An Introduction to How Genes and Environments Interact Through Development to Shape Differences in Mood, Personality, and Intelligence.* Washington, D.C.: American Association for the Advancement of Science, 2004. Available online: www.aaas.org/spp/bgenes/publications.shtml. Access date: Feb. 4, 2008.

Baldridge, J. V. *Power and Conflict in the University.* New York: Wiley, 1971.

Baldridge, J. V., and Deal, T. E. (eds.). *Managing Change in Educational Organizations.* Berkeley, Calif.: McCutchan, 1975.

Bales, F. *Personality and Interpersonal Behavior.* Austin, Tex.: Holt, Rinehart and Winston, 1970.

Balkundi, P., and Harrison, D. A. "Ties, Leaders, and Time in Teams: Strong Inference About the Effects of Network Structure on Team Viability and Performance." *Academy of Management Journal,* 2006, *49,* 49–68.

Bandler, R., and Grinder, J. *Frogs into Princes: Neuro Linguistic Programming.* Boulder, Colo.: Real People Press, 1979.

Barbaro, M. "Home Depot Gets a Fresh Coat of Less-Glossy Paint." *New York Times,* Feb. 8, 2007, pp. C1, C4. Available online: http://tiny.cc/depot. Access date: Apr. 21, 2008.

Barboza, D. "My Time as a Hostage, and I'm a Business Reporter." *New York Times,* June 24, 2007, sec. 4, p. 3.

Bardach, E. *The Implementation Game: What Happens After a Bill Becomes Law.* Cambridge, Mass.: MIT Press, 1977.

Barley, S. R. "The Alignment of Technology and Structure Through Roles and Networks." *Administrative Science Quarterly,* 1990, *35,* 61–103.

Barnes, L. B., and Kriger, M. P. "The Hidden Side of Organizational Leadership." *Sloan Management Review,* Fall 1986, pp. 15–25.

Barnett, W. P., and Freeman, J. "Too Much of a Good Thing? Product Proliferation and Organizational Failure." *Organization Science,* 2001, *12,* 539–558.

Barry, D. "The Giuliani Years: The Overview; A Man Who Became More Than a Mayor." *New York Times,* Dec. 31, 2001, p. A1. Available online: http://tiny.cc/rudy. Access date: Apr. 21, 2008.

Barstad, A., Ellingsen, D., and Hellevik, O. "Wealthier, But So What?" Oslo: Statistics Norway, 2005. Available online: www.ssb.no/english/magazine/art-2005-02-07-01-en .html. Access date: Feb. 4, 2008.

Barstow, D., and Bergman, L. "At a Texas Foundry, an Indifference to Life." *New York Times,* Jan. 8, 2003a, pp. A1, A14–A15.

Barstow, D., and Bergman, L. "Family's Profit, Wrung from Blood and Sweat." *New York Times,* Jan. 9, 2003b, pp. A1, A14–A15.

Barstow, D., and Bergman, L. "Deaths on the Job, Slaps on the Wrist." *New York Times,* Jan. 10, 2003c, pp. A1, A14–A15.

Bartlett, C. A. "Philips vs. Matsushita: A New Century, a New Round." Case # 9-302-049. Boston: Harvard Business School Case Services, 2006.

Bass, B. M. *Leadership and Performance Beyond Expectations.* New York: Free Press, 1985.

Bass, B. M. *Bass & Stogdill's Handbook of Leadership: Theory, Research, and Managerial Application.* (3rd ed.) New York: Free Press, 1990.

Bass, B., Avolio, B., and Atwater, L. "The Transformational and Transactional Leadership of Men and Women." *Applied Psychology: An International Review,* 1996, *45,* 5–34.

Bateson, G. *Steps to an Ecology of Mind.* New York: Ballantine, 1972.

Batstone, D. *Saving the Corporate Soul—and (Who Knows?) Maybe Your Own.* San Francisco: Jossey-Bass: 2003.

Beer, M., and Nohria, N. "Resolving the Tension Between Theories E and O of Change." In M. Beer and N. Nohria (eds.), *Breaking the Code of Change.* Boston: Harvard Business School Press, 2001, pp. 1–34.

Belkin, L. "*The Feminine Critique.*" *New York Times,* Nov. 1, 2007. Available online: www .nytimes.com/2007/11/01/fashion/01WORK.html. Access date: Feb. 4, 2008.

Bell, T. E., and Esch, K. "The Fatal Flaw in Flight 51-L." *IEEE Spectrum,* Feb. 1987, pp. 36–51.

Bellow, G., and Moulton, B. *The Lawyering Process: Cases and Materials.* Mineola, N.Y.: Foundation Press, 1978.

Benedict, R. *The Chrysanthemum and the Sword: Patterns of Japanese Culture.* New York: Mariner Books, 1989.

Bennis, W. G. *Why Leaders Can't Lead: The Unconscious Conspiracy Continues.* San Francisco: Jossey-Bass, 1989.

Bennis, W. G. "The Secrets of Great Groups." *Leader to Leader,* no. 3, Winter, 1997. Available online: www.leadertoleader.org/knowledgecenter/journal.aspx?ArticleID=140. Access date: Apr. 21, 2008.

Bennis, W. G., and Nanus, B. *Leaders: Strategies for Taking Charge.* New York: HarperCollins, 1985.

Bennis, W. G., and Nanus, B. *Leaders: Strategies for Taking Charge.* New York: HarperCollins, 2007.

Bensimon, E. M. "The Meaning of 'Good Presidential Leadership': A Frame Analysis." *Review of Higher Education,* 1989, *12,* 107–123.

Bensimon, E. M. "Viewing the Presidency: Perceptual Congruence Between Presidents and Leaders on Their Campuses." *Leadership Quarterly,* 1990, *1,* 71–90.

Berenson, A. "Survey Finds Profit Pressure Is Leading to Poor Decisions." *New York Times,* Feb. 7, 2004, p. C2.

Bergquist, W. H. *The Four Cultures of the Academy: Insights and Strategies for Improving Leadership in Collegiate Organizations.* San Francisco: Jossey-Bass, 1992.

Bernstein, A. "Why ESOP Deals Have Slowed to a Crawl." *Business Week,* Mar. 18, 1996, pp. 101–102.

Bettelheim, B. *The Uses of Enchantment.* New York: Vintage Books, 1977.

Bethune, G., and Huler, S. *From Worst to First: Behind the Scenes of Continental's Remarkable Comeback.* New York: Wiley, 1999.

Bianco, A. "Wal-Mart's Midlife Crisis: Declining Growth, Increasing Competition, and Not an Easy Fix in Sight. *Business Week,* Apr. 30, 2007, pp. 46–56.

Bion, W. R. *Experiences in Groups.* London: Tavistock, 1961.

Birnbaum, R. *How Colleges Work: The Cybernetics of Academic Organization and Leadership.* San Francisco: Jossey-Bass, 1988.

Birnbaum, R. *How Academic Leadership Works: Understanding Success and Failure in the College Presidency.* San Francisco: Jossey-Bass, 1992.

Blair, M. M., Kruse, D. L., and Blasi, J. R. "Employee Ownership: An Unstable Form or a Stabilizing Force?" In M. M. Blair and T. Kochan (eds.), *The New Relationship: Human Capital in the American Corporation.* Washington, D.C.: Brookings Institution Press, 2000. Available online: http://ssrn.com/abstract=142146. Access date: Feb. 4, 2008.

Blake, R., and Mouton, J. S. *Building a Dynamic Corporation Through Grid Organizational Development.* Reading, Mass.: Addison-Wesley, 1969.

Blake, R., and Mouton, J. S. "A Comparative Analysis of Situationalism and 9, 9 Management by Principle." *Organizational Dynamics,* Spring 1982, pp. 20–42.

Blake, R., and Mouton, J. S. *Managerial Grid III.* Houston, Tex.: Gulf, 1985.

Blanchard, K., and Johnson, S. *The One-Minute Manager.* New York: Morrow, 1982.

Blank, W., Weitzel, J. R., and Green, S. G. "A Test of the Situational Leadership Theory." *Personnel Psychology,* 1990, *43,* 579–597.

Blasi, J. R., Kruse, D., and Bernstein, A. *In the Company of Owners: The Truth About Stock Options (and Why Every Employee Should Have Them)*. New York: Basic Books, 2003.

Blau, P. M., and Scott, W. R. *Formal Organizations: A Comparative Approach*. Novato, Calif.: Chandler & Sharp, 1962.

Block, P. *The Empowered Manager: Positive Political Skills at Work*. San Francisco: Jossey-Bass, 1987.

Blum, A. "Collective Bargaining: Ritual or Reality." *Harvard Business Review,* Nov.-Dec. 1961, pp. 63–69.

Blumberg, P. *Industrial Democracy: The Sociology of Participation*. New York: Schocken Books, 1968.

Blumer, H. *Symbolic Interaction: Perspective and Method*. Upper Saddle River, N.J.: Prentice Hall, 1969.

Bodily, S., and Bruner, S. "Transformation of Enron 1986–2000." Multimedia Case, Darden School, University of Virginia, 2002.

Boje, D. M., Luhman, J. T., and Cunliffe, A. L. "A Dialectic Perspective on the Organization Theatre Metaphor." *American Communication Journal*, 2003, 6.

Bok, S. *Lying: Moral Choice in Public and Private Life*. New York: Vintage Books, 1978.

Bolman, L. G., and Deal, T. E. *Modern Approaches to Understanding and Managing Organizations*. San Francisco: Jossey-Bass, 1984.

Bolman, L. G., and Deal, T. E. "Leadership and Management Effectiveness: A Multi-Frame, Multi-Sector Analysis." *Human Resource Management,* 1991, *30,* 509–534.

Bolman, L. G., and Deal, T. E. "Leading and Managing: Effects of Context, Culture, and Gender." *Education Administration Quarterly,* 1992a, *28,* 314–329.

Bolman, L. G., and Deal, T. E. "Reframing Leadership: The Effects of Leaders' Images of Leadership." In K. E. Clark, M. B. Clark, and D. Campbell (eds.), *Impact of Leadership*. Greensboro, N.C.: Center for Creative Leadership, 1992b.

Bolman, L. G., and Deal, T. E. *Leading with Soul: An Uncommon Journey of Spirit*. (2nd ed.) San Francisco: Jossey-Bass, 2001.

Bolman, L. G., and Granell, E. "Versatile Leadership: A Comparative Analysis of Reframing in Venezuelan Managers." Paper presented at the World Conference of the Ibero-American Academy of Management, Madrid, Dec. 1999.

Bower, J. L. *Managing the Response Allocation Process*. Boston: Division of Research, Harvard Business School, 1970.

Boyatzis, R., and McKee, A. *Resonant Leadership: Renewing Yourself and Connecting with Others Through Mindfulness, Hope, and Compassion*. Boston: Harvard Business School Press, 2005.

Boyle, M. "Why Costco Is So Addictive." *Fortune,* Oct. 25, 2006. http://money.cnn.com/magazines/fortune/fortune_archive/2006/10/30/8391725/index.htm?postversion=2006102515. Access date: Apr. 21, 2008.

Bradford, D. L., and Cohen, A. R. *Managing for Excellence*. New York: Wiley, 1984.

Brescoll, V. L., and Uhlmann, E. L. "Can an Angry Woman Get Ahead? Status Conferral, Gender, and Expression of Emotion in the Workplace." *Psychological Science,* 2008, *19*(3), 268–275.

Briand, M. "People, Lead Thyself." *Kettering Review,* Summer 1993, pp. 38–46.

Brief, A. P., and Downey, H. K. "Cognitive and Organizational Structure: A Conceptual Analysis of Implicit Organizing Theories." *Human Relations,* 1983, *36*(12), 1065–1090.

Broder, J. M., and Schmitt, E. "U.S. Attacks on Holdouts Dealt Iraqis Final Blow." *New York Times,* Apr. 13, 2003, p. B1.

Broughton, I. *Hangar Talk: Interview with Fliers 1920s to 1990s.* Spokane: Eastern Washington University Press, 1988.

Brown, L. D. *Managing Conflict at Organizational Interfaces.* Reading, Mass.: Addison-Wesley, 1983.

Brown, L. D. "Power Outside Organizational Paradigms: Lessons from Community Partnerships." In S. Srivastva and Associates, *The Functioning of Executive Power: How Executives Influence People and Organizations.* San Francisco: Jossey-Bass, 1986.

Brown, P., and Hesketh, A. *The Mismanagement of Talent: Employability and Jobs in the Knowledge Economy.* New York: Oxford University Press, 2004.

Bryan, L. L., and Joyce, C. I. "Better Strategy Through Organizational Design." *McKinsey Quarterly,* May 2007. Available online with registration: www.mckinseyquarterly. com/article_page.aspx?ar=1991&l2=18&l3=30&pid=1869&srid=333&gp=1. Access date: Feb. 4, 2008.

Bunker, B. B., and Alban, B. T. *Large Group Interventions: Engaging the Whole System for Rapid Change.* San Francisco: Jossey-Bass, 1996.

Bunker, B. B., and Alban, B. T. "Large Group Interventions and Dynamics." In J. V. Gallos (ed.), *Organization Development: A Jossey-Bass Reader.* San Francisco: Jossey-Bass: 2006.

Burke, K. *Attitudes Toward History.* Boston: Beacon Press, 1937.

Burke, K. *A Grammar of Motives.* Berkeley: University of California Press, 1945.

Burke, K. *Dramatism and Development.* Barre, Mass.: Clark University Press, 1972.

Burke, W. "Where Did OD Come From?" In J. V. Gallos (ed.), *Organization Development: A Jossey-Bass Reader.* San Francisco: Jossey-Bass: 2006.

Burnes, B. "Kurt Lewin and the Planned Approach to Change: A Reappraisal." In J. V. Gallos (ed.), *Organization Development: A Jossey-Bass Reader.* San Francisco: Jossey-Bass: 2006.

Burns, J. M. *Leadership.* New York: HarperCollins, 1978.

Burns, N., and Kiley, D. "Executive Churn: Hello, You Must Be Going." *Business Week,* Feb. 12, 2007, pp. 30–32.

Burrough, B., and Helyar, J. *Barbarians at the Gate: The Fall of RJR Nabisco.* New York: HarperCollins, 1990.

Burrows, P. "Carly's Last Stand? The Inside Story of the Infighting at Hewlett-Packard." *Business Week,* Dec. 24, 2001. Available online: www.businessweek.com/magazine/content/01_52/b3763001.htm. Access date: Feb. 4, 2008.

Burrows, P., and Elstrom, P. "HP's Carly Fiorina: The Boss." *Business Week,* Aug. 2, 1999, pp. 76–84.

Burt, R. *Structural Holes: The Social Structure of Competition.* Cambridge, Mass.: Harvard University Press, 1992.

Business Week. "Customer Service Champs." Mar. 5, 2007, cover story. Available online: www.businessweek.com/magazine/content/07_10/b4024001.htm?chan=innovation_ special+report+-+customer+service_customer+service. Access date: Feb. 4, 2008.

Business Wire. "Fewer Women Represented in the 'C-Suite' of Fortune Global 100 Companies Than in the Boardroom, Study Finds." Sept. 24, 2007. Available online: home. businesswire.com/portal/site/google/index.jsp?ndmViewId=news_view&newsId= 20070924005524&newsLang=en. Access date: Feb. 4, 2008.

Butcher, D., and Clarke, M. *Smart Management: Using Politics in Organizations.* London: Palgrave MacMillan, 2001.

Byrne, J. A. "The Shredder: Did CEO Dunlap Save Scott Paper—or Just Pretty It Up?" *Business Week,* Jan. 15, 1996, pp. 56–61.

Byrne, J. A. "Inside McKinsey." *Business Week,* July 8, 2002(a), pp. 66–76.

Byrne, J. A. "Joe Berardino's Fall from Grace." *Business Week,* Aug. 12, 2002(b), pp. 50–56.

Byrne, J. A., France, M., and Zellner, W. "At Enron, 'The Environment Was Ripe for Abuse.'" *Business Week,* Feb. 25, 2002. Available online: www.businessweek.com/ magazine/content/02_08/b3771092.htm. Access date: Feb. 4, 2008.

Byrnes, N., and Arndt, M. "The Art of Motivation." *Business Week,* May 1, 2006, pp. 57–62. Available online: www.businessweek.com/@@6VWdbocQayYCfQYA/magazine/content/ 06_18/b3982075.htm. Access date: Feb. 4, 2008.

Byrnes, N., Byrne, J. A., Edwards, C., and Lee, L. "The Good CEO." *Business Week,* Sept. 23, 2002, pp. 80–88.

Cable, J. P., and DeRue, D. S. "The Convergent and Discriminant Validity of Subjective Fit Perceptions." *Journal of Applied Psychology,* 2002, *87,* 875–884.

Campbell, D. "If I'm in Charge, Why Is Everyone Laughing?" Paper presented at the Center for Creative Leadership, Greensboro, N.C., 1983.

Campbell, J. *The Power of Myth.* New York: Doubleday, 1988.

Campbell, J. P., and Dunnette, M. D. "Effectiveness of T-Group Experiences in Managerial Training and Development." *Psychological Bulletin,* 1968, *70,* 73–104.

Carless, S. A. "Gender Differences in Transformational Leadership: An Examination of Superior, Leader, and Subordinate Perspectives." *Sex Roles: A Journal of Research,* Dec. 1998, 1–10. Available online: www.findarticles.com/cf_dls/m2294/11–12_39/53590324/p1/ article.jhtml?term=. Access date: Feb. 4, 2008.

Carlson, S. *Executive Behavior.* Stockholm: Strombergs, 1951.

Carlzon, J. *Moments of Truth.* New York: Ballinger, 1987.

Cascio, W., and Boudreau, J. *Investing in People: Financial Impact of Human Resource Initiatives.* Philadelphia: Wharton School Publishing, 2008.

Cascio, W., Young, C. E., and Morris, J. R. "Financial Consequences of Employment-Change Decisions in Major U.S. Corporations." *Academy of Management Journal,* 1997, *40,* 1175–1189.

Case, J. *Open Book Management: The Coming Business Revolution.* New York: HarperBusiness, 1995.

Champy, J. M. *Reengineering Management: The Mandate for New Leadership.* New York: HarperCollins, 1995.

Chandler, A. D., Jr. *Strategy and Market Structure.* Cambridge, Mass.: MIT Press, 1962.

Chandler, A. D., Jr. *The Visible Hand: The Managerial Revolution in American Business.* Cambridge, Mass.: Harvard University Press, 1977.

Chandler, S. "United We Own." *Business Week,* Mar. 18, 1996, pp. 96–100.

Charan, R. "Home Depot's Blueprint for Culture Change." *Harvard Business Review,* Apr. 2006, pp. 1–11.

Charan, R., and Useem, J. "Why Companies Fail." *Fortune,* May 27, 2002, pp. 50–62.

Cherniss, C. "Emotional Intelligence: What It Is and Why It Matters." Paper presented at Annual Meeting of the Society for Industrial and Organizational Psychology. New Orleans, Oct. 2000.

"China Says 'No' to Pirated Software." *People's Daily,* Apr. 5, 2002, Available online: english.peopledaily.com.cn/200204/05/eng20020405_93534.shtml.

Christensen, C. M. *The Innovator's Dilemma: When New Technologies Cause Great Firms to Fail.* Boston: Harvard Business School Press, 1997.

Ciulla, J. B. "Leadership and the Problem of Bogus Empowerment." In J. B. Ciulla (ed.), *Ethics: The Heart of Leadership.* Westport, Conn.: Praeger, 1998.

Clark, B. R. "The Organizational Saga in Higher Education." In J. V. Baldridge and T. E. Deal (eds.), *Managing Change in Educational Organizations.* Berkeley, Calif.: McCutchan, 1975.

Clark, E. *Around the Corporate Campfire: How Great Leaders Use Stories to Inspire Success.* Sevierville, Tenn.: Insight Publishing, 2004.

Cleveland, H. *The Knowledge Executive: Leadership in an Information Society.* New York: Dutton, 1985.

Clifford, D. K., and Cavanagh, R. E. *The Winning Performance.* New York: Bantam Books, 1985.

Cochran, S. *Encountering Chinese Networks: Western, Japanese and Chinese Corporations in China, 1880–1937.* Berkeley: University of California Press, 2000.

Cohen, M., and March, J. G. *Leadership and Ambiguity.* New York: McGraw-Hill, 1974.

Cohen, P. S. "Theories of Myth." *Man,* 1969, *4,* 337–353.

Cohen, S. G., and Bailey, D. E. "What Makes Teams Work: Group Effectiveness Research from the Shop Floor to the Executive Suite." *Journal of Management,* 1997, *23*(3), 239–290.

Cohen, S. G., and Ledford, G. E., Jr. "The Effectiveness of Self-Managing Teams: A Quasi-Experiment." *Human Relations,* 1994, *47,* 13–43.

Coles, T. "How Rudy Rallied Us." *New York Post,* Sept. 9, 2002.

Collins, B. E., and Guetzkow, H. *A Social Psychology of Group Processes for Decision Making.* New York: Wiley, 1964.

Collins, J. C. *Good to Great: Why Some Companies Make the Leap and Others Don't.* New York: HarperCollins, 2001.

Collins, J. C., and Porras, J. I. *Built to Last: Successful Habits of Visionary Companies.* New York: HarperBusiness, 1994.

Collinson, D. L., and Collinson, M. "Sexuality in the Workplace: The Domination of Men's Sexuality." In J. Hearn, D. L. Sheppard, P. Tancred-Sheriff, and G. Burrell (eds.), *The Sexuality of Organization.* London: Sage, 1989.

Columbia Accident Investigation Board. *Final Report.* Washington, D.C.: National Aeronautics and Space Administration, 2003. Available online: http://caib.nasa.gov/news/report/default.html. Access date: Feb. 4, 2008.

Colvin, G. "The 50 Best Companies for Asians, Blacks, and Hispanics." *Fortune,* July 19, 1999, pp. 53–58.

Conger, J. A. *The Charismatic Leader: Behind the Mystique of Exceptional Leadership.* San Francisco: Jossey-Bass, 1989.

Congressional Budget Office. "What Accounts for the Decline in Manufacturing Employment?" Washington, D.C.: CBO, 2004. http://www.cbo.gov/doc.cfm?index=5078&type=0. Access date: Apr. 21, 2008.

Conley, C. *Peak: How Great Companies Get Their Mojo from Maslow.* San Francisco: Jossey-Bass, 2007.

Conlin, M., and Greene, J. "How to Make a Microserf Smile." *Business Week,* Sept. 10, 2007, pp. 57–59.

Coonan, C. "China Sets Fire to Pirated Material: Authorities Destroy 42 Million Illegal Goods." *Variety,* Apr. 16, 2007. Available online: www.variety.com/article/VR1117963184.html?categoryid=18&cs=1. Access date: Feb. 4, 2008.

Cooper, C., and Block, R. *Disaster: Hurricane Katrina and the Failure of Homeland Security.* New York: Henry Holt, 2006.

Corwin, R. "Organizations as Loosely Coupled Systems: Evolution of a Perspective." Paper presented at the Conference on Schools as Loosely Coupled Organizations, Stanford University, Nov. 1976.

Covey, S.M.R., and Merrill, R. R. *The SPEED of Trust: The One Thing That Changes Everything.* New York: Free Press, 2006.

Cox, H. *The Feast of Fools.* Cambridge, Mass.: Harvard University Press, 1969.

Cox, T., Jr. *Cultural Diversity in Organizations: Theory, Research, and Practice.* San Francisco: Berrett-Koehler, 1994.

Crawford, G. *The Last Link: Closing the Gap That Is Sabotaging Your Business.* Austin, Tex.: Greenleaf, 2007.

Cronshaw, S. F. "Effects of Categorization, Attribution, and Encoding Processes on Leadership Perspectives." *Journal of Applied Psychology,* 1987, *72*(1), 91–106.

Crosby, P. *Let's Talk Quality.* New York: McGraw-Hill, 1989.

Crozier, M., and Friedberg, E. *L'acteur et le système* [The actor and the system]. Paris: Points/Politique Seuil, 1977.

Cyert, R. M., and March, J. G. *A Behavioral Theory of the Firm.* Upper Saddle River, N.J.: Prentice Hall, 1963.

Dalton, M. *Men Who Manage.* New York: Wiley, 1959.

Dane, E., and Pratt, M. G. "Exploring Intuition and Its Role in Managerial Decision Making." *Academy of Management Review,* 2007, *32*(1), 33–54.

Daniels, C., Hickman, J., Chen, C. Y., Harrington, A., Lustgarten, A., Mero, J., and Tkaczyk, C. "50 Best Companies for Minorities." *Fortune,* June 28, 2004. Available online: http://money.cnn.com/magazines/fortune/fortune_archive/2004/06/28/374393/index.htm. Access date: Feb. 4, 2008.

David, G. "Can McDonald's Cook Again?" *Fortune,* Apr. 14, 2003, pp. 120–129.

Davis, M., and others. "The Structure of Educational Systems." Paper presented at the Conference on Schools as Loosely Coupled Organizations, Stanford University, Nov. 1976.

Deal, T. E., and Jenkins, W. A. *Managing the Hidden Organization: Strategies for Empowering Your Behind-the-Scenes Employees.* New York: Warner Books, 1994.

Deal, T. E., and Kennedy, A. A. *Corporate Cultures.* Reading, Mass.: Addison-Wesley, 1982.

Deal, T. E., and Key, M. K. *Corporate Celebration: Play, Purpose and Profit at Work.* San Francisco: Berrett-Koehler, 1998.

Deal, T. E., and Nutt, S. C. *Promoting, Guiding, and Surviving Change in School Districts.* Cambridge, Mass.: Abt Associates, 1980.

DeBecker, G. *The Gift of Fear.* New York: Dell, 1997.

De Geus, A. "Companies: What Are They?" *RSA Journal,* June 1995, pp. 26–35.

Deming, W. E. *Out of the Crisis.* Cambridge, Mass.: MIT Center for Advanced Engineering Study, 1986.

Denning, S. *The Leader's Guide to Storytelling: Mastering the Art and Discipline of Business Narrative.* San Francisco: Jossey-Bass: 2005.

DePree, M. *Leadership Is an Art.* New York: Dell, 1989.

Dillingham, D. L. "Air Traffic Control: Role of the FAA's Modernization Program in Reducing Delays and Congestion." Testimony to Congress, May 10, 2001. Washington, D.C.: General Accounting Office. Available online: www.gao.gov/new.items/d01725t.pdf. Access date: Feb. 4, 2008.

DiMaggio, P. J., and Powell, W. W. "The Iron Cage Revisited: Institutional Isomorphism and Collective Rationality in Organizational Fields." *American Sociological Review,* Apr. 1983, *48,* 147–160.

Dittmer, L. "Political Culture and Political Symbolism: Toward a Theoretical Synthesis." *World Politics,* 1977, *29,* 552–583.

Doktor, J. "The Early Implementation of the Family Resource and Youth Services Centers of Kentucky: Multi-Frame Perspective." Unpublished doctoral dissertation, Vanderbilt University, 1993.

Dornbusch, S., and Scott, W. R. *Evaluation and the Exercise of Authority.* San Francisco: Jossey-Bass, 1975.

Downer, L. *The Brothers: The Hidden World of Japan's Richest Family.* New York: Random House, 1994.

Drucker, P. F. "Peter Drucker's 1990s: The Futures That Have Already Happened." *Economist,* Oct. 21, 1989, pp. 19–20, 24.

Drucker, P. F. *Managing the Future: The 1990s and Beyond.* New York: Plume, 1993.

Druskat, V. U., and Wheeler, J. V. "Managing from the Boundary: The Effective Leadership of Self-Managing Work Teams." *Academy of Management Journal,* 2003, *46,* 435–457.

Duesenberry, J. Comment on "An Economic Analysis of Fertility." In Universities-National Bureau Committee for Economic Research (ed.), *Demographic and Economic Change in Developed Countries.* Princeton, N.J.: Princeton University Press, 1960.

Dukes v. Wal-Mart. No. 04-16688 (9th Cir. 12/11/2007) (withdrawing and replacing 474 F.3d 1214). Available online: www.walmartclass.com/staticdata/pleadings/Revised_9th_Circ_Panel_Opinion.pdf. Access date: Apr. 21, 2008.

Dumaine, B. "The Trouble with Teams." *Fortune,* Sept. 5, 1994. Available online: www.mph.ufl.edu/events/seminar/TroublewithTeams.pdf. Access date: Feb. 4, 2008.

Dunford, R. W., and Palmer, I. C. "Claims About Frames: Practitioners' Assessment of the Utility of Reframing." *Journal of Management Education,* 1995, *19,* 96–105.

Dwyer, J., Flynn, K., and Fessenden, F. "9/11 Exposed Deadly Flaws in Rescue Plan." *New York Times,* July 7, 2002, pp. A1, A10–11.

Eagly, A. H., and Carli, L. L. "The Female Leadership Advantage: An Evaluation of the Evidence." *Leadership Quarterly,* 2003, *14,* 807–834.

Eagly, A. H., and Johnson, B. T. "Gender and Leadership Style: A Meta-Analysis." *Psychological Bulletin,* 1990, *111,* 233–256.

Eagly, A. H., and Karau, S. J. "Role Congruity Theory of Prejudice Toward Female Leaders." *Psychological Review,* 2002, *109,* 573–598.

Eckholm, E. "China's New Leader Works to Set Himself Apart." *New York Times,* Jan. 12, 2003, p. A6.

Edelman, M. J. *Politics as Symbolic Interaction: Mass Arousal and Quiescence.* Orlando, Fla.: Academic Press, 1971.

Edelman, M. J. *The Symbolic Uses of Politics.* Madison: University of Wisconsin Press, 1977.

Edmondson, G. "BMW's Dream Factory." *Business Week,* Oct. 16, 2006, pp. 70–80. Available online: www.businessweek.com/magazine/content/06_42/b4005072.htm?chan=search. Access date: Feb. 4, 2008.

Edwards, M. R. "In-Situ Team Evaluation: A New Paradigm for Measuring and Developing Leadership at Work." Paper presented at conference on "The Impact of Leadership," Center for Creative Leadership, Colorado Springs, May, 1991.

Eichenwald, K. "Audacious Climb to Success Ended in a Dizzying Plunge." *New York Times,* Jan. 13, 2002a, pp. A1, A26–27.

Eichenwald, K. "For WorldCom, Acquisitions Were Behind Its Rise and Fall." *New York Times,* Aug. 8, 2002b, pp. A1, C6.

Eichenwald, K. "Flinging Billions of Dollars to Buy Assets No One Else Would Touch." *New York Times,* Oct. 3, 2002c, p. C4.

Eichenwald, K., and Richtel, M. "Enron Trader Pleads Guilty to Conspiracy." *New York Times,* Oct. 18, 2002, pp. C1, C9.

Elden, M. "Client as Consultant: Work Reform Through Participative Research." *National Productivity Review,* Spring 1983, pp. 136–147.

Elden, M. "Sociotechnical Systems Ideas as Public Policy in Norway: Empowering Participation Through Worker-Managed Change." *Journal of Applied Behavioral Science,* 1986, *22,* 239–255.

Elmore, R. F. "Organizational Models of Social Program Implementation." *Public Policy,* 1978, *26,* 185–228.

Emery, C. R., and Fredendall, L. D. "The Effect of Teams on Firm Profitability and Customer Satisfaction." *Journal of Service Research,* 2002, *4,* 217–229.

Enderud, H. G. "The Perception of Power." In J. G. March and J. Olsen (eds.), *Ambiguity and Choice in Organizations.* Bergen, Norway: Universitetsforlaget, 1976.

Engardio, P., and DeGeorge, G. "Importing Enthusiasm." *Business Week,* 1994 (21st Century Capitalism Special Issue), pp. 122–123.

Esposito, F., Garman, S., Hickman, J., Watson, N., and Wheat, A. "America's 50 Best Companies for Minorities." *Fortune,* July 9, 2002, pp. 122–128.

Ewing, J., Baker, S., Echikson, W., and Capell, K. "Eager Europeans Press Their Noses to the Glass." *Business Week International Edition,* Apr. 19, 1999. Available online: www .businessweek.com/1999/99_16/b3625014.htm. Access date: Feb. 4, 2008.

Farkas, C. M., and De Backer, P. *Maximum Leadership: The World's Leading CEOs Share Their Five Strategies for Success.* New York: Henry Holt, 1996.

Fayol, H. *General and Industrial Management.* (C. Stours, trans.) London: Pitman, 1949. (Originally published 1919.)

Feinberg, M., and Tarrant, J. J. *Why Smart People Do Dumb Things.* New York: Simon & Schuster, 1995.

Fiedler, F. E. *A Theory of Leadership Effectiveness.* New York: McGraw-Hill, 1967.

Fiedler, F. E., and Chemers, M. *Leadership and Effective Management.* Glenview, Ill.: Scott, Foresman, 1974.

Fiedler, K. "Casual Schemata: Review and Criticism of Research on a Popular Construct." *Journal of Personality and Social Psychology,* 1982, *42,* 1001–1013.

Fielder, J. H. "The Vioxx Debacle." *Engineering in Medicine and Biology Magazine, IEEE,* 2005, *24*(2), 106–109.

"Fire and Forget." *Economist,* Apr. 20, 1996, pp. 51–52.

Firestone, D. "Senate Votes, 90–9, to Set Up Homeland Security Department Geared to Fight Terrorism." *New York Times,* Nov. 20, 2002, pp. A1, A12.

Firestone, W. A. "Butte-Angels Camp: Conflict and Transformation." In R. Herriot and N. Gross (eds.), *The Dynamics of Planned Educational Change.* Berkeley, Calif.: McCutchan, 1977.

Fisher, R., and Ury, W. *Getting to Yes.* Boston: Houghton Mifflin, 1981.

Fishman, C. "The Wal-Mart Effect and a Decent Society: Who Knew Shopping Was So Important." *Academy of Management Perspectives,* Aug. 2006, pp. 6–27.

Fiske, S. T., and Dyer, L. M. "Structure and Development of Social Schemata: Evidence from Positive and Negative Transfer Effects." *Journal of Personality and Social Psychology,* 1985, *48*(4), 839–852.

Fisman, R., Iyengar, S. S., Kamenica, E., and Simonson, I. "Gender Differences in Mate Selection: Evidence from a Speed Dating Experiment." *Quarterly Journal of Economics,* 2006, *121*(2), 673–697.

Fleishman, E. A., and Harris, E. F. "Patterns of Leadership Behavior Related to Employee Grievances and Turnover." *Personnel Psychology,* 1962, *15,* 43–56.

Floden, R. E., and Weiner, S. S. "Rationality to Ritual." *Policy Sciences,* 1978, *9,* 9–18.

Follett, M. P. *The New State: Group Organization and the Solution of Popular Government.* London: Longmans, 1918.

Forsyth, J. "AT&T CEO Says Hard to Find Skilled U.S. Workers." Reuters, Mar. 26, 2008. Available online: www.reuters.com/article/technologyNews/idUSN2634980620080327. Access date: Apr. 21, 2008.

Foucault, M. *Surveiller et punir* [Supervise and punish]. Paris: NRF-Gallimard, 1975.

Frangos, S. *Team Zebra.* New York: Wiley, 1996.

Freiberg, K., and Freiberg, J. *Nuts: Southwest Airlines' Crazy Recipe for Business and Personal Success.* New York: Broadway, 1998.

French, J.R.P., and Raven, B. H. "The Bases of Social Power." In D. Cartwright (ed.), *Studies in Social Power.* Ann Arbor, Mich.: Institute for Social Research, 1959.

Frensch, P. A., and Sternberg, R. J. "Skill-Related Differences in Chess Playing." In R. J. Sternberg and P. A. Frensch (eds.), *Complex Problem Solving.* Hillsdale, N.J.: Erlbaum, 1991.

Freud, S. *The Interpretation of Dreams.* New York: HarperCollins, 1980. (Originally published 1899.)

Freudenberg, W. R., and Gramling, R. "Bureaucratic Slippage and Failures of Agency Vigilance." *Social Problems,* 1994, *4*(1), 214–239.

Fried, I. "HP Board Slams Walter Hewlett." C|Net News.Com, Jan. 18, 2002. Available online: http://news.com.com/2100-1001-818687.html?tag=bplst. Access date: Feb. 5, 2008.

Friedman, R. A. *Front Stage, Backstage: The Dramatic Structure of Labor Negotiations.* Cambridge, Mass.: MIT Press, 1994.

Frontline. "Two Companies, Two Visions." 2003. Available online: www.pbs.org/wgbh/pages/frontline/shows/workplace/mcwane/two.html. Access date: Feb. 5, 2008.

Frost, P. J. *Organizational Culture.* Thousand Oaks, Calif.: Sage, 1985.

Frost, P. J. "Power, Politics, and Influence." In L. W. Porter and others (eds.), *The Handbook of Organizational Communication.* Thousand Oaks, Calif.: Sage, 1986.

Fulghum, R. *From Beginning to End: The Rituals of Our Lives.* New York: Villard Books, 1995.

Galbraith, J. R. *Designing Complex Organizations.* Reading, Mass.: Addison-Wesley, 1973.

Galbraith, J. R. *Organization Design.* Reading, Mass.: Addison-Wesley, 1977.

Galbraith, J. R. *Designing Organizations: An Executive Briefing on Strategy, Structure, and Process.* (rev. ed.) San Francisco: Jossey-Bass, 2001.

Gallos, J. V. (ed.). *Organization Development: A Jossey-Bass Reader.* San Francisco: Jossey-Bass: 2006.

Gallos, J. V., Ramsey, V. J., and Associates. *Teaching Diversity: Listening to the Soul, Speaking from the Heart.* San Francisco: Jossey-Bass, 1997.

Gamson, W. A. *Power and Discontent.* Florence, Ky.: Dorsey Press, 1968.

Ganitsky, J., and Sancho, A. "Martín Varsavsky (A)." *Revista de Empresa,* July–Sept. 2002, *1*(1),97–126. Available online: www.revistadeempresa.com/REVISTA/Public.nsf/index?OpenFrameSet. Access date: Feb. 5, 2008.

Gardner, H. *Frames of Mind: The Theory of Multiple Intelligences.* (10th anniversary ed.) New York: Basic Books, 1993.

Gardner, J. W. *Handbook of Strategic Planning.* New York: Wiley, 1986.

Gardner, J. W. *The Moral Aspects of Leadership.* Washington, D.C.: Independent Sector, 1987.

Gardner, J. W. *On Leadership.* New York: Free Press, 1989.

Garland, H. "Throwing Good Money After Bad: The Effect of Sunk Costs on the Decision to Escalate." *Journal of Applied Psychology,* 1990, *75,* 728–731.

Gegerenzer, G., Hoffrage, U., and Kleinbölting, H. "Probabilistic Mental Models: A Brunswikian Theory of Confidence." *Psychological Review,* 1991, *98,* 506–528.

Gertz, D., and Baptista, J.P.A. *Grow to Be Great: Breaking the Downsizing Cycle.* New York: Free Press, 1995.

Ghoshal, S., and Bartlett, C. A. "The Multinational Corporation as an Interorganizational Network." *Academy of Management Review,* 1990, *15,* 603–625.

Gibb, J. R. "A Research Perspective on the Laboratory Method." In K. D. Benne, L. P. Bradford, J. R. Gibb, and R. O. Lippitt (eds.), *The Laboratory Method of Changing and Learning.* Palo Alto, Calif.: Science and Behavior Books, 1975.

Giroux, H. "The Business of Public Education." *Z Magazine,* Aug. 1998. Available online: www.zmag.org/ZMag/articles/girouxjulyaug98.htm. Access date: Feb. 5, 2008.

Giuliani, R., and Kurson, K. *Leadership.* New York: Miramax, 2002.

Gladwell, M. *Blink: The Power of Thinking Without Thinking.* New York: Little, Brown, 2005.

Glanz, J., and Schwartz, J. "Dogged Engineer's Effort to Assess Shuttle Damage." *New York Times,* Sept. 26, 2003, p. A1. Available online: http://tiny.cc/dogged. Access date: Apr. 21, 2008.

Goffman, E. *The Presentation of Self in Everyday Life.* New York: Anchor, 1959.

Goffman, E. *Frame Analysis.* Cambridge, Mass.: Harvard University Press, 1974.

Goldberg, L. R. "The Development of Markers for the Big Five Factor Structure." *Psychological Assessment,* 1992, *4,* 26–42.

Goleman, D. *Emotional Intelligence.* New York: Bantam, 1995.

Goleman, D., Boyatzis, R. E., and McKee, A. *Primal Leadership: Learning to Lead with Emotional Intelligence.* Boston: Harvard Business School Press, 2004.

Goleman, D., McKee, A., and Boyatzis, R. E. *Primal Leadership: Realizing the Power of Emotional Intelligence.* Boston: Harvard Business School Press, 2002.

Goodman, D. "Doctor Fights Order to Quit Maine Island." *Boston Globe,* Oct. 15, 1983, pp. 1, 8.

Graeff, C. L. "The Situational Leadership Theory: A Critical View." *Academy of Management Review,* Apr. 1983, pp. 321–338.

Granovetter, M. S. "Economic Action and Social Structure: The Problem of Social Embeddedness." *American Journal of Sociology,* 1985, *91*(3), 481–510.

Greenleaf, R. K. "The Servant as Leader." Newton Center, Mass.: Robert K. Greenleaf Center, 1973.

Gregory, K. L. "Native View Paradigms: Multiple Cultures and Cultural Conflict in Organizations." *Administrative Science Quarterly,* 1983, *28,* 359–376.

Greiner, L. E. "Evolution and Revolution as Organizations Grow." *Harvard Business Review,* July–Aug. 1972, pp. 37–46.

Greising, D. "Quality: How to Make It Pay." *Business Week,* Aug. 8, 1994, pp. 54–59.

Griffin, E. *The Reflective Executive: A Spirituality of Business and Enterprise.* New York: Crossroad, 1993.

Grinder, J., and Bandler, R. *The Structure of Magic* (Vols. 1 & 2). Science and Behavior Books: Palo Alto, Calif.: 1975.

Grinder, J., and Bandler, R. *The Structure of Magic.* Science and Behavior Books: Palo Alto, Calif.: 1989.

Groopman, J. *How Doctors Think.* Boston: Houghton Mifflin, 2007.

Grow, B. "Out at Home Depot: Behind the Flameout of Controversial CEO Bob Nardelli." *Business Week,* Jan. 9, 2007. Available online: www.msnbc.msn.com/id/16469224/. Access date: Feb. 5, 2008.

Guéhenno, J.-M. *La fin de la démocratie* [The end of democracy]. Paris: Flammarion, 1993.

Gulick, L., and Urwick, L. (eds.). *Papers on the Science of Administration.* New York: Columbia University Press, 1937.

Gunther, M. "Queer Inc.: How Corporate America Fell in Love with Gays and Lesbians. It's a Movement." *Fortune,* Dec. 11, 2006, pp. 94–110. Available online: money.cnn.com/magazines/fortune/fortune_archive/2006/12/11/8395465/index.htm. Access date: Feb. 5, 2008.

Hackman, J. R. (ed.). *Groups That Work (and Those That Don't): Creating Conditions for Effective Teamwork.* San Francisco: Jossey-Bass, 1989.

Hackman, J. R. *Leading Teams: Setting the Stage for Great Performances.* Boston: Harvard Business School Press, 2002.

Hackman, J. R., and Oldham, G. R. *Work Redesign.* Reading, Mass.: Addison-Wesley, 1980.

Hackman, J. R., Oldham, G. R., Janson, R., and Purdy, K. "A New Strategy for Job Enrichment." In L. E. Boone and D. D. Bowen (eds.), *The Great Writings in Management and Organizational Behavior.* New York: Random House, 1987.

Hackman, J. R., and Wageman, R. "Total Quality Management: Empirical, Conceptual, and Practical Issues." *Administrative Science Quarterly,* 1995, *40,* 309–342.

Hakim, C. *We Are All Self-Employed.* San Francisco: Berrett-Koehler, 1994.

Hall, R. H. "The Concept of Bureaucracy: An Empirical Assessment." *American Journal of Sociology,* 1963, *49,* 32–40.

Hall, R. H. *Organizations: Structures, Processes, and Outcomes.* (4th ed.) Upper Saddle River, N.J.: Prentice Hall, 1987.

Hallinger, P., Bickman, L., and Davis, K. *What Makes a Difference? School Context, Principal Leadership, and Student Achievement.* Occasional Paper # 3, National Center for Educational Leadership, 1990.

Hambleton, R. K., and Gumpert, R. "The Validity of Hersey and Blanchard's Theory of Leader Effectiveness." *Group and Organization Studies,* June 1982, pp. 225–242.

Hambrick, D. C., and Mason, P. A. "Upper Echelons: The Organization as a Reflection of Its Top Managers." *Academy of Management Review,* 1984, *9,* 193–206.

Hamel, G., and Prahalad, C. K. *Competing for the Future: Breakthrough Strategies for Seizing Control of Your Industry and Creating the Markets of Tomorrow.* Boston: Harvard Business School Press, 1994.

Hamm, S. "Linux Inc." *Business Week,* Jan. 31, 2005, pp. 60–68. Available online: www .businessweek.com/magazine/content/05_05/b3918001_mz001.htm. Access date: Feb. 5, 2008.

Hammer, M., and Champy, J. *Reengineering the Corporation.* New York: HarperCollins, 1993.

Hammonds, K. H. "Size Is Not a Strategy." *Fast Company,* Sept. 2002, pp. 78–86.

Hampden-Turner, C. *Creating Corporate Culture: From Discord to Harmony.* Reading, Mass.: Addison-Wesley, 1992.

Hamper, B. *Rivethead: Tales from the Assembly Line.* New York: Warner Books, 1992.

Hampton, W. J., and Norman, J. R. "General Motors: What Went Wrong—Eight Years and Billions of Dollars Haven't Made Its Strategy Succeed." *Business Week,* Mar. 16, 1987, p. 102.

Handlin, H. C. "The Company Built upon the Golden Rule: Lincoln Electric." In B. L. Hopkins and T. C. Mawhinney (eds.), *Pay for Performance: History, Controversy, and Evidence.* Binghamton, N.Y.: Haworth Press, 1992.

Handy, C. *Understanding Organizations.* New York: Oxford University Press, 1993.

Hannaway, J., and Sproull, L. "Who's Really Running the Show: Coordination and Control in Educational Organizations?" *Administrator's Notebook,* 1979, *27*(9), 1–4.

Hansot, E. "Some Functions of Humor in Organizations." Unpublished paper, Kenyon College, Gambier, Ohio, 1979.

Harrison, J., and Freeman, R. E. "Special Topic: Democracy in and Around Organizations." *Academy of Management Executive,* 2004, *18,* 49–53.

Heath, C., and Heath, D. *Made to Stick: Why Some Ideas Survive and Others Die.* New York: Random House, 2007.

Heath, C., and Gonzalez, R. "Interaction with Others Increases Decision Confidence but Not Decision Quality." *Organizational Behavior and Human Decision Processes,* 1995, *61,* 305–326.

Hedberg, B.L.T., Nystrom, P. C., and Starbuck, W. H. "Camping on Seesaws: Prescriptions for a Self-Designing Organization." *Administrative Science Quarterly,* 1976, *21,* 41–65.

Heffernan, M. "The Female CEO." *Fast Company,* Aug. 2002, pp. 58–66.

Heffron, F. *Organization Theory and Public Organizations: The Political Connection.* Upper Saddle River, N.J.: Prentice Hall, 1989.

Heifetz, R. A. *Leadership Without Easy Answers.* Cambridge, Mass.: Belknap Press, 1994.

Heifetz, R. A., and Linsky, M. *Leadership on the Line: Staying Alive Through the Dangers of Leading.* Boston: Harvard Business School Press, 2002.

Heimovics, R. D., Herman, R. D., and Jurkiewicz Coughlin, C. L. "Executive Leadership and Resource Dependence in Nonprofit Organizations: A Frame Analysis." *Public Administration Review,* 1993, *53,* 419–427.

Heimovics, R. D., Herman, R. D., and Jurkiewicz Coughlin, C. L. "The Political Dimension of Effective Nonprofit Executive Leadership." *Nonprofit Management and Leadership,* 1995, *5,* 233–248.

Helgesen, S. *The Female Advantage: Women's Ways of Leadership.* New York: Doubleday, 1990.

Helgesen, S. *The Web of Inclusion: A New Architecture for Building Great Organizations.* New York: Currency/Doubleday, 1995.

Henderson, R. M., and Clark, K. B. "Architectural Innovation: The Reconfiguration of Existing Product Technologies and the Failure of Established Firms." *Administrative Science Quarterly,* 1990, *35,* 9–30.

Hersey, P. *The Situational Leader.* New York: Warner Books, 1984.

Hersey, P., and Blanchard, K. H. *The Management of Organizational Behavior.* (3rd ed.) Upper Saddle River, N.J.: Prentice Hall, 1977.

Hersey, P., Blanchard, K. H., and Johnson, D. E. *The Management of Organizational Behavior.* (9th ed.) Upper Saddle River, N.J.: Prentice Hall, 2007.

Herzberg, F. *Work and the Nature of Man.* Cleveland, Ohio: World, 1966.

"Hewlett-Packard Merger Pitch Awarded Top Honor." *Corporate Financing Week,* June 16, 2002.

Hill, L. A., and Farkas, M. T. "Meg Whitman at eBay, Inc." Boston: Harvard Business School Publishing, 2000.

Hindo, B. "At 3M, A Struggle Between Efficiency And Creativity." *Business Week,* June 11, 2007, pp. 8–12. Available online: www.businessweek.com/magazine/content/07_24/b4038406.htm?chan=search. Access date: Feb. 5, 2008.

Hofstede, G. *Culture's Consequences: International Differences in Work-Related Values.* Thousand Oaks, Calif.: Sage, 1984.

Hogan, R., Curphy, G. J., and Hogan, J. "What We Know About Leadership." *American Psychologist,* 1994, *49,* 493–504.

Hoge, W. "Crashing, and Saving, the Old Lads' Front Office." *New York Times,* Sept. 14, 2002, p. A14.

Holland, J. H. *Hidden Order.* Reading, Mass.: Addison-Wesley, 1995.

Hollander, E. P. *Leadership Dynamics.* New York: Free Press, 1978.

Holusha, J. "No Utopia, but to Workers, It's a Job." *New York Times,* Jan. 29, 1989, sec. 3, p. 1.

Hoskisson, R. E., Hitt, M. A., Johnson, R. A., and Grossman, W. "Conflicting Voices: The Effects of Institutional Ownership Heterogeneity and Internal Governance on Corporate Innovation Strategies." *Academy of Management Journal,* 2002, *45*(4), 697–716.

House, R. J. "The Path-Goal Theory of Effectiveness." *Administrative Science Quarterly,* 1971, *16,* 321–338.

House, R. J., Hanges, P. J., Javidan, M., Dorfman, P. W., and Gupta, V. (eds.). *Culture, Leadership, and Organizations: The GLOBE Study of 62 Societies.* Thousand Oaks, Calif.: Sage, 2004.

Iacocca, L., and Novak, W. *Iacocca.* New York: Bantam Books, 1984.

Iansiti, M., and Levien, R. *The Keystone Advantage: What the New Dynamics of Business Ecosystems Mean for Strategy, Innovation, and Sustainability.* Boston: Harvard Business School Press, 2004.

Ishikawa, K. *What Is Total Quality Control? The Japanese Way.* Upper Saddle River, N.J.: Prentice Hall, 1985.

Jackall, R. *Moral Mazes: The World of Corporate Managers.* New York: Oxford University Press, 1988.

Jehn, K. A. "A Multimethod Examination of the Benefits and Detriments of Intragroup Conflict." *Administrative Science Quarterly,* 1995, *40,* 256–282.

Jensen, C. *No Downlink: A Dramatic Narrative About the Challenger Accident and Our Time.* New York: Farrar, Straus & Giroux, 1995.

Jensen, M. C., and Meckling, W. H. "Theory of the Firm: Managerial Behavior, Agency Costs, and Ownership Structure." *Journal of Financial Economics,* 1976, *3,* 305–360.

Jensen, M. C., and Meckling, W. H. "The Nature of Man." *Journal of Applied Corporate Finance,* 1994, *7*(2), 4–19.

John, O. P. "The 'Big Five' Factor Taxonomy: Dimensions of Personality in the Natural Language and in Questionnaires." In L. A. Pervin (ed.), *Handbook of Personality: Theory and Research.* New York: Guilford Press, 1990.

Johnson, K. "Divorced from the Job, Still Wedded to the Culture." *New York Times,* June 16, 1996, p. F11.

Johnson, S. *Who Moved My Cheese?* New York: Putnam, 1998.

Judge, T. A., Bono, J. E., Ilies, R., and Gerhardt, M. W. "Personality and Leadership: A Qualitative and Quantitative Review." *Journal of Applied Psychology,* 2002, *87*(4), 765–780.

Jung, C. *Memories, Dreams, and Reflections.* New York: Random House, 1965. (Originally published 1912.)

Juran, J. M. *Juran on Leadership for Quality: An Executive Handbook.* New York: Free Press, 1989.

Kacmar, K. M., Andrews, M. C., Van Rooy, D. L., Steilberg, R. C., and Cerrone, S. "Sure Everyone Can Be Replaced . . . but at What Cost? Turnover as a Predictor of Unit-Level Performance." *Academy of Management Journal*, 2006, *49*(1), 133–144.

Kahn, J. "Diversity Trumps the Downturn." *Fortune*, July 9, 2001, pp. 114–115.

Kahn, J. "Party of the Rich: China's Congress of Crony Capitalists." *New York Times*, Nov. 10, 2002, sec. 4, pp. 1, 4. Available online: www.nytimes.com/2002/11/10/weekinreview/10KAHN.html. Access date: Feb. 5, 2008.

Kahneman, D., and Tversky, A. "Prospect Theory: An Analysis of Decisions Under Risk." *Econometrica*, 1979, *47*, 263–291.

Kamens, D. H. "Legitimating Myths and Education Organizations: Relationship Between Organizational Ideology and Formal Structure." *American Sociological Review*, 1977, *42*, 208–219.

Kanter, R. M. *Men and Women of the Corporation*. New York: Basic Books, 1977.

Kanter, R. M. *The Change Masters: Innovations for Productivity in the American Corporation*. New York: Simon & Schuster, 1983.

Kanter, R. M. *When Giants Learn to Dance*. New York: Simon & Schuster, 1989a.

Kanter, R. M. "The New Managerial Work." *Harvard Business Review*, Dec. 1989b, pp. 85–92.

Kanter, R. M., Stein, B. A., and Jick, T. D. *The Challenge of Organizational Change: How Companies Experience It and Leaders Guide It*. New York: Free Press, 1992.

Karr, J-B. A. "*Plus ça change, plus c'est la même chose* [The more things change, the more they stay the same]." *Les Guêpes*, Jan. 1849.

Katzell, R. A., and Yankelovich, D. *Work, Productivity, and Job Satisfaction*. New York: Psychological Corporation, 1975.

Katzenbach, J. R., and Smith, D. K. *The Wisdom of Teams: Creating the High-Performance Organization*. Boston: Harvard Business School Press, 1993.

Kaufer, N., and Leader, G. C. "Diana Lam (A)." Case. Boston University, 1987a.

Kaufer, N., and Leader, G. C. "Diana Lam (B)." Case. Boston University, 1987b.

Kauffman, E. M. "Creating the Uncommon Company." In R. W. Smilor and D. L. Sexton (eds.), *Leadership and Entrepreneurship: Personal and Organizational Development in Entrepreneurial Values*. Westport, Conn.: Quorum/Greenwood, 1996.

Kavilanz, P. B. "Best Buy to Circuit City: Employees Matter." CNN.com, Apr. 4, 2007. Available online: http://tiny.cc/bestbuy606. Access date: Apr. 21, 2008.

Kegan, R. *In Over Our Heads: The Mental Demands of Modern Life*. Cambridge: Harvard University Press, 1998.

Keidel, R. W. "Baseball, Football, and Basketball: Models for Business." *Organizational Dynamics*, Winter 1984, pp. 5–18.

Keller, B. "While Gorbachev Gives In, the World Marvels at His Power." *New York Times*, Feb. 11, 1990, sec. 4, p. 1.

Keller, B. "Women Superintendents: Few and Far Between." Education Week, Nov. 10, 1999. Available online with registration: www.edweek.org/ew/ewstory.cfm?slug=11women.h19. Access date: Feb. 5, 2008.

Kidder, T. *The Soul of a New Machine.* New York: Little, Brown, 1981.

Kidder, T. *Among School Children.* Boston: Houghton Mifflin, 1989.

Killian, K., Perez, F., and Siehl, C. "Ricardo Semler and Semco, S. A." Glendale, Ariz.: Thunderbird, The American Graduate School of International Management, 1998.

Kirkman, B. L., and Shapiro, D. L. "The Impact of Cultural Values on Employee Resistance to Teams: Towards a Model of Globalized Self-Managing Work Team Effectiveness." *Academy of Management Review,* 1977, *22,* 730–757.

Kleinfeld, N. R. "The Company as Family No More." *New York Times,* Mar. 4, 1996, pp. A1, A8–A10.

Kochan, T. A., Lansbury, R. D., and MacDuffie, J. P. (eds.) *After Lean Production: Evolving Employment Practices in the World Auto Industry.* Ithaca, N.Y.: Cornell University Press, 1997.

Kohlberg, L. "The Claim to Moral Adequacy of a Highest Stage of Moral Judgment." *Journal of Philosophy,* 1973, *70,* 630–646.

Komives, S. R. "Gender Differences in the Relationship and Hall Directors' Transformational and Transactional Leadership and Achieving Styles." *Journal of College Student Development,* 1991, *32,* 155–164.

Kopelman, R. E. "Job Redesign and Productivity: A Review of the Evidence." *National Productivity Review,* 1985, *4,* 237–255.

Korten, D. C. *When Corporations Rule the World.* San Francisco: Berrett-Koehler, 1995.

Kotter, J. P. *The General Managers.* New York: Free Press, 1982.

Kotter, J. P. *Power and Influence: Beyond Formal Authority.* New York: Free Press, 1985.

Kotter, J. P. *The Leadership Factor.* New York: Free Press, 1988.

Kotter, J. P., and Cohen, D. S. *The Heart of Change: Real Life Stories of How People Change Their Organizations.* Boston: Harvard Business School Press, 2002.

Kotter, J. P., and Heskett, J. L. *Corporate Culture and Performance.* New York: Free Press, 1992.

Kouzes, J. M., and Posner, B. Z. *The Leadership Challenge.* (2nd ed.) San Francisco: Jossey-Bass, 1987.

Kouzes, J. M., and Posner, B. Z. *The Leadership Challenge.* (4th ed.) San Francisco: Jossey-Bass, 2007.

Kruger, J., and Dunning, D. "Unskilled and Unaware of It: How Difficulties in Recognizing One's Own Incompetence Lead to Inflated Self-Assessments." *Journal of Personality and Social Psychology,* 1999, *77,* 1121–1134.

Kruse, D. L. "Does Profit Sharing Affect Productivity?" NBER Working Paper No. W4542. Washington, D.C.: National Bureau of Economic Research, Nov. 1993. Available online: http://papers.ssrn.com/sol3/papers.cfm?abstract_id=375304. Access date: Feb. 5, 2008.

Kühberger, A. "The Framing of Decisions: A New Look at Old Problems." *Organizational Behavior and Human Decision Processes,* 1995, *62,* 230–240.

Kuhn, T. S. *The Structure of Scientific Revolutions.* (2nd ed.) Chicago: University of Chicago Press, 1970.

Labaton, S. "Downturn and Shift in the Population Feed Boom in White Collar Crime." *New York Times,* June 2, 2002. Available online: www.nytimes.com/2002/06/02/business/02CRIM.html? Access date: Feb. 5, 2008.

Labich, K. "Is Herb Kelleher America's Best CEO? *Fortune,* May 2, 1994, pp. 44–52.

Lagarde, D. "Benazir Bhutto: My Country Is in Danger." *L'Express,* Jan. 3, 2008, pp. 8–13.

Lakoff, G. *Don't Think of an Elephant: Know Your Values and Frame the Debate—The Essential Guide for Progressives.* White River Junction, Vt.: Chelsea Green, 2004.

Langer, E. *Mindfulness.* Reading, Mass.: Addison-Wesley, 1989.

Latham, G. P., and Pinder, C. C. "Work Motivation Theory and Research at the Dawn of the Twenty-First Century." *Annual Review of Psychology,* 2005, *56,* 485–516.

Lawler, E. E., III. *High-Involvement Management: Participative Strategies for Improving Organizational Performance.* San Francisco: Jossey-Bass, 1986.

Lawler, E. E., III. *From the Ground Up: Six Principles for Building the New Logic Corporation.* San Francisco: Jossey-Bass, 1996.

Lawler, E. E., III, and Shuttle, J. L. "A Causal Correlation Test of the Need Hierarchy Concept." *Organizational Behavior and Human Performance,* 1973, *7,* 265–287.

Lawler, E. E., III, and Worley, C. *Built to Change: How to Achieve Sustained Organizational Effectiveness.* San Francisco: Jossey-Bass, 2006.

Lawrence, A. T., and Weckler, D. A. "Can NUMMI's Team Concept Work for You? Part I: A Bicultural Experiment." *Northern California Executive Review,* Spring 1990, pp. 12–17.

Lawrence, P., and Lorsch, J. *Organization and Environment.* Boston: Division of Research, Harvard Business School, 1967.

Lax, D. A., and Sebenius, J. K. *The Manager as Negotiator.* New York: Free Press, 1986.

Leavitt, H. J. *Managerial Psychology.* (4th ed.) Chicago: University of Chicago Press, 1978.

Leavitt, H. J. "The Old Days, Hot Groups, and Managers' Lib." *Administrative Science Quarterly,* 1996, *41,* 288–300.

Ledford, G. E. "Employee Involvement: Lessons and Predictions." In J. R. Galbraith, E. E. Lawler III, and Associates (eds.), *Organizing for the Future: The New Logic of Managing Complex Organizations.* San Francisco: Jossey-Bass, 1993.

Lee, A. *Call Me Roger.* Chicago: Contemporary Books, 1988.

Lesgold, A., and Lajoie, S. "Complex Problem Solving in Electronics." In R. J. Sternberg and P. A. Frensch (eds.), *Complex Problem Solving.* Hillsdale, N.J.: Erlbaum, 1991.

Levering, R., and Moskowitz, M. *The 100 Best Companies to Work For in America.* New York: Plume, 1993.

Levering, R., and Moskowitz, M. "The 100 Best Companies to Work For." *Fortune,* Jan. 20, 2003, pp. 127–152.

Levine, D. I., and Tyson, L. D. "Participation, Productivity, and the Firm's Environment." In A. S. Blinder (ed.), *Paying for Productivity: A Look at the Evidence.* Washington, D.C.: Brookings Institution, 1990.

Levinson, H. *The Exceptional Executive.* Cambridge, Mass.: Harvard University Press, 1968.

Levinson, H., and Rosenthal, S. *CEO: Corporate Leadership in Action.* New York: Basic Books, 1984.

Levinthal, D. A., and March, J. G. "The Myopia of Learning." *Strategic Management Journal,* 1993, *14,* 95–112.

Lewin, K., Lippitt, R., and White, R. "Patterns of Aggressive Behavior in Experimentally Created Social Climates." *Journal of Social Psychology,* 1939, *10,* 271–299.

Lewis, N. A. "This Mr. Smith Gets His Way in Washington." *New York Times,* Oct. 12, 1996, pp. A17, A30.

Lifson, T., and Takagi, H. *Mitsubishi Corporation: Organizational Overview.* Boston: Harvard Business School Case Services, 1981.

Likert, R. *New Patterns of Management.* New York: McGraw-Hill, 1961.

Likert, R. *The Human Organization.* New York: McGraw-Hill, 1967.

Lingle, C. "China's Economy Faces Severe Pain." *Taipei Times,* Feb. 3, 2002. Available online: www.taipeitimes.com/news/2002/02/03/story/0000122610. Access date: Feb. 5, 2008.

Lipsky, M. *Street-Level Bureaucracy.* New York: Russell Sage Foundation, 1980.

Locke, E. A., and Latham, G. P. "Building a Practically Useful Theory of Goal Setting and Task Motivation." *American Psychologist,* 2002, *9,* 705–717.

Locke, E. A., and Latham, G. P. "What Should We Do About Motivation Theory? Six Recommendations for the Twenty-First Century." *Academy of Management Review,* 2004, *29,* 388–403.

Longworth, R. C. "Old Rules of Economics Don't Work the Way Textbooks Say They Should." *Kansas City Star,* Oct. 27, 1996, sec. K, pp. 1, 4.

Lopez, B. *Crow and Weasel.* New York: North Point, 1998.

Lord, R. G., and Foti, R. J. "Schema Theories, Information Processing, and Organizational Behavior." In H. P. Sims Jr., D. A. Gioia, and Associates (eds.), *The Thinking Organization.* San Francisco: Jossey-Bass, 1986.

Love, E. G., and Kraatz, M. "How Do Firms' Actions Influence Corporate Reputation? The Case of Downsizing at Large U.S. Firms." *Academy of Management Proceedings,* 2005.

Love, J. F. *McDonald's: Behind the Arches.* New York: Bantam Books, 1986.

Lubans, J. "More Than a Game," 2001. Available online: www.lubans.org/morethana game.html. Access date: Apr. 21, 2008.

Lukes, S. *Power: A Radical View.* New York: Macmillan, 1974.

Luthans, F. "Successful vs. Effective Real Managers." *Academy of Management Executive,* 1988, *2*(2), 127–132.

Luthans, F., Yodgetts, R. M., and Rosenkrantz, S. A. *Real Managers.* Cambridge, Mass.: Ballinger, 1988.

Lynch, P. "In Defense of the Invisible Hand." *Worth,* June 1996, pp. 86–92.

Lynn, L. E., Jr. *Managing Public Policy.* New York: Little, Brown, 1987.

Maccoby, M. *The Leader.* New York: Ballantine, 1981.

Maccoby, M. *The Productive Narcissist: The Promise and Peril of Visionary Leadership.* New York: Broadway, 2003.

Machan, D. "DEC's Democracy." *Forbes,* Mar. 23, 1987, pp. 154, 156.

Machiavelli, N. *The Prince.* New York: Penguin Books, 1961. (Originally published 1514.)

Maier, N. "Assets and Liabilities in Group Problem Solving." *Psychological Review,* 1967, *74,* 239–249.

Malavé, J. *Gerencia en salud: Un modelo innovador* [Health management: An innovative model]. Caracas, Venezuela: Ediciones IESA, 1995.

Manes, S., and Andrews, P. *Gates.* New York: Touchstone, 1994.

Mangham, I. L., and Overington, M. A. *Organizations as Theater: A Social Psychology of Dramatic Appearances.* New York: Wiley, 1987.

Manning, P. *Police Work: The Social Organization of Policing.* Cambridge, Mass.: MIT Press, 1979.

Manz, C. C., and Sims, H. P., Jr. *Business Without Bosses: How Self-Managing Teams Are Building High Performance Companies.* New York: Wiley, 1995.

March, J. G. "The Technology of Foolishness." In J. G. March and J. Olsen (eds.), *Ambiguity and Choice in Organizations.* Bergen, Norway: Universitetsforlaget, 1976.

March, J. G., and Olsen, J. (eds.), *Ambiguity and Choice in Organizations.* Bergen, Norway: Universitetsforlaget, 1976.

March, J. G., and Simon, H. A. *Organizations.* New York: Wiley, 1958.

Markels, A., and Murray, M. "Call It Dumbsizing: Why Some Companies Regret Cost-Cutting." *Wall Street Journal,* May 14, 1996, p. 1.

Marshall, M. V. "An Introduction to the Marketing Concept of Managing an Institution's Future." Cambridge, Mass.: Institute for Educational Management, 1984.

Marx, R., Stubbart, C., Traub, V., and Cavanaugh, M. "The NASA Space Shuttle Disaster: A Case Study." *Journal of Management Case Studies,* 1987, *3,* 300–318.

Maslow, A. H. *Motivation and Personality.* New York: HarperCollins, 1954.

Matthews, C. *Hardball.* New York: Free Press, 1999.

Mayo, E. *The Human Problems of an Industrial Civilization.* New York: MacMillan, 1933.

Mayo, E. *The Social Problems of an Industrial Civilization.* Boston: Division of Research, Graduate School of Business Administration, Harvard University, 1945.

McCall, M. W., Lombardo, M. M., and Morrison, A. M. *Lessons of Experience: How Successful Executives Develop on the Job.* New York: Free Press, 1988.

McCaskey, M. B. *The Executive Challenge: Managing Change and Ambiguity.* Marshfield, Mass.: Pitman, 1982.

McClelland, D. C. *Human Motivation.* Glenview, Ill.: Scott, Foresman, 1985.

McConnell, M. *Challenger: A Major Malfunction.* New York: Doubleday, 1987.

McConnell, M. *Into the Mouth of the Cat: The Story of Lance Sijan, Hero of Vietnam.* New York: Norton, 2004.

McGrath, J. E. *Groups: Interaction and Performance.* Upper Saddle River, N.J.: Prentice Hall, 1984.

McGregor, D. *The Human Side of Enterprise.* New York: McGraw-Hill, 1960.

McIntyre, M. G. *Secrets to Winning at Office Politics: How to Achieve Your Goals and Increase Your Influence at Work.* New York: St. Martin's Griffin, 2005.

McLean, B. "Why Enron Went Bust." *Fortune,* Dec. 24, 2001, pp. 58–68.

McLennan, R. *Managing Organizational Change.* Upper Saddle River, N.J.: Prentice Hall, 1989.

McNamee, M., and Borrus, A. "Out of Control at Enron." *Business Week,* Apr. 8, 2002, pp. 32–33.

McNamara, R., with VanDeMark, B. *In Retrospect: The Tragedy and Lessons of Vietnam.* New York: Random House, 1995.

Mellahi, K., and Wilkinson, A. "The Impact of Downsizing on Innovation Output." *Academy of Management Proceedings,* 2006.

Mendelson, H., and Korin, A. "The Computer Industry: A Brief History." Palo Alto, Calif.: Stanford Business School, n.d. Available online: http://faculty-gsb.stanford.edu/mendelson/computer_history/intro.htm. Access date: Apr. 21, 2008.

Meredith, R. "New Blood for the Big Three's Plants: This Hiring Spree Is Rewarding Brains, Not Brawn." *New York Times,* Apr. 21, 1996, sec. 3, pp. 1, 3.

Messick, D. M., and Ohme, D. K. "Some Ethical Aspects of the Social Psychology of Social Influence." In R. M. Kramer and M. A. Neale (eds.), *Power and Influence in Organizations.* Thousand Oaks, Calif.: Sage, 1998.

Meyer, J. W., and Rowan, B. "The Structure of Educational Organizations." In M. W. Meyer and Associates, *Environments and Organizations: Theoretical and Empirical Perspectives.* San Francisco: Jossey-Bass, 1978.

Meyer, J. W., and Rowan, B. "Institutionalized Organizations: Formal Structure as Myth and Ceremony." In J. W. Meyer and W. R. Scott (eds.), *Organizational Environments: Ritual and Rationality.* Thousand Oaks, Calif.: Sage, 1983a.

Meyer, J. W., and Rowan, B. "The Structure of Educational Organizations." In J. W. Meyer and W. R. Scott (eds.), *Organizational Environments: Ritual and Rationality.* Thousand Oaks, Calif.: Sage, 1983b.

Michelli, J. *The Starbucks Experience: 5 Principles for Turning Ordinary into Extraordinary.* New York: McGraw-Hill, 2006.

Mihalopoulos, D., and Kimberly, J. "Inside Daley's Machine." *Chicago Tribune,* June 21, 2006. Available online: http://tiny.cc/daley. Access date: Apr. 21, 2008.

Miller, D., and Friesen, P. H. *Organizations: A Quantum View.* Upper Saddle River, N.J.: Prentice Hall, 1984.

Mintzberg, H. *The Nature of Managerial Work.* New York: HarperCollins, 1973.

Mintzberg, H. *The Structuring of Organizations.* Upper Saddle River, N.J.: Prentice Hall, 1979.

Mintzberg, H. *The Rise and Fall of Strategic Planning: Reconceiving Roles for Planning, Plans, Planners.* New York: Free Press, 1994.

Mirvis, P. H. "Organization Development, Part I: An Evolutionary Perspective." *Research in Organizational Change and Development,* 1988, *2,* 1–57.

Mirvis, P. H. "Revolutions in OD: The New and the New, New Things." In J. V. Gallos (ed.), *Organization Development: A Jossey-Bass Reader.* San Francisco: Jossey-Bass: 2006.

Mitroff, I. I. *Stakeholders of the Organizational Mind: Toward a New View of Organizational Policy Making.* San Francisco: Jossey-Bass, 1983.

Mitroff, I. I., and Kilmann, R. H. "Stories Managers Tell: A New Tool for Organizational Problem Solving." *Management Review,* July 1975, pp. 18–28.

Moeller, J. "Bureaucracy and Teachers' Sense of Power." In N. R. Bell and H. R. Stub (eds.), *Sociology of Education.* Florence, Ky.: Dorsey Press, 1968.

Mohr, R. D., and Zoghi, C. "Is Job Enrichment Really Enriching?" Washington, D.C.: Bureau of Labor Statistics, 2006. Available online: www.bls.gov/ore/abstract/ec/ec060010.htm. Access date: Feb. 5, 2008.

Montgomery, L. "Earning Loyalty: Pay Is Only One Issue When It Comes to Retaining Employees." Insidebiz.com, 2000.

Moore, J. F. "Predators and Prey: A New Ecology of Competition." *Harvard Business Review,* May-June 1993, pp. 75–86.

Moore S., and Meyerhoff, B. *Secular Ritual.* Assen, Netherlands: Van Gorcum, 1977.

Morgan, A. *Prescription for Success: The Life and Values of Ewing Marion Kauffman.* Kansas City, Mo.: Andrews & McMeel, 1995.

Morgan, G. *Images of Organization.* Thousand Oaks, Calif.: Sage, 1986.

Morganthau, T. "Saying 'No' to New Coke." *Newsweek,* June 23, 1985, pp. 32–33.

Morris, B. "Trophy Husbands." *Fortune,* Oct. 14, 2002, pp. 79–98.

Morrison, A. M. *The New Leaders: Guidelines on Leadership Diversity in America.* San Francisco: Jossey-Bass, 1992.

Morrison, A. M., White, R. P., and Van Velsor, E. *Breaking the Glass Ceiling.* Reading, Mass.: Addison-Wesley, 1987.

Mosser, N. R., and Walls, R. T. "Leadership Frames of Nursing Chairpersons and the Organizational Climate in Baccalaureate Nursing Programs." *Southern Online Journal of Nursing Research,* 2002, *3*(2). Available online: www.snrs.org/publications/SOJNR_articles/iss02vol03.pdf. Access date: Apr. 21, 2008.

Murphy, J. T. *Managing Matters: Reflections from Practice.* Monograph. Cambridge, Mass.: Graduate School of Education, Harvard University, 1985.

Myers, I. *Introduction to Type.* Palo Alto, Calif.: Consulting Psychologists Press, 1980.

Nadler, D. A., Gerstein, M. S., and Shaw, R. B. *Organizational Architecture: Designs for Changing Organizations.* San Francisco: Jossey-Bass, 1992.

Neil, D. "Starbucks Nation." *Los Angeles Times West Magazine,* Apr. 1, 2007, p. 46. Available online: http://tiny.cc/starbucks945. Access date: Apr. 21, 2008.

Nelson, R. R., and Winter, S. G. *An Evolutionary Theory of Economic Change.* Cambridge, Mass.: Harvard University Press, 1982.

Neuman, J. "Former President Reagan Dies at 93." *Los Angeles Times,* June 6, 2004, p. 1. Available online: www.latimes.com/news/specials/obituaries/la-reagan,1,5246827,full.story. Access date: Apr. 21, 2008.

Nickerson, J. A., and Silverman, B. S. "Why Firms Want to Organize Efficiently and What Keeps Them from Doing So: Inappropriate Governance, Performance, and Adaptation in a Deregulated Industry." *Administrative Science Quarterly,* 2003, *48,* 433–465.

Niemann, G. *Big Brown: The Untold Story of UPS.* San Francisco: Jossey-Bass, 2007.

O'Grady, S. *Basher Five-Two.* New York: Yearling, 1998.

Ohmae, K. *The Borderless World: Power and Strategy in the Interlinked Economy.* New York: HarperBusiness, 1990.

O'Keefe, D. L. *Stolen Lightning: The Social Theory of Magic.* New York: Vintage Books, 1983.

Oliver, T. *The Real Coke, the Real Story.* New York: Random House, 1986.

"On a Clear Day You Can Still See General Motors." *Economist,* Dec. 2, 1989, pp. 77–78, 80.

Oppel, R. A. "How Enron Got California to Buy Power It Didn't Need." *New York Times,* May 8, 2002, p. A1.

O'Reilly, C. A., III, and Chatman, J. A. "Working Smarter and Harder: A Longitudinal Study of Managerial Success." *Administrative Science Quarterly,* 1994, *39,* 603–627.

Organ, D. W., and Ryan, K. A. "A Metaanalytic Review of Attitudinal and Dispositional Predictors of Organizational Citizenship Behavior." *Personnel Psychology,* 1995, *48,* 775–802.

Orgogozo, I. *Les paradoxes du management* [The paradoxes of management]. Paris: Les Éditions d'Organisation, 1991.

Ormerod, P. *Why Most Things Fail: Evolution, Extinction and Economics.* New York: Wiley, 2007.

Ortner, S. "On Key Symbols." *American Anthropologist,* 1973, *75,* 1338–1346.

Oshry, B. *Seeing Systems: Unlocking the Mysteries of Organizational Life.* San Francisco: Berrett-Koehler, 1995.

Osterman, P. "Work-Family Programs and the Employment Relationship." *Administrative Science Quarterly,* 1995, *40,* 681–700.

O'Toole, J. *Leading Change: Overcoming the Ideology of Comfort and the Tyranny of Custom.* San Francisco: Jossey-Bass, 1995.

O'Toole, P. *Corporate Messiah: The Hiring and Firing of Million-Dollar Managers.* New York: Morrow, 1984.

Owen, H. *Spirit: Transformation and Development in Organizations.* Potomac, Md.: Abbott, 1987.

Owen, H. *Open Space Technology.* Potomac, Md.: Abbott, 1993.

Owen, H. *Tales from Open Space.* Potomac, Md.: Abbott, 1995.

Palmeri, C., and Epstein, K. "Fear and Loathing at the Airport." *Business Week,* Sept. 10, 2007. Available online: http://tiny.cc/fear450. Access date: Apr. 21, 2008.

Palumbo, G. *Gerencia participativa: Un caso exito en el sector salud* [Participative management: A successful case in the health sector]. Caracas, Venezuela: Fundación Antonio Cisneros Bermudez, 1991.

Paré, T. P. "Jack Welch's Nightmare on Wall Street." *Fortune,* Sept. 5, 1994, pp. 40–48.

Pande, P. S., Neuman, R. P., and Cavanagh, R. R. *The Six Sigma Way: How GE, Motorola and Other Top Companies Are Honing Their Performance.* New York: McGraw-Hill, 2000.

Pape, R. *Dying to Win: The Strategic Logic of Suicide Terrorism.* New York: Random House, 2006.

Parker, S., and Wall, T. D. *Job and Work Design: Organizing Work to Promote Well-Being and Effectiveness.* Thousand Oaks, Calif.: Sage, 1998.

Pasquier, S., with Chevelkina, A. "Gasprom: L'Arme de Pression [Gazprom: The Pressure Weapon]." *L'Express*, Jan. 25, 2007, pp. 43–49. Available online: http://tiny.cc/gasprom. Access date: Apr. 21, 2008.

Paulson, E. *Inside Cisco: The Real Story of Sustained M&A Growth.* New York: Wiley, 2001.

Peck, S. *The Different Drum: Community Making and Peace.* New York: Touchstone, 1998.

Perrow, C. *Complex Organizations: A Critical Essay.* (2nd ed.) Glenview, Ill.: Scott, Foresman, 1979.

Perrow, C. *Complex Organizations: A Critical Essay.* (3rd ed.) New York: Random House, 1986.

Peters, B. G. *American Public Policy: Promise and Performance.* New York: Chatham House, 1999.

Peters, T. J., and Austin, N. *A Passion for Excellence.* New York: Random House, 1985.

Peters, T. J., and Waterman, R. H. *In Search of Excellence.* New York: HarperCollins, 1982.

Petzinger, T. *Hard Landing: The Epic Contest for Power and Profits That Plunged the Airlines into Chaos.* New York: Times Business, 1995.

Pfeffer, J. *Organizational Design.* Arlington Heights, Ill.: AHM Publishing, 1978.

Pfeffer, J. *Power in Organizations.* Boston: Pitman, 1981.

Pfeffer, J. *Managing with Power: Politics and Influence in Organizations.* Boston: Harvard Business School Press, 1992.

Pfeffer, J. *Competitive Advantage Through People: Unleashing the Power of the Work Force.* Boston: Harvard Business School Press, 1994.

Pfeffer, J. *The Human Equation: Building Profits by Putting People First.* Boston: Harvard Business School Press, 1998.

Pfeffer, J. *What Were They Thinking? Unconventional Wisdom About Management.* Boston: Harvard Business School Press, 2007.

Pfeffer, J., and Salancik, G. *The External Control of Organizations.* New York: HarperCollins, 1978.

Pichault, F. *Ressources humaines et changement stratégique: Vers un management politique* [Human resources and strategic change: Toward a political approach to management]. Brussels, Belgium: DeBoeck, 1993.

Port, O. "Quality." *Business Week*, Nov. 30, 1992, pp. 66–72.

Porter, E. "Notes for the Looking for Leadership Conference." Paper presented at the Looking for Leadership Conference, Graduate School of Education, Harvard University, Dec. 1989.

Powell, B. "Trade: No Faking It." *Time*, Thursday, Apr. 12, 2007. Available online: www .time.com/time/magazine/article/0,9171,1609466,00.html. Access date: Feb. 5, 2008.

Powell, W. W., Koput, K. W., and Smith-Doerr, L. "Interorganizational Collaboration and the Locus of Innovation: Networks of Learning in Biotechnology." *Administrative Science Quarterly*, 1996, *41*, 116–145.

Pressman, J. L., and Wildavsky, A. B. *Implementation.* Berkeley: University of California Press, 1973.

Pyzdek, T. *The Six Sigma Handbook: The Complete Guide for Green Belts, Black Belts, and Managers at All Levels.* New York: McGraw-Hill, 2003.

Quinn, R. E. *Beyond Rational Management: Mastering the Paradoxes and Competing Demands of High Performance.* San Francisco: Jossey-Bass, 1988.

Quinn, R. E., and Cameron, K. "Organizational Life Cycles and Shifting Criteria of Effectiveness." *Management Science,* 1983, *29,* 33–51.

Quinn, R. E., Faerman, S. R., Thompson, M. P., and McGrath, M. R. *Becoming a Master Manager: A Competency Framework.* New York: Wiley, 1996.

Rallis, S. "Different Views of Knowledge Use by Practitioners." Unpublished paper, Graduate School of Education, Harvard University, 1980.

Rao, P., and Kulkarni A. "Perceived Importance of Needs in Relation to Job Level and Personality Make-Up." *Journal of the Indian Academy of Applied Psychology,* 1998, *24,* 37–42."

Rappaport, C. "A Tough Swede Invades the U.S." *Fortune,* Jan. 29, 1992, pp. 76–79.

Reddin, W. J. *Managerial Effectiveness.* New York: McGraw-Hill, 1970.

Reed, K. "Rituals of Combat: Air War." Unpublished manuscript, University of Southern California, 2001.

Reed, S., and Sains, A. "Outraged in Europe over ABB." *Business Week,* Mar. 4, 2002. Available online: www.businessweek.com/magazine/content/02_09/b3772140.htm. Access date: Feb. 5, 2008.

Reichheld, F. F. "Loyalty-Based Management." *Harvard Business Review,* Mar.-Apr. 1993, pp. 64–73.

Reichheld, F. F. *The Loyalty Effect: The Hidden Force Behind Growth, Profits, and Lasting Value.* Boston: Harvard Business School Press, 1996.

Reingold, J., and Yang, J. L. "The Hidden Workplace." *Fortune,* July 18, 2007. Available online: http://tiny.cc/hidden. Access date: Apr. 21, 2008.

Rice, A. K. *The Enterprise and Its Environment.* London: Tavistock, 1953.

Ricks, D. *Blunders in International Business.* (3rd ed.) New York: Blackwell, 1999.

Ricks, T. *Making the Corps.* New York: Touchstone, 1998.

Ridout, C. F., and Fenn, D. H. "Job Corps." Boston: Harvard Business School Case Services, 1974.

Riebling, M. *Wedge: From Pearl Harbor to 9/11—How the Secret War Between the FBI and CIA Has Endangered National Security.* New York: Touchstone, 2002.

Ritti, R. R., and Funkhouser, G. R. *The Ropes to Skip and the Ropes to Know.* (2nd ed.) Columbus, Ohio: Grid, 1982.

Roberts, J. L., and Thomas, E. "Enron's Dirty Laundry." *Newsweek,* Mar. 11, 2002.

Roberts, M. "Southwest CEO's 2006 Pay Less Than $1M." Forbes.com, Mar. 30, 2007.

Robinson, G. "Survey of School Choice Research, Spring, 2005." Milwaukee: Marquette University, 2005. Available online: www.itlmuonline.com/_incoming/ITLSCSurvey2005.pdf. Access date: Feb. 5, 2008.

Rosen, C., Case, J., and Staubus, M. *Equity: Why Employee Ownership Is Good for Business.* Boston: Harvard Business School Press, 2005.

Rosener, J. B. "Ways Women Lead." *Harvard Business Review*, 1990, *68*, 119–125.

Rosenthal, R., and Jacobson, L. *Pygmalion in the Classroom: Teacher Expectations and Pupils' Intellectual Development*. Austin, Tex.: Holt, Rinehart and Winston, 1968.

Rossiter, C. *1787: The Grand Convention*. New York: New American Library, 1966.

Roush, C. *Inside Home Depot*. New York: McGraw-Hill, 1999.

Rubin, A. J. "Cleric al-Sadr Blurs the Line Between Rebel and Politician." *San Diego Union-Tribune*, July 19, 2007. Available online: http://cfx.signonsandiego.com/uniontrib/20070719/news_1n19alsadr.html. Access date: Feb. 5, 2008.

Rundall, T., Starkweather, D., and Norrish, B. "If It Ain't Broke, Fix It: Beth Israel Hospital." Seattle: Cascade Center for Public Service, University of Washington, 1998.

Russ, J. *Les théories du pouvoir* [Theories of power]. Paris: Librairie Générale Française, 1994.

Salancik, G. R., and Pfeffer, J. "An Examination of Need-Satisfaction Models of Job Attitudes." *Administrative Science Quarterly*, 1977, *22*, 427–456.

Salovey, P., Bedell, B., Detweiler, J. B., and Mayer, J. D. "Coping Intelligently: Emotional Intelligence and the Coping Process." In C. R. Snyder (ed.), *Coping: The Psychology of What Works*. New York: Oxford University Press, 1999.

Salovey, P., and Mayer, J. "Emotional Intelligence." *Imagination, Cognition, and Personality*, 1990, *9*(3), 185–211.

Sapolsky, H. *The Polaris System Development*. Cambridge, Mass.: Harvard University Press, 1972.

Saubaber, D. "Sienne: La cavalcade infernale [Siena: The horse race from hell]." *L'Express*, Sept. 8, 2007, pp. 42–45. Available online: www.lexpress.fr/voyage/destinations/dossier/vitalie/dossier.asp?ida=459154. Access date: Feb. 5, 2008.

Schein, E. H. *Process Consultation*. Reading, Mass.: Addison-Wesley, 1969.

Schein, E. H. *Organizational Culture and Leadership*. (2nd ed.) San Francisco: Jossey-Bass, 1992.

Schein, V. E. "Relationships Between Sex Role Stereotypes and Requisite Management Characteristics Among Female Managers." *Journal of Applied Psychology*, 1975, *75*, 340–344.

Schein, V. E. "The Relationship Between Sex Role Stereotypes and Requisite Management Characteristics: A Cross-Cultural Look." Paper presented at the Twenty-Second International Congress of Applied Psychology, Kyoto, Japan, July 1990.

Schelling, T. *The Strategy of Conflict*. Cambridge, Mass.: Harvard University Press, 1960.

Schlender, B. "The Man Who Built Pixar's Incredible Innovation Machine." *Fortune*, Nov. 15, 2004, pp. 207–212.

Schlesinger, L., Eccles, R., and Gabarro, J. *Managerial Behavior in Organizations*. New York: McGraw-Hill, 1983.

Schlesinger, J. M. "NUMMI Keeps Promise of No Layoffs by Setting Nonproduction Workdays." *Wall Street Journal*, Oct. 29, 1987, p. 30.

Schmidt, E., and Varian, H. "Google: Ten Golden Rules." *Newsweek*, Dec. 2, 2005. Available online: http://tiny.cc/golden. Access date: Apr. 21, 2008.

Schneider, B., and Alderfer, C. "Three Studies of Measures of Need Satisfaction in Organizations." *Administrative Science Quarterly*, 1973, *18*, 498–505.

Schuler, D. A., Rehbein, K., and Cramer, R. D. "Pursuing Strategic Advantage Through Political Means: A Multivariate Approach." *Academy of Management Journal*, 2002, *45*(4), 659–672.

Schutz, A. *The Phenomenology of Social Relations.* Chicago: University of Chicago Press: 1970.

Schwartz, H. S. "The Clockwork or the Snakepit: An Essay on the Meaning of Teaching Organizational Behavior." *Organizational Behavior Teaching Review*, 1986, *11*, 19–26.

Schwartz, J. "The Former C.E.O.: Darth Vader. Machiavelli. Skilling Set Intense Pace." *New York Times*, Feb. 7, 2002, pp. C1, C7.

Scott, W. R. *Organizations: Rational, Natural, and Open Systems.* Upper Saddle River, N.J.: Prentice Hall, 1981.

Scott, W. R. "The Organization of Environments: Network, Cultural, and Historical Elements." In J. W. Meyer and W. R. Scott (eds.), *Organizational Environments: Ritual and Rationality.* Thousand Oaks, Calif.: Sage, 1983.

Scott, W. R., and Davis, G. F. *Organizations and Organizing: Rational, Natural, and Open Systems Perspectives.* Upper Saddle River, N.J.: Prentice Hall, 2007.

Seeger, J. A., Lorsch, J. W., and Gibson, C. F. "First National City Bank Operating Group (A) and (B)." Boston: Harvard Business School Case Services, 1975.

Seely Brown, J., Denning, S., Groh, K., and Prusak, L. *Storytelling in Organizations: Why Storytelling Is Transforming 21st Century Organizations and Management.* Burlington, Mass.: Butterworth-Heinemann, 2004.

Sellers, P. "Home Depot: Something to Prove." *Fortune*, June 27, 2002. Available online: www.mutualofamerica.com/articles/Fortune/2002_06_27/homedepot1.asp. Access date: Feb. 5, 2008.

Selznick, P. *Leadership and Administration.* New York: HarperCollins, 1957.

Semler, R. *Maverick: The Success Story Behind the World's Most Unusual Workplace.* New York: Warner Books, 1993.

Senge, P. M. *The Fifth Discipline: The Art and Practice of the Learning Organization.* New York: Currency/Doubleday, 1990.

Sennett, R. *Authority.* New York: Knopf, 1980.

Seper, J. "CIA Didn't Tell FBI About 9/11 Hijackers." *Washington Times*, June 10, 2005.

Sérieyx, H. *Le big bang des organisations* [The organizational big bang]. Paris: Calmann-Lévy, 1993.

Sherman, J. *The Rings of Saturn.* New York: Oxford University Press, 1994.

Shu Li and Adams, A. S. "Is There Something More Important Behind Framing?" *Organizational Behavior and Human Decision Processes*, 1995, *62*, 216–219.

Simmel, G. *The Sociology of Georg Simmel.* New York: Free Press, 1950.

Simmons, A. *The Story Factor.* (2nd ed.) New York: Perseus Books, 2006.

Simmons, A. *Whoever Tells the Best Story Wins: How to Use Your Own Stories to Communicate with Power and Impact.* New York: AMACOM, 2007.

Simon, H. *Hidden Champions: Lessons from 500 of the World's Best Unknown Companies.* Boston: Harvard Business School Press, 1996.

Simon, H. A. *Administrative Behavior.* New York: Macmillan, 1947.

Simon, H. A., and Chase, W. G. "Skill in Chess." *American Scientist,* 1973, *61,* 394–403.

Sirianni, C. "Tavistock Institute Develops Practices of Contemporary Work Reform." Civic Practices Network, Brandeis University, 1995. Available online: www.cpn.org/topics/work/tavistock.html. Access date: Apr. 21, 2008.

Sloan, A. P., Jr. *My Years with General Motors.* New York: Macfadden, 1965.

Smith, C. S. "China Faces Problems Creating Jobs, Officials Say." *New York Times,* Apr. 30, 2002, p. A8.

Smith, H. *The Power Game.* New York: Random House, 1988.

Snook, S. *Friendly Fire: The Accidental Shootdown of U.S. Black Hawks over Northern Iraq.* Princeton, N.J.: Princeton University Press, 2000.

Sobel, R. *When Giants Stumble: Classic Business Blunders and How to Avoid Them.* Upper Saddle River, N.J.: Prentice Hall, 1999.

Solomon, R. C. *Ethics and Excellence: Cooperation and Integrity in Business.* Oxford, England: Oxford University Press, 1993.

Sorkin, A. R. "Tyco Details Lavish Lives of Executives." *New York Times,* Sept. 18, 2002, p. C1.

Spector, R., and McCarthy, D. *The Nordstrom Way: The Inside Story of America's #1 Customer Service Company.* New York: Wiley, 1995.

Springarn, N. D. "Primary Nurses Bring Back One-to-One Care." *New York Times,* Dec. 26, 1982. Available online: http://tiny.cc/nurses166. Access date: Apr. 21, 2008.

Stack, J., and Burlingham, B. *The Great Game of Business.* New York: Currency/Doubleday, 1994.

Staw, B. M., and Hoang, H. "Sunk Costs in the NBA: Why Draft Order Affects Playing Time and Survival in Professional Basketball." *Administrative Science Quarterly,* 1995, *40,* 474–494.

Staw, B. M., and Epstein, L. D. "What Bandwagons Bring: Effects of Popular Management Techniques on Corporate Performance, Reputation, and CEO Pay." *Administrative Science Quarterly,* 2000, *45*(3), 523–556.

Stein, N. "Winning the War to Keep Top Talent." *Fortune,* May 29, 2000, pp. 132–138.

Stern, R. N., and Barley, S. R. "Organizations and Social Systems: Organization Theory's Neglected Mandate." *Administrative Science Quarterly,* 1996, *41,* 146–162.

Sternberg, R. J. *Beyond IQ: A Triarchic Theory of Human Intelligence.* New York: Cambridge University Press, 1985.

Steward, T. A. "Managing in a Wired Company." *Fortune,* July 11, 1994, pp. 44–56.

Stires, D. "Fallen Arches." *Fortune,* Apr. 29, 2002, pp. 74–76.

Stogdill, R. *Handbook of Leadership.* New York: Free Press, 1974.

Stone, L. M., and Chung, J. S. "Title IX Turns 35, Yet Hasn't Reached Its Prime." *Seattle Times,* July 18, 2007. Available online: http://seattletimes.nwsource.com/html/opinion/2003793504_lisastone18.html. Access date: Feb. 5, 2008.

Strauss, G., and Hansen, B. "CEO Pay Soars in 2005 as a Select Group Break the $100 Million Mark." *USA Today,* Apr. 11, 2006. Available online: www.usatoday.com/money/companies/management/2006-04-09-ceo-compensation-report_x.htm. Access date: Feb. 5, 2008.

Stross, R. E. "Microsoft's Big Advantage—Hiring Only the Supersmart." *Fortune,* Nov. 25, 1996, pp. 159–162.

Sunderman, G. L. "The Unraveling of No Child Left Behind: How Negotiated Changes Transform the Law." The Civil Rights Project at Harvard University, 2006.

Tagliabue, J. "McDonald's Gets a Lesson in, Well, the French Fry." *New York Times,* Dec. 11, 1999. Available online: http://tiny.cc/lesson. Access date: Apr. 21, 2008.

Taleb, N. *The Black Swan: The Impact of the Highly Improbable.* New York: Random House, 2007.

Taylor, F. W. *The Principles of Scientific Management.* New York: Harper, 1911.

Taylor, M., Ramaya, K., and Puia, G. "Outback Steakhouse, Inc: Fueling the Fast Growth Company." In J. R. Schermerhorn, *Management.* (6th ed.) New York: Wiley, 2003.

Terkel, S. *Hope Dies Last.* New York: New Press, 2004.

Tetlock, P. E. "Cognitive Biases and Organizational Correctives: Do Both Disease and Cure Depend on the Politics of the Beholder?" *Administrative Science Quarterly,* 2000, *45,* 293–326.

Thompson, J. D. *Organizations in Action.* New York: McGraw-Hill, 1967.

Thorndike, E. L. "Intelligence and Its Uses." *Harper's Magazine,* 1920, 140, 227–235.

Thornton, E., Arndt, M., and Weber, J. "Why Consumers Hate Mergers." *Business Week,* Dec. 6, 2004. Available online: www.businessweek.com/magazine/content/04_49/b3911074_mz017.htm?chan=search. Access date: Feb. 5, 2008.

Toffler, B. L., with Reingold, J. *Final Accounting: Ambition, Greed, and the Fall of Arthur Andersen.* New York: Doubleday, 2004.

Tomsho, R. "How Greyhound Lines Re-Engineered Itself Right into a Deep Hole." *Wall Street Journal,* Oct. 20, 1994, p. A1.

Topoff, H. R. "The Social Behavior of Army Ants." *Scientific American,* Nov. 1972, pp. 71–79.

Treacy, M., and Wiersema, F. *The Discipline of Market Leaders: Choose Your Customers, Narrow Your Focus, Dominate Your Market.* Reading, Mass.: Addison-Wesley, 1995.

Trieschmann, J. S., Dennis, A. R., and Northcraft, G. B. "Serving Multiple Constituencies in the Business School: MBA Program vs. Research Performance." *Academy of Management Journal,* 2000, *43,* 1130–1142.

Trist, E., and Bamforth, K. "Some Social and Psychological Consequences of the Longwall Method of Coal Getting." *Human Relations,* 1951, *4,* 3–38.

Trost, A. H. "Leadership Is Flesh and Blood." In L. Atwater and R. Penn (eds.), *Military Leadership: Traditions and Future Trends.* Annapolis, Md.: Naval Institute Press, 1989.

Uchitelle, L. "We're Leaner, Meaner and Going Nowhere Faster." *New York Times,* May 12, 1996, sec. 4, pp. 1, 4.

Uchitelle, L. "The End of the Line as They Know It: Detroit's Displaced Are Struggling to Build New Lives." *New York Times*, Apr. 1, 2007, sec. 3, pp. 1, 9, 10.

Urwick, L. "Organization as a Technical Problem." In L. H. Gulick and L. Urwick (eds.), *Papers on the Science of Administration*. New York: Columbia University Press, 1937.

Vaill, P. B. "The Purposing of High-Performance Systems." *Organizational Dynamics*, Autumn 1982, pp. 23–39.

Vaill, P. B. *Managing as a Performing Art: New Ideas for a World of Chaotic Change*. San Francisco: Jossey-Bass, 1989.

Valian, V. *Why So Slow? The Advancement of Women*. Cambridge, Mass.: MIT Press, 1999.

Vaughan, D. "Autonomy, Interdependence, and Social Control: NASA and the Space Shuttle *Challenger*." *Administrative Science Quarterly*, 1990, *35*, 225–257.

Vaughan, D. *The Challenger Launch Decision: Risky Technology, Culture, and Deviance at NASA*. Chicago: University of Chicago, 1995.

Vella, M. "German Throwdown: BMW vs. Mercedes-Benz." *Business Week Online*, May 5, 2006. Available online: www.businessweek.com/autos/content/may2006/bw20060505_131772.htm. Access date: Feb. 5, 2008.

Voss, J. F., Wolfe, C. R., Lawrence, J. A., and Engle, R. A. "From Representation to Decision: An Analysis of Problem Solving in International Relations." In R. J. Sternberg and P. A. Frensch (eds.), *Complex Problem Solving*. Hillsdale, N.J.: Erlbaum, 1991.

Vroom, V. H., and Yetton, P. W. *Leadership and Decision Making*. Pittsburgh: University of Pittsburgh Press, 1973.

Wahba, M. A., and Bridwell, L. G. "Maslow Reconsidered: A Review of Research on Need Hierarchy Theory." *Organizational Behavior and Human Performance*, 1976, *15*, 2123–2140.

Wald, M. L., and Schwartz, J. "NASA Management Failings Are Linked to Shuttle Demise." *New York Times*, July 12, 2003a, p. A1. Available online: http://tiny.cc/failings. Access date: Apr. 21, 2008.

Wald, M. L., and Schwartz, J. "Part by Part, Investigators Relive the Shuttle's Demise." *New York Times*, July 22, 2003b, p. A1. Available online: http://tiny.cc/partbypart. Access date: Apr. 21, 2008.

Waldrop, M. M. *Complexity: The Emerging Science at the Edge of Order and Chaos*. New York: Simon & Schuster, 1992.

Walker Information. "The Walker Loyalty Report for Loyalty in the Workplace." Nov. 2005. Available online: www.walkerinfo.com/what/loyaltyreports/studies/employee05/factsheet.cfm. Access date: Feb. 5, 2008.

Ward, W. A. "Manufacturing Productivity and the Shifting U.S., China and Global Job Scenes—1990–2005." Clemson, S.C.: Clemson University Center for International Trade Working Paper 052507, 2005. Available online: http://business.clemson.edu/cit/Documents/Mfg%20Employment%20Working%20Paper%20draft%208%202005.pdf. Access date: Apr. 21, 2008.

Waterman, R. H., Jr. *What America Does Right: Learning from Companies That Put People First*. New York: Norton, 1994.

Watson, T. *In Search of Management: Culture, Chaos and Control in Managerial Work.* (rev. ed.) London: Thompson Learning, 2000.

Wayne, L. "Starbucks Chairman Fears Tradition is Fading." *New York Times,* Feb. 24, 2007. Available online: www.nytimes.com/2007/02/24/business/24coffee.html. Access date: Apr. 21, 2008.

Weatherford, J. M. *Tribes on the Hill: The United States Congress—Rituals and Realities.* Westport, Conn.: Bergin & Garvey, 1985.

Weber, M. *The Theory of Social and Economic Organization.* (T. Parsons, trans.) New York: Free Press, 1947.

Weddle, C. J. "A Study of Leadership Styles and Personality of Successful Women Administrators in Higher Education: Implications for Organizations and Training." Paper presented at conference on "The Impact of Leadership," Center for Creative Leadership, Colorado Springs, 1991.

Wegmans. "What We Believe." n.d. Available online: www.wegmans.com; go to Latest News, Media Room, Company Overview. Access date: Mar. 4, 2008.

Weick, K. E. "Educational Organizations as Loosely Coupled Systems." *Administrative Science Quarterly,* 1976, *21,* 1–19.

Weick, K. E., and Bougon, M. G. "Organizations as Cognitive Maps." In H. P. Sims Jr., D. A. Gioia, and Associates (eds.), *The Thinking Organization.* San Francisco: Jossey-Bass, 1986.

Weisbord, M. R., and Janoff, S. *Future Search: An Action Guide to Finding Common Ground in Organizations and Communities.* San Francisco: Berrett-Koehler, 1995.

Weiss, C. H. *Social Science Research and Decision Making.* New York: Columbia University Press, 1980.

Wellins, R. S., Wilson, R., Katz, A. J., Laughlin, P., Day, C. R., Jr., and Price, D. "Self-Directed Teams: A Study of Current Practice." Pittsburgh: Development Dimensions International, 1990.

Westerlund, G., and Sjostrand, S. *Organizational Myths.* New York: HarperCollins, 1979.

White, R. W. "Competence and the Psychosexual Stages of Development." In M. R. Jones (ed.), *Nebraska Symposium on Motivation, 1960.* Lincoln: University of Nebraska Press, 1960.

Whitmyer, C. *In the Company of Others.* New York: Putnam, 1993.

Whyte, W. F. *Money and Motivation.* New York: HarperCollins, 1955.

Whyte, W. H. *The Organization Man.* New York: Simon & Schuster, 1956.

Williamson, O. *Markets and Hierarchies.* New York: Free Press. 1975.

Wilson, C., and Wilson, J. "The Impact of Personality, Gender and International Location on Multi-Level Management Ratings." Paper presented at conference on "The Impact of Leadership," Center for Creative Leadership, Colorado Springs, July, 1991.

Wimpelberg, R. K. "Managerial Images and School Effectiveness." *Administrators' Notebook,* 1987, *32,* 1–4.

Wolf, C. "China's Rising Unemployment Challenge." Rand Corporation online commentary, 2004. Available online: www.rand.org/commentary/070704AWSJ.html. Access date: Feb. 5, 2008.

Woodward, J. (ed.). *Industrial Organizations: Behavior and Control*. Oxford, England: Oxford University Press, 1970.

WuDunn, S. "When Lifetime Jobs Die Prematurely." *New York Times*, June 12, 1996, pp. D1, D8.

Yorks, L., and Whitsett, D. A. *Scenarios of Change: Advocacy and the Diffusion of Job Redesign in Organizations*. New York: Praeger, 1989.

Yukl, G. *Leadership in Organizations*. (6th ed.) Upper Saddle River, N.J.: Prentice Hall, 2005.

Zachary, G. P. "Climbing the Peak: Agony and Ecstasy of 200 Code Writers Beget Windows NT." *Wall Street Journal*, May 26, 1993, pp. A1, A6.

Zachary, G. P. *Showstopper! The Breakneck Race to Create Windows NT and the Next Generation at Microsoft*. New York: Free Press, 1994.

Zott, C., and Huy, Q. N. "How Entrepreneurs Use Symbolic Management to Acquire Resources." *Administrative Science Quarterly*, 2007, *52*, 70–105.

THE AUTHORS

Lee G. Bolman holds the Marion Bloch Missouri Chair in Leadership at the Bloch School of Business and Public Administration, University of Missouri–Kansas City. He received a B.A. (1962) in history and a Ph.D. (1968) in administrative sciences, both from Yale University. Bolman's interests lie in the intersection of leadership and organizations, and he has published numerous articles, chapters, and cases. He is coauthor of *Escape from Cluenessness: A Guide for the Organizationally Challenged*. Bolman has been a consultant to corporations, public agencies, universities, and public schools in the United States, Asia, Europe, and Latin America. For twenty years, he taught at the Harvard Graduate School of Education, where he also chaired the Institute for Educational Administration and the School Leadership Academy. He has been director and board chair of the Organizational Behavioral Teaching Society and Director of the National Training Laboratories.

Bolman lives in Kansas City, Missouri, with his wife, Joan Gallos, the youngest of his six children, Brad, and a spirited Theory Y Cockapoo, Douglas McGregor.

Terrence E. Deal retired as the Irving R. Melbo Professor at the University of Southern California's Rossier School of Education. Before joining USC, he served on the faculties of the Stanford University Graduate School of Education, the Harvard Graduate School of Education, and Vanderbilt University's Peabody College of Education. He received his B.A. (1961) from LaVerne College in history, his M.A. (1966) from California State University at Los Angeles in educational administration, and his Ph.D. (1972) from Stanford University in education and sociology. Deal has been a policeman, public school teacher, high school principal, district officer administrator, and university professor. His primary research interests are in organization symbolism and change. He is the author of thirty books, including the best-seller *Corporate Cultures* (with A. A. Kennedy, 1982) and *Shaping School Culture* (with K. Peterson, 1999). He has published numerous articles on organizations, change, and leadership. He is a consultant to business, health care, military, educational, and religious organizations domestically and in Europe, Scandinavia, the Middle East, Canada, South America, Japan, and Southeast Asia.

Deal lives in San Luis Obispo's Edna Valley, California, with his wife, Sandy, and their cat, Max. Along with writing, his current avocation is wine-making as a member of the Edna Ranch Vintner's Guild.

Bolman and Deal first met in 1976 when they were assigned to co-teach a course on organization at Harvard University. Trained in different disciplines on opposite coasts, they disagreed on almost everything. It was the beginning of a challenging but very productive partnership. They have written a number of other books together, including *Leading with Soul: An Uncommon Journey of Spirit*. Their books have been translated into multiple languages for readers in Asia, Europe, and Latin America.

For five years, Bolman and Deal also co-directed the National Center for Educational Leadership, a research consortium of Harvard, Vanderbilt, and the University of Chicago.

The authors appreciate hearing from readers and welcome comments, questions, suggestions, or accounts of experiences that bear on the ideas in the book. Stories of success, failure, or puzzlement are all welcome. Readers can contact the authors at the following addresses:

Lee Bolman
Bloch School-UMKC
5100 Rockhill Road
Kansas City MO 64113
lee@bolman.com

Terry Deal
6625 Via Piedra
San Luis Obispo CA 93401
sucha@slocoast.net

Clark, K. B., 64, 89
Clarke, M., 219
Clarke, R., 29
Cleveland, H., 344, 369
Clifford, D. K., 345, 346
Clifford, J., 94–96
Clinton, B., 6, 189
Clinton, H. R., 263, 340, 354
Cochran, S., 58
Cohen, A. R., 360
Cohen, B., 400–401
Cohen, D. S., 345, 348, 382, 394
Cohen, M., 303, 306, 307
Cohen, P. S., 254
Cohen, S. G., 113, 180, 186
Cohen, W., 315–316
Coles, T., 341
Collins, B. E., 180
Collins, J. C., 140, 145, 146, 256, 269, 320–322, 345, 346, 356, 401, 436, 443
Collinson, D. L., 169
Collinson, M., 169
Colvin, G., 157
Condit, P., 266–267
Conger, J. A., 345
Conley, C., 125
Conlin, M., 376
Coonan, C., 197
Cooper, C., 54, 72
Corwin, R., 253
Covey, S.M.R., 15, 443
Cox, H., 278
Cox, T., Jr., 406
Cramer, R. D., 241
Crawford, G., 14
Crimmons, D., 418–419, 420, 432

Cronshaw, S. F., 22*n*.2
Crosby, P., 159
Cross, I., 108
Crozier, M., 197
Cunliffe, A. L., 296
Curphy, G. J., 8
Cutler, D., 211–213, 215, 221, 222
Cyert, R. M., 34, 49, 198–199, 200–201, 243, 384, 441
Czepak, F., 416, 417, 418, 419, 420, 432

D

Daley, R., 203
Dalton, M., 208
Dane, E., 11, 37
Daniels, C., 157
Darwin, C., 384, 385
David, G., 61
Davis, G. F., 297
Davis, K., 353
Davis, M., 253
Day, B., 258
De Backer, P., 33, 140, 143, 345, 400
De Castro, E., 282–283, 284
De Gaulle, C., 437
De Gues, A., 399, 401
Deal, G., 45, 140
Deal, T. E., 14, 19, 67–68, 114, 115, 234–235, 261, 266, 269, 325, 326, 352, 387, 403
Debbs, E., 421, 425
DeBecker, G., 38
DeGeorge, G., 160
Dell, M., 33
Demarco, H., 29–31, 32–33, 36, 319–320

Deming, W. E., 159
Denning, S., 259, 260
Dennis, A. R., 439
DePree, M., 409
DeRue, D. S., 122
Descarpentries, J.-M., 149
Detweiler, J. B., 176
Dewey, 10
Dillingham, D. L., 239
DiMaggio, P. J., 296, 297–299, 440, 441
Dittmer, L., 253
Doktor, J., 326
Donahue, P., 319
Donovan, "W. B.", 17
Dorfman, P. W., 272
Dornbusch, S., 54, 64, 66
Downer, L., 241, 266
Downey, H. K., 22*n*.2
Drucker, P. F., 67, 68, 133, 157, 254
Druskat, V. U., 186
Duesenberry, J., 167
Dula, B., 420–421, 422, 423–424, 425, 426–427, 430–431, 432–433
Dumaine, B., 112
Dunford, R. W., 19
Dunlap, "C. A.", 34, 134
Dunnette, M. D., 162
Dunning, D., 8
Durant, W., 357, 359
Dwyer, J., 46
Dyer, L. M., 22*n*.2

E

Eagly, A. H., 352–353, 354
Eastman, G., 93
Ebbers, B., 90, 257
Eccles, R., 279
Eckholm, E., 372

Edelman, M. J., 253, 267, 306–307

Edison, T., 80

Edmondson, G., 51

Edmunson, 270, 271

Edwards, C., 257

Edwards, M. R., 353

Eichenwald, K., 90, 398, 399

Einstein, A., 25

Elden, M., 155

Ellingsen, D., 155

Elmore, R. F., 9, 22n.3

Elstrom, P., 364

Emery, C. R., 113

Emery, F., 153

Enderud, H. G., 306

Engardio, P., 160

Engle, R. A., 22n.2

Epstein, K., 238–239

Epstein, L. D., 296

Esch, K., 193, 218

Esposito, F., 157

F

Faerman, S. R., 22n.3

Farkas, C. M., 33, 140, 143, 345, 400

Farkas, M. T., 180

Fastow, A., 398

Fayol, H., 48

Feinberg, M., 4, 7

Feinstein, D., 355

Fenn, D. H., 366

Fessenden, F., 46

Fiedler, F. E., 348, 361

Fiedler, K., 22n.2

Fielder, J. H., 399

Fiorina, C., 352, 363–367, 371

Firestone, D., 74

Firestone, W. A., 385–386

Firth, N., 288

Fisher, R., 214, 221–222

Fishman, C., 229, 237–238, 242, 245–246

Fiske, S. T., 22n.2

Fisman, R., 354

Fleishman, E. A., 178

Fletcher, J., 192

Floden, R. E., 304

Flynn, K., 46

Fogel, J., 261

Follett, M. P., 121

Ford, H., 357, 359

Ford, H., II, 364

Forsyth, J., 133

Foti, R. J., 22n.2

Foucault, M., 201

France, M., 398

Frangos, S., 94

Franklin, B., 185, 279

Fredendall, L. D., 113

Freeman, J., 377, 442

Freeman, R. E., 156

Freiberg, J., 143, 255

Freiberg, K., 143, 255

French, J.R.P., 203, 204

Frensch, P. A., 22n.2

Freud, S., 252, 253

Freudenberg, W. R., 9

Fried, I., 367

Friedberg, E., 197

Friedman, R. A., 305

Friedman, T. L., 443

Friesen, P. H., 90–91

Frost, P. J., 204, 208

Fry, A., 376

Fulghum, R., 261–262, 265

Funkhouser, G. R., 262

G

Gabarro, J., 279, 434n.1

Galbraith, J. R., 53, 67, 112

Galileo, 18

Gallos, J. V., 163, 340, 406

Gamson, W. A., 201–202, 233

Gandhi, M., 225, 368, 371

Ganitsky, J., 361

Gardner, H., 177

Gardner, J. W., 343–344, 346, 348

Garland, H., 40

Garman, S., 157

Gates, B., 139, 143, 211–213, 222–223

Geertz, C., 299

Gegerenzer, G., 40

Gerhardt, M. W., 179

Gerstein, M. S., 51

Gerstner, L., 369–370, 401

Gertz, D., 134, 159–160

Ghoshal, S., 59

Giamatti, A. B., 319

Gibb, J. R., 162

Gibson, C. F., 92

Giroux, H., 131

Giuliani, R., 311–312, 341–342, 344, 348, 368

Gladwell, M., 11, 39, 443

Glanz, J., 218

Goffman, E., 10, 253, 269, 296

Goizueta, R., 388–389

Goldberg, L. R., 179

Goleman, D., 176–177, 187, 361

Gonzalez, R., 40

Goodman, D., 315–316

Goodnight, J., 145

Moore, J. F., 235, 236

Morgan, A., 136

Morgan, G., 22n.3

Morganthau, T., 389

Morris, B., 354, 355

Morris, J. R., 134

Morrison, A. M., 12, 340, 352, 406

Moskowitz, M., 137, 140, 143, 340, 400–401, 404

Moss, F., 192

Moulton, B., 214

Mouton, J. S., 178, 246–247, 350

Mulcahy, A., 199

Murphy, J. T., 344

Murray, M., 134

Myers, I., 178

N

Nadler, D. A., 51

Nanus, B., 201, 343, 345, 346, 369

Nardelli, R., 3–4, 6, 8, 135, 376

Natividad, I., 353

Neil, D., 277

Nelson, R. R., 384–385, 441

Neuman, J., 406

Neuman, R. P., 375

Nickerson, J. A., 377

Nickles, D., 263

Niemann, G., 50

Nixon, R., 6

Nohria, N., 374

Nordstrom, E. (Elmer), 275

Nordstrom, E. (Everett), 275

Nordstrom, J., 275

Nordstrom, L., 275

Norman, J. R., 161, 360

Norrish, B., 96

Northcraft, G. B., 439

Novak, 365, 368

Nutt, S. C., 234–235, 387

Nystrom, P. C., 85

O

Obama, B., 340

O'Grady, S., 258

Ohmae, K., 68

Ohme, D. K., 224

O'Keefe, D. L., 253

O'Keefe, G., 315–317

Oldham, G. R., 153

Oliver, T., 388–389

Olsen, J., 253, 301

Olson, J., 399

Omidyar, P., 87, 256–257

O'Neill, T. P., 220, 405–406

Oppel, R. A., 227

O'Reilly, C. A., III, 346

Organ, D. W., 179

Orgogozo, I., 131–132

Ormerod, P., 377

Ortner, S., 253, 254

Osborne, P., 29–31, 32–33, 319–320

Oshry, B., 34, 35, 344

Osterman, P., 144

O'Toole, J., 140, 398

O'Toole, P., 364

Overington, M. A., 293, 299

Overstreet, D., 389

Owen, H., 162, 391–392

Owen, R., 139–140

P

Packard, D., 79, 364, 371

Palmer, I. C., 19

Palmeri, C., 238–239

Palumbo, G., 151

Pande, P. S., 375

Pape, R., 203

Parker, S., 154

Pasquier, S., 199

Paterson, T., 222

Paulson, E., 280

Peck, D., 281

Peck, S., 207

Pelosi, N., 355

Perez, F., 155

Perkins, B., 415, 416, 418–419, 432

Perrow, C., 22n.3, 48, 54, 240, 242, 299

Peters, B. G., 9

Peters, T. J., 320–322, 345, 346, 362, 402

Petzinger, T., 400

Pfeffer, J., 122, 135, 140, 141, 143, 146, 148, 149, 154, 155, 156, 196, 203, 204, 214–215, 232, 243–244, 441

Pichault, F., 214, 216

Pinder, C. C., 125

Porras, J. I., 140, 146, 256, 269, 320–322, 345, 356, 401, 436

Port, O., 160

Porter, E., 227–228

Posner, B. Z., 345, 346, 362–363, 369

Powell, B., 197

Powell, C., 158, 258

Powell, W. W., 59, 296, 297–299, 440, 441

Prahalad, C. K., 400

Pratt, M. G., 11, 37

Pressman, J. L., 9

Weisbord, M. R., 162
Weiss, C. H., 304
Weitzel, J. R., 349
Welch, J., 3, 4, 162–163, 205, 257, 375, 443
Wellins, R. S., 113
West, C., 83
West, T., 280–281, 282–283, 284–285, 288
Westerlund, G., 66
Wheat, A., 157
Wheeler, J. V., 186
White, R., 177–178
White, R. P., 352
White, R. (Robert), 92–93
White, R. W., 123
Whitman, M., 87
Whitmyer, C., 404
Whitsett, D. A., 154
Whyte, W. F., 150

Wiersema, F., 400
Wildavsky, A. B., 9
Wilkinson, A., 134
Williamson, O., 168, 442
Wilson, C., 353
Wilson, J., 353
Wilson, T., 231–232
Wilson, W., 225
Wimpelberg, R. K., 19, 325–326
Winter, S. G., 384–385, 441
Witt, J. L., 72
Wolf, C., 145
Wolfe, C. R., 22n.2
Woodruff, R., 389
Woodward, J., 299
Worley, C., 135
Wozniak, S., 80
Wright, R., 259–260
WuDunn, S., 132

Wyatt, J. B., 259–260, 278n.1

Y

Yang, J. L., 220
Yankelovich, D., 151
Yeltsin, B., 199
Yetton, P. W., 348, 361
Yodgetts, R. M., 320, 323, 324
Yorks, L., 154
Young, C. E., 134
Yukl, G., 178, 346

Z

Zachary, G. P., 211, 212–213, 215
Zellner, W., 398
Zoghi, C., 154
Zott, C., 252, 307

SUBJECT INDEX

A

"Above the Call" citizen award, 258
Absenteeism, 128
Academy of Management Journal (AMJ), 439–440
Accessibility, of human resource leaders, 362–363
Accountability: need for personal, 153; team, 112, 115, 186
Accreditation review, as symbol, 303
Action planning, 56
Action theories, 169–175, 187
Activism, 233–235
Adaptability: human resource dilemmas and, 132–138; and values, 435–443
Adhocracy, 85–86, 88, 89
Administrative component, 78
Administrative Science Quarterly (ASQ), 439–440
Adversarial tactics, 222–224
Adversaries: appealing to self-interests of, 335–336; coercive tactics with, 333–334, 386, 425; letting go of, 225
Advertisements, plans as, 303
Advocacy and inquiry, 172–173
Advocates, 363–367
Afghanistan, 46, 101, 312
Age, organizational, 63–64
Agency problem, 76–77, 384
Agenda setting, 204, 214–216, 425

Agreeableness, 179
Aircraft carrier organization, 45–46, 54
Aircraft industry, 89
Airline industry: aviation ecosystem and, 238–239; cultural turnaround in, 272, 274–275; human resource practices in, 136, 143
Al Quaeda, 24, 29, 101, 248
Alcohol, 129
Alignment: of frames with situations, 12, 317–320; of rewards with business success, 146–148; structural, 382–383
All-channel network, 105–106, 107
Alliances, 204, 218–220
Alternative scenarios, for reframing in action, 328–339. *See also* Scenarios
Ambiguity: in adhocracy, 85; coping with, 36–41; cultural differences in tolerance for, 273; framing and, 36–41; level of, and choice of frame, 318, 319; in organizational change, 383; as organizational characteristic, 32–33; of performance assessment, 208; self-protection and, 33, 173; symbols and, 253. *See also* Uncertainty
American Cast Iron Pipe (Acipco), 137
American Customer Satisfaction Index, 144
American flag, 248
American football teams, 108, 110

Ceremonies, 264, 265–267, 276–277, 286–288, 393, 396, 408–409. *See also* Rituals

Challenger space shuttle, 8, 191–194, 195–196, 207, 208, 213, 218

Change: agenda setting for, 214–216, 425; conflict and, 385–388; culture and, 388–393; difficulties of, 374–379, 393–394; economics' view of, 384–385; emotional intelligence and, 176; getting others to, 171, 184; human resource frame for, 378, 379–382, 394–396; and loss, 388–393; model of, 393–396; political activism and, 233–235; political frame for, 378, 385–388, 395–396; political mapping for, 216–218; power volatility and, 205, 230–232, 245; reframing, 373–396; research and models of, 374; restructuring and, 87–91, 300; stages of, 394–396; structural frame for, 378, 382–383, 395–396; and structural progression in teams, 110, 116; symbolic frame for, 378, 388–393, 394–396; symbols and, 254; systemic approach to, 378–379; systemwide, job enrichment and, 151, 152, 154

Change, rapid. *See* Turbulence and rapid change

Change agents, 219–220, 374, 382, 393

Change strategy, 393–396

Chaos, 254

Charisma, 203–204, 205, 321

Charter, team, 111

Charter schools, 239–240

Chase Manhattan, 321

Cheerleaders, cultivating, 219

Chess masters, 11

Chevrolet, 357, 359

Chief executive officers (CEOs): compensation of, 157; as heroes and heroines, 257, 260–261, 344; politics and, 197. *See also* Senior executives

Children: as partisans, 202; treating workers like, 127, 130–131, 150

China: anti-piracy efforts of, 197–198; Communist Party leaders in, 371–372; contradictory directions in, 34; economic reform in, 133, 145; human rights abuses in, 404–405; isolation of, 220; job security loss in, 145; political opposition in, 202; social networks in, 58; unemployment in, 145

Choice, 435–443

Chrysler Corporation, 360; political leadership in, 363–367

"Cindy Marshall" case study, 327–338, 340, 361

Circle network, 105, 106

Circuit City, 145

Circular causality, 34–35

Cisco Systems, 280

Citibank, 91–93, 321

Civil rights movement, 233

Classic Coke, 388–390

Cluelessness, 3–10, 21

CNN, 6, 73, 295

Coaching, leadership through, 349–350

Coal miners, 152–153

Coalitions: building, 214, 218–220, 387; organizations as, 194, 195, 197, 198–201, 209; power and decision making in, 201–206

Coca-Cola, 157, 197, 388–390

Coercion, 126, 203, 334–335, 366, 386, 425

Coercive isomorphism, 298

Cognitive maps, 22*n*.2

Cola wars, 388–390

Colgate Palmolive, 257

Collaboration, political, 201, 224

Collective bargaining, 304–305. *See also* Labor unions

Collective unconscious, 252, 253

Collectivism, 273

Colleges and universities: downsizing in, 132; isomorphism among, 298; politics of, 196; storytelling in, 259–260; symbolic planning of, 303; symbolic structure of, 300

Colleges and universities, presidents: attitudes of, toward planning, 303; female, 355; power of, 205, 214, 306, 307; presidents of, multiframe thinking of, 325, 326

Columbia Accident Investigation Board, 191, 193–194

Columbia space shuttle, 191–194, 207, 213, 218

COMDEX, 212, 222

Comedy, 295

Commando team, 100–101, 102, 116

Commitment: authorship and, 403; downsizing and, 135, 145; of leaders, 346; requirements, and choice of frame, 318, 319; in teams, 186. *See also* Loyalty

Committees, 180

Common ground: symbols to unite, 318–319, 427; in teamwork, 185

Communication: of belief in people, 362; determining channels of, 216; multiframe approach to, 315; open, 172; in organizational change, 382, 395; through rituals and ceremonies, 266, 286–288; self-protective, 173–175; through stories, 259–261, 270, 370–371; through symbols, 254, 346; of vision, 346, 369–370

Communities of practice, 220

Community, 256

Compaq, 86, 236, 363–367

Compensation, executive, 157

Competing for the Future (Hamel and Prahalad), 400

Competition: human resource frame and, 132–137; myth of fair, 208; playful, 281, 285–286; political frame and, 16, 208, 245. *See also* Conflict

Competitive advantage: diversity as, 282–283; government policy as, 240–241

Complexity: coordination and, 73; coping with, 36–41; environmental, 27; framing and, 36–41; human resource choices and, 132–137; managerial thinking and, 23–42; organizational change and, 378–379; as organizational characteristic, 31; organizational decision making and, 26–27; organizational learning and, 33–36; of organizations, 23–42; and peculiarities of organizations, 29–33; proliferation of, 6–7; rapid cognition and, 12, 37, 38, 39–40; team structure and, 102

Computer engineering team, 280–290

Conditional openness, 224, 225

Conflict: as asset, 185–186, 206–207; avoidance of, 126, 182, 184, 386, 420; centrality of, 195–196, 206, 225; cultural, 207; employee-management, 128–132; eruption of suppressed, 385–386, 420–421; ethics and, 405–407; in groups and teams, 184–186; horizontal, 207; inner, 259; interface, 207; interpersonal, 165–179, 184–186; level of, and choice of frame, 318–319, 320; management of, 207, 333–336; multiframe approach to, 314; multiple lenses and, 313; organizational change and, 385–388; politics and, 195–196, 225, 385–388; in public school case study, 413–434; quasi-resolution of, 200; scenario for handling, 333–336; structural view of, 206, 422–423; vertical, 207. *See also* Politics

Customer-based groupings, 53

Customer satisfaction: employee satisfaction and, 275–277; hiring for, 143; reengineering for, 93–94

Customer service: organizational culture for, 275–277; storytelling about, 261, 276

Cynicism: about dramaturgical/institutional approach, 299; about politics, 189–190, 213, 214, 220, 339

D

Daimler Benz, 367

Dallas Cowboys, 108

Data General, Eagle Group, 280–290

"David King" case study, 411–434

Death notification ritual, 264

Decentralization: coordination and, 73; globalization and, 68; goals and, 65; human resource requirements and, 132–133; in lateral coordination, 60, 62, 73; of operations, 357–358; in self-organized teams, 101. *See also* Lateral coordination

Deception: by frustrated employees, 129–130; in organizations, 29–31, 32, 33, 36; about rules of the game, 226–227; self-protection and, 173

Decision making: access to, as source of power, 204, 406; bargaining and, 221–224, 225; complexity of, 27, 312–313; ethical, 225–227; framing effect and, 40; in groups and teams, 186–187; with Model I theory-in-use, 170, 171, 174–175; multiframe view of, 314; negotiation and, 221–224, 225; participation in, 155–157, 363; planning and, 303; political dynamics in, 195, 196, 200–206; power and, 201–206; reactive and crisis-oriented, 90; relational concepts of, 200–201;

relationships and, 168; role models and, 258–259; "satisficing" view of, 26–27; structure and, 168

Defensiveness, 169–171, 173–175, 424

Delegation, leadership through, 349–350

Dell Computer Corporation, 33, 86, 236

"Delta Corporation," 391–393

Democratic leadership style, 178

Democratic presidential candidates, 340, 354

Democratic workplace, 155–157

"Den mother," 289

Denny's Restaurants, 157

Dependency: and leadership, 343; and power, 196–197, 219. *See also* Interdependence

Deregulation, 89

Developing countries: corporate power in, 246; ethical outsourcing in, 404–405; skill gap in, 133

Diagnosis, making an accurate, 36–41

Differentiation: integration *versus*, 73; in structural design, 52, 69, 422

Digital Equipment (DEC), 86, 89, 212, 366

Dilbert, 121, 131

"Dilbert principle," 8

Dilbert Principle, The (Adams), 443

Directing, leadership through, 349–350

Direction setting: as political skill, 214–216; spiritual leadership and, 436–437; in teams, 186

Discipline of Market Leaders, The (Treacy and Wiersema), 400

Discrimination lawsuits, 157–158

Disk drive industry, 64

Distribution of power, 205–206, 365

Divergent interests. *See* Interests

Diversity: appearance of, 300; as group asset, 185–186, 282–283; politics and, 194; power and, 406; promotion and management of, 157–159, 406

Diversity officer, 300

Division of labor, 47, 52, 59

Divisionalized form, 83–85, 88, 90, 92–93

"Doctor Fights Order to Quit Maine Island," 315–317

Double bind, 36

Doubling up, 129

Doubt, 185

Downsizing: alternatives to, 145–146; benefits and costs of, 134–135; and dumbsizing, 134; reengineering and, 91; trends in, 132, 134, 145

Drama, organizational, 293–308

Dramaturgical theory, 16, 249, 294, 296–299. *See also* Theater

Dreamliner, 266–267

Duke University, women's basketball team, 109

Dukes *vs.* Wal-Mart, 158

Dumpster Ball, 129

DuPont, 93

E

Eagle Group, 280–290

Early wins, 395

Eastern cultures, 40–41

Eastern Europe, 202, 206

Eastman Kodak, 93–94

EBay, 87, 256–257

"Economic Action and Social Structure" (Granovetter), 167–168, 441

Economic Institutions of Capitalism, The (Williamson), 442

Economic theory, 15, 122, 167, 384–385

Ecosystems: business-government, 240–241; organizational fields and, 298; organizations as political agents in, 230, 235–246; political dynamics of, 236–246; public sector, 238–240; society, 242–246

Effective Executive, The (Drucker), 254

Effectiveness: criteria for success *versus*, 324–325; dramaturgical/institutional view of, 297; in human resource leadership, 362–363; leadership, 345–351; managerial, 322–326; of multiframe approaches, 320–325; organizational, 320–322; in political leadership, 364–367; political view of, 232; in structural leadership, 359–360

Effort, 346

Egalitarianism, 155–157, 160

Egg McMuffin, 61

Egypt, 221–222

E-mail, 66

Elite schools, 300

Elites, 204

Emotional intelligence (EI), 175–177, 187, 361

Emotional Intelligence (Goleman), 176–177

Emotions: symbols and, 247–248; theater and, 295

Employee-management conflict, 127–132, 304–305, 319. *See also* Labor unions

Employee orientation rituals, 262, 271, 275, 282

Employee stock ownership plans (ESOPs), 147

Employees: empowering, 93–94, 114, 115, 149–157; frustrated, 127–131; hiring the right, 143; keeping, 143–159. *See also* Human resource management; People

Employment contract, changes in, 132–137

Empowerment: bogus, 152; in high-school principal case study, 424; human resource leadership and, 361, 363; in organizational change, 395, 396; organizational culture for, 270–271; power and, 201; practices

Empowerment: *(Continued)*
for, 149–157, 331; reengineering for, 93–94, 150–151; in self-managing teams, 114, 115, 154–155, 160, 161; self-protection *versus*, 225

Enron: culture of, 269; deception in, 32, 36, 75, 226–227; ethical laxity of, 397–399; executive compensation at, 157; explanations for demise of, 25, 26, 28; financial secrecy of, 149–150; loss of soul of, 397–399, 400; McKinsey and, 9; and politics of getting ahead, 208; preexisting beliefs and, 40; surprise at demise of, 31–32

Enterprise Rent-a-Car, 143

Entrepreneurial culture, 270–271

Entrepreneurs: funding of, symbolic view of, 307–308; internal, 214; myths and stories about, 254–255, 260–261. *See also* Start-up companies

Environment: complexity of, 27; dramaturgical and institutional views of, 297; human needs and, 123–124; organizational ecosystems and, 235–246; organizational power and, 242–246; restructuring due to shifts in, 89, 300, 359–360; as source of uncertainty, 49–50; structure and, 49–50, 51–52, 63, 65, 89, 359–360

Environmental activism, 233, 234

Environmental sustainability, 406–407

Equity model, 147–148

Errors of omission, 182

Ethics: Aristotelian, 401–402; conversations about, 227–228; human resource frame for, 402, 403–405; and moral reasoning, 225–227; political frame for, 402, 405–407; and politics, 207–209, 224–228; principles for, 225–227; reframing, 397–409; soul and, 399–409; structural frame for,

402–403; symbolic frame for, 402, 407–409

Evaluation: multiframe view of, 314; symbolic view of, 304

Evolution, 384–385

Evolutionary Theory of Economic Change, An (Nelson and Winter), 384–385, 441

Excellence: ethic of, 402–403, 427–428, 430; research on organizational, 320–322

Execution (Bossidy and Charan), 443

Executive committees, 57

Executive compensation, linking, to stock price, 77

Existing goals, 66

Expectations: perception and, 36–37, 38, 39–40; performance and, 126; power of, 40; for women *versus* men, 353–354

Experience: openness to, 179; reflection on, 12; as source of power, 203; structural leadership effectiveness and, 359; symbolic leaders' interpretation of, 367, 369

"Experimental Schools Project," 385–386, 387

Experimentation, 185, 360

Expertise: fluid, 12; in high-performing teams, 111–112; structural leadership effectiveness and, 359

External Control of Organizations, The (Pfeffer and Salancik), 243–244, 441

External pressures, 65

Extroversion, 178–179

Exxon, 163, 199

F

Factories: employee autonomy in, 150–151; employee frustration in, 127–131; organizations as, 15–16, 402–403

Failure: of change efforts, 374–379, 393–394; due to cluelessness, 3–10, 18; covering up, 32; fallacious explanations of, 25–29; due to lack of imagination, 19–20; due to political pressures, 191–194, 195–196, 197–198, 207, 213; to prevent catastrophe, 19–20, 23–25; systemic causes of, 25, 28, 378–379; of top-down control, 234–235

Fairy tales, 258

Faith, 407–409, 427, 431

Families: informal norms of, 182–183; as organizations, 7; organizations as, 16, 403–405; power in, 202; socialization in, 166; women executives and, 354–355

Favoritism, 76

Feast of Fools, The (Cox), 278

Featherbedding, 129–130, 138*n*.1

Federal Aviation Administration (FAA), 24–25, 238–239

Federal Bureau of Investigation (FBI): Department of Homeland Security and, 74; relationship of CIA and, 16–18, 29; whistleblower of, 208

Federal Emergency Management Agency (FEMA), 53–54, 72–73, 295

Federal Express (FedEx): human resource management of, 125, 142–143, 146, 362; political strategy of, 241

Federal Register, 373

Feedback, 153, 163

Feeling, as personality dimension, 178–179

Feminine cultures, 273

Fields, organizational, 297–299

Fighter pilots, 258, 263–265

Filters, 11. *See also* Frames

Financial reports, sharing, with employees, 149–150

First impressions, 215–216

Fit: people-organization, 122, 137, 143; structure, 47, 89

Flatter structures, 67

Followers: and power of leaders, 306–307; readiness and maturity of, 349–350; and servant-leadership, 361, 369, 436

FON, 361

Football teams, American, 108, 110

Ford Motor Company, 51, 128, 270, 271, 357, 359, 360, 364

Foreign Corrupt Practices Act, 401

Fortune, 149; America's most admired companies, 4; best companies for minorities, 157; best companies to work for in America, 122, 137, 275; global 100 companies, 353; most admired global airlines, 275; most admired global company, 275

Founders: myths and stories about, 254–255, 260–261, 371, 391–392; as social architects, 356

Four-frame model: applied, in high-school principal case study, 428–433; development of, 14; government agency illustration of, 16–18; in management books, 14–15; multiframe thinking with, 18–20, 22, 41; overview of, 18, 21; pluralistic approach to, 41. *See also* Frames; Human resource frame; Multiframe thinking; Political frame; Structural frame; Symbolic frame

Frames and framing: breaking, 12–14; changing *versus* conserving, 39–41; concept of, 10–12; for coping with ambiguity and complexity, 36–41; error and, 12, 37; for ethics, 402–409; influence of, on reality, 40, 42*n*.2; integrating, 311–326, 393–396, 411–434; leadership according to, 355–372; managers' preferences in, 325–326; matching, to situations, 12, 317–320,

Frames and framing: *(Continued)* 338–340; model of four organizational, 14–21; multiframe thinking and, 18–20, 22, 41; for organizational change, 377–396; pluralistic approach to, 40–41; rapid cognition and, 11–12, 37, 38, 39–40; as source of power, 204; terms and metaphors for, 10–11, 22*n*.2. *See also* Four-frame model; Human resource frame; Multiframe thinking; Political frame; Reframing; Structural frame; Symbolic frame

Framing effect, 40

France, 131–132

Free-market capitalism, 245–246

Friendly-fire incident, 36–37, 38, 39, 182, 193

Friends, 204, 218–220, 225, 421–422

Frontline, 120

Frustration, employee, 127–131

Funders, managing impressions with, 307–308

Future: leadership and, 435–443; and letting go of past, 390–391; vision and, 255–256, 369–370

Future search, 162

FzioMed, 110

G

Gain-sharing plans, 147

Games, plans as, 303

Garbage-can scripts, 301–302

Gay employees, 158–159

Gazprom, 199

Geico, 254

Gender: culture and, 273; discrimination and, 158, 328, 340, 354; interpersonal dynamics and, 169, 263, 328; and leadership, 351–355; organizational structure and, 86; power and, 353–354; and reframing, 338–339; stereotypes, 352, 353

General Electric (GE), 3, 80, 199, 205, 321; Six Sigma at, 374, 375; survival of, 245; Work-Out conferences of, 162–163

General managers, 322, 323

General Managers, The (Kotter), 320, 322, 323, 324

General Motors (GM), 93, 163, 246, 270, 271, 346; management by wandering around in, 362–363; NUMMI joint venture of, 160–161, 360; Saturn division of, 113–115, 360; structural leaders of, 356–360

Generality, 227

Genetic predispositions, 123–124

Geographically-based groupings, 53

Geographically-dispersed groupings, 67–68

Germany, 143, 367

Gillette, 245

Glasnost, 205–206

Glass ceiling, 340, 353–355

Global corporations: cultural differences and, 272–274; power of, 229–230, 237–238, 242–246; structural design of, 58, 59, 65, 68

Globalization: organizational complexity and, 6, 438; and person-organization relationship, 132–138, 145; and society-organization relationship, 242–246

GLOBE, 272

GM, 51

Goal-setting theory, 122

Goals and goal-setting: defining specific and measurable performance, in teams, 111, 114–115; multiframe approach to, 315; performance control and, 56; politics and, 196, 197, 198–199, 200–201; shared, 172; structure and, 63, 65–66, 76, 198–199; in teams, 111, 185; unstated types of, 66; vague or fuzzy, 297, 298, 318; values *versus*, 255

Goldman Sachs, 113

Good to Great (Collins), 269, 320, 321, 346, 443

Google: creation of, 279–280; and FON, 361; human resource management at, 139, 143, 377; structure of, 10, 113

Google Scholar (GS), 440

Gore, W. L., 113

Government: ecosystems of, 238–241; failure of, to improve organizations, 9–10; politics and, 197–198, 199, 234–235, 238–241; women leaders in, 355. *See also* Public sector

Government agencies: bumbling of, 4–5; bureaucratic rigidity in, 76; deception in, 29–31, 32–33, 36; ecosystems of, 238–241; flaws of restructured, 72–73; goal setting in, 198, 199; political mapping of, 216–218; politics and, 192–193, 195–196, 198, 199, 238–241; strategies for influencing, 241; suboptimization of, 53–54; as theaters, 301. *See also* Public sector

Grassroots action, 233–235

Great Depression, 360, 367

Greatest hits, from organization studies: *Behavioral Theory of the Firm, A* (Cyert and March), 200–201; citation analysis of, 42*n*.1, 439–440; "Economic Action and Social Structure" (Granovetter), 167–168; "Evolutionary Theory of Economic Change, An" (Nelson and Winter), 384–385; *External Control of Organizations, The* (Pfeffer and Salancik), 243–244; "Iron Cage Revisited, The" (DiMaggio and Powell), 297–299; *Organization* (March and Simon), 26–27; *Organizations in Action* (Thompson), 49–50; "Theory of the Firm" (Jensen and Meckling), 76–77

Green activism, 233, 234

Grieving, 252–253, 264. *See also* Loss

Griping, 393

Group interventions, 162–163

Groupings, in structural design, 52–54

Groups: assets and liabilities of, 180; culture of, 279–291; decision making in, 186–187; forms of, 103–106, 180; in high-school principal case study, 416–434; informal networks in, 183–184; informal norms in, 182–183; informal roles in, 181–182, 288–289; interpersonal conflict in, 184–186, 424; leadership of, 186–197; process and dynamics of, 180–187; task and process levels of, 180. *See also Team headings*

Guiding team, 395

Gulf War, early 1990s, 46

H

Hardball, 194

Hardy Boys, 283, 284, 285, 286

Harley-Davidson, 113, 252

Harvard Business Review, 176

Harvard Business School, 144

Harvard University: attempted restructuring of, 71, 83; female president of, 355; structure of, 60, 62, 64, 65, 68, 82–83; symbolic elements of, 254, 300

Headless giants, 90

Headquarters: divisional managers' relationship with, 84–85; local managers' relationship with, 81–82

Healing, 252–253, 390–391

Health care insurers, 240

Heart: ethics and, 402; giving as a matter of, 308; symbols and, 248. *See also* Soul; Spirit and spirituality

Heart of Change, The (Kotter and Cohen), 394

"Helen Demarco" case study, 29–31, 32–33, 36, 319–320

Heroes and heroines: leaders and, 342, 344, 437; as symbolic elements, 257–259, 260–261, 264, 276; values and, 437

Hertz, 143

Hewlett-Packard (HP), 321; Compaq merger negotiations in, 363–367; founders of, 356, 364, 371; human resource management in, 362; political leadership in, 363–367; structure of, 75, 79, 83

Hierarchy: decision making and, 168; of motives, 225–226; of needs, 124–125, 126, 424; promotion in, 130; system blindness in, 35; in teams, 104–105; web of inclusion *versus*, 86–87

High-performing teams: characteristics of, 111–112, 114–115; culture and, 279–291; political frame for, 281; secrets of success of, 281–282, 289–290; structure and, 111–113, 280–281; symbolic frame for, 279–291. *See also* Teams

High-school principal case study, 411–434

High-technology firms: adhocracy in, 86; lateral coordination forms in, 57, 59, 65

Higher education institutions. *See* Colleges and universities

Hillcrest Corporation, 165–166

Hippocratic Oath, 11

Hiring, 143, 270–271

History: lack of, in culture, 426–427; releasing negative, 393; symbolic use of, 336, 370, 371–372, 391–393

Home Depot, 3–4, 135, 257

Homeland Security, Department of: Hurricane Katrina and, 5, 53–54, 72–73; structural flaws of, 72–73,

74. *See also* U.S. homeland defense organizations

Homework, structural leadership effectiveness and, 359

Honesty, 346

Honorific goals, 66

Hope, 252, 308, 369

Hope Dies Last (Terkel), 308

Horse trading, 219–220, 221, 426

Hospitals: client-based groupings in, 53; divisionalized form in, 83; redundancy in, 74; restructuring of, 94–96

House-system school, 411–434

How to Get Rich (Trump), 443

Human capacity: and employment contract, 132–137; and work redesign, 152–154

Human needs: hierarchy of, 124–125, 126, 424; for self-actualization, 127–131, 226; theories of, 122–126

Human psyche, 252, 253

Human resource frame, 117–187; assumptions of, 121–132, 136; for ethics, 402, 403–405; for FBI-CIA relationship, 17; global forces and dilemmas in, 132–138, 145; for high-school principal case, 424, 429, 432; interpersonal dynamics in, 165–179, 187; leadership in, 356, 360–363; management book based on, 15, 16; for managerial effectiveness, 323, 324–325, 326; for organizational change, 378, 379–382, 394–396; for organizational effectiveness, 321, 322; organizational metaphor for, 16, 18, 402; to organizational processes, 314–315; overview of, 18, 21, 117–118; pioneers of, 121–122, 139–140; for power, 201; scenario for, 331–333; situations appropriate for, 318–320; strengths and weaknesses of, 339, 356, 360–363. *See also* Employees; People

Human resource management: barriers to progressive, 141, 161–162; basic strategies for, 142; comprehensive approach to, 159–161; credo or philosophy for, 141–143, 424; global forces and, 132–138, 145; high-involvement practices for, 141–164; improving, 139–164; invest-in-people approach to, 135–138, 139–164; lean-and-mean approach to, 134–135, 136–138; for loyalty *versus* adaptability, 132–138; organization development and, 162, 163–164; traditional, assembly-line practice of, 127–132. *See also* Employees; People

Human resource requirements: changes in, 67–68, 132–134; gap in availability and, 133

Humility, 346

Humor, 268–269, 285–286, 400, 403

Hurricane Katrina: bumbled response to, 5–6, 72–73, 295; Homeland Security organization and, 53–54, 72–73; U2 video about, 295

Hustlers, 356, 363

Hygiene factors, 153

I

"I Have a Dream" speech (King), 255–256, 369, 426

IBM, 274; ecosystem of, 236; Microsoft and, 211, 222–223; organization development and, 163; structure of, 75; values of, 369–370, 401

Image. *See* Appearance and image

Imagination: failure of, 19–20; for restructuring, 93

Imitation, 297–299

Implementation, structural leadership and, 360

Implicit theories, 22*n*.2

Impressions, managing, 307–308. *See also* Theater

Improvisational jazz, 109

Impulsive organizations, 90

In Search of Excellence (Peters and Waterman), 320–321

Inclusion, web of, 86–87, 95–96, 105

Incompetence, 8

Indifference, zones of, 205

Individualism, 273

Industrial analysts, 48

Infallibility, doubting one's, 185, 186

Influence: of authorities and partisans, 201–202, 204, 209, 233, 235; building, through networking and coalitions, 218–220, 425–426; inquiry and, 366; with Model I theory-in-use, 170, 171; of organizations *versus* environment, 242–246; sources of power and, 203–205, 233–235. *See also* Power

Informal cultural players, 288–289

Informal exchanges, 57, 286–288

Informal group norms, 182–183

Informal networks, 183–184, 220. *See also* Networks

Informal roles, 181–182, 288–289

Information: agenda setting and, 214–215; ambiguity and, 33, 173–175; ignoring or misinterpreting, 3–10, 174–175; political influence and, 218; providing, for employees, 149–150; as source of power, 203

Information revolution: job changes and, 133; lateral networks and, 58–59; organizational complexity and, 6

Information technology: decision making and, 312; structure and, 63, 64, 66–67

Initiating-structure style, 178

Initiation rituals, 262–263, 271, 275, 282

Innovation: conflict and, 207; control and, 375–376; culture for, 270–271,

Innovation: *(Continued)*
  376–377; process of, 374–379; symbolic frame for, 391–393. *See also* Creativity
Inquiry, advocacy and, 172–173
Inspiration, leadership for, 346
Institutional Shareholders Services (ISS), 366
Institutional theory, 249, 296–297
"Institutionalized Organizations" (Meyer and Brown), 441
Institutions and Organizations (Scott), 442
Integration: differentiation *versus*, 73; of frames, 311–326, 393–396, 411–434; structural, 52, 69, 422–423. *See also* Coordination
Intel, 236
Intellectual property protection, 197–198
Intelligence, 346
Interdependence: *versus* autonomy, 75; and politics, 194, 196–197, 213; teamwork and, 106–109. *See also* Autonomy
Interdisciplinary care teams, 96
Interests: and centrality of conflict, 194, 195–196, 206, 225; and coalitions, 198–199, 209–210; focus on, *versus* positions, 221–222; mapping, 217–218
Interface conflict, 207
Internal schemata, 38–39
International Harvester, 149
Interorganizational coordination: complexity of, 31; networks for, 58–59; suboptimization and, 53–54
Interpersonal competence, 169, 175, 187
Interpersonal relationships, 165–179; building political, 214, 218–220, 365–366; dynamics of, 168–177, 187, 424; emotional intelligence and, 175–177, 187; in groups and teams, 180–187; key questions of, 168–169; Model I, 169–171, 173–175, 184, 424;

Model II, 172–175; negotiation and bargaining in, 221–224; personal contact in, 416–420; social embeddedness and, 167–168
Intimidation, 334–335
Introversion, 178–179
Intruder story, 12–13
Intuition: personality dimension, 178–179; in reading or responding to situations, 38, 313, 317, 319, 411
Invest-in-people strategy: barriers to, 141, 161–162; benefits of, 135–136, 140, 141; human resource management for, 139–164; *versus* lean-and-mean strategy, 136–138; pioneer of, 139–140
Iran-Contra scandal, 17
Iraq: antiwar movement and, 234; complexity of change in, 378; contractors in, 148; friendly-fire incident over, 36–37, 38, 39, 182, 193; lack of authority in, 202, 206; soccer team of, 279; stories in, 371; technology and resistance in, 66–67
Iron Cage Revisited, The (DiMaggio and Powell), 297–299, 441
Islam, 248
Isomorphism, 297–299
Israel, 221–222
Issue framing, 204
Ivy League schools, 300

J

J. D. Power Award, 275
Japan: business-politics intersection in, 241; manufacturing processes of, 160; manufacturing standards in, 55; religious pluralism in, 40–41; Seibu ceremony in, 265–266
Jazz, improvisational, 109

Leadership *(Continued)* 211–228, 333–336, 356, 363–367; rational-technical approach to, 20–21; reframing, 341–372, 435–443; shared, 186–187; structural, 329–331, 356–360; symbolic, 336–338, 356, 367–372. *See also* Management

Leadership styles: in human resource frame, 356, 360–363; models of, 177–179, 348–350; in political frame, 356, 363–367; in structural frame, 356–360; in symbolic frame, 356, 367–372; of women *versus* men, 352–353

Lean-and-mean strategy, 134–135, 136–138

Learning: in complex organizations, 33–36; individual *versus* organizational, 34; with Model I theory-in-use, 170; in organizations, 148–149. *See also* Organizational learning

Lebanon, 202

Legitimacy: appearance and, 296; authority and, 330, 343; isomorphism and, 299

Lenses: frames and, 11. *See also* Frames

Leveraged buyout (LBO), 236–237, 318

Levi Strauss, 404–405

Liberia, 202

Likert Scale, 164*n*.1

Lincoln Electric, 145–146

Linux, 10, 87

Listening, 332, 366, 382, 404, 416–420

Literary criticism, 296

Lobbying, 241

Longwall method, 152, 153

Loss, 388–393. *See also* Grieving

Lotus, 236

Love, 400, 401, 403–405

Loyalty: downsizing and, 135, 138; human resource dilemmas and, 132–138;

organizational culture and, 270–271. *See also* Commitment

M

Machine bureaucracy, 80–82, 88, 89, 90; restructuring, to divisionalized form, 92–93. *See also* Bureaucracy

Mackey Middle School, 368

Magic, 253

Mahdi army, 203

Managed health care, 75–76, 240

Management: artistic approach to, 20–21, 433–434, 435–443, 437–438; cultural differences and, 273–274; failed efforts to upgrade, 9; leadership *versus*, 343–344; multiframe thinking and, 19–20; rational-technical approach to, 20–21; shortcomings of, in complexity, 23–42; theatrical approach to, 293–308; traditional, and self-actualization needs, 127–131. *See also* Leadership

Management books: best-sellers, 380–381, 400, 441–443; four frames represented in, 14–15; on stories and leadership, 259

Management by wandering around, 362–363

Management science, 15

Management styles, 177–179

Managerial grid, 346–347, 350

Managers: ambivalence of, toward progressive human resource practices, 161–162; assumptions of, about people, 125–126; cluelessness problem of, 3–10, 18; compensation of, 157; ethical principles for, 224–228; frame preferences of, 325–326; group dynamics and, 180–187; interpersonal relationships and, 165–179; leaders *versus*, 343–344; multiframe thinking of, 311–326, 411–434; myth of "super," 312–313; personal styles of, 177–179; as politicians, 211–228, 244; power gap of, 204; realities of life for, 312–313, 411; reengineering failures and, 91; reframing in action for, 327–340, 411–434; research on effectiveness of, 322–326; sense-making by, 36–41; symbolic role of, 244. *See also* Leaders; Senior executives

Managing Public Policy (Lynn), 320, 322–323, 324

Manipulative strategies, 225, 226–227, 334–335, 340

Manufacturing jobs, decline in, 133

Maps and mapping: for coping with ambiguity and complexity, 36–41; frames and, 11, 22n.2; political, 214, 216–218, 365, 426; rapid cognition and, 12, 37; system, 34. *See also* Frames

March of Dimes, 76

Marion Laboratories, 136

Marketing concept, 244, 245–246

Markets and Hierarchies (Williamson), 442

Marriott Hotels, 260–261

Mary Kay Cosmetics, 266

Masculine cultures, 273

Maslow's hierarchy of needs, 124–125, 126, 424

Matrix structures, 58, 60, 358, 422

Matsushita, 68

Matthew 16:26, 409n.1

Mazda, 146

McDonald's: action planning at, 56; structural dilemma of, 81–82; structure of, 60–61, 63–64, 65, 68, 74, 80; symbols of, 254

McKinsey & Co., 9

McWane, 120–121, 137

Meaning: rituals and, 261–262, 286–287; spirit and, 290–291, 409; symbols and, 248, 252, 253, 277, 389–390, 427. *See also* Sense-making; Spirit; Symbolic frame; Symbols

Meaningful work, 153–154, 407–409

Medal of Honor, 256

Medical diagnosis, 11–12

Meetings: conflict in, 420–421; formal and informal, 57; ground rules for, 423; for lateral coordination, 57, 60; multiframe approach to, 315; symbolic focus of, 287, 301–302

Memos, 218

Men: culture and, 273; interpersonal dynamics and, 169, 263, 328; leadership styles and, 352

Men and Women of the Corporation (Kanter), 442

Mental maps. *See* Frames; Maps

Mental models: for ambiguous and complex situations, 36–41; concept of frames and, 10–11, 22n.2; tenacity of, 8. *See also* Frames

Mercedes, 270, 271

Merck, 321, 399, 400

Mergers: political leadership for, 363–367; politics in, 231–232

Messes, 41. *See also* Ambiguity; Complexity

Metaphors: for frames, 10–11, 22n.2, 402; for organizations, 15–16, 18, 296, 402; root, 22n.2; as symbolic elements, 268–269, 274

Metric system adoption, 9–10, 373–374

Microkids, 281, 284

Microsoft, 197; ecosystem of, 236; human resource management at, 143, 376–377; IBM and, 211, 222–223; political management at, 211–213, 221, 222–223; structure of, 34, 113

Microsoft Windows, 87; NT, 211–213, 221, 222

Middle East negotiations, 221–222

Middle managers, restructuring and, 88

Might-makes-right approach, 184

Mimetic isomorphism, 298

Mindlessness, 19

Minorities, 340, 406

Mintzberg's model, 78–87, 88, 93, 97

Misanthrope, The (Molière), 220

Mission, team, 111, 115

Mission statements, 255, 302

Model I theory-in-use, 169–171, 173–175, 184, 424

Model II theory-in-use, 172–175

Model T, 357, 359

Modern management techniques, dramaturgical view of, 293–294, 296, 297

Modern Times, 127

Moments of truth, 363

Monocratic bureaucracy, 48

Moral mazes, 208

Moral reasoning: conversation about, 227–228; questions and tests of, 226–227; stages of, 225–226

Morale: downsizing and, 134, 135; job redesign and, 153–154, 156; organizational change for, 376–377; participation and, 150–152; structure and, 48, 50–51, 96, 104, 105, 113

Morality: politics and, 207–209, 224–228; taught in stories, 260. *See also* Ethics

Morton Thiokol Corporation, 192–193, 195–196, 208, 218

Motivation: in invest-in-people approach, 136; job enrichment and, 153–154; leadership style and, 350; in lean-and-mean approach, 135; multiframe view of, 315; requirements, and choice of frame, 318; team performance and,

280, 281; in traditional assembly-line management, 130–131

Motivators, 153

Motorola, 148, 160, 374

MS-DOS, 211, 222–223

Multicentric organization, 59

Multiframe thinking: concepts of, 18–20, 21, 22, 41; for leaders and managers, 309, 311–326, 411–434, 437–438; and matching frames to situations, 317–320; for organizational processes, 313–317; research on effectiveness and, 320–326. *See also* Four-frame model; Frames; Reframing

Multinational corporations. *See* Global corporations

Music, 408–409

Mutual gains bargaining, 305

Mutuality, 226–227

Myers-Briggs Type Indicator, 178–179

"Myopia of Learning, The" (Levinthal and March), 442

Myths and legends: leadership models as, 350–351; as symbolic elements, 254–257, 370–371

N

Nabisco, 231–233, 236–237

Naïveté, 213, 221

Narcissism, 346

National Aeronautics and Space Administration (NASA), 192–193, 195–196, 221

National Bureau of Standards, 373

National Health Service Corps (NHSC), 315–317

Natural selection, 384–385

Nature-nurture interplay, 123–124

NBC, *Nightly News*, 258

Near-death experiences, 270

Need, human, 122–126

Negotiation: dramaturgical view of, 305; ethical issues of, 224–228; in political frame, 196, 197, 209, 366; skill of, 214, 221–224

Nepotism, 32

Networks: all-channel or star, 105–106, 107; building, 214, 218–220, 425–426; circle, 105, 106; geographically dispersed, 67–68; human resource requirements and, 132–133; informal, 183–184, 220; information technology and, 67; as lateral coordination form, 58–59, 60; political, 204, 214, 218–220, 425–426; as source of power, 204, 425–426

Neurolinguistic programming, 253

Neuroticism, 179

New Coke, 388–390

New Lanark, Scotland, knitting mill, 140

New Patterns of Management (Likert), 163

New United Motors Manufacturing, Inc. (NUMMI), 160–161, 360

New York City: fire and police departments, 46, 53, 342; Mayor Giuliani and, 311–312, 341–342, 348, 368. *See also* World Trade Center

New York Stock Exchange, 227

New York Times, 83, 137, 198, 241

Newcomers: in reframing case studies, 327–338, 411–434; reframing for, 340; rituals for, 262, 271, 275, 282; symbols and, 337, 391–393

Newsweek, 258

9/11 terrorist attacks: agency restructuring after, 72–73; antiwar movement and, 234; failure to prevent, 19–20, 23–25, 27–28, 29; FBI-CIA relationship and, 17, 29; heroes of, 258, 342, 344; Mayor Giuliani and, 311–312, 341–342, 348, 368; organizational complexity and, 31, 33; organizational deception and, 32; police and fire department coordination in, 46, 53; standard operating procedures and, 55; symbols and, 252–253, 319. *See also* World Trade Center

No Child Left Behind Act, 239, 240

Nordstrom, 275–277

Normative isomorphism, 298

Norms, informal group, 182–183

North American Aerospace Defense Command (NORAD), 24–25

Northern Commercial, 276

Norway: Industrial Democracy Project of, 153; participative decision making in, 155

Novo-Nordisk, 10

Nucor Corporation, 119–120, 121, 147, 156

NUMMI, 160–161, 360

Nursing, restructuring of, 94–96

O

OAG (Official Airline Guide), 275

Office, The, 131

Offshoring, 133, 404–405

One-the-job training, 148–149

Open-book management, 149–150

Open space, 162

Open systems, organizations as, 31

Openness: conditional, 224, 225; in ethical decision making, 227; to experience, 179; of human resource leaders, 362–363

Operating core: defined, 78; of machine bureaucracy, 81–82; of professional bureaucracy, 82–83; and restructuring, 88; of simple structure, 79

Opinion leaders, 204

Opportunity structures, 340

Organization chart: egalitarianism and, 156; of interconnected teams, 154; traditional, 44, 78, 86

Organization development (OD), 162, 163–164

Organizational change. *See* Change

Organizational design: political dimension of, 232–233; restructuring and, 71–97; as stage design, 299–301; structural assumptions and, 47; structural configurations for, 78–89. *See also* Structure

Organizational Ecology (Hannan and Freeman), 442

Organizational fields, 297–299

Organizational learning: complexity and, 33–36; evolution to, 201; need for, 33; perspectives on, 34–35

"Organizational Learning" (Levitt and March), 442

Organizational processes: multiframe perspective on, 313–317; political dimensions of, 232–233; as theater, 301–308

Organizational theory: consolidation of, into four-frame model, 14, 41; pluralistic approach to, 41; symbolic frame and, 253

Organizations: ambiguity of, 32–33, 173; autonomy *versus* influence of, 242–246; as coalitions, 194, 195, 197, 198–201, 209; complexity of, 6–10, 12, 23–42; dark side of, 7, 242–246; deception in, 29–31, 32, 33, 36; democracy in, 155–157; ecosystems of, 230, 235–246; failure of improvement strategies for, 8–10; fit between people and, 122, 137, 143; goal-setting in, 198–201; metaphors for, 15–16, 18, 296, 402; as multiple realities, 313–317; new models of, 10; people and, 119–138; as political agents, 230, 235–246; as political arenas, 230–235, 246, 386–387; power distributions in, 205–206; power of, 229–230, 237–238, 242–246;

reframing change in, 373–396; relationships in, 166–167; research on effective and successful, 320–322; soul and spirit in, 399–409, 428–433; symbolic elements in, 251–269; as temples, 16, 367–372, 407–409; as theaters, 293–308, 367; universal peculiarities of, 29–33; virtues and drawbacks of, 6–10. *See also* Large organizations

Organizations (March and Simon), 26–27, 442

Organizations in Action (Thompson), 49–50, 441

Orientations, 11. *See also* Frames

OS/2, 211, 212

OSHA, 137

Outsiders: power sharing with, 406; reframing for, 340

Outsourcing, trends in, 132, 135, 137

Overbounded systems, 205–206

Oversight: in divisionalized form, 84–85; by stock analysts, 77

Oversimplification: and complexity, 27, 200; in explaining organizational problems, 25–29

Ownership: agency problem and, 77; barriers to, 147, 161–162; downside of, 148; open-book management and, 147, 150; reward practices of, 146–148

P

Palio, 251–252

Paradigms, 22*n*.2

Part-time employees, 132, 137

Participation: in decision making, 155–157, 363; encouraging, 150–152; failure of, 152; in high-school principal case study, 424; in organizational change, 379–382; ownership and, 147; in self-managing teams, 114, 154–155, 160, 161

Particularism, 54–55

Parties, 287

Partisans: authorities and, 201–202, 204, 209, 233, 235; sources of power of, 203–205, 233–235

Passion, 346, 428

Passivity, 129

Patriarchal organizations, 48

Patterns, changing *versus* conserving, 39–41

Pay differentials, 157

Pay for skills, 155

Pay practices, 144–145

Peace Corps, 369

Peak performance, 279–280. *See also* High-performing teams

People: blaming, 25–27, 28, 32, 73, 193, 194, 422; dimension of, in leadership styles, 348–350, 352; dimension of, in managerial grid, 346–347; exploitation of, 120–121, 122; fit between organizations and, 122, 137; good practices for, 141–159; hiring the right, 143; investing in, 135–138, 139–164; needs of, 122–131, 424; and organizations, 119–138; self-actualization needs of, 127–131, 226; as source of uncertainty, 50. *See also* Employees; Human resource frame; Human resource management

Pepsi, 388

Perceiving, as personality dimension, 178–179

Perception, expectations and, 36–37, 38, 39–40

Performance: assessment of, ambiguity of, 208; dramaturgical view of, 296; expectations and, 126; overestimating, 8; peak, 279–280; profit-sharing plans and, 147; review, 377; team culture and, 269, 279–291; team structure and, 111–113, 280–281. *See also* High-performing teams

Personal computer industry, 236, 366–367

Personal power, 203–204

Personal roles, 181

Personality: blaming failure on flawed, 7, 25–26, 28, 32; informal group roles and, 181–182; and organization, 126–132; styles, 177–179; tests, 178–179

Perspectives: frames and, 11. *See also* Frames

Persuasion, 171, 366–367

Petrochemical industry accidents, 148

Pfizer, 321

Pharmaceutical industry: business-government ecosystems of, 240; conflict management in, 387; human resource practices in, 136; research and development process in, 110

Philadelphia Eagles, 108

Philips, 68

Philosophy, 296

Physicians, rapid cognition of, 11–12

Pilots, 39, 55. *See also* Fighter pilots

Pipe manufacturing, human resource approaches in, 137

Piracy, 197–198

Pixar, 57

Placebo effect, 40

Plans and planning: multiframe view of, 313, 314; symbolic/dramaturgical view of, 296, 302–303; in vertical coordination, 56

Play, 268–269, 281, 285–286

Pluralism, in worldview, 40–41

Point-of-sale terminals, 56

Polaris missile project, 293–294

Policies, in vertical coordination, 54–55

Policymaking: corporate influence on, 240–241; and organizational improvement, 8, 9–10

Political action: bottom-up, 233–234; top-down, 234–235
Political action committees, 241
Political agents, organizations as, 230, 235–246
Political appointees, research on effectiveness of, 322–323, 324, 325
Political arenas, 230–235, 246, 386–387
Political conventions, 267
Political correctness, 208
Political frame, 189–246; assumptions of, 194–198, 201; centrality of conflict in, 195–196, 205, 206; for ethics, 402, 405–407; for FBI-CIA relationship, 17, 29; goals and, 63, 65–66, 76, 198–201; for high-school principal case study, 425–426, 429, 432; leadership in, 356, 363–367; management book based on, 15, 16; for managerial effectiveness, 323, 324, 325, 326; for managers, 211–228; morality in, 207–209, 224–228; for organizational change, 378, 385–388, 395–396; for organizational effectiveness, 321–322; organizational metaphor for, 16, 18, 402; for organizational processes, 314–315; for organizations as arenas, 230–235, 246, 386–387; for organizations as political agents, 230, 235–246; overview of, 18, 21, 189–190; scenario for, 333–336; situations appropriate for, 318–320; strengths and weaknesses of, 339, 356; for team performance, 281
Political maps, 214, 216–218, 365, 426
Political science, 14, 16, 253
Politicians: female, 355; managers as, 211–228, 244, 333–336; principles for effective, 364–367; skills of, 211–224, 235–236; team leader as, 285
Politics: authorities and, 201–202, 209, 233, 235; blaming, for organizational

problems, 28; constructive, 169, 208–209, 210, 211–228, 425–426; ethics and, 207–209, 224–228; of getting ahead, 207–209; managers and, 211–228; negative attitudes toward, 189–190, 213, 220, 405; organizational failures and, 191–194, 195–196; partisans and, 201–205, 233; positive, 225–226, 228; as realistic and inevitable process, 190, 194, 201, 213, 220, 225; relational concepts and, 200–201; suppression of, 205–206. *See also* Power
Population ecology, 385
Position: jockeying for, 196, 197–198, 231; leadership and, 343, 344–345, 361; power, 202, 203, 204, 209, 361
Positional bargaining, 221
Post-it notes, 256, 376
Postconventional moral reasoning, 225
Power: as asset, 195–197; authority and, 201–202, 209, 233, 235, 343; building coalitions of, 218–220; corporate, 229–230, 237–238, 242–246; and decision making, 201–206; defined, 196; dependency and, 196–197, 219; distribution of, 205–206, 365; dramaturgical view of, 306–307; ethics and, 405–407; gender and, 353–354; in high-school principal case study, 425–426; human resource perspective on, 201; leadership and, 343, 366; mapping and assessing, 217–218, 220, 365; negative attitudes toward, 190; in overbounded and underbounded systems, 205–206; partisan, 201–205, 233; political frame and, 16, 195–197, 201–206; reality of, 201; scenarios for using, 333–336; self-protection and, 225; sharing, 405–407; sources and types of, 203–205, 233–235; structural

perspective on, 201; team performance and, 281; thirst for, as source of organizational problems, 28, 29; volatility of, 205, 230–232, 245. *See also* Authority; Influence; Political frame; Politics

Power distance, 272

Power-sharing, ownership and, 147

Preconceptions, 39–41. *See also* Frames; Mental models

Preconventional moral reasoning, 225

Presentation. *See* Appearance and image

Presentations, 219–220, 307–308

Presidents. *See* Colleges and universities, presidents; U.S. presidents

Pret à Manger, 10

"Price pyramid" cars, 359

Pride, 120

"Priest" or "priestess" role, 288

Primal Leadership (Goleman, McKee, Boyatzis), 177

Prince, The (Machiavelli), 16, 377–378

Princeton University, 300, 355

Prisms, 11. *See also* Frames

Prisoners of war (POWs), 258

Private sector, public sector intersection with, 240–241

Problem solving: bargaining and, 221–224, 225; with Model I theory-in-use, 170, 171, 184; negotiation and, 221–224, 225; relational concepts of, 200–201

Problemistic search, 201

Problems, solutions as future, 32

Process-based groupings, 53

Procter & Gamble (P&G), 220, 245

Product-based groupings, 53

Product cycle time, rapid, 31, 132

Productivity: job enrichment and, 154; participation and, 151–152; under

traditional management practices, 127–131

Professional bureaucracy, 82–83, 88, 89

Profit-sharing plans, 147–148

Program Evaluation Review Techniques (PERT), 293

Program Planning and Budgeting Systems (PPBS), 293

Program reviews, symbolic, 304

Programs, to deal with complexity, 27

Promotion: from within, 146; in factory, 130

Prophets, 367–372

Psychological withdrawal, 129

Psychology, 14, 16, 26; of human needs and motivation, 122–132, 424; and personality/management styles, 177–179; of self-actualization needs, 126–131; and symbolic frame, 253

Public schools: ecosystems of, 239–240; employee skill deficits and, 133; external pressures on, 65; goals of, 66; heroes in, 257; house-system approach to, 411–434; isomorphism among, 298; power in, 210; reform efforts for, 9, 82, 234–235, 239–240, 385–386, 387; reframing case study in, 411–434; symbolic structure of, 299–300; women's positions in, 353. *See also* School principals

Public sector: ecosystems of, 238–241; goal-setting in, 199; politics in, 197–198, 199, 238–240; private sector intersection with, 240–241; symbolic evaluation in, 304. *See also* Government; Government agencies

Publix, 145

Q

QDOS, 211, 222

Quadgraphics, 408–409

Quality, job enrichment and, 154
Quality movement and programs, 55, 159–161, 374–376
Quitting, 128

R

R. J. Reynolds, 231–233, 318
Racial discrimination, 157, 158
Racial tensions, 420–421, 425, 431
Ranking system, 377
Rapid change. *See* Turbulence and rapid change
Rapid cognition (blink process): accuracy in, 37, 38; characteristics of, 11–12; personal theories and, 39–40
Rashomon, 19
Rational approach: artistic approach *versus*, 20–21, 437; characteristics of, 20; dramaturgical approach *versus*, 296, 297; to explaining organizational problems, 28–29; illusion of, 312–313; political approach *versus*, 220; of structural frame, 15–16, 47, 48, 49, 339
"Rational man" view, 26–27
Raytheon, 158–159
"Reach and Grasp" case study, 327–338
Readiness, of subordinates, 349–350
Real Managers (Luthans, Yodgetts, Rosenkrantz), 320, 323, 324
Realists, 364–365
Recognition, of heroes and heroines, 257–258, 276–277
Red tape, 27–28, 68, 76
Redundancy, 74
Reengineering: concept and practice of, 91; principles of successful, 96–97; successful cases of, 91–96, 150–151
Reengineering Management (Champy), 91
Referent power, 204
Reflection, 12, 421, 432, 433–434, 437

Reframing: in action, 327–340, 411–434; artistry and, 21, 433–434, 437–438; benefits and risks of, 338–340; case studies of, 327–340, 411–434; change, 373–396; cluelessness problem and, 3–10, 18; concept of frame breaking and, 12–14; of ethics and spirit, 397–409, 428–434; four-frame model and, 18–20, 41; gender differences and, 338–339; integrative case study of, 411–434; leadership, 341–372, 435–443; for new and tough situations, 12, 311–326, 327–340, 411–434; for newcomers, 340; organizations as political arenas, 230–235, 246, 386–387; for outsiders, 340; power of, 3–22, 41; reflecting and, 421–434; scenarios for, 328–338. *See also* Frames and framing; Multiframe thinking
Regime fall, 202
Relational concepts, 200–201
Relationship management, 177
Relationships. *See* Interpersonal relationships
Remember the Titans, 183–184
Reorganizing, multiframe view of, 314
Representations, 22*n*.2
Republicans, 204
Reputation, as source of power, 203
Resistance: assessing potential, 217, 219, 365; by frustrated employees, 129–130, 164; to organizational change, 378–379, 381–382
Resource allocation, 195, 196
Resource scarcity: conflict and, 206, 425; level of, and choice of frame, 318–319, 320; politics and, 16, 194, 195, 196, 213; power and, 201; simplification and, 27
Responsibility charting, 112, 383, 423

Responsibility taking: for interpersonal conflict in groups, 186; with Model I theory-in-use, 171

Restructuring, 71–97; generic issues in, 87–91; perils of, 71–73, 90–91, 97, 358–360; principles of, 96–97; reasons for, 89–91, 319; reengineering and, 91–96; structural configurations and, 87–89; structural deficiencies and, 47; structural dilemmas and, 73–76, 97; successful cases of, 91–96; tensions in, 87–89; theatrical, 300; troubled organizations and, 90. *See also* Structure

Review committees, 57

Rewards: for cultural turnaround, 274–275; in human resource frame, 144–145, 146–148; as power base, 203, 219–220

Rigidity, 76, 435–436

Rise and Fall of Strategic Planning, The (Mintzberg), 302

Rites of passage, 262–263

Rituals, 261–265; for building significance, 408–409; in case examples, 271, 275, 276, 282, 286–288; of initiation, 262–263, 271, 275, 282; of loss, 390–391; of transition, 266–267, 390–391. *See also* Ceremonies

Ritz-Carlton, 261

Rivet Hockey, 129

RJR Nabisco, 231–233, 236–237

"Robert F. Kennedy High School" case study, 411–434

Role definition: in aircraft carrier, 46; autonomy *versus* interdependence dilemma in, 75, 82; clarity *versus* creativity dilemma in, 74–75, 81, 127–131; gap *versus* overlap dilemma in, 74; in high-performing teams, 112, 115; in structural frame, 47, 52, 69, 74, 181; underuse *versus* overload dilemma in, 74

Role models: heroes and heroines as, 257–259; leading by example and, 283–284, 368, 428

Roles: change and realignment of, 382–383; formal, 181; informal, 181–182, 288–289

Rolex, 197

Rolls-Royce, 271

Roman Catholic Church, 262

Romania, 202

Routine: to deal with complexity, 27; machine bureaucracy and, 81; work, 154

Rules: blaming, for failure, 27–28; ground, 423; mutual understanding of, 226–227; taught in stories, 260; in vertical coordination, 54–55

Russia, natural gas company in, 199

S

Sabotage, 126, 129–130, 381

Safety needs, 424

Safety problems, workplace, 120–121, 137, 148

"Saints Are Coming, The," 295

Sam's Club, 144

Sarbanes-Oxley Act (SOX), 401

Satisficing, 26–27

Saturn, 113–115, 360

Savings and loan crisis, 227

Scandals: in Catholic Church, 262; ethics and, 208, 226–228, 387–398, 401; heroes and heroines and, 257; loss of soul and, 397–399, 401; reactions and remedies for, 401

Scandinavian Air Systems (SAS), 144–145, 363

Scanlon plans, 147

Scenarios: gender differences and, 338–339; human resource, 331–333; political, 333–336; for reframing in

Single-loop learning, 170

Situational analysis, 38

Situational leadership, 345, 348–350

Situations: context of leadership and, 344–345; definitions of, 22*n*.2; matching frames to, 317–320, 338–340; misreading, 3–10; reading ambiguous and complex, 36–41, 313; reframing in new or tough, 12, 311–326, 327–340, 411–434

Six Sigma, 55, 374–376

Size, organizational: restructuring and, 89; structure and, 63–64, 80, 87

Size, team, 103, 111

Skilled incompetence, 175

Skills: gap between needs and, 132–133; for interpersonal conflict in groups, 184–185; invest-in-people strategy for, 135–138, 139–164; investing in training of, 148–149; lean-and-mean strategy for, 134–135, 136–138; pay for, 155; political, 190, 213–224, 235–236

Slack resources, 67

Sleeper cells, 101

Smoothing tactics, 184

Soccer coach, 351–352

Social architecture: importance of, 51–52; structural frame and, 44, 297; structural leadership and, 356–360

Social awareness, 177

Social categorizations, 22*n*.2

Social constructivist perspective, 42*n*.2

Social control, 202

Social embeddedness, 167–168

Social intelligence, 175–176

Social networking, 220. *See also* Networks

Social psychology, 162

Social sciences: four-frame model and, 14, 15–16; power and, 203; structure and, 49

Socialization, 166

Society: corporate power and, 242–246; as ecosystem, 242–246; symbols in, 251–252

Sociology, 14, 15, 167–168, 253

Sociotechnical systems approach, 153, 154

Software industry: good human resource practices in, 144–145; turnover rates in, 144

Solutions, win-win, 221–222, 224, 336

Somalia, 202

Sony, 197, 321, 356

Soul, 289–290, 397–399. *See also* Culture, organizational; Spirit; Values

Soul of a New Machine, The (Kidder), 280–289

Southwest Airlines: authorship at, 403; executive compensation at, 157; human resource management at, 136, 143, 400; launching of, 254–255; self-directed teams at, 113; soul and spirit at, 400, 403, 404; symbolic elements at, 254–255, 257–258, 400

Southwest Bell, 89

Soviet Union, 205–206

Space shuttle disasters, 8, 191–194, 195–196, 207, 208, 213, 218, 221

Specialization: in high-performing teams, 111–112; self-actualization needs *versus*, 127–131; structure and, 47, 52, 53; team diversity and, 283

SPEED of Trust, the (Covey and Merrill), 15, 16

Spinelessness, 435–436

Spinning mills, 140

Spirit and spirituality: discipline of, 433–434, 436–437; innovation and, 376–377; organizational culture and, 269, 288, 290–291; in organizations, 399–409; reframing, 397–409, 428–434; symbolic frame and, 16; theater and, 295

Sports teams, 106–109, 110, 116, 279

Springfield Remanufacturing (SRC Holdings), 149

SRC Holdings, 149

Stagnant bureaucracy, 90

Stakeholders: agenda setting and, 214–216; bargaining and negotiation with, 221–224, 225; building relationships with, 214, 218–220, 365–366; organizations as political agents and, 235–246; political frame and, 196, 199

Standard Brands, 231–232

Standard operating procedures (SOPs), 55, 80–81

Standards and standardization: in machine bureaucracy, 80–81; in public education, 131; in Six Sigma, 375–376; technostructure and, 88; in vertical coordination, 55, 61, 62

Star network, 105–106

Starbucks, 277, 397, 400, 401

Starbucks Experience, The (Michelli), 15, 16

Start-up companies: myths about, 254–255; simple structure of, 79–80, 90. *See also* Entrepreneurs

Status differences, reducing, 156

Status quo, 435–436

Stereotypical goals, 66

Stock analysts' role, 77

Stories and storytelling: negative, 426–427; role of, in organizational change, 391–392, 394; as symbolic elements, 259–261, 270, 276, 284–285, 408; symbolic leadership and, 370–371

Straight from the Gut (Welch), 443

Strategic apex: defined, 78; in machine bureaucracy, 80; in professional bureaucracy, 82, 83; and restructuring, 88, 89; in simple structure, 79. *See also* Senior executives

Strategic planning: dramaturgical view of, 302–303; multiframe view of, 314

Strategy: flexible, and core values, 435–443; for organizational change, 393–396; structure and, 63, 65–66, 359–360; vision and, 214, 215–216

Strategy of Conflict, The (Schelling), 223

Street fights, 386

Structural configurations, 78–89

Structural frame, 43–118; assumptions of, 47; basic concepts of, 45–69; on conflict, 206, 422–423; for ethics, 402–403; for FBI-CIA relationship, 17; goals and, 63, 65–66, 76, 198–199; for groups and teams, 99–116; for high-school principal case, 422–433, 429, 432; intellectual origins of, 48–50; key questions of, 47, 52–54; leadership in, 356–360; management book based on, 14, 15–16; for managerial effectiveness, 323, 324, 325, 326; for organizational change, 378, 382–383, 395–396; for organizational effectiveness, 321, 322; organizational metaphors for, 15–16, 18, 402; for organizational processes, 314–315; overview of, 18, 21, 44; on power, 201; rational approach of, 15–16, 47, 48, 49; scenario for, 329–331; situations appropriate for, 318–320; strengths and weaknesses of, 339, 356–360

Structural Holes (Burt), 442

"Structural Inertia and Organizational Change" (Hannan and Freeman), 442

Structural realignment, 382–383

Structure: configurations for, 78–89; coordination methods and, 54–59, 73; decision making and, 168; design issues and options for, 47, 52–68, 69, 73–76; different, for unique circumstances, 62–68, 69; dilemmas of, 73–76, 97; fit of, 47, 89; forms and functions of, 50–52; group and team, 99–116, 280–281; for high-performing teams, 111–113; imperatives of, 62–68; lateral, 56–59, 60, 73, 85; Mintzberg's model of, 78–87, 88, 93, 97; parameters in determining, 62–68; pathologies and pitfalls in, 73–76; political dimension of, 232–233; restructuring and, 71–97; strategy and, 63, 65–66, 359–360; as theater, 299–301; tight *versus* loose, 50–51, 68, 75–76; vertical, 54–56, 59; vertical *versus* lateral, 60–68, 73. *See also* Restructuring

Suboptimization, 53

Subway, 261

Success: celebrating early, 395; ceremonies of, 266–267; criteria for effectiveness *versus*, 324–325; culture and, 269, 280–290; research on multiframe approaches and, 320–325; spirit and, 400–401, 436–437; symbolic explanations of, 269, 280–290, 294–295

Suicide attacks, 203

Supervisors, employee-centered *versus* job-centered, 163

Support: attracting, through presentation, 297, 299–300, 307–308; friends and, 204, 218–220, 225, 421–422; leadership style of, 349–350; during organizational change, 382; providing, 331–333, 349

Support staff, 78, 88

Surgical team, 99–100

Surprises. *See* Unexpected events

Survey research approach, 163

Survey Research Center, 163

Sustainability, 406–407

Symbolic frame, 247–308; assumptions of, 253–254; dramaturgical theory and, 293–308; for ethics, 402, 407–409; for FBI-CIA relationship, 17–18; for high-school principal case study, 426–428, 429, 430–433; leadership in, 356, 367–372; management book based on, 15, 16; for managerial effectiveness, 323, 324, 325, 326; for managerial role, 244; for organizational change, 378, 388–393, 394–396; for organizational effectiveness, 321, 322; organizational metaphors for, 16, 18, 296, 402; for organizational processes, 314–315; overview of, 18, 21, 247–249, 251–253; scenario for, 336–338; situations appropriate for, 318–320; strengths and weaknesses of, 339–340, 356. *See also* Culture; Culture, organizational; Symbols

Symbols: for building significance, 408–409, 431; defined, 252; emotions and, 247–248; forms of organizational, 249, 251–269, 408–409; funding and, 307–308; ineffective use of, 336–337, 339–340; negative, 267, 393, 426–427; organizational culture and, 266–277, 279–291; pervasiveness of, 251–253; plans as, 303; status, 156, 160; symbolic frame and, 16, 249; uses of, 252–253, 346, 372

System maps, 34

Systems: complex, 34–36, 378–379; gaming the, 213; overbounded and underbounded, 205–206, 423

Systems model with delay, 34–35

T

T-groups, 162, 163

Taboo goals, 66

Taming of the Shrew, The (Shakespeare), 354

Target, 254

Task forces, 57, 60

Through the Looking Glass (Carroll), 254
Tiger 01. *See* Friendly-fire incident
Time, 208, 231
Time-based units, 53
Tipping Point, The (Gladwell), 443
Titan (Chernow), 443
Tools: frames and, 11; wise use of, 13–14. *See also* Frames
Top-down change, 319, 377
Total quality management (TQM), 159–161, 374–376
Town hall meetings, 162–163
Toy factory, 150–151, 152, 154
Toyota, 34; NUMMI joint venture of, 160–161, 360
Tragedy, 295
Training: ethics, 401; in high-school principal case study, 424; investing in, 148–149; for organizational change, 379–382; for progressive human resource practices, 161–164; for self-managing teams, 155; for team-building, 162
Transactional leaders, 368
Transforming leaders, 368
Transition rituals and ceremonies, 266–267, 390–391
Trophy husbands, 355
Trust: bargaining styles and, 223, 225; and leadership, 346; organizational change and, 383
Tube wars, 281
Turbulence and rapid change: ad hoc structures in, 86; leadership and, 435–443; managers' realities and, 312–313, 411; and need for organizational learning, 33; and need for structural change, 65; and person-organization relationship, 132, 145. *See also* Uncertainty
Turf conflict: blaming, for organizational problems, 28; between FBI and CIA, 17, 29

Turnover: costs of, 143–144; poor fit and, 143; poor human resource management and, 120, 121, 137; in software industry, 144
Tyco, 77
Tylenol, 256
Tyrants, 356

U

U2, 295
Uncertainty: avoidance, 200, 273; coping with, 36–41; decision making in, 168; information technology and, 67; level of, and choice of frame, 318; organizational complexity and, 6, 32–33; politics and, 223; sources of organizational, 33, 49–50; structure and, 49–50, 65; symbols and, 253. *See also* Ambiguity; Turbulence and rapid change; Unexpected events
Unconscious, 252, 253
Underbounded systems, 205–206, 423
Unexpected events: dealing with, 36–41; failure to imagine, 19–20; as organizational characteristic, 31–32; reframing for, 311–312; standard operating procedures and, 55
Unilateral action, 170, 171
United Airlines, 148, 157
United Automobile Workers (UAW): and NUMMI, 161; and Saturn, 114
United Parcel Service, 50, 56
United States: corporate failures in, 8; diversity in, 158; failed policy initiatives of, 9–10; founders of, 279; metric system adoption in, 9–10, 373–374; multinational managers from, 273; space program of, 191–194. *See also* Government; Government agencies
U.S. Air Force, 258, 264–265
U.S. Army, 56, 100–101, 158

U.S. Congress: General Motors and, 365; initiation into, 262–263; lobbying of, 241; metric system legislation and, 9–10; 9/11 and, 252; politics in, 01, 220; space shuttle disasters and, 191, 192, 193, 195

U.S. Congressional Budget Office, 133

U.S. Congressional Medal of Honor, 258

U.S. Department of Education, 240

U.S. Food and Drug Administration, 110

U.S. General Accounting Office, 239

U.S. Health and Human Services, 316

U.S. homeland defense organizations: deception in, 32; failure of, to prevent 9/11 terrorist attacks, 19–20, 23–25, 27–28, 29; flawed restructuring of, 72–73, 74; organizational complexity and, 31, 33; squabbling among, 16–18; suboptimization of, 53–54

U.S. House of Representatives, 355

U.S. Internal Revenue Service, 163

U.S. Justice Department, 17

U.S. Marine Corps, 264–265

U.S. Navy, 163, 294–295, 390–391

U.S. Postal Service, 163

U.S. presidents: campaign promises of, 374; election ceremonies and, 267; personal power of, 204; politics and, 189, 214, 215–216; 2008 Democratic candidates and, 340, 354

U.S. Senate, 192, 241, 262–263

Units: conflict between, 207; quasi-resolution of conflict in, 200

Universities. *See* Colleges and universities

University of California, Berkeley, 205

University of Michigan, Survey Research Center, 163

Uplifting vision and strategy, 395

"Upper Echelons" (Hambrick and Mason), 442

Urgency, sense of, 394–396

USS Kennedy, 45–46, 54, 69*n*.1

V

Value: claiming, 221, 222–224; creating, 221–222, 224

Values: adaptability and, 435–443; appealing to, 337–338, 369–370, 427–428, 428, 430; loss of soul and, 397–399; as symbolic elements, 254–257, 408, 427–428; transmitting, through stories, 260–261, 270, 284–285, 370–371. *See also* Culture, organizational

Vanderbilt University, 41, 259

Venezuela, health care participation in, 151

Vertical coordination, 54–56, 59; centralized organizations and, 358; lateral coordination *versus*, 60–68, 73

Vietnam War, 233–234, 258

Vinalhaven, Maine, 315–317

Violence, 414, 415, 417, 435

Vision: for change, 395; communicating, 346, 369–370, 395; effective leadership and, 345–346, 369–370; political leadership and, 214–216, 225; strategy and, 214, 215–216; as symbolic element, 254–257; symbolic leadership and, 369–370

Visionary companies, 320–321, 322, 436

Vivendi, 205

Volkswagen, 132

Volvo, 10

W

Wal-Mart: discrimination lawsuit against, 158; ecosystem of, 237–238; image problems of, 229–230; power of, 229–230, 237–238, 245–246; Retail Link, 237; Sam's Club, 144

Wal-Mart, Dukes *vs.*, 158

"Wal-Mart effect," 229

Walker Information, 135

Washington Redskins, 108

Web of inclusion, 86–87, 88; restructuring to, 94–96; star network and, 105

Wegmans, 122–123

Western cultures, unilateral worldview in, 40

Westinghouse, 321

Whistleblowers, 32, 208

White House, 104, 216

Who Moved My Cheese? (Johnson), 380–381, 440, 443

Whole Foods: executive compensation at, 157; self-managing teams of, 113, 154

Wikipedia, 10

Wimps, 356, 360

Win-win approaches, 221–222, 224, 336

Windows NT, 211–213

"Wintel," 236, 237

Wisdom of Teams, The (Katzenbach and Smith), 111–112

Women: culture and, 273; discrimination against, 158, 328, 354; glass ceiling for, 340, 353–355; interpersonal dynamics and, 169, 263, 328; as leaders, 351–355; power and, 353–354; prevalence of, in high positions, 353; reframing for, 340; structure and, 86

Work ethic, 131

Work-Out conferences, 162–163

Work redesign, 152–154, 156

Workforce characteristics: change in requirements and, 132–133; diversity and, 158; organizational structure and, 63, 67–68; women and, 355

Workforce reduction strategies, 132, 137–138. *See also* Downsizing; Outsourcing

Workplace: accidents in, 148; democratic, 155–157; diversity in, 157–159

World Is Flat, The (Friedman), 443

World Trade Center: Mayor Giuliani and, 311–312, 341–342, 348, 368; rescue efforts at, 46, 258, 341–342; symbolic value of, 319. *See also* 9/11 terrorist attacks

World Trade Organization, 197

World War II, 279

WorldCom, 8, 22*n*.1, 90, 208

X

Xerox, 199

Y

Yale University, 300, 319

Z

Zealots, 356, 367

Zones of indifference, 205